Street by Street

NEWCASTLE UPON TYNE
SUNDERLAND
DURHAM, GATESHEAD,
SOUTH SHIELDS, TYNEMOUTH

Blyth, Chester-le-Street, Cramlington, North Shields, Peterlee, Ponteland, Seaham, Stanley, Washington, Whitley Bay

GW01471512

Ist edition May 2001

© Automobile Association Developments Limited 2001

This product includes map data licensed from Ordnance Survey® with the permission of the Controller of Her Majesty's Stationery Office. © Crown copyright 2000. All rights reserved. Licence No: 399221.

Published by AA Publishing (a trading name of Automobile Association Developments Limited, whose registered office is Norfolk House, Priestley Road, Basingstoke, Hampshire, RG24 9NY. Registered number 1878835).

Mapping produced by the Cartographic Department of The Automobile Association.

A CIP Catalogue record for this book is available from the British Library.

Printed by G. Canale & C. S.P.A., Torino, Italy

Ref: MD051

Key to map pages   ii-iii

Key to map symbols   iv-1

Enlarged scale pages   2-5

Street by Street   6-209

Index – towns & villages   210-211

Index – streets   212-264

Index – featured places   265-273

JEDBURGH

BERWICK-UPON-TWEED

Morpeth

A696

A192

A1

JEDBURGH

| 7 |

| 13 |

| 19 | 21 |

Cramlington

A68

A6079

| 29 | 31 | 33 |

Ponteland

Dudle

Newcastle

CARLISLE

| 43 | 45 | 47 |

Gosforth

A1

| 57 | 59 | 61 | 63 |

Corbridge

A69

NEWCASTLE

Hexham

| 75 | 77 | 79 | 2 | 3 |

UPON TYNE

| 81 |

| 99 |

A695

| 93 | 95 | 97 |

GATESHEAD

A694

| 113 | 115 | 117 |

| 111 |

| 129 | 131 | 133 | 135 |

A692

A693

| 147 | 149 | 151 |

A68

Stanley

Consett

| 165 |

Lanchester

A691

| 179 |

| 193 |

Durham

PENRITH

| 203 |

A690

A689

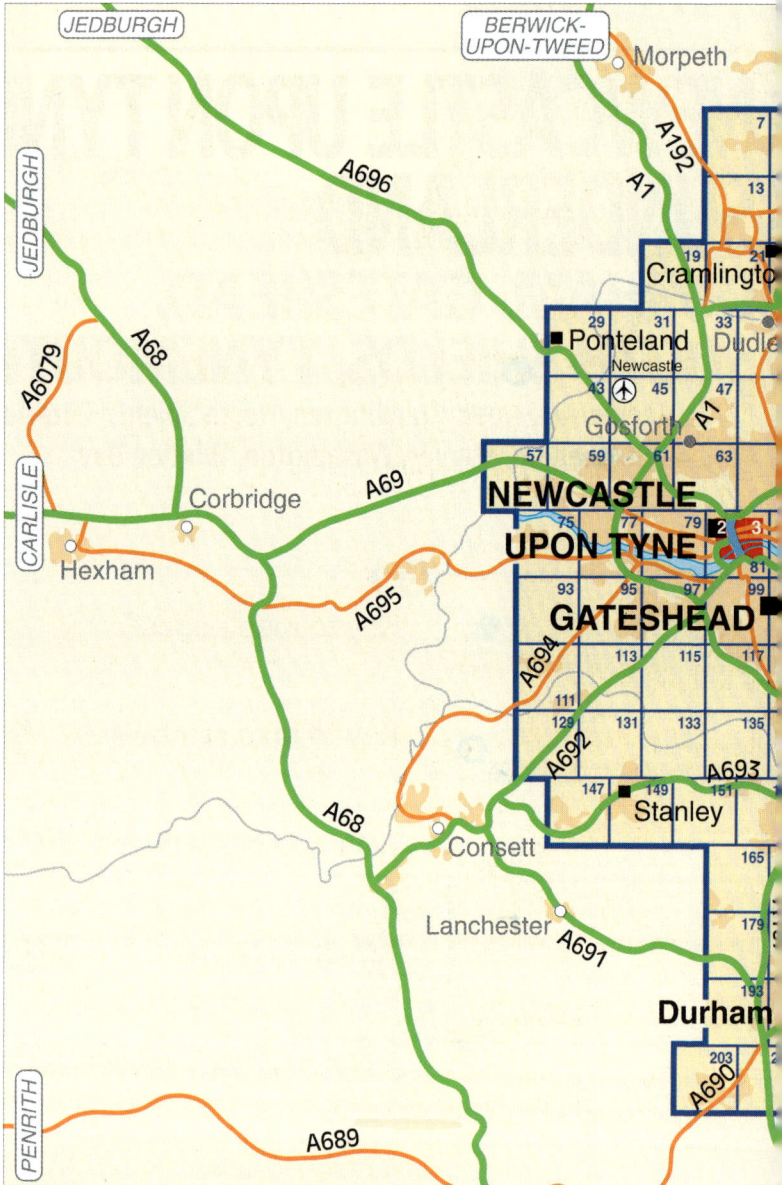

0   1/4   miles   1/2

0   1/4   1/2   kilometres   3/4   1

A189

11 Blyth
17

25 27

37 39 41
Whitley Bay
A19
51 53 55 **Tynemouth**
Jorth Shields
67 58 69 71 73
A1058 **SOUTH SHIELDS**

85 87 89 91
Jarrow
103 105 107 A183
A194(M) A184
123 125 127 109
A194(M)
121 4 5 **SUNDERLAND**
139 141 143 145
Washington

155 157 159 161 163
Chester-le-Street A19
169 171 173 175 177
Seaham
A1(M) A690
183 185 187 189 191
62
197 199 201
Peterlee
207 209
A19 A1086
61
DARLINGTON HARTLEPOOL

3.6 inches to 1 mile **Scale of main map pages** 1:17,500

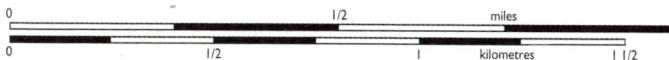

0 1/2 miles 1
0 1/2 1 kilometres 1 1/2

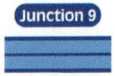

Junction 9	Motorway & junction		**P+** 🚌	Park & Ride
Services	Motorway service area		🚌	Bus/coach station
	Primary road single/dual carriageway			Railway & main railway station
Services	Primary road service area			Railway & minor railway station
	A road single/dual carriageway		⊖	Underground station
	B road single/dual carriageway		⊖	Light railway & station
	Other road single/dual carriageway		+++++++++	Preserved private railway
	Restricted road		_LC_	Level crossing
	Private road		•—•—•—	Tramway
← ←	One way street		– – – – – –	Ferry route
	Pedestrian street		....	Airport runway
	Track/ footpath		— · — · — ·	Boundaries- borough/ district
	Road under construction		\\\\\\\\	Mounds
	Road tunnel		**93**	Page continuation 1:17,500
P	Parking		**7**	Page continuation to enlarged scale 1:10,000

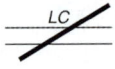

River/canal lake, pier		Toilet with disabled facilities
Aqueduct lock, weir		Petrol station
465 ▲ Winter Hill — Peak (with height in metres)		PH — Public house
Beach		PO — Post Office
Coniferous woodland		Public library
Broadleaved woodland		Tourist Information Centre
Mixed woodland		Castle
Park		Historic house/ building
Cemetery		Wakehurst Place NT — National Trust property
Built-up area		Museum/ art gallery
Featured building		Church/chapel
City wall		Country park
A&E — Accident & Emergency hospital		Theatre/ performing arts
Toilet		Cinema

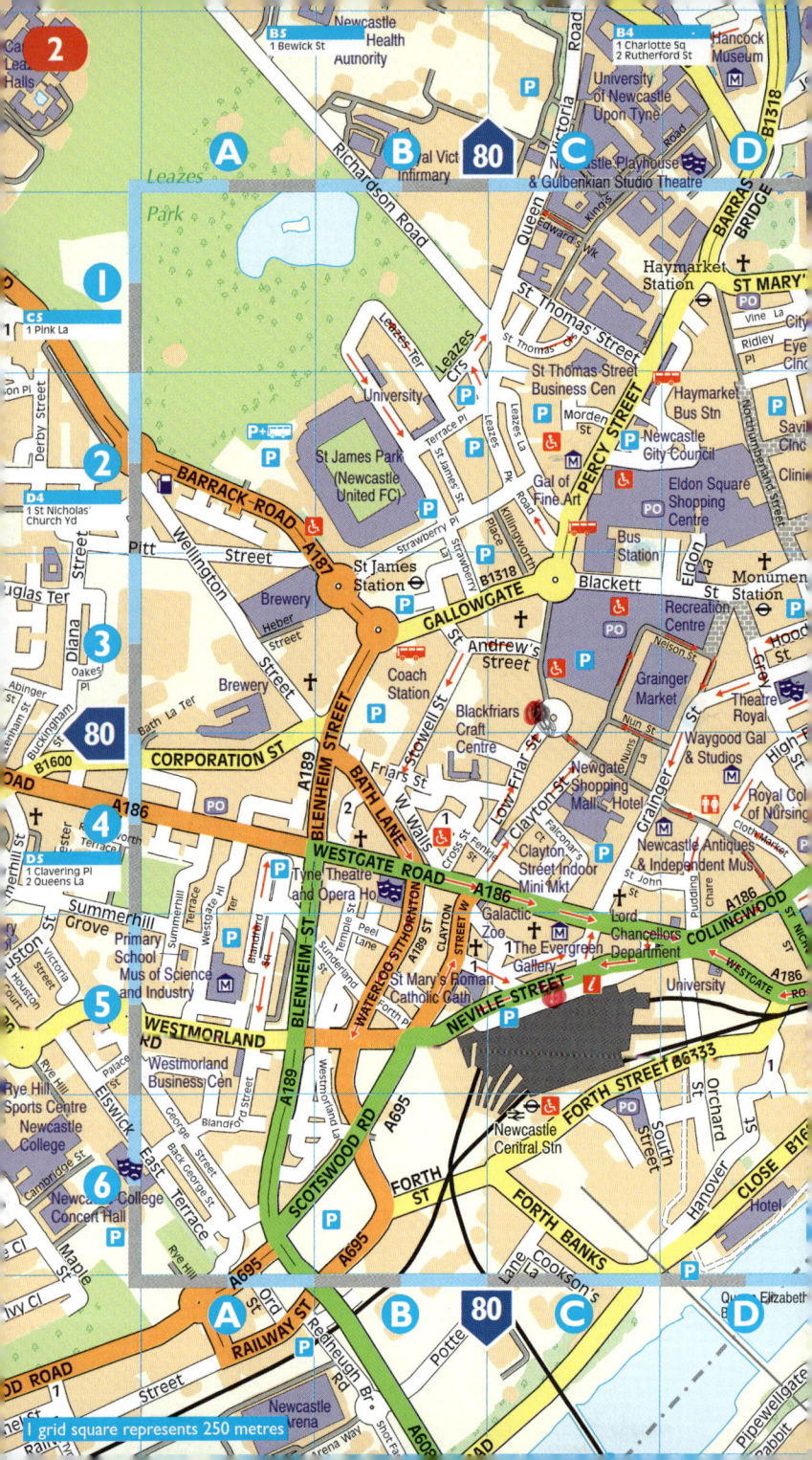

2

Can...
Lea...
Halls

B5
1 Bewick St

Newcastle
Health
Authority

B4
1 Charlotte Sq
2 Rutherford St

Hancock
Museum

Leazes
Park

A

B Royal Vict
Infirmary

80

Victoria Road

C

University
of Newcastle
Upon Tyne

Newcastle Playhouse
& Gulbenkian Studio Theatre

D

BARRAS BRIDGE

B1318

Richardson Road

I

C5
1 Pink La

Queen
Edward's
Wk

King's
Rd

Leazes Ter

Leazes Crs

Leazes La

St Thomas

St Thomas' Street

Haymarket
Station

ST MARY'

Vine La

Ridley
Pl

Eye
Clin

Savil
Clin

Derby Street

Diana Street

Douglas Ter

Pitt Street

2

BARRACK ROAD

A187

University

St James Park
(Newcastle
United FC)

Terrace Pl

St James St

Leazes Pl

St Thomas Street
Business Cen

Gal of
Fine Art

Morden
St

Newcastle
City Council

PERCY STREET

Haymarket
Bus Stn

Eldon Square
Shopping
Centre

Clinic

Clinic

D4
1 St Nicholas'
Church Yd

Wellington Street

St Nicholas Street

3

Brewery

Heber Street

Brewery

Bath La Ter

St James
Station

Strawberry Pl

Strawberry St

Killingworth Place

GALLOWGATE

Killingworth Road

B1318

Blackett St

Bus Station

PO

Recreation
Centre

Eldon St

Grey St

Monumen
Station

80

B1600

CORPORATION ST

A189

BLENHEIM STREET

BATH LANE

Stowell St

Friars St

W Walls

Coach
Station

Blackfriars
Craft
Centre

St Andrew's
Street

Low Friar St

Clayton St

Nun St

Newgate
Shopping
Mall

Grainger
Market

Nelson St

Hotel

Newcastle Antiques
& Independent Mus

St John St

Grainger St

Theatre
Royal

Waygood Gal
& Studios

High St

Royal Col
of Nursing

Cloth Market

A186

A186

Terrace

Westgate Hl

Summerhill
Terrace

4

WESTGATE ROAD

A186

Cross St

Fenkle St

Falconar's St

Clayton
Street Indoor
Mini Mkt

Pudding Chare

COLLINGWOOD

A186

WESTGATE

D5
1 Clavering Pl
2 Queens La

Summerhill
Grove

Primary
School

Mus of Science
and Industry

Tyne Theatre
and Opera Ho

BLENHEIM ST

WATER ST

ST THORNTON

Peel Lane

Temple

Sunderland

Galactic
Zoo

Clayton St W

St Mary's Roman
Catholic Cath

NEVILLE STREET

The Evergreen
Gallery

Lord
Chancellors
Department

University

St John St

Victoria

Houston St

Houston
Court

5

WESTMORLAND RD

A189

Westmorland
Business Cen

Westmorland Terrace

Blandfo

Forth Pl

B6333

FORTH STREET

PO

Orchard Street

A186

N St

Rye Hill
Sports Centre
Newcastle
College

Elswick

East Terrace

Palace

George

Back George St

Forth Banks

Newcastle
Central Stn

South Street

Hanover

CLOSE

B16

Hotel

Cambridge St

6

Newcastle College
Concert Hall

Maple St

Rye Hill

SCOTSWOOD RD

A695

FORTH ST

A695

FORTH BANKS

Cookson's

Quee Elizabeth

IVY CI

Ord St

RAILWAY ST

A

Redheugh Br

B

80

Potte

C

A69

D

Pipewellgate

Rabbit

OD ROAD

Street

Newcastle
Arena

Arena Way

A69

Shot Fac

1 grid square represents 250 metres

E2
1 Higham Pl
2 New Bridge St West

University of Northumbria at Newcastle

81

City Council

E3
1 Erick St

Warwick Street

E4
1 City Rd

University of Northumbria at Newcastle

Northumberland Road

A167(M)

College St

Ellison Place

Laing Art Gal

Hotel

Plummer Tower

Durant Rd

Dobson St

Police Station

A187 NEW BRIDGE STREET

Manors Station

Barker St

Shieldfield Health Centre

Napier St

Rock Terrace

Falconer Street

Camden St

Byron St

Milton Close

Milton Pl

PORTLAND ROAD

Rosedale Terrace

Dinsdale Pl

STODDART ST

Coppice W

Gosforth St

Wretham Pl

Beadnell Pl

Copland Ter

SHIELDFIELD

Field Cl

LA

Simpson Terrace

Albert Street

Back New Br St

CLARENCE ST

Union St

Union St

B1600

B1600

Portland Rd

Bermondsey St

BYKER BRIDGE

Stepney Road

A1

Newcastle City Council

2

F3
1 Trafalgar St

3

St Ann's

3
1 Queen's Close

Tarset

Stepney Lane

Stepney St

Argyle St

Meibourne Street

Howard St

Red Barnes

CRAWHALL RD

B1600

Breamish St

GIBSON ST

B1600

81

CITY ROAD

Quayside

Manors Stn

Pandon Bank

Tower St

Sallyport Twr

Garth Heads

Calvey

Jubilee Rd

Tyne Tees TV Studios

St Ann's St

4

F5
1 Pilgrim St

A186

PILGRIM ST

MELBOURNE ST

CITY ROAD

A186

MILK MARKET

Sandgate

Quayside

Sandgate Hotel

NEWCASTLE U

A167

St Nicholas

The Side Gallery

Trinity Maritime Mus

Mnr Chare

Broad Chare

Pandon Law Courts

QUAYSIDE B1600

Quayside

Baltic Millennium Bridge

5

F6
1 Cannon St
2 Half Moon La

Castle Keep Hotel

Crown Court

Guildhall

Swing Bridge

Bessie Surtees Ho

Live Theatre

Queen St

Custom House

Tyne Bridge

River Tyne

HMS Calliope Cadet Training Centre

South Shore Road

Mill Road

G2
1 Henry Sq
2 Prince Albert Ter
3 Russell Ter

6

H3
1 Coquet St

High Level Bridge

BRIDGE ST

HIGH STREET

Bottle Bank

Mirk La

Bankwell La

Church St

A167

Oakwellgate

Hillgate

Abbot's Rd

Hawks Rd

Hawks Road

Quarryfield Road

B1307

E

F

81

G

H4
1 The Swirle

H

Swinburne St

Nelson St

West St

Ellison St

A167

GATESHEAD

Greenesfield Business Cen

4

SUNDERLAND

Ayres Quay

Bishopwearmouth

Ashbrooke

A3
1 Hind St

A2
Bar 1 Ayre's Quay Rd
2 Paley St
Str 3 Silksworth Rw

B1
1 Queen St

B2
1 Dun Cow St
2 Garden Pl
3 Middle St

B4
1 Mary St
2 Stockton Rd

B5
1 Worcester St
2 Worcester Ter

C1
1 Cumberland St

C2
1 Charman St
2 Prince St

C3
1 Maritime St

C5
1 St George's Wy

C6
1 Carlyon St

D2
1 John St
2 Little Villiers St

D3
1 Frederick St

A B 126 C D
144

Trimdon St
Farringdon
Place
Row
Gilley's Gill Road
Washington Street N
Brooke St
Richmond St
Wilson St North
Easington Street
Street
NORT
A2
Monk
Wearmouth
Railway
Station
Museum
Bonner's Field
DAME DOROTHY STREET
Char
Palmer's Road

A1018
Wearmouth
Bridge
W-Wear Street
Bridge Crs
Panns
River
Hou
Cen

Fontaine Road
Gill Road
Brewery
Castle street
Dunning St
Matlock street
Green St
Back-Br
Br St
Bridge St
Bedford
High
Street
West
PO

LIVINGSTONE ROAD A183
SILKSWORTH ROW
ST MICHAELS WAY A1231
Johnson street
Rail
Eden st W
Empire Thtr
High Street
Tax Office
West St
Crowtree Road
King St
College
Union St
Station St
York St
Middle street
South street
Sunderland AFC
Club Shop
Fawcett street
St Thomas' Street
University
for Industry
University

Fire Station
Waterworks Road
Gilhurst Gra
Clanny street
Hope street
Police Headquarters and
DSS
Magistrates Court
Bridges
Shopping
Centre
PO
Sunderland City Council
Sunderland
Station
ATHENAEUM ST
John St
Sunderland Co
Court
FREDERICK

University of Sunderland
Green
Crowtree
Leisure
Centre
Crowtree Terrace
University
Terrace
BROUGHAM STREET
The Art Gallery
HOLMESIDE
Cinema
WATERLOO PL
FAWCETT STREET
Sunderland Museum
& Art Gallery
War Memorial

126
CHESTER ROAD
Rosedale Stre
Westbourne Road
The Leazes
Cleft
Rd
Royalty Thtr
University Technology Park
University of Sunderland (Library)
A690 ALBION PL VINE PL
DERWENT ST
A690
Mary St
Olive St
Park Lane
Bus Station
Civic Centre
BURDON ROAD A1018
TOWARD RUAD
Mowbray Park

NEW DURHAM ROAD
Tunstall Ter W
Elwin St
Derby St
Tunstall Terrace
Tunstall Rd
A1231 STOCKTON ROAD
Cowan Ter
University of Sunderland

A&E
Sunderland Royal Inf
Shakespeare Ter
Havelock St
Thornhill Terrace
Alice St
Princess St
Grange Terrace Surg
Azalea Ter
Argyle street
Argyle Sq
PARK ROAD A1018
Masonic Temple
High School

BURN PARK ROAD
Beechwood
Elmwood
Ashwo
Ashwood
Thornhill
St Anthonys RC School
Abbotsford Ter
Beresford park
Belvedere
Woodside
Ashmore St
Lorne Ter
Gorse Road
A1018
University of Sunderland
gray

wood Ter
Wood Ter
nwood Terrace
Argyle House School
Thornhill Park
Valebrooke Gdns
Azalea Ter
The Avenue
Cloisters
High School
Mowrai

Thornhill Comprehensive School
Belle Vue Park
Thornhill Gdns
brooke Avenue
Cross Vale Rd
verdale
Briery V
Sunderland A
Health Autho
Meadow Vale
Tunstall
The Grove
georges Gardens
High School
HOPE ROAD
University

1 grid square represents 250 metres

St Peter

National Glass Centre

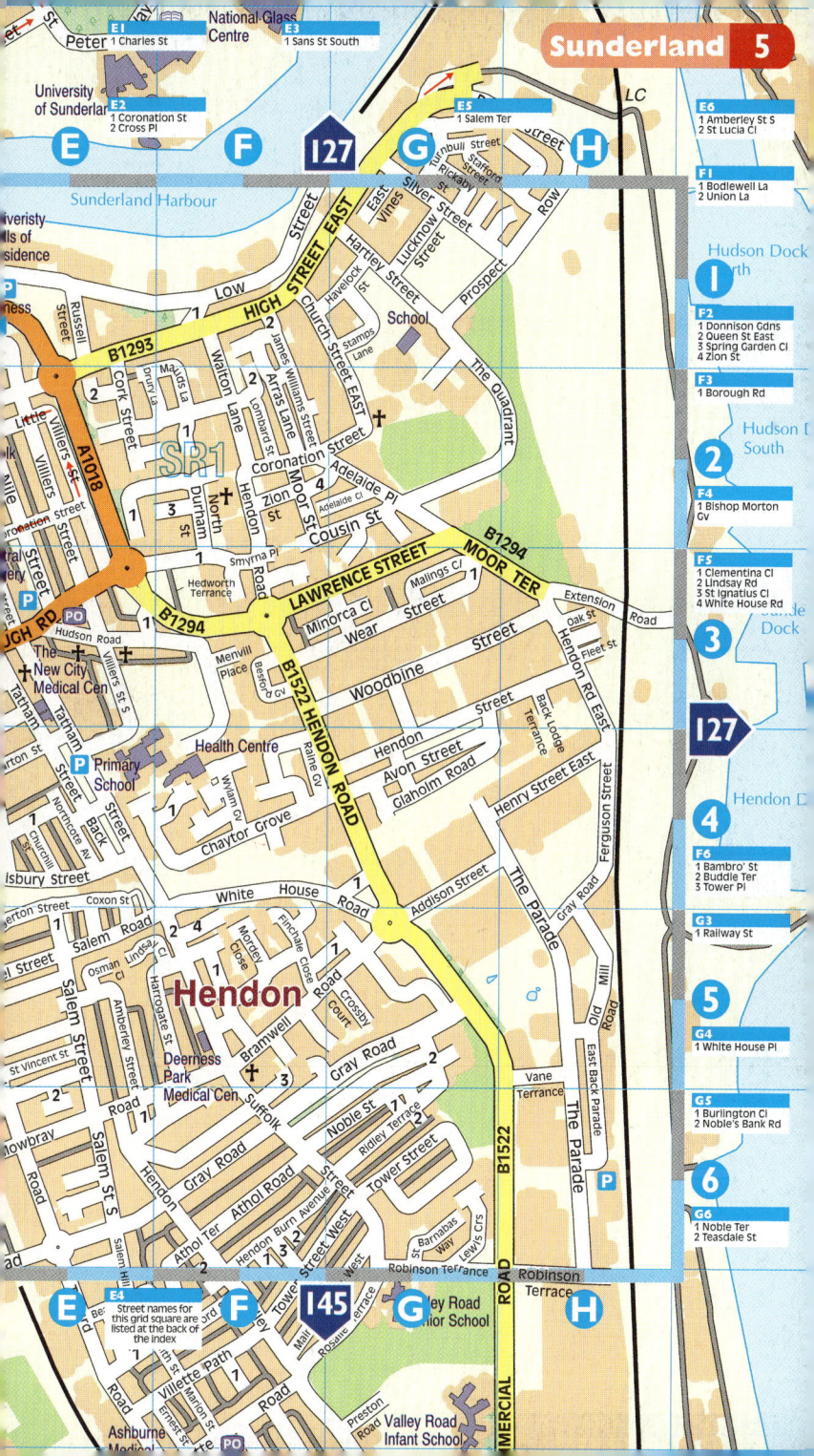

University of Sunderland

Sunderland Harbour

iversity lls of esidence

Hudson Dock North

Hudson Dock South

Hendon Dock

LC

I 27

I 45

SR1

Hendon

Deerness Park Medical Cen

New City Medical Cen

Health Centre

Primary School

Low Row
HIGH STREET EAST
B1293
A1018
Russell Street
Villiers Street
Cork Street
Drury La
Maids La
Walton Lane
Arras Lane
Lombard St
James Williams Street
Durham St
North
Hendon
Zion St
Coronation Street
Moor St
Adelaide Pl
Adelaide Cl
Cousin St
Smyrna Pl
Hedworth Terrace
LAWRENCE STREET
MOOR TER
B1294
B1294
B1522 HENDON ROAD
Minorca Cl
Wear Street
Malings Cl
Woodbine Street
Menvill Place
Beston Gv
Hendon Avon Street
Glaholm Road
Raine Gv
Wylam Gv
Chaytor Grove
White House Road
Coxon St
Salem Road
Northcote Av
Churchill St
Back
Street
Tatham St
Tatham Street Back
Villiers St S
Street
Salem Street
St Vincent St
Amberley Street
Osman Lindsay
Mortley Close
Finchale Close Road
Harrogate St
Bramwell
Suffolk
Gray Road
Crosby Court
Noble St
Ridley Terrace
Tower Street
Athol Ter
Athol Road
Hendon Burn Avenue
Street West
West
Barnbas St Way
Lewis Crs
Robinson Terrace
Vane Terrace
The Parade
B1522
Henry Street East
Back Lodge Terrace
Hendon Rd East
Fleet St
Oak St
Extension Road
Addison Street
Gray Road
Ferguson Street
Dio Mill Road
East Back Parade
Robinson Terrace
COMMERCIAL ROAD

School

Stamps Lane

Church Street EAST

Hartley Street

Lucknow Street

Silver Street

East Vines

Havelock St

Prospect Row

The Quadrant

Turnbull Street

Stafford St

Rickaby St

ley Road Junior School

Valley Road Infant School

Ashburne Medical

Villette Path
Marion St
Ernest St
Preston Road
Rosanne Terrace
Villette Road
Tower Mill
Rosa St

6

A   B   C

C3
1 Chipchase Cl
2 Durham Cl
3 Netherdale

I

Burnt House

2

Netherton

Blue House Farm

Ripley Cl

Aytoro

Knaresborough Cl

Skipton

Warwick Gr

Dover Close

Hylton Cl

3

Conway Ct

NETHERTON LANE

Lane

North Farm

B1331

North   Ridge

Meadowdale

Dunstanbu

The Grange

Oakdale

Hallwood Cl

South Farm

Nedderton

Netherton   Lane

Red House Farm

Ceme

4

Westlea

5

HARTFORD

6

ROAD

Netherton Moor Farm

A   **I2**   B   C

A 192

DS

I grid square represents 500 metres

Plessey Woods

D **E** **F**

D3
1 Bishops Meadow
2 Cloverdale
3 Cumberland Av
4 Netherton La

Gooch Av

Stephenson Wy

Long Ri Way

Barrington Road

E2
1 Lanchester Gn

I

LC

Glebe Farm

CHOPPINGTON ROAD

A1068

E3
1 Fountain Cl
2 Glebe Ms
3 John Brown Ct

Be **Station** **n**

2

therstone Gv

Octavia Cl

Augustus Dr

Bonchester Close

Chichester Gv

Winchester Rd

Corchester Rd

Thorn Tree Dr
Yew Tree Dr
Ash Tree Dr

Rowan Cl

Cedar

Carisbrooke

Cherry Tree

Hassop Way

BEDLINGTON

Centurian Way

The Wynding

mond Cl

NE22

The Crest

The Wynding

Meadow Ct

Court Road

Cleland Road

Glebe Road

Oakapple Close

Schalksmuhle

Cholverton Drive

Aconda

Shaley Ct

B1331

E4
1 Church Cl
2 Nether Riggs
3 W End Front St

Wood Lane

Wansbeck Rd

lin Park

Stanley Gv

Trevelyan Av

STEAD

Poplar

Dene

ra View

 Rosevale

Forster Avenue

Braeside

Northumberland Av

Nesmondale Ay

Deanery St

Health Authority

PO

Milline Ct

Road

VULCAN PLACE

Park Road

Doggsing Av

Millf

Haig Road

Beatty Road

Millba

Kn

8

F4
1 Barrington Ct
2 Brook Ct

RIDGE TERRACE

irst chool

St Benet Biscops RC High School

Catholic Row

Hartford Ct

Clovelly Gdns

5 Riggs
W Riggs

Windsor Dr

Windsor Gdns

Church Ct

Wansbeck District Council

FRONT ST EAST

Front Street East

Whitley Memorial Sch

Bell Pl

Hollywood St

Spring Pk

BEDLINGTON BANK

A193

4

edlingtonlane arm

Hartford Crs

Hartlands

Hartlands

Acorn Avenue

Demesne Dr

Elm Dr

Hotspur

Russell Ter

Avenue

Tower's Ct

Church Lane

Millfield N

Millfield Ct

Millfield

Millfield E

Millfield

A1068

A193

Millfield South

Humford Way

Church Lane

Golf Course

5

6 Humford Mill

Church Lane

8

A4
1 Cornweli Crs

A3
1 Wanny Rd

B2
1 Lampton Ct
2 Lumley Ct
3 Waverley Av

Bedlington Station

BEDLINGTON

B3
1 Clement Av
2 Edgewood Av
3 Trotter Gv

Burnside

† Bedlington
Station Co
First Sch

The Gables
Medical Group

Bedlington
Communi
High Sch

Roslin
Park

The Oval
Park

Roslin
Park

Roslin
Park

Wood Lane

Roslin

7

Bedlington
Stead County
First School

STEAD LANE B1331

B1331

Stanley Gv

Trevelyan
Av

Poplar
Grove

Dene View
West

Dene View
East

Woodside

C1
1 Greenwood Av
2 Sleekburn Av

Whitley
Memorial Sch

FRONT ST EAST

Church

Millfield N

Millfield

Millfield

C2
1 Cherrytree Ct
2 Edward Rd
3 George Rd
4 Knox Cl

Humford
Way

BEDLINGTON BANK

Church Lane

Bebside Social
Club House

A193

BEBSIDE ROAD A193

FRON

Bebside
Hall

Hathery
Lane

Humford
Mill

Church Lane

HORTON

A   **I4**   **B**   **C**

I grid square represents 500 metres

D
1 Burt Rd
2 Moorland Ct
3 Moorland Crs

E1
1 Havelock Crs

**East
Sleekburn**

Brock Lane

Havelock Mews

Barrington Park

Sleek Burn

I

E4
1 Avondale Cl

Park Av

Park Parkside

Park Avenue

Legg Avenue

Greenway Avenue

A189

Moorland Av

Moorland
3 Moorland Vis
Moorland Dr

2

Mount Pleasant
Farm

2

E5
1 Chase Ms

River Blyth

Blyth Valley
Borough Council

Cowley Road

Spencer Road

3

Spencer
Court

Cowley Rd

Kitty Brewster
Farm

Coniston Road

Ennerdale Rd

Loweswater
Cl

Coniston Road

Ullswater

Grasmere Wy

Thirlmere

Buttermere
Way

10

F4
1 Cowpen Rd
2 Ferndale Cl
3 Greendale Cl
4 Ribblesdale Av
5 Thorndale Pl
6 Tweedy St

Northumberland
County Council

Close

Glendale Av

Avondale

Kitty Brewster

Bells

Crescent

Maple

Weardale

Wensleydale

Teesdale
Pl

Craigmill
Park

COWPEN

Wensdall Rd

Nidderdale
Cl

Craigmill

ROAD

Cowpen

4

The Orchards

Langley
Av

Edendale Avenue

Malvins Road

A193

LC

Lyndon
Wk.

A193

Chase Farm Dr

A189

**Middle
School**

First School

Inglewood Cl

Thorntree Way

Humford
Grn

Beaumont Manor

Eskdale Av

Wharfedale

Doveedale Av

Patterdale
Av

Cloverdale

Cowpen Hall

Norfolk

Nordale

Brandreth

Bankdale
Gdns

Devonworth

Worth
Place

Easton

Dunston
Rd

Dean Vw

Brierley

Green

Hortondale Grove

Garreston
Dr

Axwell

Ingram Drive

F5
1 Callerdale Rd
2 Coverdale Av
3 Milldale Av

F6
1 Moordale Av
2 Warkdale Av

Bebside

**Blyth Tynedale
Co High
School**

Tynedale

Ravensdale Grove

Kingsdale Av

Swaledale Avenue

**Middle
School**

Lynndale Av

Prestdale Av

Wettondale Av

Peltondale Av

Bigsodale Av

Monkdale

Stardale
Av

Castledale

Drive

Brookside Av

Rookery Cl

Hallside Road

5

Northumberland
Hlth Authority

6

NE24

Rothbury Av

St Mary's Dr

Chillingham Rd

Cresswell Crs

Drurindge

Pecket Cl

Wallsand

Whittington

Stanton

Drive

Beadnell

Otterburn Av

PO

Golf

D   A189   E   15   F

A4
1 Burnside Cl

A3
1 Buttermere Wy

A5
1 Cragton Gdns
2 Hartleigh Pl
3 Malton Cl
4 Redesdale Pl

xkburn

B4
1 Earl's Gdns

B5
1 Belsay Ct
2 Thorneyburn Wy
3 Whithorn Ct

B6
1 Amber Ct
2 Bebdon Ct
3 Fallow Park Av
4 Hargrave Ct
5 Haven Ct
6 Hepple Ct
7 Mitford Av
8 Thropton Ct

C3
1 Grieve St
2 Millfield Gdns

C4
1 Goschen St
2 Hambledon St
3 Sweethope Av
4 Thompson St

C5
1 High St
2 Rosebery Av

C6
1 Cherry Trees
2 Elm Trees
3 Fourth Av
4 Kendal Av
5 Rowan Ct
6 Second Av

First School

A4
A3

Brock Lane

Blyth Valley
Borough Council

Cowley Road

Spencer Road
Spencer Court

Coniston Road

COWPEN   ROAD

A193   HODGSON'S ROAD

Cowpen Road

Cemetery

Lindsay Av

Alwinton
Close

Walton Avenue

COWPEN   ROAD

Cowpen

The Orchards

Langley Av

Edendale Avenue

King's Gdns

Queen's Gdns

Prince's Gdns

Malvins
Close County
First School

St Andrews RC
Aided First School

Dean View Drive

Albion Way

Brierley Road

Hortondale Grove

Beal Cl

Ingram
Dr

Matfen
Cl

Elsdon
Cl

Cambo
Cl

Budle Cl

Craster Cl

Ingoe Cl

Ogle

Bamburgh

Ford Drive

Norham
Drive

Bolam   Avenue

Harper St

Sidney St

Lynn St

Claremont Ter

Blyth Valley

Blyth
Sports Centre

St Wilfrids
Middle School

Blyth Valley
Borough
Council

Princess Louise
First School

Prs Louise   Road

Blyth Tynedale
Co High
School

Middle
School

Northumberland
Area Hlth Authority

Garestone

Arwell

Brookside Av

Hallside Road

Rookery

Isabella Rd

Southend
Av

Leaholme Crs

Trevelyan

Newsham   Road

BLYTH

NE24

Monkdale Av

Bishopdale Av

Skardale
Av

St Mary's Dr

Golf

A   B   C

16

**Isabel
Pit**

Middle
School

1 grid square represents 500 metres

D3
1 Goschen St
2 Thompson St
3 Worsdell St

D4
1 Arthur St
2 Boyne Ct
3 Cummings St
4 Davison St
5 French St
6 Gatacre St
7 Kerry Cl
8 Merton Sq
9 Seaforth St
10 Simpson St
11 Thompson St

D5
1 Aidborough St
2 Back Croft Rd
3 Barnard St
4 Crofton St

D6
1 Broadway Crs
2 Columbia Ter
3 Eleventh Av
4 George St
5 Kingsway
6 Rutherford St

E4
1 Ballast HI
2 Beaconsfield St
3 Plessey Rd
4 Post Office St
5 Quay Rd
6 Quayside
7 Ridley St
8 Sussex St
9 Tate St

E5
1 Carlton St
2 Coburg St
3 Crown St
4 Hawthorne Rd
5 Oxford St
6 Percy St South
7 Rosamond Pl
8 St Cuthberts Ct
9 Wellington St

E6
1 Chamberlain St
2 Nixon St
3 Twizell St
4 Woodside

North Blyth

DALE ST
GRAY ST

REGENT STREET
BURT
WATERLOO ROAD
B1329
B1328
B1327
MADDISON ST
Dr Reg
Carrs Surg
Phoenix
Junior Sch
First School
UNION ST
PLESSEY RD
Northumberland Co Council
BROADWAY
Blyth Spartans AFC
First School
Kingsway

BRIDGE ST
RIDLEY AVENUE
LOW QUAY
Pol Stn
Headway
East Pk View
Park Vw
WENSLEYDALE TERR
Dent St
Rosemary Ter
Braewood Rd
Hunter Av
Grantham Ter

A193 ROTARY WAY
B1523
Wolmer Rd
Estate
Wandbeck Av
Solingen

17

D   E   F

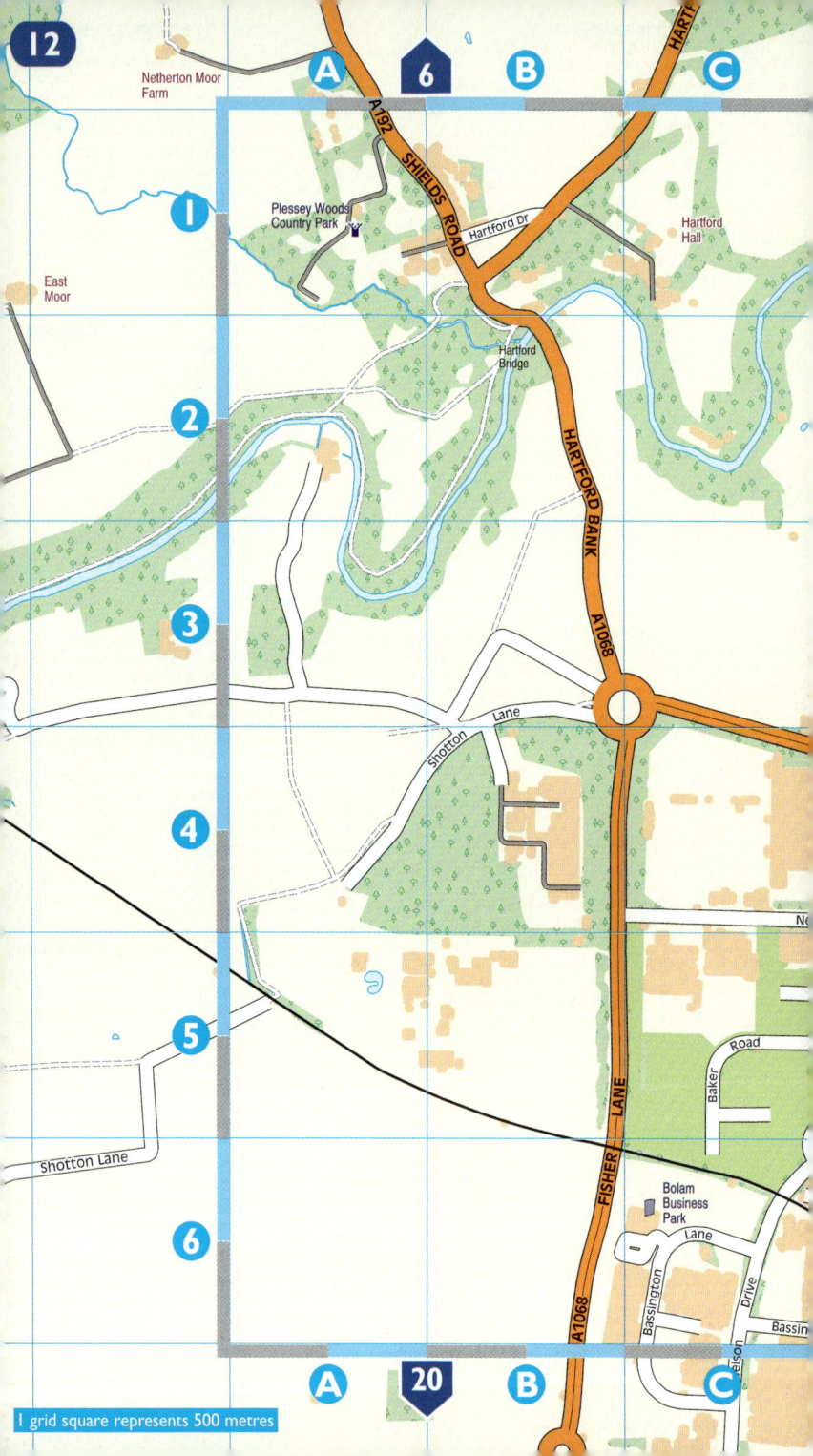

A   6   B   C

I

Netherton Moor
Farm

Plessey Woods
Country Park

SHIELDS ROAD

A192

Hartford Dr

Hartford
Hall

East
Moor

2

Hartford
Bridge

HARTFORD BANK

A1068

3

Shotton   Lane

4

Ne

Baker   Road

5

Shotton Lane

FISHER LANE

Bolam
Business
Park

Lane

Bassington

Drive

Bassin

6

A1068

Nelson

A   20   B   C

Humford

Church

F4
1 Colbury Ci
2 Denholm Av
3 Hanover Pl
4 Hartside Crs

D E **7** F

F5
1 Carmel Gv
2 Castleton Cl
3 Cheadle Av
4 Ilford Av
5 Ingham Gv
6 Whitehill Rd

River Blyth

I

F6
1 Yardley Gv
2 Yeovil Cl

River Blyth

2

East Hartford

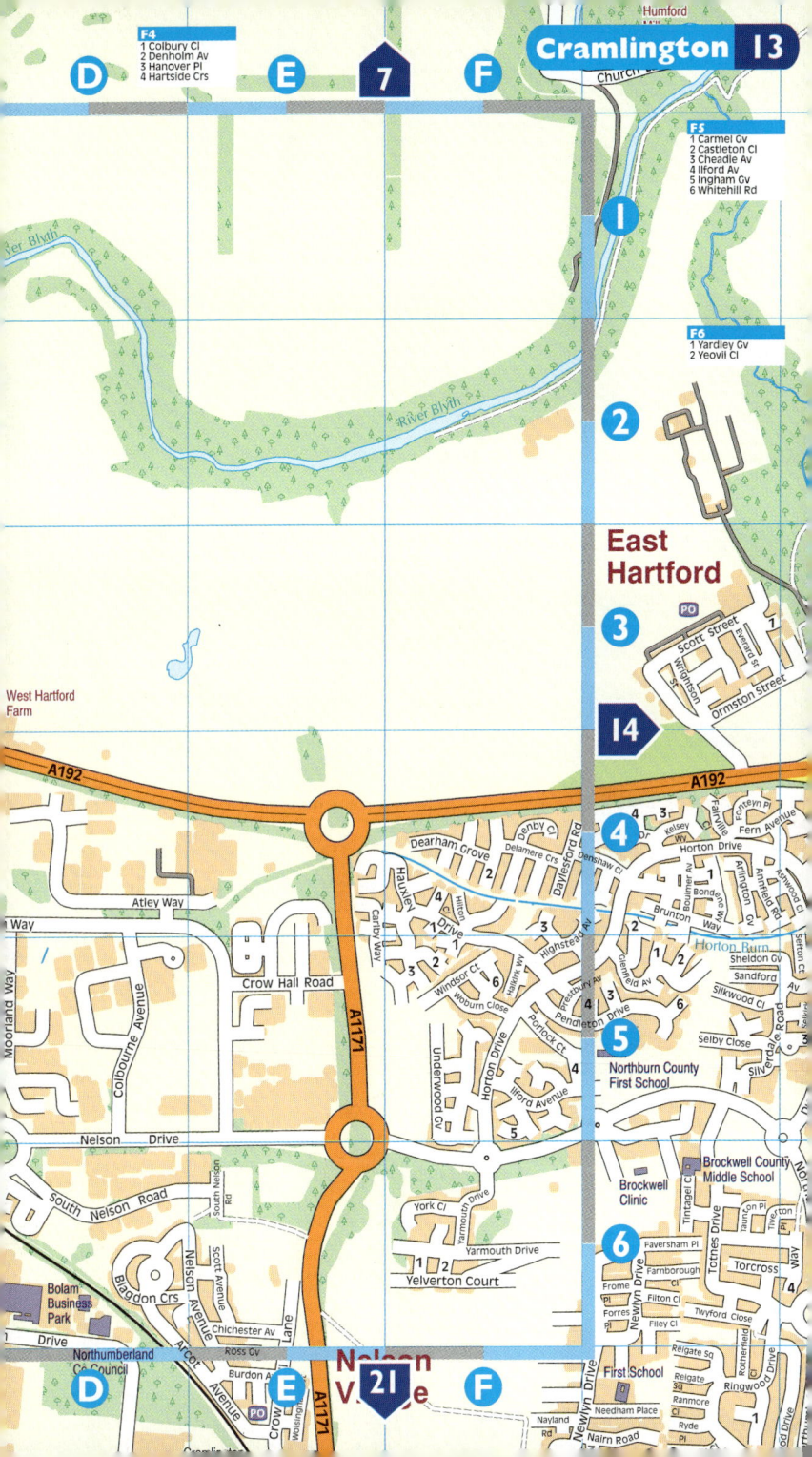

West Hartford Farm

PO

3

Scott Street
Wrightson St
Everard St
Ormston Street

14

A192

A192

Atley Way

Denby Cl
Dearham Grove
Delamere Crs
Daylesford Rd
Denshaw Cl

Kelsey
Fairvile
Fonteyn Pl
Fern Avenue

Hauxley
Hilton
Horton Drive
Wightson

4

Arlington
Annfield Cl
Boulmer Av
Bonde
Way
Brunton

Way

Cardew Way

Carbw Way

Horton Farm

Crow Hall Road

Colbourne Avenue

Moorland Way

Way

A1171

Windsor Ct
Woburn Close

Hawk Wy
Highstead Rd

Prestbury Av
Clenfield Av
Pendleton Drive

Sheldon Gv
Sandford
Silkwood Cl

Porlock Ct

5

Selby Close

Northburn County First School

Silverdale Road

Underwood Gv

Horton Drive

Ilford Avenue

Brockwell Clinic

Brockwell County Middle School

Tintagel Cl
Totnes Drive
Taunt on Pl
Tiverton
Torcross

Nelson   Drive

York Cl
Yarmouth Drive

Faversham Pl

6

Frome
Pl
Forres Pl

Farnborough Cl

Filton Cl

Filey Cl

Twyford Close
Newlyn Drive
Way

South Nelson Road

South Nelson Rd

Scott Avenue

Nelson Avenue

Yelverton Court

Yarmouth Drive

Newlyn Drive

Rotherfield

Ringwood Drive

Bolam Business Park

Blagdon Crs

Chichester Av

Ross Gv

Arcot Avenue

Lane

Relgate Sq
Relgate
Cl
Ranmore
Ryde
Pl

Drive

D E **21** F

Nelson Village

PO

Woolsington

Nayland
Rd
Needham Place
Nairn Road

A1171

14

A   8   B   C

Humford Mill

Church Lane

HORTON ROAD

B1505

A3
1 Mortimer Cha

Hathery Lane

A4
1 Bellevue Crs
2 Greenholme Cl
3 Kelfield Gv
4 Kemble Cl

1

A5
1 Gilsland Gv
2 Glynwood Cl
3 Parkham Cl
4 Pentland Cl
5 Pinewood Av
6 Plaistow Wy

River

2

A189

HORTON ROAD

East Hartford

PO

Scott Street
Wrightson
Everest St
Ormston Street

B4
1 Eastwood Pl
2 Ellerton Wy
3 Eton Cl

3

13

B5
1 Lincoln Rd
2 Lydbury Cl
3 Skipton Cl

A192

B1505

B1505

Dearham Grove
Delamere Crs
Daylesford Rd
Debenshaw Cl
Keston Dr
Kelsey
Fairville
Fern Avenue
Fotheryn Pl
Eastburn Gv
Edgefield Drive
Ellerton Wy

4

Hauxley
Hilton
Drive
Horton Drive
Boultmer Av
Bondee Wy
Arlington
Annfield Rd
Sefton Cl
Melrose

Brunton
Way
Horton Burn
Langton Drive
Millbrook Rd
Hastings Ter

Highsteel Cr
Glenfield Av
Sheldon Gv
Sandford
Lapford Dr

B6
1 Kettering Pl
2 Kinloss Sq
3 Kirkbride Pl
4 Tenby Sq

Hawk Wy
Astbury Av
Pendleton Drive
Silkwood Cl
Silverdale Road
Slaterk Ct
Durham Road
Avebury Place

5

Underwood Gv
Horton Drive
Ilford Avenue
Selby Close
Abingdon Sq
Aldenley Way

Cambo Way

A1171

Northburn County
First School
Burnside County
First School
Axminster Ct

A1061

A189

C5
1 Albion Wy

Shankhouse

York Cl
Yarmouth Drive
Yarmouth Dr

Brockwell County
Middle School
Brockwell
Clinic
Kirton Way
Kendal
Drive

6

C6
1 Bellburn Ct
2 Bowmont Dr
3 Cadleston Ct
4 Cairnglass Gn
5 Canonbie Sq
6 Drybeck Wk

Faversham Pl
Farnborough
Frome Cl
Filton Cl
Forres
Tintagel Cl
Totnes Drive
Torcross
Twyford Close
Taunton Pl
Twerton
Kendal
Wood
Rd
Eastlea First
School
Drybeck Ct
Dunsdale Drive

Nelson Village

First School
Reigate Sq
Rotherfield
Ringwood
Ryde Pl
Nairn Road
Newlyn Drive
Filey Cl
Northumbrian Road
Porchester Drive
Pent
Hayton
Hertford
Henley
Oxted Cl
Hazelmere
Hickstead
Huntington Drive

A   22   B   C

1 grid square represents 500 metres

D   E   9   F

A189

Golf
Course

1

Ortdridge Crs
St Mary's Dr
Welham
Chillingham Cl
Otterburn Ov
Cresswell Dr
Southfi

Pecket Cl
Witton Cl
Drudge
Stainton Av
Beatmen Rd
PO
Drive
Kreider Close
Horsforde

Low Horton
Farm

Blyth New
Delaval County
First School
PO
Winsna Cl
Warwick Cl

2
Beatrice Av
Plessey Road
2
1
Id
St Bede
Park Dr
Delaval Crescent
3
Winsna Cl
Delaval St

NEWCASTLE RD

**New
Delaval**

2
1
The Oval

3

Laverock Hall Road

16

Cottingwood

Cottingwood

A192

Laverock
Hall

LAVEROCK HALL ROAD

A1061

4

5

A192

Stickley
Farm

6

D   E   23   F

North Moor

A2
1 Beatrice Av
2 Cosser St
3 Horton Pl
4 St Bedes Rd

A3
1 Etal Rd
2 Laverock Pl

B1
1 Byron Av
2 Eighteenth Av
3 Embleton Dr
4 Keats Av
5 Thropton Av
6 Twentysecond Av

B2
1 Brockwell Ct
2 Cramlington Ter
3 Delaval Crs
4 East Dr
5 Hartley Ter
6 West Dr

C1
1 Eighth Av
2 Fenwick Av
3 Newlands Av
4 Newlands Pl
5 Twentieth Av
6 Twentyfifth Av

C2
1 Clifton Gdns
2 Glendford Pl

C3
1 Elstree Gdns

A1
1 Thorp Cl

NE24

10

A   B   C

Isabella Pit

Middle School

PLESSEY ROAD

Barras Av West

South View

New

Blyth New Delaval County First School

Beatrice Av

Plessey Road

New Delaval

First School

Warwick St

Carr Street

NEWCASTLE ROAD

SOUTH NEWSHAM ROAD

Newsham Surgery

Carlton Av

Seaton Av

Delaval Crescent

Park Drive

The Oval

Laverock Hall Road

Cottingwood Gn

South Newsham

A1061

A1061

Sandringham Drive

Lysdon Farm

15

Gc Co

Rothbury Av

St Mary's Cl

Chillingham Cl

Druridge Crs

Druridge Drive

Stanton Av

Wharton Street

Burns Av

Wordsworth Av

Newsham Rd

Newlands Rd

Seventh Av

Sixth Av

Ninth Av

Twelfth

Eighth

Fifteenth Av

Third Av

Twentysixth Av

Melville Av

Gosport Wy

Carsdale Av

Grately Av

Amershm

Earlswood

Esher Gdns

Eastwood

Epsom Wy

Dewberry Cl

Sweetbriar Wy

Juniper Cl

Hamstead Cl

Honister Wy

Hadrian Rd

Ingleston Gdns

Blagdon Dr

LC

LC

LC

LC

LC

LC

PO

PO

I grid square represents 500 metres

A   24   B   C

D E F

I

South Beach

2

3

4

5

6

B1523

A193 ROTARY WAY

Warkworth Av
Wansbeck Av
Acomb Av

Solingen

Estate

Wolmer Rd

Matthew Rd

O Solingen Est

Ashledore Rd
Atkinson Rd

Grebe

Amersham Rd

Guillemot

Osprey

Plover

Curlew Way

Dunlin

Kingfisher
Sandpiper Cl

Petrel Wy

shearwater
Cormorant

Deal

Dorking
Close

Shearwater
Way

Heron
Close

Tern Cl

Elder Close

Fulmar Drive

Mallard Wy

Avocet
Way

Kittiwake Close

Gull Albatross

ROTARY WAY A193

LINKS ROAD

B1329

Link House

Beachway

Links Road

NEWSHAM   ROAD

A193

Cemetery

LINKS ROAD

A193

Gloucester Lodge
Farm

LINKS

ROAD

A193

Hartley
Links

D E **25** F

Seaton Red
House Farm

Seaton Sluice
Middle School

Conway Grove

Alston
Grove

Astley Gr

18

A
B
Home
Farm
C

North Woo

I

Blagdon
Hall

Bog
House

2

Blagdon
Park

Leages Drive

3

Milkhope

Northumberland County

4

Newcastle upon Tyne

5

Brenkley

6

Gardener's Houses
Farm

A
31
B
C

I grid square represents 500 metres

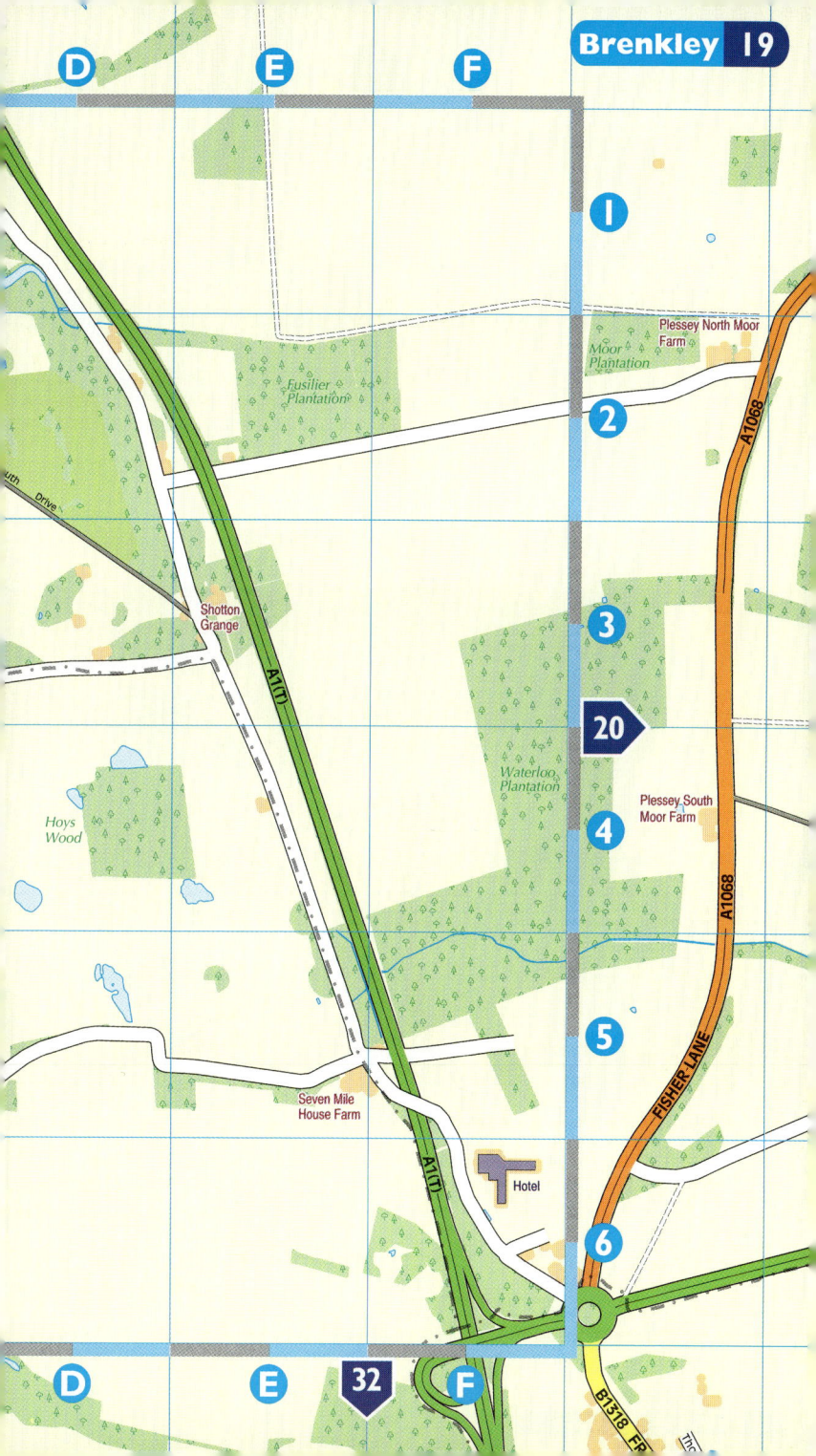

D   E   F

I

Plessey North Moor Farm

Moor Plantation

A1068

2

Fusilier Plantation

South Drive

3

20

Shotton Grange

Waterloo Plantation

Plessey South Moor Farm

4

A1068

Hoys Wood

A1(T)

5

FISHER LANE

Seven Mile House Farm

6

Hotel

A1(T)

D   E   32   F

B1318 FR

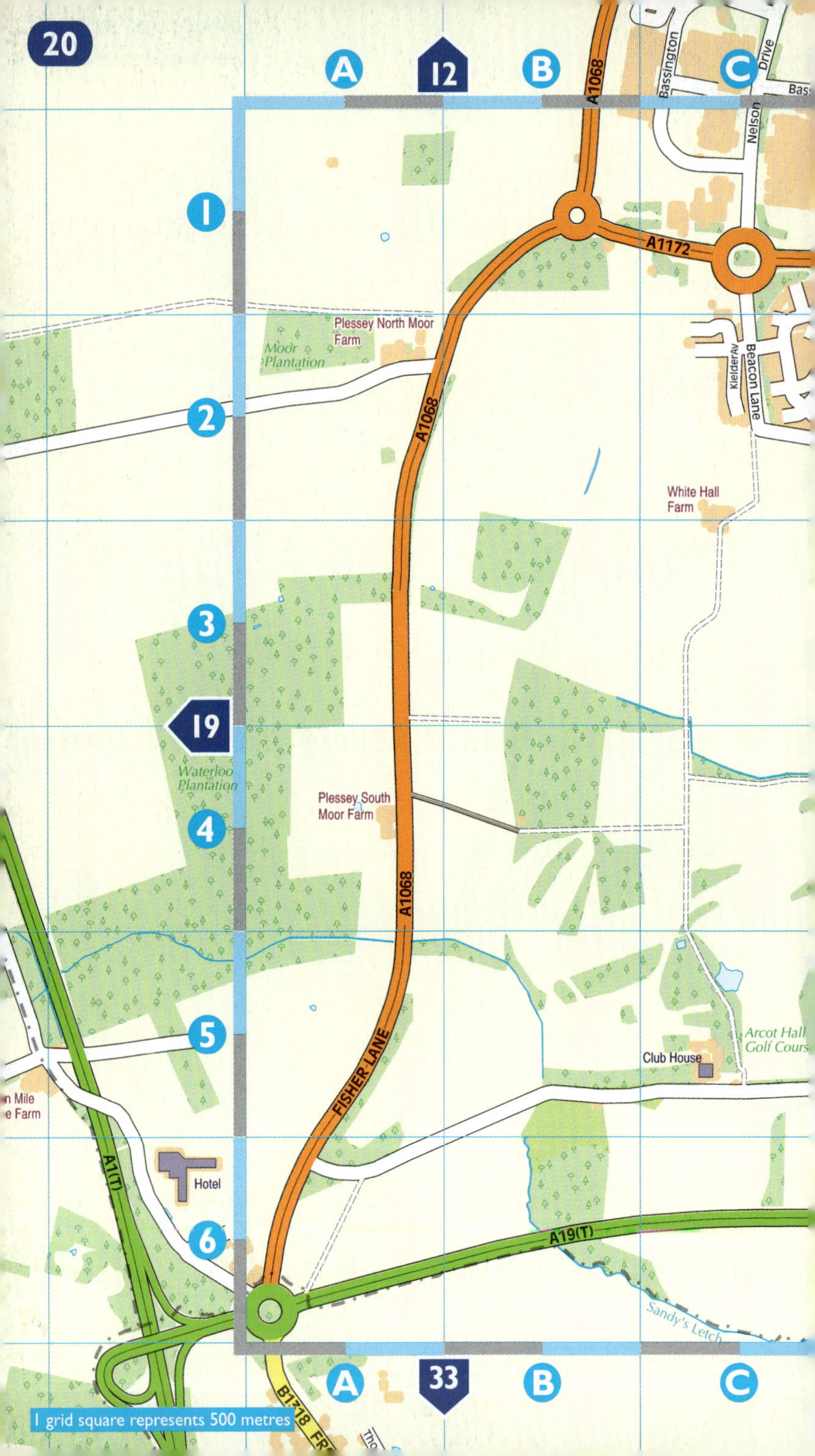

A

12

B

A1068

C

Bassington

Drive

Bas

Nelson

I

A1172

Plessey North Moor
Farm

Moor
Plantation

A1068

Kielder Avenue

Beacon Lane

2

White Hall
Farm

3

19

Waterloo
Plantation

Plessey South
Moor Farm

4

A1068

5

Arcot Hall
Golf Cours

Club House

n Mile
e Farm

A1(T)

Hotel

6

A19(T)

Sandy's Letch

B1318 FR

FISHER LANE

1 grid square represents 500 metres

D **E** **13** **F**

Yarmouth Drive
Faversham Pl

1 2 Yelverton Court

D2
1 Ladykirk Wy
2 Lytham Cl
3 Selbourne Cl
4 Shanklin Pl
5 Southwold Wy

Bolam Busin Park

Northumberland Co Council

Ross Gv
Burdon La

Blagdon
Winchester Av

A1171 Avenue
Alcot Dr
Crow Hall

Cramlington Station

Nelson Village

Forret
Filey Cl

Twyford Close
Orford Close

New

First School

Needham Place

Nayland Rd
Nail

Newm Drive

Ryde Pl
Romsey C

E2
1 Larriston Pl
2 Lindean Pl
3 Lochcraig Pl

Ran

Reigate
Rel

Ringwood Drive

Bassington Avenue
A1172

STATION ROAD

Sudbury Way
3 Safford Cl
Shiel Gdns
Salisbury
Sheringham Dr
5
4

Loughrigg Avenue

Longridge Way

Langdale Dr
Lindean Drive
Langdale Drive

Beaconhill

Beaconhill County First School

CRAMLINGTON

Melling Road

Malden Cl

Minting

Mirlaw Road
Morwick Cl
Melkridge Place
Mirlaw Rd

Medstone Avenue

Herdlaw

Hebron Way
Harwood Cl
Harnh

Hareside

Lancastrian Road

PO

Northumberland County Council
Forum

Way

Dudley Lane

B1326

Northumberland Mental Health NHS Trust

Parkside Middle

3

2

Dewsgreen

Allensgreen
Anstead Cl
Allensgreen

E3
1 Mirlaw Rd

Hillcrest Day Special School

2

Dipton Gv
3 2

Adderstone Av

F2
1 Mainstone Cl

St Pauls RC First School
Alexandra Way

Dewley
Anton Pl
Aller

Northumbria Road

Coanwo

Cornhill
Chipchase Av
Cambo

3

Doxford Place
1

Cateran Way

NORIAN RD

22
Peters Middle School

F3
1 Manningford Cl

Crofthead Dr

Cramond Way

Cragside
Cornford Way

Co

Beacon Lane

Stonelaw County Middle School

NE23

Grassington Drive
Carforth Close

4

Ripley Drive

Raynham Cl
7

6

Glenluce Drive
Ganton Av
Grey Av
Glencoe Av

First School
PO

Westerkirk

Gerrard Cl

F4
1 Grantham Pl

Cunn

Waterbeck Cl
Walkerburn

2 5

Grindon Cl

Richmond Way
Riabon
Richmond Way

Ripon Cl
Ruislip Place
Rochford Gv

Windermere

Windburgh Drive

Southlands Middle School

Westloch Rd
Waverton
Waverton

Wasdale
Whitburn Cl
Whitburn P

5

Southfield

Damdykes

LC

A19(T)

A1171

F5
1 Gilderdale Wy
2 Glenmuir Av
3 Gowanburn
4 Grosvenor Cl
5 Richmond Wy
6 Romford Cl
7 Roslin Wy

6

B1505

DUDLEY LANE

Hedgefield View

Orange Gv

Clover

A2
1 Aisgill Cl
2 Dalton Cl
3 Debdon Pl
4 Paradise Rw

A3
1 Doxford Pl
2 Dukesfield

A5
1 Gilderdale Wy
2 Whernside Pl

B1
1 Ormskirk Gv

B2
1 Brinkburn Av
2 Carham Av

B3
1 Barrasford Rd
2 Brownrigg Dr
3 Carlcroft Pl
4 Coldbeck Ct
5 Cranshaw Pl

B4
1 Cobden Rd
2 Coomside
3 Warenford Cl
4 Weetwood Rd
5 Whitelaw Pl
6 Wilkwood Cl
7 Woodhill Cl

C1
1 Hampton Cl

A1
1 Ringwood Dr
2 Station Rd
3 West Farm Ct

STATION ROAD

MORLAND WAY

A1171

MELLING ROAD

Lancastrian Road

DUDLEY LANE

NE23

Mayfield

Collingwood

Southfield

VILLAGE ROAD

Northumberland
County
Council Forum

Northumberland
Mental Health
NHS Trust

Parkside
Middle
School

Hillcrest Day
Special
School

First School

St Pauls
RC First
School

St Peters RC
Middle
School

Southlands
Middle
School

First
School

Cramlington
Football
Club

Cemetery

A189

A19(T)

B1505

B1326

I grid square represents 500 metres

D **E** **15** **F**

D3
1 Weldon Rd

E6
1 Meadow Cl
2 Murrayfield
3 Taynton Gv

I

North Moor Farm

A192

2

East Cramlington

B1326

A192

ood Crs

3

Double Re

24

School

A19

4

Middle School

Whytrigg Close

Linden Road

Western Avenue

E
E
W

Prospect Aven

Ancroft Road

5

Middle Farm

Atkinson House School

Thornbury Av

Whiteford Pl

Trinity Gv

Kestmere

Deneside

Dene Grove

Burnley

6

Front Street

Twickenham

Front Street

Hatfield Drive

Winton Cl

Kirkwood Cl

Murrayfield

Carrington Close

Hill Av

A190

Seghill County First School

PO

Forest Way

Front St

36

Barrowb

Yard Gdns

D **E** **STATIO** **F**

Barrass Av

The Close

The Crescent

A 16 B A5
1 St Stephen's Cl C

B5
1 Astley Gdns
2 Rothley Gv
3 Starlight Crs

I

C2
1 Maple Ct
2 Wansbeck Gv

2

C5
1 Ambleside Cl
2 Kearsley Cl
3 Wallington Ct

3

23

C6
1 Vanborough Ct

A192

PT326

First
School

4

SEATON
DELAVAL

Middle
School

Double Row

Allenheads

ASTLEY ROAD

A192

A190

Blyth St

Prospect Av

Mitford
Av

Doctors Surg

PO

Blyth Valley
Borough Council

Greenlands

Avenue Head
Farm

Seaton
Terrace

Western Avenue

Linden Road

Wynthrop Close

Park
Road

Sinclair Gdns

View PK

Park

Whitton

Prospect
Avenue

Glanton Av

Avenue
Road

AVENUE ROAD

Ridsdale Ct

Astley
Community
High School

A190

Elsdon

Fontburn Road

Nelington
Dr

Bavington
Road

Swinburn
Road

Mindrum Wy

Avenue

Swarland Road

Ancroft Road

Trinity Gv

Kenmere

Pine Grove

Burnley
Hill Av

Deneside

Hatfield Drive

Winton Cl

Kirkwood Cl

Trevors Cl

Twickenham
Whitleyford Pl

Thornbury Av

A190

A190

Newburgh
Av

Ashkirk Wy

Kyloe
Av

Acomb

Steward Av

Paston

Woodside Cl

Denham

Thornhill

Front St

ROAD

Barrowburn

Sandown Cl

A 37 B C

E6
1 Bardon Crs
2 Horsley Gdns

D E 17

A193

Hartley
Links

Seaton Sluice
Middle School

Conway Grove

Alston
Grove

Astley Gdns

Astley Gardens

I

Benfield
Grove

Denway
Grove

Franklyn
Avenue

Waring
Av

Romsey
St

Romsey
Dr

7
2
1

Astley
Gv

Seaton Red
House Farm

Naylor
Pl

Meadow

7
1

Derwent
Rd

New Hartley

Lookout
Farm

FOUNTAIN HEAD BANK

Westlands

St   Michael's   Avenue

St. Michael's Avenue

LCh

2

Lysdon Burn

A190

Seaton

+

3

26

AVENUE

4

5

Holywell County
First School

Holywell

6

Medburn Rd

Dunsdale   Rd

Northside
Pl

Tranwell

Kenshaw
Grove

Valley Rd

Seaton Crs

2

Holywell
Grove

Holywell Avenue

East Gra

Crow Hall
Farm

Brentwood

Avenue

Hedley

Hollinghill

Wylam Av

Choleford

Branchland
Dr

Holywell Dene Road

North T
Northumbe

North Ty

Southward Wy

Ridge Way

Dale
Top

Seaton Burn

Bank Top

D E 38 F

A   Hartley Links   B   C

A1
1 Hastings Av
2 Marden Ct

A2
1 Aidan Av

1

Seaton Sluice Middle School

Conway Grove
Benfield Grove
Denway Grove
Franklyn Avenue

Alston Grove
Waring Av
Ronan's St
Naylor Pl
Ronan's Dr
Meadow Rd

Astley Gdns
Astley Gardens
Astley Gv
Derwent Rd

C2
1 Collywell Ct
2 Waterford Cl

2
A190

Lookout Farm

FOUNTAIN HEAD BANK

Park Field Ter
Easdale
Westlands
Cresswell
The Seaburn Gv

The Links

West Ter
Collywell

PH

A193
Ponteland
Albert Rd
Taylor

Bay

C3
1 Southward Cl

Seaton

Seaton Sluice

Queens Road
PO
Southward
Clarence St
Elwin Road
Millway

3

25

Elwin Bd
Budworth Av
Malvern Road
Dereham
Granville Av

Melton Crs
Dereham Rd
Simonside
Greenwood Crs
The

4

NE26

Seaton Burn

5

Hartley West Farm

HARTLEY LANE

Holywell

East Gra
ne Road

6

Crow Hall Farm

A   39   B   C

North Ty
Northumbe

1 grid square represents 500 metres

D   E   F

1

2

3

Crag
Point

2

St Mary's
Wynd   **Hartley**

East End

A193

BLYTH

St Mary's or
Bait Island

St Mary's
Lighthouse

ROAD

5

6

Cemetery

D   Gerrard Road   E   40   F

The Links

Cranes

Brier

Road

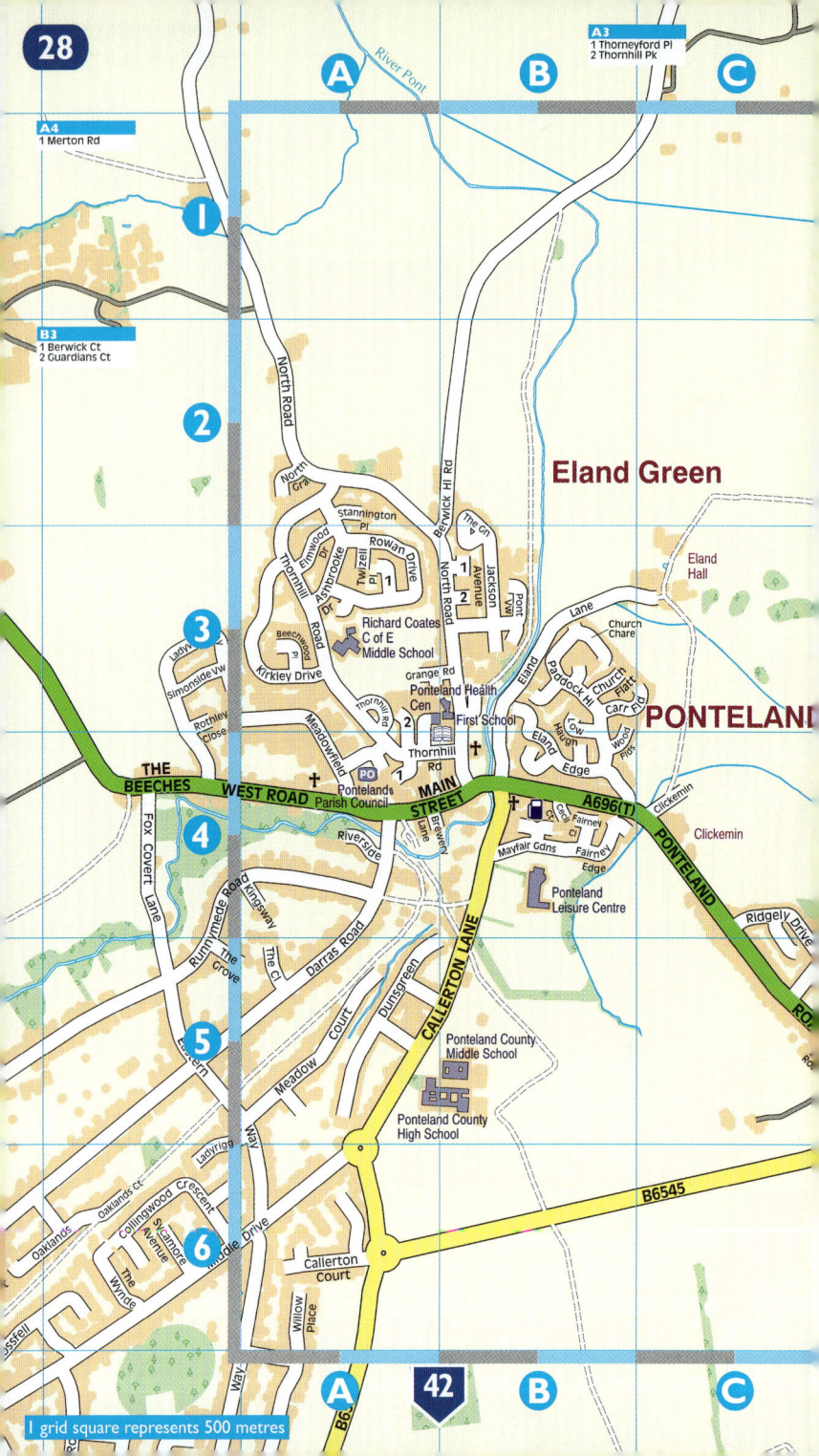

River Pont

A3
1 Thorneyford Pl
2 Thornhill Pk

A4
1 Merton Rd

1

B3
1 Berwick Ct
2 Guardians Ct

2

North Road

Eland Green

North Gra

Stannington Pl

Berwick Hi Rd

Eland Hall

The Gn

Elmwood Dr

Ashbrooke Dr

Twizell Pl

Rowan Drive

1

Jackson Avenue

North Road

Pont Vw

Lane

Church Chare

Thornhill Road

2

Richard Coates C of E Middle School

1

2

Eland

Paddock Hi

Church

Flatt

Carr Rd

PONTELAND

3

Ladywood

Beechwood Ct

Kirkley Drive

Grange Rd
Ponteland Health Cen

First School

Low Haugh

Wood Fids

Simonside Vw

Thornhill Rd

Eland Edge

Rothley Close

Meadowfield

Thornhill Rd

THE BEECHES

WEST ROAD

Ponteland
Parish Council

PO

MAIN STREET

A696(T)

Clickemin

PONTELAND

Clickemin

4

Fox Covert Lane

Riverside

Brewery Lane

Mayfair Gdns

Cess Ct

Fairney Ct

Fairney Edge

Ridgely Drive

RD

Runnymede Road

Kingsway

The Cl

The Grove

Darras Road

Dunsgreen

Ponteland Leisure Centre

5

Eastern

Meadow

Court

Way

CALLERTON LANE

Ponteland County Middle School

Ponteland County High School

B6545

Oaklands

Oaklands Ct

Collingwood Crescent

Sycamore Avenue

Ladyrigg

Middle Drive

6

The Wynde

Willow Place

Callerton Court

Rossfell

Way

B6

1 grid square represents 500 metres

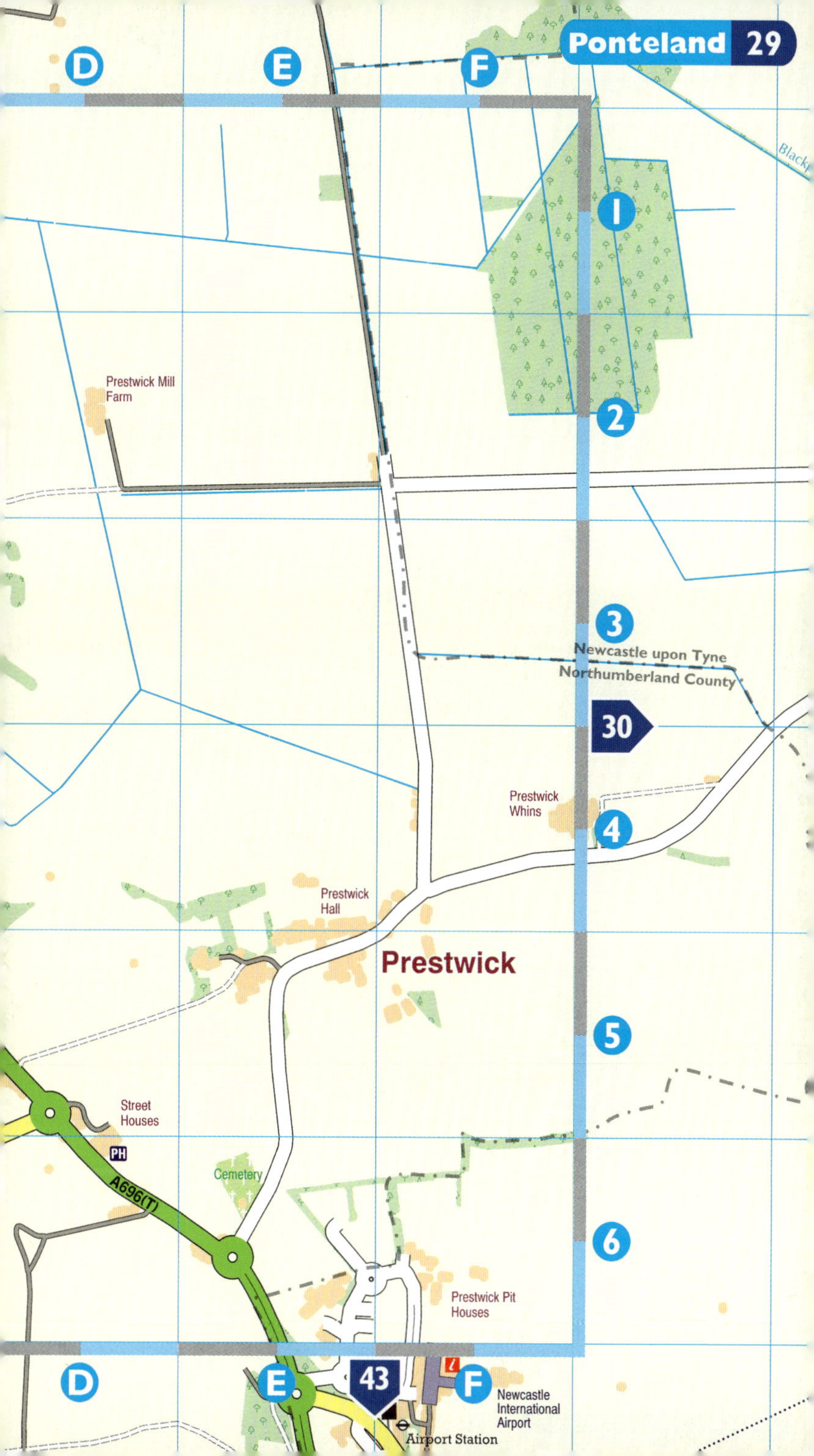

Black

I

2

Prestwick Mill
Farm

3

Newcastle upon Tyne
Northumberland County

30

Prestwick
Whins

4

Prestwick
Hall

Prestwick

5

Street
Houses

PH

A696(T)

Cemetery

6

Prestwick Pit
Houses

D **E** **43** **F**

Newcastle
International
Airport

Airport Station

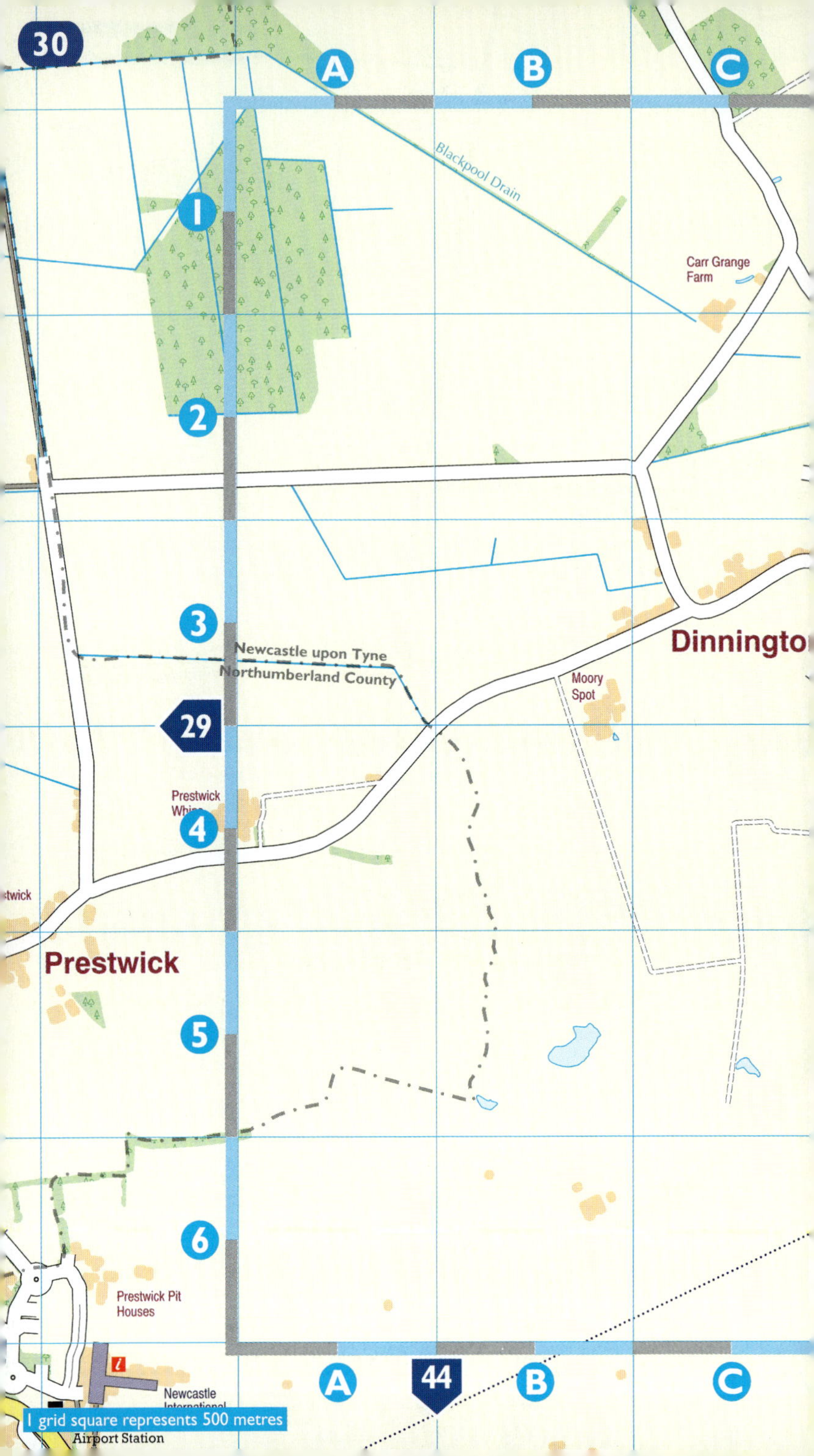

30

A **B** **C**

Blackpool Drain

1

Carr Grange
Farm

2

3

Newcastle upon Tyne
Northumberland County

Dinningto

Moory
Spot

29

Prestwick
Whins

4

stwick

Prestwick

5

6

Prestwick Pit
Houses

i

Newcastle
International
Airport Station

A **44** **B** **C**

1 grid square represents 500 metres

D
E
18
F

D2
1 West Acres

D3
1 Brenkley Cl
2 Farndale Cl
3 Horton Crs
4 The Winding

I

Gardener's Houses
Farm

D4
1 Havannah Crs
2 Merlay Dr

2

Mason

Mason Lodge

East Acres

Oakfield Grange
PO
North Vw
Front Street
Beech Avenue
Elm Av
Ash Av
Oak Av
Poplar Av
Pine Av
Sycamore Av

NE13

Hartley Burn

3

The Crest
Mitford Way
Castleway
Dunsley Gdns
Church Cl
Way
cken

Dinnington
Village
First School

Mill Hill

32

Sandy

4

Hack Hall

Main Road

Morley Hill
Farm

5

Coach Lane

6

D
E
45
F

32

A **19** B C

B5
1 Lola St

C4
1 Brunswick Gv
2 Grey St

1

C5
1 Arundel Cl
2 Austral Pl
3 Charles St
4 Highfield Pl
5 Norham Cl
6 Priory Pl
7 Simon Pl
8 Thorn Cl
9 Willows Cl
10 Windt St

2

North East Mason
Farm

NE13

Hartley Burn

C6
1 Belsay Av
2 Enid St
3 Lieven St
4 Ogle Av

● Big Waters
Nature Reserve

3

31

Mill Hill

4

Lane

Hack Hall

Waterford Pk

Drysdale Creser

Westfield Av

Dene Av

Cheviot View

Special
School

Darre

Wallington Avenue

Hawthorn Av

Brookside Av

Seaton Av

Sandison
Court

5

Morley Hill
Farm

**Brunswick
Village**

Sandford Ms

Mayfield
Pl

2
4

Beacon Dv

6

1
7
5

8

2

Meiness

PO

1

3 2

3 10

Coach Lane

6

Coach Lane

4

1

Newham Av

Arkle St

Fergu

Cas

Coach Lane

Hazlerigg

A **46** B C

A1(1)

Newcast

1 grid square represents 500 metres

D

E

20

F

D1
1 Garden Cl

D2
1 Brenkley Ct

I

High Barnes

D4
1 Aidan Cl
2 Elvet Cl
3 Netherton Gdns
4 Ovingham Gdns

2

Seaton Burn

B1318 FRONT STREET

Thorntree Avenue

Brenkley Way

Brenkley Ct

PO

BRIDGE STREET

B1318

DUDLEY LANE

Russlels Ct

Patience Av

Meadow

Six-Mile Bridge

Rookwood Dr

Drive

B1321

Cemetery

Green's Houses Farm

Green Cl

Seaton Burn Hall

D5
1 Dempsey Rd
2 High Rdg
3 Hornsea Cl
4 Norwich Av
5 Pader Cl
6 Remus Cl

3

McCracken Dr

Leigh Drive

Ravy

Chantry Drive

Gray Av

Swindoe Gdns

Ravleigh Drive

Havant Gdns

Hayes Walk

Boulmer Gdns

Ewesley Cl

Cranwell Drive

woodhorn Gdns

Morpeth Avenue

Warkworth Drive

Taylor Av

34

D6
1 Chelton Cl

4

A1(T)

Stalks Road

Winchester Wk

Canterbury

Longhirst Dr

Barrasford Dr

Harrow Gdns

Hazlewood Community Primary School

Woodlands Park Health Centre

Way

Worcester Way

Birchwood Av

Limewood Gv

Elmwood Av

Larchwood Av

Oakwood Av

Ashwood Gv

Pinewood Avenue

Wide Open

Cem

Cem

Cem

Pinewood Avenue

E2
1 Nearlane Cl

5

SANDY LANE

A1(T)

E3
1 Alnwick Ter
2 Wooler Sq

6

Farm Cottages

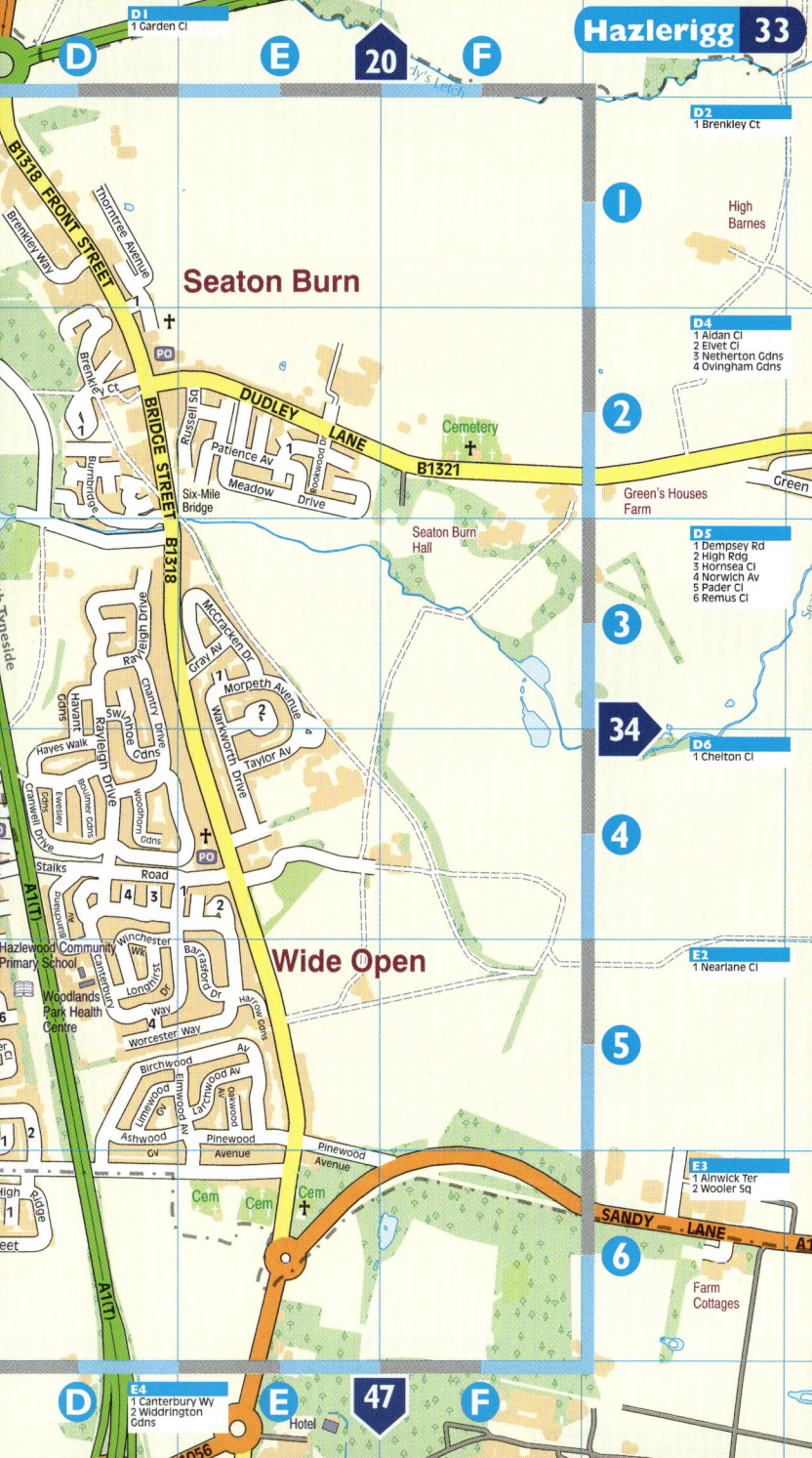

D

E

47

F

E4
1 Canterbury Wy
2 Widdrington Gdns

Hotel

A1056

Sandy's Letch

B2
1 Bamborough Ct
2 Green Crs

DUDLEY LANE

Hedgefield View

C2
1 Southfields

I

High
Barnes

Cloverhill Close

GRIEVES' ROW B1319

Ford View

Croft Cl

Primrose Clc

2

Cemetery

West Park VW

Elizabeth Cresent

Fordley

Dudley

B1321

Western Ter

2

Coquet Ter

Green Crs

Station Rd

MARKET ST

Ashkirk

Brookside

PO

Ashkirk

Green's Houses
Farm

Wansbeck Rd

Blyth Close

Wright D

B132

Seaton Burn
Hall

3

Seaton Burn

WEETSLADE ROAD

DUDLE

Weetslade Crs

33

B1319

Ethel St

4

LIME ROAD

A18

5

High
Weetslade

GREAT

KILLINGWOR

6

SANDY   LANE   A1058

Farm
Cottages

Great Lime Road

Newcastle

A189

North T

I grid square represents 500 metres

A19(T)

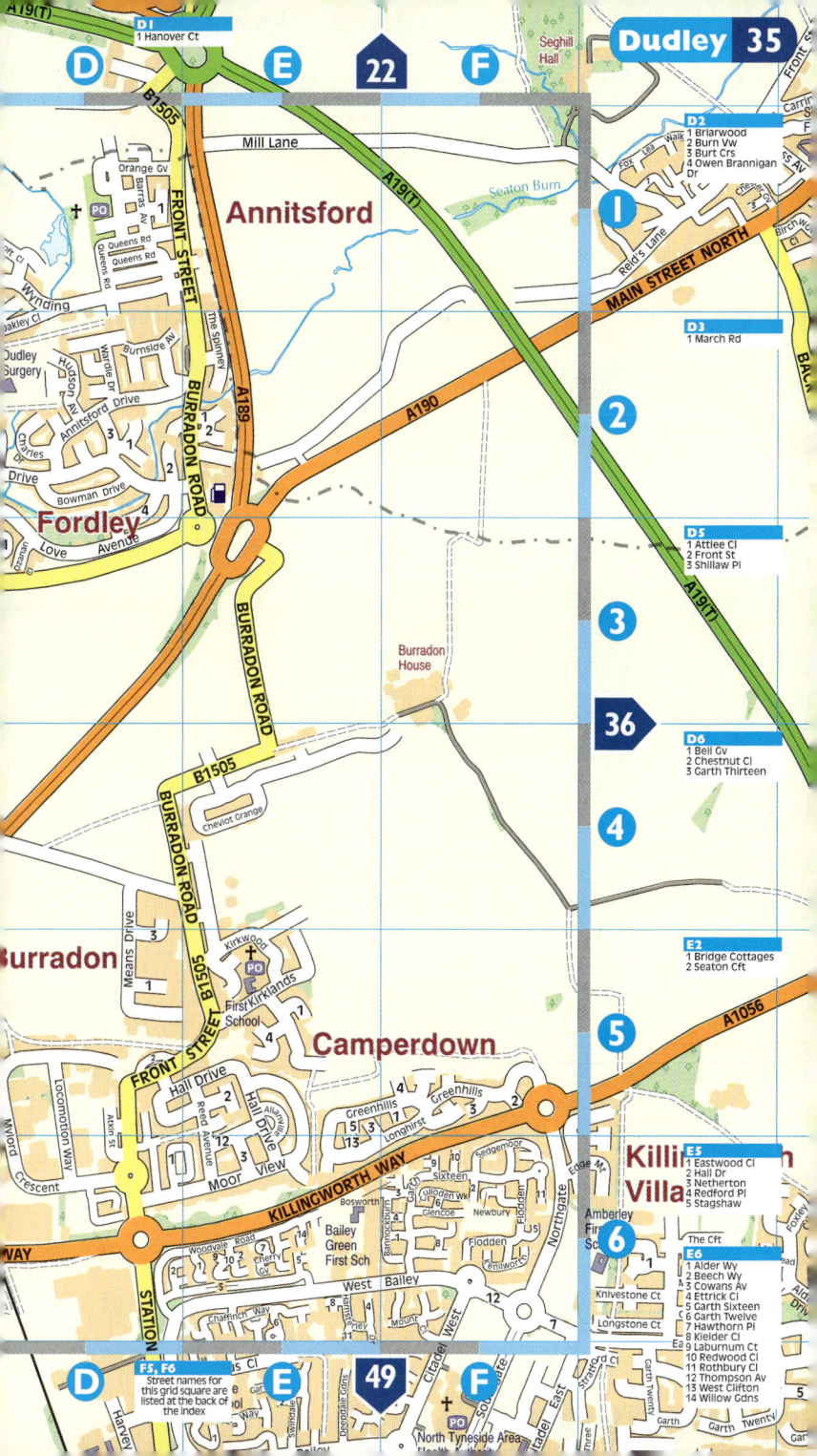

Dudley 35

D1
1 Hanover Ct

D2
1 Briarwood
2 Burn Vw
3 Burt Crs
4 Owen Brannigan Dr

Mill Lane

Annitsford

Seghill Hall

Seaton Burn

MAIN STREET NORTH

Reid's Lane

D3
1 March Rd

Orange Gv
Barras Av
Queens Rd
Queens Rd
PO
B1505
FRONT STREET
The Spinney
A189
A19(T)

Dudley Surgery
Hudson Dr
Wardle Dr
Burnside Av
Annitsford Drive
Charles Drive
Bowman Drive

Fordley
Love Avenue

BURRADON ROAD

A190

D5
1 Attlee Cl
2 Front St
3 Shillaw Pl

A19(T)

Burradon House

36

D6
1 Bell Gv
2 Chestnut Cl
3 Garth Thirteen

B1505
BURRADON ROAD
Cheviot Grange

E2
1 Bridge Cottages
2 Seaton Cft

Burradon
Meadow Drive
B1505
FRONT STREET
Kirkwood
PO
Kirklands
First Kirklands School

Camperdown

A1056

Killi... Villa...

E5
1 Eastwood Cl
2 Hall Dr
3 Cowans Av
4 Redford Pl
5 Stagshaw

Hall Drive
Reed Avenue
Allerwash
Moor View

Greenhills
Greenhills
Longhirst
Sixteen
Gilpeden Wk
Glencoe
Newbury
Edgemoor
Flodden
Northgate
Edge Mr

KILLINGWORTH WAY

Locomotion Way
Mylord Crescent
Atkin St
Bosworth
Bailey Green First Sch
Woodvale
Cherry
Kenilworth
Flodden
West Bailey
STATION

Amberley First Sch

The Cft

6

E6
1 Alder Wy
2 Beech Wy
3 Cowans Av
4 Ettrick Cl
5 Garth Sixteen
6 Garth Twelve
7 Hawthorn Pl
8 Kielder Cl
9 Laburnum Ct
10 Redwood Cl
11 Rothbury Cl
12 Thompson Av
13 West Clifton
14 Willow Gdns

Knivestone Ct
Longstone Ct

F5, F6
Street names for this grid square are listed at the back of the index

49

PO
North Tyneside Area Health
Chaffinch Way

A 23 B C

A6
1 Amberley Cha

A1
1 Burnside Vw
2 Hazelmere Dene
3 Warwick Cl

Kenmere
Deneside
Twickenham
Murrayfield
Wicket
Kirkwood Ci
Winton
Leyone Pl

Seaton Burn

A19(T)

I

Seghill Hall

Fox Lea Walk
Reid's Lane
Chester Rd
Carrington Close
Barrass Av

Seghill County
First School
PO

Forest Way
Front St
STATION ROAD

The Close
The Crescent
Oakfield Way
Birch Wood Cl

Barrowburn Pl
Bannard Gdns

Seghill

MAIN STREET NORTH

B6
1 Cragside Gdns
2 Cranham Cl
3 Darden Cl

A190

2

BACKWORTH LANE

Northumberland County
North Tyneside

B1322

C1
1 Esmaralda Gdns
2 Hazlitt Pl

A19(T)

3

Burradon House

35

4

B1322 BACKWORT

mperdown

5

A1056

High Farm

Greenhills
Greenhills
Longhirst
Sedgemoor
Sixteen
Gilpin Wk
Glencoe
Newbury
Flodden
Kenilworth
Edge Mr
Porthgate

TH WAY
2

Killingworth Village

Amberley First School

The Cft

Knivestone Ct
Megstone Ct
Longstone Ct

Crumstone Ct
East Bailey

Ahmead
Foley
Berkeley Ct
Ashley Close
Alderley Drive

Simonside Way
Blueburn Dr
Harwood Drive

KILLINGWORTH LANE B1317

Bailey
Mount
Citadel West
West
Southgate
East
Stratford Cl

North Tyneside Area

A 50 B C

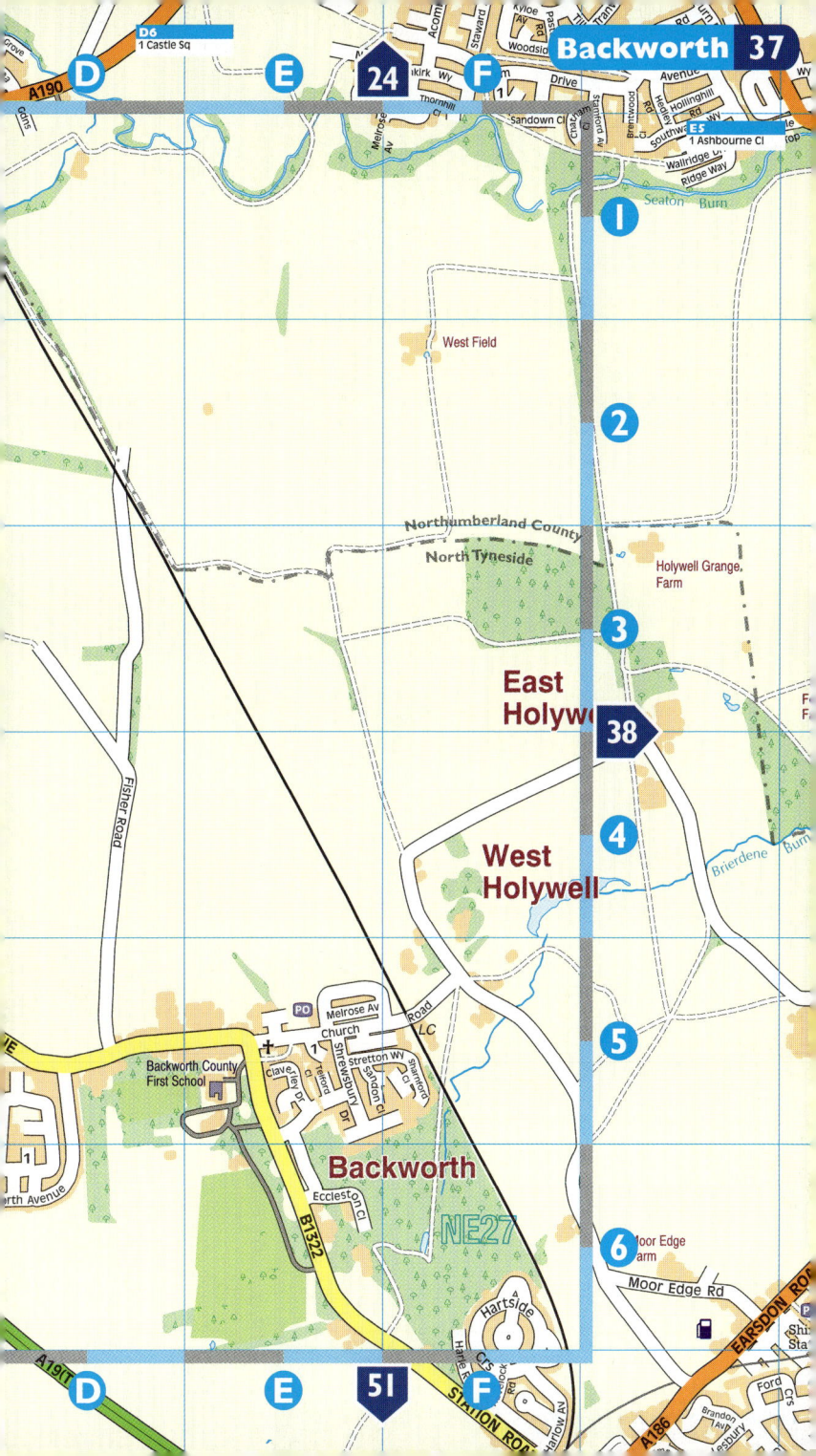

A190

D6
1 Castle Sq

D   E   24   F

Acom
Kyloe
Past
Tran

Woodsid

Avenue

Stamford Av

Hollinghill
Rd

southwa

E5
1 Ashbourne Cl

Wallridge Dr

Ridge Way

Drive

Sandown Cl

kirk Wy

Thornhill

Seaton Burn

I

West Field

2

Northumberland County

North Tyneside

Holywell Grange,
Farm

3

East
Holyw

38

Brierdene Burn

4

West
Holywell

Fisher Road

5

PO

Melrose Av

Church

Road

LC

Backworth County
First School

Clave
Vw Dr

Shrewsbury

Stretton Wy

Shretford

Shafford Cl

rth Avenue

1

Eccleston Cl

Backworth

NE27

B1322

Moor Edge
Farm

6

Moor Edge Rd

EARSDON ROAD

Shi
Sta

A19(T)

D   E   51   F

Hartside

Hare

STATION ROAD

Harlow Av

Ford

Brandon
Av

lesbury

A186

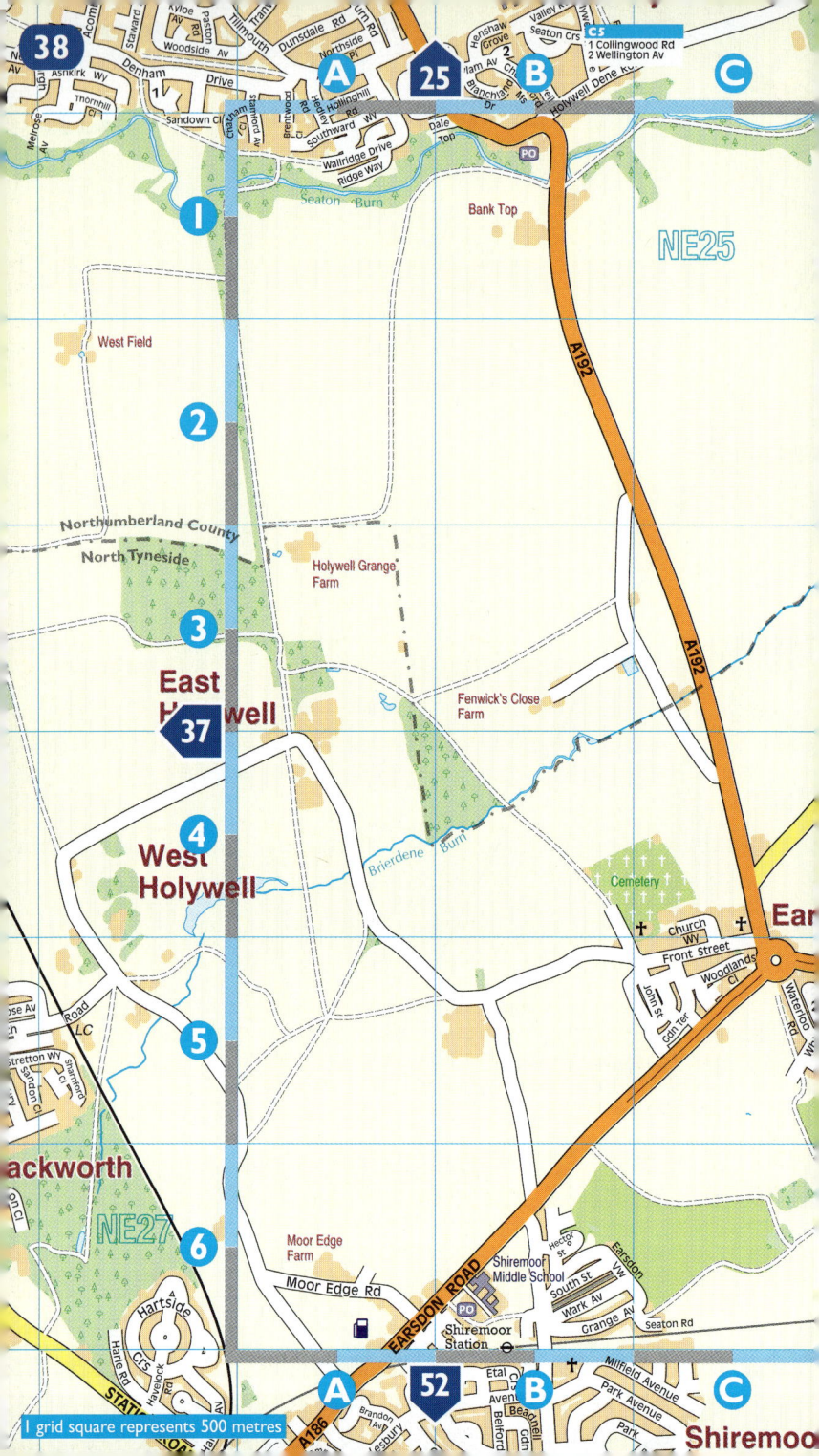

25

C5
1 Collingwood Rd
2 Wellington Av

A

B

C

Acomb
Kyloe
Stoward
Tranwell
Tillmouth
Dunsdale Rd
Northside Pl

Denham
Woodside Av
Thornhill Ct

Aslkirk Wy

Brentwood Rd
southward Wy
Hollinghill Rd
Wallridge Drive
Ridge Way
Dale Top

Sandown Cl

Seaton Burn

Henshaw Grove
Valley Vw
Seaton Crs
Branch End
Wham Av
Chevi

Holywell Dene Rd

PO

Bank Top

NE25

I

West Field

A192

2

Northumberland County

North Tyneside

Holywell Grange Farm

3

East
Holywell

37

Fenwick's Close Farm

A192

4

West
Holywell

Brierdene Burn

Cemetery

Ear

Church Wy
Front Street
John St
Gdn Ter
Woodlands Cl

LC

5

Stretton Wy
Stamford Cl
Sandon Cl

Waterlo Rd

ackworth

NE27

6

Moor Edge Farm

Moor Edge Rd

Hartside

Harle Rd
Havelock Cl

EARSDON ROAD

Shiremoor Middle School

PO

Hector St
Eardon Vw
South St
Wark Av
Grange Av
Seaton Rd

Shiremoor Station

STATION

A186

A
52
B
C

Brandon Av
Aylesbury
Etal Cl
Beach Gdn
Belford

Milfield Avenue
Park Avenue
Park

Shiremoo

26

D E F

I

D6
1 Harewood Crs

Crow Hall Farm

North Tyneside
Northumberland County

B1325

Brier Dene Farm

Gerrard Road
Garsdale Road
Westley
Westley Aver
Unton
Gerrard Cl
Brierdene
PO
Gorse
Hastings Av

ne Cres

Brierdene Burn

2

Whitley Lodge First School

St Lucia Close

Glebe School

Claremont
St David's Wy
PO

Claremont Surgery

Woodburn
Square
Woodburn Drive
Nevis
Carolyn Wy
Willoughby Drive
Carolyn Crs
Cragside
Longridge Drive
Monkridge
Rothey
Ross Wy

Ashton Rd
Grenville Dr
Woodburn Drive

Beaumont Drive
Beaconsdale
Darian
Dipton
Dachet Rd
Chevington
Grenville St
Martins
Claremont
Dene
Shaftesbury

3

40

Huntly Rd
Earnshaw
Haddington
Hillsden Way
Cranleigh
Craster Av
Chesters
MONKSEATON DRIVE

Beaumont
Calnsborough
Well Ridge Cl
Hertford Cl
Hascombe
Cl
First School

Whitley Bay High School

Well Rdg
Red House
Caterton
Close
Hepscott St

Westgate
Ashbury
Meldon
Thornbury
Dr
Cheldon
Dene Gdns
Holywell

The Ridings
Mill Dyke Cl
Beckwill Gv

Beaumont Park Surgery

4

Alder Gv
Denehom
Ivanhoe
Denebank
The Dene
Langdale
Hartley Avenue

Monkseaton

North
MONKSEATON DRIVE
Churchill St
1
Bilkdale
Valley Gardens
Haselene
Hillfield
Hermison
Uplands
The Dene
2
Windsor Road
Seaton Crs
Mor Stat

A192
Hesleyside Rd
EARSDON ROAD
Carnoustie Ct
Turnberry Newsteads
Fairways
Lythe
Murfield
Ashbrooke
Back La
Pykerley
Petron Ter
Percy
Seaton
Front
Street

5

Seaton Rd
Burnbank
Warwick Rd
Wilton
Haddon
Dve
Wentworth Cl
West Monkseaton Station
Sandown
Brantwood Avenue
Beechwood Av
Woodleigh Rd
Monkseaton Clinic
Middle School
St George's

Kielder Road
Ludlow Dr
Wilton Cl
Arundel Drive
Church
Sandringham Drive
Marina Drive
Marina Drive
Mitchell Av
Oakland Av
Elmwood Rd
Crawford

First School
PO
Thorntree
Harewood Crs
Grange Park

EARSDON ROAD

Eastward Gn
Horn
Fairfield Gn
Fairfield Drive
Brantwood Avenue
Beaumont Av
Eastfield Av
Westfield
Homwood Rd
Meadow Rd
Dale Rd
Paignton
Cauldwell Cr
Wembley Av
The Lane
Closefield Grove

6

First School

Medical Cen
PO
Monks Av
Camberra
Seatonville
Crs
Melbourne Ct
Springfield
Churchill Av
Haig
Roker
Vernon
Beverley

A192

Caulwell Av
Drumoyne
Townsville Av
Selwyn Av
Langley Av
Gardens
Oaktree Gdns
Cedar

D E F

West Monkseaton

MONKSEATON
A192

A5
1 Highbury
2 Holmlands

B2
1 Grenada Cl
2 Grenada Pl
3 St John's Cl
4 St John's Pl
5 St Vincent's Pl
6 St Vincent's Wy

C4
1 Marine Av

Brier Dene Farm

Cemetery

The Links

Gerrard Road
Garsdale Road
Westley Avenue
Gorsedene Road
Hastings Avenue
Brier Dene Crescent
Craneswater
Brierdene Rd
Grenada Drive

Brierdene Burn

Whitley Lodge First School

Glebe School

Claremont Footcare Surgery
St Mary's Avenue
Links Avenue
Kingston Drive
Hamilton Drive
Western Way
Woodburn Drive

Claremont Drive

Astley Drive

THE LINKS

A193

Whitl
Sand

A1148

Madeira Avenue
Claremont Avenue
Brighton Rd
Eversham Rd
Davison
King's Road
Queen's Avenue
Windsor Gdns
Kew Gdns
Eastbourne Gdns
Cliftonville Gdns
Glendale
Bournemouth Gdns
Ventnor Gdns
Cromer Gdns

First School
Beaumont Park Surgery

Monkseaton

MONKSEATON DRIVE

Whitley Bay High School

39
First School

Valley Gardens
Hillcrest
The Dene
Hartley Avenue
Langdale
Monkseaton Station
Norham

West Monkseaton Station

EARSDON ROAD

Brantwood Avenue
Belmont Av
Mitchell Av
Westfield Av
Eastfield Av
Dale Rd

Windsor Road
Back La
Pykerley Road
Front Street
Monkseaton Clinic
Middle School
St Ronan's Rd
Kenilworth Road
The Gardens
St Georges
Beverley
Queen's Dr
Grosvenor Drive

A192 SEATON

A191 HILLHEADS ROAD

PARK ROAD
Elmwood Grove
Doctors Surg
First School
Marine Avenue Medical Cen
Holly Av
Beach Av
Park Pde
Roxburgh Ter
Doctors Surgery

Medical Cen

First School

Marden Bridge Middle School
Lovaine Av
Hotspur Avenue

Whitley Bay Cricket Club
Whitley Bay Rockcliff RFC
Whitley Bay Ice Rink
Whitley Bay Football Club

54

I grid square represents 500 metres

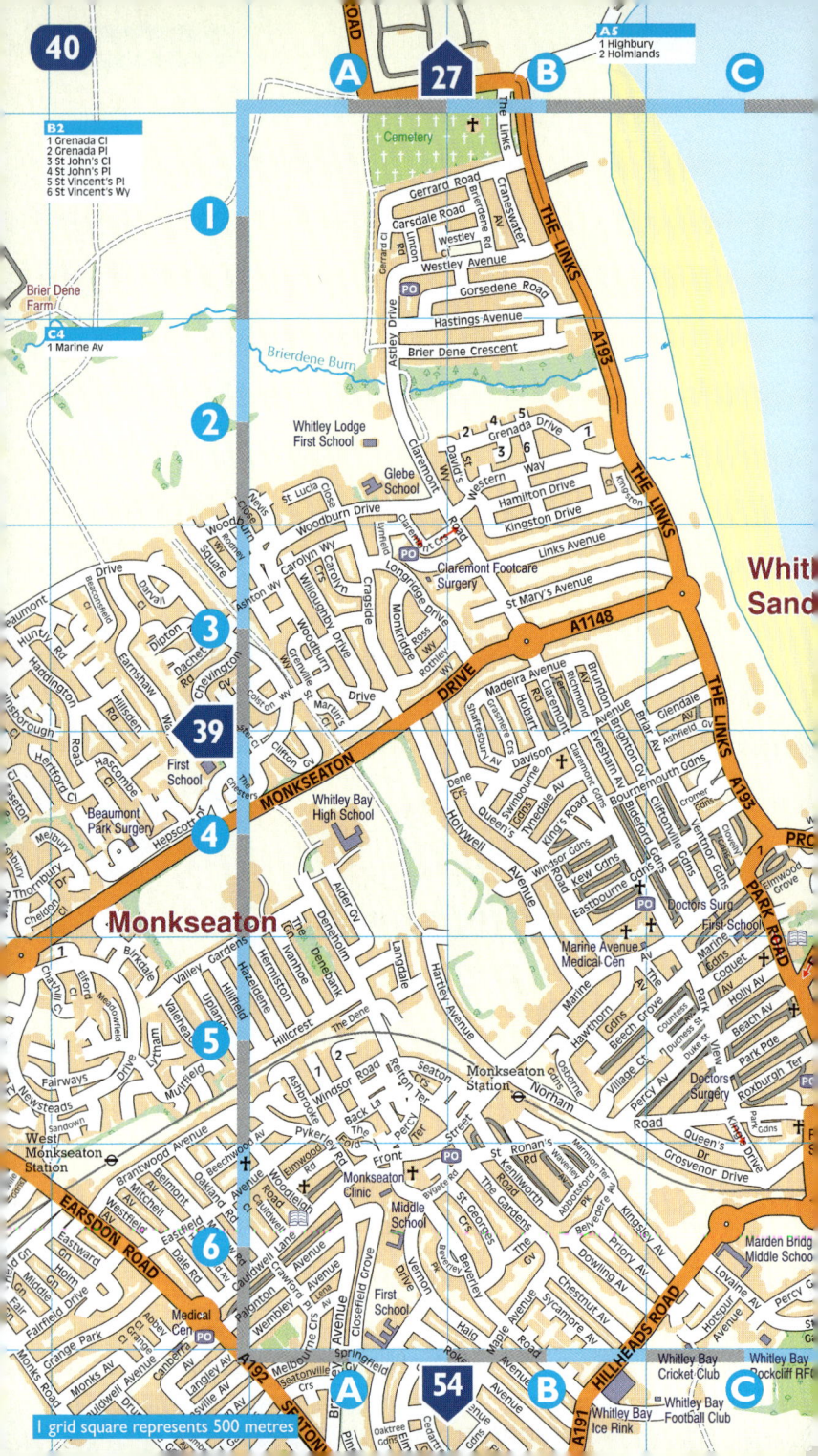

D **E** **F**

1

2

3

4

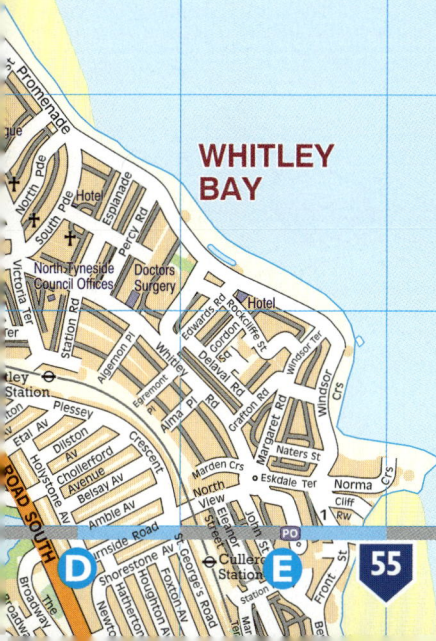

**WHITLEY
BAY**

Promenade

North Pde

South Pde

Esplanade

Percy Rd

Victoria Ter

Station Rd

North Tyneside
Council Offices

Doctors
Surgery

Hotel

Edwards Rd

Rockcliffe St

Gordon
Rd

Delaval Rd

Windsor Ter

Windsor
Crs

Whitley Rd

Algernon Pl

Earsdon

Station

Piessey

Eta Av

Dilston
Av

Chollerford
Avenue

Belsay Av

Amble Av

Crescent

Alma Pl

Marden Crs

North
View

Eskdale Ter

Margaret Rd

Grafton Rd

Naters St

Norma
Cliff
Rw

Burnside Road

Shoreston Av

Houghton Av

Hatherton

Newc

The

Broadway

ROAD SOUTH

St George's Road

Foxton Av

Cullercoats
Station

PO

John St

Elsdon St

Bella St

Front St

Mar

5

6

D **E** **55** **F**

Callerton
Court

Willow Place

A

28

B

C

The Wynde

Oak...

Middle...

more

CROSSFELL

Willow Way

B6323

CALLERTON LANE

1

Eastern Way

Whinfell Road

Hawthorn Way

Woodlands

Whinbank

Queensway

High View

Edge Hill

Edgewood

Deyncourt Close

Woodend

Whinbank Way

Woodvale

2

Callerton Hall

High
Callerton

Hill Pk

Callerton Hall

Hold House
Farm

Northumberland C...

Newcastle upon...

3

Northumberland County

Newcastle upon Tyne

B6323

4

Black
Callerton

Callerton
Grange

5

Calle...on
Lane End

Broomhall
Farm

6

Crescent Fa...

Lough
House

STAMFORDHAM ROAD

B...

B6323

A

58

B

C

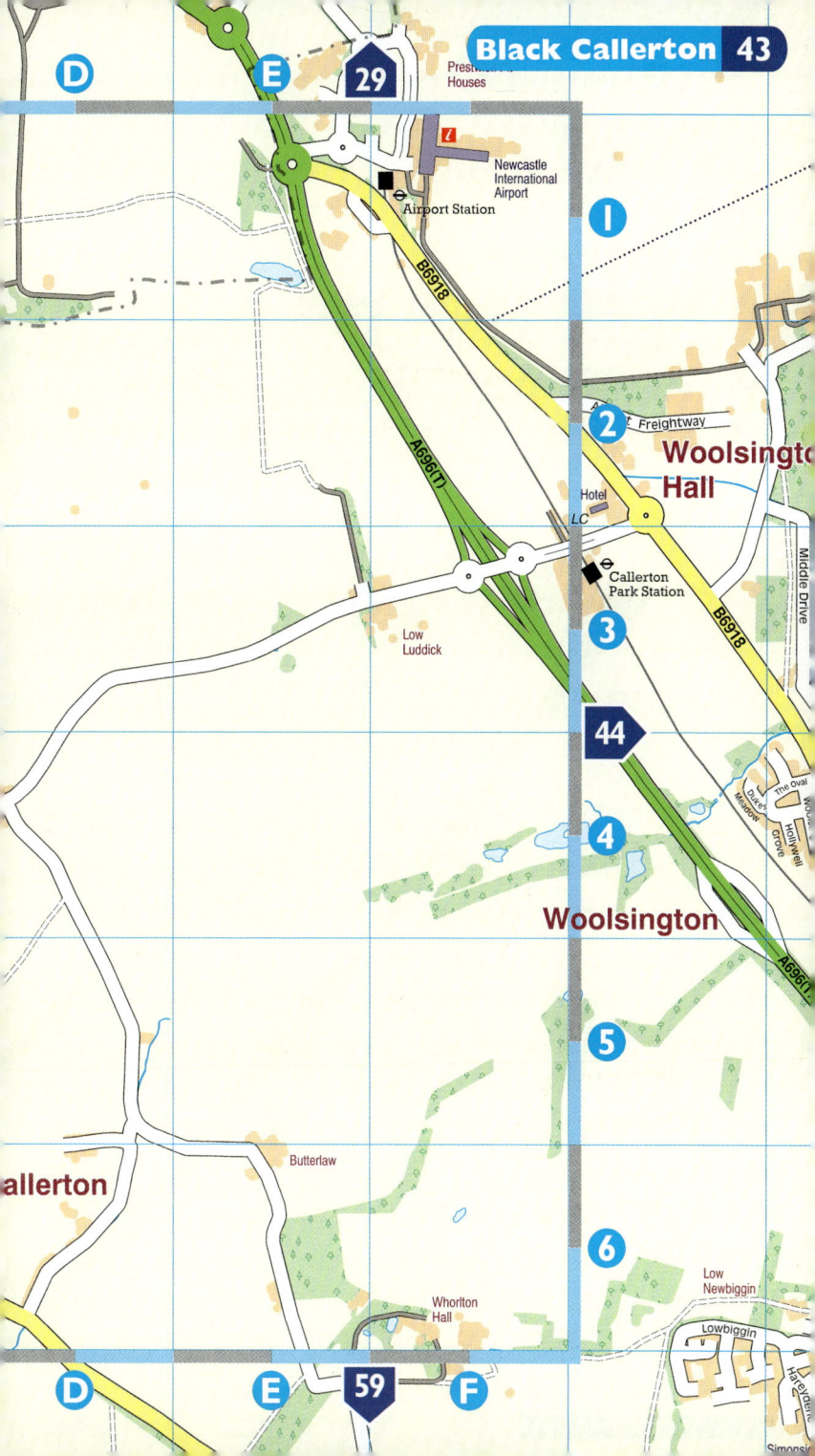

D

E

29

Prestwick
Houses

i

Newcastle
International
Airport

Airport Station

I

B6918

A696(T)

2

Airport Freightway

Woolsington
Hall

Hotel

LC

Callerton
Park Station

3

Middle Drive

Low
Luddick

44

4

The Oval

Duke's Meadow

Hollywell Grove

Woolsington

B6918

A696(T)

5

allerton

Butterlaw

6

Low
Newbiggin

Lowbiggin

Whorlton
Hall

Haydales

Simonsi

D

E

59

F

Prestwick Pit
Houses

A 30 B C

Newcastle
International
Airport

Airport Station

I

B6918

A696(T)

Woolsington
Hall

Airport Freightway

**Woolsington
Hall**

2

Hotel

LC

Callerton
Park Station

3

Low
Luddick

Middle Drive

B6918

South Drive

43

4

The Oval

The Paddock

Duke's
Meadow

Hollywell

Woolsington Gdns

Woolsington
Park South

South Drive

Woolsington

Green Lane

A696(T)

PONTELAND ROAD

Bullock
Steads

5

**Kenton
Bankfoot**

6

Whorlton
Hall

Low
Newbiggin

Lowbiggin

Newbiggin Lane

Bluebell
Dene

Eastgarth

Meadowdene

Simonside

Road

A 60 B C

D **E** **31** **F**

D5
1 Elstree Ct

D6
1 Honiton Ct

I

West Brunton Farm

E4
1 Hersham Cl

2

Sunnyside

Middle
Brunto
Farm

Brunton Lane

E5
1 Kirkham Av

3

46

E6
1 Belvedere Pkwy
2 Ilminster Ct

Ouse Burn

4

Brunton Bridge
Farm

Kingston

Park

Launceston Ct

Huntingdon Ct
1 2

Hereford

Farm Ct

Road

Fawdon
1

Woodend Way

Soulby Ct

Skelton Ct

F4
1 Aberdeen Ct
2 Hersham Cl

Chicheste Ct

2 4

8 5
Wercop

Newcastle
Falcons Rugby
Football Club

Epsom Ct

Brunton

Fawdon Lane

Hastings Av

Windsor Way

7
6

Lichfield Cl

Drive
Cresswel
Sch
Pri

Brunton Rd

Road

Lancing Ct

Chesleigh Av

Windsor Way

Hersham Ct

Colnbrook

Marlborough

Warwick Ct

5

Fawdon

Hazlew

Dykefield Avenue

Fawdon

Amherst Road

Derrington Road

Ferrisdale

F5
1 Faversham Ct
2 Hawkshead Ct
3 Lancaster Ct
4 Ousby Ct
5 Wraysbury Ct

Tedmorton Cl

1

Brunton Rd

Brunton
Road

Minverton Ct

Stuart

Kingston
Park Station

LC

Kingston
Park

Witton Rd

6

MAIN ROAD

The Crs

Wilmington Ct

Kingston Park
Primary School

PO

Belvedere
Retail Park

Redland

Rowan

Hillview
Surgery

Emden Rd

Bank Foot
Station

erton Road

The Gables

Vexille

Linacre Cl

Thornbury Cl

Tudor
Way

Tudor Way

Kyaford Ct

Somerton

Penterton Ct

Kingston Pk
Av

1

Brodrick

Carstaile Rd

Saxforms

Hillview

1

Apsley

Crs

Avenue

2

3

Kinros

Rowan Road

D **E** **61** **F**

696(T)

PONTELAND ROAD

Beaminster
Wy

Brunton Lane

A1(T)

Avenue

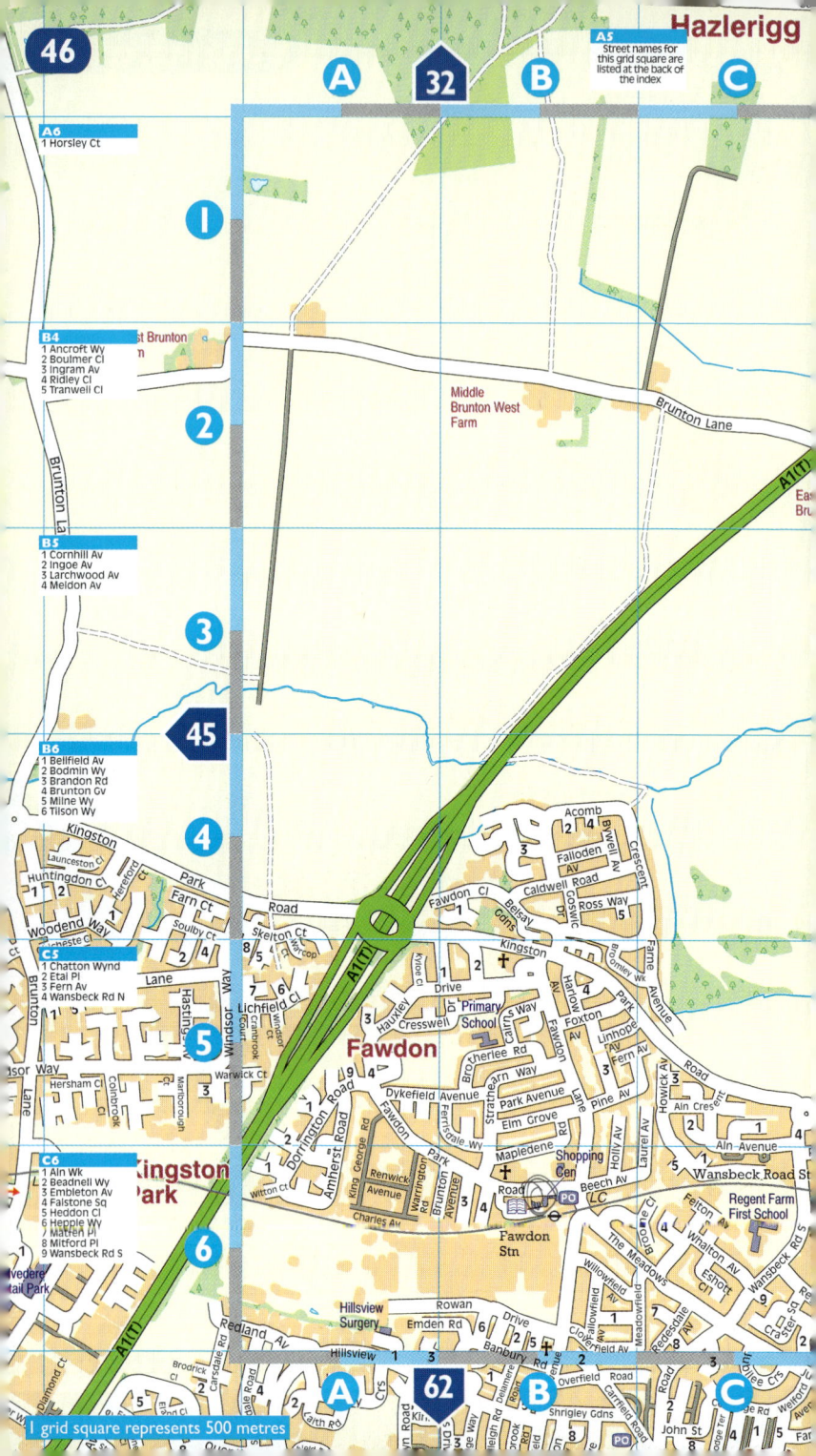

46

A 32 B

A5 Street names for this grid square are listed at the back of the index

C

1

A6
1 Horsley Ct

B4
1 Ancroft Wy
2 Boulmer Cl
3 Ingram Av
4 Ridley Cl
5 Tranwell Cl

2

Middle Brunton West Farm

Brunton Lane

Brunton La

A1(T)

East Bru

B5
1 Cornhill Av
2 Ingoe Av
3 Larchwood Av
4 Meldon Av

3

45

B6
1 Belfield Av
2 Bodmin Wy
3 Brandon Rd
4 Brunton Gv
5 Milne Wy
6 Tilson Wy

4

Kingston

Launceston Cl
Hereford Cl
Huntingdon Cl
Park
Farn Ct
Road

Acomb
Bywell Av
Failoden Av
Crovic Dr
Caldwell Road
Ross Way
Crescent

Woodend Way
Soulby Ct
Skelton Ct
Mercop

C5
1 Chatton Wynd
2 Etal Pl
3 Fern Av
4 Wansbeck Rd N

Lane
Hastings Way
Windsor Way
Lichfield Court
Crabtrook
Kirton Ct

Fawdon Cl
Belsay Gdns
Kingston
Kyloe Ct
Drive
Primary School
Harlow Av
Foxton Av
Fawdon
Broomley Wk
Farne Avenue
Linhope Av
Fern Av

5

Hersham Cl
Colnbrook
Warwick Ct
Marlborough

Hauxley
Cresswell
Kherlee Rd
Strathearn Way
Park Avenue
Pine Av

Fawdon

Dykefield Avenue
Elm Grove
Holly Av
Laurel Av

Howick Av
Aln Cresct
Road
Aln Avenue

C6
1 Aln Wk
2 Beadnell Wy
3 Embleton Av
4 Falstone Sq
5 Heddon Cl
6 Hepple Wy
7 Matfen Pl
8 Mitford Pl
9 Wansbeck Rd S

Kingston Park

Dorrington Road
Amherst Road
King George Rd
Renwick Av
Warrington Rd
Brunton Avenue
Beech Av
Mapledene

Shopping Cen
PQ
LC
Wansbeck Road

Feiton Av
Whatton Av
Eshott Cl
Regent Farm First School

Belvedere Retail Park

A1(T)

Witton Ct
Charles Av

Fawdon Stn

Willowfield
Meadowfield
Redesdale Cl

The Meadows

6

Hillsview Surgery
Rowan
Redland Rd
Carsdale Rd
Emden Rd
Drive
Banbury Rd
Clover Field Av

A1(T)
Brodrick Cl
Hillsview

A 62 B

Overfield Road
Shrigley Gdns
PQ
John St

C

33

D2
1 Beverley Cl
2 Clinton Pl
3 Melrose Cl

D E F

D5
1 Berkeley Sq
2 Kielder Wy

Hotel

A1056

North Brunton

Newcastle Racecourse

I

D6
1 Amble Wy

High Gosforth Park

2

GREAT NORTH ROAD

B1318

Sherwood Place

Northumberland County Council

E2
1 Queens Ct

Queensway

Grenville Dr

Norwood Avenue

Brunton Lane

Easdale Avenue

Glanton Avenue

Gosforth Lake

3

Lincoln Gr

Westwood Road

Polwarth Road

Polwarth Drive

PO

Davenport Dr

Ferndale Av

Kingsley Avenue

Newlands

Brackenfield

Summerhill

Belmont

Bellingham Av

Ferndale Av

South Bend

Greenfield Rd

Princes

Waterbury Rd

Clayworth Road

Layfield Rd

Park Drive

Polwarth Crs

South Ridge

Milford Gdns

Princes Cl

Fairway Close

The Fairway

Golf Course

Northern Rugby Club

48

E3
1 Hartside Pl
2 Inglewood Pl
3 Linwood Pl

McCracken Close

Greystoke park

Bridge Park

Fencer Ct

Saxilby Dr

Willerby Drive

Exelby Close

Flaxby Cl

Swainby Cl

Rugby Close

Melmerby Cl

Ousel Burn

NE3

Cresmere Pl

Whitebridge

4

E5
1 Langholm Rd
2 Marlborough Ap
3 Whitebridge Ct

Sinderby Cl

Burnside

Reay

Broadway E

Celandine

5

Grange Road

Granville Road

Linthorpe Road

Strathmore Road

Broadway East First School

Hartford Road

Heathery Lan

Woodlea Gardens

Briarwood Av

F3
1 Beech Cl
2 Chapel Pl
3 Heathfield Pl
4 Juniper Cl
5 Kilnshaw Pl
6 Low Gosforth Ct

West Avenue

Broadway

Marlborough

Cranbrook Av

Kingsway Av

Princes Avenue

Westbourne Av

Kielder Way

B1318

PO

Harewood Road

Links Green

Fernwood Avenue

Rosewood Av

Hollywood Drive

Hollywood Avenue

6

Glanton Wynd

Kirkley Cl

Coquet Av

Norham Av

Park

Leesbury

Rothbury

Whitton Wy

Holystone Av

Ware Cl

Grange First School

St Charles RC Primary School

Knightsbridge

Gosforth High School

Regent Centre Station

The Open University

Middle School

Christon

Regent Farm Rd

Hollywood Crs

Hollywood

Carnt Close

Cheswick

Archbishop Runcie C of E School

Gosforth Industrial Est

Rydal Road

GOSFORTH

D E **63** F

F4
1 Charleswood
2 Ferriby Cl
3 Navenby Cl
4 Scalby Cl

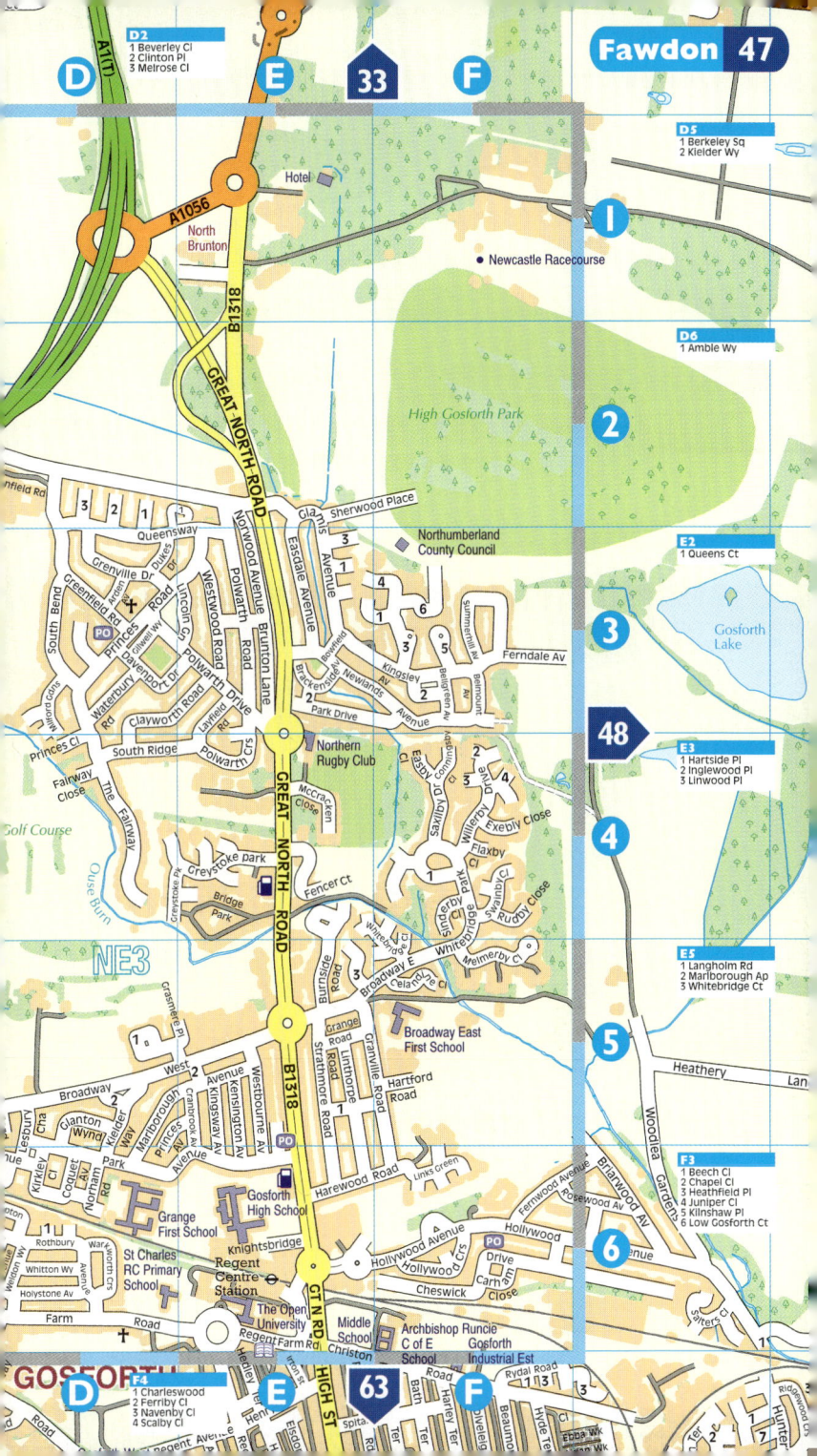

Farm Road

HIGH ST

Spital

Hedley

Harley Ter

Bath

Bewick

Ivy Ter

Hyde Ter

Ebba Wk

Hunter

A 34 B C

Farm
Cottages

A6
1 Turnberry Wy

B5
1 Kingsbridge
2 Queensbridge
3 Rossendale Pl

Great Lime Road

Newcastle upon Tyne

A189

North Tyneside

● Newcastle Racecourse

The L...

B6
1 Bilsdale Pl
2 Camsey Cl
3 Mendip Wy
4 Troutdale Pl
5 West Farm Av

High Gosforth Park

2

Gosforth
Wood

Sherwood Place

Gosforth
Lake

C2
1 Dene Av

Northumberland
...Council

3

3

1

6

Summerhill Gr

Ferndale Av

Salters Lane

1

3

Kingsley Av

Bellgreen Av

Benmount

Newlands Avenue

2

Drive

47

thern
by Clu...

C5
1 Curlew Cl
2 Heron Pl

2

Saxilby Dr

Kirby

Willerby

Exebridge Close

4

Balliol Business
Park

Flaxby

Gosforth Park Way

Singleby

Ingleby

Swanby Cl

Rugby Close

Broadway East
First School

C6
1 Bishop Rock Rd
2 Blackdown Cl
3 Cardinal Cl
4 Greyfriars La
5 Quantock Cl

Selmerby Cl

Newcastle upon Tyne

North Tyneside

5

Peregrine

Grassholm Pl

Stonechat

Shearwater Av

Merlin

Stoneleigh

Aven

Granville Road

Hartford
Road

Linthorpe

1

2

Heathery   Lane

Kingsdale

Runswick Av

Merlin Pk Wy

Pennine Way

Bishop Rock

Blackfriars

North

Links Green

Woodlea Gardens

Briarwood Av

Byland

Monks Pk Wy

Tyneside

4

Council

wood Road

3

Fernwood Avenue

Rosewood Av

Avenue

Byland

Falcon

Whitefriars Way

Lutterworth...

PO

Hollywood Avenue

Drive

6

Fairfield

Farm
Doctors
Surgery

Chester

Av

2

5

Avenue

PO

Hollywood Crs

Carn...

Vicars

Whitefriars Way

The Stow

Cheswick

Close

Glent Wy

Lutterworth

Middle
School

Archbishop Runcie
C of E
School

Gosforth
Industrial Est

Rydal Road

1

3

Salters Cl

West Farm Wynd

Chest...

Longbento...
Station

...riston

...thwell

Bath

Road

3

Lealholm Rd

A 64 B C

Paxford

I grid square represents 500 metres

D **E** **35** **F**

D3
1 Cotswold Av
2 Grampian Pl

Killingworth

Forest Hall

West Moor

LONGBENTON

George Stephenson High School

Killingworth Middle School

North Tyneside Area Health Authority

North Tyneside Council

Moor Edge First School

Angus Cl

West Bailey

East Bailey

West Lane

Northumbrian Way

West Moor First School

GREAT LIME ROAD

Westmoor Middle School

Westmoor Drive

Chiltern Drive

Greenhaugh

Georgian Ct

Samson Cl

Comet Row

Planet Place

Armstrong Dr

Hazel Gv

STATION ROAD

B1505

KILLINGWORTH DRIVE

BENTON LANE B1505

Harvey Combe

Station Rd

Arrow Cl

Sharp Cl

Reynolds Av

Northfield Dr

LC

PO

Albert Terrace

Kings Road

Balliol Av

Myrtle Crs

Holly Av

Glebe

Glebe Villas

Glebe Crs

Firtree Crs

Delaval Rd

Police Stn

Charles Av

Briar Edge

Weardale Av

Linden School

North Tyneside Council

STATION ROAD

Clydedale

Allandale

Clifton Ter

Northumberland Av

Victoria Av

Lyndhurst

Midhurst

Longbenton Community College

Basingstoke Place

Edenbridge Crs

Glenfield Rd

Hailsham Avenue

Goathland Av

Wheatfield Grove

Tenbury Crs

Ongar Wy

Altan Pl

BENTON LANE

Stephens RC Primary School

Glenfield Road

Benton Ln

Elmsford Gv

Lambourn

Goathland Av

Ashleigh Gv

Beech Gv

Benton Stn

Cemetery

Goathland Primary School

Yewburn

Lythe Wy

Whitley Crs

Eastfield Rd

Southfield Rd

College Rd

Sandringham Av

Whitfield Drive

Maddox Rd

Carlton Rd

North Av

East Av

Thornhill Rd

The Covers

The Grange Av

The Oval

Doctors Surgery

Rowanberry Rd

Balliol First School

Four Lane Ends Station

FRONT STREET

WHITLEY

STATION ROAD

GRANGE ROAD

Civil Service Sports Club

BENTON LANE

A191

65

D5, F4, F6
Street names for these grid squares are listed at the back of the index

D **E** **65** **F**

D6
1 The Byeways
2 Clipsham Cl
3 Doulting Cl
4 Ketton Cl
5 Lutterworth Cl
6 Meadow Cl

E1
1 Coniston Cl
2 Grasmere Ct

E4
1 Redesdale Cl

E5
1 Deerbolt Pl
2 Radstock Pl
3 Ringwood Gn
4 Roseden Ct

E6
1 Carolyn Cl

F1
1 Bolam Rd
2 East Bailey
3 West Bailey

F3
1 Ruskin Av

F5
1 Hastings Av

1 **2** **3** **4** **5** **6**

KILLINGWORTH ROAD

B1317

FOREST HALL ROAD

STATION ROAD

Granville Drive

Granville Crs

Cresswell Av

Primary School

50

36

A 1
1 Green La

A2
1 East Stoneycroft
2 West Stoneycroft

North Tyneside Area
Health Authority
PO

A3
1 Clousden Gra
2 Earlington Ter
3 Errington Ter
4 Willowdene

Killingworth

henson
School

Killingworth
Middle School

A4
1 Ashwood Cl
2 Cedar Wy
3 East Forest Hall
Rd

**Killingworth
Moor**

West Lane

WEST LANE B1317

Leybourne
Avenue

Elm Grove

**Forest
Hall**

Denewood

Palmersville

Bento

Laurel Av

Laurel Av

Laurel Av

Crossley Terrace

GREAT LIME ROAD

Palm
Stati

Police
Sth

Cresswell Av

Young
Road

PO

49

A5
1 Studley Vls

NE12

Ivy Road
Primary School

Farne Rd

Briar Edge

PO

4

North Tyneside
Council

Linden School

Mead

Mead
Way

Feetham

North Tyne
Industrial Est

Chollerton

B1
1 Applewood
2 Downswood
3 Garleigh Cl
4 Garth Twenty
Five
5 Garth Twenty
Four
6 Goodwood
7 Greenwood
8 Hazelwood
9 Rosewood

Clifton Ter

Northumberland
Av

Westcroft
Road

Granville Drive

Ashcroft
Dr

Bellingham

Bellway
Industrial
Est

Megabowl

Cemetery

5

Lyndhurst
Rd

North Cft

Granville Drive

WHITLEY ROAD

C3
1 Roseberry Gra

Midhurst Rd

Station Rd

The Covers

The
Oval

The Grange Av

ROAD

Sandringham Av

Maddox Rd

6

WHITLEY

East
Benton Farm

Eastfield
Rd

Southfield Rd

TREET

Civil
Serv
Sports Club

A

66

B

C4
1 Humshaugh Cl
2 Margaret Dr
3 William Cl

C

1 grid square represents 500 metres

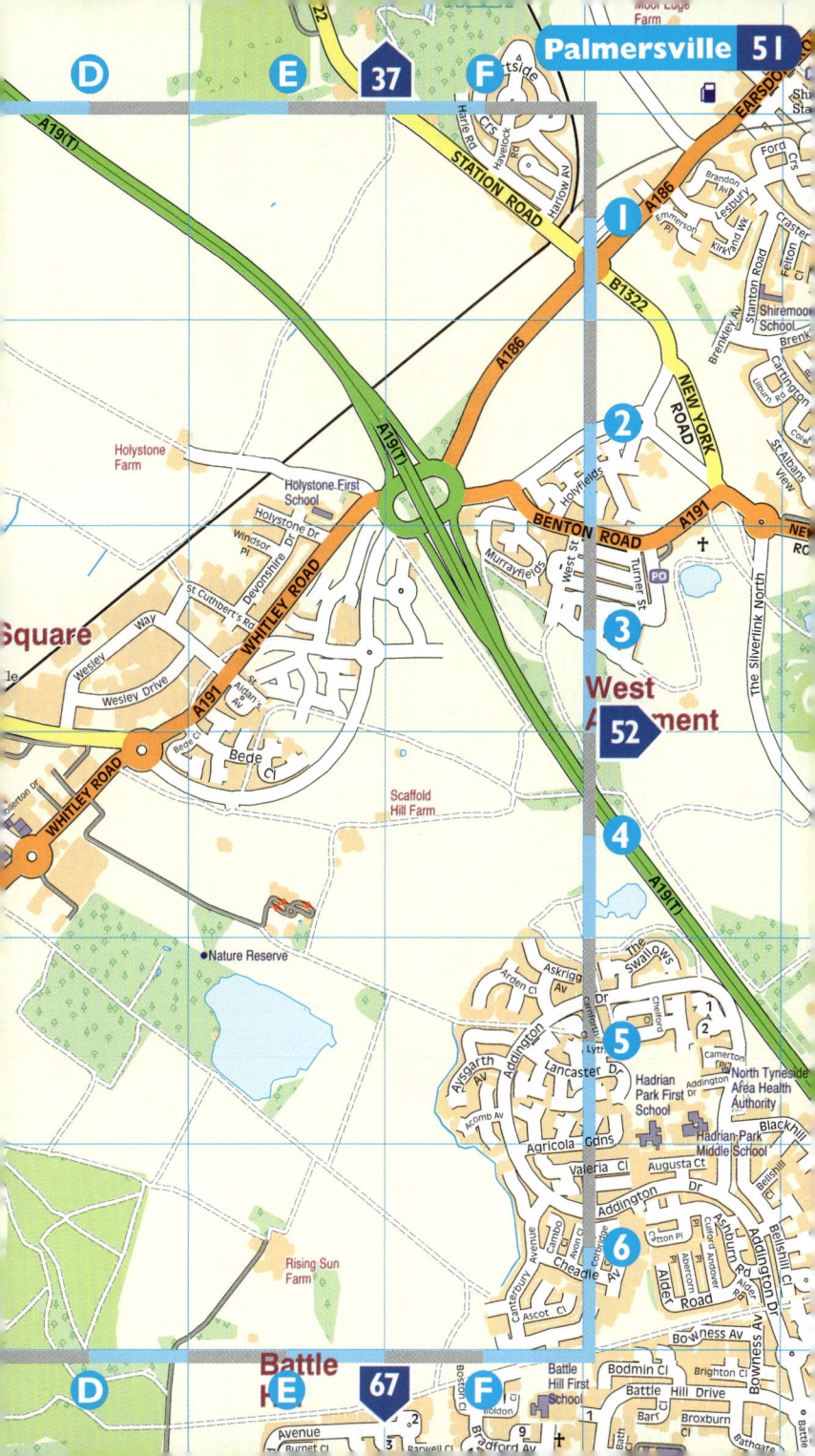

D   E **37** F

EARSDON

Moor Edge Farm

STATION ROAD

Hare Rd
Harlow Av
Havelock Rd
Crs
tside

A186

Emmerson
Kirk and W
Brandon
Av
Lesbury
Ford Crs
Craster
Felton
Crs

B1322

Brenkley Av
Stanton Road
Shiremoor
School
Cartington
Lilburn
Brenk
cote
St Albans
View

NEW YORK ROAD

2

Holystone
Farm

A19(T)

A186

Holystone First
School

Holystone Dr

Windsor
Pl

Devonshire Dr

Highfields
Murrayfields
West St
West Av

BENTON ROAD

A191

NEW
RO

PO
Turner St
Turner St

The Silverlink North

3

West
A....ment
52

Square

St Cuthbert's Rd

WHITLEY ROAD

Wesley
Way

Wesley Drive

A191

St Aidan's Av

Bede Cl

Bede Cl

Bede Cl

ollerton Dr

WHITLEY ROAD

Scaffold
Hill Farm

4

A19(T)

• Nature Reserve

The
SWALLOWS

Arden Cl
Askrigg
Av

Chelford

Cameron

1
2

5

Lythe

Addington

Aysgarth
AV

Lancaster Dr

Addington Dr

North Tyneside
Area Health
Authority

Acomb Av

Hadrian
Park First
School

Hadrian Park
Middle School

Blackhill

Agricola Gdns

Valeria Cl

Augusta Ct
Dr

Augusta

Addington

Belishill

Cambo
Cl

Coxlodge
Av

6

Canterbury Avenue

Cheadle
Av

Otton Pl

Clifford Av
Ando....

Catburn Rd

Alder

Abercorn

Road

Alder

Bellshill Cl

Addington Dr

Ascot
Cl

Bowness Av

Bowness Av

D   E **67** F

Battle
H...

Battle
Hill First
School

Bodmin Cl
Brighton Cl
Battle Hill Drive
Bart
Broxburn Cl
Bathgate

Boston Cl
Boldon

Avenue

Burnet Cl

Barwell Cl

Bradford Cl

9
1

Rising Sun
Farm

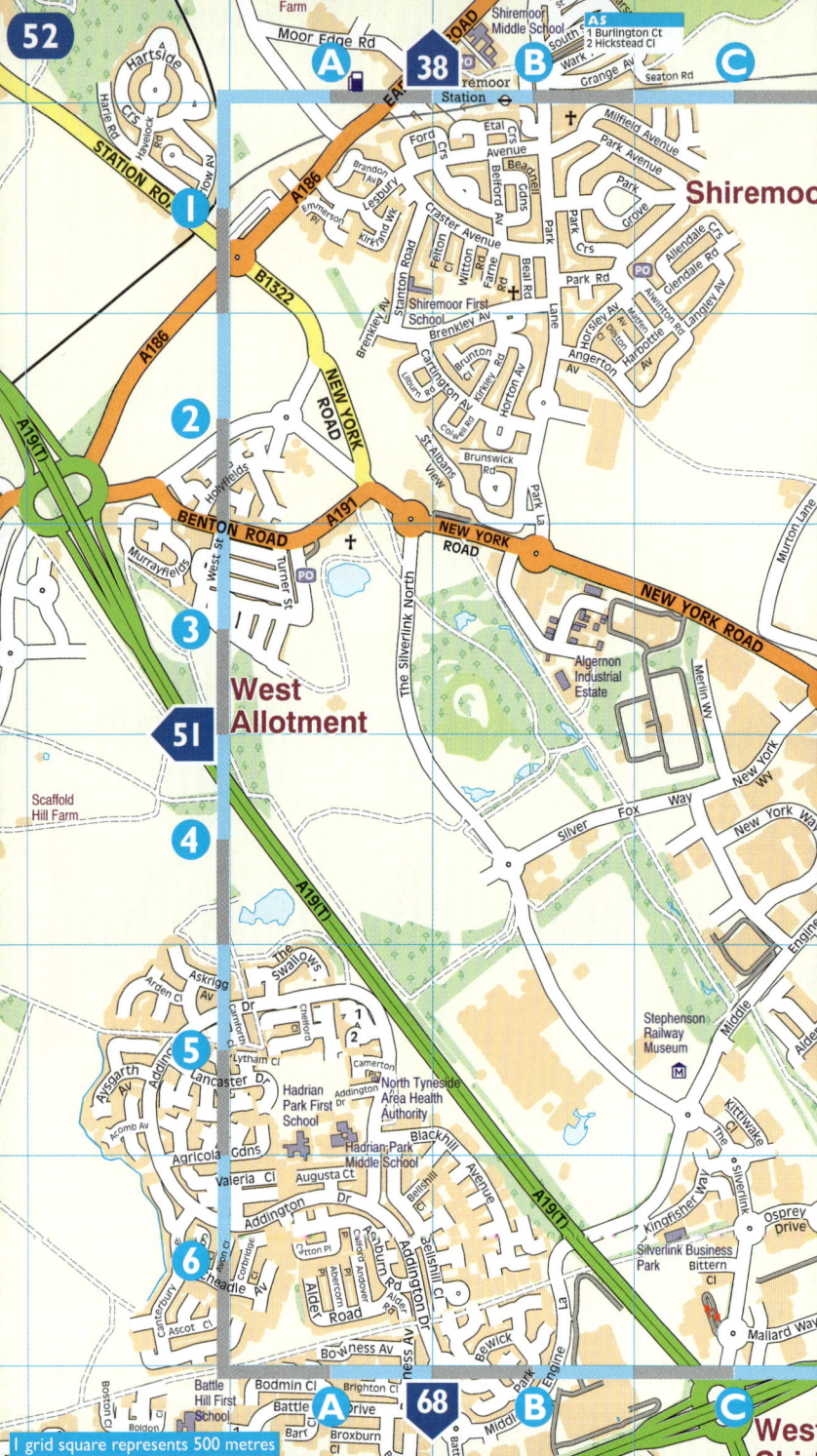

Moor Edge Farm

Moor Edge Rd

Shiremoor Middle School

A

38

Shiremoor Station

South Wark

B

Grange Av

Seaton Rd

As
1 Burlington Ct
2 Hickstead Cl

C

Hartside

Harle Rd

Havelock Rd

STATION RD

Low Rd

A186

I

Brandon Av

Emmerson Pl

Lesbury

Kirk and Wk

Ford

Etal Crs

Avenue

Beaufield

Belford St

Mifield Avenue

Park Avenue

Park Grove

Park Crs

Shiremoor

B1322

Brenkley Av

Stanton Road

Felton

Witton

Craster Avenue

Farne

Beal Rd

Park Lane

Park Rd

Allendale Crs

Glendale Rd

Langley Av

PO

Swinton Rd

Hetton Rd

Harbottle

A186

NEW YORK ROAD

2

Howfields

Shiremoor First School

Brenkley Av

Cardrona Av

Lisburn

Brunton Av

Kinley Rd

Colwell Rd

Horton Rd

St Johns View

Brunswick Rd

Horsley Av

Angerton Av

Dillston

Park La

BENTON ROAD

A191

NEW YORK ROAD

Murrayfields

West St

Turner St

PO

3

The Silverlink North

West Allotment

NEW YORK ROAD

Algernon Industrial Estate

Merlin Wy

51

Scaffold Hill Farm

4

A19(T)

Silver Fox Way

New York Wy

New York Way

Askrigg Av

The Swallows

Arden Cl

Dr

Cherton

Lytham Cl

Lancaster Dr

Camerton

Addington Dr

North Tyneside Area Health Authority

Stephenson Railway Museum

M

Middle

Engine

Alder

5

Aysgarth Av

Addington

Acomb Av

Hadrian Park First School

Blackhill

Kittiwake

The Silverlink

Agricola Gdns

Valeria Cl

Augusta Ct

Hadrian Park Middle School

Bellshill

Avenue

Bewick

A19(T)

Silverlink Business Park

Kingfisher Way

Osprey Drive

6

Canterbury

Cheadle

Corbridge Av

Ascot Cl

Acton Pl

Alder Road

Clifford

Ashburn Rd

Addington Dr

Bellshill Cl

Silverlink

Bittern Cl

Battle Hill First School

Bodmin Cl

Battle Bart

Brighton Drive

Broxburn Cl

A

68

Middi

Park

Engine

B

Mallard Way

C

West Chirt

Bowness Av

Bathgate

West Monkseaton

Murton

New York

Billy Mill

Chirton

39

54

69

2

3

4

5

6

E4
1 Bodmin Rd
2 Coldstream Wy
3 Elgin Cl
4 Perth Cl

E5
1 Alston Cl
2 Hexham Cl
3 Moorhouses Rd

E6
1 Humshaugh Rd
2 Norham Rd
3 Nunwick Gdns

F4
1 St Aidan's Cl
2 Sherborne Av
3 Somerset Gv
4 Taunton Av

F5
1 Hedgeley Rd
2 Lynn Rd
3 Netherton Gv
4 Thirston Pl
5 Whitton Gdns

F6
1 Bellister Rd
2 Berkley Rd
3 Glendower Av
4 Gunnerton Pl
5 Juliet Av
6 Mortimer Av
7 Surrey Rd

Medical Cen

Monkseaton High School

St Anselm's RC High School

Whitehouse Primary School

Formica Social & Sports Club

Primary School

RAKE LANE
SEATONVILLE ROAD
BEACH ROAD
BILLY MILL AVENUE
REGENT TER
COAST ROAD
LYNN ROAD
BILLY MILL LANE
A191
A192
A1058
NE29

Well Lane
Murton Lane
The Bridle
Sherwood Close
Adderstone Gdns
Warenton Place
New York Road
Tiverton Avenue
Barnstaple Rd
Falmouth Rd
Abbots Way
Whitehouse La
Elm Road
Norham Road N
Westminster Av
Moor Park Rd
St Anselm Road
Woolington Dr
Cumberland Rd
Westmorland Rd
Gloucester Rd
Chollerford Avenue
Redesdale Rd
Wark Avenue
Denton Rd
Langley Rd
Alexandra
Alexandra Gdns
Kimberley Av
Lansdown

54

A

40

B

C

A6
1 Rutland Pl

B2
1 Quantock Cl

2

B3
1 Langdon Cl
2 Pentland Cl
3 Pevensey Cl

3

53

B4
1 Westbury Rd

4

B5
1 Hawthorn Gdns

5

B6
1 Glendale Gv
2 Milton Gv
3 Milton Pl

6

C4
1 Argyle Pl
2 Bulman's La
3 Pennyfine Cl
4 Popplewell Ter
5 Post Office La

A

70

B

C5, C6
Street names for
this grid square are
listed at the back of
the index

C

1 grid square represents 500 metres

Preston
Grange

Preston

Billy
Mill

Chirton

Monkseaton
High School

Whitley Bay
Cricket Club

Whitley Bay
Rockcliff RFC

Whitley Bay
Ice Rink

Whitley Bay
Football Club

John Spence
Community
High School

North Shields
Rugby Club

Whitehouse
Primary School

Cemetery

Tynemouth
College

St Anselm's
RC High School

SEATONVILLE ROAD

SHIELDS ROAD

RAKE LANE

BEACH ROAD

PRESTON RD N

NORTH ROAD

PRESTON ROAD

WALTON AV

HAWKEY'S LA

BILLY MILL AVENUE

REGENT TER

CHIRTON GN

A192

A191

A1058

B1304

A4

HILLHEADS ROAD

Cullercoats

TYNEMOUTH

NE30

Marden

D1
1 Cranbourne Gv

D2
1 Ellersmere Gdns
2 Grange Cl

D5
1 Kensington Gv
2 Rosedale Ter

D6
1 Church St
2 Kensington Gdns
3 Kielder Ter
4 Suez St
5 Upper Norfolk St
6 Upper Pearson St

E4
1 Monkstone Av
2 Monkstone Cl

E6
1 Bird St
2 Brewhouse Bank
3 Walker Pl

F4
1 Argyle St
2 Back Percy Gdns
3 Birtley Av
4 Manorway
5 Prudhoe Ter
6 Stanwick St
7 Warkworth Ter

F5
Street names for this grid square are listed at the back of the index

Cullercoats Station
Cullercoats Primary School
Marden High School
Monkhouse School
Tynemouth Cricket Club
Ronald Moore Gallery
King Edward Junior & Infant School
Tynemouth Station
Tynemouth Castle
North Tyneside Council
Tynemouth Business Cen
Ashleigh Sch
Long Sands

BEACH ROAD A193
THE BROADWAY
BROADWAY
MANOR RD
TYNEMOUTH RD A193
Grand Parade
Percy Gardens

B4
1 Calvus Dr

A
B
C

East Heddon

1

Allerburn

Sunny
Side

A69(T)

Heddon
Mill

2

Blackrow

Mill
Lane

3

MILITARY ROAD B6318

First
School

Taberna Cl
PO

Midras Gdns

The Towne Gate

Camilla Rd

B6528

Remus Av

Calvus Dr

Valerian Av

Martius Av

Antonine Walk

Hill
Head

Aquila Drive

Campus

Martius

Banks

Centurion
Way

Heddon
Banks Farm

Station Road

4

Killiebrigs

Heddon Banks

Heddon

**Heddon-on-
the-Wall**

Heddon
Hall

Close

5

Station Road

Close
House

6

A
B
C

Maryside
Hill

E4
1 The Briary
2 Clipstone Cl

D **E** **F**

Crescent Farm

Heddon
Birks

E5
1 Holeyn Rd

I

B6323

PONTELAND ROAD

Dewley Burn

F4
1 The Crescent
2 Mount Pleasant
Ct

Dewley Farm

2

Lane

Drove Road

F5
1 The Causeway
2 Collier Cl
3 Hawkwell Rl
4 Isabella Wk
5 The Wynd

Throckley Industrial
Estate

3

PONTELAND ROAD

Westway

Northway

Alston

Laurel St

Sycamore St

Wesley Wy

Brampton
Gdns

Limecroft Gdns

Arncliffe

58 ▶

Throck

Ingleton Drive

Ainderby Road

Throckley
Middle
School

A6085

Talbot
House Special
School

Ollerton Drive

Sheringham Gardens

Horncliffe Place

The Mount

Hill House Road

Coquet Grove

Valeside

Wilsway

Coquet Cv

Stuart Gardens

Broomy

1

HEXHAM ROAD

Northam Rd

B6528

4

Vale Rd

4

2

Woodside Av

Bank Top

Throckley
First
School

Coach Road

Reeth Wy

Wellfield Close

Tillmouth

The By-Way

Park Road

Hill Road

Throckley
Surgery
PO

2

Loraine

Newcastle
City Council

Mayfield Avenue

A6085

Callerton Road

Wal

Throckley
House

1

3

4

Longgate

2

The Willows

Hewley Crescent

Hallow Drive

1

3

Newburn

2

Rd

3

Fosse
Law

1

2

Parkside

5

Leazes Pkwy

Richard Browell
Road

Tyne Riverside
Country Park

Grange
Farm

6

NEWBURN ROAD

Townfield

Doctors Surgery

7

Lovaine St

Boyd St

Davison St

Newcastle upon Tyne
Northumberland County

Coach Road

Grange Rd

Newburn
Leisure
Centre

New
City
Cou

Station

PO

D **E** **74** **F**

A 42 B C

A4
1 Appian Pl
2 Elmfield Rd
3 Eversleigh Pl
4 St Mary's Pl

Crescent Farm

Lough House

A5
1 Briar La
2 Mayfield Gdns
3 Rye Cl

1

PONTELAND ROAD

A6
1 Westmacott St

Dewley Burn

Dewley Farm

Fell House Farm

2

B5
1 Bankhead Rd

Throckley Industrial Estate

North Walbottle

3

PONTELAND ROAD

NORTHWAY

Westway

Laurel St
Sycamore St

57

Gdns
Ambleside
Brampton Gdns

Throckley

Oak Gdns

HEXHAM ROAD B6528

Talbot House Special School

B6
1 Berkley St
2 Millfield Cl

Stuart Gardens
Broomy

Throckley Surgery
PO

4

Hadrian Pl
Callerton Road
Vallum Rd
Portland Rd

Woodside Av

A6085

Primary School

George Street

N Walbottle Rd
North Walbottle Road

HAWTHORN

C5
1 Village Farm

Throckley
st
school

Hill
Tillmouth Av
Park Road
Hallow
Leazes Pkwy

Long Gate
The Willows
Hewley Cresent
Dri

Newcastle City Council

Mayfield Avenue

Newburn Rd

Walbottle

The Green
PO

Grove Rd
Whitehall Rd

The Paddock

Percy Way
Queen's Ct
Queens Road

Walbottle

5

Richard Browell Road

Fosse Law

Parkside

NEWBURN ROAD

New Burn

Tyne Riverside Country Park

6

Grange Farm

Doctors Surgery

Townfield Gdns
Ovens St
Davison St

Park Rd

Newburn Hall Motor Mus
M
First School

Newburn

Grange Rd

Newburn Leisure Centre

Newcastle City Council

Millfield Lane

Walbottle Road

A 75 B C

PO

Station Rd

HIGH ST

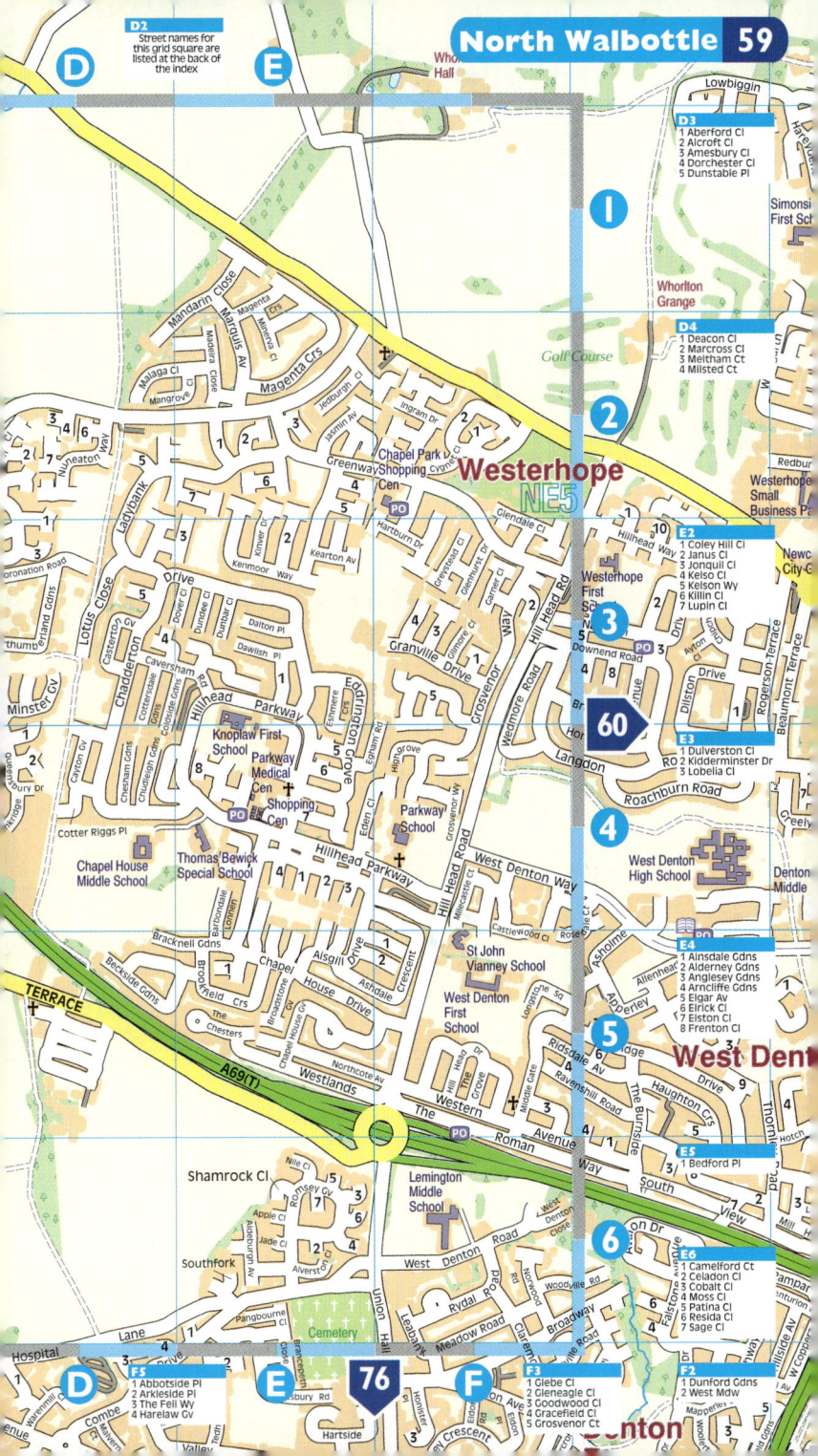

D2
Street names for this grid square are listed at the back of the index

D

E

D3
1 Aberford Cl
2 Alcroft Cl
3 Amesbury Cl
4 Dorchester Cl
5 Dunstable Pl

Lowbiggin

Simons
First Sc

Whorlton
Grange

I

D4
1 Deacon Cl
2 Marcross Cl
3 Meltham Ct
4 Milsted Ct

Golf Course

2

Westerhope
NE5

Chapel Park
Shopping
Cen
PO

Redbur

Westerhope
Small
Business

Mandarin Close
Marquis Av
Magenta
Madeira Av

Malaga Cl
Mangrove

Magenta Crs

Nuneaton

Ingram Dr

Jedburgh
Jasmin Av

Greenway

Hartburn Dr

Glendale Av

Westerhope
First
Sch

Hillhead Way

E2
1 Coley Hill Cl
2 Janus Cl
3 Jonquil Cl
4 Kelso Cl
5 Kelson Wy
6 Killin Cl
7 Lupin Cl

Newc
City C

Ladybank

Lotus Close

Kinver Dr

Kenmoor Way

Kearton Av

Crossdale Dr
Glenhurst Dr

Garner Cl

Grosvenor
Way

Hill Head Rd

Downend Road

Ayton

Dilston
Drive

Roperson Terrace

Beaumont Terrace

Coronation Road

Minster Gv

Chadderton
Drive

Casterton Gv

Dover Cl
Dundee Cl
Dunbar Cl

Dalton Pl

Dawlish Pl

Granville Drive

Gilmore Cl

Gilmore Cl

Wedmore Road

3
PO

8

60

thumb

Caversham Rd
Cottesdale Gdns
Coldside Gdns
Colside Gdns

Chesham Gdns
Chudleigh Gdns

Hillhead

Parkway

Edgington Grove

Eshmere Cres

Esham Rd

High Grove

Horl

Langdon

E3
RO 1 Dulverston Cl
2 Kidderminster Dr
3 Lobelia Cl

Queensbury Dr

Cayton Gv

Knoplaw First
School
Parkway Medical
Cen

Shopping
Cen
PO

Parkway
School

Roachburn Road

4

West Denton
High School

Denton
Middle

Cotter Riggs Pl

Thomas Bewick
Special School

Barfondale
Birtley...

Hillhead Parkway

Grosvenor Wy

West Denton Way

Millcastle Ct
CastleWood Dr

Asholme

Allenhea...

E4
1 Ainsdale Gdns
2 Alderney Gdns
3 Anglesey Gdns
4 Arncliffe Gdns
5 Elgar Av
6 Eirick Cl
7 Elston Cl
8 Frenton Cl

Chapel House
Middle School

Bracknell Gdns

Beckside Gdns

Brookfield

Chapel
House
Drive

Broadstone

Alsgill Drive

Ashdale

St John
Vianney School

West Denton
First
School

Ravenshill Road

Ridsdale Av

Denton Gate

Aperley

West Dent

TERRACE

A69(T)

The
Chesters

Northcote Av

Westlands

Middle Gate

The
Western

Roman

Avenue

South

Haughton Crs

The Burnside

Drive

Thornley

9

5

E5
1 Bedford Pl

Shamrock Cl

Nile Cl

Romsey Gv

Apple Cl
Jade Cl

Alverston

Lemington
Middle
School

West
Denton
Close

West
View

6

Southfork

Aldeburgh Av

West Denton
Road

Pangbourne La

Cemetery

Rydal Road

Meadow Road

Union Hall

Leabank

Norwood Av

Broadway

Claremon...

Woodville Rd

E6
1 Camelford Ct
2 Celadon Cl
3 Goodwood Cl
4 Moss Cl
5 Patina Cl
6 Resida Cl
7 Sage Cl

Falston

Dr

Cantur

Hospital

Warrenm...

Combe

F5
1 Abbotside Pl
2 Arkleside Pl
3 The Fell Wy
4 Harelaw Gv

D

E

76

F

F3
1 Glebe Cl
2 Gleneagle Cl
3 Goodwood Cl
4 Gracefield Cl
5 Grosvenor Cl

Denton

F2
1 Dunford Gdns
2 West Mdw

Valley

Hartside

Crescent

Mapp...

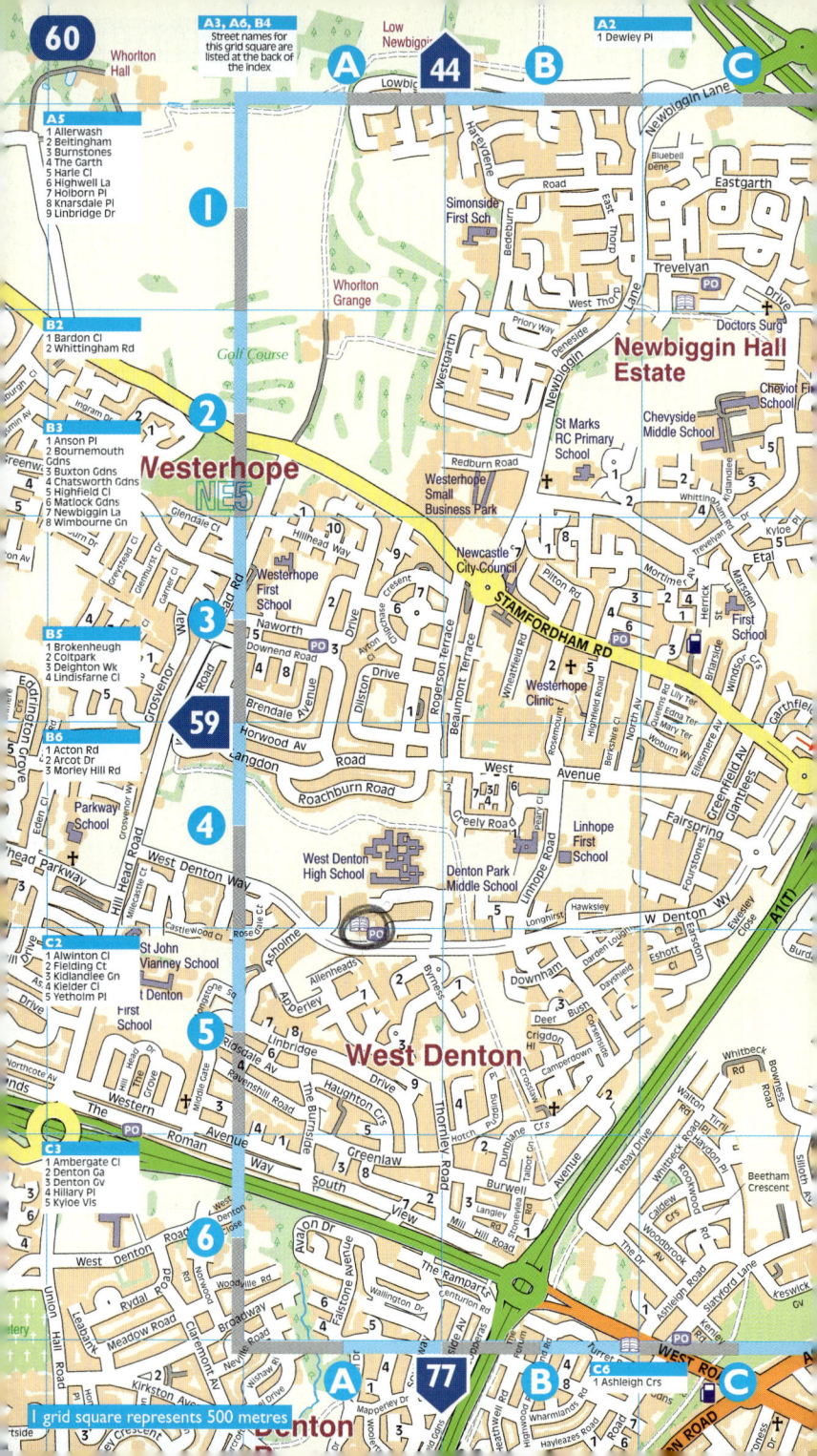

60

Whorlton Hall

A3, A6, B4
Street names for this grid square are listed at the back of the index

Low Newbiggin

A **44** **B** **C**

A2
1 Dewley Pl

Lowbiggin

Newbiggin Lane

A5
1 Allerwash
2 Beltingham
3 Burnstones
4 The Garth
5 Harle Cl
6 Highwell La
7 Holborn Pl
8 Knarsdale Pl
9 Linbridge Dr

I

Hareydene

Bedeburn Road

East Thorp

Bluebell Dene

Eastgarth

Simonside First Sch

Trevelyan

PO

Doctors Surg

Whorlton Grange

Priory Way

West Thor

Deneside

Newbiggin Lane

Westgarth

Newbiggin Hall Estate

Cheviot Fi School

Golf Course

St Marks RC Primary School

Chevyside Middle School

Whittingdale

Kyloe

Etal

B2
1 Bardon Cl
2 Whittingham Rd

Redburn Road

2

Westerhope
NE5

Glendale Cl

Westerhope Small Business Park

Trevelyan Dr

Mortimer Av

Herrick

First School

B3
1 Anson Pl
2 Bournemouth Gdns
3 Buxton Gdns
4 Chatsworth Gdns
5 Highfield Cl
6 Matlock Gdns
7 Newbiggin La
8 Wilmbourne Gn

Hillhead Way

Newcastle City Council

Pilton Rd

Windsor Dr

Brunside

Carthfield

3

Westerhope First School

Naworth

PO

STAMFORDHAM RD

PO

Westfield Rd

Highfield Road

North Av

Westerhope Clinic

Downend Road

Ayton Close

Berridge

Queens Rd

Lilly Ter

Edna Ter

Mary Ter

First School

B5
1 Brokenheugh
2 Coltpark
3 Deighton Wk
4 Lindisfarne Cl

59

Brendale Avenue

Diston Drive

Rogerson Terrace

Beaumont Terrace

Wheatfield Dr

Rosemount

Woburn Way

Ellesmere Av

Greenfield Av

Glantees

B6
1 Acton Rd
2 Arcot Dr
3 Morley Hill Rd

Horwood Av

Langdon Road

Roachburn Road

West Avenue

Fairspring

Foustoome

Eddrington Grove

Grosvenor Way

Head Parkway

Parkway School

Hill Head Road

West Denton Way

4

West Denton High School

Denton Park Middle School

Greely Road

Linhope Road

Linhope First School

Hawksley

Eshott

W Denton Wy

Elvesley Close

Burd

Castlewood Cl

Rose Gdns

PO

Downham

Garden Leigh

Eshott Cl

Deanfield

C2
1 Alwinton Cl
2 Fielding Ct
3 Allandlee Gn
4 Kielder Cl
5 Yetholm Pl

St John Vianney School

Denton

Asholme

Allenheads

Apperley

Byrness

Deer Bush

Crigdon Pl

Camperdown

Crossne

Whitbeck Rd

Bowness Road

First School

5

Hill Head Rd

The Grove

Middle Gate

Ravenshill Road

Linbridge Drive

Haughton Crs

Thorney Road

Pl

Dunbiane Crs

Walton Tarn

Whitbeck Road

Haydon Cl

Rookwood Road

Beetham Crescent

Northcote Av

Ridesdale Av

The Burnside

Hotch

Tebay Drive

Caldew Crs

Woodcroft

The Dr

Western Avenue

Roman Way

PO

C3
1 Ambergate Cl
2 Denton Ga
3 Denton Gv
4 Hillary Pl
5 Kyloe Vls

Greenlaw

Burwell

Langley

Avenue

Ashleigh Road

Kettle

Keswick Gv

6

West Denton Road

Norwood Rd

Woodville Rd

Avalon Dr

Falstone Avenue

Wallington Dr

Centurion Rd

The Ramparts

View

Mill Hill Road

Denton Road

Rydal Rd

Meadow Road

Claremont Rd

Broadway

Newington

The Dr

WEST ROAD

PO

Union Hall Road

Leabank

Kirkston Av

A **77** **B**

C6
1 Ashleigh Crs

C

Mapperley Dr

Heathwell Rd

Wharmlands Rd

Hayleazes Rd

N ROAD

Denton

I grid square represents 500 metres

D1
1 Knowsley Ct

D 45 E F

D2
1 Brecon Cl
2 Caernarvon Cl
3 Dereham Ct
4 Haggerston Cl
5 Haggerston Ct
6 Hensby Ct
7 Lampeter Cl
8 Reedham Ct
9 Rhuddlan Ct
10 Rollesby Ct
11 Shawdon Cl
12 Shearwater Cl
13 Tredegar Ct
14 Wroxham Ct

1

PONTELAND ROAD

Belvedere Retail

Hotel

Tudor Way

Hillsview Surgery

Redland Av

Emden Rd

Hillsview

Mountfield Primary School

Meadow Rise

Beaumaris Way

D4
1 Abercrombie Pl
2 Amersham Pl
3 Blakelaw Rd
4 Bonington Wy
5 Chandra Pl
6 Curzon Pl
7 Lawmill Wy
8 Waltham Pl
9 Wellfield La

2

KENTON LA

Primary School

Kenton Comprehensive School

Kenton Bar

Etal Lane

PONTELAND RD

A191

Kenton

The Rise
The High Gate
The West Rig

D6
1 Allonby Wy
2 Elrington Gdns
3 Farlam Rd
4 Windermere Rd

3

Ashbrooke

Burnfoot

E1
1 Pensford Ct

Cowgate Leisure Cen

Scafell Dr
Wansfell Av
Crossbank
Harenills AV

Grasswell Drive

Highland Rd

62

Montagu Junior & Infant School

E2
1 St Austell Cl

Yatesbury Avenue

Blakelaw

CRAGSTON AV

Hilton Av

Blakelaw School

Blakelaw Health Centre

Hillsleigh Road

Deepdale

4

Whitehorn Crescent

PONTELAND ROAD

E3
1 Avonlea Wy
2 Broxburn Cl
3 Coleridge Cl
4 Creland Wy
5 Lothian Ct

Primary School

STAMFORDHAM RD

Newcastle City Council Drive

Yewvale Road
Brookside Crs
Arden Crs

Chestnut Avenue

E4
1 Cragston Cl
2 Rothay Pl
3 Roundhill Av
4 Wilbury Pl
5 Wychcroft Wy

5

Newcastle City Council

A696 SPRINGFIELD ROAD

Rose Hill Way

Southmead Avenue

Bavington

STAMFORDHAM ROAD

B6324

E5
1 Blakemoor Pl
2 Deepbrook Rd
3 Hadstone Pl
4 Houndelee Pl
5 Oakwood Pl
6 Springfield Rd
7 Togstone Pl

Newcastle City Council

Cowgate Primary School

E6
1 Friars Wy
2 Lindale Rd

Friarside Rd

Netherby

B6326

Heatherslaw Grove

Greenway

Queensway

Royal Crs

6

Redewater Road

Kingsway

F1
1 Bellingham Cl
2 Bodley Cl
3 Castle Cl
4 Dunnykirk Av
5 Gunnerston Gv
6 Hazeley Wy
7 Laverock Pl
8 Thirston Wy

SILVER

ALL LONNEN

LONNEN

Hesleyside Drive

Willow Av

Alder Av

Mimosa

Fenham Hall Drive

Primary School

Bourne Av

D F4, F5, F6
Street names for this grid square are listed at the back of the index

Cemetery

D3, D5
Street names for this grid square are listed at the back of the index

F3
1 Beaufort Cl
2 Bowfell Cl
3 Murrayfield Rd
4 Spenfield Rd

Boys School

62

C2 street names for this grid square are listed at the back of the index

A **46** **B**

A1
1 Afton Wy
2 Columbia Gra
3 Harvard Rd
4 Shandon Wy

C

A2
1 Carnforth Gn
2 Runnymede Wy

I

Coxlo

A3
1 Dene Bank Vw
2 Woodleigh Vw

Primary School

Kenton Comprehensive School

2

Mountfield Primary School

Kenton Bar

A191

Kenton

KENTON LANE

Mountfield Gardens

Newcastle Reform Synagogue

KENTON RD

A4
1 Link Rd

Cowgate Leisure Centre

3

The Uplands

Newcastle City Council

61

Montagu Junior & Infant School

A5
1 Howat Av
2 Mayfield Ter
3 Revell Ter

Blakelaw Health Centre

4

Newcastle City Council

Nuns Moor

B1
1 Ambridge Wy
2 Carrfield Rd
3 Colgrove Wy
4 Crantock Rd
5 Hillsview Av
6 Kirkwood Dr
7 Shilmore Rd
8 Winton Wy

SPRINGFIELD ROAD

PONTELAND ROAD

5

Arden Crs

STAMFORDHAM ROAD   B6324

Newcastle City Council

Cowgate Primary School

Ponteland Road

A167

PONTELAND ROAD

GRANDSTAND ROAD

A1

B3
1 Aylyth Pl
2 Braebridge Pl
3 Millgrove Vw
4 Montpellier Pl

6

Ridgeway

Doctors Surgery

A187

C1
1 Agnes Maria St
2 George St
3 Leagreen Ct
4 Mary Agnes St
5 Nelson Av
6 Rea Pl
7 Souter Rd
8 South St
9 Turner Crs

Fenham Hall Drive

Fenham Hall Drive

PONTELAND ROAD

Fenham

Primary School

St Marys

A **79** **B**

Dame Allans Boys School

C3
1 Carlton Cl
2 Hardwick Pl
3 Wyndsail Pl
4 Wyndtop Pl

C

Tongues

I grid square represents 500 metres

GOSFORTH

South Gosforth

West Jesmond

Town Moor

NE2

St Charles
D2
1 Bloomsbury Ct
2 The Firs
3 Meadowfield Rd
4 Thornfield Rd

D3
1 Richmond Ms

D6
1 Cross Morpeth St
2 Dunn's Ter
3 Hunter's Pl
4 Limewood Ct

E1
1 Edward St

E2
1 Gordon Av
2 Linden Av
3 Roseworth Av
4 St Nicholas Av

E3
1 Leslie Crs

E6
1 Windmill Ct

F1
1 Cambo Cl
2 Manor Cl
3 Rothley Cl

F2
1 Grove Av

F3
1 Albemarle Av
2 Kingswood Av
3 Treherne Rd

F4
1 Holmwood Gv
2 Lyndhurst Gdns
3 Mayfair Rd
4 Mildmay Rd
5 Oakland Rd

Gosforth West Middle School
Regent Centre Station
Archbishop Runcie C of E School
Gosforth Industrial Est
Archibald First School
Gosforth Memorial Health Cen
Sanderson Hosp
Ascham House Sch
Police Stn
The Surg
Gosforth Cricket Club
The Hobart Gallery
Eastcliffe Grammar School
South Gosforth First School
Ilford Road Stn
Newcastle City Council
La Sagesse Convent High School
Westfield School
Kenton Lodge Residential School
The Poplars The Avenues Medical Practice
Moorfield
Towers Avenue
Tyne Clinic
Doctors Surg
Osborne Rd
The Toco Gal
Browns Gallery
West Jesmond Station
The Brandling Medical Practice
Century
Corrymaela Scott Gallery
University of Newcastle upon Tyne
Newcastle Nuffield Hospital
University of Newcastle upon Tyne
Split-Level Way

Salters' Road
Church Av
Station Road
Haddricksmill
Great North Road
Jesmond Dene Road
Grandstand Road
A167
A189
Osborne Road
Clayton Road
B1318
B1309
A10

47   64   80

64

A2
1 Alnmouth Dr
2 Balmoral Av
3 Craghall Dene
4 Craghall Dene Av
5 Hill Crest Gdns
6 Willowbank Gdns

A4
1 Coniston Av
2 Newborough Crs
3 N Jesmond Av
4 Sanderson Rd
5 W Jesmond Av

A5
1 Henshelwood Ter
2 Holly Av West
3 Norham Pl
4 Tankerville Rd
5 Thornleigh Rd

A6
1 Eskdale Ter
2 Kingsland

B1
1 Cloister Garth
2 The Cloisters
3 Gallalaw Ter
4 Lartington Gdns

B2
1 Cornwell Ct
2 Kingham Ct
3 Westwell Ct

B4
1 Castleton Cl
2 Dunira Cl
3 The Grove
4 Reid Park Cl
5 Sycamore Cl

B5
1 The Grove
2 Hartside Gdns
3 Jesmond Gdns

C1
1 Glaisdale Rd
2 Lealholm Rd

C2
1 Cleveland Gdns
2 Longborough Ct

C3
1 Gretton Pl
2 Kirkstone Gdns
3 Winchcombe Pl

C5
1 Churchill Gdns

A1, C6
Street names for
this grid square are
listed at the back of
the index

1 grid square represents 500 metres

NE2

JESMOND

49 **66** **82** **I** **2** **3** **4** **5** **6**

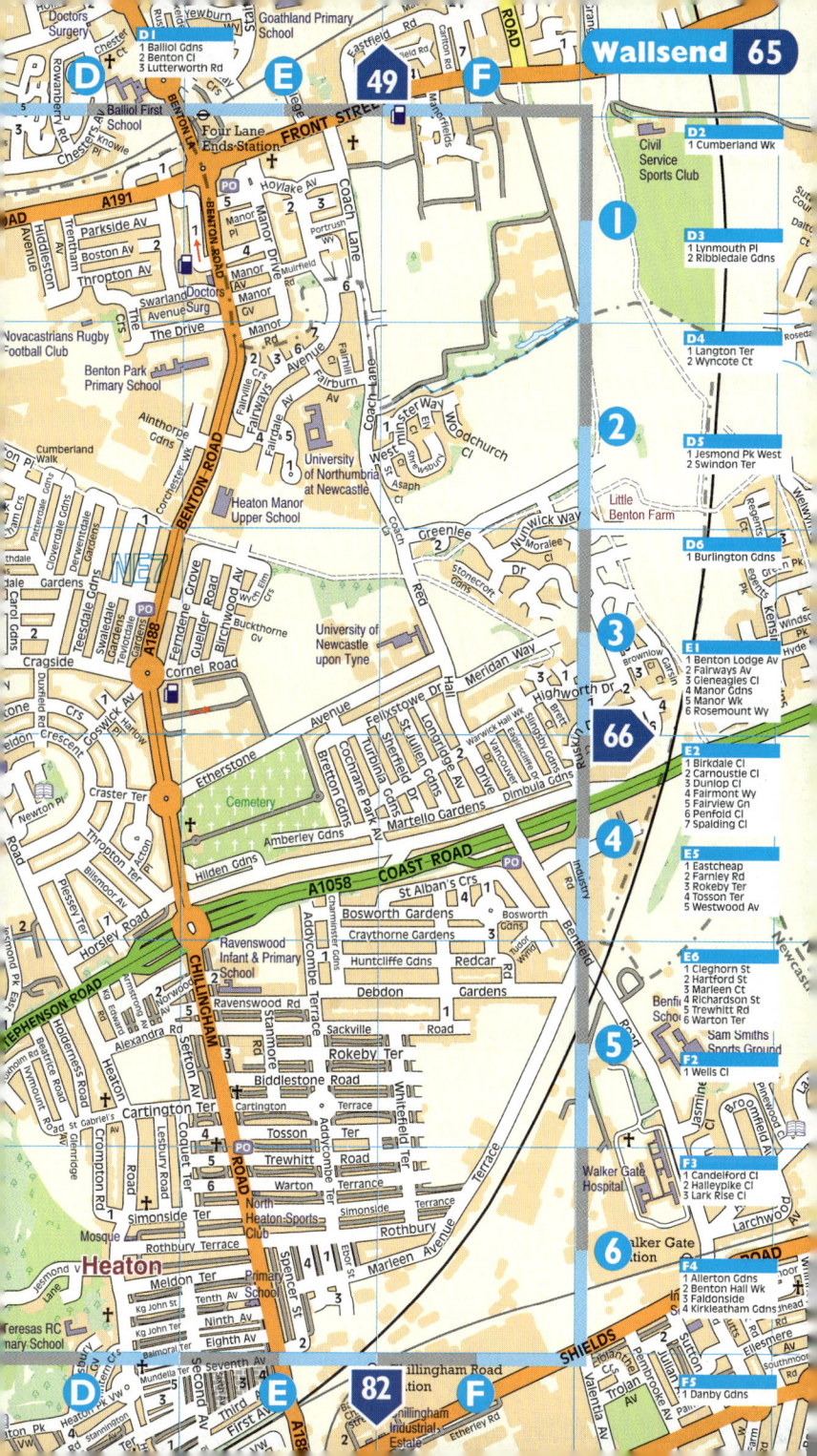

D1
1 Balliol Gdns
2 Benton Cl
3 Lutterworth Rd

D2
1 Cumberland Wk

Civil Service Sports Club

D3
1 Lynmouth Pl
2 Ribbledale Gdns

D4
1 Langton Ter
2 Wyncote Ct

D5
1 Jesmond Pk West
2 Swindon Ter

D6
1 Burlington Gdns

E1
1 Benton Lodge Av
2 Fairways Av
3 Gleneagles Cl
4 Manor Gdns
5 Manor Wk
6 Rosemount Wy

E2
1 Birkdale Cl
2 Carnoustie Cl
3 Dunlop Cl
4 Fairmont Wy
5 Fairview Gn
6 Penfold Cl
7 Spalding Cl

E3
1 Eastcheap
2 Farnley Rd
3 Rokeby Ter
4 Tosson Ter
5 Westwood Av

E6
1 Cleghorn St
2 Hartford St
3 Marleen Ct
4 Richardson St
5 Trewhitt Rd
6 Warton Ter

F1
1 Wells Cl

F3
1 Candelford Cl
2 Halleypike Cl
3 Lark Rise Cl

F4
1 Allerton Gdns
2 Benton Hall Wk
3 Faldonside
4 Kirkleatham Gdns

F5
1 Danby Gdns

Goathland Primary School

Four Lane Ends Station

FRONT STREET

ROAD

Eastfield Rd

A191

Parkside Av
Boston Av
Thropton Av

Hoylake Av
Manor Pl
Manor Drive
Coach Lane
Portrush Rd
Muirfield

Swarland Av
Manor Surg
The Drive
Manor Av
Manor Gv
Manor Rd

BENTON ROAD

Novacastrians Rugby Football Club

Benton Park Primary School

Ainthorpe Gdns

Cumberland Walk
Cragside

Corchester Wk
Fairways
Fairgate

University of Northumbria at Newcastle

Woodchurch Cl
Coxlodge Way
West Fm
St Asaph

Heaton Manor Upper School

Greenlee Dr
Moraine
Stonecroft Gdns
Nunwick Way

Little Benton Farm

Teesdale Gdns
Swaledale Gdns
Tewcotdale
Ferndene Grove
Guelder Av
Birchvood Av
Buckthorne Gv
Wch Elm

A188

University of Newcastle upon Tyne

Brownlow
Catsin
Highworth Dr
Meridan Way
Longridge Dr
Avenue
Felixstowe Dr
St Julien Dr
Shenfield
Turbinia Gdns
Cochrane Park
Bretton Gdns
Cornel Road

Cemetery

Etherstone
Craster Ter
Thropton Ter
Bismoor Av

Warwick Hall Wy
Vancouver Dr
Eaglescliffe Dr
Slingsby Gdns
Dimbula Gdns

Coast Road
A1058 COAST ROAD

St Alban's Crs
Addycombe Terrace
Amberley Gdns
Hilden Gdns

Bosworth Gardens
Craythorne Gardens
Bosworth Gdns

Ravenswood Infant & Primary School
Ravenswood Rd
Alexandra Rd
Stannmore
Sefton Av

Huntcliffe Gdns
Redcar Gardens
Debdon Gardens
Sackville Road

STEPHENSON ROAD
CHILLINGHAM ROAD

Rokeby Ter
Biddlestone Road
Cartington Ter
Cartington Terrace
Tosson Ter
Trewhitt Road
Warton Terrace
North Heaton Sports Club

Whitefield Ter
Addycombe Ter
Simonside Terrace
Rothbury Terrace
Rothbury Avenue
Marleen Avenue
Spencer St

Holderness Road
Beatrice Road
Wymount Road
Glenridge
Crompton Rd
Coquet Ter
Lesbury Rd
Simonside Ter
Mosque
Rothbury Terrace

Heaton

Meldon Ter
Kg John St
Kg John Ter
Ninth Av
Eighth Av
Seventh Av
First Av
Second Av

Teresas RC mary School
Mundella Ter

Chillingham Road Station

Chillingham Industrial Estate

Walker Gate Hospital

Walker Gate Station

SHIELDS ROAD

Sam Smiths Sports Ground

Civil Service Sports Club

D E F

66

A B C

50

83

65

WALLSEND

East Benton Farm

Civil Service Sports Club

Little Benton Farm

Redesdale First School

Parkside School

Wallsend Sports Centre

Benfield Comprehensive School

Sam Smiths Sports Ground

Walker Gate Hospital

Walker Gate Station

Chillingham Road Station

STATION ROAD

COAST ROAD

A1058

A187

SHIELDS ROAD

FOSSWAY

HIGH ROAD

Newcastle Upon Tyne

North Tyneside

1 grid square represents 500 metres

D2
1 Birkdale Cl
2 Glendale Av
3 Hollings Crs
4 Weardale Av

Rising Sun Farm

D **E** 51 **F**

Battle Hill

Battle Hill First School

Bodmin Cl

D3
1 Henderson Rd

Battle Hill Drive

Broxburn

Avenue
Burnet Cl

Barwell Cl

Boldon

Bradford Av

Broomfield

Blackthorn Dr

Bracken Av

Bristol Av

I

North Tynside

D4
1 Albert Av
2 Clifton Av
3 Diamond St
4 Harle St
5 Harrington St
6 Hopper St
7 Thompson Gdns
8 Victoria Av

St Bernadettes RC First School

High Farm Middle School

Eskdale Av

Dinsdale

Battle Hill Dr

Boscombe

The Surg
PO

Belm

Willing High S

Rose Gdns

Rae Av

Lauderdale Av

Ridsdale

Milfield

Avenue

COAST ROAD   A1058

Willington

Prospect Av N

View N

Allendale Av

Kings Road

Battle Hl

NE28

Oswald's Rd

Norfolk Gdns

Whitby Gdr

St Peter's Road

Suffolk Gdns

St Cuthbert's Rd

Bede Crs

2

D6
1 Carvill Gdns
2 Maurice Rd
3 Philiphaugh
4 Plantation St
5 Praetorian Dr
6 Wilberforce St

Prospect Gdns

Selby Gdns

Fitzsimmons

Rd

Kings Road

The View

Holy Cross

Cemetery

St Cuthbert's

Essex Gdns

Sussex Gdns

E1
1 Barnwood Cl
2 Basildon Gdns
3 Baywood Gv
4 Beamish Cl
5 Beaufort Gdns
6 Beckford Cl
7 Bedale Cl
8 Belford Cl
9 Belper Cl
10 Belsay Cl
11 Berry Cl
12 Briar Cl

3

Dees Av

Irwin St

South

Queens Ter

Deneholm

Valley Gdns

Lindisfarne Pl

B1315   AR

68

E4
1 Alexandra St
2 Croft Av
3 Durham St West
4 Hunters Ct
5 Sunningdale Av

93

Willington Ter

PO

Shafto
S

Chester

North Tyneside Area Hlth Authority

Civic Hall

Lily Bank

Hunters Ldg

Park Av

Park Ter

Sir G B Hunter Memorial Hosp

Doctors Surgery

Crow Bank

Boyd Crs

Boyd

Alnwick St

Cumberland

Church Bank

ST PETER'S RD

Primary

4
Sch

Cem

Willing

E5
1 Chestnut St
2 Sycamore St

North Rd

Laburnum Av

Woodbine Av

Richardson St

Durham St

Dene Crs

Burnside High School

Central First School

North

South Ter

A187

Police Stn

Coronation St

First School

Limekiln

Church Vw

Hotel

F1
1 Banbury Gdns
2 Barmouth Cl
3 Barnstaple Cl
4 Barton Cl
5 Bewley Gdns
6 Boreham Cl
7 Bridlington
8 Bromley Gdns
9 Buxton Cl

David St

Elton St E

Hedley

Frank St

HIGH ST E   A193

Laurel St

Park Rd

Ferndale

Town Hall

PO
LC

Oak

Cedar Gv

Coach

Wagon Wy

Hadrian Road Station

Rd

5

Warwick Road

Brussels Rd

Sedley Rd

Hugh St

Holly

Vine

HADRIAN ROAD   A187

Davy Bank

Davy Bank

North Tyneside Council

Wallsend Business Cen

North Tyneside Council

First School

BUDDLE ST

Wallsend Station

Atkinson Ter

Wooley Street

Station Rd

Ind Est

Segedunum Business Cen

North Tyneside Council

F3
1 Haggie Av
2 Parkside
3 Swan Av

North Tyn
South Tyn

NEPTUNE RD

Benton Way

Buddle Industrial Estate

Wagonway Industrial Estate

F5
1 Brentwood Gv

6

Cecil Ct

Neptune Field

Hebburn Colliery

D **E** 84 **F**

Abingdon Rd

WAGONWAY ROAD

School Str

D5, E2, F2
Street names for this grid square are listed at the back of the index

A3
1 Ashbrooke Gdns
2 St Hilda's Av

A1
1 Bromsgrove Cl

Silverlink Business Park
Bittern Cl

Wes Chir

Mallard Way

A4
1 Bishops Cl

A
52
B
C

Bowness Av

Bewick Park

Engine La

Battle Hill First School

Bodmin Cl
Brighton Cl
Battle Hill Drive
Broxburn Cl
Bathgate Cl
Embleton Av

Battle Hill Bar
Bart
Bingley
Bath
Barr
Belmont

A1058

Tiverton Ct
3
Gardens
Mitford
Matfen Gdns
Langdale Gdns
Kendal Gdns
Aston
Coniston
Brough
Derwent Gdns
Appleby Gdns
Brampton Gdns
Keswick Av

Holy Cross RC Primary School

B1
1 Ingram Cl
2 Sandholm Cl
3 Tarrington Cl

Boldon
Barwell Cl
Bradford

Wick Dr
The Surg
PO

North Tyneside College

Willington High School

Coast Rd

Bristol Dr

COAST ROAD
A1058

B2
1 Garden Pk
2 Perth Cl

Willington

Engine Inn Rd
Octavia
Churchill Road
Perth Gdns
Oban Gdns
Garden Park Surg
Denbigh

B3
1 Cragside Gdns
2 Craster Gdns
3 Eversley Pl
4 Kingsley Pl

28

2

St Peter's Road

St Oswald's Rd
Norfolk Gdns
Suffolk Gdns
Whitby Gdns
Essex Gdns

Bede Crs

West Farm Road
Edward Road
Wilam Street
Simonside Av

Windsor Drive
PO
Camberley Gdns
Monmouth Av
Pembroke
Kelso Gdns

Howdon

St Cuthbert's

B4
1 Angle Ter

Cemetery

St Hilda's Gdns

Cuthbert's
St

Richmond Gdns
Ripon Gdns
Savory Rd
Edward Rd
Rothbury Rd
Lesbury Av
Greno Rd
Elton Av

Malvern Road
Lisle Road
Harrison Rd
Coldstream Gdns

Denbigh Community First School
Grosvenor Gdns
Edwin Gv
Caroline Cres

B5
1 Meadow Rd

3

McNamara Rd
Newton Av

Archer St Av

ARCHER STREET
B1315

Doctors Surg
Merlin Cl
PO
Benjamin Rd

Hazelwood Ter

Lindisfarne Pl

C2
1 Amberley Cl
2 Ennerdale Gdns
3 Windsor Cottages

67

Shafto
St

Willington Ter
Priors Wy

Chester St
Beasley

Stanley St

TYNEMOUTH

Bewicke Health Cen

Howdo Statio

ROSEHILL A193

Rosehill
Bamburgh Dr
Ravensworth

Kent Rd
Martin
Road

CHURCH BANK

Central First School

C of E Primary Sch

Vts
Northumberland
Roland Ter
Viaduct St

Ropery
Willington Cut

Lane

Headlam View

Burnside High School

Dene Crs

First School

Oak
Cedar Gv
Limekiln
WAGONWAY

North Ter
South Ter
A187
Church Vw
North

Point Pleasant
Ford
Western Road
Marina View
Quay

Armstrong Rd
Bewicke
Station

C3
1 Watson Gdns

LC

HADRIAN
ROAD

Wallsend Business Cen
North Tyneside Council

Hadrian Road Station
Hotel

Rosehill

4

5

A187 **ROAD**

Davy Bank
Davy Bank

Potter Street

North Tyneside Council

North Tyneside
South Tyneside

River Tyne

C4
1 Holme Gdns
2 Rosewood Ter

6

Wagonway Industrial Estate
Windmill Wy

Tedco Business Centre

Tedco Business Park

Coach
Tyne
Rolling Mi Rd

C5
Street names for this grid square are listed at the back of the index

Hebburn Colliery

BLACKETT ST

B1297
Witton Rd
High La
Hanlon Ct

WESTE

A
85
B
C

NWAY RD
School Street

Berkley Wy
Riley Wy
Newmarket

St Oswalds C of E

Palmer St

1 grid square represents 500 metres

Howdon 69

Chirton

53

D3
1 Cleveland Gdns
2 St Julien Gdns
3 Saltburn Gdns
4 Tynemouth Rd

D5
1 Clavering St
2 Cumberland St
3 Gladstone St
4 Westmorland Av

D6
1 Milton St
2 Shakespeare St
3 Spenser St

E1
1 Bournemouth Rd
2 Eyemouth Rd
3 Lynmouth Rd
4 Norham Rd

E4
1 Mitford St

E5
1 Barrasford St
2 Lesbury St

E6
1 Commercial Rd
2 Pearson Pl
3 Priory Rd

F1
1 Biddlestone Crs
2 Craster Rd
3 Plessey Gdns
4 Tosson Pl

F2
1 Chillingham Dr

F3
1 Cockburn Ter
2 Nelson Crs
3 St John's Wk

Bugatti Industrial Park

Norham Community High School

Percy Main Station

Meadow Well Station

Percy Main

Primary School

Cricket Club

HOWDON ROAD

Howdon Green Industrial Estate

North Tyneside Council

Howdon Pans

Howdon Dock Road

Northumberland Dock Road

Jarrow Slake

CHAYTOR ST

B1297

St Peters JMI Sch

WALLSEND RD

A193

A187

A19(T)

BEWICKE STREET

TYNE VIEW TER

70

Chirton

54

Percy Main

69

87

Hi Sh

A2
1 Coventry Gdns
2 Didcot Av
3 Meadow Well Wy
4 Wincanton Pl

A1
1 Millbrook
2 Mill Cl
3 Thorncliffe Pl

A3
1 Woodlea Ct

B1
1 Appleby Ct
2 Carlton Ter
3 Chirton Gn
4 Lovaine Pl West

B2
1 Morcott Gdns

B3
1 Hackworth Wy
2 Stockton Rd

C1
1 Beaumont St
2 Bedford St
3 Brannen St
4 Gardner Pl
5 Lovaine Av
6 Newcastle St
7 Nile St
8 Railway Ter
9 Rudyerd St
10 Saville St West
11 S Preston Gv
12 Spencer St
13 Stanley St
14 W Percy St
15 W Wellington St
16 William St

C2
1 Coronation St
2 Elsdon Pl
3 Elsdon St
4 Hylton St
5 Penman Pl
6 Penman St
7 Thrift St
8 Trinity Pl
9 Upper Elsdon St
10 West Lawson St

C3
1 Atkinson Gdns
2 Hendon Cl
3 Kingdom Pl
4 Watch House Cl

North Tyneside
Area Hlth
Authority

North Tyneside
Metropolitan
Borough Council

Norham Community
High School

Meadow Well
Station

Percy Main
Station

The Parks Sports
Centre

Jarrow
Slake

Ferry
Termin

1 grid square represents 500 metres

A193 WALLSEND RD A187 HOWDON ROAD HOWDON RD FRONT ST CHIRTON GN ALBION RD COACH LA PRUDHOE ST BOROUGH RD

55

D1
1 Bedford St
2 Camden St
3 Dockwray Cl
4 Lwr Rudyerd St
5 Sibthorpe St

D2
1 Tennyson Ter

D3
1 Coble Landing

D4
1 Brewery La
2 Carpenter St
3 Riverside Ct

D5
1 Cornwallis Sq
2 Weetman St
3 Windmill Hl

D6
1 Barnes' Rd
2 Elizabeth Diamond Gdns
3 Temple St West

E2
1 Hedley St
2 Morton St
3 Petrel Cl
4 Roman Rd North

E3
1 Barrington St
2 Brigham Pl
3 Burrow St
4 Cornwallis St
5 Nelson St
6 Russell St
7 Salem St
8 Smithy St
9 Station Ap
10 Thomas St
11 Wallis St
12 Waterloo Sq
13 Waterloo V

E5
1 Dixon St
2 Havelock St
3 New Green St

E6
1 Beaufront Ter
2 Chichester Pl
3 Gilbert St
4 Hampden St
5 Laygate

F2
1 George Scott St
2 Henry St
3 Livingstone St

F3
1 Brodrick St
2 Catherine St
3 Eastbourne Gv
4 Saville St
5 Shortridge St
6 Sydenham Ter
7 Winchester St
8 Woodbine St

E4, F4, F5, F6
Street names for this grid square are listed at the back of the index

NORTH SHIELDS

The Lawe

SOUTH ...D

Westo

88

A4
1 Aldwych St
2 Fitzpatrick Pl

A3
1 Wouldhave Ct

A5
1 August Pl
2 Catherine Cookson Ct
3 Gleneagles
4 Ingham Gra
5 Sunningdale
6 Turnberry

A6
1 College Dr

B6
1 Eastfield Rd
2 North Vw

C5
1 Bideford Gdns

SOUTH SHIELDS
NE33

Westoe

Horsley Hill

South Pier

Herd Sand

The Lawe

The Bents

Amphitheatre

Promenade

SEA ROAD A183

OCEAN RD

CHICHESTER RD

SUNDERLAND ROAD

COAST ROAD A183

HORSLEY HL RD B1301

DEAN RD B1301

HIGHFIELD ROAD

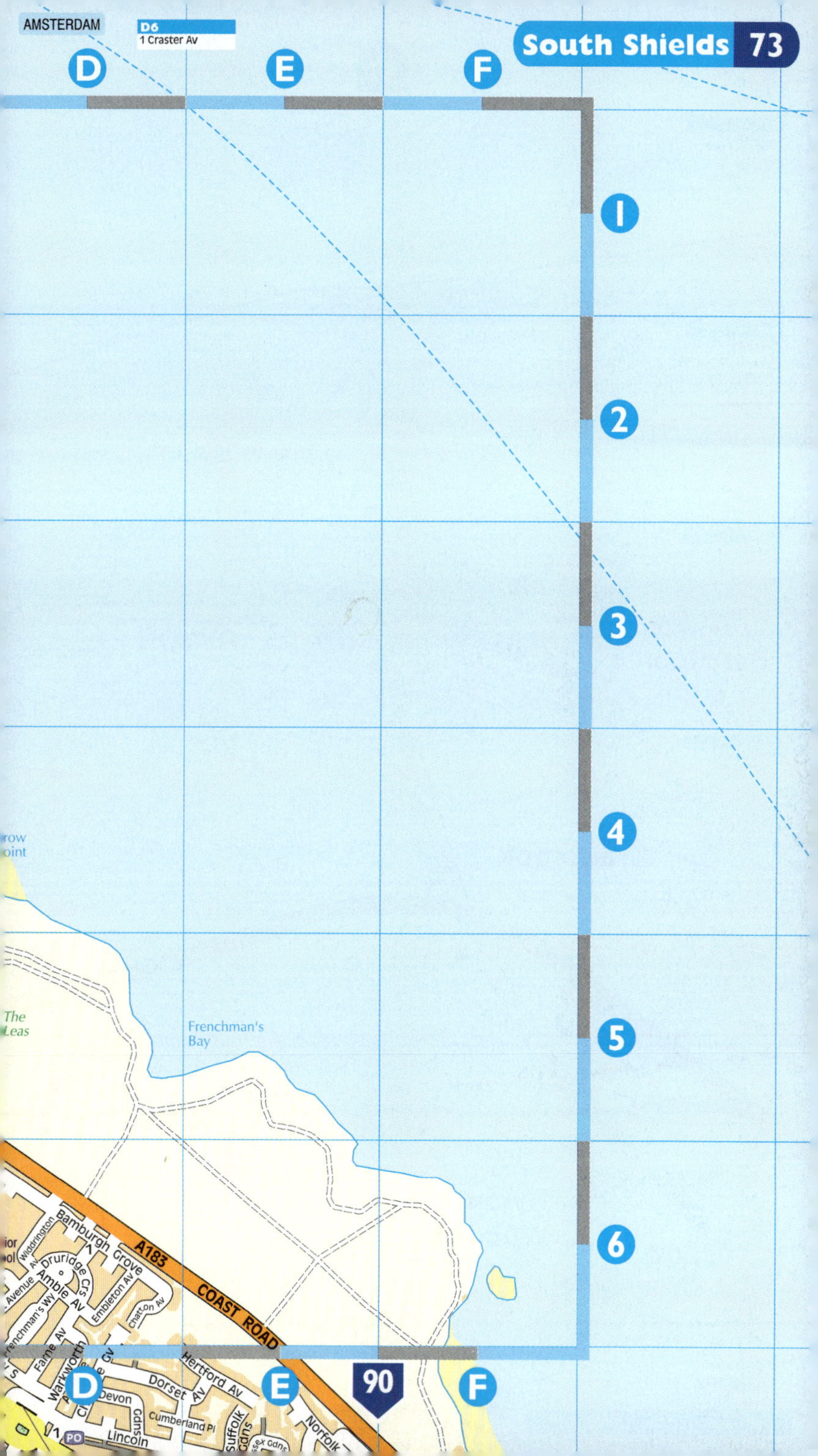

D E F

1
2
3
4
5
6

row
oint

The
Leas

Frenchman's
Bay

A183
COAST ROAD

Bamburgh Grove
Druridge Av
Embleton Av

Avenue
Amble Av
Fane

Warkworth

Devon
Dorset
Hertford Av
Suffolk Gdns
Norfolk

Cumberland Pl

Lincoln
PO

90

D E F

74

A · 57 · B · C

B2
1 Cypress Gv
2 Holly Av
3 Ivy Av
4 May Av
5 Ryton Hall Dr

I

B4
1 Southern Wy

2

C3
1 Holburn Cl
2 Holburn Ct

Ryton
Grange

Ryton Junior
& Infant School

3

Ryton
Comprehensive
School

Bar Moor

RYTON

MAIN ROAD   B6317   B6315

C4
1 Ferndown Ct
2 Sandpiper Cl
3 Whernside Wk

Ryton
Rugby Club

4

Crawcrook

WOODSIDE LA

Hexham Old Road

Cemy

5

A695   B6315

LANE

NE40

Ryton
Woodside

Star

Maiden Lane

WOODSIDE

Cemetery

6

Low
Greenside

Stephen's
Hall

Greenside
Cricket Club

A · 92 · B · C

1 grid square represents 500 metres

Doctors Surgery

First School

D4
1 Clifton Cl
2 Curlew Cl
3 Dunlin Cl
4 Sanderling Cl

D

E

58 Newburn

F

Newburn Leisure Centre

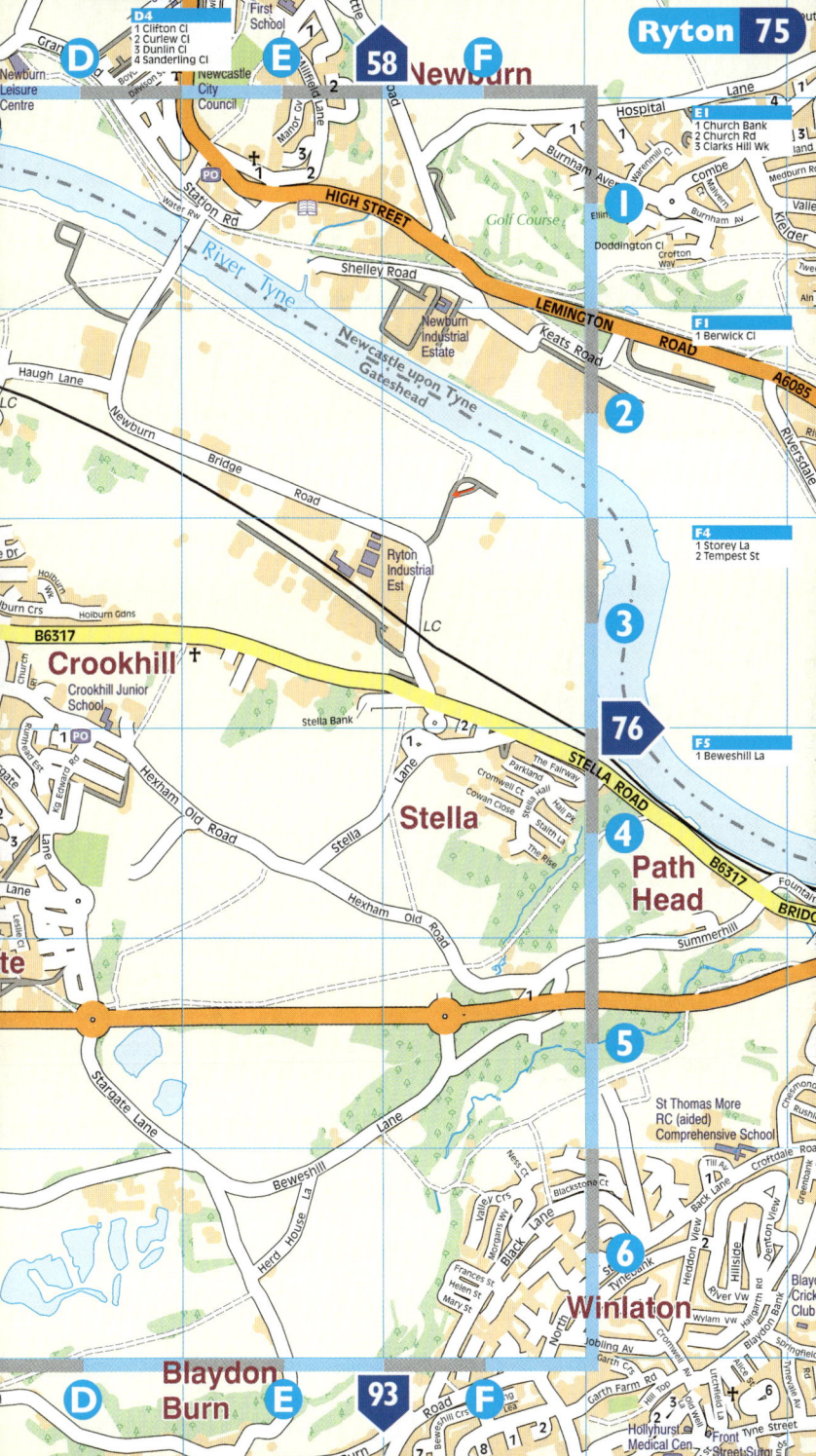

Gran

Newcastle City Council

Hospital

E1
1 Church Bank
2 Church Rd
3 Clarks Hill Wk

I

Burnham Ave

Combe

Doddington Cl
Crofton Way

Burnham Av

PO

Station Rd

Water Rw

HIGH STREET

LEMINGTON ROAD

A6085

Kielder

Riversdale

F1
1 Berwick Cl

Shelley Road

Golf Course

Keats Road

River Tyne

Newburn Industrial Estate

Newcastle upon Tyne
Gateshead

2

Haugh Lane

LC

Newburn

Bridge

Road

F4
1 Storey La
2 Tempest St

3

Dr

Holburn Crs

Holburn Gdns

B6317

Ryton Industrial Est

LC

76

Crookhill

Crookhill Junior School

Church

PO

1

Stella Bank

Hexham Old Road

Stella
Lane

The Fairway

Parkland

Cromwell Ct

Hall Pk

Cowan Close

Stella Hall

Statlh La

The Rise

F5
1 Beweshill La

STELLA ROAD

B6317

4

Path Head

Stella

Hexham Old Road

Summerhill

BRIDG

Fountain

5

St Thomas More RC (aided) Comprehensive School

Chesmond

Rushlea

Stargate Lane

Lane

Blackstone Ct

Back Lane

Croftdale

Greenhaugh

Ness Ct

Valley Crs

Morgan Wy

Beweshill La

Herd House La

Black Lane

Heddon View

Hillside

River Vw

Denton View

6

Winlaton

Frances St

Helen St

Mary St

Jobling Av

Garth Cl

Tynebank

North

Cromwell Rd

Wylam Vw

Wylam St

Blaydon Bank

Springfield

Blaydon Cricket Club

D

Blaydon Burn

E

93

F

Carth Farm Rd

Burn

Beweshill Crs

Road

7

8

1

Hollyhurst

Medical Cen

PO

Litchfield Ct

Front Tyne St

Street Sutro

Tynevale Rd

76

Newburn

A6
1 Lanercost Av
2 Westway

A1
1 Allerdean Cl
2 Grasmoor Pl
3 Hamsterley Crs
4 Helston Ct

B1
1 Blyth Ct
2 Bridgewater Cl
3 Cranfield Pl
4 Henlow Rd
5 Woodburn St

B2
1 Gladstone St
2 Johnson St
3 Loraine Ter
4 Maud St
5 Northumberland Rd
6 Percy St
7 Quarry Rd
8 Store St

B5
1 Clifford St
2 Garden St
3 Horse Crofts
4 Lawrence Ct
5 Loup St
6 Lynwood Av
7 Shop Spouts

B6
1 Burnley St
2 Crowley Gdns
3 Ethel Av
4 Pine Rd

C1
1 Addison Rd
2 The Crossway
3 Honister Cl
4 Woodlands Rd

Stella

C2
1 The Orchard
2 Wedgewood Cottages

C5
1 George St

B4
Street names for this grid square are listed at the back of the index

Winlaton

C6
1 Shibdon Crs
2 Shibdon Park Vw

Newcastle upon Tyne Gateshead

Industrial Estate

Golf Course

Hospital

Southfork

Cemetery

Burnham Avenue

LEMINGTON ROAD

A6085

NORTHUMBERLAND ROAD

Doctors Surg

Lemington Clinic

First School

St Georges RC Primary School

STELLA ROAD

Path Head

B6317

BRIDGE STREET

Blaydon Station

BLAYDON

CHAINBRIDGE

HWY

St Thomas More RC (aided) Comprehensive School

Primary School

Gateshead Metropolitan Borough Council

Blaydon Cemetery

Blaydon Cricket Club

A 59 **B** **C**

A 75

2

3

4

5

6

I

A 94 **B** **C**

l grid square represents 500 metres

D1
1 Carlton Gdns
2 Flexbury Gdns
3 Shelford Gdns
4 Styford Gdns
5 West Copperas

D2
1 Lintzford Gdns
2 Malton Cl
3 Maple Cl
4 Matfen Cl
5 Norfolk Wy

D3
1 St George's Pl
2 St George's Rd
3 St George's Ter

D6
1 Napier Wy

E1
1 Castlenook Pl
2 Copperas La
3 Hextol Gdns
4 Legion Gv
5 Legion Rd
6 Overdene
7 Rockcliffe Gdns
8 West Vallum

E2
1 Ravenburn Gdns

E3
1 Langham Rd
2 Parmontley St

F2
1 Inglemere Pl
2 Muscott Gv

F3
1 Sandmere Pl

F4
1 Lightwood Av
2 Pretoria St

Denton Burn

Lemington

Bell's Close

Blaydon Haughs

Scotswood

Benwell

60 78

2 3 4 5 6

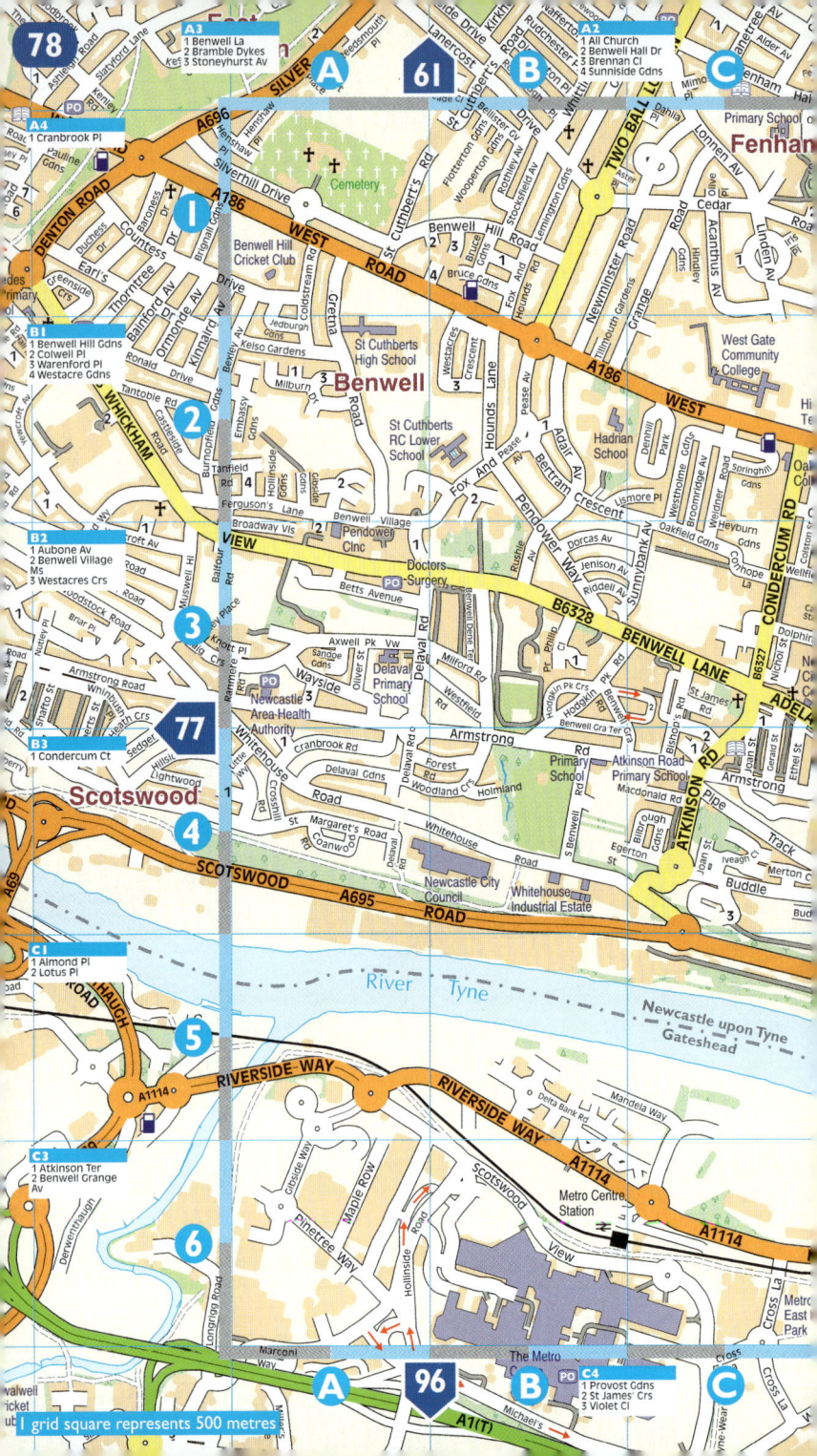

A3
1 Benwell La
2 Bramble Dykes
3 Stoneyhurst Av

61

A2
1 All Church
2 Benwell Hall Dr
3 Brennan Cl
4 Sunniside Gdns

A **B** **C**

A4
1 Cranbrook Pl

B1
1 Benwell Hill Gdns
2 Colwell Pl
3 Warenford Pl
4 Westacre Gdns

B2
1 Aubone Av
2 Benwell Village Ms
3 Westacres Crs

B3
1 Condercum Ct

C1
1 Almond Pl
2 Lotus Pl

C3
1 Atkinson Ter
2 Benwell Grange Av

77

96

C4
1 Provost Gdns
2 St James' Crs
3 Violet Cl

Fenham

SILVER

Cemetery

Benwell Hill Cricket Club

WEST ROAD

Benwell

St Cuthberts High School

St Cuthberts RC Lower School

West Gate Community College

Hadrian School

WHICKHAM

Benwell Village

Pendower Clnc

Doctors Surgery

Betts Avenue

Newcastle Area Health Authority

Wayside

Delaval Primary School

Atkinson Road Primary School

Scotswood

Newcastle City Council

Whitehouse Industrial Estate

River Tyne

Newcastle upon Tyne Gateshead

RIVERSIDE WAY

SCOTSWOOD ROAD A695

A1114

Metro Centre Station

The Metro Centre

A1(T)

BENWELL LANE B6328

CONDERCUM RD

WEST ROAD A186

DENTON ROAD A686

A186

Silverhill Drive

1 grid square represents 500 metres

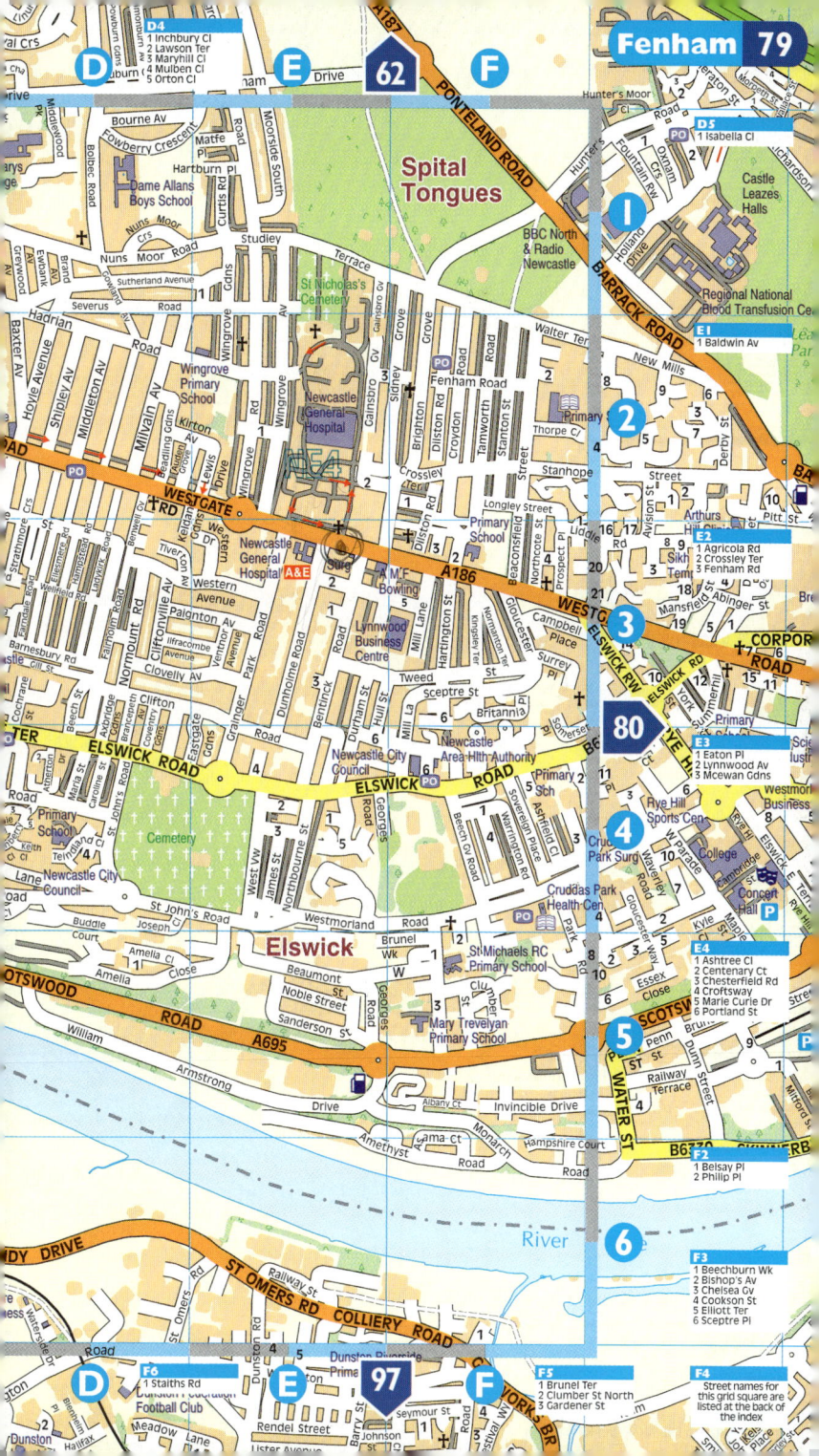

80

A2, A4, A5, B5
Street names for
this grid square are
listed at the back of
the index

A   63   B   C

A1
1 Ancrum St
2 Belle Gv West

A3
1 Buckingham St
2 Colliery La
3 Cookson Cl
4 Cottenham
  Chare
5 Cottenham St
6 Cross Villa Place
  No 4
7 Cross Villa Place
  No 5
8 Douglas Ter
9 Edward Pl
10 Elswick St
11 High Swinburne
   Pl
12 Lancaster St
13 Mansfield Pl
14 Quarry Bank
15 Ravensworth
   Ter
16 St Philips Cl
17 St Philips Wy
18 Tindal Cl
19 Tindal St
20 Worley Cl
21 Worley St

B1
1 Claremont St
2 Windmill Ct

B2
1 St James' St

B3
1 Rutherford St
2 Swinburne Pl

79

B4
1 Back George St
2 Blandford Sq
3 Churchill St
4 Forth Pl
5 Lord St
6 Neville St
7 Peel St
8 Sunderland St
9 Westmorland Rd

C1
1 Devonshire Ter

C2
1 Morden St
2 Northumberland
  Rd
3 Vine La

C3
1 Cloth Market
2 Grey St
3 St Nicholas'
  Church Yd
4 Shakespeare St

C4
1 Clavering Pl
2 Orchard St
3 Queens La
4 South St
5 Stephenson's La

A   98   B   C

1 grid square represents 500 metres

D1, D4, D5, E3
Street names for
this grid square are
listed at the back of
the index

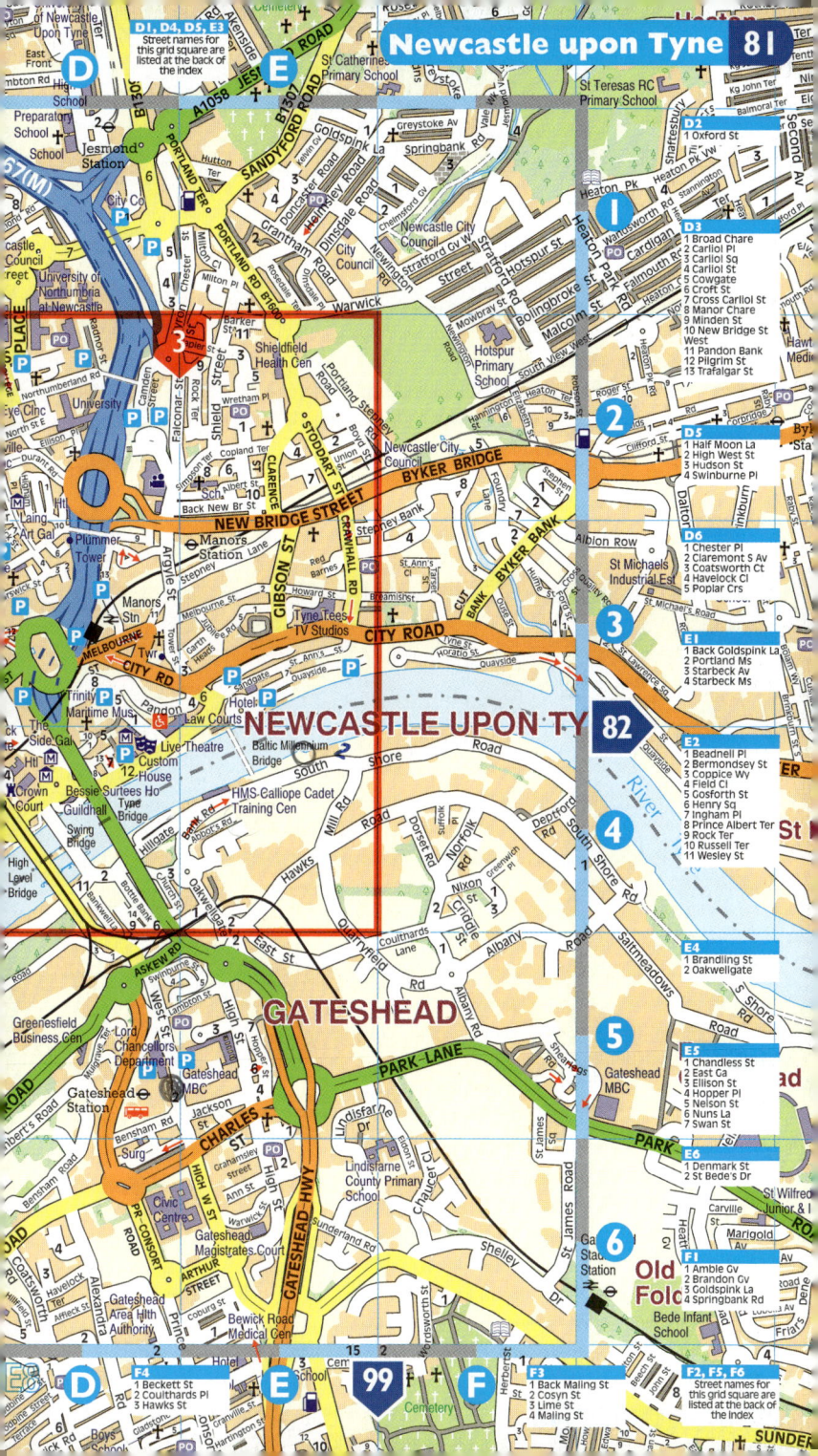

D2
1 Oxford St

D3
1 Broad Chare
2 Carliol Pl
3 Carliol Sq
4 Carliol St
5 Cowgate
6 Croft St
7 Cross Carliol St
8 Manor Chare
9 Minden St
10 New Bridge St West
11 Pandon Bank
12 Pilgrim St
13 Trafalgar St

D5
1 Half Moon La
2 High West St
3 Hudson St
4 Swinburne Pl

D6
1 Chester Pl
2 Claremont S Av
3 Coatsworth Ct
4 Havelock Cl
5 Poplar Crs

E1
1 Back Goldspink La
2 Portland Ms
3 Starbeck Av
4 Starbeck Ms

82

E2
1 Beadnell Pl
2 Bermondsey St
3 Coppice Wy
4 Field Cl
5 Gosforth St
6 Henry Sq
7 Ingham Pl
8 Prince Albert Ter
9 Rock Ter
10 Russell Ter
11 Wesley St

E4
1 Brandling St
2 Oakwellgate

E5
1 Chandless St
2 East Ga
3 Ellison St
4 Hopper Pl
5 Nelson St
6 Nuns La
7 Swan St

E6
1 Denmark St
2 St Bede's Dr

F1
1 Amble Gv
2 Brandon Gv
3 Goldspink La
4 Springbank Rd

F2, F5, F6
Street names for
this grid square are
listed at the back of
the index

F4
1 Beckett St
2 Coulthards Pl
3 Hawks St

F3
1 Back Maling St
2 Cosyn St
3 Lime St
4 Maling St

Ⓐ 65 Ⓑ Ⓒ

Heaton

St Teresas RC Primary School

Chillingham Road Station

Chillingham Industrial Estate

Heaton Pk

Hotspur Primary School

Doctors Surgery

Raby Cross Medical Centre

Hawthorn House Medical Cen

Ⓑ Ⓡ Ⓘ Ⓓ Ⓖ Ⓔ

BYKER BANK

Byker Station

St Lawrence RC Primary School

Byker

Welbeck Primary School

Albion Row

St Michaels Industrial Est

Primary School

WELBECK ROAD

81

St Peter's

Newcastle City Council

WALKER ROAD

River Tyne

The Ropery

Chandlers Quay

PARK LANE

Gateshead MBC

East Gateshead

Gateshead International Stadium

PARK ROAD

Felling Business Cen

Felling Business Centre

Gateshead Stadium Station

St Wilfreds RC Junior & Infant School

Old Fold

Bede Infant School

ABBOTSFORD ROAD

Ⓐ 100 Ⓑ Ⓒ

SUNDERLAND

Station

D1
1 Christopher Rd

D · E · 66 · A187 · F

FOSSWAY

Rutland Avenue

WAVERDALE AVENUE

BATH STREET

WELBECK ROAD

Walker

STATION ROAD

WALKER ROAD

River Tyne

St Anthony's

elling hore

Tyneview Primary School

St Anthonys Health Centre

West Walker School

Newcastle City Council

Pelaw · 101

Bill Quay

D2
1 Musgrave Ter

D3
1 Cullercoats St

D5
1 Jellicoe Rd
2 Portman Pl

E1
1 Keebledale Av

2

E2
1 Allendale Ter
2 Cowen St
3 Hedgeley Ter
4 Jackson St

3

E3
1 Horsley Ter
2 Melton Av
3 Troutbeck Av
4 Tweedy St

84

E4
1 Carnaby Rd
2 Staward Ter
3 Wetheral Ter

4

E5
1 Gaughan Cl
2 Mafeking St
3 Sandwich St

F2
1 Ingram Ter
2 Iona Pl
3 Langdale Gdns
4 Sunningdale Av
5 Winslow Cl
6 Yorkdale Pl

5

F3
1 Beverley Ter
2 Lamb St
3 Park Vw
4 Proctor St
5 Saffron Pl
6 Whitworth Cl

F4
1 Back Walker Rd
2 Caledonia St
3 Cobham Pl
4 Crossfield Ter
5 Hailing Cl
6 Hibernia Rd
7 Highfield Ter
8 Kingsmere Gdns
9 Royston Ter
10 Southfield Ter

6

F5
Street names for this grid square are listed at the back of the index

84

A187

A **67** **B** **C**

A3 1 Mitchell St

A2 1 Ambrose Pl

A6
1 Bamburgh Dr
2 Brack Ter
3 Braemar Ct
4 Christon Wy
5 Elgin Ct
6 Hainingwood Ter
7 Hall Ter
8 Wood Ter

I

B1
1 Edward St
2 Lamport St
3 Pinewood
4 Price St
5 St Andrew's St

2

B3
1 Longdean Cl

Walker

3

83

C1
1 Albert St
2 Ashwood Cft
3 Carr St
4 Cosserat Pl
5 Hazelmoor

4

West Walker School

C2
1 Coquet St
2 Ellison St
3 Ropery La

5

C4
1 Cradock Av
2 Garden Dr
3 High Croft Cl
4 Hospital Dr
5 Penshaw Vw

6

Bill Quay

Bill Quay Cricket Club

Hebburn New Town

Hebburn Station

Victoria Medical Cen

Mountbatten Medical Centre
South Tyneside Borough Council

Cemetery

Victoria Industrial Est

South Tyneside College

Newcastle upon Tyne
South Tyneside

A **102** **B** **C**

C5
1 Birtwistle Av
2 St Joseph's Ct
3 Wilkinson Av

1 grid square represents 500 metres

Pelaw

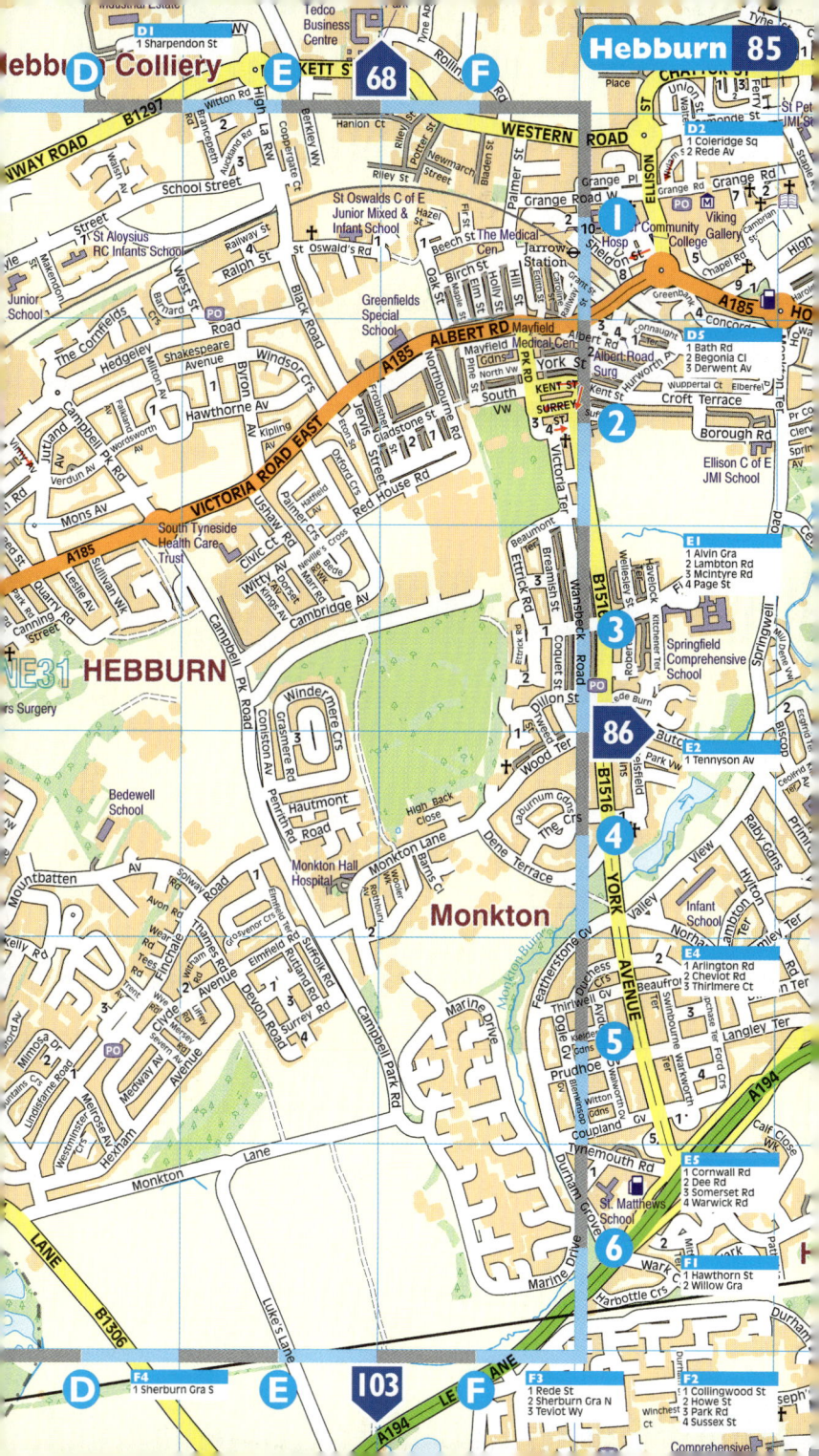

D1
1 Sharpendon St

Hebburn Colliery

D **E** KETT St **68** Rollin **F**

Tedco Business Centre

B1297
CONWAY ROAD
Witton Rd High La Rw Copperate Ct Berkley Wy
Branogarth Auckland Rd
Walsh Av
School Street
School Street
Makerion Ct Railway St Hanlon Ct
St Aloysius RC Infants School Ralph St
West St Black Rd
Road St Oswalds C of E Junior Mixed & Infant School
The Cornfields Barnard St Riley St Newmarch Street
Hedgeley PO St Oswald's Rd Potter St Bladen St Palmer St
Shakespeare Avenue Greenfields Special School Beech St Hazel St The Medical Cen
Windsor Crs Milton Rd Birch St Oak St Hill St Jarrow Station
Campbell Rd Byron Hawthorne Av Kipling ALBERT RD Elm St HOLY St Mayfield
Junior School Jutland Av Wordsworth Jervis St Northbourne Mayfield Gdns Medical Cen
Verdun Av Gladstone Rd York St North Vw Albert Road Surg
Mons Av VICTORIA ROAD EAST Oxford Crs South Vw KENT St SURREY St
Leslie Av Usraw Rd Palmer Crs Red House Rd Hatfield PK RD
A185 Civic Ct Witty Rd Dorset Neville's Cross Beaumont St
Sullivan Wk South Tyneside Health Care Trust Brede Breamish St Wansbeck Road
Quarry Rd Campbell Pk Road Cambridge Av Ettick Rd B1516
Canning Street Coquet St
NE31 HEBBURN Windermere Crs Dillon St Springfield Comprehensive School
rs Surgery Grasmere Rd Conjston Av rde Burn PO Butcher 86
Bedewell School Hautmont Road Penrith Rd Wood Ter Park Vw B1516
Monkton Hall Hospital Monkton Lane High Back Close Laburnum Gdns The Crs York Av
Mountbatten Solway Rd Monkton Barns Cl Dene Terrace Valley Infant School
Avon Rd Grosvenor Rd Elmfield Rd Monkton Featherstone Gv Beaufort
Penchale Thame Rd Suffolk Rd Rothbury Wk Thirlwell Odle Gdns Kleiner
Clyde Av Tees Rd Rutland Rd Campbell Park Road Prudhoe Bamborough
Wear Surrey Rd Marine Drive Coupland Witton Gdns
Mimosa Dr Medway Av Devon Road Monkton Lane Tynemouth Rd Durham Grove
Lindisfarne Road Avenue St. Matthews School Ward
Westminster Road Melrose Av Hexham Monkton Lane Marine Drive Harbottle Crs
LANE B1306 Luke's Lane LE LANE A194

D F4 1 Sherburn Gra S **E** **103** **F** F3
1 Rede St
2 Sherburn Gra N
3 Teviot Wy

D2
1 Coleridge Sq
2 Rede Av

CHARLTON St
Ormonde St St Pet
Grange Pl Ellison Water St Ferry
WESTERN ROAD Grange Rd Grange Rd
Grange Road PO M Viking Gallery
Hosp Community College Chapel Rd
Sheldon St Greenbank A185 Concorde
A185 Connaught HO
Albert Rd **D5**
1 Bath Rd
2 Begonia Cl
3 Derwent Av
Wuppertal Ct Elberfel
Croft Terrace
Borough Rd
Ellison C of E JMI School

E1
1 Alvin Gra
2 Lambton Rd
3 McIntyre Rd
4 Page St
Havelock Wellesley Ter
Kitchener Ter
3
PO

E2
1 Tennyson Av
Raby Gdns
View

E4
1 Arlington Rd
2 Cheviot Rd
3 Thirlmere Ct
Swinbourne Ter Langley Av
Norham Warkworth A194
Calf Close

5
Ford Crs

E5
1 Cornwall Rd
2 Dee Rd
3 Somerset Rd
4 Warwick Rd

F1
1 Hawthorn Rd
2 Willow Gra

6

F2
1 Collingwood St
2 Howe St
3 Park Rd
4 Sussex St

MONKTON

2

4

Hebburn

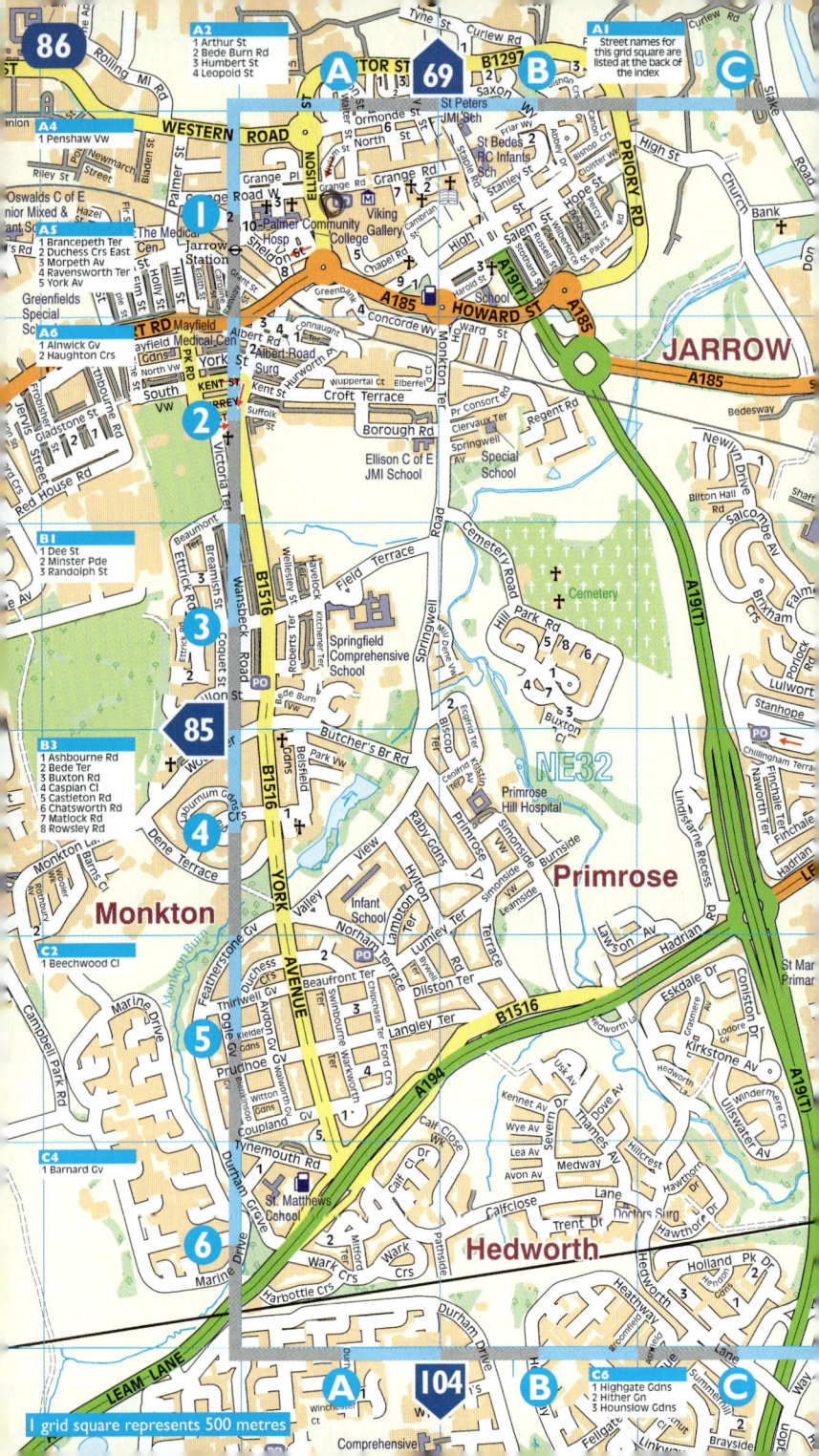

86

A2
1 Arthur St
2 Bede Burn Rd
3 Humbert St
4 Leopold St

A
VICTOR ST

69
B1297
St Peters
JMI Sch

B

3

C
Street names for this grid square are listed at the back of the index

A4
1 Penshaw Vw

WESTERN ROAD

Rolling Ml Hill

Palmer St
Bladen St
Hazel
Newmarch St
Street
Riley St

Oswalds C of E
nior Mixed &
ant Sch

A5
1 Brancepeth Ter
2 Duchess Crs East
3 Morpeth Av
4 Ravensworth Ter
5 York Av

The Medical Cen
Jarrow Station

Grange Pl
Grange Road W
10 Palmer Community
Hosp
Grange Rd
Grange Rd

Sheldon St

Viking Gallery

Jarrow Community College

St Bedes
RC Infants
Sch

Friar Wy
Abbey Rd
Bishop
High St

Priory Rd

High St
Church Rd
Bank

Greenfields
Special
Sch

ST RD Mayfield
Mayfield Medical Cen

A6
1 Alnwick Gv
2 Haughton Crs

North Vw
York

Albert Rd
Albert Road
Surg

Connaught
Elberfel

Hope St
Stanley St

Salem St
St Paul's

A185

HOWARD ST
A185

JARROW
A185

Bedesway

KENT ST

SURREY

South
Vw

Kent St

Croft Terrace

Hurworth

Wuppertal Ct Elberfel

Clervaux Ter
Springwell
Special
School

Pr Consort
Regent St

Newlyn Drive

Bilton Hall

Salcombe Dr

Victoria Ter

Borough Rd

Ellison C of E
JMI School

Monkton Rd

A19(T)

Blaxham
Crs
Falm
Pordock
Lulwort

B1
1 Dee St
2 Minster Pde
3 Randolph St

Beaumont
Ter

Ettrick Gdns

Wansbeck Road

B1516

Field Terrace

Wellesley St
Havelock

Kitchener Ter

Roberts

Springwell Road

Cemetery Road

Cemetery

Hill Park Rd

5 8 6
4 7
3

Buxton
Cl

Stanhope

B3
1 Ashbourne Rd
2 Bede Ter
3 Buxton Rd
4 Caspian Cl
5 Castleton Rd
6 Chatsworth Rd
7 Matlock Rd
8 Rowsley Rd

3

85

Coquet Gv

Ettrick Gv

PO

Bede Burn
Vw

Butcher's Br Rd

Belsfield
Park Vw

Laburnum Gdns

Crs

4

Dene Terrace

Monkton

Manors

Woodburn

C2
1 Beechwood Cl

Marine Drive

Monkton Burn

YORK

B1516

AVENUE

Biscop
Cecil Rd
Kirkstone

Primrose
Hill Hospital

NE32

Rably Gdns

Primrose

Simonside

Burnside

Simonside
Leamside
Terrace

Primrose

Lindisfarne Recess

Nawforth Ter
Finchale
Finchale

Featherstone Gv

Duchess
Thirlwell Gv
Ogle Gv

PO

Beaufront Ter
Swinbourne Ter
Warkworth

Kielder
Gdns

Chipchase Ter
Dilston Ter

View
Valley

Infant
School

Lambton
Norham Terrace

Hylton
Lumley
Terrace

Langley Ter

B1516

Lawson Av
Hadrian

Eskdale Dr

Grasmere

Coniston Av

St Mar
Primar

5

Prudhoe Gv

Witton
Gdns

Coupland
Gv

Avon Gv
Aydon Gv

Ford Crs

A194

Kennet Av

Usk Av

Wye Av

Thames Av

Dove Av

Severn

Lea Av

Medway

Avon Av

Hedworth La

Lodore
Av

Kirkstone Av

Hillcrest

Hawthorn Rd

Windermere Av

Ullswater Av

A19(T)

C4
1 Barnard Gv

Durham Drive

Tynemouth Rd

St Matthews
School

Calf Close

Calf Dr

Calf Cr

Calfclose

Trent Dr

Lane

Doctors Surg

Hawthorn Dr

6

Marine

Ward Crs

Mitford
Crs

Wark Crs

Pathside

Hedworth

Heathway

Holland Pk Dr

Hendon

Harbottle Crs

Durham Grove

LEAM LANE

Comprehensive

A

104

W

B

C6
1 Highgate Gdns
2 Hither Gn
3 Hounslow Gdns

Summerhill

Brayside

Feligate

Linkway

I grid square represents 500 metres

D4
1 Melrose Gv

D
E
70
F

Jarrow
Slake

D5
1 Balmoral Av
2 Mull Gv

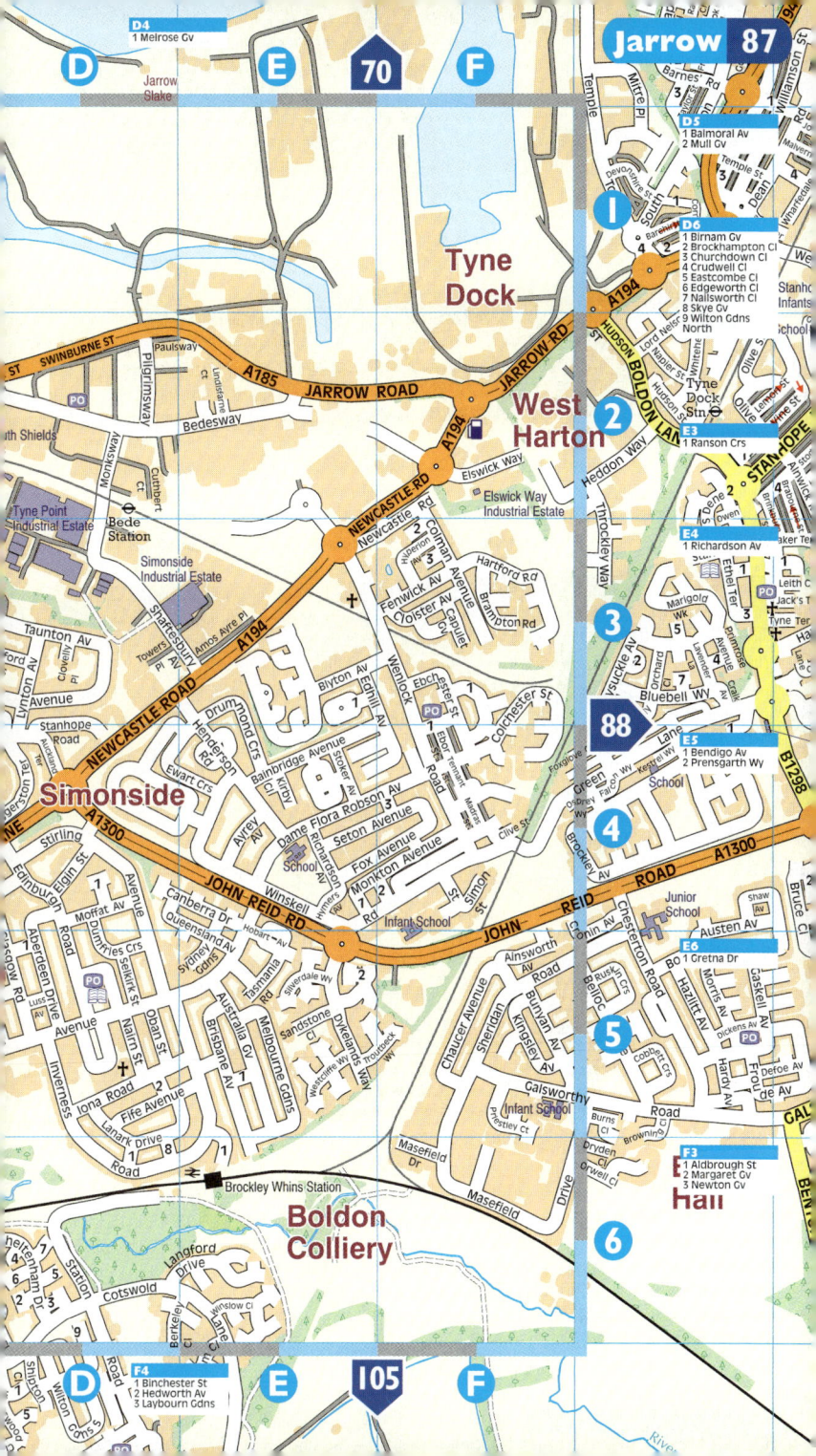

I

D6
1 Birnam Gv
2 Brockhampton Cl
3 Churchdown Cl
4 Crudwell Cl
5 Eastcombe Cl
6 Edgeworth Cl
7 Nailsworth Cl
8 Skye Gv
9 Wilton Gdns
North

Stanhope
Infants

**Tyne
Dock**

SWINBURNE ST
Paulsway
Pilgrimsway
Lindisfarne
A185
JARROW ROAD
A194
JARROW RD
HUDSON
BOLDON LANE

**West
Harton**

2

Tyne
Dock
Stn

E3
1 Ranson Crs

STANHOPE

PO

Bedesway
th Shields
Monkway
Cumbert
Ct

A194

Elswick Way

NEWCASTLE RD
Newcastle Rd
Colman Avenue
Alnerton
Elswick Way
Industrial Estate

Heddon Way

Throckley Way

E4
1 Richardson Av

Tyne Point
Industrial Estate

Bede
Station

Simonside
Industrial Estate

Fenwick Av
Oyster Av
Hartford Rd
Brampton Rd

Marigold
Wk

Ysuckle Av
Bluebell Wy

Ethel Ter

Avenue
Lavender
PO
Jack's

Leith Ct
Tyne Ter

3

Taunton Av
Clovelly Av
ford Av

Towers
Pl
Amos Ayre Pl
A194

Blyton Av
Edhill Av
Wenlock
Ebch

Colchester St

88

Lane

School

E5
1 Bendigo Av
2 Prensgarth Wy

B1298

Lynton
Av
Avenue

Stanhope
Road
Auckland

Drummond Crs
Henderson
Rd

Bainbridge Avenue
Kirby

Chester St
Ebor St
Tempest
Maltravers

Foxglove
Wy
Green
Fairy
Kestrel Wy
Vestel Wy

School

4

Simonside

A1300

Ewart Crs

Dame Flora Robson Av
Richardson

Avrey
Av
Seton Avenue

Clive St

Brockley
Av

JOHN REID ROAD
A1300
Shaw
Av

Junior
School

Austen Av

Stirling

Canberra Dr
Queensland Av

Hobart

Fox Avenue
Monkton Avenue
Winter's

St Simon
Rd

JOHN REID

Chesterton Road
Conin Av

E6
1 Gretna Dr

Edinburgh Elgin St
Moffat Av
Dumfries Crs
Selkirk St
Sydney
Gdns

Tasmania
Rd
Silverdale Wy

Infant School

Ainsworth
Av

Ruskin
Av
Belloc

Norris Av
Hazlitt Av

Caskel
Av
Defoe Av

Bruce Cl

Aberdeen Drive
Luss Av

PO

Australia Av
Brisbane Av
Melbourne Gdns
Sandstone
Dykelands Rd
Troutbeck
Westcliffe Wy

Sheridan

Bunyan Av
Kingsley
Av

Cobbett's Cl

PO
Hardy Av
Froude Av

5

Avenue
Inverness
Nairn St
Iona Road

Chaucer Avenue

Galsworthy
Infant School
Priestley Ct

Road
Burns
Browning

Fife Avenue
Lanark Drive
1
8

Road

Masefield
Dr

Dryden
Cl
Orwell Cl

F3
1 Aldbrough St
2 Margaret Gv
3 Newton Gv

E
Hall

Brockley Whins Station

**Boldon
Colliery**

Masefield
Drive

6

Cotswold

Langford
Drive

nham
Dr

Station

Berkeley Cl
winslow Cl
Lane

Wilton
Gdns

D
E
105
F

F4
1 Binchester St
2 Hedworth Av
3 Layburn Gdns

PO

River

88

71

106

87

A2
1 Belle Vue Crs
2 Rutland St
3 Union St

A1
1 Dean Rd
2 Greathead St
3 S Frederick St
4 Whitehead St

A3
1 Beattie St
2 Hope St
3 Lucock St
4 Primrose Av
5 School Loaning
6 Thompson St
7 Watling St

A4
1 Swallow Tail Ct

Tyne Dock

West Park

B1
1 Clifton Ter
2 Pembroke Ter
3 Shrewsbury Ter
4 Wharfedale Dr

B2
1 Burnham St
2 Farnham Rd
3 Revesby St
4 Stoddart St

West Harton

Stanhope County
Infants School

Tyne Dock Stn

Farnham
Medical Cen

St Wilfrids RC
Comprehensive
School

Ashley Road County
JMI School

St Tyne Dock

Elswick Way
Industrial Estate

B3
1 Afton Ct
2 Awnless Ct
3 Bensham Ct
4 Browntop Pl
5 Claypool Ct
6 Coxford Ct
7 Eavers Ct
8 Eskdale St
9 Hardyards Ct
10 High Moor Pl
11 Loudon St
12 Newland Ct
13 Windlass Ct

A&E
South Tyneside Health
Care Trust

The Wynde

B5
1 Brodie Cl
2 Cameron Cl

Boldon
Lane
Health
Centre

C1
1 Lismore Av
2 Newbury St

Infant School

Whiteleas

C2
1 Haweswater Cl

Junior
School

C3
1 Broadfield Pl
2 Bryden Ct
3 Homestall Cl
4 Moorhouse Cl

Infant School

C5
1 Romney Av
2 Sandalwood

Biddick Hall

Albert Elliott County
Junior Mixed School

B4
Street names for
this grid square are
listed at the back of
the index

C6
1 Sutherland Ct

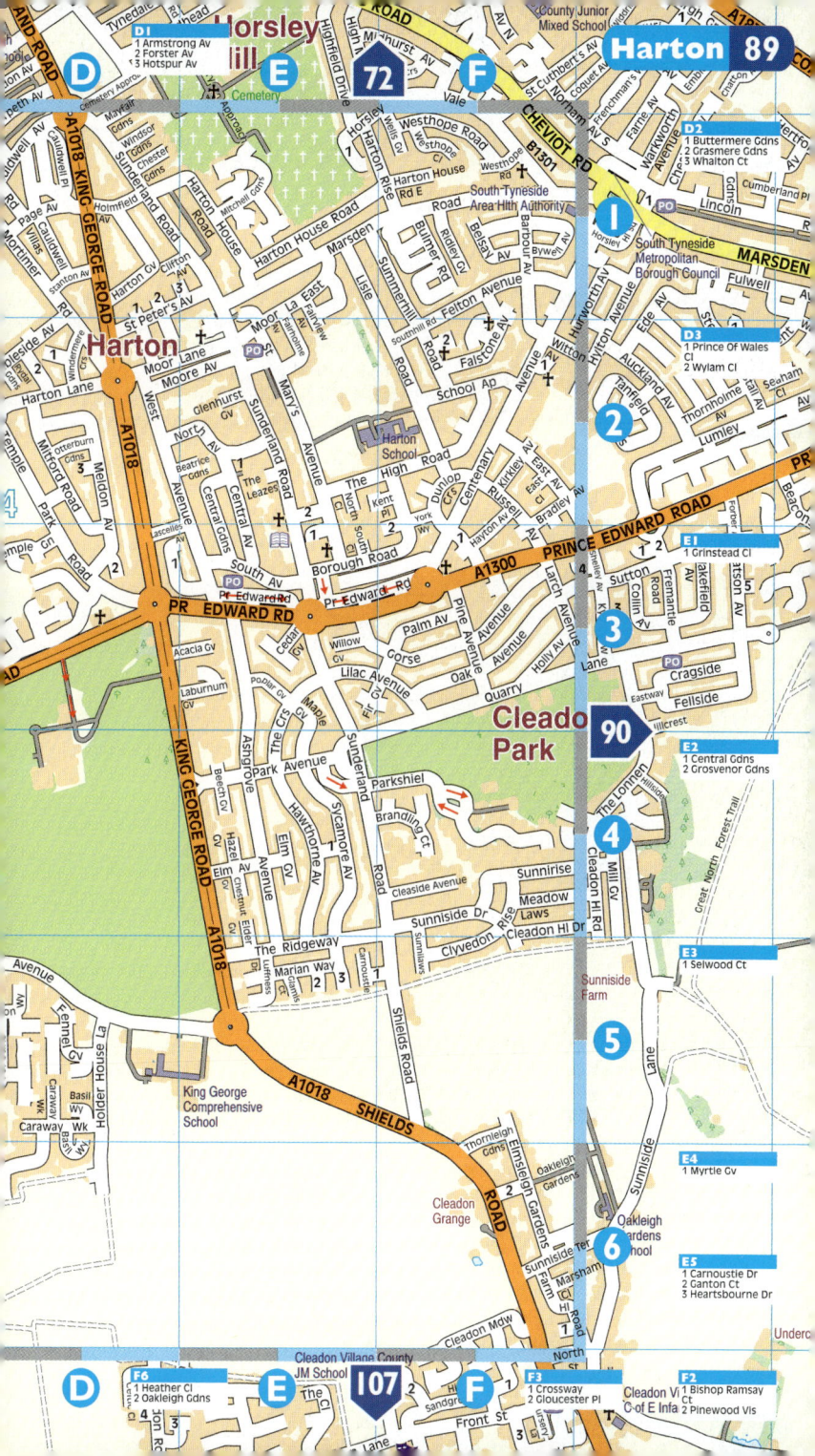

Horsley Hill

D1
1 Armstrong Av
2 Forster Av
3 Hotspur Av

72

F

County Junior Mixed School

CHEVIOT RD

St Cuthbert's Av

D2
1 Buttermere Gdns
2 Grasmere Gdns
3 Whalton Ct

Cumberland Av

Lincoln

MARSDEN

Cemetery

Horsley Vale

Westhope Road

Harton House Rd E

South Tyneside Area Hlth Authority

Barbour Av

South Tyneside Metropolitan Borough Council

Fulwell

D3
1 Prince Of Wales Cl
2 Wylam Cl

Harton House Road

Marsden

Ridley Av

Belsay

ByWell

Tanfield

Lumley

Thornholme Av

Seaham Av

Harton

Harton Gv

Clifton

Moor Lane

Burnet Road

Witton Gdns

Auckland Av

PR

Beacon

Harton Lane

Moore Av

Mary's Gv

Feltom Avenue

School Ap

Falstone Av

2

Fremantle Road

akerfield

tson Av

Glenhurst Gv

Harton School

Dunlop

Centenary

E1
1 Grinstead Cl

Sutton

The Leazes

The High Road

Kent Pl

Russell Av

Bradley Av

PRINCE EDWARD ROAD

Colin Av

South Av

Borough Road

York Wy

Hayton Av

A1300

3

Cragside

PR EDWARD RD

Pr Edward Rd

Pr Edward Rd

Larch Avenue

Eastway

Fellside

Acacia Gv

Palm Av

Pine Avenue

Holly Av

Willow Gv

gorse

Oak

Lilac Avenue

Fir

Quarry

Cleadon Park

90

illcrest

E2
1 Central Gdns
2 Grosvenor Gdns

Laburnum Gv

Poplar Gv

Maple

Sunderland

Park Avenue

Parkshiel

The Lonnen

Ashgrove

Sycamore Av

Brandling Ct

4

Cleadon Hl Gv

Great North Forest Trail

Hawthorne Av

Elm Gv

Cleaside Avenue

Sunnirise

Meadow Laws

Cleadon Hl Rd

E3
1 Selwood Ct

The Ridgeway

Marian Way

Sunniside Dr

Clyvedon

Cleadon Hl Dr

Sunniside Farm

5

Sunniside Lane

E4
1 Myrtle Gv

Avenue

KING GEORGE ROAD

A1018

Shields Road

Fennel Gv

Holder House La

Caraway

Basil Wy

Caraway Wk

King George Comprehensive School

A1018 SHIELDS ROAD

Thornleigh Gdns

Elmsleigh Gdns

Oakleigh Gardens

Oakleigh Gardens School

6

E5
1 Carnoustie Dr
2 Ganton Ct
3 Heartsbourne Dr

Cleadon Grange

Sunniside Ter

Marsham

Cleadon Mdw

North Road

Undercliff

D

F6
1 Heather Cl
2 Oakleigh Gdns

E

Cleadon Village County JM School

107

F

F3
1 Crossway
2 Gloucester Pl

Front St

F2
1 Bishop Ramsay Ct
2 Pinewood Vls

Cleadon Vil C of E Infa

90

73

A185 COAST ROAD

A1

A

B

C

County Junior Mixed School

St Cuthbert's Av
Coquet Avenue
Ambleside
Druridge Cl
Appleton Cl
High Grove

A1 1 Horsley Hill Sq

CHEVIOT RD
B1301

A2 1 Charles Baker Wk

Westhope
Rd E
Harton House
Harton Rise
Road

South Tyneside Area Hlth

Northam Av
Frenchman's
Fane
Warkworth Avenue
Cheshire
Devon Gdns
Dorset Cl
Lincoln
Cumberland Pl
Suffolk Gdns
Essex Gdns
Hertford Av

Norfolk Road

PO

South Tyneside Metropolitan Borough Council

MARSDEN LANE
Fulwell Avenue
B1301

Westmorland Rd

REDWELL
Grotto La
Grotto Gdns
Grotto Rd

COAST ROAD A1

Great North Forest

A3
1 Ashridge Cl
2 Carden Av
3 Flaunden Cl
4 Shilton Cl
5 Watson Pl

Belsay Av
Ridley Av
Bulmer Rd
Byhwell
Hulworth Av
Hylton Avenue
Witton Av
Auckland Av
Tanfield Gdns

Steward Crescent
Walworth Av
Seaham Cl
Tunstall Av
Thornolme
Lumley

Chirton Av
Valley
Lake Grn Hi
Beacon Old
Lake Av
Cliffside
Lizard
Fallow Rd
Grotto Rd

Gt North Forest Trail

Marsden Hall

Harton School
The High Road

Dunlop Crs
Centenary
Kirkley
Kent
York
Russell
East Av
Bradley Av

Hayton Av
Larch Avenue

PRINCE EDWARD ROAD EAST

Beaconside
Beacon Old
Lake
Quarry

Lane

Gt North Forest Trail

Marsden

B1
1 Hampshire Wy
2 Redwell Ct

A1300 PRINCE EDWARD ROAD

Foxter Av
Wy
Watson Av

Edward Rd
Palm Av
Pine Avenue
Gorse
Oak
Lilac Avenue
Holly Av
Avenue
Lane
Quarry
Kyffin Av
Collin Av
Fremantle Av
Wakefield Av
Sutton Av
Shelley Av

Cragside
Eastway
Fellside
PO

89

Cleadon

B2
1 White Horse Vw

Parkshiel
Brandling Ct
Road
Sunderland
more Av

Sunnirise
Meadow Laws
Sunnside Dr
Sunnside Rise
Cleadon Hl Dr
Cleadon Hl Rd
Mill Gv

The Lonnen
Hillside
Hillside Road

Great North Forest Trail

C2
1 Quarry La

Sunniside Farm

Cleadon Hills Farm

SHIELDS
Shields Road

Sunniside Lane

Thornleigh Gdns
Elmsleigh Gdns
Oakleigh Gardens

Cleadon Grange

ROAD

Oakleigh Gardens School

Sunniside Ter
Marsham Cl
Hl Road
Farm

Cleadon Mdw
North St
High Sandgrove
PO

Cleadon Age C of E Infant School

Undercliff

A

108

B

C

1 grid square represents 500 metres

D E F

I

2

3

COAST ROAD

Souter Lighthouse

Lizard Lane

Kitchener Road

4

Whitburn Colliery

Arthur St

Lizards Farm

White Rocks

Grove

Shearwater

5

MILL LANE

Lilac Av

Lily Crs

May St

Marsden Av

Rose Crs

Rose Crs

Rose Crs

Fairfield Dr

Wheatall Drive

Fern Avenue

Lizard Lane

Fulmar Wk

Wellands Farm

Cedar Gv

6

Poplar Drive

Chick's

Farrow Dr

Wellands

Geoffrey St

Birch St

Sycamore Rd

Maple

Parry Drive

A183

D E **109** F

WHITBURN

Low Greenside

Woodside

A1
1 The Oaks

Fo...
Lan
Alma Ter
Long
Ridge

B4
1 Barlow Crs

Cricket Club
Gardens
Heathfield

John Av
Jasper Av
Lead Road
Berry Hill
The Pines
1

PO

Lead
Burnhills Gdns

I

Whiteley Cl

Greenside

Burnhills Lane

Reeley Mires
Farm

2

SPEN LANE

3

Ricklees
Farm

Barlow Burn

Barlow

Barlow Lane

4

B6315 ROGUES LANE

1

Barlow Fell Road

Spen
...rial Estate
...rothers Rd

5

Pawston Road

Ashtree Lane

COLLINGFORD RD

PO

High Spen
Court

6

Compton Gn

Ashfield Ct

Fell View
...enlea
1 2

Spen Burn

Spen Lane

Spen Banks

Sherburn T...
Farm

Hookergate

Spen Burn

I grid square represents 500 metres

Blaydon
Burn

75

F1
1 Birchgate Cl
2 Brockwell Cl
3 The Close
4 Daryl Cl
5 Greenwell Cl
6 Herd Cl
7 Milner Crs
8 Owlet Cl
9 Waterloo St

F2
1 Barlowfield Cl
2 Brandon Cl
3 Burnthouse Cl
4 Cresswell Cl
5 Lyndhurst Cl
6 Stampley Cl
7 Whinney Cl
8 Woodburn Cl

E2
1 Farndale Cl
2 Waverley Cl

Hollyhurst
Medical Cen

The Clnc

NE21

West Lane Junior
& Infant School

Norman's Riding
Farm

94

Winlato

Low
Thorney

Thornley Bank

Hollin Hill

2
3
4
5
6

Frances St
Helen St
Mary St
Winlaton

Barlow Lane
Glendale Close
Barlow Lane
Knoblyends Lane
Gatesfield Lane
Thornley Lane
Beverley Drive
Meldon Way
Harside Drive
Farmdown
Huntley Crs
Colstream
West Lane
Long Cair
Scotland Head
Church Street
Rectory La
Parkgate
Park Lane
Stephenson Wy
Derwent View
California
Borrowdale Crs
Rydal Cl

Hollinhill
Denneway
Thornley La
Glamis Crs
West Horse Close Wood
High Horse Close Cl
High Horse Cl
Hollinhill Lane
HAUGH ROAD
Sherburn
Sherburn Pk Dr
Bowlands Gill
Ashtree
A694
River Derwent

Winlato

A 76 **B** **C**

Snibston

A1
1 Back St
2 Branch St
3 Mount Pleasant
4 Northlands
5 Ramsay St
6 Weatherside

A2
1 Buttermere Crs
2 Coniston Crs
3 Ennerdale Crs
4 Grasmere Crs
5 Thirlmere Crs
6 Ullswater Crs
7 Waskdale Crs
8 Windermere Crs

B1
1 Beech Ter
2 East Park Gdns
3 Myrtle Rd
4 Poplar Rd
5 Simonside Rd

Frances St
Helen St
Mary St

M Bla
Tynebank
Street
Heddon
Hillside
Blaydon
icket
Laburnum Road
Cypress
Rockmore Road

NE21

Hollyhurst
Medical Cen
Front
Street Surg

Winlaton
Vulcans
Rugby Club

Axwell P

West Lane Junior
& Infant School

Winlaton Park
Junior School

Scotland

93

3

Mill Lane

Thornley Lane

Derwent Walk
Country Park

Hagg
Hill

A694

Manor Ter
Noel Ter
May Avenue
June Av
Holly Av
Clover Av
Noel Av
Naylor Avenue

River Derwent

Derwent Walk

4

Winlaton Mill

A694

**Low
Thornley**

5

Hollinhill

Thornley La

Glamis Crs

A694

Deneway

High Horse
Close Wood
High Horse CL
West
Horse Cl

LOCKHAUGH ROAD

6

Thornley Woodlands
Centre

A 112 **B** **C**

Snipes
Wood

River Derwent

Hollin Hill

I grid square represents 500 metres

D5
1 Clockburnsyde Cl
2 Hunt Lea
3 Ravenscar Cl
4 Springsyde Cl

D **E** 77 **F**

D6
1 Redhill Dr
2 Rookery La
3 Woodhouses La

F4
Street names for this grid square are listed at the back of the index

I

E1
1 Lake Ap

2

E4
1 Thornhaugh Av

3

WHICK

Gateshead Area
Health Authority

Gateshead
MBC

96

F1
1 Brewery Bank
2 Brewery La
3 Hood St
4 Jubilee Ter
5 Long Rigg
6 Napier Rd
7 Quality Row Rd
8 Ridley Gdns
9 Spencers Bank

4

F2
1 Brinkburn Av
2 Burns Crs
3 Henderson Av
4 Phillips Av
5 Stubbs Av
6 Tennyson Crs

5

F3
1 Axwell Vw
2 Castle Cl
3 Fellside Ct
4 George St
5 Hawksbury
6 Heathwood Av
7 James St
8 Kestrel Ms
9 Laburnum Gv
10 Sandringham Dr
11 Thomas St
12 William St

6

Wickham Fell

F6
1 Ladyhaugh Dr

D **E** 113 **F**

F5
1 Warwick Cl

Swalwell

Fellside

Swalwell Cricket Club

Blaydon Rugby Football Club

Trinity School

Comprehensive School

Primary School

Whickham Parochial C of E Junior & Infant School

Gibside School

Infant School

Golf Course

96

78

A   **B**   **C**

A1
1 Clavering Rd
2 Coalway La North
3 Masefield Av
4 Shield Av

A2
1 East View Ter
2 Heathwell Gdns
3 Kipling Ct
4 Spencer Gv

A3
1 Church Chare

A4
1 Greystoke Wk
2 Oakfield Dr

A5
1 Birchfield
2 Cheam Cl
3 Cloverdale Gdns
4 Mayfield

B2
1 Crowley Av
2 Duckpool La
3 Horncliffe Gdns

B3
1 Crawley Gdns
2 Dockendale La
3 The Orchard
4 Whickham Pk

C3
1 Bowness Rd
2 Coniston Av

The Metro Centre

A1(T)

Marconi Way

Market Lane

Cross Lane

Metro East Park

Tyne-Wear Trail

Swalwell

HEXHAM RD

B6317

FELL BANK

Clavering Rd

Beverley Dr

Cemetery

Whickham Thorns

Market Lane

Dunston Hill Hospital

I
2
3
95
4
5
6

Village Gallery

St Marys RC Primary School

WHICKHAM

Gateshead MBC

Gateshead Area Health Authority

B6317

RECTORY LA

Millfield Road

WHAGGS LANE

B6316

Oakfield Road

Hollinside Cl

Grange Lane

SUNNISIDE RD

Wickham Fell

Burnthouse Lane

Comprehensive School

Primary School

Marshall Lands Farm

Washingwell

Washingwell Lane

B6317

A692
ROAD

Black Burn

A   **114**   **B**   **C**

B6316

1 grid square represents 500 metres

D
E
F

79

D1
1 Federation Wy
2 Halifax Pl

E1
1 Fairfield Cl
2 Kingsley Pl
3 Meadow La
4 Nelson St
5 Newton St
6 Ruskin Av

E2
1 Clavering Sq
2 Dixon Pl
3 Willow Av

E4
1 Finchale Cl
2 Gibside Ct
3 Hexham Ct
4 Knightside Gdns
5 Westminster Dr

I

Teams

Dunston Riverside
Primary School

Dunston Federation
Football Club

Railway St

Wellington

Seymour St

Rendel Street

Johnson

Lister Avenue

Victoria St

Ross Avenue

Clephan St

Spoor Street

Dunston

Renforth St

Parkside

Doctors
Surg

Dr Rannus
Surg

Kingsmeadow
Comprehensive
School

A1(T)

Dunston Stn

Ravensworth

2

DERWENTWATER RD

GAS WORKS BR ROAD

CLOCKMILL RD

Infant School

Dunston
Health Centre

Dunston Swimming
Pool

Dunston Hill

Elsdon Gdns

Holmside Av

West Wy

Cypress Crs

Myrtle Av

Holly Av

Poplar
Crs

Cedar

Oak Avenue

Maple Av

Horsley
Rochester

Forge Road

A1(T)

F1
1 Athol Gn
2 Castlegate Gdns
3 Ravensworth Ct
4 Riverside Ct
5 Seymour Ct
6 Swan Dr
7 Wallace St

3

WHICKHAM

Park Av

Dunston Bank

Hillcrest Drive

Hillside

Dene Side

Knoll Rise

Bracken Drive

HIGHWAY

Valley
Drive

Mount

Mountside Gardens

Redesdale Gardens

Monkridge
Gdns

Woodside Gardens

Spinneyside
Gdns

Braeside

Knightside
Gdns

Percy Gdns

Douglas Gdns

Knightside

Moorfoot
Gdns

Scafell
Gdns

Catswold

Chiltern

Pennine Gdns

Cotswold
Gdns

Mourne
Gdns

98

F2
1 Kent Av

4

Norwood

Lobley Hill

LOBLEY HILL ROAD

Woodburn Gdns

Lobley Gdns

Malvern

Oakfield

Road

Whickham
Hill

Emmanuel
College

Gateshead Area
Hlth Authority

Lobley
Hill Junior &
Infant School

Elmwood
Gdns

Thornwood
Gdns

Elderwood
Gdns

Oakwood Gdns

Beechwood Gdns

Larc

Pinewood

Birwell
Gdns

Rowanwood
Gdns

Holly wood

Alder wood
Gdns

Elmwood

Laurelwood
Gardens

Craigside Gdns

Rothbury Gardens

Mitford Gdns

Meldon Gdns

Alwinton
Gardens

A692

CONSETT ROAD

Trench
Hall

F3
1 Cheviot Gdns
2 Malvern Gdns
3 Murray Gdns
4 Otterburn Gdns
5 Pentland Gdns
6 Raylees Gdns

5

F4
1 Braeside
2 Fountains Cl
3 Hillhead Gdns
4 Malvern Gdns
5 Snowdon Gdns

6

D
E
F

115

F5
1 Belford Gdns
2 Belsay Gdns
3 Greenwood Gdns

Cross

Lane

River Tyne

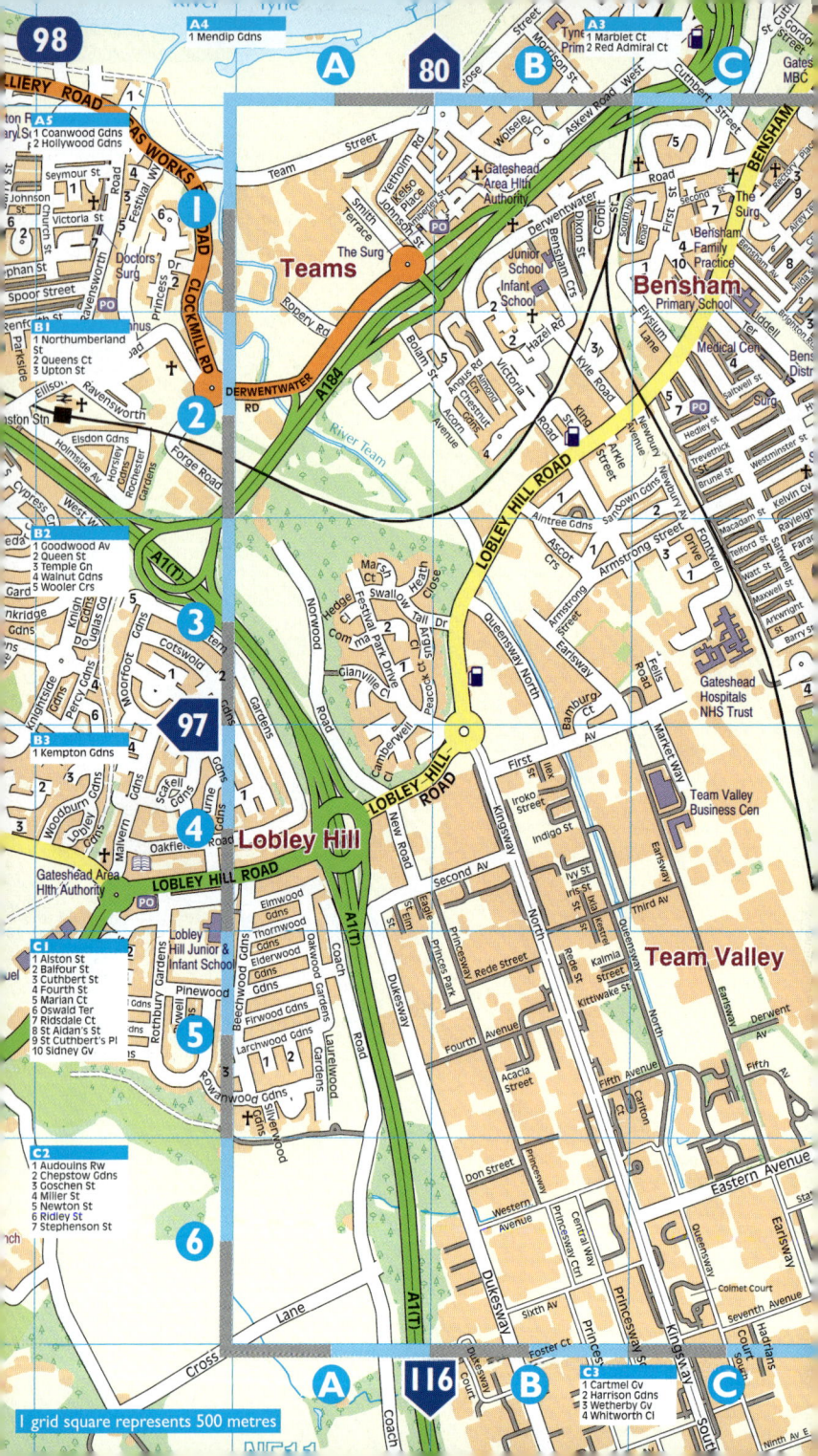

A4
1 Mendip Gdns

A3
1 Marblet Ct
2 Red Admiral Ct

80

A

B

C

A5
1 Coanwood Gdns
2 Hollywood Gdns

Gateshead
Area Hlth
Authority

Bensham
Family
Practice

Bensham
Primary School

Teams

The Surg

Junior
School

Infant
School

Doctors
Surg

Medical Cen

B1
1 Northumberland
St
2 Queens Ct
3 Upton St

DERWENTWATER
RD

River Team

LOBLEY HILL ROAD

B2
1 Goodwood Av
2 Queen St
3 Temple Gn
4 Walnut Gdns
5 Wooler Crs

Aintree Gdns

Ascot
Crs

Gateshead
Hospitals
NHS Trust

B3
1 Kempton Gdns

97

Marsh
Ct

Swallow
Cl

Heath
Close

LOBLEY HILL ROAD

Lobley Hill

Team Valley
Business Cen

Gateshead Area
Hlth Authority

LOBLEY HILL ROAD

Elmwood
Gdns

Thornwood
Gdns

Elderwood
Gdns

Team Valley

C1
1 Alston St
2 Balfour St
3 Cuthbert St
4 Fourth St
5 Marian Ct
6 Oswald Ter
7 Ridsdale Ct
8 St Aidan's St
9 St Cuthbert's Pl
10 Sidney Gv

Lobley
Hill Junior &
Infant School

Beechwood Gdns

Oakwood Gardens

Laurelwood
Gardens

Pinewood

Firwood Gdns

Larchwood Gdns

Second Av

Princess Park

Fourth Avenue

Fifth Avenue

Acacia
Street

C2
1 Audouins Rw
2 Chepstow Gdns
3 Goschen St
4 Miller St
5 Newton St
6 Ridley St
7 Stephenson St

Rowanwood Gdns

Silverwood

6

Don Street

Western
Avenue

Sixth Av

Eastern Avenue

Seventh Avenue

Colmet Court

116

A

B

C

C3
1 Cartmel Gv
2 Harrison Gdns
3 Wetherby Gv
4 Whitworth Cl

l grid square represents 500 metres

Bensham

Magistrates Court

81

D Gateshead Area Hlth Authority

E Bewick Medical Cen

F

Bede Infant School

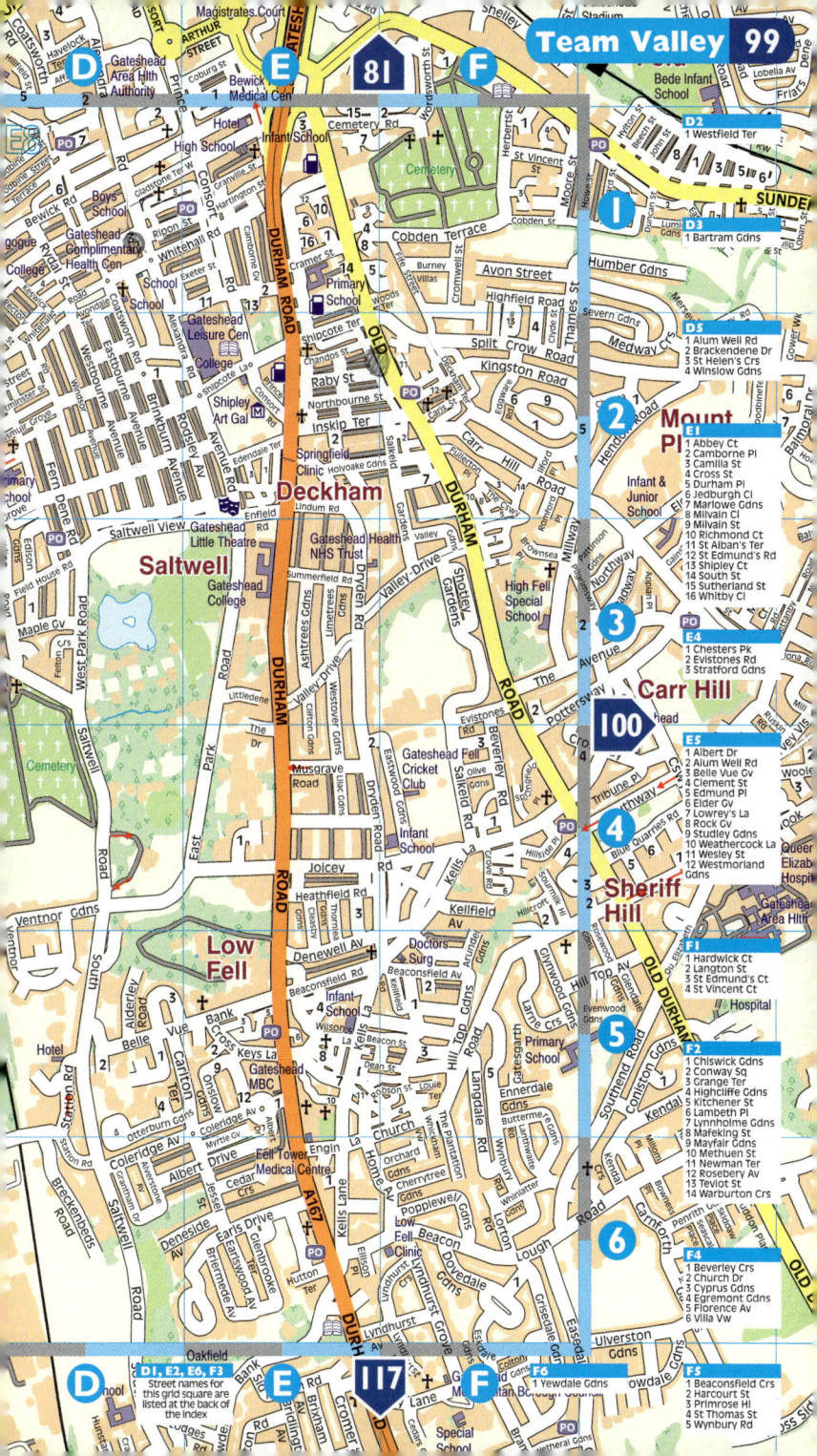

D2
1 Westfield Ter

1

D3
1 Bartram Gdns

Cobden Terrace

Avon Street

Highfield Road

Humber Gdns

Split Crow Road

Medway

Kingston Road

D5
1 Alum Well Rd
2 Brackendene Dr
3 St Helen's Crs
4 Winslow Gdns

2

Mount Pl

1 Abbey Ct
2 Camborne Pl
3 Camilla St
4 Cross St
5 Durham Pl
6 Jedburgh Cl
7 Marlowe Gdns
8 Milvain Cl
9 Milvain St
10 Richmond Ct
11 St Alban's Ter
12 St Edmund's Rd
13 Shipley Ct
14 South St
15 Sutherland St
16 Whitby Cl

Infant & Junior School

3

E4
1 Chesters Pk
2 Evistones Rd
3 Stratford Gdns

High Fell Special School

Carr Hill

100

E5
1 Albert Dr
2 Alum Well Rd
3 Belle Vue Gv
4 Clement St
5 Edmund Pl
6 Elder Gv
7 Lowrey's La
8 Rock Gv
9 Studley Gdns
10 Weathercock La
11 Wesley St
12 Westmorland Gdns

4

Sheriff Hill

Gateshead Area Hlth

F1
1 Hardwick Ct
2 Langton St
3 St Edmund's Ct
4 St Vincent Ct

Hospital

5

F2
1 Chiswick Gdns
2 Conway Sq
3 Grange Ter
4 Highcliffe Gdns
5 Kitchener St
6 Lambeth Pl
7 Lynnholme Gdns
8 Mafeking St
9 Mayfair Gdns
10 Methuen St
11 Newman Ter
12 Rosebery Av
13 Teviot St
14 Warburton Crs

6

F4
1 Beverley Crs
2 Church Dr
3 Cyprus Gdns
4 Egremont Gdns
5 Florence Av
6 Villa Vw

D **E** **117** **F**

F6
1 Yewdale Gdns

F5
1 Beaconsfield Crs
2 Harcourt St
3 Primrose Hl
4 St Thomas St
5 Wynbury Rd

D1, E2, E6, F3
Street names for this grid square are listed on the back of the index

Deckham

Saltwell

Gateshead Little Theatre

Gateshead College

Gateshead NHS Trust

Gateshead Cricket Club

Gateshead Fell Cricket Club

Musgrave Road

Infant School

Low Fell

Gateshead MBC

Bell Tower Medical Centre

Gateshead Leisure Cen

Shipley Art Gal

Springfield Clinic

Boys School

High School

Infant School

Primary School

Gateshead Complimentary Health Cen

Gateshead College

Primary School

Doctors Surg

Infant School

Primary School

Low Fell Clinic

Special School

Street names for this grid square are listed at the back of the index

100 **82** A **B** C

FELLING

Mount Pleasant

Carr Hill

Sheriff Hill

Windy Nook

Whitehills

Beacon Lough

ABBOTSFORD ROAD

SUNDERLAND

Felling ROAD

Church Place
Primary School

St Oswalds Clinic

Gateshead M Borough Cou

St Albans Medical Group

Infant & Junior School

Gateshead MBC

Queen Elizabeth Hospital

Gateshead Area Hlth Authority

A&E

Queen Elizabeth Hospital

Windy Nook Primary School

Larkspur Primary School

St Edmunds RC Comprehensive School

Gateshead Metropolitan Borough Council

118

Moss Side

OLD DURHAM ROAD

1 grid square represents 500 metres

D **E** **83** **F**

D1
1 High House Gdns

Felling 101

D2
1 Bondene Av
2 Chilside Rd
3 Maple Gv

SHIELDS ROAD

Pelaw

SHIELDS ROAD

I

D3
1 The Cotgarth
2 The Haynyng
3 Highfield Ct
4 Monksfeld
5 Parkin Gdns
6 Prestmede
7 Thornygarth

Heworth
Station

Cartmel
Business
Cen
Pelaw Station

D4
1 Dornoch Crs
2 Medham Cl

2 **Wardley**

Heworth

Heworth Grange
Comprehensive
School

Wardley
Primary Sch

D5
1 Pianesway
2 Prestwick
3 Yewtrees

NEW

D6
1 Medomsley Gdns

A195

3
Primary
School

E1
1 Durham St
2 George St
3 John St

102

E3
1 Chilcrosse
2 Longrigg

Lean
Lane

Longrigg
Medical Centre

St Augustines
RC Infant
School

4
Gate
Health
Care

E4
1 Bleachfeld

Ridgeway

E5
1 Felldyke
2 Fossdyke
3 Kellsway
4 Wealcroft

5

LEAM LANE

F1
1 Cartmel Pk
2 Portland St
3 Princess St
4 Salisbury St

Roman Road
Primary School

The
Leam

F2
1 Bevan Gdns
2 Macmillan Gdns
3 Pankhurst Gdns
4 Rydal
5 Thirlmere
6 Webb Gdns

LEAM LANE B1288

Hill Top
School

6

F3
1 Thorne Brake

D **E** **119** **F**

F5
1 Bavington

F4
1 Chevington
2 Redemarsh
3 Staynebrigg

84

A B C

Pelaw

King Street

DS ROAD

PO

Cartmel
Business
Cen

Pelaw Station

2 Bill Quay
Cricket Club

Davidson Rd

Tyne St

Coxon St

Kinross Ct

Morven

Woodgate

Richmond av

Woodgate
Gdns

Shaw RD A185

Windermere Av

Coniston

Pelaw Wy

Broadside

Broadgr

Wardley

Broadside

Kirkwood

Laski
Cottrell

Baker
Gdns

Toberty Gdns

Parklands Ct

Parklands Wy

Manor Gdns

White Gdns

Wyredale

Leam
Gdns

Moare
Gdns

West Crs

Wardley Ct

Wardley La

Wardley Dr

Lane

Landbury
Gardens

Kerr

Cole Gdns

Hardie
Av

Henderson

Lowness

Stileford

2

PO

Thorne Av

Cripps Av

Morris Gdns

Penshaw

Lindsey Gdns

PO

Julian
Dr

Briardene Dr

Silverdale

3

Field La
Road

th Grange
rehensive

Lane

Bolburn

Warrenmoor

Fossefeld

Longhirst

Longrigg

Fallowfield

Coles

Whinstone

Mereside

Whinbrook

SUNDERLAND RD

KIRKWOOD GDNS

A184

A195

Tuneside

Longsha

Steverdon

Ridgeway

Millford
Primary
School

Hazelgrove

Graystones

Lincey Lane

Havercroft

Haydock Cl

Whalton Cl

Prest
wick

Montrose Dr

Cendrick
Dr

Oliston

Montrose Drive

Follingbot Dr

Slaley Cl

Sherburn Wy

Montrose Dr

Haydock
Dr

Seaton Cl

Clanton

Bowburn

Slaley Cl

Thropton Cl

Conforth

Stanton Cl

Haswell

Leam Lane

B1288

101

eam
Lane

St Augustines
RC Infant
School

Wealcroft

Cotemede

Coverdale

Coverdale

Whinbrooke

Gateshead
Health
Care

Ridgeway

Millford

Ridgeway

Langley Avenue

LEAM

LANE

New

Road

A195

NEW ROAD

Follingsby

A194(M)

Hopedene

Cotemede

Millford

Sheraton

Sheraton

Belmy

Falstone

staindro

LEAM

River Don

B1288

The
Leam

Roman Road
Primary School

churchills

Follingsby

A194(M)

A195

NORTHUMBERLAND

A B

120

C

D · B1306 · E · **85** · F

LEAM LANE

A194 LEAM LANE

Marl...

Durham Dr

St Joseph
WY

Winchester
Ct

I

Comprehensive
School

Fellgate

Fellgate JMI
School

Red Barns
Farm

A194

LEAM LANE

Durham Drive

2

A184(T)

Laverick Hall
Farm

Pikes Hole
Farm

3

High House
Farm

NEWCASTLE

ROAD

Scot's House

104

Strother House
Farm

Shotton
WY

4

Jillingsby
Avenue

Road

5

Follingsby Lane

LC

6

South Tyneside

Sunderland

East House

D · E · **121** · F

Waterlo... ...d

Hedworth

A2
1 The Bower

A194

LEAM LANE

Marine Dr

Harbottle Crs

Wark Crs

Wark Crs

A1
1 Don Dixon Dr

Holland Pk Dr

Hedon

Durham Dr

Heathway

Heathway

PO

Winchester Ct

St Joseph's Wy

Comprehensive School

Fellgate JMI School

Fellgate

PO

Fellgate

Avenue

Chestnut Ct

Linkway

Linkway

Brayside

Firbanks

Westlands

Southlands

Moorlands

Summerhill

2

Abingdon

Abingdon

A19(T)

I

C1
1 Badminton Cl
2 Fieldway

The Gd

Limecroft

Limecroft

Fieldway

2

Brooklands Way

3

Pike Farm

NEWCASTLE

House

ROAD

Scot's House

A184(T)

West House Farm

A19(T)

◀ **103**

Strother House Farm

4

West Pastures

West Pastures

5

6

South Tyneside

Sunderland

Downhill

Lane

Hylton Grove Farm

A1290

1 grid square represents 500 metres

87

New Town

West Boldon

NE35

NE36

Downhill

106

123

The Medical Centre

Boldon Comprehensive School

NEW ROAD

B1298

River Don

HENLEY WAY

HUBERT ST

Smiths Surgery

ABINGDON WAY

Witney Way

Hotel

Didcot Way

Didcot Wy

NCASTLE RD

A184

Mount Pleasant

Lawn Drive

Down Hill Farm

Downhill Lane

Hylton Lane

ADDISON ROAD

A184 WESTERN TERRACE

West Boldon Junior Mixed School

Hindmarch

Hardie Drive

Boker Lane Health Centre

Lyndon Cl

Lyndon Drive

Lyndon Grove

Aviemore Road

The Folly

Hall Gdns

Dipe

Cemetery

Bridle

Kingsway Road

St John Bosco RC Primary School

Townend Primary School

Bradford Avenue

Brunswick Road

Bexhill Primary School

Downhill Primary School

Kidderminster Road

Rutherford Rd

Bradwater Avenue

106

88

A   B   C

A3
1 Alpine Gv
2 Claremount Ct
3 Everest Gv
4 Grampian Gv
5 Rosemount Ct
6 Snowdon Gv
7 Stewart Dr

1

A2
1 Wilson Dr

Albert Elliott County
Junior Mixed School

River Don

BOLDON LANE

LC

Heaton Gdns

Millais

Raeburn Rd

Landseer Gdns

Cotman

Tilesheld   Lane

New
ow

B2
1 Borrowdale Cl

Boldon
Comprehensive
School

ROAD   B1298

NEW

Gn N Forest Trail

Boldon
North Bridge

LC

2

West
Boldon

Morris Crs

Ernest St

Sidney St

red Street

Byron Av

Rustin Dr

Shelley
Av

Tracey

Owen

Dunelm Dr

Hindmarch

Reay Crs

Burns

Dr

Kipling Av

Tennyson Av

Brooke Av

Boker Av

Keats Av

Hardie Dr

Lilburn Cl

Langdale Av

Kendal Dr

Lonsdale Wy

Rydal
Cl

1

East
Boldon

Ravensbourne Av

Beckenham Av

Langholm

The
Hawthorns

Burnham Gv

Road

Boker Lane
Health Centre

West Boldon Junior
Mixed School

North Rd

North Road

North

Junior School

2

B3
1 Bowness Cl
2 The Fairways
3 Patterdale Cl

es Trail

Boldon

Don

Hardie Drive

Hardie Drive

WESTERN TERRACE

A194

Lyndon Cl

Lyndon Drive

Lyndon Grove

Bride

Pm

PO

FRONT STREET   A184

South   Lane

Mundles La

Gordon

Airey

Claremont
Gdns

Whitburn

Ferndale La

Ferndale
Gv

St Ge

3

ADDISON ROAD

Mill Vw

Hall Gdns

1

New
Gv

Aviemore Road

Lane

Lane

Hunter Cl

Wiram Ct

105

B6
1 Reedling Ct

Cemetery

4

Down
Hill Farm

Hylton

Lane

Belle
Vue Villa

Mundles

Lane

C3
1 Beatrice Gdns
2 Charlcote Crs
3 Coulton Dr
4 Grange Ter
5 St Chad's Vls

5

Mundles

Hylton

Lane

St John Bosco
RC Primary
School

6

Kingsway

Road

Kenton

Kenya Road

Kenilworth Sq

Kentchester Road

Hylton
Red House

Bradford

Avenue

Bowness Rd

Brunswick Road

Blyth

Brunton Av

Braemar

Blyth

Downhill

Primary School

Brantwood Av

Blyth Sq

PO

Bradshaw St

Bayswater

Kidderminster Road

A

Rutherford Rd

Rutherford
Sq

124

esdale Road

PO

4   3

B

Rishton
Sq

Rhodesia

Riddings

4   3

3

C

1 grid square represents 500 metres

D
E
89
F

89

D1
1 Celtic Crs
2 Kelvin Gv
3 Paddock Cl
4 Saxon Cl

D2
1 Beckenham Cl

Cleadon Village County JM School

Cleadon Village C of E Infant School

High Sandgrove

Front St

Cleadon Mdw

North St

Little Theatre

Cleadon

D3
1 Bede Ter
2 Crossways

Laburnum Grove

West Pk Rd

Buttermere

Crasmere

Boldon Lane

Underhill Road

Boldon Road

Windsor Drive

North Grosvenor

West Drive

Burdon Road

The Cl

Burdon Crs

Celtic Cl

Burdon Cl

Boldon La Dr

Boldon Rd

East Dr

The Crs

Marsden Road

Cleadon Lane

WHITBURN   ROAD   B1299

Bywell Road

Charlton

Woodlands

Woodlands Dr

Trevor Road

West Farm Rd

West Meadows Road

Bywell

2

D6
1 Wiltshire Cl

Moor Lane

Broadlands

W Moor Dr

Moor Lane

West Mdw

SUNDERLAND ROAD

3

STATION AP

East Boldon Station

Glencourse

Colfere Av

Burnside

Y's Ter

Natley Avenue

St John's Terrace

St John's

PO

LC

Moor Lane

Blue House Lane

Blue House Farm

108

E1
1 East Boldon Rd
2 South Dr

SUNDERLAND

ROAD   A184

Bell House Road

4

A1018 SHIELDS RDA

Crizedale Cl

Shield Cl

Alston Rd

NEWCASTLE ROAD

Field House

E6
1 Fontburn Ct
2 Rothley Ct
3 Waterlow Cl
4 Watford Cl
5 Westport Cl
6 Whitchurch Cl
7 Wiltshire Rd
8 Woodford Cl

Havelock

5

F1
1 Low Meadow
2 Sandgrove
3 Windermere

6

F2
1 Old Course Rd

Witherwack

Whitchurch Rd

Wessex Road

Woolwich Road

Westmorland Cl

Witherwack Primary School

Wendover Close

PO

Wendover Way

Old House Rd

Ellenmoor Lane

Carley Hill

Wiltshire Road

Roxburgh Rd

Rosyth Road

Everglen Rd

Cemetery

Marley

D
E
125
F

125

F3
1 Moorfield Gdns

Otley Rd

Everton Rd

Old La

Emsworth Rd

Broomshields Cl

Viewforth

Carley Hill Road

A 90 B C

A2
1 Mayfield Dr

B5
1 Barton Ct
2 Cumbrian Av
3 Dalegarth Gv
4 Gatesgarth Gv
5 Skiddaw Dr
6 Threlkeld Gv
7 Troutbeck Rd
8 Wasdale Ct

Little Theatre

B6
1 Cairns Rd
2 Cairns Sq
3 Patterdale Gv
4 Ullswater Gv
5 Windmill Sq

eadon

B1299

C6
1 Atkinson Rd
2 Bower St
3 Dene La
4 Dudley Av
5 Moran St
6 Prince George Av
7 Thorburn St
8 Whitburn Ter

Cleadon Village C of E Infant School

Cleadon Lane

West Hall

SR6

MOOR LANE B1299

Sea View Park

Moor Lane

Moor Farm

Dene Lane

107

Blue House Farm

A184

NEWCASTLE ROAD A184

Bell House Road

SUNDERLAND ROAD

A1018

SHIELDS ROAD

Staveley

Lunedale Av

Dovedale

Kentmere Av

Stainton Gv

Grizedale Ct

Alston Crescent

Shield Rd

Torver

Borrow

Crs

Seaburn Dene Primary School

Mere Knolls Cemetery

Deepdene

Bampton Rd

Martindale Av

Ummock Av

Ambleside Ter

Keswick Av

Fulwell
Fulwell Medical Centre

DYKELANDS ROAD

Drayton Rd
Dacre Rd
Denham Av
Darnford Rd

King Rd

Sea Road

Laws Lee Rd

Dent St

NEWCASTLE RD A1018

Haversham Pk

Penrith Gv

Coniston Rd

Cairns Road

Alston Avenue

STATION ROAD

Seaburn Station

Mill Bank

Maywood Rd

Browne Road

Neale St

Carle

A 126 B C

View worth

School

CARLTON RD

Kirkstone Av

Grasmere Avenu

Mayfield Av

Side Cliff Ro

WHITBURN

Grid references and street listings

D1
1 Highcroft Dr

D2
1 Moor Vw

D4
1 Hawthorn Ter

D5
1 Cuthbertson Cl
2 Princes Gdns

D6
1 Calderbourne Av
2 Cambourne Av
3 Chapman St
4 Cliftonbourne Av
5 Cressbourne Av
6 Rockville
7 Seaburn Hl

E1
1 Buckingham Cl
2 Marina Ter
3 Robinson Gdns

E2
1 Cornthwaite Dr
2 Staffords La

E3
1 Whitburn Bents Rd

E4
1 Hart Ter

E6
1 Seaburn Ter
2 Westcliffe Rd

F2
1 Ash Gv

Map labels

Wella Farm
Cedar Gv
Poplar Drive
Chick's Lane
Farrow Dr
Parry Drive
Welland Dr
Geoffrey
Rupert St
Birch St
Sycamore Rd
Maple St
High Crs
High St
Bryers
Bowman St
Myrtle
Avenue
Larch Av
Elm Dr
Whitburn Cem
Myrtle Av
Oak Crs
Beech
Holly Av
Hillside
Central Av
West Av
Moor Ct
Welland La
Fieldside
Croftside Av
Rackly Wy
Adophurst
Whitburn Junior Mixed School
B1299
Redhill
Orchard Gdns
North
Front St
FRONT STREET
Church Lane
EAST STREET
A183
East
Fids
Whitburn Surgery
Whitburn Cricket Club
Whitburn Comprehensive School
Markham
Newark Dr
Nicholas Av
Hill Vw
WHITBURN BENTS ROAD
Weardale Av
Birkdale Av
Lonsdale Av
Lingdale Av
Rosedale Av
Bransdale Av
Bildale
Swaledale Av
Glassdale
Farndale Av
Eskdale Rd
Ryedale
South Bents Av
Cleveland Vw
Huntcliff Avenue
South Bents
Whitby Av
Sparfields
Lowry Rd
Lowry
Stepgene Rd
Redene
DYKELANDS ROAD
Drayton Rd
Dunblane Rd
Danville Rd
Derry
Mere Knolls Rd
Queens Av
Princes Av
Kings Rd
Kingarth Av
Hotel
Douglas Rd
Sea La
Junior School
Chichester Rd
Clifton Road
Mere Av
Gloucester
Ashgill Gv
Stanhope Rd
Helen Av
Peareth Rd
Ritson St
Hugh
Maud St
Rosedale Ter
Atkinson
Wedgrove Rd
Peareth
Browne Road
Elvington
Clarendon
Talbot Rd
Neale St
Rock Lodge Gdns
David
A183
WHITBURN ROAD

High Spen Court

Ashfield Ct

C2
1 Briar Rd
2 Hollinside Ter
3 Park Rd
4 Townley Rd

Spen Burn

Spen Lane

HOOKERGATE

Fleywood Crescent

School Lane

1

Hookergate Comprehensive School

Sherburn Tower Farm

Spen Burn

C3
1 Cross Ter
2 West Av
3 Wingrove

Hookergate Lane

LANE

2

Low Spen Farm

Low Spen Burn

William Morris Av

B6315

St Josephs School

Cemetery

Highfield Junior & Infant School

SMAILES LANE

Cowell Gv

Wellfield Road

Barkwood

Postop Vw

Leazes Vw

Whinfield

Valley View

Burnside Rd

Terrace

PO

Gateshead Metropolitan Borough Council

Highfield

C4
1 Bowes Lyon Cl

Margaret Ter

Highfield Road

Whinfield Way

Smailes Lane

Dene Crs

Dene Av

ST

3

Whinfield Industrial Estate

Woodside Walk

Whinfield Road

Low West Av

Dene Rd

3

Orchard

2

Orchard Dene

Orchard Road

Orchard Ct

Orchard Av

Dipwood Way

Friarside Crs

DIPWO

Riverside

4

Lintzford Lane

Lintzford Wood

Holmewood Drive

River Derwent

Low Friarside

5

Lintzford

Lintz Green Lane

A694

LINTZFORD ROAD

A694

6

LINTZFORD ROAD

Mill Farm

High Ham

Lodge Cl

Hig

High Ham Mill

Lintz Green

Lintz Green

Road

HOUGH ROAD

West High
Horse Close
High Horse Close

A6
1 Chapel Av
2 Watson St

A

94

B

A5
1 The Larches

C

Thornley Woodla
Centre

River Derwent

Snipes Dene
Wood

Hollin Hill
Farm

I

B6
1 Broom Ter

2

Cut
Thorn

Gibside
Hillhead

Hillhead Lane

West Lane

3

Gibside
(NT)

III

B6314

BUSTY BANK

4

LOBLEYHILL

Byermoor RC Aide
Junior & Infant Sch

Byer

Fellside Road

Sandypath La

5

Busty

Sheep
Hill

Gateshead
Durham County

NEW ROAD

Westwood
Cl

Bank

The Close

Oakfields

The Fold

Valley Vw
Elm Gr

Hill
Crest

Sheep Hi

Raglan Pl

A692

Primary
School

FRONT STREET

PO

Crookbank
Farm

Ch

Crescent

6

Barcusclose Lane

Crookgate
Bank

A

130

B

C

Field Fare
Court

Power b

D **E** **95** **F**

Broadway

Fell

Golf Course

B6316 **SUNNISIDE ROAD**

Kingsway

Wansbeck Cl

Plenmeller

Carlton Gv

Longwood Cl

Avenue

Fellside

Granby Close

I

Sidegate Gallery

Fellside

Waskerley Cl

Dunnock Dr

Waskerley Wy

Lambley Cl

Calder Vw

Clover Hl

Gladeley Wy

Sunniside

Laburnum Gv

Coronation Road

Prinn Pl

Neill Dr

St

Princes

Queens

Elm St W. Elm St.

PO

Burdon

Fellside

Fellside Road

Fellside Farm

Byermoor

Sunniside

2

Farm

Kingsway

Fell Cl

Road

A692

Bowes Cl

A6076

GATESHEAD ROAD

3 **Marley Hill**

Cuthbert St

CHURCH STREET

St. Cuthbert's Pk

114

A6076

4

Marley Hill Primary School

ROAD A692

Schoolhouse Lane

NE16

or

Longfield House Farm

St. Cuthbert's Road

5

Tanfield Railway

BURDON PLAIN

A6076

6

Hedley House F

D **E** **131** **F**

Hotel

Broadway

Wickham Fell

96

A2
1 Old Farm Ct

ROAD

A69

Carrhouse Lane

B6316

SUNNISIDE ROAD

Kingsway

Highfield

Granby Close

GATESHEAD

Street Ga Pk

Shepton Cottages

Street Gate

Plenmeller

Carnwood Wy
Longwood Ct

Catton Cv

Felside

Pennyfine Road

I

Durmock
Tgh

Wackerley

Lambley
Cl

Sunniside
Ct

Laburnum
Gr

Sidegate
Gallery
M

Calder
Wk

Clover
Hill

Gladeley Wy

Prinn Pl

Neill Dr

St
Princess

Elm St W Elm St

Burdon
Rd

B Tcnes

Burdon Lag

2

Sunniside

Farm Cl

Coronation
Dr

Fernville Av

Kingsway

Queens
St

A692

PO

Fell Ln

Boves Cl

A6076

GATESHEAD ROAD

**Marley
Hill**

3

Cuthbert
St

CHURCH STREET

113

Marley Hill
Primary School

4

Cuthberts
Pk

A6076

BURDON PLAIN

Birkland Lane

St Cuthbert's Road

5

Tanfield Railway

A6076

6

Hedley West
House Farm

Hedley Lane

132

1 grid square represents 500 metres

Hotel

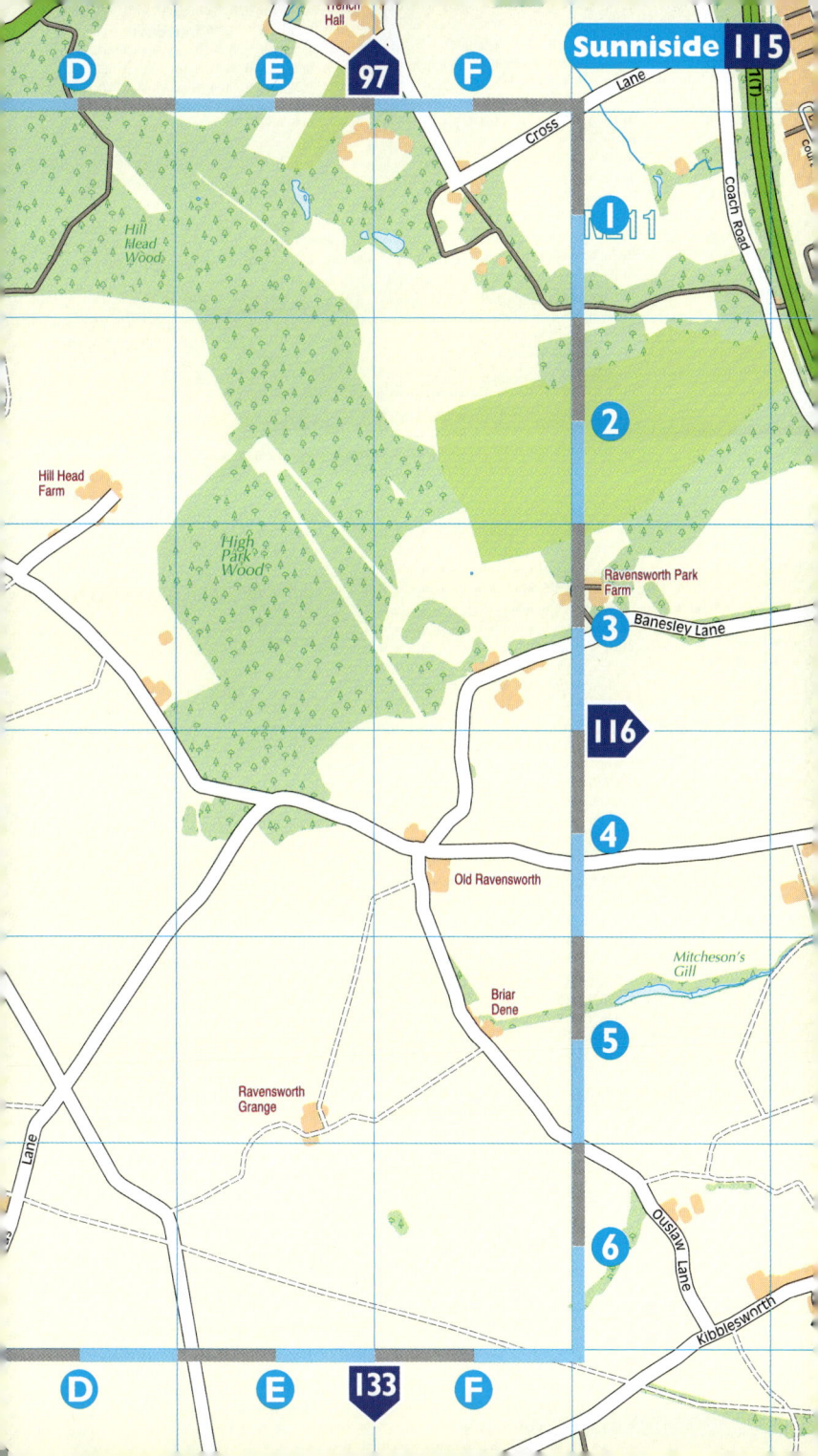

Trench Hall

D E 97 F

Cross Lane

Coach Road

11

Hill Head Wood

2

Hill Head Farm

High Park Wood

Ravensworth Park Farm

3 Banesley Lane

116

4

Old Ravensworth

Mitcheson's Gill

Briar Dene

5

Ravensworth Grange

Lane

6 Ouslaw Lane

Kibblesworth

116

98

A

B

C

1

NE11

Cross Lane

Coach Road

Dukesway

Foster Ct

Princesway

Princesway South

Kingsway

Street Court

Tenth Avenue

Hadrians Court South

Dukesway Court

Eighth Av

Ninth Av

Octavian Way

Gateshead Metropolitan Borough Council

Marquisway

Ninth Av

Mayoral Way

2

Dukesway W

Tenth Avenue West

Tenth Avenue

Dukesway

A1(T)

Lady Park

Ravensworth Park Farm

3

Banesley Lane

Lan

115

4

Old Ravensworth

Mitcheson's Gill

5

Briar Dene

6

Ouslaw Lane

Primary School

PO

West View

Hollydene

Coltspo

Bank

Ashvale Av

Laburnum Crs

Moorhill

Greenford

Ouselaw

Kibblesworth

Grange Est

A

134

B

C

I grid square represents 500 metres

D E **99** F

F2
1 Rotherfield Gdns

Old Dur

Lough

Dovedale

Ullerston Gdns

Borrowdale

Hutton

Wyndhurst Grove

Clinic

Ellison Pl

Escale

Crisedale Gdns

Easedale Gdns

Moss Bank

Moss Side

DURHAM ROAD

Lynn Dr

Oakfield Junior School

Ivy Lane

Colton Gdns

Gateshead
Metropolitan Borough Council

Wetheral Gdns

PO

South Road

The Lodges

Bank Sid

mouth Rd

Brixham Av

Linton Rd

Bridlington

Cromer

Bude Gdns

A167

Special School

Brampton Gdns

Mardale Gdns

1 **Wrekenton**

School

Hunstanton Ct

Cremond

Lynmouth

Gleneagles Rd

Ravenswood Gdns

Chowdene Bank

Dartmouth

Bideford Gdns

Dawlish Gdns

Torquay Gdns

Oakwood Av

Calderwood Crs

Beechwood Gdns

Ashwood Gdns

Birchfield Gdns

Harlow Grn La

wdene

St Andrew's Dr

Berkdale Rd

Avenue

Frome

St Austell Gdns

Portland Gdns

Dorchester

Newquay Gdns

Weymouth Gdns

Flaxbury Gdns

Harlow Grn Vw

Kenilworth

Shoe

Woodstock Rd

Seaham Gardens

Waverley Road

Silksworth La

Av

PO

Bank

Salcombe Gardens

Hertford

Harlow Green Infant School

St Ronans Vw

2 **Harlow Green**

m Valley Trading
ate Post Office

Chowdene

North Farm

PO

Rokeby Vw

Waverley Road

Rokeby Vw

Black La

A1(T)

Woodford

Trafford

Smithyford

DURHAM

3

Smithy Lane

Deneford

Cowen Gdns

118

ey

River Team

Angel of the North

A1(T)

ROAD

Low Eighton

4

Greenford Lane

Moor Mill Farm

A6127 NEWCASTLE BANK

Long Bank

5

Long Acre Farm

The Hollys

Windsor Road

Moormill Lane

Longshank Lane

Cemetery

Valley Vw

Leyburn Pl

Lansbury

Lansbury Dr

Mary

Elisabeth

Devon Crs

Glamis Vis

ibblesworth

6

Lansbury

Lansbury Dr

Rutland

Avenue

Drive

Elizabeth

Edward Road

118

100 A   B   B2 1 Springwell Av   St Edmunds RC Comprehensive School C

Beacon Lough

B6 1 Newcastle Rd
Metropolitan Borough Council

Wrekenton

Hamsterley Gdns
Plawsworth Gdns
Wrekenton Health Centre
Infant & Junior School
Doctors Surgery
Infant School

B1296

I

Special School

Oakwood Av

Calderwood Crs

C1 1 Brandon Gdns
2 Marsden Gv

2

Harlow Infant School

Rokeby

C2 1 Cypress Rd

3

Harlow Green

Black Lane

Stanley Gdns
Wrekenton Row
Tanfield Rd
Tanfield Place

Springfield Av

Jubilee Av

117

Angel of the North

4

A1(T)

Dunkirk Farm

Low Eighton

LONG BANK
B1296

5

A6127 NEWCASTLE BANK

A1(T)

Long Acre Farm

The Hollys
Long Bank
Northdene
Dene Ct

Cemetery

Valley Vw
Leyburn Pl

Birtley East Primary School

6

Windsor Road

Lansbury Dr
Lansbury

Glamis Vis
Devon Crs

Selkirk

Carlside Avenue

BIRTLEY

Wilson Av

136 A   Edward Road   B   C

1 grid square represents 500 metres

D **E** **101** **F**

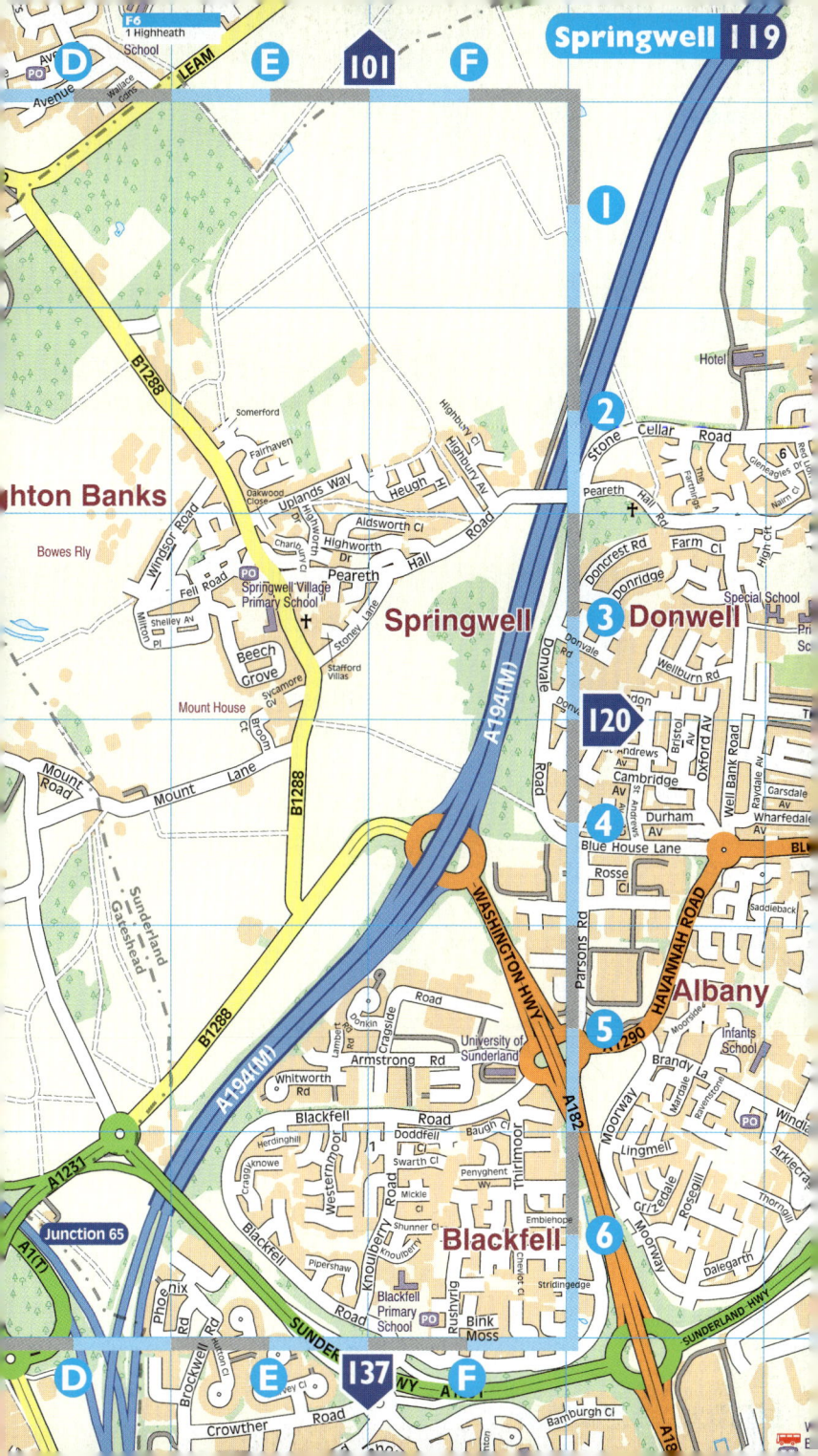

F6
1 Highheath
School

LEAM

Av
PO
Avenue
Wallace Gdns

I

Hotel

Somerford

Fairhaven

hton Banks

Bowes Rly

Windsor Road

Oakwood Close

Uplands Way

Highworth

Charlbury
Dr

Aldsworth Cl

Heugh

Highbury Cl

Highbury Av

Road

Highbury Cl

Stone Cellar Road

Gleneagles Cl

6

The
Farthings

Nairn Cl

High Cft

Peareth Rd

Peareth

Hall

†

2

Doncrest Rd

Donridge

Farm Cl

Donvale

3 **Donwell**

Special School

Pri
Sc

Fell Road
PO

Springwell Village
Primary School
†

Pearech
Hall

Stoney Lane

Stafford
Villas

Springwell

Beech
Grove

Sycamore
Gv

Broom

A194(M)

Donvale

Road

Wellburn Rd

120

St Andrews
Av

Bristol
Av

Oxford Av

Cardon

Cambridge
Av

Durham
Av

St Andrews

Well Bank Road

Raydale Av

Carside

Wharfedale
Av

Saddleback

Mount House

Mount
Road

Mount Lane

Sunderland
Gateshead

B1288

4

Blue House Lane

Rosse
Cl

Parsons Rd

HAVANNAH ROAD

Albany

Shelley Av

Milton
Pl

WASHINGTON HWY

A290

A182

5

Infants
School

Brandy La

Maypole

Ravenscome

Marsh

Grizedale

Rosegill

Thornlo

Arkleton

Windla

Road

Donkin

Crapside

Lambert
Rd

University of
Sunderland

Moorway

Lingmell

PO

A1231

Whitworth
Rd

Armstrong Rd

Blackfell

Road

Herdinghill

Craigs

Knowe

Doddfell
Cl

Swarth Cl

Mickle

Thirlmoor

Baugh
Cl

Penyghent
Wy

Emblehope

Blackfell

Moorway

Dalegarth

6

Junction 65

A1(T)

A194(M)

B1288

Phoenix
Rd

Brockwell Rd

Hutton Cl

Blackfell

Road

Pipershaw

Westernmoor

Knoulberry Road

Shunner Cl

Knoulberry

Blackfell
Primary
School

PO

Rushyrig

Cheviot Cl

Bink
Moss

Stridingedge

SUNDERLAND HWY

D **E** **137** **F**

SUNDER   HWY   A1

Crowther   Road

Ney Cl

Bamburgh Cl

A18

A 102 B C

B2
Street names for
this grid square are
listed at the back of
the index

UMBERLAND WAY

B4
1 Heworth Gv
2 Wensleydale Av

1

C1
1 Downfield

Longniddry
The Fairway
Gullane
Foxton
Hall

2

Highbury Av
Highbury Cl

Heugh Hl

Way

Peareth Hall Rd

Stone Cellar Road

Peareth

Carnoustie Dr

Road

Hotel

Wentworth

Stone

Silloth Dr

Cellar Dr

Road

Usworth
Secondary
School

Muirfield Dr

Heworth Road

Norfolk Dr

Wiltshire Rd

Essex

Warwick

Westmorland Av

St B
RC
Dr

C2
1 Cumberland Wy
2 Rutland Pl

Highway
Dr

Peareth
Ha

Gleneagles

Red Lion Lane

Potthca'wl Drive

Nairn

Coach

Doncrest Rd

Farm Cl

Road

High Ct

Troon

Springwe   3

Donwell

Usworth

Monter
Road

Donvale Rd

Donridge

Special School

Primary
School

Inkerman Road

Tyne Gardens

A194(M)

119

Denvale Road

Wellburn Rd

The   Drive

Park Gv

Concord

Viola Dr

House Ter

Manor

C3
1 Essex Dr
2 Hampshire Pl
3 Sussex Pl

Road

London
Av

Bristol
Av

Oxford Av

St Andrews
Av

Cambridge
Av

St Andrews

Durham

Well Bank Road

Reydale Av

Garsdale
Av

Weardale

Wharfedale

Victoria Road
Health Centre

Victoria Rd

4

Blue
House
Cl

Rosse
Cl

Blue House Lane

BLUE HOUSE LANE

Saddleback

VE

Spout La

C4
1 Laurens Ct

Road

Lambert

Craigside

Donkin

Armstrong   Rd

University
of Sunderland

5

Parsons Rd

HAVANNAH ROAD

A1290

WASHINGTON HWY

Way

M Washington
Pit Museum

Washington
Football
Club

Albany

Infants
School

Brandy La

Mardale Av

Moorside

Ravenstonedale

Albany Av

Blencathra

Windlass Lane

Washington
Secondary
School

Spout
Lane

C6
1 Trenton Av

Westmoor

Westmoor
Road

Baugh Cl

Doddfell

Penyghent
Wy

Mickle
Cl

Shunner Cl

Thirlmoor

Knoulberry

Knoulberry
Road

A182

Moorway

Lingmell

Grizedale

Roseditt

Dalegarth

Thornhill

Arklecrag

Moorway

SUNDERLAND HIGHWAY

Richmond Av

Boston Av

Valley Forge

Dene
Bede

Village

Lane

Spout
Lane

Blackfell   6

Stridingedge

Bink
Moss

Blackfell
Primary
School

PO

Rushyrig

Chev.ot Cl

Glenope

SUNDERLAND HWY

A1231

Elvang Cl

Thornton
Ct

St Jos
School

ERLAND HWY

A1231

A   138   B   C

Washington
Bus Station

Latercost

Primary
School

Parkwa

Was

D2
1 Marwell Dr
2 Whitbourne Cl
3 Wimpole Cl

D **E** **103** **F**

Sunderland

East House

Waterloo Road

D3
1 Wylam Cl

1

Northumbria
Sports
Centre

North Moor
Farm

Merevale Cl

Barton
Cl

Marwell Dr

D4
1 Front St
2 Hall Rd
3 Usworth Station Rd

Stephenson Road

Waterloo Road

Usworth
Hall
Road

2

Barton Cl

Rutherford

Rainhill Road

Rainhill

E2
1 Watcombe Cl

NE37

Sulgrave Road

Waterloo Rd

3 A690

Clayton Rd

Brackley

Usworth Colliery
Junior School

Usworth Grange
Primary School

Cherry Blossom Way

Marlborough Road

122

NORTHUMBERLAND WAY

Silverstone Road

Helmsdale

Sulgrave

E3
1 Shalstone
2 Trafalgar Rd

Foxley

Bamburgh

PO

Station Rd

Barmston

Usworth

Mandeville

Cherwell

LC

4

Lane

Mnr Vw

Edgecote

GLOVER ROAD

Nissan Way

E6
1 Thornhope Cl

Industrial Road

Bridgewater Road

Tower Rd

Spire Road

Glover
Industrial
Estate

5

Lindley Road

1231

Washington
Village Primary School

Rise

WASHINGTON

NORTHUMBERLAND WAY

Burnhope Road

Glebe

SUNDERLAND HIGHWAY A1231

Barmston Way

Stockley Rd

Horsley Road

Pattinson Road

6

Alston Road

Lee Rd

Faraday Cl

Cemetery

Avenury Dr

PO

Barmston
Medical Centre

Primary
School

Westerhope

erley Road

Barmston Road

Welton Rd

Barmston

Cresc

D **E** **139** **F**

ton

South Tyneside
Sunderland

Downhill
Lane

Hylton Grove
Farm

1

North Moor
Farm

A1290

North B
Aircraft
Museu

2

West Moor
Farm

3 A1290

121

Cherry Blossom Way

Barmston

Peepy
Plantation

Nissan Way

4

LC

Lane

Nissan

Way

5

Spire

Road

WASHINGTON

Barmston Lane

SUNDERLAND HIGH

SUNDERLAND HIGHWAY   A1231

Horsley Road

Stockley Rd

Pattinson Road

Barmston Lane

Barmston Li

Low
Barmston
Farm

6

Alston Road

Lee Cl

Faraday Cl

Barmston

erley Road

Rd

ne

Wildfowl and
Wetlands

West

1 grid square represents 500 metres

Castletown 123

D **E** 105 **F**

E2
1 Caithness Sq
2 Capetown Rd
3 Conway Sq
4 Cramlington Sq
5 Crieff Sq

I

E3
1 Calais Rd
2 Cardiff Sq
3 Caspian Rd
4 Clacton Rd
5 Cullercoats Rd
6 Hepburn Gv

2

Hylton
Castle

E4
1 Macmerry Ci
2 Maydown Ci

3

E1, F6
Street names for
this grid square are
listed at the back of
the index

124

F1
1 Baird St
2 Balmoral Ct
3 Bayswater Sq
4 Bodmin Sq
5 Bootle St
6 Brentford Sq
7 Burke St
8 Chelmsford Sq
9 Cotswold Sq

of Sunderland

4

The Medical
Centre

F2
1 Cheltenham Rd
2 Cheltenham Sq
3 Cook Sq
4 Corinthian Sq
5 Cranberry Sq

5

F3
1 Donnington Ci
2 Shannon Ci

Hylton

6

F4
1 Haggerstone Dr
2 Stanstead Ci

North
Hylton

Hylton
Castle

Castletown

South
Hylton
Primary School

F5
1 Dalla St
2 John St
3 Pottery La

D **E** 141 **F**

124

A2
1 Coleridge Rd
2 Robertson Sq

A1
1 Rennie Sq

Downhill

Hylton

Red House

106

A   **B**   **C**

A3
1 Alder St
2 Ashwood Gv
3 Elizabeth St
4 The Grove
5 Jennifer Av
6 Joyce Ter
7 Sheppard Ter
8 Stanley St
9 Thompson Crs
10 West Vw

A6
1 Coronation Ter
2 King Edward Rd

B1
1 Harthope Av
2 Raeburn Rd
3 Rangoon Rd
4 Rawmarsh Rd
5 Rishton Sq
6 Rochford Rd
7 Rockingham Sq
8 Rotherfield Sq

Hylton Castle

Castletown

B3
1 Barron St South
2 Castle St South
3 Colima Av
4 East Vw
5 Park St South
6 Robin Gv
7 Thrush Gv
8 Wren Gv

123

B5
1 Flax Sq
2 Pelaw Sq
3 St Luke's Rd

B6
1 Frome Sq
2 Pennant Sq
3 Plaistow Sq
4 Polebrook Rd
5 Pontop Sq
6 Poole Rd

C1
1 Redditch Sq
2 Redruth Sq
3 Regina Sq
4 Riddings Sq
5 Ringwood Sq
6 Rochdale Wy

C6
1 Fenton Sq
2 Fordenbridge Rd
3 Priestman Ct

A5, B2, B4
Street names for this grid square are listed at the back of the index

South Hylton

142

A   **B**   **C**

Hylton Castle Health Centre

Hylton Castle

Hylton Dene Burn

SR5

Castletown

River Wear

WESSINGTON WAY

University of Sunderland

A1231

The Medical Centre

Riverside Park

South Hylton Primary School

St Annes RC Primary School

Sunderland Counselling Services

Red House Junior Mixed School

City of Sunderland College

Castle View School

Riverbank Road

1 grid square represents 500 metres

D1
1 Raydale

107

D2
1 Redcar Sq

Carley Hill

I

D4
1 Lyndhurst Ter

High Southwick

D5
1 Margaret Alice St
2 Minton Sq
3 Onslow St
4 Plantation Sq
5 Stratfield St
6 Tanfield St
7 Warennes St
8 Wilfred St

D6
1 Fordenbridge Sq
2 Fordhall Dr

Marley Pots

E1
1 Wimbledon Ci

2

Southwick

3

E2
1 Pinewood Sq
2 The Poplars
3 Walter Thomas St

126

E3
1 Clockwell St

E6, F2, F5
Street names for this grid square are listed at the back of the index

E4
1 Merle Ter
2 Pallion Subway

Deptford

4

E5
1 Amethyst St
2 Enfield St
3 Garfield St
4 Jacques St
5 Lincoln St
6 Maxwell St
7 Meldon Rd
8 Percival St
9 Pine St
10 Prudhoe St
11 Reginald St

Millfield

5

F1
1 Ellis Rd
2 John Taylor Ct
3 Okehampton Sq

6

F3
1 Camden St
2 Church Bank
3 Dickens St
4 Kingsley Ci
5 Kipling St
6 Lilburn Pl
7 Malaburn Wy
8 Mount Pleasant
9 Park Rw
10 Stoney La
11 Wessington Wy

143

F6
1 Brunton Ter
2 Catharine St West
3 Chester St West
4 Duke St

WESSINGTON WAY A1231

NORTHERN WAY

QUEEN'S ROAD

KEIR HARDIE

B1405 PALLION NEW ROAD

CHESTER ROAD A183

Sunderland District General Hospital

Sunderland Royal Hospital

University of Sunderland

Alexandra Business Park

English Martyrs RC Primary School

Maplewood School

A2, A4, A6, C1
Street names for
this grid square are
listed at the back of
the index

A 108 **B** **C**

A3
1 Attwood Gv
2 Close St
3 Lee St
4 Maypole Cl
5 Pemberton Cl
6 Queen's Rd
7 South Ter
8 Suddick St
9 Usher St
10 Vedra St

A5
1 Alliance Pl
2 Alliance St
3 Cirencester St
4 Dryborough St
5 Hyacinth Ct
6 Hylton Rd
7 Jasmine Ct
8 Lansdowne st
9 Marguerite Ct
10 Marigold Ct
11 Millburn St
12 North
Ravensworth St
13 Queensberry St
14 St Cuthbert's
Ter

SUNDERLAND RD

B1
1 Bywell Av
2 Elizabeth St
3 Honister Dr
4 Joannah St

B2
1 Boundary St
2 Edith St
3 Newbridge Av
4 Northwood Ct

B3
1 Chilton St
2 Crozier St
3 Empress St
4 Finsbury St
5 Hood Cl
6 North St
7 Ross St

B4
1 Easington St N
2 Stadium Wy

ROAD

B5
1 Dun Cow St
2 Dunning St
3 Eden St West
4 Galley's Gill Rd
5 Garden Pl
6 Middle St
7 Paley St
8 Queen St

B6
1 Clanny St
2 Crowtree Rd
3 Crowtree Ter
4 Elwin Ter
5 Green Ter
6 Hope St
7 Mary St
8 St Michaels Wy
9 Silksworth Rw
10 Stockton Rd
11 Tunstall Rd
12 Tunstall Ter W

C2
1 Burscough Crs
2 Edgeworth Crs
3 Fairlands East
4 Leeds St
5 Moreland St
6 Wearmouth Av

C3, C4, C5, C6
Street names for this grid square are listed at the back of the index

I grid square represents 500 metres

Carley Hill

High Southwick

Southwick

SUNDERLAND

Deptford

Millfield

Monkwearmouth

Ayres Quay

Bishopwearmouth

KEIR HARDIE WAY

QUEEN'S ROAD

Sunderland Football Club

Wearmouth Bridge

Mowbray Park

1 Burnhope Dr
2 Clarendon Sq

A 144 **B** **C**

109

D1
1 Claremont Av
2 Lyn-thorpe Gv
3 Merryfield Gdns

D2
1 Association Rd
2 Clockstand Cl
3 St Andrew's Ter

D3
1 Brandling St
South
2 Cooper St

D4
1 Huddlestone Ri

D5
1 Cross Pl
2 Donnison Gdns
3 Russell St
4 Spring Garden Cl
5 Zion St

D6
1 Besford Gv
2 Bishop Morton
Gv
3 Churchill St
4 Menvill Pl
5 Winifred Ter

E4
1 Stafford St

E5
1 Adelaide Cl
2 Stamps La

Rokder

WHITBURN ROAD

Peareth Rd
Peareth

Claremont
Rd
Rock Ldg
Talbot
Road
David

ROKER TERRACE A183

Park Ga
Craigievar School
PK
Rok
Sea
View
Gdns
North
Gill Side Gv

ROKER PARK ROAD

HARBOUR VIEW
St George's Ter
Featherstone
Benedict Rd
Park Pde
Bede street
Marine

Lonsdale Rd
Grantham
Roker
Baths
Branding St
Givens
Street
Cooper St
Horatio St

Pier
Walk
Police
Station
Barbary Dr
VW

Ripon St
Brandling
University
Av
Whickham St
Zetland St

DAME DOROTHY STREET

Wickham
Dock St
School

North Sands
Business Centre

National Glass
Centre

University
Sunderland

Barrack

B1293
LC

5

HIGH STREET EAST
Low Street
Church St
Prospect Row

The Qd
School

SR1

Coronation St

LAWRENCE ST
MOOR TER
Extension
Rd

HENDON ROAD
B1294
Hudson Rd
Wear Street
Woodbine Street
Hendon Street
Avon St
Glaholm
Road
Henry St
East

The New City
Medical Cen
Primary
School

Addison
Street

White House

Docks

B1522

145

Hendon

Deerness Park

128

A

110

B

C

Lodge Cl

High Hamsterley Rd

Ig Close Road

Mill Farm Road

High Mill Road

Road

1

Road

Lintz Green

Lintz Lane

Green

B6310

ands

Lintz Hall Farm

Loft House

Li

2

Hamsterley Hall

Low Ewehurst

3

Field

Straightneck Wood

Ewehurst Wood

4

Pont Bu

5

Collierley

Collierley Lane

FR C

6

South Meadow

Dipton

Surgery

Collierley County Primary School

Co-operative Te

PO

Catchwell Road

A

A692

FRONT STREET

B

C

Delight Bank

lyde

Pontesyde

1 grid square represents 500 metres

D4
1 Heather Lea

BU OPFIELD

Lintz

I

D5
1 Meadow Vw
2 The Moorlands
3 Mount Pleasant

Golf Cours

D6
1 Bradley Lodge Dr

Hobson

2

Syke Road

Craglea

FRONT STREET

Pickering Nook

F4
1 Westhills
2 White Le Head Gdns

3

Clough Dene

130

A692

EWEHURST ROAD

173

4

B6311

Unity Terrace
PO

Chapel St

Tantobie

South View

Alder Crs

Road

Ewehurst Pde

Ewehurst

Hill op

A692

Front St

Ewehurst Crs

FLINT HILL BANK

B6311

WEST ROAD

Larch Terrace

5

Flint Hill

mer Rd

Palmer Rd

Plunkett Rd

Wyndways Dr

NORTH ROAD

Lily Gardens

White-le-Head

Harperley Lane

Ta
Co
& I

The

6

Bush des

146

Bush

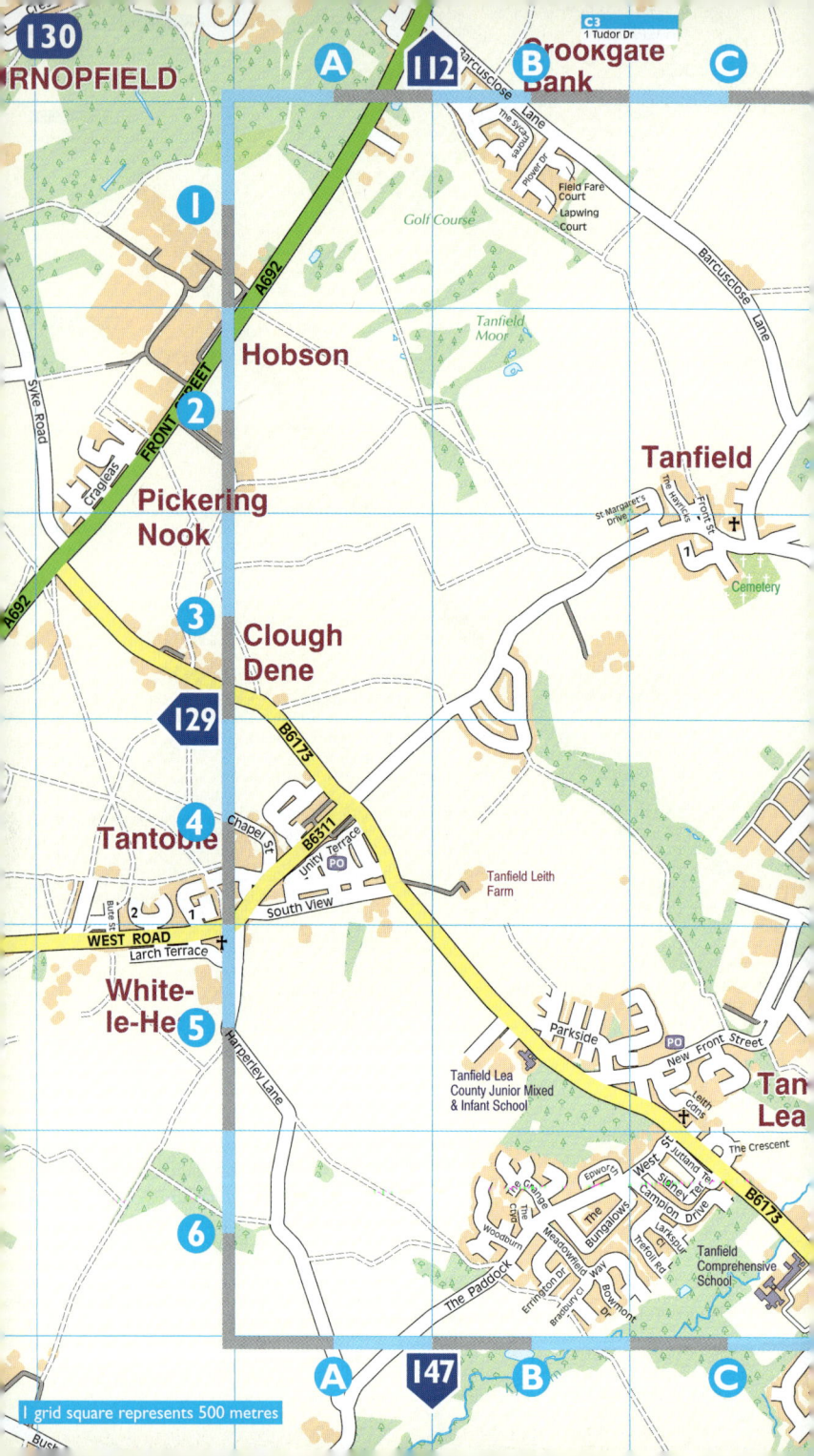

RNOPFIELD

A

112

B

rookgate
Bank

C

1

Syke Road

A692

FRONT STREET

2

Craglea

Hobson

Golf Course

The Sycamores

Piper Dr

Field Fare
Court
Lapwing
Court

Barcusclose Lane

Barcusclose Lane

Tanfield
Moor

Tanfield

St Margaret's
Drive

The Hawicks

Front St

Cemetery

Pickering
Nook

A692

3

Clough
Dene

129

B6173

Chapel St

4

Tantobie

B6311

Unity Terrace
PO

Bute St

2

1

South View

WEST ROAD

Larch Terrace

Tanfield Leith
Farm

White-
le-He

5

Harperley Lane

Parkside

New Front Street

PO

Tanfield Lea
County Junior Mixed
& Infant School

Leith
Gdns

Tan
Lea

St Jutland Ter

The Crescent

6

The Grange

The Cloves

Woodburn

Epworth

Meadowfield

The
Bungalows

West

Sidney Ter

Campion Drive

Larkspur

Trefoil Rd

B6173

The Paddock

Errington Dr

Bradbury Cl

Way

Bowmont

Tanfield
Comprehensive
School

A

147

B

C

1 grid square represents 500 metres

Bush

D   E   **113**   F

E6
1 The Birches
2 Catherine Ter
3 Ernest Ter
4 Pearson St
5 Robert Ter
6 Ryton Crs
7 Wylam Ter

Beckley

Causey
Arch

I

Causey

Tanfield Grange
Farm

CAUSEY ROAD

Beamishburn Road

2

A6076

Causey Burn

Causey Burn

Tanfield Railway

3

Causey Hall
Farm

132

Beamish
Burn

4

Houghwell Burn

CAUSEY ROAD

Beamishburn Road

5

Kip Hill

Stanelaw
Way

St Andrew's
Road

Station Field
Rd

Oakus Road

Alderman Wood Rd

Argyle Ct

A6076

Causey Dr

Kiphill
Ct

Shield Row Junior &
Infants School

6

Ryton Crs

Hillside
Gdns

Newburn
Rd

Wylam Road

Beaslaw Av

Shield Row

Id

WOOD STREET

SUNNY
TERRACE

The Birches

The Barns

Duncombe

Iveston Ter

STATION ROAD

A6076

PO

Sylvia Ter

Quarry Rd

Wesson

View
Ter

Ray St

Argyle Gardens

Benson St

BARN HILL

CHURCH

Ridley St

Cemetery

church st

D   E   **148**   F

**East
Stanley**

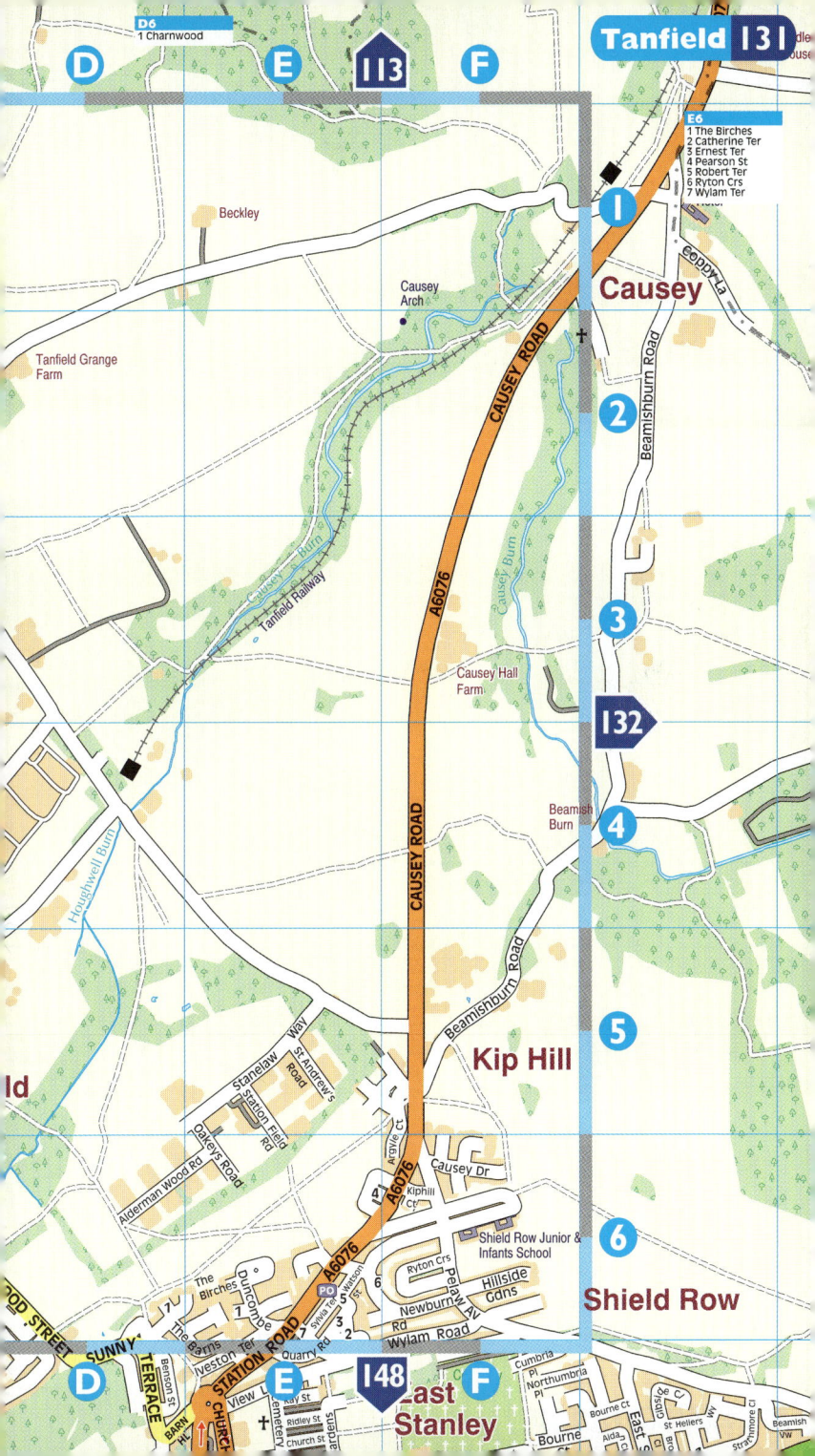

Cumbria
Pl

Northumbria
Pl

Bourne Ct

St Heliers

Gildas Ct

Strathmore Cl

Beamish
VW

Bourne

Aida

East

St Helliers Ct

132

A 114 B C**

1

Hedley Lane

Causey

Causey
Arch

2

Gateshead
Durham County

A6076

3

Causey Hall
Farm

Coppy

131

Coppy
Lane

4
Beamish
Burn

Beamish
Hall

Beamish Burn

Beamish Park
Golf Club

CAUSEY ROAD

Beamishburn Road

5

Kip Hill

Beamish Open
Air Museum

A6076
Kiphill
Ct

Causey Dr

6
Shield Row Junior &
Infants School

Ryton Crs

Hillside
Gdns

Newburn
Rd

Wylam Road

Shield Row

**East
Stanley**

Cemetery

Cumbria
Pl
Northumbria
Pl

A 149 B

Beamish
Vw

Beamish County

A6

Roseberry St
John Street
Gladstone
St

Co-operative
Villas

Beamish
Hills

C

1 grid square represents 500 metres

D
E
115
F

Kibblesworth

Hedley Hall
Farm

I
Kibblesworth
Grange

Cooper House

2
Riding Lane

3
Kibblesworth
Common

134

Beamish
East Moor

4

Pockerley
Buildings

River Team

**High
Forge**

Hammer Square Bank

5

Mount
Escob

High Urp

Birchwood Cl

6

Stony Lane

station Road
Peggy's
Wicket
Abbots Wk

**High
Handenhold**

Bean D sh
E
150
F

Sydney St
Arthur St
Road

134

116

A

Kibbles Lane

Bank

B

Grange Est

Ashvale Av

Laburnm Crs

Moorhill

Greenford

Coltspo

C

Ouselaw

1

Kibblesworth Grange

Cooper House

2

Riding Lane

Riding Farm

Kibblesworth Common

3

133

Pockerley Buildings

4

Summer square Bank

Abbot

Walden Cl

Leyburn Cl

Mill La

River Team

5

Mount Escob

High Urpeth

6

Stony Lane

New Road

High Handenhold

A

Bart Te

La

Arthur St

151

B

C

Fairfield

A693

I grid square represents 500 metres

D4
1 Bellerby Dr

ibbleDworth

E

117

F

Lansbury
Lansbury Dr

Drive

Avenue

Elisabeth

Edward Road

St Josephs
Infant
School

I

Poplar
Crs

Ravensworth Road

Pine St

Kings St

George St

Jones St

Morris St

Lane

2

Station

Rowletch Burn
Industrial
Estate

Birt
RC

Rowletch Burn

River Team

Low Urpeth

3

Bir
Gre

136

4

Ouston

Ba
Mo

Bellerby Dr

Melbeck Dr

Carlton
Crt

Tradley Ct

The Oval

The Oval

The Oval

Abernethy

Athull

Viola

Crs

Angus

Alford

Turnberry

Coldstream

Calander

Cannock

Cromarty

Ross

Coldstream

Iris Crs

PO

Urpeth

Ouston
Junior
School

Winchenham Cl

Wensley Cl

Reginvere

Penhill
Close

Arfsaig

Ardrossan

Aberdeen

Rothsay

Aberfoyle

Carnoustie

Carnoustie

Ouston
County
Infant
School

Byron

Milbanke Close

Milbanke
Close

St Benets
Primary
RC School

5

Institute
W

Ter

Lyne Cl

Colquit Dr

Tweed

Alloa St

Allooch Pl

Conway Pl

Ouston Lane

Brecon
Pl

Carlloch Dr

6

Road

Drum

First Av

Second
Av

Drum

Third
Av

Ro

Perkinsville

D

A693

Wanseck Dr

diefiield

IVYWAY

Health

Constance St

Barbary

Ernest St

PO

E

152

F

Pelton

136

A

118

PO

B

B2
1 Birtley La
2 Holyoake Gdns
3 Ruskin Rd

C

BIRTLEY

1

Lansbury Dr

Mary

Elisabeth

Lansbury Drive

Avenue

Glamis

Carlisle

Wilson Av

Crs

Ruskin Rd

Avenue

Edward Road

St Josephs
Infant
School

DURHAM ROAD

Mt Pleasant

Mount Rd

Gateshead Metropolitan
Borough Council

FELL BANK

The

Primrose

Hillside

Poplar Crs

Ravensworth Road

Pine St

May St

Birtley
Lane Surg

Orchard St
Orchard
Pk

south Vw

Junior

ter

Portland

King St

George St

Jones St

Morris St

Lane

The Av

St John's Rd

St John's

Birtley Lane

Primary
School

Portobello

2

A6127

PO

Station

Rowletch Burn
Industrial
Estate

Rowletch Burn

Birtley St Josephs
RC School

School

Harras
Bank

Lord Lawson of
Beamish
Secondary School

Birtley Medical
Group Practice

Birtley
Swimming
Baths

Leafield House
School

Radcliffe
St

Wilfrid St

3

135

Portobello
County Junior
Infant School

Colebrooke

Hartla

Polpero

Tamerto

A6127

DURHAM ROAD

Barley
Mow

4

Ouston

Turnberry

Coldstream

Ross

Callander

Cannock

Cromarty

Coldstream

York Rd

Dorset Avenue

Pembroke Av

Barley Mow
Primary School

Athlone
Pl

Errol

Kirkstone

Colebrooke

Sandray

McIvorCl

Swint Cl

The Dr

Suffolk Pl

5

Ouston
County
Infant School

Byron

Close

Milbanke Close

Carnoustie

Norfolk Avenue

Cambridge
Pl

Oxford Pl

Cheshire Av

Cumberland

Durham
Pl

Bedford Avenue

Vigo La

Milbanke
Close

PO

6

Road

Drum

Pelaw Cr

Park View
Comprehensive
School

Sinclair
Drive

First Av

Second
Av

Drum

A

153

B

A6127

C

Leander

Lombard Drive

1 grid square represents 500 metres

Blackfell

Junction 63

A1(1)

E2
1 Hexham

Blackfell
Pipershaw

119

Blackfell
Primary
School

Bink
Moss

F5
1 Harwood Cl

SUNDERLAND HWY

A1231

A182

SUNDERLAND HWY

Bamburgh Cl

Crighton

Lumley

I

A1288

Brockwell Rd
Phoenix Rd
Hutton Cl
Harvey Cl
Crowther Road
Stanhope

Crowther Road

Tilley Road

Ayton

Greenhead

Raby Rd

Raglan

Primary
School

Oxclose

Dunstanburgh Cl
Warkworth Cl

Castle Road

Langley Cl

Dunstanburgh Cl

Cambrian Way

2

Mitford

Brancepeth Rd

Chipchase

Diston Cl

Close

Morpeth Cl

Poneland

Berwick

Oxclose
Community
School

Ayton Road

Mallard Cl
Lapwing Cl

Partridge

Fulmar Drive
Glendurn

Turnstone Dr

Ayton

Kittiwake Drive
Dunlin Dr

Goosander's Rd

Greenwich Cl

Teal

Primary School

Lambton

Chiltern Cl

Bredon Cl

Penhamb Cl

Cairnsmore Dr

Cleveland Dr

Cullin

Hambleton Rd

Howarden Cl

3

Cambrian Way
Pennine Way

138

Glenorrin Cl

Cairngorm

Helvellyn
Avenue

Primary
School

Kestrel

Redshank
Cl

Crake Wy

Hotel

Dunvegan

Thirlmere

Shadon Way

Birtley La

Hotel

Washington Birtley Service Area

Heron
Cl
Curlew

Wigeon

Monkside Cl

Ayton Road

WESTERN HIGHWAY   A195

WESTERN HWY

4

Sedling

A1(M)

Junction 64

Harraton

Harraton
Primary
School

Road

Lonsdale

Lodge

Lea Gn

Rickleton Way

Coquet

The Chase

Alwin

Wanbeck

Taylor

Sheridan
Gn

Larchwood

5

Rickleton Way

Linburn

Westward
Larchwood
Alderwood

North

West Av

South Crs

Hope
Shield

Redburn

Winston

Petrel

Vigo Lane

Hargill

Setting
Stones

Breamish Dr

Vigo Lane

Washington
Hospital

Morningside

Harthope

Rickleton
Primary
School

Danby Cl

Rockhope

Forest Dr

Woodlands

Bonemill Lane

Swinhope

Bonemill Lane

6

Rickleton

154

Sunderland
Durham County

Picktree

Picktree Lane
Lampton Rd

D   E   F

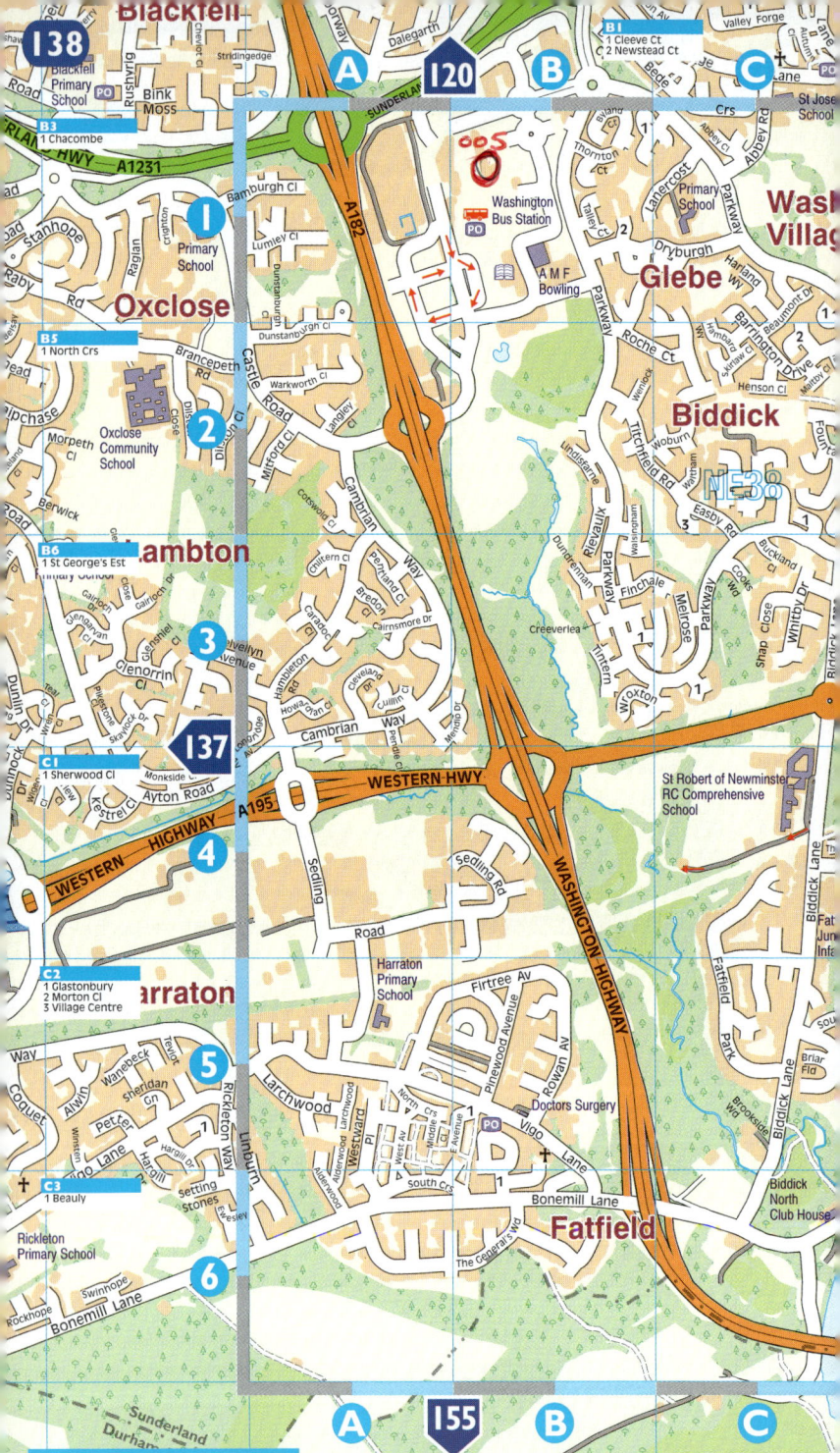

Blackfell

1 Blackfell
Primary School

Bink
Moss

B3
1 Chacombe

CUMBERLAND HWY A1231

Road

Stanhope

Raby Rd

Oxclose

I
1 Primary
School

B5
1 North Crs

Morpeth
Cl

Berwick

Oxclose
Community
School

2

Lambton

B6
1 St George's Est
Primary School

3

137

C1
1 Sherwood Cl

Ayton Road

WESTERN HIGHWAY

WESTERN HIGHWAY A195

4

Harraton

C2
1 Glastonbury
2 Morton Cl
3 Village Centre

C3
1 Beauly

Rickleton
Primary School

Bonemill Lane

Rockhope

Swinhope

5

6

B1
1 Cleeve Ct
2 Newstead Ct

Valley Forge

Bede

Crs

St Jose
School

Abbey Rd

Washington
Bus Station

A M F
Bowling

Thornton
Ct

Lanercost

Primary
School

Dryburgh

Parkway

Harland
Wy

Was
Village

Glebe

Roche Ct

Parkway

Biddick

NE38

Lindisfarne

Dunmerman

Parkway

Finchale

Melrose

Parkway

Wroxton

Creeverlea

St Robert of Newminster
RC Comprehensive
School

WESTERN HWY

WASHINGTON HIGHWAY

Sedling

Sedling Rd

Road

Harraton
Primary
School

Firtree Av

Pinewood Avenue

Rowan Av

Larchwood

Rickleton Way

Unburn

Sheridan

Alwin

Peter

Harpill

Setting
Stones

North
Crs

West Av

Middle

Avenue

South Crs

Doctors Surgery

Vigo

Lane

Bonemill Lane

Fatfield

Biddick
North
Club House

Fatfield
Park

Biddick Lane

Brookside
Wy

Biddick Lane

Barmston

D1
1 Park Chare

D2
1 Beech Sq

D3
1 Freesia Gra

D4
1 Hawkhurst
2 Lanchester Pk

D5
1 High Pasture
2 Longacre
3 Rivermead Wy

D6
1 Baysdale
2 Bishopdale
3 Kildale
4 St Stevens Cl

E2
1 Bell St
2 Brady Sq
3 Hillthorne Cl
4 Hugh St

E5
1 Spartylea

E6
1 Chandlers Ford
2 Ladywood Pk

F6
1 Ennerdale Crs
2 Eskdale
3 Wharfedale

F2
1 Frensham
2 Purley

F1
1 Athelhampton
2 Kinlett

121

140

156

Cemetery

Barmston Medical Centre

Primary School

Waskerley Road

Horsley Road

Station Road

NORTHUMBERLAND WAY

Columbia

Oxclose Road

Reynolds Avenue

Romney Av

Biddick Villas

Biddick School

Tweed Rd

Eddison Rd

Swan Road

Albert Pl

Widen Road

Pattinson

Staithes Road

The Willows

Barmston Road

Beckford Road

Thornbridge

Pattinson Rd

Alston Road

Faraday Cl

Lee Cl

Waltz

Cox Green

The James Steel Park

Coxgreen Road

Low Lambton Farm

Shepherd Way

Brinkburn

Falstone

Cowanburn

Slaley

Whitton

Carrgill

Allenhead

Blanchland

Fallowfield

South View

Beatrice Ter

Sandwell Drive

Winston Gn

Station Road

St Pauls Rd

Branston Dale

Westerdale

Stonesdale

Dentdale

Gliardale

Ferndale Road

Teesdale

Langdale

Swaledale Crs

Wensleydale

Avenue

Coxgreen Road

Allendale

Primary School

Fenwick

The Limes

Back

Rainton

Penshaw La

Pensh Monur

Weardale

Avondale

Tyne Crs

Clydesdale

140

Barmston

A

122

B

C

A6
1 Fenwick Cl
2 Wallis St

Alston Road

Lee Lane

Faraday Cl

Pattinson Road

Barmston

Kimblesworth

Walton Road

Wildfowl and
Wetlands
Trust

River Wear

Talgarth

Barmston Road

Pattinson Rd

Lane

Thornbridge

Barmston Road

Beckford

Pendeford

Corndean

Otterington

Wydcott

2

Stirling Cl

Wilden Road

Pattinson Road

Road

Staithes Road

3

Cox
Green

139

The James
S
P

4

Coxgreen Road

Low
Lambton
Farm

5

Hill Lane

Penshaw
Monument (NT)

A183

Coxgreen Road

Ferndale Road

Teesdale

Road

Back

The Limes

Monument Ter

Langdale

Borrowdale Crs

Allendale

Primary
School

Fenwick St

Rainton St

Penshaw La

CHESTER

ROAD

Bell St

Rose St W

PO

Swaledale Crs

Wensleydale Avenue

6

A

157

B

C

1 grid square represents 500 metres

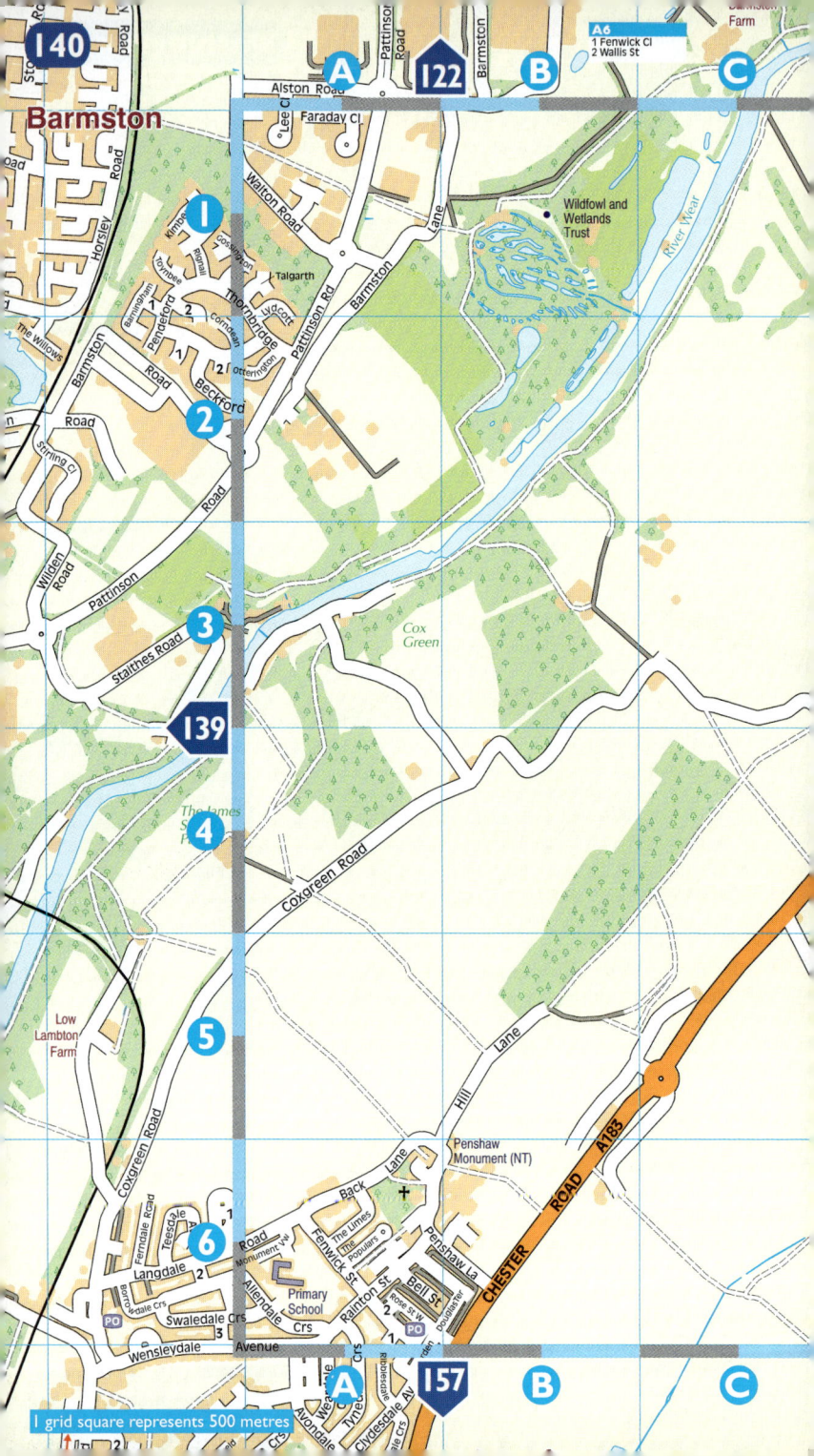

F1
1 Hylton Wk
2 Pennycross Sq
3 Pennygate Sq
4 Pennygreen Sq

123

F2
1 Dellfield Dr
2 Pennymore Sq
3 St Johns V

F3
1 Goodwood Rd
2 Parkmore Rd

Penny

F4
1 Rosewood Sq
2 Selsdon Av
3 Woodhurst Gv

Comprehensive School

South Hylton Primary School

Offerton

CHESTER ROAD

A183

Hasting Hill

Flinton Hill Farm

Grindo

142

Middle Herrington

West Herrington

158

Offerton Lane

Foxcover Road

A19(T)

124

A2 1 Penman Sq

A1 1 Grindon Cl
2 Hylton Wk
3 Romaldskirk Cl

Friar

A **B** **C**

South
Hylton
Primary School

A3
1 Galway Rd
2 Gardiner Sq
3 Geneva Rd
4 Gerrard Rd
5 Glanmore Rd
6 Pickhurst Sq
7 Pontefract Rd
8 Portadown Rd

A4
1 Gambia Rd
2 Gambia Sq
3 Gladwyn Rd
4 Gleneagles Sq
5 Gravesend Rd
6 Greenock Rd
7 Grenfell Sq
8 Northfield Dr

St Annes
RC Primary
School

Sunderland
Counselling
Services

Petersham Road

Padgate

I

Pennywell

SR4

Comprehensive
School

PO

B1
1 Pegwood Rd
2 Pinner Rd

2

B2
1 Glasbury Av
2 The Greenway
3 Hampstead Sq
4 Nookside Ct
5 Partick Sq
6 Pelton Rd

Pickering

Pickhurst

Palmerston

THE BROADWAY

Broadway
Junior
School

Broadstairs
Ct

3

B3
1 Galashiels Sq
2 Glanton Sq
3 Gleneagles Rd
4 Grindon Pk

STER ROAD

141

Grindon
Infants
School

Grindon

Geddes Rd

Galashiels
Rd

Gainsborough Road

Grindon Lane

Simonside

Grindon Lane

Sunn

B4
1 Gravesend Sq
2 Teddington Sq

B5
1 Tamworth Sq
2 Thorne Rd
3 Thorpeness Rd
4 Tyldesley Rd

4

Gordon Road

Greenshields Rd

Gravesend

Goldsmith Road

Goldsmith
Avenue

Torrens
Rd

Toronto Rd

Tunbridge

Torquay

**asting
Hill**

B6
1 Munslow Rd
2 Tenby Rd
3 Thames Rd
4 Tilbury Gdns

**Thorney
Close**

Tay Road

Telford Road

Taunton Road

C1
1 Huntley Sq

5

Tadcaster Road

Tintagel Close

Tadcaster Road

Tuscan Road

Townend Road

PO

C2
1 Broadmayne
Gdns
2 Holborn Sq
3 Medway Gdns
4 Southmayne Rd

Tasman Road

6

**Middle
Herrington**

Beckwith Road

DURHAM ROAD

C3
1 Selkirk Sq
2 Somerset Sq
3 Springbank Sq

Farringdon Road

Arbroath Road

Farring
Junior
School

A5, C5, C6
Street names for
this grid square are
listed at the back of
the index

A191

Hillcrest

A **159** **B**

DURHAM ROAD

C4
1 Shaftoe Sq
2 Silloth Rd
3 Thirsk Rd

C

PO

I grid square represents 500 metres

125

160

144

Street names for this grid square are listed at the back of the index
D2, D6, F5

Royal Hospital
A&E
A183

Cemetery

CHESTER ROAD

ORMONDE STREET

BARNES PARK ROAD

Junior Schools

Childrens Hospital

Humbledon
Wearside Coll

Springwell

Barnes Burn

DURHAM RD

DURHAM ROAD

Ashbr
Ashby

Thornhill Comprehensive

Barbara Priestman

RC Primary School
Alexandra Pk

Crosslea

Copley Dr

Harperley Dr

Plains Farm
Portland School

Silksworth La

Silksworth Lane

The Crs

Dene Street

Warwick Terrace
Westgate

N. Moor Road
North Allendale Sq

The Strand

Infants School

Tunstall Village

D3
1 Seymour Sq
2 Shoreham St
3 Swindon St

D4
1 Grindon La
2 Paignton Sq
3 Paisley Sq
4 Plymouth La
5 Polmuir Sq
6 Pretoria Sq
7 Strathmore Sq
8 Tunis Rd

E1
1 Dilston Gdns
2 General Graham St
3 Swaledale Gdns

E3
1 Ettrick Gv
2 Portland Sq
3 Sacriston Av

E4
1 Perth Sq
2 Polworth Sq
3 Powis Sq
4 Proctor Sq

E6
1 Sandown Gdns
2 Silksworth Cl
3 Southwold Gdns
4 Symington Gdns

F1
1 Burnaby St
2 Co-operative Ter
3 Cranford Ter
4 High Barnes Ter
5 Ingleby Ter
6 Oaklands Ter
7 Wolseley Ter

F2
1 Chatsworth Crs
2 Chatsworth St South
3 Georgian Ct

F3
1 Albyn Gdns
2 Alpine Wy
3 Hanby Gdns
4 Harewood Gdns
5 Haslemere Dr
6 Hatfield Gdns
7 Hathaway Gdns
8 Horsham Gdns
9 Hovingham Gdns
10 Huntingdon Gdns

F6
1 Bedford Pl
2 Cypress Sq
3 Minehead Gdns
4 Newport Gv
5 North Ter
6 West St

Farringdon
SR3
New

144

126

143

161

A1, A4, B4
Street names for this grid square are listed at the back of the index

A2
1 Birchfield Rd
2 Silksworth La
3 Wayside
4 Wenham Sq

A5
1 Bamburgh Gdns
2 Bowbank Cl
3 Braemar Gdns
4 Brentwood Gdns
5 Fernsway
6 Greenrigg Gdns
7 Heatherlea Gdns
8 Meadow Gdns
9 Pemberton Gdns

A6
1 Hazel Av
2 Winslade Cl

B1
1 Argyle Sq
2 Argyle St
3 Azalea Ter North
4 Valebrooke Gdns
5 Worcester St
6 Worcester Ter

B2
1 Avenue Ter
2 Brookside Gdns
3 Holmlands Pk N
4 Holmlands Pk S

B3
1 Ashbrooke Cross
2 Ashbrooke Range
3 Fairholme Rd
4 Greystoke Gdns
5 Hillside Gdns
6 Linden Gdns
7 Linden Rd
8 Lulworth Gdns
9 Lynford Gdns
10 Willow Bank Rd

B6
1 Camberley Cl

C1
1 Ashmore St
2 Burdon Rd
3 St George's Wy

C2
1 Ashburne Ct
2 Corby Ga
3 Corby Hall Dr

C3
1 The Glen
2 Langport Rd

C4
1 Longridge Sq

C5
1 Halidon Sq
2 Harcourt Rd
3 Hereford Ct
4 Hereford Sq

Ashbrooke

Hillview

Thornhill Comprehensive School

Thornhill Pk

St Anthonys RC School

Argyle House School

Barbara Priestman School

St Marys RC Primary School

Sunderland Cricket & Rugby Football Club

St Aidans RC Comprehensive School

University of Sunderland

Sunderland Eye Infirmary

Hillview Infant School

Portland School

Primary School

Infants School

Mowbray Park

Civic Centre

Masonic Temple

Sunderland Mus & Art Gallery

War Memorial

Sunderland Royal Hospital

1 grid square represents 500 metres

127

Hendon

Deerness Park
Medical Cen

Ashburne
Medical Cen

Valley Road
Junior School

Valley Road
Infant School

Grangetown
Junior & Infant
School

Southmoor
School

Grangetown
Family Dental
Health Cen

City of
Sunderland
College

Cemetery

Grangetown

SR2

Toll Bar Road

162

Ryhope Colliery

C5
1 Leeholme Ct

B3
1 Sandringham Dr

Catchwell Road

Co-operative Ter

Del Ban

Fondlyset Lane

Bush Blades

Bushblades Lane

Peter's Ba

1

House

Unity Ter

B6168

Harelaw Gdns

Harelaw

Harperley

Kyo Heugh Road

2

Cemetery

Cemetery

Carrmyers

Harperley Rd

Riding Hill Road

3

NORTH ROAD

Police Station

PO

Taylor Street

Swan Street

West Kyo

Kyo Road

Windsor Drive

Manor Dr

Hexham Dr

Annfield

Catchgate

Annfield House

Catchgate Primary School

Street

Blackett Street

Hamsterley Gardens

ANNFIELD PLAIN

4

Greencroft Comprehensive School

Annfield Pl

NEW FRONT

Welsh Ter

A693

Greencroft

West Road

Doctors Surgery

PO

School

Railway

STATION RD

DURHAM RD

SHIELDROW LA

Annfield Plain Cricket Club

Larwood Ct

Doctors Surgery

Crs

Park Cl

5

Douglas Ct

St Aidan's

Annfield Plain Infants School

The Avenue

A693

A693

ngingstone Lane

Derwents District C

A6076

6

Parkhead

Parkhead

Greencroft Parkway

Amos Drive

Tower Road

Lane

Park ad

1 grid square represents 500 metres

D   E   **130**   F

F2
1 Lyndhurst Rd

The Paddock

F3
1 Palmer St
2 School La

STATION RD

BARN

I

DH9

East
Kyo

F4
1 Greenlands

Tanfield View
Surgery

Durham County
Council

Louisa
Surgery

Stanley
Health
Centre

PO

Royal Rd

2

Oxhill

Carmel Road

Grange
Rd

Conscliffe

Front St

A693

B6532

Spen St

Smailes St

Derby Rd

Tyne Rd

Lindon Rd

3

South
Stanley

Comprehensive
School

Junior Mixed
School

Tyne Rd East

Mandela Cl

Geoffrey Ter

Gladstone St

King St

Salisbury St

B6313 PARK ROAD

School Ter

Gale St

Eyre St

148

Charles St

Orwell Gdns

Waverley Gdns

Keswick Rd

Rydal Av

John St

Mitchell St

Pine
Street

Poplar Street

Elm Street

Maple Street

Mundell St

Bridge St

South
Moor

Sandgate Lane

Sheldrow Lane

Greencroft
Comprehensive
School

New
Kyo

A693

PO

4

HUSTLEDOWN ROAD

South Moor Road

5

Muriel
Street

Wardle St

Stanley Burn

The Fairways

6

Quaking
Houses

Newacres Road

New
Acres

Kyo Lane

Kyo Burn

Perley Lane

D   E   F

148

131

147

East Stanley

STANLEY

Oxhill

South Stanley

Moor

The Middles

Quaking Houses

DH9

A2
1 Ritson St

A3
1 Joseph St

A4
1 Coquet Gdns
2 Moore St
3 Oliver St
4 Parmeter St

B1
1 Agnes St
2 Beaconsfield St
3 Front St
4 Joicey Gdns
5 Manor Rd
6 Mona St
7 Slaidburn Rd

B4
1 Hustledown Gdns

A1
1 Beamish St

Tanfield Comprehensive School

GOOD STREET

SUNNY TERRACE

STATION ROAD

Wylam Road

Newburn

Chester Rd

CHESTER ROAD

The Garrick Gallery
Durham County Council

Tanfield View Surgery

Louisa Surgery

Stanley Health Centre

Police Station

Derwentside District Council

A693

WEAR ROAD

B6532

DURHAM

Comprehensive School

Junior Mixed School

The Shopping Centre

Holly Hill

Holly Hill Gdns E

HUSTLEDOWN ROAD

B6313

St Marys Junior & Infant School

Holmside & South Moor Hospital

Bloemfontein Co Junior Mixed School

South Moor Road

Stanley Burn

The Fairways

Golf Course

Newacres

New Acres

Ousterley Road

Wagtail

West

1 grid square represents 500 metres

D1
1 St Aubyn's Wy

hield Dow E F 132

A693

D3
1 Pankhurst Pl

Beamish

We

1

2

3

4

5

6

Eden Hill Farm

Tw

Twizell Lane

150

Twizell Hall

Stanley Wood
Stanley Burn

Twizell Burn

Beamish County School
Beamish Villas

Co-operative Villas

HILL TOP

Roseberry St
John Street
Gladstone St
Beamish Hills

St Heliers Wy
Strathmore Cl
Broom
Beamish Vw

PO
Masefield Ct

Thorntree Cl

Acton Dene

East St

Gilpside Cl
1
orne Ct

Rusland

Ballater Ct
Colville Ct
Clare
Elgin Cl
Girvan

Aberfoyle Cl
Kinross
Culzane Cl
Hawick
Harwick Ct
Brentwood

Forrest Court

Fontery Nightingale
Pl
1
Bronte

B6532

Woodside Gardens

ROAD

PO

ES

Hazel Ter
Oak Terrace
Palm
Beech
Ter

Dr Dhuny's Surgery

B6313
Front St
PO
Thomas St
Thomas St
John St

CRAGHEAD LAN

EDWARD ST
Wylam St
Wagtail Lane
Railway St

Ousterley

Wagtail Ter
Ousterley Ter

Craghead

D E F

LOWER

LANE

White House Farm

Humblebum

B

side
ol
1

D Dow E 132 F

150

Station ad

Peggy's Wicket

Stor La

A693

Beamish County School

Beamish

Beamish Hills

o-operative illas

Roseberry St
John Street
Gladstone St

High
Hande

New

Road

A693

Sydi

1

West Pelton †

Edenfield

Green's

Bank

†

PO

Whernield

2

Plantation View

County Junior
Middle & Infant
School

Orchard
Cl

Eden Hill
Farm

Twizell
Lane

Gra
Vill

3

Twizell Lane

Albert St
Queen St
Pine

Stone Row

149

Twizell
Hall

PO

4

Newbridge Banks

Twizell Burn

5

BLUEHOUSE BANK

White Ha
Farm

B6313
Thomas St

CRAGHEAD   LANE

Thomas St

John St

6

Craghead

Lane

LOWERY

A

Humbleburn

B

C

White House
Fa

LAN

1 grid square represents 500 metres

D E **134** F

A693

A693 PO

Fairfield
Thornton Middleton
Lea King's Lane
Front Street
Elm Av
Cemetery
Oak Ter
The Pde
Heathmeads

Fieldside
Southfield
The Wynd

PELTON

Pelton
Lane
Pelton Ms
Lovaine St
Holyoake St
Alexandra St
Provident St
Industrial St
Roseberry
Primary
School
Roseberry Vls

2

Station Lane

PO
Front Street

Newfield

3

Pelton Lane

152

Blndy Burn

Twizell Burn

4

Miller
New Grange Terrace Plunkett Ter Gdns
VIEW
B6313 BEAMISH

Fellrose
Surgery

Whitehill
Pelton Fell Rd
Surgery
Briarwood Fell Rd
Av
Crs

DH2

Valley Rd

Shelley
Ct

Hett
Hills

5

Wordsworth Avenue
Shakespeare
Terrace
Ruskin Av
Henley
Av
Avenue
Brown

Tribley Farm

6

D E **164** F **Waldridge**

Golf Course

Broomy

Perkisville A | 135 | B | C

A1
1 Vicarage Cl

B6
1 Banks Holt

A693

Fairfield
Mosswood
King's Lane
Thornton
Lea
Snacres
Sandyford
Middlefield
Health
Centre
Ivyway
Constance St
Ernest St
Barbary
PO
Brecon Pl
Alice St
Lyne Cl
Oustonye
Conway Pl
Ascot
Jansbeck Cl
Garloch Dr

Cemetery
Front Street
Orchard St
Elwin St
Grange St
Wood St
The Wynd
Fieldside
Southfield
Brackendale Close
Pelton Health Clinic
Pelton County Junior & Infant School

Heathmeads
Oak Ter

PELT 2

Station Lane

Pelton Lane

High Flats

Front Street

3

151

Twizell Burn

Pelton Fell

PELTON

Lilac G
Eln
Briarhill
Hazel
Holly
Oaklea
Cragside

4

New Grange Terrace
Plunkett Ter
Millor Gdns
Fellrose Surgery
Burnthouse Bank
B6313
Whitehill Gdns
Lingholme

IEW

DH2

Pelton Fell Surgery
Valley Rd
Briarwood Av
Fell Rd
PO
Whitehill Crs
Tennyson Rd
Shelley Cl
CHESTER-LE- STREET

5

Byron
Avenue
Shakespere
Tennyson
Ruskin Av
Shelley Gdns
Long Burn
Wordsworth Avenue
Henley Av
Graythwaite
Brinkburn
Branwood
Auckland
Gibside
Wynard
Che
Stre
Galne

6

Waldridge Lane
Meadow Drive
West Dr
Long Burn Dr
Netherton
Clifton
Oastia Health Centre
Long Burn Dr
Cartmel Ct
Waldridge La
Redesdale Road
Fenton Cl
Norton
Dronfield
Lesbury Ct
Chester
Alwinton Ct
Duncan Cl
Millfield Ct

Wald A **lge** | 165 | B | C

l grid square represents 500 metres

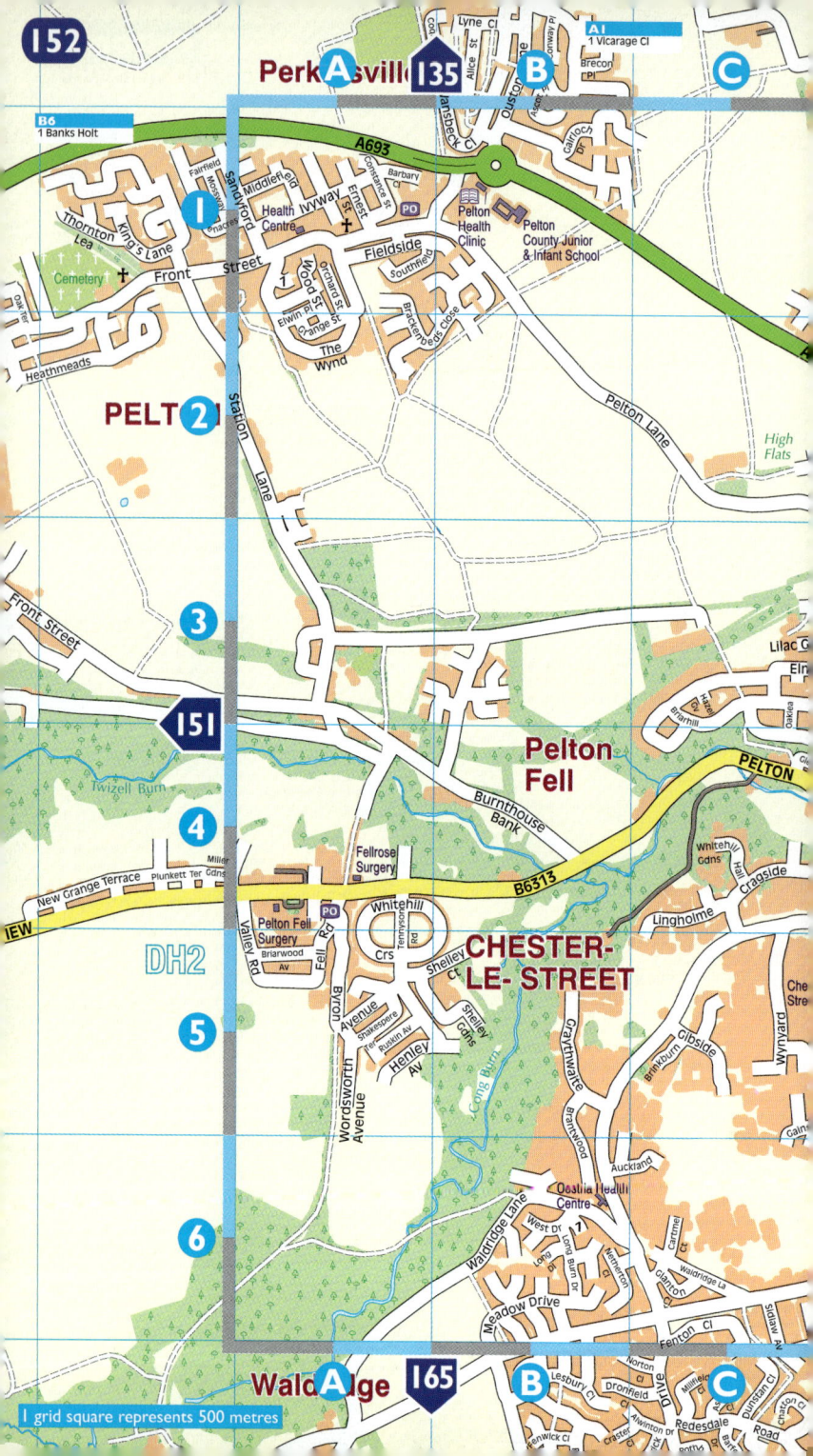

136

Drum Road
First
Second
Drum AV
Third Road
Drum Rd
Drum AV

E
Pelaw Cres
Kingsmere
Queensway
Wear Edg Rd
A6127 NORTH ROAD
Long Dean Pk

Park View Comprehensive School
Lombard Drive
Leander Av
Hampton
Merlin Dr
Sinclair Drive

F
Ash Mdw
North Drive
Lintfort
Picktree

I

Ri

Vigo Lane

2

A1(M)

South Pelaw

Low Flatts Rd
Lyndhurst Avenue
Lyndhurst Av

Pelaw House
Blind La
BLIND LANE A183

Pelaw Rd
Beechwoods
Firtrees
Convers Avenue
Myrtle Convers
Gdns Convers Road
Pelaw Av
Pelaw Pl

Highfield Hospital

Newcastle
Highfield Crs
Highfield Rd
Broadway
Arcadia Av
Tudor Rd
Springfield Rd
Castle View
Hillside
Pelaw Bank

PARK ROAD NORTH B6290
Campderton Av
Shields Rd
Rickleton
Cherry Banks

Junction 63

3
A167(T)

PICKTREE LANE
NEWBRID

Hilda Pk
Infant School
Laurel
PO
Pelaw Square
Junior School
Glencoe AV
Glen Barr
Glencoe Gdns
Glenmore
South St

Atkinson
Hadrian Av
Appledore Gdns
Chester-le-Street Health Cen
Civic Centre
PO
Chester-le-Street District Council
B6313 PICKTREE LANE
Hogarth Gdns

154

4

ROAD
North Rd
B6313
N BURNS
S Burns
Ashley Ter

Twelfth Av
Seventh Av
Eighth Av
Ninth Av
Jacques Ter
Murray Crd
Bede Ter
The Avenue
Cookson Ter
Station Rd
Tuart Street
Bede St
Elm St
Front Street
High Ch
Low Chare

Doctors Surgery
Park View Community School

Chester-le-Street Leisure Centre

5

Fourth Av
Third Gdns
The Crs
The Gdns
Lane
Chester-le-Street Station
Avondale Ter
Clarence Ter
Victor Ter
West
Primary School
St Cuthberts Av
Roman Avenue
Unostairne Av
Earfourn Av
Lindom Av

PARK RD CTRL

Bullion
Primary School
Newker Junior & Infant School
Yetholm AV
Second Avenue
Ashton
Boulmer Ct
South St
Vivian St
Station Rd
Poplar St
West
Waldridge Road
Wear
Chester-le-Street Cricket Club
St Cuthberts RC Primary School
Ropery Lane
Lumley Ter
Lancaster Ter
Castle Cl

6

B1284
LUM

Cleveland Av
Mendip Avenue
Moorfoot
North Durham NHS Trust
Relton Ter
Ramsey Ter
Melville Ter
Allen St
Baden Ter
Benson Rd
Weldon Ter
George St
York Ter
Coronation Av
Beverley Gdns
PARK ROAD SOUTH
Bridgman Drive
Lanwood
Drive

Durham County Cricket Club

River Wear

D
PO
Esperwater Rd
Grasmere
Dunvegan
Thirlmere
Rydal
Road

E
Windermere Av
Hawes
Orchard Ter

166

F
Red Rose Primary School
Crichton
Av

DI

A

137

B

C

Sinclair

Hampton Ct

Park View
Comprehensive
School

Leander Av

Merlin Dr

Lombard Drive

North Drive

Ash Mdw

Picktree

Rickleton

Danby Ct

Forest Dr

Bonemill Lane

Rockhope

Swinhope

Bonemill Lane

Sunderland
Durham County

1

Lintfort

Longdean Pk

Pelaw House

Blind La

2 A1(M)

Vigo Lane

River Wear

Lambton
Park

Black Drive

BLIND LANE A183

Highfield Crs

Park
Road

Camperdown Av

Rickleton

Cherry Banks

Junction 63

3

Broadway

Atkinson

Hadrian Av

Tudor Rd

PARK ROAD NORTH B6290

A161

PICKTREE
LANE

NEWBRIDGE BANK

A183 CHESTER

Appledore

Chester-le-Street
Health Cen

153

A1(M)

Civic
Centre

PO

Chester-le-Street
District Council

B6313 PICKTREE LANE

PARK RD NORTH

4

White
House

Hopgarth Gdns

Chester-
le-Street
Leisure Centre

A167(T)

DH3

Doctors
Surgery

High
Chare

Low
Chare

Park View
Community School

Front
Street

Primary
School

St Cuthbert's Av

Lindisfarne La

Earsdon Av

Lindom Av

Roman Avenue

PARK RD CTR L

5

West
Mains

Park Rd

Weldon Ter

St Cuthberts
RC Primary School

St Cuthberts Av

Ropery
Lane

B1284 LUMLEY

Chester-
le-Street
Cricket Club

Benson St

Ramsey St

Lumley Ter

George St

Beverley Gdns

Castle Cl

PARK ROAD SOUTH

6

Durham County
Cricket Club

River Wear

Lumley Park Burn

Ropery Lane

York
Ter

Coronation
St

Clifford
Ter

Jolliffe
St

Red Rose
Primary
School

Crichton
Av

Braeman
Drive

Larwood
Av

A

167

B

NEW

C

ROAD

D E **138** F

I

Road

2

The Avenue

Durham County

Sunderland

ence

3

River Wear

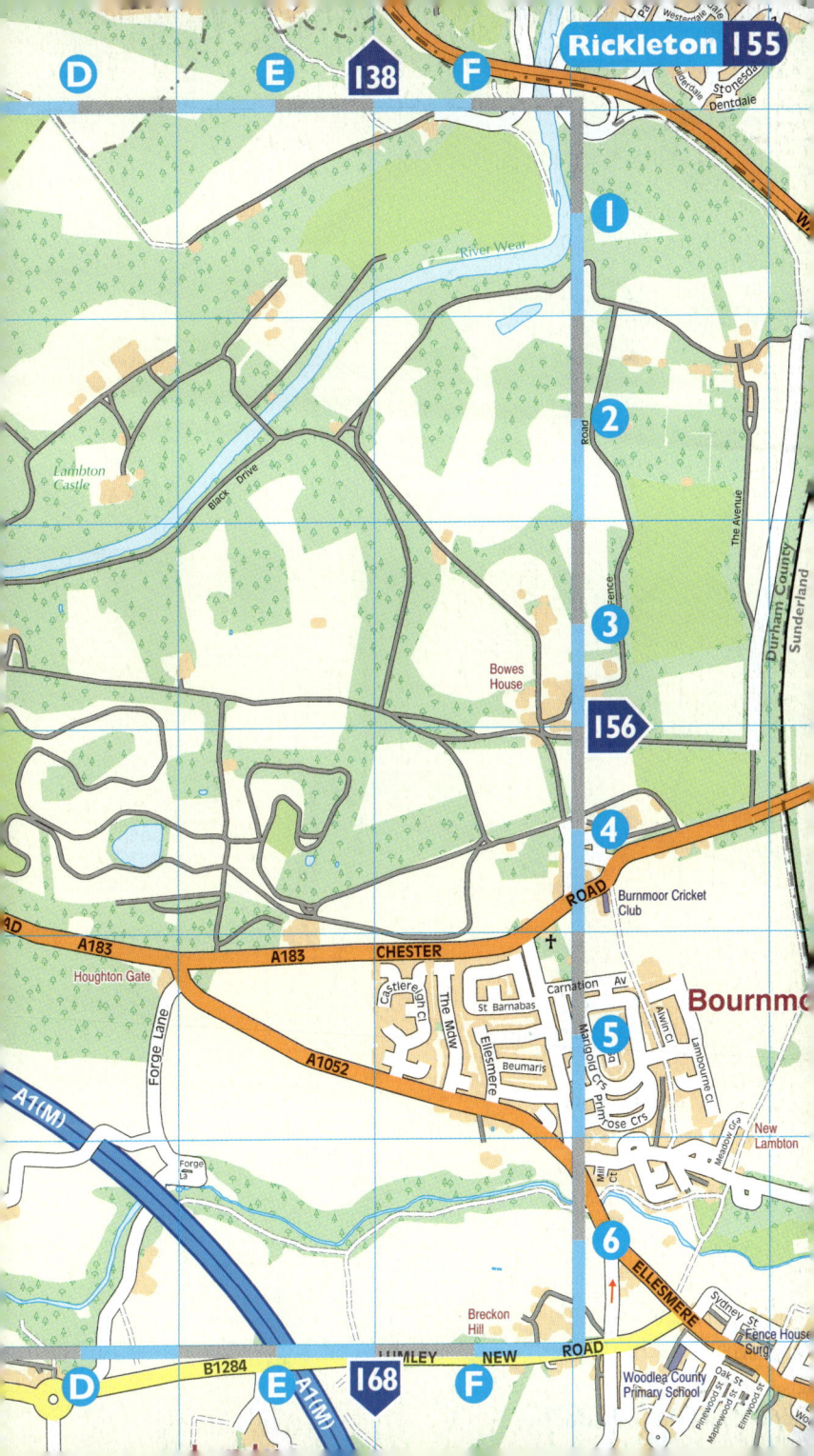

Lambton
Castle

Black Drive

Bowes
House

156

4

ROAD

Burnmoor Cricket
Club

A183

Houghton Gate

A183

CHESTER

Castlereigh Cl

The Mdw

St Barnabas

Carnation Av

Bournmo

A1052

Forge Lane

Ellesmere

Beumaris

Marigold Crs

Primrose Crs

Alwin Cl

Lambourne Cl

5

Meadow Cl

New
Lambton

A1(M)

Forge
Cl

Mill Ct

6

ELLESMERE

Sydney St

Fence House
Surg

Breckon
Hill

LUMLEY NEW ROAD

Oak St

B1284

Woodlea County
Primary School

156 **139** B C1
1 Cross Rigg Cl
2 Frederick Gdns

C2
1 Craighill
2 Kelso Gv
3 Station Rd

C3
1 Larkfield Crs

I

2

3

155

4

5

6

A

139

B

C

River Wear

WASHINGTON HIGHWAY

Our Lady
of Peace
RC School

Station Road

Langdale

Swaledale

Wensleydale

Westbourne
Grangewood
Surg

Gainsborough
Crescent

CHESTER ROAD

Larkfield
Crescent

Hunter St

Paddock
Close

Bowes Lea

Golf
Course

Briar

Road

Birkdale Dr

Lytham
Grange

Woodhall
Spa

Bowes
House

Burnmoor Cricket
Club

CHESTER ROAD

St Barnabas

Beumaris

Ellesmere

The Mdw

Castlereigh Cl

Carnation Av

Marigold Crs

Lilac Sq

Primrose Crs

Alwin Cl

Lambourne Cl

Bournmoor

New
Lambton

Breckon
Hill

ELLESMERE ROAD

Sydney St

Fence Houses
Surg

Woodland
Primary School

LUMLEY NEW ROAD

A

169

B

C

Fence Hou

Avenue

Vivian

DH4

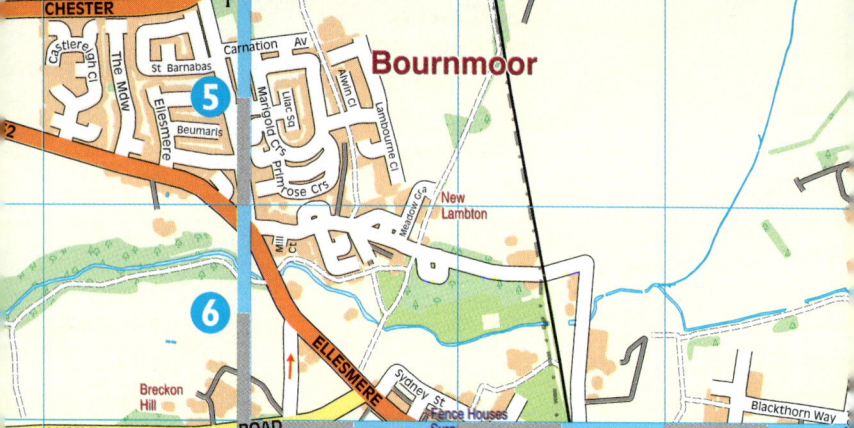

I grid square represents 500 metres

Penshaw

Shiney Row

New Herrington

Philadelphia

Sunniside

Newbottle

Burnside

Grassw

CHESTER ROAD

PHILADELPHIA LANE A182

HOUGHTON ROAD

NEWBOTTLE STREET

Primary School

Herrington Medical Centre

City of Sunderland College

Philadelphia Cricket Club

Newbottle Primary School

Burnside Primary

D1
1 Chislehurst Rd
2 Cricklewood Dr
3 Thirkeld Pl

D2
1 Council Av
2 The Harbour
3 The Haven
4 Jedburgh Rd
5 Mill Pit
6 Oakmere Cl

D3
1 Beaufort Cl
2 Coldstream Cl
3 Galashiels Gv

D6
1 Holystone Cl

E1
1 Chingford Cl

E2
1 Cricklewood Dr

E3
1 Connaught Cl
2 Goodrich Cl

E4
1 Bigbury Cl
2 Elfordleigh
3 Fowler Cl
4 Honiton Cl
5 Sidmouth Cl
6 Torrington Cl
7 Warren Cl

E5
1 Bickington Ct
2 Lydford Ct
3 Saunton Ct
4 Tavistock Ct

E6
1 Byland Cl
2 Littleburn Cl
3 Rosedale Crs
4 Thorneyburn Cl

F2
1 Sutherland Gra

F4
1 Green Av
2 Sparkwell Cl
3 Voltage Ter

F5
1 Garden St
2 Hartoft Cl
3 Hillview Crs
4 Hillview Gv
5 Hillview Rd
6 Kirk Vw
7 St Cuthbert's Rd
8 Springfield Rd

F6
1 Gertrude St
2 Hylton St

A

141

B

C

A2
1 Hill Ter

FOXCOV

A19(T)

West Herrington

I

Manor Grove

McClaren Way

The Paddock

Vardy Terrace

Cresent

Fletcher

ST AIDAN'S TERRACE

HERRINGTON ROAD

Street

Lanton

PO

B1286

Catherine Rd

Langley St

Kirkside

Freezemoor Road

2

New Herrington

Herrington Hill Ho

Philadelphia

3

157

Stony Gate

PHILA

LANE A182

4

The Crs

North St

Front St

Hampton Drive

5

Grange View

Union Rd

2

Coaley Lane

4

5

3

South Street

PO

8

The Dell

Leas

Cathedral View

5

Newbottle

Sunderland Road

High Lane

Over the Hill Farm

DURHAM ROAD

A690

HOUGHTON ROAD

ottle

ary School

Adventure St

Chestnut

Lumley

Ruby St

Blind Lane

6

G—sswell

NEWBOTTLE STREET

Newburn Cr

2

A

171

Balfour St

HOUGHTON CUT

B

C

Primary

Middle
Herring...

D1 1 St Chad's Crs

D **E** **142**

DURHAM

Farri

E1
1 Algiers Rd
2 Berkeley Cl
3 Lambton Ct
4 Lulworth Ct
5 Lumley Ct

SR3

Hillcrest
Summerhill
Hillview
Foxcove Lane
St Chad's Road
Careen Crs
Crow Lane
Herrington Road

A690

Charter Drive
Carlton Crs
Raby Drive
Avonmouth Sq
Appleby Rd
Ashdown Road
Andrew Road
Farringdon Av
Brynie
Steep Hill
Beckwith Road
ROAD

Aruna
Ambrose Rd
Avalo
Archer
School
Anthony
Arden Square
The
Amsterdam Rd

Anthony
10 PO
Allendale Rd
Anglesey Rd
Adercare Rd

East Herrington Primary School
Warwick
Launceston Drive
Augusta Road
Ardrossan Rd

Farringdon School

Amelia Gdns
Silksworth
Balmer
Arundel Gdns
Dudley Gdns
Caernarvon Dr
Aldwych Sq

PO

B1286

Elmfield
Drumoyne Close
Oakfield Cl
Briardene
Clendale Close
Ashton
Longmeadows
Woodside Terrace
Camborne

East Herrington

Silksworth Road

Silksworth Road

E2
1 Braemar Gdns

Brenlynn Cl
Raclynn
Goldly
Nasmont
Corbery Dr
Rise
Woodland

2

DOXFORD PK

DOXFORD PK Way

Meadow Dr
Meadow View
Broadmeadow
Glendale Close

CITY WAY

Morpeth
Midhurst
Morval Cl
Manston
Marcross Dr
Margrove Dr
Melvin
Marlee
Masnmmford

E3
1 Grayling Ct

Chantry Cl
Flaxfield Cl
Bishops

CITY WAY

Admiral
Victory Way
Hendon Way
Camberwell Way

Benedict Biscop C of E School

Moorside

Morval Cl
Harlow Dr

3

Moorley Dr
Moorside Road

Ledenham Way
160 Lancepark
7 10

F1
1 Aldershot Rd
2 Aldershot Sq
3 Aldwych Rd
4 Allendale Rd
5 Anglesey Sq
6 Anthony Rd
7 Appleby Sq
8 Ashford Rd
9 Ashwell Rd
10 Aston Sq
11 Conway Gdns

4

Low Haining

A19(T)

F2
1 Maidstone Cl
2 Marbury Cl
3 Matfen Dr
4 Melsonby Cl
5 Merrington Cl
6 Merrion Cl

5

Hangmans Lane

F3
1 Maplebeck Cl
2 Maxton Cl
3 Midsomer Cl
4 Milsted Cl
5 Minskip Cl
6 Montford Cl

6

Warden Law North Farm

Salter's

ining

D **E** **172** **F**

160

143

A   B   C

Farringdon

SR3

New Silksworth

East Herrington

CITY WAY

DOXFORD PK WY

DOXFORD PARK WAY

159

Farringdon Junior School

Silksworth Road

Benedict Biscop C of E School

173

A   B   C

C3
Street names for this grid square are listed at the back of the index

Old Burdon

Thristley House Farm

Hangmans Lane

Burdon Lane

Hall Farm Road

1 grid square represents 500 metres

144

F

Holly Av
Hawthor
Infants School
Paddock La

D1
1 Ainthorpe Cl
2 Fairways
3 Quarry Rd
4 Tunstall Vls

TUNSTALL VILLAGE

TUNSTALL BANK

Withernsea Gv

Ryemount Rd

Tunstall

BURDON ROAD

B1286

Nettles

Lane

Ravensworth

Ramilies

Rothbury

Goathland Cl

Rachel
Rowell
Cl

Richmond
Runcorn
Ridgeway

Rushford

Tunstall Lodge Farm

Lodgeside Meadow

Burdon Lane

East Farm

Burdon Road

ord Park

Burdon

Burn Hall Farm

A19(T)

Pacific Hall Farm

Colliery

D2
1 Closeburn Sq
2 Danby Cl
3 Drybeck Sq
4 Monkswood Sq

Bankside Cl

Brick Rw

sbury Av

Western Hl

B1286

RYHOPE STREET

Cheviot La

Back Ryhope St

Ryhope Health Centre

Infant Scho

D3
1 Leyfield Cl

Stewart
Bevan
Av

Blyton Avenue

Burdon

Escdale

Smith Gv Lane

2

E1
1 Boulby Cl
2 Hawsker Cl
3 Hilltop Gdns
4 Houlskye Cl
5 Levisham Cl

3

162

E2
1 Rodney Cl

4

F1
1 Runnymede

5

6 A1018

Ryhope
Cemete

Ry

I

PO

161

D E 174 **F**

Sunderland
Durham Count

A 145 B A1 C
1 Murphy Gv

Orkney Dr
Hewitt Ave
Lynthorpe
Linskell
Leechmere
Lansdowne

Rye View Road
Ocean Vw
Ridley Av
Pentaile Dr
Callington Dr
Trevarren Dr
Pelperro Cl
Queen
Lanvet

Ryhope Colliery

.L BANK
Withernsea Gv
Ryemount Rd
Bankside Cl
Brick Rw
Shaftesbury Av
Western Hl
Ryhope Health Centre
Rosslyn Avenue
Roselea Av
Atholstan
Rigg

Runcorn
Richmond
Ravensworth
Ridgeway
Rothbury
Rushford

B1286
Back Ryhope St.
RYHOPE STREET
Cheviot La
Blyton Avenue
Infant School
Trottet Ter
Dincaite Hl
Smith Street
Thomas Street
Colin Ter
Primary School
Stockton Rd
Station Road
Ethel Richardson Ter
Brewer Terrace

Stewart Avenue
Bevan Avenue
Smith Gv
Lane
Esdale
Burdon
Smith Avenue
School
Ryhope Cemetery

Ryhope

Dwyer Ter
Thomas A St
Feather Bed La
Marville W
Marville E
Arthur Av
Atrol Gdns
Country
Regent Road
Cliff Road

Markington
Viewforth Rd
STOCKTON ROAD
A1018

Ryhope General Hospital

THE VILLAGE
B1287
SEA VIEW
Scotland
George

161

Sunderland
Durham County

Hall

A1018
ROAD

Seaham Grange

STOCKTON
A1018
STOCKTON
South Cra Pk

LC

A 175 B C
Lord Byrons Walk
B1285
Burdon
Neash
Rd

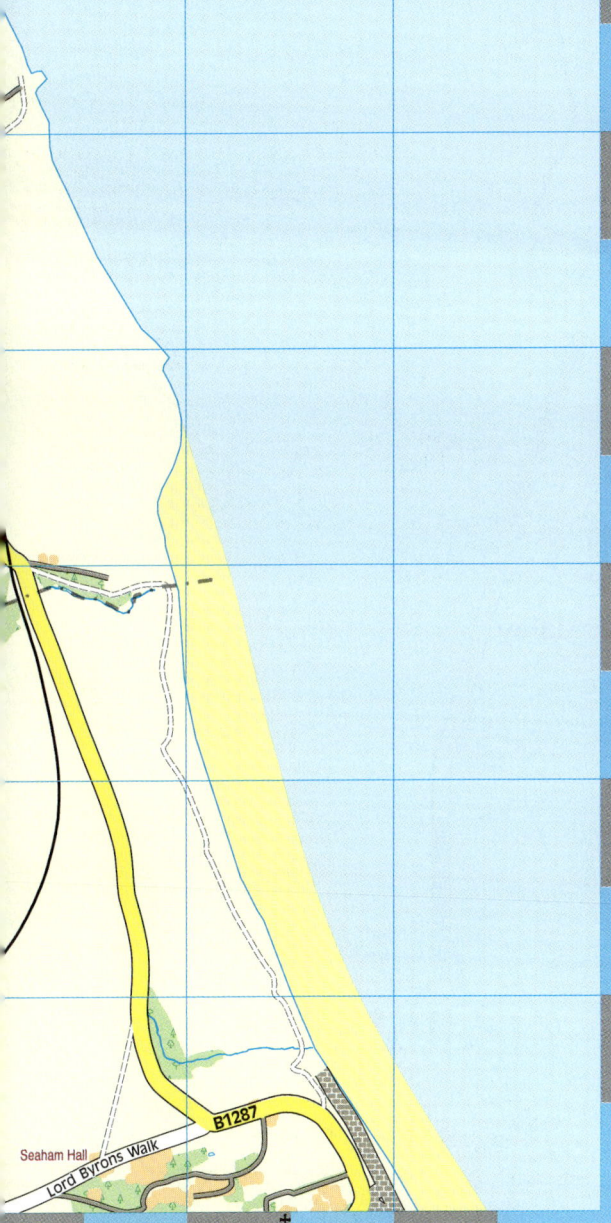

D　　　E　　　F

1

2

3

4

5

6

B1287

Seaham Hall

Lord Byrons Walk

D　　　E　　176

F

I

A3
1 Stobart St

Broomy
Holm

Little Burn

Grove

ole Burn

2

Congburn
Bridge

CONGBURN BANK

Edmondsley
JMI School

3

Tyzack

Street

B6532

Jubilee Cl

Edmondsley

4

Sacriston
Wood

Bruce St
Hamilton
Terrace

EDMONDSLEY LANE

Nettlesworth
West House

5

Westhills

Close

Daleside

Cross

Ashford
Dr

Black Burn

6

Charlaw

Close

Acorn Close

B6532

Deneside

Lane

Morningside

Brookside

Parkside

SACRISTON

RCJMI
School

Derwent Terrace

Springside

Rydal
Close

St Cuthberts

Cemetery

Sacriston

Ripon Cl

FRONT STREET

Baths

Fleming

Gregson St

Avenue

Front Street

Rose

ROAD

Plawsworth Road
County Infant School

Barras Hill

1 grid square represents 500 metres

D E F
152

F2
1 Chillingham Dr

Waldridge

Meadow Rd
Long Burn Dr
Netherby Cl
Clarton Cl
Waldridge
Fenton Dr

Lesbury Cl
Norton Cl
Dronfield Cl
Millfield
Eshkirk
Duntson Cl
Charton Cl
Road

Fenwick Cl
Craster Cl
Alwinton Cl
Redesdale
Road

Falstone
Almwick
Bamford

Floden Cl
Ingram

Warkworth Drive

Embleton Drive
Hawley Dr
Lilburn Cl

Chillingham Drive

Denwick
Close
Cheviot
Vw
Bywell Dr

Warkworth
Close

Hawkin
Cl
Prendwick
Cl
Bewick Cl

South Burn

Waldridge Fell
Country Park

The Crs
Waldridge Lane

Beaney Lane

Darley Court

Nettlesworth

Ugly Lane

PARK VIEW
Nettlesworth
Primary School

Hillmeads

B6312

Tanmeads

B6312

Tan
Hills

Hawthorn

Sycamore
Rd
Briar
Elm

D E F
179

PO
Caerwater Rd
Road
Grasmere Av
St
Marys
Rd
Thirlmere
AV
Rydal

Lomond
Pl
Ullswater Rd
Dunvegan
Cagh
Rd
Car

The Hermitage

2

A167(T)
The
Dene
The
Oval

Chester
Moor

3
Union Lane
The Gallery

166

4

5

Plawsworth

6

Mill Lane
Mill House

B6312
A167(T)

I

Kinloch

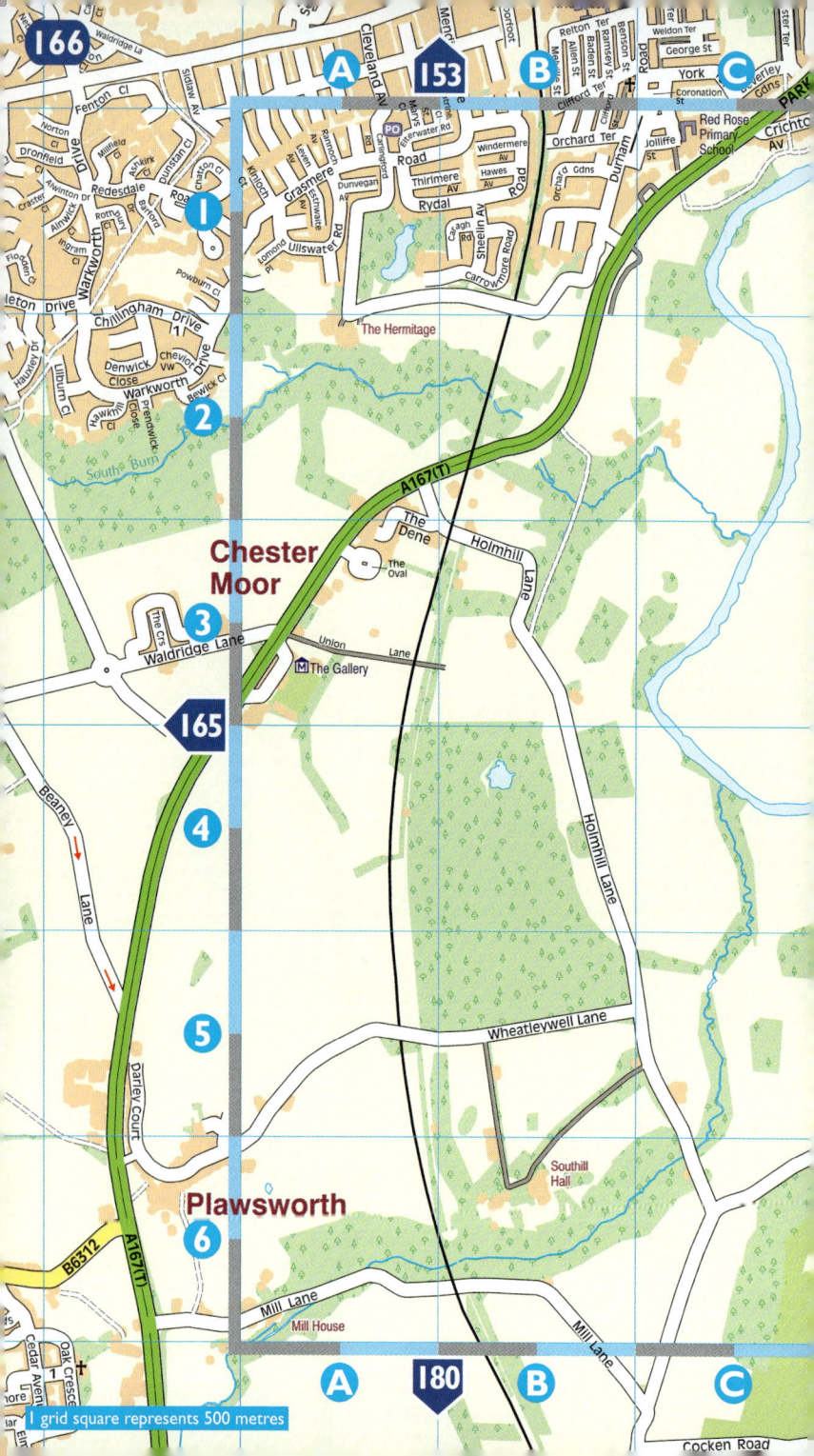

166
153
A
B
C

Cleveland Av
Menceforth
Reiton Ter
Weldon Ter
George St
Beverley Gdns
PARK

Waldridge La
Fenton Cl
Ramsey St
Allen St
Baden St
Benson St
York
Coronation St
Crichton Av

Norton
Dronfield
Millfield
Duncan Cl
Ramcroft Rd
Carmington
PO
Road
Windermere Av
Orchard Ter
Red Rose Primary School

Redesdale
Shilaw Av
Warkworth Road
Jewitt
Grasmere Av
Etchwells
Thirlmere Av
Hawes Av
Orchard Gdns
Durham Road
Jolliffe St

Craster
Alnwick Dr
Ingram Dr
Rothley
Lomond Pl
Ullswater Rd
Rydal
St Mary's Rd
Cragagh Rd
Sheelin Av
Carrowmore Road

1

Flodden
Cedar Dr
Warkworth Road
Powburn Cl

Chillingham Drive
The Hermitage

Lilburn Cl
Denwick Close
Chevlot Drive
Chevlot Drive
Warkworth
Prenwick Close
Bewick Cl

2

Haydon
Hawkhills

South Burn
A167(T)

Chester Moor

The Dene
Holmhill Lane
The Oval

The Crs
Waldridge Lane
3
Union Lane
Lane
The Gallery

165

Beaney Lane

4

Holmhill Lane

5

Darley Court

Wheatleywell Lane

Southill Hall

Plawsworth

6

B6312
A167(T)

Mill Lane
Mill House
Mill Lane

A
180
B
C

Cocken Road

1 grid square represents 500 metres

D Durham
Club

F4
1 Canterbury Cl
2 Lichfield Cl

E

154

F

Lu
Th

NEW ROAD

B

Lumley Riding

I

Lumley Park Burn

Lumley Park Lane

2

Scoper's Lane

Lumley County Infant School

Durham County Council

GREAT LUMLEY

Back Lane

Scott Street

3 Lumley JMI School

4

Scoper's Cl

Nenthead Cl

Fenton Lumley Grange

Well Lane

Front Street

PO

Norwich Cl

168

Cairnmore Drive

Brignall Cl

Lartington Close

River Wear

Old Mill Lane

Winchester Cl

Salisbury Cl

Gloucester Cl

Exeter

Cambridge

Worcester Drive

Cocker

4

Harbour House Farm

5

Charles Pit Cottages

Cocken White House Farm

6

Cocken Lane

D Low Cocken Farm

E

181

F

168

A

155

B

A3
1 Eggleston Cl
2 Hamsterley Cl
3 Mickleton Cl
4 Startforth Cl

C

Cocken
Hill

A4
1 Lunedale Dr

B1284   LUMLEY   NEW

ROAD

1

A1(M)

Lumley
Thicks

Scorer's

2

Lumley
County
Infant School

Lane

Lane

Back

Durham
County Council

3

Scott Ct Street

Lumley
JMI School

4

Prospect

Front

PO

Hazelgarth

Norwich
Cl

Winchester
Cl

167

1

Salisbury
Cl

Gloucester
Cl

2

Cambridge

Water

Drive

4

Cocken Lane

Stainmore Drive

Prospect

Cl

3

Cl

Nenthead
Cl

Lartington
Close

Brignall Cl

Pea Flatts Lane

George   Pit   Lane

A1(M)

5

Prior's
Close

Charles Pit
Cottages

Cocken White
House Farm

6

Cocken   Lane

A

182

B

C

1 grid square represents 500 metres

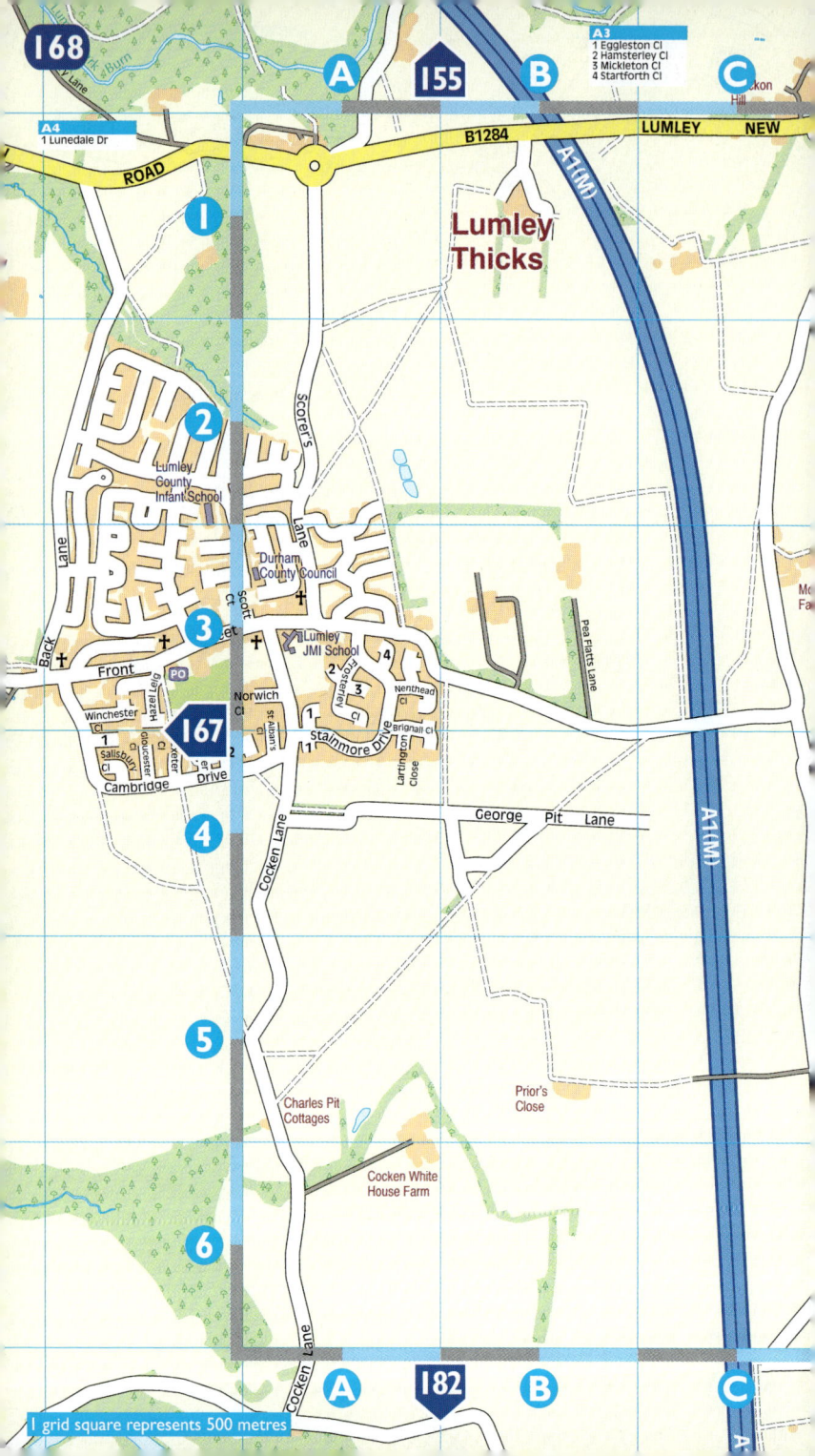

ELLE

D

E

156

F
Blackthorn Way
Sedgeler

AD

F1
1 Brancepeth Av
2 Murray Av
3 Raby Cl

Stoney St

Fence Houses
Surg

Woodlea County
Primary School

Oak St

Pinewood St

Maplewood St

Elmwood St

Woodland Gra

PO

LC

A1052

Avenue

Fence Houses

DH4

Vivian

Ravensworth Av

Grange Av

3
Rose Avenue

Acacia Av

Morley Ter

Cherry Way

I

F2
1 Chilton Gdns
2 Cross St

Lindisfarn
Cl

um

Morton
House

Durham St

Dubmire
County Junior
& Infant School

A1052

PO

Bankhead Ter

Dubmire Ccl

Park Keld

Hardie

Moor

F3
1 Maiden Law
2 The Mews
3 Stretton Cl

Du

Moorsfield

2
DAIRY LANE

South View Ter

St Michaels

St
Andrews

2

C
R

Chilton
Gdns

Dubmire
Cottages

John
Street

James Ter

Wynyard
Street

Thalmes Crs

Avon Crs

Wear Street

Syston
Close

FRONT STREET

Highfield
Drive

St

3

Chilton
Moor

LC

Newbottle Lane

Relton

Atherton
Dr

2

3

PH

Black Boy Road

170

4

Lumley Moor
Farm

Nature
Reserve

range

5

Sunderland

Durham County

6

Mark's Lane

Meadows
Lane

D

E
Stables
Farm

183

F

170

157

A3
1 Highfield Gra

Burnside

A2
1 Churchill Sq

NETTLE STREET

Grass

Newminster Close

Fountains Close

Blackthorn Way

Sedgeletch

Cherry Way

Moors Burn

ce Houses

DH4

B1
1 Stoneleigh Cl

Vivian

Ravensworth Av

Morley Ter

Banl

A1052

B2
1 Redburn Cl
2 Southburn Cl

Otterburn Crs

Burnside Avenue

Woodburn Dr

Moorburn

Newburn Crs

Sherburn Grove

Houghton Colliery Welfare Cricket Club

Leyburn Gv

Leyburn Av

Larch Av

Beech Av

Burnside Primary School

Gas House Lane

Station Rd

B3
1 Crimdon Gv

Moorsfield

Moors

High Dubmire

Burn

Park

Road

Dickens

Dubmire County Junior & Infant School

A1052

PO

Kell

Hardie

Discroll St

Gladstone Street

DAIRY LANE

South View Ter

DAIRY LANE

Longacre

Longacre

Lime Av

Seaburn Dr

Lime

Greenwood Av

Bernard St

Gilpin St

Wallace

Thornhill Street

Houghto

Kepier S

B6
1 Mingary Cl
2 South St

Thames Crs

Avon Crs

Street

St Michaels

St Andrews

Colliery Row

Alreys

Nine

Lands

Willow

Whicham

Hixton

Marion

Dunelm

The Oval

Finchale

Ferrand Ter

Castle Dene Grove

HOUGH LE-SPR

Dubmire Cottages

C1
1 Cross St

Wear Street

FRONT STREET

Highfield

Drive

Witton Grove

Dunelm

Drive

Dunelm

Wingate Close

Stanhope Close

A690

C2
1 Linden Gv

Syston Close

Atherton

Dr

Chilton Moor

Phoenix Way

Mercantile

Road

169

C3
1 Brandon Cl

Arena Business Park

Lister

Mill Hill

Dixon Rd

B1284

North Pit Farm

Burn Close

DURHAM RD

DURHAM

C4
1 Millbeck Gv
2 Rotherham Cl

Nature Reserve

Durham Road

Ryehill View

Markle Grove

North St

Grange View

Sunderland

Durham County

C5
1 Summerhouse Farm

PO

East Rainton JMI School

South St

Quarry St

Road

House

East Rainton

Holly Haven

Meadows Lane

Meadow St

Durham Road

Pontop Street

Lloyd

Pontop Street

Mournhill

House

184

Fieldside

C6
1 Emmbrook Cl
2 Waterford Cl

Middle

1 grid square represents 500 metres

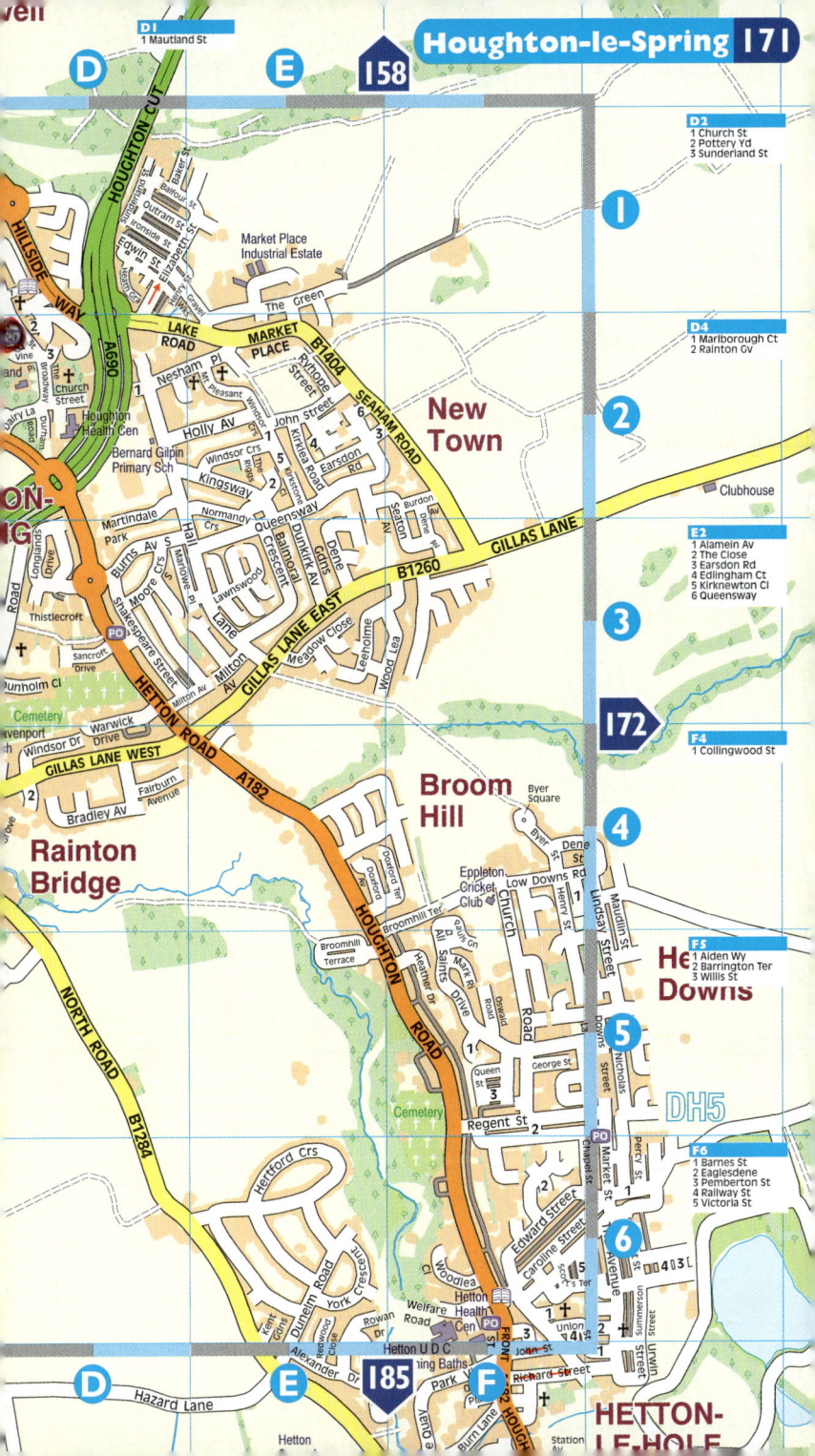

D1
1 Mautland St

158

D2
1 Church St
2 Pottery Yd
3 Sunderland St

I

D4
1 Marlborough Ct
2 Rainton Gv

2

Clubhouse

Market Place
Industrial Estate

The Green

LAKE
ROAD

MARKET
PLACE

B1404

**New
Town**

SEAHAM ROAD

Nesham Pl

Mt Pleasant

Holly Av

Houghton
Health Cen

Bernard Gilpin
Primary Sch

Windsor Crs

Kingsway

Windsor
The

John Street

Kirklea Road

Earsdon
Rd

Burdon
Av

Seaton

Dene Rd

GILLAS LANE

B1260

E2
1 Alamein Av
2 The Close
3 Earsdon Rd
4 Edlingham Ct
5 Kirknewton Cl
6 Queensway

3

172

F4
1 Collingwood St

Martindale
Park

Longlands

Drive

Burns Av

Moore

Marlowe Pl

Normandy

Queensway

Dunkirk Av

Balmoral
Crescent

Dene
Gdns

GILLAS LANE EAST

Lawnswood

Milton
Av

Meadow Close

Wood Lea

Leeholme

Thistlecroft

Sancroft
Drive

Shakespeare Street

Milton Av

Lane

HETTON ROAD

GILLAS LANE WEST

Warwick
Drive

Windsor Dr

A182

Cemetery

Davenport

Fairburn
Avenue

Bradley Av

**Rainton
Bridge**

NORTH ROAD

B1284

HOUGHTON ROAD

Broomhill
Terrace

Broomhill Ter

Oxxford Ter

Dodena

All Saints Way

Heather Dr

**Broom
Hill**

Byer
Square

Byer St

Dene
St

Eppleton
Cricket
Club

Low Downs Rd

Henry St

Church
Road

Oswald
Road

Ralph Gn

Mary Rd

Lindsay Street

Mauldin St

He
Downs

F5
1 Aiden Wy
2 Barrington Ter
3 Willis St

4

5

Downs
Street

Nicholas
Street

Queen
St

George St

Regent St

Cemetery

DH5

Hertford Crs

Kent
Gdns

Dunelm Road

York Crescent

Rowan
Dr

Welfare
Road

Woodlea

Hetton
Health
Cen

PO

Hetton U D C
ning Baths

Park Lane

Edward Street

Caroline Street

Chapel St

Market St

Percy St

6

Barnes St

Union

John St

Richard Street

Burn Lane

FRONT ST

HOUGH

Station

Summerson
Street

Urwin Street

Avenue

F6
1 Barnes St
2 Eaglesdene
3 Pemberton St
4 Railway St
5 Victoria St

185

D **E** **F**

Hazard Lane

Hetton

Alexander

**HETTON-
LE-HOLE**

A **159** B

A6
1 Eppleton Rw
2 Stephenson Cl
3 Victory St East
4 Victory St West

C

den Law
n Farm

1

2 New Town

Warden Law

B1404

Clubhouse

GILLAS LANE

B1260

Golf Course

3

Leeholme
Wood Lea

◄**171**

Broom Hill

Byer Square

4

Dene St Rd

Eppleton Cricket Club

Low Downs Rd

Henry St

Maudlin St

Lindsay Street

Hetton Downs

Broomhill Ter

Church

All Saints

Mark Rd

Heather Dr

Oswald Road

HOUGHTON

Downs Street

Nicholas Street

Downs Pit Lane

5

George St

ROAD

Queen St

Great Eppleton

Cemetery

Regent St

DH5

Edward Street

Chapel St

PO

Market St

Percy St

S Market St

The Avenue

6

Caroline

Scott

Joseph Street

4 3

Woodlea

Hetton Welfare Health Cen

PO

Union

Simpson Street

Urwin Street

Rowan Dr

Hetton U D C Swimming Baths

Park View Place

John St

Richard Street

Alder Cl

Station

A **186** B C

TTON-LE-HOLE

Burdon

Hall Farm

D

E

160

F

Salter's

Lane

Sharpley
Hall
Farm

I

B1404

2

Durham County

Sunderland

High
Sharpley

Seaton Moor
House

Seaton
Bank
Top

3

174

Green Lane

Salter's Lane

4

Slingley
Hill

5

Carrhouse

Lane

6

MUR

Carr House
Farm

Davison
Crs

Station

Est

Stephens

Terrace

Bevan

Square

Clarke

D

E

187

F

Short

N

Row

Cairns Road

Farmer

Crs

Wetherburn

Av

Rowland

Metcalfe

2

Wellfield

Est

Shinwell

Ter

Luke

Ter

1

Hill Cr

Barnes

4

Down

174 Burdon

Hall Farm

A **161** **B** **C** 1 Mann Crs

Sunderland
Durham County

1 Sharpley
Hall
Farm

B1404

Seaton
Grove

Hall Cl
Hillrise Crs
Avoncroft
Close

Seaton

2

Seaton
Bank
Top

Seaton Moor
House

3

173

Stotfold

4

Haverley
House

Slingley
Hill

5

Dalton
Moor

6

MURTON

Davison
Crs

Burnip Road

Truro Avenue

Bude

Penzance Bungs

Greenhill

Tregoney Av

Station Est Stephens
Short N

A

Wetherburn Av

Clarke Terrace
Bevan Square
Clarke

Webb Av

188

Barnes Road

B

Cedars Crs
Ash Ter
Toft Crs

Durham Co
Council

Primary
School
Infant

C

Penryn Crs
Maude
Terrac

Police
Station

Luke Cr

Rowland
Metcalfe Crs
Wellfield

1

2

Cairn Gv
E

Tudkin Crs
Ter

1 grid square represents 500 metres

162

D   E   F

D2
1 Pacific Hall
2 Slingley Cl

E4
1 Bournemouth Dr
2 Galfrid Cl
3 Plymouth Cl

I

Northlea

Lord Byrons Walk

B1285

SEATON LANE

New Seaham School Primary

Seaham Comprehensive School

Burnhall Drive

Neasham Rd

Norfolk Close

Normanby Close

NeWark Crs

Napier Road

Northlea Road

E5
1 Overdene

Embankment

Sutherland Street

Stockton St

Durham St

St Aldwyn Rd

Parkland Terrace

Seaham Station

2

STATION ROAD

Church Court

PO

Kingfisher Industrial Est

B1404

Station Road

Cheviot Gdns

Cheviot Court

Westlea Junior School

PO

Enfield Road

Malvern Crescent

F4
1 Brixham Cl
2 Dartmouth Cl
3 Exmouth Cl
4 Falmouth Cl
5 Salcombe Cl
6 Yarmouth Cl

Windsor Road

B1285

Evesham Road

Eastlea Road

Eastlea Crescent

Ryton Crescent

Malvern Crescent

Portland Avenue

The Avenue

3

PO

Easington District Council

Easington District Leisure Centre

Deneside Medical Centre

176

Laurel Avenue

WAY

Doctors Surgery

Deneside Junior & Infant School

West Lea

Wordsworth Av

Windermere Road

Wells Crs

Watling Avenue

Walton Avenue

B1285

Weymouth Drive

GRAHAM

THE

4

Bowes Av

Escaldona Drive

B1287

Deneside

SR7

South View

Overdene

A19(T)

B1285

Dene Road

5

Parkside Infant School

Dalton-le-Dale

6

Sea View Walk

A19(T)

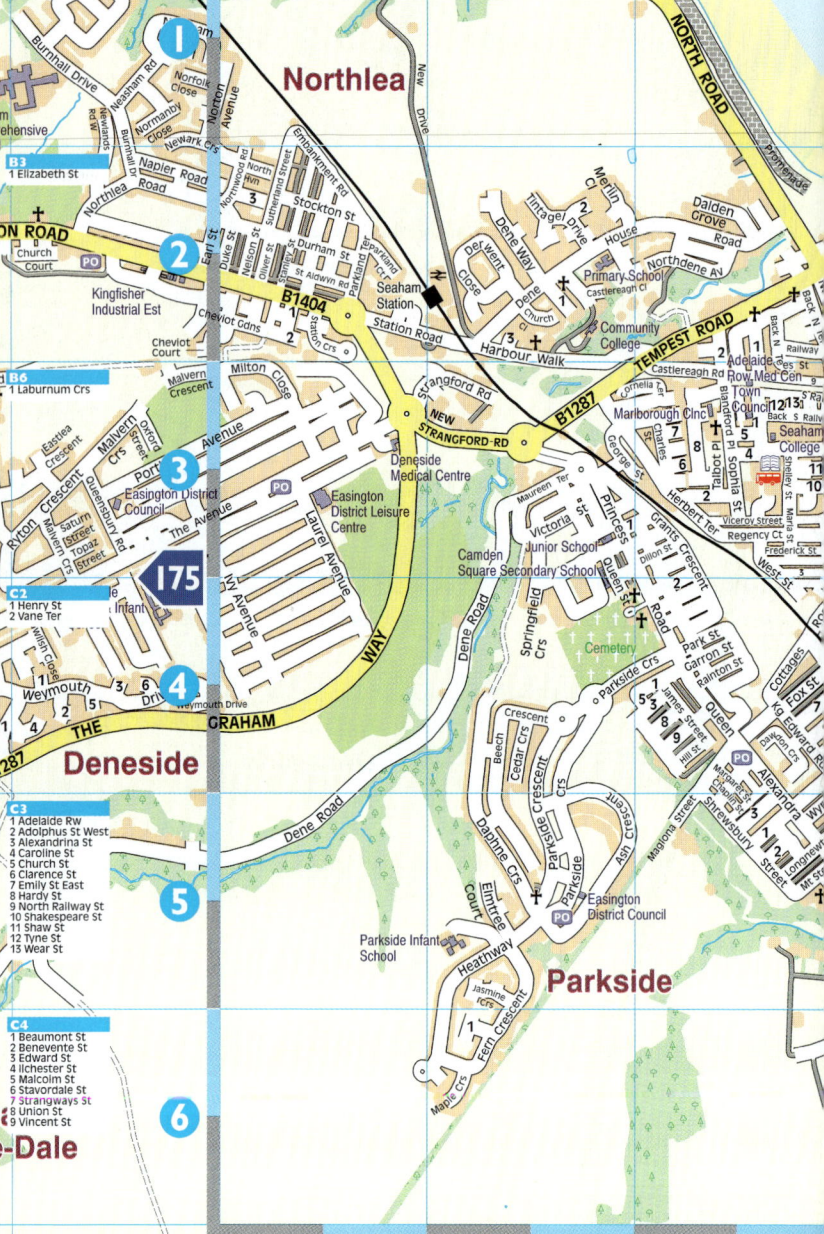

B1287

A **B** **C**

A2
1 Clara St
2 Hambleton Dr
3 Newlands Rd E

Seaham Hall Dene Lyons Walk

LC

B2
1 Antrim Gdns
2 Camelot Cl
3 Church Gn

NORTH ROAD

Burnhall Drive

Nesham Rd

Norfolk Close

Norton Avenue

Normanby Close

Newark Crs

Newlands Rd W

Northlea

New Drive

Promenade

Seaham Comprehensive School

B3
1 Elizabeth St

Napier Road

Northlea Road

Embankment Rd

Northwood Rd

North Tyn

Sutherland Street

Stockton St

Duke St

St Durham St

St Aldwyn Rd

Terpandral

Derwent St

Dene Way

Tintagel Drive

Merlin Cl

House

Dalden Grove Road

Northdene Av

I

Primary School

Castlereagh Cl

STATION ROAD

Church Court

PO

2

Kingfisher Industrial Est

Earl St

Nelson St

Oliver St

Cheviot Gdns

Station Crs

North Hm

B1404

Station Crs

Station Road

Station Road

Strangford Rd

Seaham Station

Dene Close

Dene Church

Harbour Walk

Community College

TEMPEST ROAD

Castlereagh Cl

Cornelia Ter

Marlborough Cln Cl

George St

Charles

Back N

Railway

Adelaide Row Med Cen

Town Council

Seaham College

Back N

St

B6
1 Laburnum Crs

Cheviot Court

Malvern Crescent

Milton Close

NEW STRANGFORD-RD

B1287

Talbot Pl

Sophia St

Viceroy Street

Regency Ct

Shelley St

Maria St

Frederick St

West St

Eastlea Road

Eastlea Crescent

Malvern Crescent

Oxford Crescent

Port Crescent

The Avenue

Ryton Crescent

Queensbury Rd

Saturn Street

Topaz Street

Deneside Medical Centre

3

Easington District Council

PO

Easington District Leisure Centre

Maureen Ter

Victoria St

Princess St

Queen St

Grants Crescent

Dillon St

Herbert Ter

Road

Park St

Garron St

Rainton St

James Street

Hill St

Queen

Fox St

Edward St

Cortanes

Davison Cs

175

C2
1 Henry St
2 Vane Ter

Infant

With Close

The Avenue

Ivy Avenue

Laurel Avenue

Dene Road

Camden Square Secondary School

Junior School

Springfield Crs

Cemetery

Parkside Crs

Alexandra Street

PO

Shrewsbury Street

Longnewm

4

Weymouth Drive

GRAHAM

WAY

Graham Dri

Beech Crescent

Cedar Crescent

Crs

Parkside Crescent

Ash Crescent

Maglona Street

Deneside

B1287

Dene Road

Daphne Crs

Parkside

Easington District Council

Parkside

PO

C3
1 Adelaide Rw
2 Adolphus St West
3 Alexandrina St
4 Caroline St
5 Church St
6 Clarence St
7 Emily St East
8 Hardy St
9 North Railway St
10 Shakespeare St
11 Shaw St
12 Tyne St
13 Wear St

5

Elmtree Court

Heathway

Parkside Infant School

Jasmine Crs

Fern Crescent

Maple Crs

C4
1 Beaumont St
2 Benevente St
3 Edward St
4 Ilchester St
5 Malcolm St
6 Stavordale St
7 Strangways St
8 Union St
9 Vincent St

Da
le-Dale

6

A **190** **B** **C**

C5
1 Embleton St
2 School St
3 Stavordale St W

I grid square represents 500 metres

D3
1 Aline St
2 Mary St
3 South Ter

D4
1 Robert St
2 Ropery Wk

D5
1 Londonderry St
2 Seaham St

D

E

F

1

2

Police Station

SEAHAM

3

Bottle Works Rd

Gas Works Road

Candlish Ter

4

Hill Crs

Road

Dawdon

5

Edith Street

LC

Nose's Point

6

A182

D

E

191

F

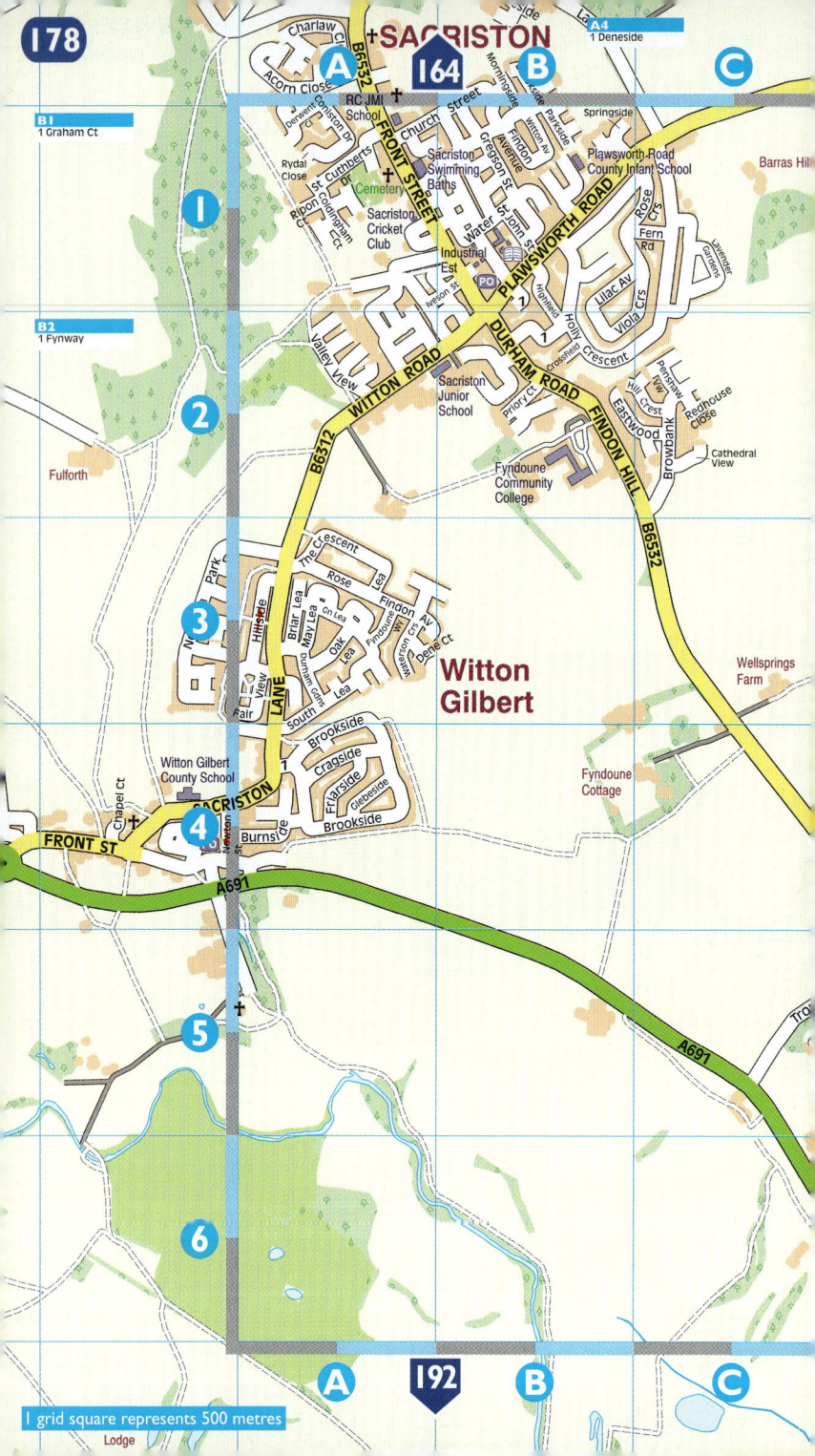

SACRISTON

164

A   B   C

Charlaw

Acorn Close

RC JMI School

Derwent Dr

Coniston Dr

Rydal Close

St Cuthberts Dr

Ripon Close

Coldingham Ct

Cemetery

Church

FRONT STREET

Sacriston Swimming Baths

Sacriston Cricket Club

Industrial Est

Water

PO

Weston St

Deneside

A4
1 Deneside

Springside

Morningside

Front Street

Parkside

Witton Av

Fundon Av

Avenue

Cregson St

St John St

Plawsworth Road County Infant School

Barras Hill

Rose Cts

Fern Rd

Lavender Gardens

Lilac Av

Viola Cts

Highfield

Holly Crescent

Crossfield

PLAWSWORTH ROAD

Fulforth

I

2

3

4

5

6

WITTON ROAD

B6312

DURHAM ROAD

Sacriston Junior School

Priory Ct

Fyndoune Community College

FINDON HILL

Eastwood

Browbank

Hill Crest

Peashaw Vw

Redhouse Close

Cathedral View

B6532

Wellsprings Farm

The Crescent

Rose Lea

Park

Hillside

Briar Lea

May Lea

Cn Lea

Findon Av

Fyndoune

Oak Lea

Waterton Cr

Dene Ct

Witton Gilbert

View

Fair

LANE

Dunham Cres

South Lea

Brookside

Cragside

Friarside

Glebeside

Brookside

Witton Gilbert County School

SACRISTON

Chapel Ct

FRONT ST

Newton St

Burnside

A691

A691

Fyndoune Cottage

Lodge

A   192   B   C

1 grid square represents 500 metres

PARK VIEW

B6312

A167(T)

F1
1 Church Vw

D
B6312

Hillheads

Tanmeads

E

165

Mill Lane

Mill House

F5
1 Littlebridge Ct

Tan
Hills

Hawthorn
Close

Cedar Avenue

Oak Crescent

Sycamore
Rd

Briar
Cl

Elm Crescent

1

Kimblesworth

I

F6
1 Aldhome Ct

N
Fa

2

Kimblesworth
Grange

A167(T)

3

180

Potter
House

Potterhouse Lane

Imex Business
Centre

4

Smithfield

Abbey

Road

1

The
Orchard

Lane

Hartside
Farm

Trouts
Lane School

Durham County
N H S Trust

Earls House
Hospital

B6532

Sniperley
Hall

A167(T)

Woodbine Rd

Anvil Ct

Hartside
View

The Avenue

Hudspeth Crs

Beaumont Cl

Augustine Cl

Aglenmere Drive

Hatfield
1

Alexandra Cl

Folly

Ter

Bishops
Way

5

Pity Me

Mere Dr

Front Street

Durham
County
Counc

6

Framwellgate Moor
Comprehensive
School

wellgate Moor
Junior & Infant School

Chastleton
Surgery

Lund Av

Newton Drive

Aykley Hid

Priory Rd

Brackenfield Rd

Caterhouse Rd

Anvil Hd

D
A691

E

193

New
Coll
Du

South
Ter

Gray Av

PO

F

Cuthberts
Av

St Aidan's
Av

Kirby Av

Finchale

Beech

Rd

Nasmeah

Durham
Co Council

Newton
Road

Frambard Rd

Frankland

Pitt

Durham
County
Counc

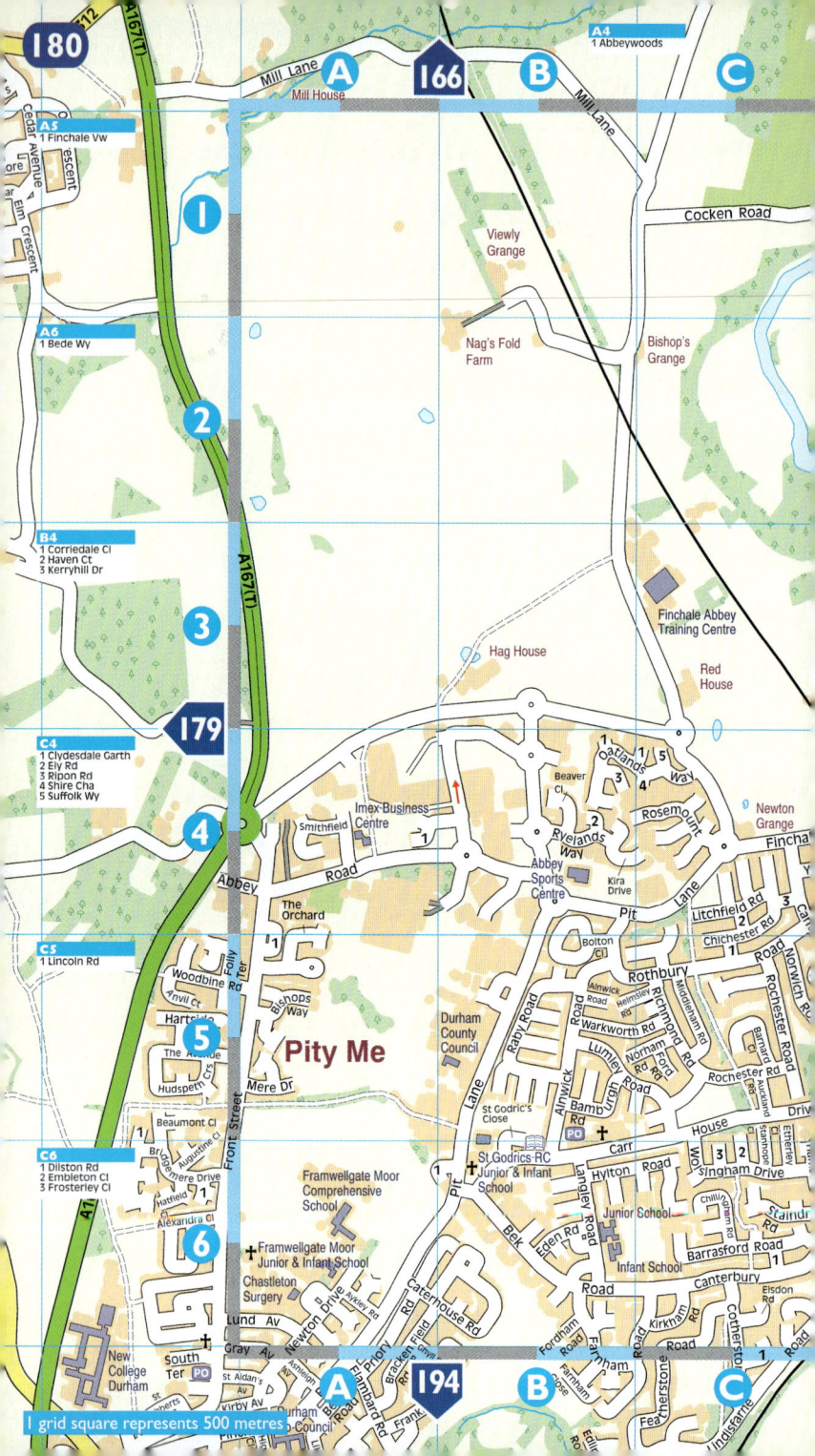

180

Mill Lane **A** **166** **B** **C**
Mill House

A4
1 Abbeywoods

A5
1 Finchale Vw

Mill Lane

Cocken Road

Viewly
Grange

1

A6
1 Bede Wy

Nag's Fold
Farm

Bishop's
Grange

2

B4
1 Corriedale Cl
2 Haven Ct
3 Kerryhill Dr

Finchale Abbey
Training Centre

3

Hag House

Red
House

179

C4
1 Clydesdale Garth
2 Ely Rd
3 Ripon Rd
4 Shire Cha
5 Suffolk Wy

Oatlands
Way
1 1 5
3 4

Beaver
Cl

4

Imex Business
Centre

Smithfield

Ryelands
Way

Rosemount

Newton
Grange

Abbey Road

Abbey
Sports
Centre

Kira
Drive

Pit Lane

Fincha

The
Orchard

Litchfield Rd

Chichester Rd

Norwich Road

Rochester Road

C5
1 Lincoln Rd

Woodbine Ter

Bishops
Way

Folly Ter

Bolton
Cl

Rothbury

Anvil Ct

Hartside

Raby Road

Ainwick
Road

Warkworth Rd

Richmond Rd

Middleham Rd

Rochester Road

Barnard

Auckland

The Avenue

Durham
County
Council

Lumley
Road

Norham
Ford

House

5

Hudspeth Crs

Mere Dr

Pity Me

St Godric's
Close

Bamb
Rd

PO

Carr

Stanhope

Etherley

Standr

C6
1 Dilston Rd
2 Embleton Cl
3 Frosterley Cl

Beaumont Cl

Augustine Drive

Front Street

St Godric's RC
Junior & Infant
School

Hylton

Road

Singham Drive

Chilli

Bromere Drive

Framwellgate Moor
Comprehensive
School

Pit Lane

Langley

Junior School

Barrasford Road

Hatfield

Alexandra Cl

6

Framwellgate Moor
Junior & Infant School

Newton Drive

Bek

Eden Rd

Infant School

Canterbury

Road

Elsdon
Road

Chastleton
Surgery

Ayley Rd

Caterhouse Rd

Fordham

Kirkham Rd

Cotherstone

Lund Av

Gray
South
Ter
PO

Bracker Field

Farnham

Featherstone

Indistarre

New
College
Durham

St Aidan's
Av

Kirby Av

Frank

Pilov

Flambard Rd

Fordham Rd

Edlin

Road

A **194** **B** **C**

Durham Council

1 grid square represents 500 metres

D   E   **167**   F

Cocken Lane

Low Cocken
Farm

I

Finchale
Priory

Finchale
Banks

River Wear

2

3

East Moor
Leazes

182

Union Hall

4

Rowan Dr

Finchale   Avenue

Beech
Close

HM Prison

River

Salisbury Rd

Finchale
Co Infant Sch

Brecon Road

Winchester
Rd

Woodwell
House

5

Carlisle
Rd

Peterborough Rd

Eggleston
Close

Blanchland Av

6

**Newton
Hall**

D   Frankland
Farm   E   **195**   F

J

182

168

Cocken Lane

1

Finchale
Priory

Finchale
Banks

Cocken Road

Cocken

A1(M)

Broom
House

2

3

Raintonpark
Wood

East Moor
Leazes

181

Union Hall

4

HM Prison

River Wear

5

Woodwell
House

Low
Grange

A1(M)

6

196
A690
Junction 62

Kirley Road
Filby Dr
Romiley Dr
ene
Falls Way

1 grid square represents 500 metres

D **E** **F**

I

2

3

184

4

5

6

E3
1 School Vw
2 Tollgate Flds

Mark's Lane

F2
1 Lea Riggs
2 St Mary's Dr
3 Sheen Cl

Stables
Farm

**West
Rainton**

The
Dene

The
Meadows

PO

Benridge
Bank

Church
Street

Cem

Adventure Lane

Finchale
View

Crescent

Benridge Bank

Rainton View

Hall Lane

Hall Cl

St
Godric's
Ct

Burns Cl

Riggs

Leamside

The Vw

Prospect

West Rainton
Primary School

Chapel Vw

Station

Low Station
Road

Woodside Lane

A690

Robin Lane

Rainton Gate

The
Surgery

Road

Hotel

LC

Wood Side
Farm

Field House
Farm

Moor House
Farm

A690

Pitfield
House

Pittington Road

The Rift
Farm

Station Rd

Front Street

High Street

Pittington

Ramside Hall
Hotel

Lady's

Piece

Coalford Lane

Elemore St

St Lawrence Rd

D **E** **F**

Fatfield
House

...ington Lane

M
R

170

A

B

C

Holly
Haven

**West
Rainton**

I

Durham R.

Lloyd

Meadows Lane

Ponton Street

Meadow St.

School

Quarry

Hollyhouse Lane

Bloomfield Rd

Hedgeley Rd

Robin Ct

1

7

**Middle
Rainton**

Fieldside

A690

The
Dene

The
Meadows

PO

Benridge

Bank

Church
street

Cem

3

Hall Lane

Hall Ln

2

Godric's

Burns Cl

7

2

ON VIEW

gery

2

2

Robin Lane

Robin
House

3

Field House
Farm

183

Pitfield
House

4

Pittington

Road

Moorsley Road

**High
Moorsley**

5

Station Rd

6

Lady's

Pittington

Front Street

High Street

Hills

Coalford Lane

Piece

A

Elemore St.

St. Lawrence

St. Lawrence
Rd.

B

Newby Lane

PO

C

field
use

I grid square represents 500 metres

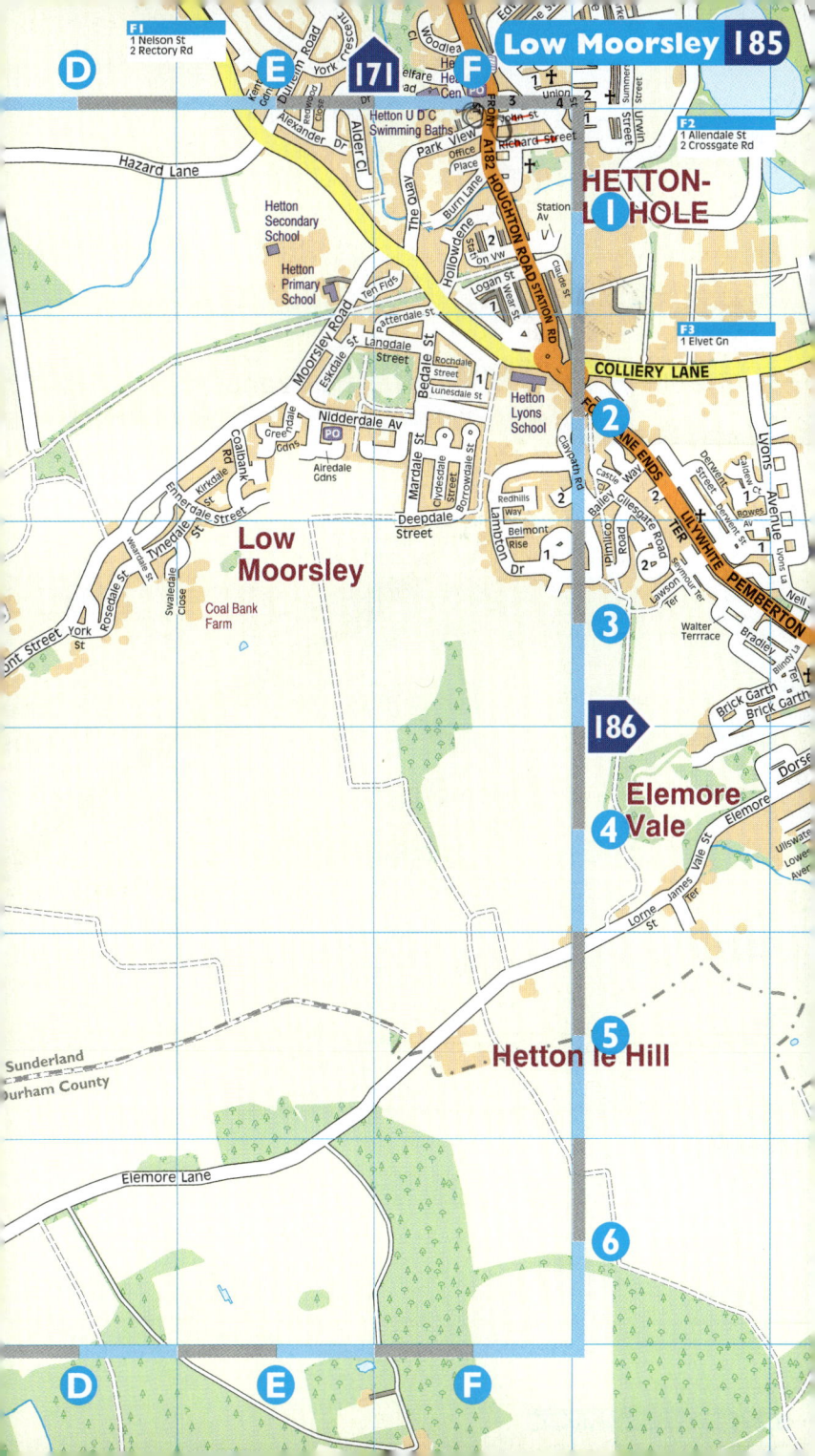

HETTON-LE-HOLE

Low Moorsley

Elemore Vale

Hetton le Hill

171

185

186

F1
1 Nelson St
2 Rectory Rd

F2
1 Allendale St
2 Crossgate Rd

F3
1 Elvet Gn

Hazard Lane

Durham Road

York

Kenton Gdns

Alexander Dr

Alder Cl

Woodlea

Welfare Hetton Centre

Park View

The Quay

Hollowdene

Burn Lane

Hetton U D C Swimming Baths

Office Place

Richard Street

Union Street

Urwin Street

COLLIERY LANE

Hetton Secondary School

Hetton Primary School

Moorsley Road

Esydale St

Eskdale St

Langdale Street

Patterdale St

Bedale St

Rochdale Street

Lunesdale St

Ten Flds

Nidderdale Av

Green Gdns

Greendale

PO

Airedale Gdns

Mardale St

Clydesdale Street

Borrowdale St

Deepdale Street

Hetton Lyons School

Redhills Way

Belmont Rise

Lambton Dr

Castle

Bailey

Pimlico Road

Gillesgate Road

Seymour Ter

Lawson Ter

Lyons Avenue

Darwen

Carden

Bowes Av

Nell

PEMBERTON

LILYWHITE TER

Walter Terrrace

Bradley Ter

Brick Garth

Dorse

Elemore

Ullswater

Lower Aver

Lorne St

James Vale St

Coalbank Rd

Kirkdale St

Ennerdale Street

Tynedale St

Swaledale Close

Rosedale St

Weirdale St

York St

Unt Street

Coal Bank Farm

Sunderland

Durham County

Elemore Lane

A182 HOUGHTON ROAD STATION RD

FAWCETT

LANE ENDS

186

A

172

B

C

A1
1 John St

Caroline
Avenue

Summerson
Street

John St

Union

Richard Street

Welfare Health
Road Cen
Hetton U.D.C PO

A2
1 Gelt Crs
2 White Gates Dr

Rowan
Dr

Alder Cl

The Quay

Tenterdale St

Burn Lane

Place

Holloweave

Logan W

Station

Ten Fld's

**HETTON-
LE-HOLE**

1

A3
1 Hornsey Ter
2 Peth Gn

Beda
Street

Lunesdale St

Derderdale Av

Mardale
St

Clydesdale
Street

Borrowdale St

Deepdale

Lyons

B1285

COLLIERY LANE

Hetton

Eppleto
Hall

2

Clavatriu Rd

FOUR LANE ENDS

Redhills
Way

Belmont
Rise

Lambton
Dr

Bailey
Castle
Way

Gillesgale Road

Pimlico
Road

Dermont
Street

Derwent St

Lyons
Av

Cumber Ct

Bowes

Lyons
Avenue

Lyons St

Neil St

B3
1 Jubilee Sq

3

Lawson
Ter

Seymour Ter

Walter
Terrrace

Bradley

LILYWHITE

PEMBERTON BANK

Brick Garth

Brick Garth

Hartside Crs

The Poplars

North
View

The Laws

The Elms

PO

Elmore
Leisure
Cen

Murton Lane

Willow Crescent

Cemetery

185

B4
1 Teviot St
2 Tweed St

4

Elemore

James Vale St

Elemore Ter

**Elemore
Vale**

Dorset St
Lane

Prospect
Crs

Thames

Rydal Av

Windermere

Cranston St

Canterbury

Thorntree

Buttermere Av

Ullswater Av

Loweswater
Avenue

White Hill Rd

Tyne
Street

Tamar St

Trent St

Tay

School St

The Elms

Qu Elizabeth

Line Ter

HIGH STREET

SOUTH HETTON

**Eas
Lan**

Easington Lane
Primary School

7 D

C3
1 Frosterley Cl

Lorne
St

James
Ter

Sheriff's Moor

Ruskin Av

South View

5

Hetton le Hill

C4
1 Coronation Gn
2 Shelley Av
3 Tees St
4 Wordsworth Av

6

Coldwell Burn

A

B

C

MUR

E5
1 Pasteur Rd

D

Carr Ho
Farm

E

173

Salter's Lane

Davison
Crs

Stephens
2

Station Est
Short
Gv

Rowland
Av

Wetherburn

Bevan
Square

Clarke
Ter

Shirwell Hill Crs

Metcalfe

Luke Crs
1

Barnes

Cairns Road

Station
Est

Station Est
South PO

STATION

STATION

ROAD

B1285

Park Lane

Calvert Ter

Station
Road

Cook
Crs
Gra

Wra

CHURC

Murton Moor
Farm

B1285

Melrose
Avenue

Winds
Est

Lonnen

Winds
Lane

2

3

188

4

Murton
Moor

ton

Windermere Road

Patrick Crs

Conishead
Terrace

Keswic Ter

Donald Av

Windsor
Dr

Argyle
Pl

Ravensworth
Court

182

FRONT

STREET

Coldwell Cl

Pinedale Drive

Elemore Vw
Plantation Vw

Bessemer
Rd

Front Street
Industrial Estate

South Hetton
Health Centre

5

Hawthorn
Cottages

Coronation
Sq

1

B1280

South
Hetton

Southy Hetton
Primary School

Frederick Terrace

PO

A182

Ashwood

Greencroft

Bevin
Sq

6

Fallowfield

SALTER'S

Ma
Driv

Catwo

D

E

F

LANE

West
Farm

MURTON

Greenhill

A1
1 Huntley Av
2 Lumsden Sq

Truro Avenue

174

A

B

C

A5
1 Grasmere Ter

Davison Crs

Clarke Road

Penzance Bungs

Tregoney Av

Penryn Dr

Claude Terra

Stephens
Station Est
Short N
Cv

Rowland

Wetherburn Av

Clarke Ter
Hill Crs
Webb Av

Cedars Crs

Trevo

Cairns
Dawn
Square

Farmer Cr

Metcalfe
Wellfield Road

Luke Crs
Calvert Ter

Barnes Road

Durham Co
Council

Ash Ter
Toft Crs

Primary
School
Infant
School

Police
Station

Doctors Surgery

Park Lane

Cook
Crs

Calvert
Ter

Calvert
Ter

Porter
Ter

6

N H S
Clinic

Woods Ter

Station Est
South

PO

Station
Road

Gray Av

Porter
Ter

2
1

Edison st

George st

STATION   ROAD   **B1285**

Williams Rd   Knaresborough
Rd

7

Ripon Ter

Federation
Sq

CHURCH LANE

Easington
District
Council

B1
1 Dobson Ter
2 Faraday St
3 Harrogate Ter
4 Lansbury Dr
5 Stephenson St
6 Watts St
7 West Av

rose
Avenue

Winds
Est
Lomen

Winds
Lane

Park
Lane

Cemetery

St Josephs
RC School

Grasmere Ter

B1285

Hawthor
Cl

2

C1
1 Treen Crs
2 Windsor Ter

3

Hesledon M
East

C2
1 Windsor Ter

187

4

Windermere Road

5

Bessemer
Rd

ront Street
dustrial Estate

South Hetton
Health Centre

A182

Greencroft

Bevin
Hawthorn
Cottages

Coronation
Sq

1

West Lane

Great Coop Ho
Farm

Frederick
Terrace

PO

Ashwood

Oakwood

6

Maythorne
Drive

A

198

B

C

West Moor House
Farm

1 grid square represents 500 metres

Sea View

D **E** **F**

Dalton-
le Dale

175

I

A182

**Cold
Hesledon**

2

CHURCH STREET

A19(T)

B1432

B1285

3

190

A19(T)

STOCKTON ROAD

Little Coop House
Farm

East Batter Law
Farm

Service Area

Letch Av

4

Belmont Av

Barn

+

West Batter Law
Farm

Hawthorn

West   Lane

5

B1432

Eagle
Hall

SUNDERLAND

ROAD

Lea Lane

Hallfield Burn

6

A19(T)

Hallfield

D **E** **199** **F**

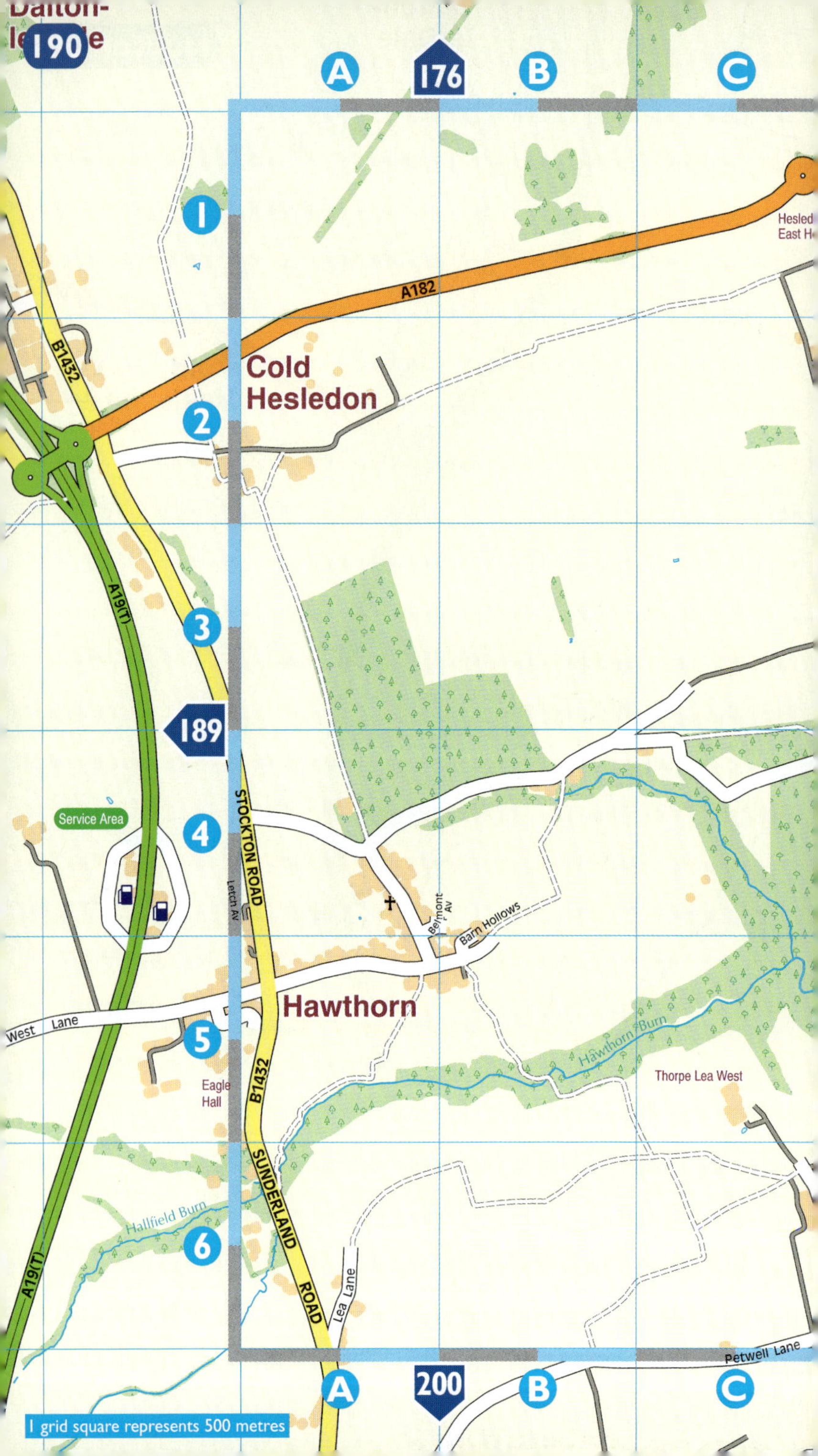

Dalton-le-Dale
190
176
A
B
C
1
2
3
4
5
6
189
200
A182
B1432
A19(T)
Cold Hesleden
Hesled East H
Service Area
STOCKTON ROAD
Letch Av
Belmont Av
Barn Hollows
Hawthorn
West Lane
Eagle Hall
Hawthorn Burn
Thorpe Lea West
SUNDERLAND ROAD
Hallfield Burn
Lea Lane
Petwell Lane
1 grid square represents 500 metres

D

A182

E

177

F

I

2

Kinley
Hill

Chourdon
Point

3

Hawthorn Burn

Hawthorn
Hive

4

Beacon
Point

Shippersea
Bay

5

6

White
Lea

Dene Av

East Rd

West Av

the Crs

D

E

201

F

EASINGTON

A

178

B

C

1

Lodge
Farm

Stotgate

2

Hedley
Ct

Hilltop Road
1 2

Blackcliffe
Way

College Vw
Park Wd Av
Beaurepaire

Woodside Av

Avenue

Bearpark Colliery Road

County Junior
& Infant School

East Side Av

Quarry Crs

Woodland Close

Ritson Avenue

Taylor Avenue

Bearpark

Kingston Avenue

Auton Stile

3

Dunelm
Medical
Practice

PO

Aldin
Grange

Lane

Deerness Valley
Comprehensive
School

Auton Stile

River Browney

Whitehouse

Hall Av

Hunter Av

New Acres

4

Aldridge
Ct

Ash Av

Flass Av

Ridge

Broom
Hall

Ushaw Moor
Junior School

St. Josephs
RC School

w Moor
et Club

Holly Pk

Lilac Pk

Maple Pk

Pine Pk

Holywell
Court

Broom Crescent

Road

Chestnut Gv

Valley View

Beech Gv

Elder

Elm Gv

Wooley Dr

Brancpeth
Close

Cemetery

5

Deerness
Sports Cen

B6302

BROOM LANE

Thornley Cl

Broom

Dowey Dr

Hall Dr
2
1

Stockley
Court

Deerness Valley
Walk

River Deerness

6

Mill Lane

Broompark

Cooke's Wood

B6302

Alum
Waters

A

203

B

C

D   E   179   F

Spinerley
F2
1 Aykley Ct

Framwelgate Moor

Lund Av
Newton
South Ter
Gray Av
St Aldan's
Kirby Av
Finchale
F3
1 Larches Rd
Durham Co-Council
I

New College Durham
St Cumberts Av

A691
Witton Gr
Westcott Dr

Dryburn Hill
DRYBURN ROAD

Aykley Vale
Dunholme Ct
Dunholme School
F5
1 Farnley Mt
2 Lyndhurst Dr

Framwelgate Moor

North End
Dryburn Hospital
A&E
B6532

Aykley Heads Business Centre
Northern Land & Leisure Cen
2

Aykley Heads

Aden Cottage

A167(T)
A691
Aykley Gn
Long Garth
St Nicholas Ct

Whitesmocks
SOUTHFIELD WY
North End

County Hall Durham
F6
1 Neville's Cross Bank
2 Newcastle Rd

Beechways
Whitesmocks Av
Springwell Rd
Fieldhouse Lane
The Grove
The Grove
St Leonards RC Comprehensive School
3

FRAMWELGATE PETH

Club Lane
Crossgate Moor Gardens
Springwell Pk
Springwell Rd
Flassburn Rd
PO
Shaw Wood Close

194

Arbour House

Durham Johnston Comprehensive School
Western Hill
County Hospital
4

Princes St
Western Road
Durham Station
P
Station Ap

Toll House Rd
A167(T)
NEWCASTLE ROAD

Redhills
Priors
Surtees
St Aidan's Crs
Monica Grove
St Bede's Close
Redhills Lane
Redhills Lane

Almer Dr
Waddington St
Mowbray St
Flass St
SUTTON ST
Atherton St
Holly St
St John St
Hawthorn Ter
Lawson Ter
New
Allergate
Crossgate

Neville Dene
Baxter Wood

Quarry House Lane
St John's Rd
St George St

Farnley Rdg
Percy Ter
Farnley Hey Rd
The Avenue
Max Rd
Laburnum Avenue
Lawson Ter
5

A690
Summerville
Bardene
Margery Lane
Orchard Priory
Grove St
Quarryheads La
Pimlico

Nevilles Cross Primary School
PO
Relly Path
Copeland Ct
Archery
St Margarets C of E Primary Sch
Infants School
Clay Lane
Durham School

Nevilles Cross
6
DURHAM

CROSSGATE PETH

NEVILLE'S CROSS BANK
DARLINGTON ROAD
Geoffrey
Lowes
Ellam Av

New College Durham
Clay La
Almond Ct
Observatory

BROOM LANE
Lowes Rise
Lowes Wynd
Kepier Bank
Hastings Av

D   E   204   F

Stone
Lowes
Bell's Folly
Potters Bank
St Cuthbert's Cemetery
Elvet

180

A   B   C

Barrasford Road

Canterbury

Elsdon Rd

A4
1 Bridge St
2 Lambton St
3 Mitchell St
4 Sutton St

Framwellgate Moor
Junior & Infant School

Chastleton
Surgery

South Ter

Lund Av

Gray Av

Newton

Finchale

Durham
Co-Council

Aykley Vale

Framwellgate Moor

Dunholme School

Dunholme

DRYBURN ROAD

A5
1 Alexandria Crs
2 Brass Thill
3 St Margaret's Ct

End

Dryburn
Hospital

B6532

2

SOUTHFIELD WY

Aykley Heads
Business Centre

Northern Land
& Leisure Cen

Aykley Heads

County Hall
Durham
County Council

DLI Museum
& Arts Centre

B4
1 Back Silver St
2 Castle Chare
3 Millburngate
4 Station Bank
5 Walkergate

North
End

The Grove
The Crescent

St Leonards RC
Comprehensive
School

FRAMWELGATE PETH / A691 FRAMWELGATE

Crook
Hall

Frankland Lane

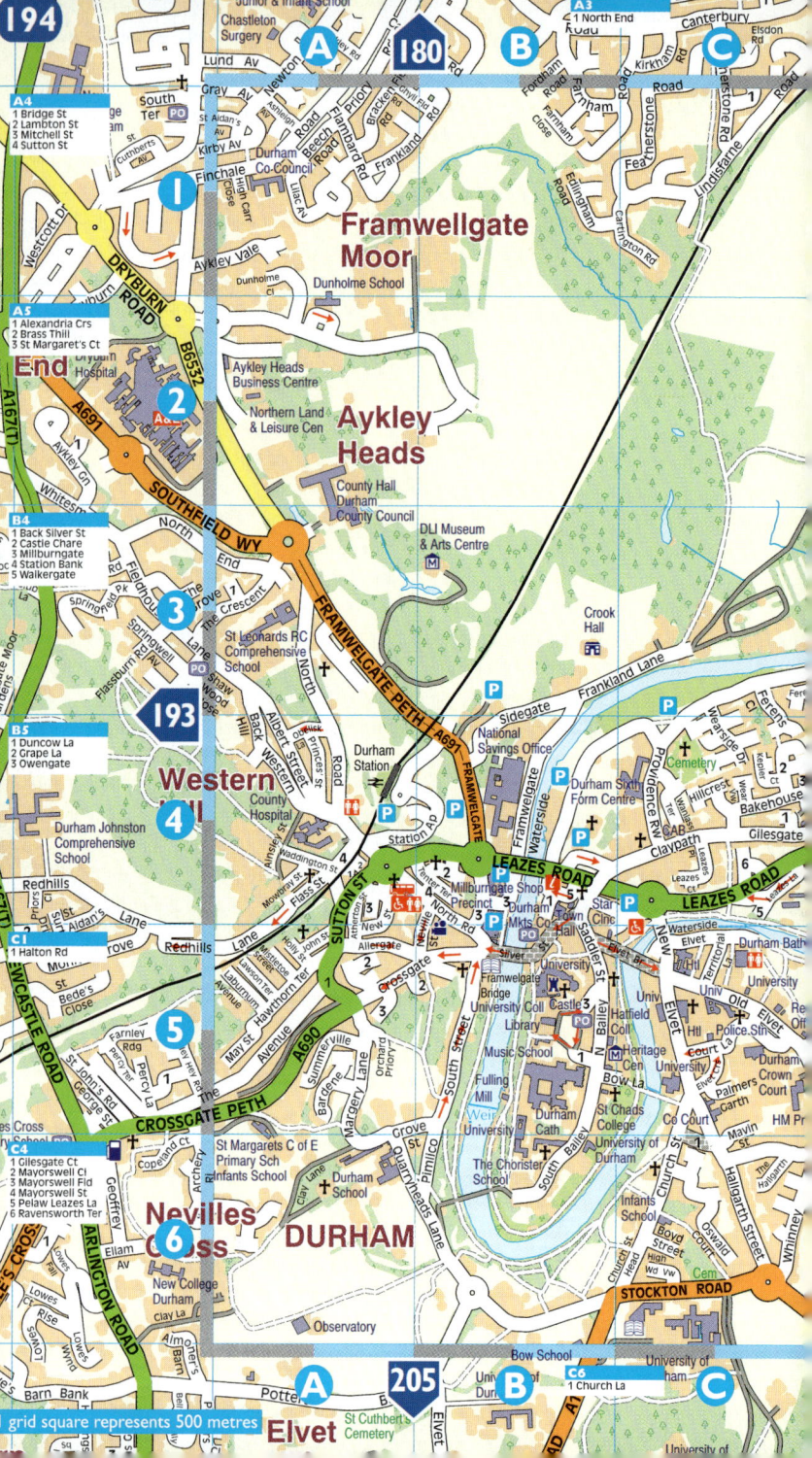

193

Flassburn Rd

Snow
Wood

B5
1 Duncow La
2 Grape La
3 Owengate

Sidegate

National
Savings Office

P

Durham Sixth
Form Centre

Cemetery

Hillcrest

Bakehouse

Gilesgate

Western Hill

Durham Johnston
Comprehensive
School

Albert Street

Back Western Road

Durham
Station

P

Framwellgate
Waterside

P

CAB

Claypath

4

County
Hospital

Station Ap

P

P

LEAZES ROAD

Star
Cinc

LEAZES ROAD

Waterside

Durham Bath

Sutton St

Millburngate Shop

Durham
Mkts Co Hall

University

Elvet

University

C1
1 Halton Rd

Redhills

St Aidan's
Lane

Redhills

New

North Rd

Silver

PO
Sadler St

Framwellgate
Bridge

Castle

Hatfield
Coll

New

Police Stn

Durham
Crown
Court

St Bede's
Close

University Coll
Library

Bailey

Heritage
Cen

Court

HM Pr

5

Crossgate

Music School

Bow La

University

Palmers
Garth

CROSSGATE PETH

A690

Orchard Priory

Fulling
Mill
Weir

Durham
Cath

St Chads
College

Co Court

A167(T) NEWCASTLE ROAD

Margery Lane

May St

Summerville

Bardene

Grove

Pimlico

South Bailey

University of
Durham

Mavin

Church St

The
Halgarth

C4
1 Gilesgate Ct
2 Mayorswell Cl
3 Mayorswell Fld
4 Mayorswell St
5 Pelaw Leazes La
6 Ravensworth Ct

St Margarets C of E
Primary Sch

St Infants School

Clay Lane

Durham
School

Quarryheads Lane

The Chorister
School

Infants
School

Boyd
Street

High

Cem

Nevilles Cross

ARLINGTON ROAD

New College
Durham
Clay La

DURHAM

Observatory

STOCKTON ROAD

VILLE'S CROSS

Lowes
Rise

Lowes Wynd

Barn Bank

Potter

A

205

Elvet

St Cuthbert's
Cemetery

Bow School

Uni
Dur

B

C6
1 Church La

University of
Durham

A1

University of

181

D4
1 Douglas Vls
2 Magdalene Hts
3 Magdalene St
4 Renny St
5 St Hild's La

D

E

F

Newton Hall

Frankland Farm

Frankland Lane

River Wear

I

E3
1 Cunningham Pl

University of Durham

Durham City Amateur Football Club

E4
1 Mcnally Pl
2 Young St

M E

2

Gilesgate

A690

Prebends Fld

Deans' Walk

Pilgrims Way

Monks'

Nuns'

Abbots

Priors

Friars

Rowan Tree Av

Willowtree

Durham Gilesgate Comprehensive School

Gilesgate County Junior School

Alder

Lea Close

Poplar Dr

Cypress Gv

Moor Crescent

Aspen

Hawthn

Cedar

Kepier Clinic

Gilesgate County Infant School

Ash

Yewbank Av

Elmfield Av

Whiteoak Av

Limecragg Av

F2
1 Fir Tree Cl

3

Kenny

Bradford

Montgomery Rd

Crs

Donning

Long Acres

Watershaw Rd

Gort Pl

1

Cooper Sq

Roosevelt

Annand Road

Sharp Crs

Mill Lane

Orchard Drive

Tealside

UW

WEST

Leazes

Green

Churchill Av

Edward

Sunderland

Edge Ct

Edge

Saint Joseph's

St Josephs RC School

Primary School

St Hild's

Renny's Lane

Frank Street

Dragon Lane

Dragonvil Park

F3
1 Beechcroft Cl
2 Conifer Cl

196

4

Durham Coun Coun

Station Lane

GILESGATE

St Giles Cl

Maynard's Rw

William Place

Dunelm Medical Practice

Gilesgate Moor

PO

Gilesgate

Church Lane

A181 SHERBURN ROAD

Police Station

Maple

Laurel Av

Laurel

Ash Av

Oak Av

Pine Av

Fir Avenue

Oak Avenue

Londonderry Cl

Bede Avenue

Oswald

Hilda

Cuthbert

Crs

BIEH

FRONT STREET

A181

F4
1 Ramsey Cl
2 Sherburn Rd

5

ypath dical ctice

5

Leazes

University rham

St Hild & St Bede College

Laurel Avenue County Junior & Infant School

DH1

River Wear

Bowling Green

Magistrates Court Green

University of Durham

Durham City Rugby Club

Durham City Cricket Club

Lane

Durham Johnston Comprehensive School

Old Durham

Old Durham Beck

Bent House Farm

Bent House Lane

6

D

A177

Houghall

University of Durham

E

F

HEE LANE

196

182

A3
1 Birchgrove Av

A   182   B   C

B2
1 Borrowdale Dr
2 Fellside Gdns

I

A690
Junction 62

A690

University of Durham

Kinley Road
Filby Dr
Romney Dr
Wantage Way

B3
1 Berkshire Cl
2 Oxfordshire Dr
3 Wiltshire Cl

Durham City Amateur Football Club

Moor End

Swinside Drive
Grange Road
High Road
Kirkstone Drive
Street
Langdale Crs
Grinstead
Bainbridge Street
Hawthorn
Brae Rd
Oakham Dr
Coronation Avenue
Broome Road
Chevele Primary

2

Carrville

Rowan Tree
Willowtree
Moor Crescent

Newlands
Magdalene Av
Mary's
Broomside Lane
Broomside Surg
Belmont Grange
Clinic
Rosedale Road
Broomside
Brackendale Rd
Ferndale
Brackendale Road

C1
1 Carrsdale
2 Carrsway
3 Ramside Vw

Gilesgate County Junior School

Alder
Lea
Poplar
Cypress Gv
Dr
Yewbank Av
Ashtown
Elmfield Av
Whiteoak Av
Limecragg Av

Infant School
Junior School
Cheveley Park Medical Cen

Riverdale
Grassdale
Lindale
Thorndale Road

Aspen Cl
Kepier Clinic
Gilesgate County Infant School
Cedar Crs

3

Buckinghamshire

Belmont Comprehensive School
School

Belmont

195

C2
1 The Links
2 Poplar Rd

ate Moor

PO

Poplar Rd
Bevan
St Hilda's Lane
Dragonville Ind Park
Penny's Lane

Primary School

Great Dragon Lane

Hampshire Road
Lincolnshire
Gloucestershire Rd
Nottinghamshire
Lancashire Dr
Cheshire Rd
Cambridgeshire Drive
Hertfordshire Drive
Devonshire
Shropshire Drive
Yorkshire Drive
Staffordshire Drive
Derbyshire Drive

Road

2

4

Saint Joseph's Cl
St Josephs RC School

4

BURN ROAD

Maple Av
Laurel Av
Oak Av

Front Street

A181

C3
1 Gorsedale Gv
2 Huntingdonshire Dr
3 Leicestershire Dr
4 Northamptonshire Dr

Oxdale Crs
Glendale Crs
Chandler
Pennag
Cundall
Donderry Av
Bede Avenue
Cuthbert Avenue

5

Durham County Council

Sherburn Grange

B1283

C4
1 Warwickshire Dr

House Lane

Bede

Bent House Farm

6

A181

Sherburn Hospital

A   B   C

I grid square represents 500 metres

B1198

183

D2
1 Borrowdale Cl
2 Ennerdale Cl
3 Patterdale Cl

D Rams Hotel

E

F

E4
1 Harrison Garth
2 Liddle Av
3 Park House Cl

PO

Pittington Lane

Fatfield House

Lady's Piece Lane

Coalfo

I

Priors Grange

St La

Rd

Chu Vale

E5
1 Blair Cl
2 Crawford Cl

2

Hallgart

Hallgarth

†

F5
1 Hallgarth Vis
2 Peart Cl

Scarside Way

Ullerdale Drive

Coniston Close

Broomside House

3

Coalford Beck

Whitegates Road

Lady Anne Rd

Dowsey Rd

Coalford Rd

Cummings Avenue

Usher Av

Forster Av

4

Cookshold Lane

Gray Avenue

Beech Road

Kidd Avenue

Liddle Av

Sports Centre

Stanley Close

1

2

Haltgarth Street

King St

Forster Av

†

George St

Milburn Rd

Whalton Cl

Sherburn

2

Railway Close

Mary's Drive

Cem

Church Wynd

St Cuthberts

St

Hope

Meldon Av

Chapel Ct

1

PO

Liddle

5

FRONT STREET

B1283

LOC

Loca

Smith

1

Talisman Wy

Talisman Close

The Crescent

Mill Lane

Sherburnhouse Beck

6

Mill Lane

D

E

F

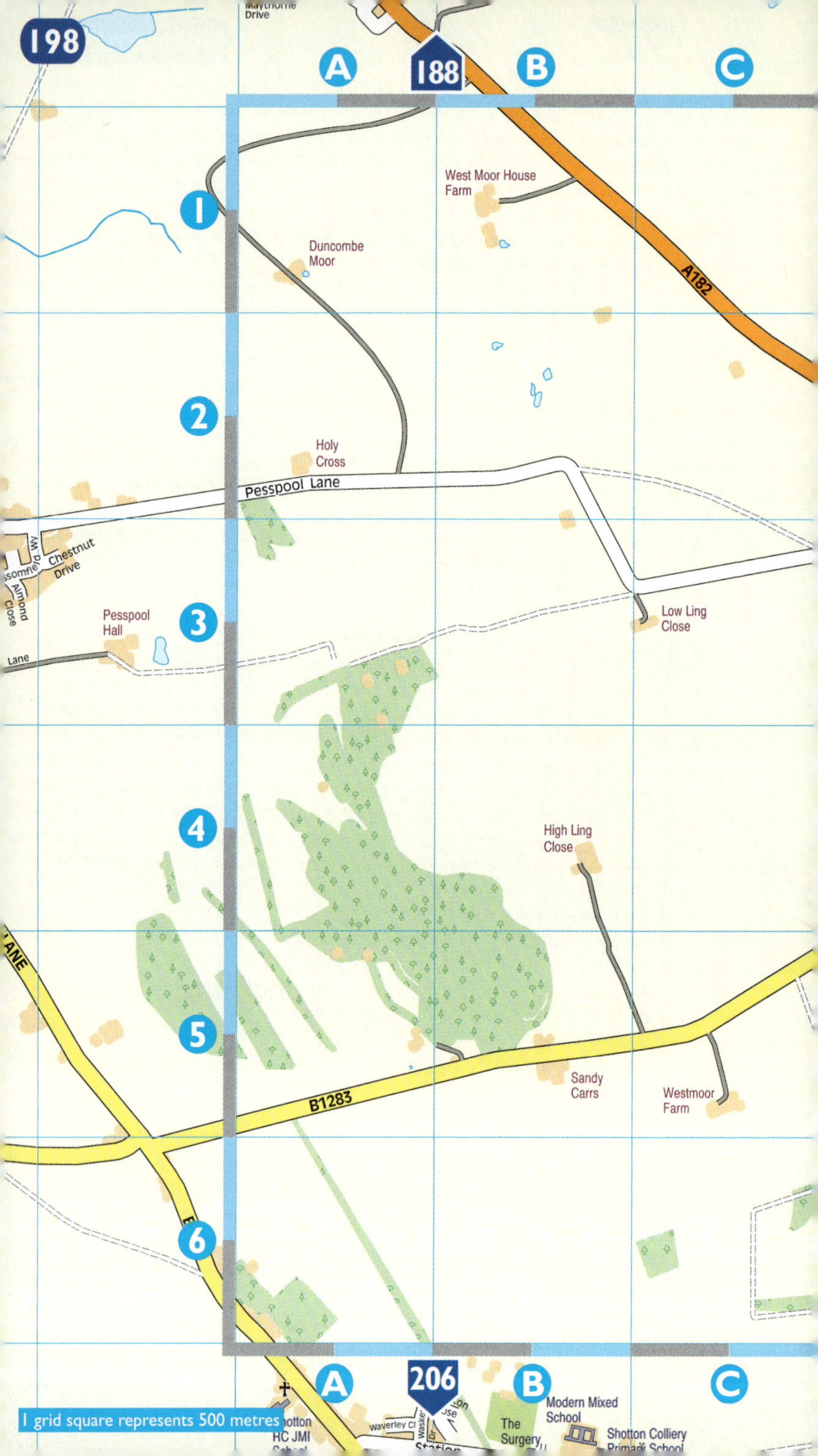

A
188
B
C

1

Duncombe Moor

West Moor House Farm

A182

2

Holy Cross

Pesspool Lane

Chestnut Drive

Almond Close

somme

3

Pesspool Hall

Lane

Low Ling Close

4

High Ling Close

5

ANE

Sandy Carrs

Westmoor Farm

B1283

6

A
206
B
C

Maythorne Drive

Waverley Cl

Wasler

The Surgery

Modern Mixed School

Shotton Colliery Primary School

RC JMI

Shotton Station

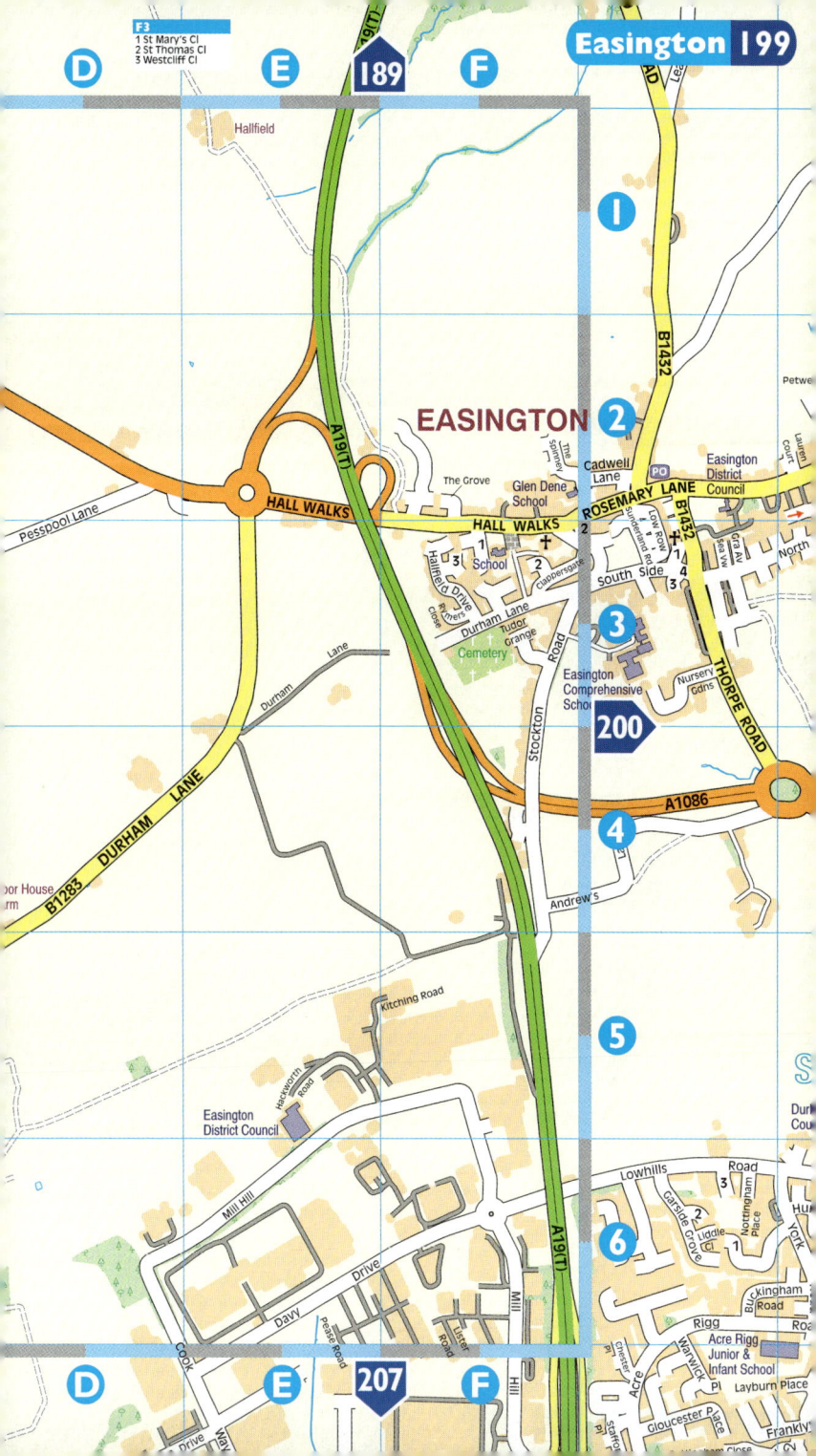

Hallfield

EASINGTON

189

The Grove

The Spinney

Cadwell Lane

Glen Dene School

Easington District Council

PO

HALL WALKS

HALL WALKS

ROSEMARY LANE

School

Hallfield Drive

Rivers Close

Clappersgate

South Side

North

Low Row

Sunderland Rd

Lauren Court

Petwe

B1432

B1432

A19(T)

Pesspool Lane

Durham Lane

Tudor Grange

Cemetery

Lane

Durham

Easington Comprehensive School

Nursery Gdns

200

THORPE ROAD

Stockton Road

A1086

Andrew's

DURHAM LANE

B1283

por House rm

Kitching Road

Haxworth Road

Easington District Council

Mill Hill

Davy

Drive

Peake Road

Lister Road

Mill

Hill

Cook

Way

Drive

A19(T)

Lowhills Road

Nottingham Place

Carlside Grove

Liddle

York

Hu

Acre Rigg Junior & Infant School

Rigg

Buckingham Road

Warwick Pl

Acre

Chester Pl

Stafford

Gloucester Place

Frankl

Layburn Place

Road

Dur Cou

S

207

A

190

A3
1 Brampton Ct
2 Church Wk
3 East Grange Ct
4 Thorpe Rd

B

C

Petwell Lane

A6
1 Barsloan Gv
2 Mitchell Cl
3 Northumberland Pl

I

Holmhill

Holme Hill Farm

James St

Cavell Square

Crawla

B2
1 Comet Dr
2 Jupiter Ct
3 Saturn Cl

2 1

PO

EASINGTON

2

Wordsworth Road

Milton Lane

Shakespeare Ter

Petwell Crs

SEASIDE LANE

Police Station

Glebe Ter

3

Primary School

Rydal Mount

Paradise Lane

Paradise Crs

Cadwell Lane

Easington District Council

PO

Lauren Court

Manisty Terrace

Glenhurst Rd

Moncrieff Terrace

The Grove

Glen Dene School

ROSEMARY LANE

HALL WALKS

Davis Terrace

B6
1 Jude Pl
2 Norfolk Wk
3 Suffolk Wk

1

School

Capbergate

Low Row

Cumberland Road

Gra Av

Sea Vw

B1432

3

1

2

North Crescent

Burn Gdns

Oak Road

Spiers

School

eld Drive

Rivers

Close

Durham Lane

Gran

South Side

1

2 3

4

5

3

Cemetery

Judd

Road

Easington Comprehensive School

Nursery Gdns

THORPE ROAD

199

C1
1 Easington St
2 Oswald Ter

A19(T)

Thorpe Burn

4

A1086

Little Thorpe

Andrew's

Lane

C2
1 St Nicholas Ter
2 Tennyson Rd
3 Whickham St

Kitching Road

THORPE

Cemetery

5

SR8

Durham County Council

Stephenson Road

Easin

Distri

C6
1 Jude Pl
2 Sledmere Cl

Lowhills Road

Nottingham Place

Huntingdon Rd

Northampton Road

Essington Way

Par

Buddle Close

Armstrong

Drive

Mill

A19(T)

Garside Grove

Liddle Cl

1

York

Cambridge Road

Bexley Rd

E S Place

2

3

Bruce Place

Jarvis

Ramsey

Fairbairn

Road

Johnson Cl

PO

Jones Cl

Bai

Close

Luser Road

Hill Road

Warwick

Gloucester Place

Acre Rigg Junior & Infant S

Rigg

Buckingham Road

Acre Rigg Road

Franklyn

Colin Close

Coast Road

Morton Square

Rise

Way

Dunelm Walk

Amersham Cres

Smith

Close

Crawford Av

Cann Rd

Wilson Cl

Westcott Road

Yoden

Robson

Rd

A

208

B

C

D2
1 Vincent St

191

D Dene Av

E

**EASINGTON
COLLIERY**

East View
Raby Av
West Av

The Crs
Lane
Cem

John Street
Thomas St
Memorial Avenue

Tower St
Abbot Street

School Street
1

Ashton St
B1283
PO

Office Street

Welfare Close

Bede Street
STATION ROAD

Memorial Avenue

Paradise

Horden Burn

SUNDERLAND ROAD

Maritime Crs

A1086

Thorpe Road
Horden & Easington
RC Primary School

Kilburn

Webb Sq
Wilkinson Rd
Beaumont Crs
Bruce
Kirkup Road
Moutter Cl
Nesbitt

Belford St
Rothbury Av
Alnwick St
Morpeth St

Timber Rd

Drive

Yoden Crs

Newcastle Av
Sunderland Av
A1086

Northumberland St
PO
Durham Av

Blackhills

Durham County
Council

Thompson St

I

2

3 Horden Point

4

5

6

en Hall
ant School

Lane
Edenhill

SUNDERLAND RD

Park Lt

Doctors Surg
PO
Eden Street
Eden Crs
Fern Cott

A PO B B5
1 Ashbrook Cl
2 Camberley Dr
C

Prospect Place
Rock Ter
Edward Ter
Prospect Ter
Cooperative Ter
Terrace

C4
1 Dove Cl
2 Palm Lea
3 Rushey Gill

1

**New
Brancepeth**

Tuscan Cl
New Brancepeth
Primary School
Rowan Ct
Pringle
Pl
Pringle
Grove
Pringle Cl
Doric Road

Lane

C5
1 Laburnam Pk

2

Stobb
House

3 Pit Lane

North
End

Cemetery

High Mdw

Pear Lea
Pine Lea
Park
Sawmill

4

BRANDON

Scripton

Maple
Court
Cherry
Pk
Beech
Park
Beech
Park
Alder
Park
Alder
Park
Alder
Park
White
Meadow
Briar
Clover
Lea

Morley
Farm

5

Brancepeth Vw
Forest
View
Scripton
Beechcroft Av
Murrayfield
Drive
Cavendish Ct
Carvis Cl

Morley Lane

6

Little
White

Quarry Hill

Startsbury
Levington
Vernon
Court
Gill
Winchester Drive
Scripton Road
Cir Rise

A B A1690 C Scripton

Wolsingham Rd

192

D E F

D4
1 Acorn Pl
2 Hawthorn Pk
3 Linden Pk
4 Vicarage Flats

Alum
Waters

D5
1 Cypress Ct

I

Langley
Hall Farm

E3
1 Hemmel Cts

Front Street

2

GROVE TERR.

La
Mo

Langley Moor
Primary School

PO

Black Road

St Cuthbert's Wk

Brandon Lane

Lyne's Dr

Langley Cts

1

Blair Ct

1

STREET

HIGH

E4
1 Allendale Rd
2 Brecken Wy
3 Chalfont Wy
4 Frensham Wy
5 Stanhope Cl

High St

S. Beck

Littlei

La

Stack
Garth

Brandon
United
Football Club

1

Tiree Cl

Brandon
Cricket
Club

Brandon &
Byshottles
Parish Council

3

Mill Road

St Patricks
RC School

Durham
Business
Centre

204

E5
1 Leesfield Rd

Deerness Heights

Midhill
Cl

3

Red Firs

Lyme Pk

Rowan
Lea

2

Holly
Rd

Carr Avenue

Victoria Avenue

Station Avenue

Chalfont
Way

Perry
Way

Arundel
Way

Chalfont
Way

3

Meadowfield
Sports Centre

Meadowfield
Clinic

Meadowfield

PO

Cemetery

St

4

Littleburn Road

Rosebay Road

Thistle

4

Silver Cts

Lowland Road

PO

1

Brandon Modern
School

7

Fir Av

Grove Road

2

3

5

1

Leesfield Gardens

Leesfield Dr

Aston
Road

1

A690

Dunelm
Gv Rd

Moor
Edge

Health
Centre

Dominion Road

Victoria Gardens

South
View

West
View

Dorlonco
Villas

Central
Av

A690

Edwardson Road

Browney County
Primary School

St John's Road

F3
1 Boyne Ct

5

Red Barns

A690

BROWNEY LANE

6

B6300

D E F

Holywell Beck

B6302 BROOM LANE

A 193 B A2 C
1 North
Brancepeth Cl

A3
1 St Bedes Wy

Stone Bridge

Lowes
Barn

Lowes Barn Bank

Hastings Av

Kings Gv

A690

Dickens

I

Langley
Hall Farm

Kings Gv

A167(T)

C1
1 Copperfield
2 Neville Sq
3 Percy Sq
4 Rokeby Sq
5 Warwick Ct

2

Front Street

GROVE TERRACE

Langley
Moor

Brandon Lane

Tyne's Dr

Langley Ct

Langley Moor
Primary School

Black Road

PO

C2
1 Deyncourt

Blair Ct

St Cuthberts Wk

HIGH STREET

High St's Back

Littleburn La

3

Brandon &
Byshottles
Parish Council

Mill Road

St Patricks
RC School

Durham
Business
Centre

Brandon
Cricket
Club

203

Meadowfield
Sports Centre

Chalfont Way

PO

4

Cemetery

Littleburn Road

Rosebay Road

Thistle Road

Meadowfield

A690

Meadowfield Clinic

Edwardson Road

St John's Road

5

Brown County
Primary School

Club House

Littleburn
Farm

BROWNEY LANE

6

B6300

Burn Hall

A B C

River Browney

A B C

River Deerness Beck

1 grid square represents 500 metres

D1
1 Pickwick Cl

D Observatory
E
194
F

CKTON ROAD

Cem

Potters   Bank

Bow School
University of Durham

University of Durham

A177

Elvet Hill

St Cuthbert's Cemetery

St Aidans College

University of Durham

Trevelyan College

University of Durham

Grey College

University of Durham

Houghall College

I

Elvet Hill Road

ROAD

Hollingside

University of Durham

University of Durham

Millhill   Lane

Van Mildert College

M

2

SOUTH

Club House

University of Durham

Botanic Gardens

Farm   Road

Houghall Farm

3

MONEY SLACK

A177

Cemetery

SOUTH   ROAD

Durham High School

Farewell Hall

4

High Houghall

Low Butterby

River Wear

5

Low Burnhall

Croxdale Wood House

6

D
E
F

206

B2
1 Hamilton Ct

I
**Fleming
Field**

C2
1 Alcote Gv
2 Cowley St
3 Dunelm Pl
4 East Gn
5 Potto St

2

**Shotton
Colliery**

3

Low Crow's
House

4

5

6

B1
1 Jubilee Pl

Wenton
Close
Waverley Cl   Waskerley Cl
Belverdere
Gdns
Westgarth
Grove
Atkinson Ct
Thornhill Rd
Whinmed Rd
Thornhill
Rd
Hawthorne
Hazel Terrace
Lilac Terrace
Terrace

Modern Mixed
School
The
Surgery
Shotton Colliery
Primary School
Southdene
Medical
Centre
Arden
Street
Tudor
Ct
East St
Windsor Pl
Eden Vw
Shotton
King St
Victoria Street
Milton Grove
West St
Milbank
Terrace
Byron Ter
Shotton
Parish
Council
Burn's Ter

Station   Road
Cem Shotton
RC JMI
School

The Surg
PO

Grove
Court

PO
Dixon
Est
Dixon
Ter
AJ
Cook
Bruce
Terrace
Glasier

Dixon Est Bungalows

SALTER'S LANE
B1280

Thornley Station
Industrial Estate

Church Pk
Watson Cl
Dodds Cl
CHURCH STREET
PATTON WALK
Weardale
Park

B1279

Green Hills

SALTER'S LANE
B1280

A181
I grid square represents 500 metres

Durham
Taylor Grove

D **E** 199

E3
1 Winchester Dr

Drive
Pease Road
Ushaw Road
Hill

Rigg
Acre Rigg
Acre Rigg Junior &
F3
1 Hambledon Pl
Layburn Place

Acre Rigg Road

Chester

Cook Way
Burdon Drive
Shotton Road

Gloucester Place
Cottingham Close
Franklyn
Willerby
Woodminster Close

Brendon Place
Cotswold Place
B1320
Cheviot Place

PETE...
URNHOPE

F5
1 Buttermere

Doxford Drive
Whitehouse Way
Brindley Road
Gresley Road

Furness
Pennine
Mendip

Cleveland Place
Howletch Lane Junior & Infant School
Balliol Close
Com...
Scho...

Whitworth Road

Bracken Hill
Swan Road
Hunter Road
Palmer Road
Shotton Lane

Blackdown Way
Quantock Place
Polden Close

Grampian
Cherwell Road
Clare Road
Passfield
Drive

Pennine
Shrewsbury Close
Girton Close
Brecon Drive
Pentland

208
Lorimers Cl
Wellan Cl
Orwell Cl
Waverley Way

Whitehouse Wy

Shadforth Cl
The Green

Pet... Town Council
Passfield

Shotton Hall Junior School

Edder Acres

A19(T)
Shotton Bank

Shotton
Corby Gv

Kendal Gv
Milton Ct
Appleby
Askerton Dr
Muncaster Ms
Brough Grove

Way
Egremont Gv

Durham

Shotton Hall Comprehensive School

Severn

Norham Dr
Berwick Chase
Dur...

Brougham Ct
Rose Ct
Barnard Gv
Gleaston
Brancepeth Chare
Monk Ct
Naworth Ct
Lowther Ct
Wynd

Edderacres Plantation

Castle Eden Burn

6

Golf Course

D A181 **E** **F**

Greenhills Est
The Maltings

A6
1 Blenkinsopp Ct

A Rigg

200

B

A4
1 Van Mildert Cl

C

PO

Acre Rigg
Junior &
Infant School

Warwick
Pl

Acre

Layburn Place

Gloucester Place

Cottingham Close

Chester

Franklyn

Willerby

Morton
square

Crawford
Av

Cann

Wilson Pl

Robson

Crescent

Stafford

Beverley

Newark Cl

Basingstoke Road

Yoden
Way

Elliott Road

Little

Eden

Harvey

B2
1 Montfalcon Cl
2 Woodfield

Brendon Place

Cotswold

Woodhorn

Weston
View

Newlie

Herton

Gilbert Rd

Beck Pl

Essington Way

Dunelm Walk

Kemp Rd

Yoden Road

Clifton Sq

Hawes
Road

Brandlings

PETERLEE

B1320

B3
1 Hulme Ct
2 Westway

Doxford

Brindley
Road

Cheviot Place

Drive

Peterlee College

Howletch Lane

Spike Hollin

Community
College

B5
1 Calley Cl
2 Norham Dr

Penrith

Furness

Cleveland Place

Burnhope Way

Stainton Way

Burnside

BURNHOPE WAY

PO

Durh
Con
Co Durham
Health Aut

Hartle
NHS T

C1
1 Adfrid Pl
2 Dunelm Wk
3 Hallam Rd
4 Lowther Cl

Howletch
Lane Junior &
Infant School

Balliol Close

Comprehensive
School

Tweed

Tweed Cl

Moor

Pray Cl

Firth

North Blunts
Primary School

Palm

Blackdown Rd

Grampian

Dinting

Shrewsbury

Drive

Cherwell Road

Drive

Isis Road

Clare Road

Way

Avon
Close

Arun
Cl

Tamar
Rd

Thames

Teign
Close

Road

Peterlee Leisure
Centre

3

Pennine

Pentland

Brecon
Close

Girton
Close

Passfield

Dart Road

Southway

C2
1 Fleming Pl

207

Shadforth Cl

The Green

Lorimers
Cl

Weiland
Cl

Skerne
Cl

Orwell

Helford Road

Medway

PO

4

Peterlee
Town
Council

Way

Wavery Rd

Tees
Cl

Oakerside

Sunny
Blunts

severn Cl

Lindisfarne

Passfield

Shotton
Hall Junior
School

Oakerside Drive

Dormand

Bywell
Dr

Durham Way

Carr

C3
1 St Cuthbert's Rd

otton

Corby
Gv

Egremont Gv

Shotton Hall
Comprehensive
School

Durham Way

Dilston Cl

Escomb
Cl

Lumley

5

Kendal

Appleby

Durham Way

Brougham Ct

Norham
Dr

Brancepeth
Chare

Garth

Morton
Court

Marwood
Grove

Bank

Askerton
Dr

Muncaster
Ms

Milton

Bywell
Group

Berwick
Chase

Rose
Cl

Naworth
Ct

Barnard
Wynd

Lambron

C4
1 Mitford Ct

Gleeson

Monk
Ct

Lowther
Ct

6

Castle Eden Burn

The
Castle

Golf Course

A

B

C5
1 Cartington Cl

C

1 grid square represents 500 metres

201

Horden

D1
1 Alston Wk
2 Ambleside Cl
3 Bowness Cl
4 Troutbeck Wy

D2
1 Burdon Pl
2 Coniston Cl
3 Duddon Cl
4 Eskdale Wk
5 Grisedale Rd
6 Kentmere Pl
7 Langdale Pl
8 Tarn Cl

D3
1 Beaumont Pl

E1
1 Cowell St
2 Hamilton St
3 Handley St
4 North Av

E2
1 Edendale Ter
2 Kell Rd

E3
1 Delavale Cl
2 Thornes Cl

F1
1 Edward Cain Ct
2 Grant St
3 John Wilson Ct
4 Nelson Cl
5 Ninth St
6 Thorpe St

F2
1 Dene Bank Av
2 Rogers Cl

Blackhills
Northumberland St
Durham Av

Council

Doctors Surg
PO
Dr Chandys Surg
Dene St

Cotsford Junior School

Cotsford Primary School

Cotsford County Infant School

Beach Gv
Windsor Ter
Alder Rd
Alder Lane
Dixon Rise

SUNDERLAND ROAD
SHOTTON RD
COTSFORD LA
COAST ROAD

Sunderland Avenue
Greenside Avenue
Shotton Road
Chapel Hill Road
Rosedale Terrace
Edward Av
Roseby
Twelfth St
Eleventh St
Warren St
South Terrace
Tees Terrace
Eighth St
Park Terrace
Hardwick St

Ellison Road
Oakeland
Keswick Road
Grasmere Rd
Rydal Road
Thirmere
Kirkstone Avenue
Scafell Close
Grisedale Rd
Wasdale
Staveley Road
Cumbrian Way

RTEES ROAD
B1320
YODEN WAY

Community Care

Church Close

Matterdale Road
Braithwaite Road

Nesbit Road
Harrison Close
Heath Close Road
Fulwell Road
Dean Cl
Granville Road
Chilton
Larchene Way
Garth Close
White Lea Close
Garth Cornfield

Manor Way
Bede Way
Drive
wthorns Hospital

Eastfield

Dene House County Mixed Modern School

Cresswell Av
Burnside Av
Eden Ter
St Murray
Sermour St
Dene Vis
Willow Gv

Castleeden Burn

Bellister Pk

Castle Eden Dene Nature Reserve

Dene Leazes

HESLEDEN ROAD

Hardwick Hall Farm

B1281
Hazel Dr
Cem
Hesleden County Junior & Infant School

A10

D · E · F · I · 2 · 3 · 4 · 5 · 6

Albany 120 A5
Annfield Plain 146 C4
Annitsford 35 E1
Axwell Park 94 C2
Aykley Heads 194 A2
Ayres Quay 126 A4
Ayton 137 E3
Backworth 37 E6
Bank Top 57 D5
Barley Mow 136 B4
Barlow 92 C4
Barmston 139 E1
Battle Hill 67 E1
Beaconhill 21 D2
Beacon Lough 100 B6
Beamish 150 A1
Bearpark 192 B3
Bebside 9 D5
Bedlington 7 F2
Bedlington Station 8 A2
Bell's Close 77 D2
Belmont 196 B3
Bensham 98 C1
Benton Square 50 C3
Benwell 78 A2
Biddick 138 C2
Biddick Hall 88 A6
Bill Quay 84 A6
Billy Mill 53 F5
Birtley 118 C6
Bishopwearmouth 126 A5
Black Callerton 42 C4
Blackfell 119 F6
Blakelaw 61 E4
Blaydon 76 C5
Blaydon Burn 93 D1
Blaydon Haughs 77 D4
Blyth 10 B6
Boldon Colliery 87 E6
Bournmoor 156 A5
Brandon 202 B4
Brenkley 18 B5
Broom Hill 171 F4
Broompark 192 C6
Brunswick Village 32 B5
Burdon 161 D5
Burnopfield 111 E6
Burnside 157 D6
Burradon 35 D5
Byermoor 112 C5
Byker 82 B3
Callerton 43 D6
Camperdown 35 E5
Carley Hill 126 A1
Carr Hill 100 A3
Carrville 196 B2
Castletown 123 F3
Causey 132 A1
Chester-le-Street 152 B5
Chester Moor 165 F3
Chilton Moor 170 A2
Chirton 54 A6
Chowdene 117 D2
Cleadon 107 F2
Cleadon Park 89 E5
Clough Dene 130 A3
Cold Hesledon 190 A4
Colliery Row 170 B2
Collingwood 22 A4
Columbia 139 D2
Concord 120 B4
Cowpen 10 A4
Coxlodge 62 C1
Craghead 149 F6
Cramlington 21 D3
Crookgate Bank 112 B6
Crookhill 75 D3
Cullercoats 55 F2
Dalton-le-Dale 175 E6
Dawdon 177 D5
Deckham 99 E2
Deneside 175 D4
Denton Burn 77 D1
Deptford 125 F4
Dinnington 30 C3
Dipton 128 B6
Donwell 120 A3
Downhill 106 A6
Doxford Park 160 C4
Dudley 34 C3
Dunston 97 E1
Dunston Hill 97 D3
Durham 194 A6
Earsdon 38 C4

Easington 199 F2
Easington Colliery 201 E1
Easington Lane 186 C3
East Boldon 106 B2
East Cramlington 23 D3
East Denton 60 C6
East Gateshead 82 A5
East Hartford 14 A3
East Herrington 159 F2
East Holywell 37 F3
East Kyo 147 D2
East Rainton 170 C6
East Sleekburn 9 F1
East Stanley 148 C1
Eighton Banks 118 C2
Eland Green 28 B2
Elemore Vale 186 A4
Elswick 79 E5
Elvet Hill 205 D1
Farringdon 160 A1
Fatfield 138 B6
Fawdon 46 A5
Felgate 103 F1
Felling 100 B2
Felling Shore 83 D6
Fellside 95 E4
Fence Houses 169 F1
Fenham 78 C1
Flint Hill 129 E5
Follingsby 102 C5
Fordley 35 D3
Forest Hall 49 F3
Framwellgate Moor 194 A1
Fulwell 108 B6
Gateshead 81 E5
Gilesgate 195 D3
Gilesgate Moor 195 E4
Glebe 138 B1
Gosforth 63 D1
Grangetown 145 D5
Grange Villa 150 C3
Grasswell 157 F6
Great Eppleton 172 C5
Great Lumley 167 E3
Greenhill 174 B6
Grindon 142 A3
Hallgarth 197 F2
Harelaw 146 A2
Harlow Green 118 A2
Harperley 146 C2
Harraton 137 F5
Hartley 27 D4
Harton 89 D2
Hasting Hill 141 F4
Hawthorn 190 A5
Hazlerigg 32 C5
Heaton 65 D6
Hebburn 85 D3
Hebburn Colliery 68 A6
Hebburn New Town 84 B2
Heddon-on-the-Wall 56 A5
Hedworth 86 B6
Hendon 5 F5
Hetton Downs 172 A5
Hetton-le-Hill 185 F5
Hetton-le-Hole 186 A1
Heworth 101 E2
High Callerton 42 A2
High Dubmire 170 A2
Highfield 110 B3
High Forge 133 D5
High Friarside 110 C6
High Handenhold 150 C1
High Moorsley 184 C4
High Shields 70 C6
High Southwick 125 F1
High Urpeth 134 A6
Hill Top 129 D4
Hillview 144 B5
Hobson 130 A2
Holy Cross 67 E3
Holywell 25 E6
Horden 209 D1
Horsley Hill 72 B6
Houghton-le-Spring 170 C2
Howdon 68 C3
Howdon Pans 69 E5
Humbledon 143 E3
Hylton Castle 123 F2
Hylton Red House 106 C6
Isabella Pit 16 C1
Jarrow 86 C2
Jesmond 64 B6
Kenton 61 F2

Kenton Bankfoot 44 C6
Kenton Bar 61 F2
Kibblesworth 117 D6
Killingworth 49 F2
Killingworth Moor 50 C2
Killingworth Village 36 A6
Kimblesworth 179 D1
Kingston Park 45 F6
Kip Hill 131 F5
Lady Park 116 C3
Lambton 137 F3
Lamesley 116 C3
Langley Moor 204 B2
The Lawe 71 F2
Leam Lane 101 F4
Leamside 183 D2
Lemington 77 D2
Lintz 129 E1
Lintzford 110 A5
Little Thorpe 200 B2
Lobley Hill 98 A4
Longbenton 49 E4
Low Eighton 118 A4
Lowes Barn 204 B1
Low Fell 99 E5
Low Moorsley 185 E3
Low Thornley 93 F5
Lumley Thicks 168 B1
Lyons 186 B2
Marden 54 C2
Marley Hill 114 A3
Marley Pots 125 E1
Marsden 90 C4
Mason 31 D2
Mayfield 22 B3
Meadowfield 203 F4
Middle Herrington 142 A6
Middle Rainton 184 B1
The Middles 148 C5
Mill Dam 70 C5
Millfield 125 F5
Monkseaton 39 E4
Monkton 85 F4
Monkwearmouth 126 A3
Moor End 196 B2
Mount Pleasant 100 A2
Murton 53 D2
Murton 174 A6
Nedderton 6 A4
Nelson Village 21 E1
Nettlesworth 165 D6
Nevilles Cross 193 F6
Newbiggin Hall Estate 60 B2
Newbottle 158 A5
New Brancepeth 202 A1
Newburn 58 C6
Newcastle upon Tyne 3 H4
New Delaval 16 A3
Newfield 151 E3
New Hartley 25 D2
New Herrington 158 A2
New Kyo 147 D4
Newsham 15 F1
Newsham 16 B1
New Silksworth 160 B1
Newton Hall 181 D6
New Town 105 E1
New Town 171 F2
New York 53 E3
North Blyth 11 D2
North End 193 E2
North Hylton 123 D5
Northlea 176 A1
North Shields 71 D1
North Walbottle 58 C3
Offerton 141 D3
Old Burdon 160 C6
Old Fold 82 A6
Ouston 135 F4
Oxclose 137 F1
Oxhill 147 F2
Pallion 124 C4
Palmersville 50 C3
Parkside 176 B5
Path Head 76 A4
Pelaw 101 E1
Pelton 151 F2
Pelton Fell 152 B4
Pennywell 142 A2
Penshaw 157 E1
Percy Main 70 A4
Perkinsville 135 D6
Peterlee 208 A2
Philadelphia 157 F3

Pickering Nook	129 F2
Pittington	184 A6
Pity Me	180 A5
Plawsworth	165 F6
Ponteland	28 C3
Portobello	136 B2
Preston	54 C4
Preston Grange	54 B2
Prestwick	29 F5
Primrose	86 B4
Quaking Houses	147 F6
Rainton Bridge	171 D4
Rainton Gate	183 D3
Rickleton	154 B1
Roker	127 E2
Rosehill	68 A5
Rowlands Gill	111 D2
Ryhope	162 B2
Ryhope Colliery	162 A1
Ryton	74 B3
Ryton Woodside	74 A6
Sacriston	164 A6
St Anthony's	83 D5
St Peter's	82 B4
Saltwell	99 D3
Scotswood	77 F4
Seaham	177 D3
Seaton	25 F3
Seaton	174 C2
Seaton Burn	33 E1
Seaton Delaval	24 B4
Seaton Sluice	26 B3
Seghill	36 B1
Shankhouse	14 B5
Sheep Hill	112 A5
Sherburn	197 F5
Sheriff Hill	100 A4
Shield Row	132 A6
Shiney Row	157 D3
Shiremoor	52 C1
Shotton	207 F5
Shotton Colliery	206 A2
Simonside	87 D4

South Beach	17 F2
South Bents	109 D4
Southfield	22 A5
South Gosforth	63 F2
South Hetton	187 E5
South Hylton	124 A6
South Moor	147 F4
South Newsham	16 B3
South Pelaw	153 D2
South Shields	71 F4
South Stanley	148 A3
Southwick	125 F3
Spital Tongues	79 F1
Springwell	119 F3
Springwell	143 D3
Stanley	148 B2
Stargate	74 C5
Stella	75 F4
Stony Gate	158 C4
Street Gate	114 C2
Sulgrave	121 D4
Sunderland	4 A1
Sunderland	125 F4
Sunniside	113 F2
Sunniside	157 E5
Swalwell	95 F1
Tanfield	130 C2
Tanfield Lea	130 C5
Tan Hills	165 E6
Tantobie	129 F4
Teams	98 A1
Team Valley	98 C5
Thorney Close	142 B5
Throckley	58 A3
Tunstall	161 E1
Tyne Dock	87 F1
Tynemouth	55 D4
Urpeth	135 D4
Usworth	120 B3
Walbottle	58 A5
Waldridge	165 D1
Walker	83 E3
Wallsend	66 B4

Wardley	102 A2
Washington	121 F6
Washington Village	138 C1
West Allotment	52 A3
West Boldon	105 F2
West Chirton	68 C1
West Denton	60 A5
Westerhope	59 F2
Western Hill	193 F4
West Harton	87 F2
West Herrington	158 B1
West Holywell	37 F4
West Jesmond	63 D4
West Kyo	146 B3
Westlea	6 C4
West Lea	175 D4
West Monkseaton	53 E1
West Moor	49 D3
Westoe	72 A5
West Park	88 B1
West Pelton	150 B1
West Rainton	183 F1
Whickham	96 A3
Whitburn	109 E1
Whitburn Colliery	91 E4
Whitehills	100 C5
Whiteleas	88 B5
White-le-Head	129 F5
Whitley Bay	41 E5
Whitley Sands	40 C3
Wickham Fell	96 A6
Wide Open	33 E5
Willington	68 A2
Willington Quay	68 C5
Windy Nook	100 C4
Winlaton	75 F6
Winlaton Mill	94 A4
Witherwack	107 D6
Witton Gilbert	178 B3
Woolsington	43 F4
Woolsington Hall	44 A2
Wrekenton	118 A1

USING THE STREET INDEX

Street names are listed alphabetically. Each street name is followed by its postal town or area locality, the Postcode District, the page number, and the reference to the square in which the name is found.

Example: **Abbey Ct** *GATE* NE8.................. **99** E1 🟦

Some entries are followed by a number in a blue box. This number indicates the location of the street within the referenced grid square. The full street name is listed at the side of the map page.

GENERAL ABBREVIATIONS

ACC	ACCESS	CON	CONVENT	FK	FORK
ALY	ALLEY	COT	COTTAGE	FLD	FIELD
AP	APPROACH	COTS	COTTAGES	FLDS	FIELDS
AR	ARCADE	CP	CAPE	FLS	FALLS
ASS	ASSOCIATION	CPS	COPSE	FLS	FLATS
AV	AVENUE	CR	CREEK	FM	FARM
BCH	BEACH	CREM	CREMATORIUM	FT	FORT
BLDS	BUILDINGS	CRS	CRESCENT	FWY	FREEWAY
BND	BEND	CSWY	CAUSEWAY	FY	FERRY
BNK	BANK	CT	COURT	GA	GATE
BR	BRIDGE	CTRL	CENTRAL	GAL	GALLERY
BRK	BROOK	CTS	COURTS	GDN	GARDEN
BTM	BOTTOM	CTYD	COURTYARD	GDNS	GARDENS
BUS	BUSINESS	CUTT	CUTTINGS	GLD	GLADE
BVD	BOULEVARD	CV	COVE	GLN	GLEN
BY	BYPASS	CYN	CANYON	GN	GREEN
CATH	CATHEDRAL	DEPT	DEPARTMENT	GND	GROUND
CEM	CEMETERY	DL	DALE	GRA	GRANGE
CEN	CENTRE	DM	DAM	GRG	GARAGE
CFT	CROFT	DR	DRIVE	GT	GREAT
CH	CHURCH	DRO	DROVE	GTWY	GATEWAY
CHA	CHASE	DRY	DRIVEWAY	GV	GROVE
CHYD	CHURCHYARD	DWGS	DWELLINGS	HGR	HIGHER
CIR	CIRCLE	E	EAST	HL	HILL
CIRC	CIRCUS	EMB	EMBANKMENT	HLS	HILLS
CL	CLOSE	EMBY	EMBASSY	HO	HOUSE
CLFS	CLIFFS	ESP	ESPLANADE	HOL	HOLLOW
CMP	CAMP	EST	ESTATE	HOSP	HOSPITAL
CNR	CORNER	EX	EXCHANGE	HRB	HARBOUR
CO	COUNTY	EXPY	EXPRESSWAY	HTH	HEATH
COLL	COLLEGE	EXT	EXTENSION	HTS	HEIGHTS
COM	COMMON	F/O	FLYOVER	HVN	HAVEN
COMM	COMMISSION	FC	FOOTBALL CLUB	HWY	HIGHWAY

IMP	IMPERIAL
IN	INLET
IND EST	INDUSTRIAL ESTATE
INF	INFIRMARY
INFO	INFORMATION
INT	INTERCHANGE
IS	ISLAND
JCT	JUNCTION
JTY	JETTY
KG	KING
KNL	KNOLL
L	LAKE
LA	LANE
LDG	LODGE
LGT	LIGHT
LK	LOCK
LKS	LAKES
LNDG	LANDING
LTL	LITTLE
LWR	LOWER
MAG	MAGISTRATE
MAN	MANSIONS
MD	MEAD
MDW	MEADOWS
MEM	MEMORIAL
MKT	MARKET
MKTS	MARKETS
ML	MALL
ML	MILL
MNR	MANOR
MS	MEWS
MSN	MISSION
MT	MOUNT
MTN	MOUNTAIN
MTS	MOUNTAINS
MUS	MUSEUM
MWY	MOTORWAY
N	NORTH
NE	NORTH EAST
NW	NORTH WEST
O/P	OVERPASS
OFF	OFFICE
ORCH	ORCHARD
OV	OVAL
PAL	PALACE
PAS	PASSAGE
PAV	PAVILION
PDE	PARADE
PH	PUBLIC HOUSE
PK	PARK
PKWY	PARKWAY
PL	PLACE
PLN	PLAIN
PLNS	PLAINS
PLZ	PLAZA
POL	POLICE STATION
PR	PRINCE
PREC	PRECINCT
PREP	PREPARATORY
PRIM	PRIMARY
PROM	PROMENADE
PRS	PRINCESS
PRT	PORT
PT	POINT
PTH	PATH
PZ	PIAZZA
QD	QUADRANT
QU	QUEEN
QY	QUAY
R	RIVER
RBT	ROUNDABOUT
RD	ROAD
RDG	RIDGE
REP	REPUBLIC
RES	RESERVOIR
RFC	RUGBY FOOTBALL CLUB
RI	RISE
RP	RAMP
RW	ROW
S	SOUTH
SCH	SCHOOL
SE	SOUTH EAST
SER	SERVICE AREA
SH	SHORE
SHOP	SHOPPING
SKWY	SKYWAY
SMT	SUMMIT
SOC	SOCIETY
SP	SPUR
SPR	SPRING
SQ	SQUARE
ST	STREET
STN	STATION
STR	STREAM
STRD	STRAND
SW	SOUTH WEST
TDG	TRADING
TER	TERRACE
THWY	THROUGHWAY
TNL	TUNNEL
TOLL	TOLLWAY
TPK	TURNPIKE
TR	TRACK
TRL	TRAIL
TWR	TOWER
U/P	UNDERPASS
UNI	UNIVERSITY
UPR	UPPER
V	VALE
VA	VALLEY
VIAD	VIADUCT
VIL	VILLA
VIS	VISTA
VLG	VILLAGE
VLS	VILLAS
VW	VIEW
W	WEST
WD	WOOD
WHF	WHARF
WK	WALK
WKS	WALKS
WLS	WELLS
WY	WAY
YD	YARD
YHA	YOUTH HOSTEL

POSTCODE TOWNS AND AREA ABBREVIATIONS

ASHBK/HED/RY	Ashbrooke/Hedon/Ryhope
BDLGTN	Bedlington
BDN/LAN/SAC	Brandon/Lanchester/Sacriston
BLAY	Blaydon
BLYTH	Blyth
BOL	Boldon
BOLCOL	Boldon Colliery
BW/LEM/TK/HW	Benwell/Lemington/Throckley/Heddon-on-the-Wall
BYK/HTN/WLK	Byker/Heaton/Walker
CLDN/WHIT/ROK	Cleadon/Whitburn/Roker
CLS/BIR/GTL	Chester-le-Street/Birtley/Great Lumley
CLSW/PEL	Chester-le-Street west/Pelton
CNUT	Central Newcastle upon Tyne
CRAM	Cramlington
DHAM	Durham
DIN/WO	Dinnington/Wide Open
DUN/TMV	Dunston/Team Valley
ELS/FEN	Elswick/Fenham
FELL	Felling
GATE	Gateshead
GOS/KPK	Gosforth/Kingston Park
HAR/WTLS	Harton/Whiteleas
HEBB	Hebburn
HLH	Hetton-le-Hole
HLS	Houghton-le-Spring
JES	Jesmond
JRW	Jarrow
LGB/HTN	Longbenton/Heaton
LGB/KIL	Longbenton/Killingworth
LWF/SPW/WRK	LowFell / Springwell/Wrekenton
MLFD/PNYW	Millfield/Pennywell
MONK	Monkseaton
NSHW	North Shields west
PLEE/EAS	Peterlee/Easington
PONT/DH	Ponteland/Darras Hall
RDHAMSE	Rural Durham south & east
RHTLP	Rural Hartlepool
ROWG	Rowlands Gill
RYTON	Ryton
SEA/MUR	Seaham/Murton
SMOOR	Shiremoor
SSH	South Shields
STKFD/GP	Stakefold/Guide Post
STLY/ANP	Stanley/Annfield Plain
SUND	Sunderland
SUNDSW	Sunderland southwest
SWCK/CAS	Southwick/Castletown
TYNE/NSHE	Tynemouth/North Shields east
WASHN	Washington north
WASHS	Washington south
WBAY	Whitley Bay
WD/WHPE/BLK	West Denton/Westerhope/Blakelaw
WICK/BNPF	Wickham/Burnopfield
WLSD/HOW	Wallsend/Howdon

Abb - Act

Index - streets

A

Abbay St SWCK/CAS SR5	125	F5
Abbey Cl MONK NE25	39	F6
WASHS NE38	138	C1
Abbey Ct GATE NE8	99	E1 🔢
Abbey Dr JRW NE32	86	B1
TYNE/NSHE NE30	55	F4
WD/WHPE/BLK NE5	59	D2 🔢
Abbey Rd DHAM DH1	179	F4
WASHS NE38	138	C1
Abbeywoods DHAM DH1	180	A4 🔢
Abbotsfield Cl SUNDSW SR3	160	B3 🔢
Abbotsford Gv ASHBK/HED/RY SR2	4	A5
Abbotsford Pk MONK NE25	40	B6
Abbotsford Rd FELL NE10	100	C1
Abbotsford Ter JES NE2	63	F6
Abbotside Cl CLSW/PEL DH2	134	C4
Abbotside Pl WD/WHPE/BLK NE5	59	F5 🔢
Abbotsmeade Cl WD/WHPE/BLK NE5	61	D6
Abbot's Rd GATE NE8	3	G6
Abbots' Rw DHAM DH1	195	E3
Abbot St PLEE/EAS SR8	201	E1
Abbots Wk STLY/ANP DH9	133	E6
Abbots Wy NSHW NE29	53	E5
Abbs St SWCK/CAS SR5	126	C3 🔢
Abercorn Pl WLSD/HOW NE28	52	A6
Abercorn Rd BW/LEM/TK/HW NE15	77	F3
SUNDSW SR3	142	C5
Abercrombie Pl WD/WHPE/BLK NE5	61	D4 🔢
Aberdare Rd SUNDSW SR3	159	F1
Aberdeen CLSW/PEL DH2	135	E5
Aberdeen Ct DIN/WO NE13	45	F4 🔢
Aberdeen Dr JRW NE32	87	D4
Aberford Cl WD/WHPE/BLK NE5	59	D3 🔢
Aberfoyle CLSW/PEL DH2	135	E5
Aberfoyle St STLY/ANP DH9	149	D2
Abernethy CLSW/PEL DH2	135	E4
Abingdon Rd BYK/HTN/WLK NE6	84	A1
Abingdon Sq CRAM NE23	14	B5
Abingdon St MLFD/PNYW SR4	143	E1
Abingdon Wy BOL NE36	105	D3
BOLCOL NE35	104	C1
Abinger St ELS/FEN NE4	80	A3
Aboyne Sq SUNDSW SR3	142	C5
Acacia Av HLS DH4	169	F1
Acacia Gv HAR/WTLS NE34	89	D3
Acacia Rd FELL NE10	82	A6
Acacia St DUN/TMV NE11	98	B5
Acanthus Av ELS/FEN NE4	79	F1
Acer Ct ASHBK/HED/RY SR2	144	C2
Acklam Av ASHBK/HED/RY SR2	145	E5
Acomb Av MONK NE25	24	C6
WLSD/HOW NE28	51	F5
Acomb Ct ASHBK/HED/RY SR2	145	E5 🔢
BDLGTN NE22	7	F3
Acomb Crs GOS/KPK NE3	46	B4
Acomb Gdns WD/WHPE/BLK NE5	61	E6
Acorn Av BDLGTN NE22	7	E4
GATE NE8	98	B2
Acorn Cl BDN/LAN/SAC DH7	164	A6
Acorn Pl BDN/LAN/SAC DH7	203	D4 🔢
Acorn Rd JES NE2	64	A4
Acre Rigg Rd PLEE/EAS SR8	208	A1
Acton Dene STLY/ANP DH9	149	E2
Acton Dr NSHW NE29	53	F4

Acton Pl LGB/HTN NE7 .... 65 D4
Acton Rd WD/WHPE/BLK NE5 ...... 60 B6 [1]
Adair Av BW/LEM/TK/HW NE15 .... 78 B2
Ada St BYK/HTN/WLK NE6 .... 83 D2
  SSH NE33 .... 71 F5
Adderstone Av CRAM NE23 .... 22 A3
Adderstone Crs JES NE2 .... 64 B4
Adderstone Gdns NSHW NE29 ...... 53 D3
Addington Crs NSHW NE29 .... 54 A6
Addington Dr BLYTH NE24 .... 17 D1
  WLSD/HOW NE28 .... 51 F5
Addison Ct WLSD/HOW NE28 ...... 68 C5 [1]
Addison Gdns FELL NE10 .... 102 A2 [1]
Addison Rd BOL NE36 .... 105 F3
  BYK/HTN/WLK NE6 .... 76 C1 [1]
Addison St ASHBK/HED/RY SR2 ...... 5 G5
  NSHW NE29 .... 70 C2
Addycombe Ter
  BYK/HTN/WLK NE6 .... 65 E5
Adelaide Cl SUND SR1 .... 5 F2
Adelaide Pl SUND SR1 .... 5 G2
Adelaide Rw SEA/MUR SR7 .... 176 C3 [1]
Adelaide Ter ELS/FEN NE4 .... 78 C3
Adeline Gdns GOS/KPK NE3 .... 62 C4
Adelphi Cl NSHW NE29 .... 53 E4
Adelphi Pl BYK/HTN/WLK NE6 .... 83 D3
Adfrid Pl PLEE/EAS SR8 .... 208 C1 [1]
Admiral Wy SUNDSW SR3 .... 159 F3
Adolphus Pl CLDN/WHIT/ROK SR6 .. 109 E2
Adolphus St West
  SEA/MUR SR7 .... 176 C3 [2]
Adventure La HLS DH4 .... 183 E1
Affleck St GATE NE8 .... 81 D6
Afton Ct HAR/WTLS NE34 .... 88 C3 [1]
Afton Wy GOS/KPK NE3 .... 62 A1 [1]
Agar Rd SUNDSW SR3 .... 142 C6
Agincourt HEBB NE31 .... 84 C1
  LGB/KIL NE12 .... 35 F6 [1]
Agnes Maria St GOS/KPK NE3 ...... 62 C1 [1]
Agnes St STLY/ANP DH9 .... 148 B1 [1]
Agricola Gdns WLSD/HOW NE28 .. 51 F6
Agricola Rd ELS/FEN NE4 .... 79 E2 [1]
Aidan Av WBAY NE26 .... 26 A2 [1]
Aidan Cl DIN/WO NE13 .... 33 D4 [1]
  STLY/ANP DH9 .... 149 D1
Aidan Wk GOS/KPK NE3 .... 63 F1
Aiden Wy HLH DH5 .... 171 F5 [1]
Ailesbury St LWF/SPW/WRK SR4 .. 125 F5
Ainderby Rd BW/LEM/TK/HW NE15 .. 57 D4
Ainsdale Gdns
  WD/WHPE/BLK NE5 .... 59 E4 [1]
Ainsley St DHAM DH1 .... 194 A4
Ainslie Pl WD/WHPE/BLK NE5 ...... 61 D5
Ainsworth Av HAR/WTLS NE34 .... 87 F5
Ainthorpe Cl SUNDSW SR3 .... 161 D1 [1]
Ainthorpe Gdns LGB/HTN NE7 .... 65 D2
Aintree Gdns GATE NE8 .... 98 B2
Aintree Rd SUNDSW SR3 .... 142 C6
Airedale WLSD/HOW NE28 .... 66 B1
Airedale Gdns HLH DH5 .... 185 E1
Aireys Cl HLS DH4 .... 170 B2
Airey Ter BYK/HTN/WLK NE6 ...... 83 F3
  GATE NE8 .... 98 C1 [1]
Airport Freightway DIN/WO NE13 .. 44 A2
Airville Mt SUNDSW SR3 .... 160 C4
Aisgill Cl CRAM NE23 .... 22 A2 [1]
Aisgill Dr WD/WHPE/BLK NE5 ...... 59 E5
Aiskell St MLFD/PNYW SR4 .... 125 F5
Aj Cook Ter RDHAMSE DH6 .... 206 B3 [1]
Akeld Ct CRAM NE23 .... 22 A3
Akenside Hl CNUT NE1 .... 3 E5
Akenside Ter JES NE2 .... 64 B6
Alamein Av HLS DH5 .... 171 E2 [1]
Alansway Gdns SSH NE33 .... 71 F6 [1]
Albany Av LGB/KIL NE12 .... 49 F4 [1]
Albany Ct ELS/FEN NE4 .... 79 F5
Albany Rd GATE NE8 .... 81 F5
Albany St East SSH NE33 .... 71 F6 [1]
Albany St West SSH NE33 .... 71 F6 [1]
Albany Wy WASHN NE37 .... 120 B5
Albatross Wy BLYTH NE24 .... 17 D3
Albemarle Av JES NE2 .... 63 F5 [1]
Albemarle St SSH NE33 .... 71 E3
Albert Av WD/WHPE/BLK NE5 ...... 67 D4 [1]
Albert Dr LWF/SPW/WRK NE9 ...... 99 E5 [1]
Albert Pl LWF/SPW/WRK NE9 ...... 99 E6 [1]
  WASHS NE38 .... 139 E3
Albert Rd BDLGTN NE22 .... 8 C2
  JRW NE32 .... 86 A1 [1]
  MLFD/PNYW SR4 .... 125 F5
  WBAY NE26 .... 26 C2
Albert St CLS/BIR/GTL DH3 .... 153 E5
  CLSW/PEL DH2 .... 150 C5
  DHAM DH1 .... 194 A3
  HEBB NE31 .... 84 C1 [1]
  JES NE2 .... 3 G2
  SEA/MUR SR7 .... 176 C4
Albert Ter LGB/KIL NE12 .... 49 E3
Albion Pl SUND SR1 .... 5 F4
Albion Rd TYNE/NSHE NE30 .... 54 C6
Albion Rd West NSHW NE29 .... 70 C1
Albion Rw BYK/HTN/WLK NE6 .... 82 A2 [1]
Albion St FELL NE10 .... 100 C4
  MLFD/PNYW SR4 .... 123 F6
Albion Ter NSHW NE29 .... 54 C6 [1]

Albion Wy BLYTH NE24 .... 10 B5
  CRAM NE23 .... 14 C5 [1]
Albury Park Rd TYNE/NSHE NE30 .. 55 E5 [1]
Albury Pl WICK/BNPF NE16 .... 95 F5
Albury Rd JES NE2 .... 63 F3
Albyn Gdns SUNDSW SR3 .... 143 F3 [1]
Alconbury Cl BLYTH NE24 .... 17 D1
Alcote Gv RDHAMSE DH6 .... 206 C2 [1]
Alcroft Cl WD/WHPE/BLK NE5 ...... 59 D3 [2]
Aldborough St BLYTH NE24 .... 11 D5 [1]
Aldbrough Cl
  ASHBK/HED/RY SR2 .... 162 B2 [1]
Aldbrough St HAR/WTLS NE34 .... 87 F3 [1]
Aldeburgh Av
  BW/LEM/TK/HW NE15 .... 59 E6
Aldenham Rd SUNDSW SR3 .... 143 D6
Alder Av ELS/FEN NE4 .... 61 F6
Alder Cl HLH DH5 .... 185 E1
Alder Crs STLY/ANP DH9 .... 129 E4
Alderdene Cl
  BDN/LAN/SAC DH7 .... 192 B5 [1]
Alder Gv MONK NE25 .... 40 A4
Alder Lea Cl DHAM DH1 .... 195 F3
Alderley Cl ASHBK/HED/RY SR2 .. 145 E4
  BOLCOL NE35 .... 105 D1 [1]
Alderley Dr LGB/KIL NE12 .... 36 B6
Alderley Rd LWF/SPW/WRK NE9 .. 99 D5
Alderley Wy CRAM NE23 .... 14 C5 [1]
Alderman Wood Rd
  STLY/ANP DH9 .... 131 D6
Alderney Gdns
  WD/WHPE/BLK NE5 .... 59 E4 [2]
Alder Pk BDN/LAN/SAC DH7 ...... 202 C5 [1]
Alder Rd NSHW NE29 .... 52 C5
  WLSD/HOW NE28 .... 52 A6
Aldershot Rd SUNDSW SR3 .... 159 F1 [1]
Aldershot Sq SUNDSW SR3 .... 159 F1 [1]
Alder St SWCK/CAS SR5 .... 124 A3 [1]
Alder Wy LGB/KIL NE12 .... 35 E6 [1]
Alderwood WASHS NE38 .... 138 A6
Alderwood Crs BYK/HTN/WLK NE6 .. 66 B3
Alderwyk FELL NE10 .... 102 A4 [1]
Aldhome Ct DHAM DH1 .... 179 F6 [1]
Aldsworth Cl LWF/SPW/WRK NE9 .. 119 E2
Aldwick Rd BW/LEM/TK/HW NE15 .. 77 E2
Aldwych Dr NSHW NE29 .... 53 D5
Aldwych Rd SUNDSW SR3 .... 159 F1 [3]
Aldwych Sq SUNDSW SR3 .... 159 F2
Aldwych St SSH NE33 .... 72 A4 [1]
Alexander Dr HLH DH5 .... 185 E1
Alexander Ter
  CLDN/WHIT/ROK SR6 .... 126 C1 [1]
Alexandra Av SWCK/CAS SR5 ...... 125 E3
Alexandra Cl DHAM DH1 .... 179 F6
Alexandra Dr WICK/BNPF NE16 .. 96 B2
Alexandra Gdns NSHW NE29 .... 54 A6
Alexandra Pk ASHBK/HED/RY SR2 .. 144 B2
  SUNDSW SR3 .... 144 A2 [2]
Alexandra Rd BYK/HTN/WLK NE6 .. 65 D5
  GATE NE8 .... 99 D2
Alexandra St CLSW/PEL DH2 ...... 151 E2
  WLSD/HOW NE28 .... 67 E4 [1]
Alexandra Wy CRAM NE23 .... 22 A3
Alexandria Crs DHAM DH1 .... 194 A5 [1]
Alexandrina St SEA/MUR SR7 ...... 176 C3 [3]
Alford CLSW/PEL DH2 .... 135 E4
Alfred Av BDLGTN NE22 .... 8 A3
Alfred St BYK/HTN/WLK NE6 ...... 83 D2
  HEBB NE31 .... 84 C3
  SEA/MUR SR7 .... 177 D4
Alfreton Cl BDN/LAN/SAC DH7 .. 202 C6
Algernon LGB/KIL NE12 .... 35 F5 [1]
Algernon Pl WBAY NE26 .... 41 D6
Algernon Rd BW/LEM/TK/HW NE15 .. 76 B2
  BYK/HTN/WLK NE6 .... 82 B2 [1]
Algernon Ter TYNE/NSHE NE30 .. 55 E4
Algiers Rd SUNDSW SR3 .... 159 E1 [1]
Alice St ASHBK/HED/RY SR2 .... 4 B5
  BLAY NE21 .... 94 A1
  CLSW/PEL DH2 .... 135 E6
  SSH NE33 .... 71 E6
Aline St SEA/MUR SR7 .... 177 D3 [1]
  SUNDSW SR3 .... 161 D1
Alison Dr BOL NE36 .... 106 C3
Allandale Av LGB/KIL NE12 .... 49 F5
Allandale Crs HLS DH4 .... 139 F6
  SMOOR NE27 .... 52 C1
Allandale Dr HAR/WTLS NE34 ...... 72 C6
Allandale Pl TYNE/NSHE NE30 .... 55 E4 [1]
Allandale Rd BDN/LAN/SAC DH7 .. 203 E4 [1]
  BLYTH NE24 .... 11 E6
  BYK/HTN/WLK NE6 .... 82 C3
  SUNDSW SR3 .... 159 F1 [1]
Allendale Sq SUNDSW SR3 .... 143 D5
Allendale St HLH DH5 .... 185 F2 [1]
Allendale Ter BYK/HTN/WLK NE6 .. 83 E2 [1]
Allenheads WASHS NE38 .... 139 D5
Allenheads MONK NE25 .... 24 B4
  WD/WHPE/BLK NE5 .... 60 A5
Allensgreen CRAM NE23 .... 22 A2
Allen St CLS/BIR/GTL DH3 .... 153 E6

Allerdean Cl
  BW/LEM/TK/HW NE15 .... 76 A1 [1]
Allergate DHAM DH1 .... 194 A5
Allerhope CRAM NE23 .... 22 A3
Allerton Gdns
  BYK/HTN/WLK NE6 .... 65 F4 [1]
Allhusen Ter GATE NE8 .... 100 A1 [1]
Alliance Pl MLFD/PNYW SR4 .... 126 A5 [1]
Alliance St MLFD/PNYW SR4 .... 126 A5 [2]
Allingham Ct LGB/HTN NE7 .... 66 A3 [1]
Alloa Rd SUNDSW SR3 .... 142 C6 [1]
Allonby Wy WD/WHPE/BLK NE5 .. 61 D6 [1]
All Saints Dr HLH DH5 .... 171 F4
Alma Pl NSHW NE29 .... 54 C6
  WBAY NE26 .... 41 D6
Alma St MLFD/PNYW SR4 .... 123 F5
Alma Ter RYTON NE40 .... 74 B6
Almond Crs GATE NE8 .... 98 B2
Almond Dr SWCK/CAS SR5 .... 123 F4
Almond Pl ELS/FEN NE4 .... 78 C1 [1]
Aln Av GOS/KPK NE3 .... 46 C6
Aln Ct BW/LEM/TK/HW NE15 ...... 76 B2
Aln Crs GOS/KPK NE3 .... 46 C5
Aln Gv BW/LEM/TK/HW NE15 ...... 76 B1
Alnham Ct GOS/KPK NE3 .... 46 A5 [1]
Alnmouth Av NSHW NE29 .... 69 F2
Alnmouth Dr GOS/KPK NE3 .... 64 A2 [1]
Aln St HEBB NE31 .... 84 C2
Aln Wk GOS/KPK NE3 .... 46 C6
Alnwick Av NSHW NE29 .... 69 F2
Alnwick Cl CLSW/PEL DH2 .... 165 F1 [1]
  WICK/BNPF NE16 .... 95 F3
Alnwick Gv JRW NE32 .... 86 A6 [1]
Alnwick Rd DHAM DH1 .... 180 B5 [1]
  HAR/WTLS NE34 .... 88 B2
  SUNDSW SR3 .... 143 D6
Alnwick Sq SUNDSW SR3 .... 143 D6
Alnwick St BW/LEM/TK/HW NE15 .. 58 B6
  PLEE/EAS SR8 .... 201 E5
  WLSD/HOW NE28 .... 67 E4
Alnwick Ter DIN/WO NE13 .... 33 E3 [1]
Alpine Gv BOL NE36 .... 106 A3 [1]
Alpine Wy SUNDSW SR3 .... 143 F3 [2]
Alresford LGB/KIL NE12 .... 35 F6 [2]
Alston Av BYK/HTN/WLK NE6 ...... 83 D2
  CRAM NE23 .... 22 C3 [1]
Alston Cl NSHW NE29 .... 53 E5 [1]
  WLSD/HOW NE28 .... 68 C2
Alston Crs CLDN/WHIT/ROK SR6 .. 108 B6
Alston Gdns BW/LEM/TK/HW NE15 .. 57 F3
Alston Gv WBAY NE26 .... 26 C2
Alston Rd MONK NE25 .... 24 C2
  WASHS NE38 .... 122 A6
Alston St GATE NE8 .... 98 C1 [1]
Alston Wk PLEE/EAS SR8 .... 209 D1 [1]
Alston Wy BDN/LAN/SAC DH7 .... 203 E4 [1]
Altan Pl LGB/KIL NE12 .... 49 D5
Alum Well Rd
  LWF/SPW/WRK NE9 .... 99 D5 [1]
  LWF/SPW/WRK NE9 .... 99 E5 [2]
Alverston Cl BW/LEM/TK/HW NE15 .. 59 E6
Alverstone Av LWF/SPW/WRK NE9 .. 99 D6 [1]
Alverthorpe St SSH NE33 .... 71 F6
Alvin Gra JRW NE32 .... 85 E1 [1]
Alwin WASHS NE38 .... 137 F5
Alwin Cl HLS DH4 .... 156 A5
Alwinton Av NSHW NE29 .... 53 F4
Alwinton Cl BLYTH NE24 .... 10 B4
  WD/WHPE/BLK NE5 .... 60 C2 [1]
Alwinton Dr CLSW/PEL DH2 .... 165 F1 [1]
Alwinton Gdns DUN/TMV NE11 .. 97 F5
Alwinton Rd SMOOR NE27 .... 52 C1
Alwinton Ter GOS/KPK NE3 .... 63 F1
Amara Sq SUNDSW SR3 .... 143 D6
Ambassadors Wy NSHW NE29 .... 53 D4
Amber Ct BLYTH NE24 .... 10 B6 [1]
Ambergate Cl
  WD/WHPE/BLK NE5 .... 60 C3 [1]
Amberley Cha LGB/KIL NE12 .... 36 A6 [1]
Amberley Cl WLSD/HOW NE28 .... 68 C2 [1]
Amberley Gdns LGB/HTN NE7 .... 65 E4
Amberley St ASHBK/HED/RY SR2 .. 5 E5
  GATE NE8 .... 98 C1 [1]
Amberley St South
  ASHBK/HED/RY SR2 .... 5 E6 [1]
Amberley Wy BLYTH NE24 .... 17 D1 [1]
Amberly Gv WICK/BNPF NE16 .... 95 F5
Amble Av HAR/WTLS NE34 .... 73 D6
  MONK NE25 .... 55 D1
Amble Cl BLYTH NE24 .... 16 B1
Amble Gv JES NE2 .... 81 F1 [1]
Amble Pl LGB/KIL NE12 .... 50 B3
Ambleside BW/LEM/TK/HW NE15 .. 58 A3
Ambleside Av HAR/WTLS NE34 .. 89 D2
  SEA/MUR SR7 .... 175 D2
Ambleside Cl MONK NE25 .... 24 C5 [1]
  PLEE/EAS SR8 .... 209 D1 [2]
Ambleside Ter
  CLDN/WHIT/ROK SR6 .... 108 B6
Amble Wy GOS/KPK NE3 .... 47 D6 [1]
Ambridge Wy GOS/KPK NE3 .... 62 B1 [1]
Ambrose Pl BYK/HTN/WLK NE6 .. 84 A2 [1]
Ambrose Rd SUNDSW SR3 .... 142 C6

Amec Wy *WLSD/HOW* NE28............... 68 A5
Amelia Cl *ELS/FEN* NE4.................... 79 D5
Amelia Gdns *SUNDSW* SR3 .... 159 D1
Amersham Ct *PLEE/EAS* SR8 .... 208 C1
Amersham Pl
    WD/WHPE/BLK NE5 .... 61 D4 **2**
Amersham Rd *BLYTH* NE24 .... 16 C2
Amesbury Cl
    WD/WHPE/BLK NE5 .... 59 D3 **3**
Amethyst Rd *ELS/FEN* NE4 .... 79 E6
Amethyst St *MLFD/PNYW* SR4 ...... 125 E5 **1**
Amherst Rd *GOS/KPK* NE3 .... 46 A6
Amos Ayre Pl *HAR/WTLS* NE34 ...... 87 E3
Amsterdam Rd *SUNDSW* SR3 .... 143 D6
Amy St *SWCK/CAS* SR5 .... 126 A2 **1**
Ancaster Av *LGB/KIL* NE12 .... 49 D6
Ancaster Rd *WICK/BNPF* NE16 .... 95 E5
Ancona St *MLFD/PNYW* SR4 .... 125 E4
Ancroft Av *NSHW* NE29 .... 54 B5
Ancroft Pl *WD/WHPE/BLK* NE5 ...... 61 D6
Ancroft Rd *MONK* NE25 .... 24 A5
Ancroft Wy *GOS/KPK* NE3 .... 46 B4 **1**
Ancrum St *JES* NE2 .... 80 A1 **1**
Anderson St *SSH* NE33 .... 71 F3
Andover Pl *WLSD/HOW* NE28 .... 52 A6
Andrew Rd *SUNDSW* SR3 .... 159 E1
Andrew's La *PLEE/EAS* SR8 .... 199 F4
Anfield Rd *GOS/KPK* NE3 .... 62 A1
Angerton Av *SMOOR* NE27 .... 52 B2
    TYNE/NSHE NE30 .... 54 C3
Angerton Gdns
    WD/WHPE/BLK NE5 .... 61 F6
Anglesey Gdns
    WD/WHPE/BLK NE5 .... 59 E4 **3**
Anglesey Rd *SUNDSW* SR3 .... 159 F1
Anglesey Sq *SUNDSW* SR3 .... 159 F1 **5**
Angle Ter *WLSD/HOW* NE28 .... 68 B4 **1**
Angram Dr *ASHBK/HED/RY* SR2 ..... 145 F5
Angrove Gdns *MLFD/PNYW* SR4..... 125 E6
Angus *CLSW/PEL* DH2 .... 135 E4
Angus Cl *LGB/KIL* NE12 .... 49 E1
Angus Crs *NSHW* NE29 .... 69 F2
Angus Rd *GATE* NE8 .... 98 B2
Annand Rd *DHAM* DH1 .... 195 E3
Anne Dr *LGB/KIL* NE12 .... 50 C4
Annfield St *STLY/ANP* DH9 .... 146 A4
Annfield Rd *CRAM* NE23................. 14 A4
Annie St *CLDN/WHIT/ROK* SR6 ...... 108 C6
Annitsford Dr *CRAM* NE23 .... 35 D2
Ann's Rw *BLYTH* NE24 .... 11 D3
Ann St *BLAY* NE21 .... 76 B5
    GATE NE8 .... 81 E6
    HEBB NE31 .... 84 B1
Annville Crs *BYK/HTN/WLK* NE6 ..... 83 F4
Anscomb Gdns *LGB/HTN* NE7 .... 64 B3
Anson Cl *SSH* NE33 .... 71 D6
Anson Pl *WD/WHPE/BLK* NE5 .... 60 B3 **1**
Anstead Cl *CRAM* NE23.................. 22 A2
Anthony Rd *SUNDSW* SR3 .... 159 F1 **8**
Anthony St *STLY/ANP* DH9 .... 148 A1
Antoine Wk
    BW/LEM/TK/HW NE15.................. 56 B4
Anton Pl *CRAM* NE23 .... 22 A3
Antrim Cl *WD/WHPE/BLK* NE5........ 61 D3
Antrim Gdns *SEA/MUR* SR7 .... 176 B2 **1**
Antwerp Rd *SUNDSW* SR3 .... 159 E1
Anvil Ct *DHAM* DH1 .... 179 F5
Apperley Av *WD/WHPE/BLK* NE5 ... 60 A5
Apperley Av *GOS/KPK* NE3 .... 61 E2
Appian Pl *BW/LEM/TK/HW* NE15 .... 58 A4 **1**
    LWF/SPW/WRK NE9 .... 100 A3
Appleby Cl *NSHW* NE29 .... 70 B1 **1**
Appleby Gdns *WLSD/HOW* NE28..... 68 C2
Appleby Pk *NSHW* NE29................. 54 B6
Appleby Rd *SUNDSW* SR3.............. 159 F1
Appleby Sq *SUNDSW* SR3 .... 159 F1 **7**
Appleby St *NSHW* NE29 .... 70 C2
Appleby Wy *PLEE/EAS* SR8 .... 207 F5
Apple Cl *BW/LEM/TK/HW* NE15 ...... 59 E6
Appledore Gdns *CLS/BIR/GTL* DH3.. 153 F3
Appledore Rd *CLDN/WHIT/ROK* SR6.. 127 D3
Appleforth Av
    ASHBK/HED/RY SR2 .... 145 F5
Appletree Gdns *BYK/HTN/WLK* NE6... 66 A6
    MONK NE25 .... 54 A1
Applewood *LGB/KIL* NE12 .... 50 B1 **1**
Appley Ter *CLDN/WHIT/ROK* SR6 ... 127 D3
Apsley Crs *GOS/KPK* NE3 .... 62 A1
Arbroath *SUNDSW* SR3 .... 142 C6
Arcadia Av *CLS/BIR/GTL* DH3 .... 153 E3
Arcadia Ter *BLYTH* NE24 .... 11 D6
Archbold Ter *JES* NE2 .... 81 D1 **1**
Archer Rd *SUNDSW* SR3 .... 142 C6
Archer Sq *SUNDSW* SR3 .... 142 C6 **2**
Archer St *WLSD/HOW* NE28 .... 68 A3
Archery Ri *DHAM* DH1 .... 193 F6
Archibald St *GOS/KPK* NE3 .... 63 E1
Arcot Av *CRAM* NE23 .... 13 D6
    MONK NE25 .... 54 A1
Arcot Dr *MONK* NE25 .... 54 A2
    WD/WHPE/BLK NE5 .... 60 B6 **2**
Arden Av *GOS/KPK* NE3 .... 47 D3
Arden Cl *WLSD/HOW* NE28 .... 51 F5
Arden Crs *WD/WHPE/BLK* NE5 ...... 61 F5
Arden Sq *SUNDSW* SR3 .... 143 D6

Arden St *RDHAMSE* DH6................ 206 B1
Ardrossan *CLSW/PEL* DH2 .... 135 E5
Ardrossan Rd *SUNDSW* SR3 .... 159 F1
Arena Wy *ELS/FEN* NE4 .... 80 B5
Argus Cl *DUN/TMV* NE11 .... 98 A3
Argyle Ct *STLY/ANP* DH9 .... 131 F6
Argyle Pl *NSHW* NE29 .... 54 C4 **1**
    RDHAMSE DH6.......................... 187 E5
Argyle Sq *ASHBK/HED/RY* SR2 ...... 4 B5
Argyle St *ASHBK/HED/RY* SR2 ...... 4 B5
    CNUT NE1 .... 3 F3
    HEBB NE31 .... 85 D1
    TYNE/NSHE NE30 .... 55 F4 **1**
Arisaig *CLSW/PEL* DH2 .... 135 E4
Arklecrag *WASHN* NE37 .... 120 B6
Arkleside Pl *WD/WHPE/BLK* NE5 ... 59 F5 **2**
Arkle St *DIN/WO* NE13 .... 32 C6
    GATE NE8................................. 98 C3
Arkwright St *GATE* NE8 .... 98 C3
Arlington Av *GOS/KPK* NE3 .... 62 B3
Arlington Gv *CRAM* NE23 .... 14 A4
    WICK/BNPF NE16....................... 95 F4
Arlington Rd *HEBB* NE31 .... 85 E4 **1**
Arlington St *MLFD/PNYW* SR4 .... 125 E6 **1**
Armstrong Av *BYK/HTN/WLK* NE6 ... 65 D5
    HAR/WTLS NE34 .... 89 D1
Armstrong Dr *LGB/KIL* NE12 .... 49 D2
Armstrong Rd
    BW/LEM/TK/HW NE15.................. 77 E3
    ELS/FEN NE4............................. 78 C4
    PLEE/EAS SR8 .... 200 C6
    WASHN NE37............................. 119 E5
    WLSD/HOW NE28....................... 68 C5
Armstrong St *DUN/TMV* NE11......... 98 B3
    GATE NE8................................. 98 B3
Armstrong Ter *SSH* NE33............... 71 E6
Arncliffe Av *MLFD/PNYW* SR4 .... 143 D2 **1**
Arncliffe Gdns
    WD/WHPE/BLK NE5 .... 59 E4 **4**
Arnham Gv *MLFD/PNYW* SR4 .... 141 E4
Arnold Cl *STLY/ANP* DH9 .... 148 C2
Arnold Rd *SUNDSW* SR3 .... 142 C6
Arnold St *BOLCOL* NE35 .... 105 E2
Arran Ct *SUNDSW* SR3 .... 160 C2 **1**
Arran Dr *JRW* NE32 .... 87 D5
Arran Pl *NSHW* NE29 .... 53 E4
Arras La *SUND* SR1 .... 5 F2
Arrow Cl *LGB/KIL* NE12 .... 49 D2
Arthur Av *ASHBK/HED/RY* SR2 ...... 162 C2
Arthur Cook Av *WICK/BNPF* NE16 ... 96 B3
Arthur St *BLYTH* NE24 .... 11 D4 **1**
    CLDN/WHIT/ROK SR6.................. 91 E4
    GATE NE8................................. 81 D6
    JRW NE32 .... 86 A2 **1**
    STLY/ANP DH9.......................... 150 C1
Arun Cl *PLEE/EAS* SR8 .... 208 B3
Arundel Cl *BDLGTN* NE22.............. 8 B1
    DIN/WO NE13 .... 32 C5 **1**
Arundel Dr *BW/LEM/TK/HW* NE15 ... 77 D1
    MONK NE25 .... 39 D6
Arundel Gdns *LWF/SPW/WRK* NE9 ... 99 F5
    SUNDSW SR3 .... 159 E1
Arundel Rd *SUNDSW* SR3 .... 142 C6
Arundel Wy *BDN/LAN/SAC* DH7 ..... 203 E4
Asama Ct *ELS/FEN* NE4 .... 79 F6
Ascot Cl *WLSD/HOW* NE28 .... 51 F6
Ascot Ct *SUNDSW* SR3 .... 159 F1
Ascot Gdns *HAR/WTLS* NE34.......... 88 C2
Ascot Pl *CLSW/PEL* DH2................ 152 B1
Ash Av *DHAM* DH1 .... 195 F5
    DIN/WO NE13 .... 31 D3
Ashberry Gv *CLDN/WHIT/ROK* SR6... 126 C3
Ashbourne Av *BYK/HTN/WLK* NE6... 83 E2
Ashbourne Cl *SMOOR* NE27 .... 37 E5 **1**
Ashbourne Rd *JRW* NE32 .... 86 B3 **1**
Ashbrook Cl *BDN/LAN/SAC* DH7 .... 202 B5 **1**
Ashbrooke *MONK* NE25.................. 40 A5
Ashbrooke Cross
    ASHBK/HED/RY SR2 .... 144 B3 **1**
Ashbrooke Dr *PONT/DH* NE20 .... 28 A3
Ashbrooke Gdns
    WLSD/HOW NE28....................... 68 A3 **1**
Ashbrooke Range
    ASHBK/HED/RY SR2 .... 144 B3 **2**
Ashbrooke Rd
    ASHBK/HED/RY SR2 .... 144 B3
Ashbrooke St *WD/WHPE/BLK* NE5... 62 A3
Ashburne Ct
    ASHBK/HED/RY SR2 .... 144 C2 **1**
Ashburn Rd *WLSD/HOW* NE28........ 52 A6
Ashburton Rd *GOS/KPK* NE3 .... 62 C2
Ashbury *MONK* NE25 .... 39 E4
Ashby St *ASHBK/HED/RY* SR2 .... 145 E3
Ash Crs *SEA/MUR* SR7.................. 176 B3 **1**
Ashcroft Dr *LGB/KIL* NE12 .... 50 A5
Ashdale *HLS* DH4 .... 139 D6
Ashdale Crs *WD/WHPE/BLK* NE5 ... 59 E5
Ashdown Av *DHAM* DH1 .... 196 A3
Ashdown Cl *LGB/KIL* NE12 .... 49 D5 **1**
Ashdown Rd *SUNDSW* SR3 .... 142 C6
Ashdown Wy *LGB/KIL* NE12 .... 49 D5 **1**
Asher St *GATE* NE8 .... 100 B1 **1**
Ashfield *JRW* NE32 .... 104 C1
Ashfield Av *WICK/BNPF* NE16 .... 96 B2

Ashfield Cl *ELS/FEN* NE4 .... 79 F4
Ashfield Gdns *WLSD/HOW* NE28 .... 66 B3
Ashfield Gv *NSHW* NE29 .... 54 C6 **2**
    WBAY NE26 .... 40 C4
Ashfield Pk *WICK/BNPF* NE16 .... 96 A2
Ashfield Ri *WICK/BNPF* NE16......... 96 A5
Ashfield Rd *GOS/KPK* NE3 .... 62 C2
    WICK/BNPF NE16....................... 96 A5
Ashford Cl *BLYTH* NE24 .... 17 D1 **3**
Ashford Dr *BDN/LAN/SAC* DH7 ...... 144 A6
Ashford Gv *WD/WHPE/BLK* NE5 ..... 59 D2 **2**
Ashford Rd *SUNDSW* SR3 .... 159 F1 **3**
Ash Gv *CLDN/WHIT/ROK* SR6 .... 109 F2 **1**
    DUN/TMV NE11......................... 97 D1
    RYTON NE40 .... 74 B2
    WLSD/HOW NE28....................... 67 F4
Ashgrove Av *HAR/WTLS* NE34........ 89 E4
Ashkirk *CRAM* NE23 .... 34 C2
Ashkirk Cl *CLSW/PEL* DH2 .... 165 F1
Ashkirk Wy *MONK* NE25................. 24 C6
Ashleigh Av *DHAM* DH1 .... 194 A1
Ashleigh Cl *BLAY* NE21 .... 94 C1
Ashleigh Crs *WD/WHPE/BLK* NE5 ... 60 C6 **1**
Ashleigh Gv *CLDN/WHIT/ROK* SR6 ... 109 D2 **1**
    JES NE2 .... 63 F4
    LGB/KIL NE12 .... 49 F5
    TYNE/NSHE NE30 .... 55 E4
Ashleigh Rd *WD/WHPE/BLK* NE5 ... 60 C6
Ashley Cl *LGB/KIL* NE12 .... 36 B6
    WASHS NE38 .... 138 C3
Ashley Rd *HAR/WTLS* NE34 .... 88 B2
Ashley Ter *CLS/BIR/GTL* DH3 .... 153 E4
Ashmead Cl *LGB/KIL* NE12 .... 36 A6
Ash Mdw *CLS/BIR/GTL* DH3 .... 154 A1
Ashmore St *ASHBK/HED/RY* SR2 ... 14 B5
Asholme *WD/WHPE/BLK* NE5 .... 60 A5
Ashridge Av *HAR/WTLS* NE34 .... 90 A3 **1**
Ashridge Ct *FELL* NE10 .... 102 A3 **1**
Ash St *BLAY* NE21 .... 94 B1
Ash Ter *SEA/MUR* SR7 .... 188 B1
Ashton Cl *RYTON* NE40.................. 74 C4
Ashton Ri *CLSW/PEL* DH2 .... 153 E6
    PLEE/EAS SR8 .... 209 D1
Ashton St *PLEE/EAS* SR8 .... 201 E2
Ashton Wy *SUNDSW* SR3 .... 159 E2
    WBAY NE26 .... 39 F3
Ashtree Cl *ELS/FEN* NE4 .... 79 E4
    ROWG NE39 .... 111 E1
Ash Tree Dr *BDLGTN* NE22 .... 7 E2
Ashtree La *BLAY* NE21 .... 92 B5
Ashvale Av *DUN/TMV* NE11 .... 116 B6
Ashwell Rd *SUNDSW* SR3 .... 159 F1 **3**
Ashwood *RDHAMSE* DH6 .... 187 F6
Ashwood Av *SWCK/CAS* SR5 .... 125 E2
Ashwood Cl *CRAM* NE23 .... 14 A4
    LGB/KIL NE12 .... 50 A4 **1**
Ashwood Crs *BYK/HTN/WLK* NE6 ... 66 B6 **1**
Ashwood Crt *HEBB* NE31 .... 84 C1 **2**
Ashwood Gdns
    LWF/SPW/WRK NE9 .... 117 F2
Ashwood Gv *DIN/WO* NE13 .... 33 D5
    SWCK/CAS SR5 .... 124 A3 **2**
Ashwood Rd *ASHBK/HED/RY* SR2 ... 144 A1
Ashwood Ter *ASHBK/HED/RY* SR2 ... 144 A1
Askern Av *ASHBK/HED/RY* SR2 ..... 145 F5 **1**
Askerton Dr *PLEE/EAS* SR8 .... 207 F5
Askew Rd *GATE* NE8 .... 80 C6
Askew Rd West *GATE* NE8 .... 98 B3
Askrigg Av *ASHBK/HED/RY* SR2 .... 145 E5
    WLSD/HOW NE28....................... 51 F5
Aspen Cl *DHAM* DH1 .... 195 D3
Aspen Ct *SUNDSW* SR3 .... 160 A2 **1**
Aspley Cl *SUNDSW* SR3 .... 160 C2
Association Rd
    CLDN/WHIT/ROK SR6.................. 127 D2 **1**
Aster Pl *ELS/FEN* NE4 .... 78 B1
Astley Dr *WBAY* NE26 .... 40 A2
Astley Gdns *MONK* NE25 .... 24 B5 **1**
    WBAY NE26 .... 26 A1
Astley Gv *WBAY* NE26 .... 26 A1
Astley Rd *MONK* NE25 .... 24 B4
Aston Sq *SUNDSW* SR3 .... 159 F1 **10**
Aston St *SSH* NE33 .... 88 C1
Athelhampton *WASHS* NE38 .... 139 F1 **1**
Athelstan Rigg
    ASHBK/HED/RY SR2 .... 162 C1 **1**
Athenaeum St *SUND* SR1................ 4 D3
Atherton Dr *ELS/FEN* NE4 .... 79 D4
    HLS DH4 .... 169 F3
Athill St *DHAM* DH1 .... 194 A5
Athlone Pl *CLS/BIR/GTL* DH3 .... 136 C5
Athol Gdns *ASHBK/HED/RY* SR2 .... 162 C2
    MONK NE25 .... 53 F1
Athol Gn *DUN/TMV* NE11 .... 97 F1 **1**
Athol Gv *SUNDSW* SR3 .... 160 C1 **3**
Atholl Gdns *LWF/SPW/WRK* NE9 ... 100 A3 **1**
Athol Rd *ASHBK/HED/RY* SR2 .... 5 F6
Athol Ter *ASHBK/HED/RY* SR2 ...... 5 F6
Athull *CLSW/PEL* DH2 .... 135 E4
Atkinson Gdns *NSHW* NE29 .... 70 C3 **1**
Atkinson Gv *RDHAMSE* DH6........... 206 A1
Atkinson Rd
    CLDN/WHIT/ROK SR6.................. 108 C6 **1**
    CLS/BIR/GTL DH3 .... 153 F3
    ELS/FEN NE4............................. 78 C4

Atkinson St *WLSD/HOW* NE28 .... 67 D5 **1**
Atkinson Ter *ELS/FEN* NE4 .... 78 C3 **1**
  WLSD/HOW NE28 .... 67 D5
Atkin St *LGB/KIL* NE12 .... 35 D5
Atlantis Rd *SUNDSW* SR3 .... 142 B6
Atley Wy *CRAM* NE23 .... 13 D4
Attlee Cl *CRAM* NE23 .... 35 D5 **1**
Attlee Gv *ASHBK/HED/RY* SR2 .... 145 D6
Attwood Gv *SWCK/CAS* SR5 ...... 126 A3 **1**
Aubone Av
  BW/LEM/TK/HW NE15 .... 78 B2 **1**
Auburn Cl *WLSD/HOW* NE28 .... 68 C4
Auburn Gdns *ELS/FEN* NE4 .... 62 A6
Auckland *CLSW/PEL* DH2 .... 152 B6
Auckland Av *HAR/WTLS* NE34 ...... 90 A2
Auckland Rd *DHAM* DH1 .... 180 C5
  HEBB NE31 .... 85 E1
Auckland Ter *JRW* NE32 .... 87 D4
Auden Gv *ELS/FEN* NE4 .... 79 D2
Audley Gdns *SUNDSW* SR3 .... 144 A3
Audley Rd *GOS/KPK* NE3 .... 64 A2
Audouins Rw *GATE* NE8 .... 98 C2 **1**
Augusta St *WLSD/HOW* NE28 .... 52 A6
Augusta Sq *SUNDSW* SR3 .... 159 F1
Augustine Cl *DHAM* DH1 .... 179 F6
August Pl *SSH* NE33 .... 72 A5 **1**
Augustus Dr *BDLGTN* NE22 .... 7 D2
Austen Av *HAR/WTLS* NE34 .... 88 A5
Austen Pl *STLY/ANP* DH9 .... 148 C4
Austin Sq *SWCK/CAS* SR5 .... 126 A2
Australia Gv *HAR/WTLS* NE34 .... 87 E5
Austral Pl *DIN/WO* NE13 .... 32 C5 **2**
Autumn Cl *WASHS* NE38 .... 120 C6
Avalon Dr *BW/LEM/TK/HW* NE15 .... 60 A6
Avalon Rd *SUNDSW* SR3 .... 142 C6
Avebury Dr *WASHS* NE38 .... 139 D1
Avebury Pl *CRAM* NE23 .... 14 B5
Avenue Rd *GATE* NE8 .... 99 E2
  MONK NE25 .... 24 B6
Avenue Ter *ASHBK/HED/RY* SR2 .. 144 B2 **1**
The Avenue *ASHBK/HED/RY* SR2 ..... 4 B6
  BLAY NE21 .... 77 D6
  CLS/BIR/GTL DH3 .... 136 B2
  CLS/BIR/GTL DH3 .... 156 A3
  CLSW/PEL DH2 .... 153 D5
  DHAM DH1 .... 179 F5
  DHAM DH1 .... 193 F5
  HLH DH5 .... 172 A6
  LWF/SPW/WRK NE9 .... 99 F3
  MONK NE25 .... 24 C4
  ROWG NE39 .... 111 E3
  SEA/MUR SR7 .... 175 F3
  STLY/ANP DH9 .... 146 A5
  WASHS NE38 .... 139 D1
  WBAY NE26 .... 40 B5
  WLSD/HOW NE28 .... 67 D5
Avenue Vivian *HLS* DH4 .... 169 E1
Aviemore Rd *BOL* NE36 .... 106 A3
Avision St *ELS/FEN* NE4 .... 80 A3
Avocet Cl *BLYTH* NE24 .... 17 D3
Avolon Pl *ELS/FEN* NE4 .... 80 A2 **2**
Avon Av *JRW* NE32 .... 86 B6
  NSHW NE29 .... 70 A2
Avon Cl *ROWG* NE39 .... 111 E1
  WLSD/HOW NE28 .... 51 F6
Avon Ct *MONK* NE25 .... 24 C3
Avoncroft Cl *SEA/MUR* SR7 .... 174 C2
Avondale *BLYTH* NE24 .... 9 D4
  HLS DH4 .... 157 D1
  LGB/KIL NE12 .... 49 F4 **2**
Avondale Cl *BLYTH* NE24 .... 9 E4 **1**
Avondale Gdns *BOL* NE36 .... 105 F3 **1**
Avondale Rd *BYK/HTN/WLK* NE6 ... 82 B2
Avondale Ter *CLSW/PEL* DH2 ...... 153 E5
  GATE NE8 .... 99 D2
Avonlea Wy *WD/WHPE/BLK* NE5 ... 61 D3 **1**
Avonmouth Rd *SUNDSW* SR3 ..... 159 E1
Avonmouth Sq *SUNDSW* SR3 ..... 159 F1
Avon Rd *HEBB* NE31 .... 85 D4
  PLEE/EAS SR8 .... 208 A3
  STLY/ANP DH9 .... 148 B3
Avon St *GATE* NE8 .... 99 F1
  SUND SR1 .... 5 G4
Awnless Ct *HAR/WTLS* NE34 .... 88 B3 **2**
Axbridge Gdns *ELS/FEN* NE4 .... 79 D4
Axminster Cl *CRAM* NE23 .... 14 B5
Axwell Dr *BLYTH* NE24 .... 10 A5
Axwell Park Rd *BLAY* NE21 .... 95 D1
Axwell Park Vw
  BW/LEM/TK/HW NE15 .... 78 A3
Axwell Vw *BLAY* NE21 .... 94 B1
  WICK/BNPF NE16 .... 95 F3 **1**
Aycliffe Av *LWF/SPW/WRK* NE9 .. 100 C6
Aycliffe Crs *LWF/SPW/WRK* NE9 .. 100 C6
Aydon Gv *JRW* NE32 .... 86 A5
Aykley Cl *DHAM* DH1 .... 193 F2 **1**
Aykley Gn *DHAM* DH1 .... 193 F1
Aykley Rd *DHAM* DH1 .... 180 A6
Aykley V *DHAM* DH1 .... 193 F1
Aylesbury Dr *SUNDSW* SR3 .... 160 C3
Aylesbury Pl *LGB/KIL* NE12 .... 49 D5 **2**
Aylesford Sq *BLYTH* NE24 .... 17 D1 **3**

Aylsham Cl *WD/WHPE/BLK* NE5 .... 59 D2
Aylsham Ct *SUNDSW* SR3 .... 160 C4 **1**
Aylyth Pl *GOS/KPK* NE3 .... 62 B3 **1**
Ayr Dr *JRW* NE32 .... 86 C5
Ayre's Quay Rd *SUND* SR1 .... 4 A2 **1**
Ayre's Ter *NSHW* NE29 .... 54 C6 **3**
Ayrey Av *HAR/WTLS* NE34 .... 87 E4
Aysgarth Av *ASHBK/HED/RY* SR2 .. 145 E4
  WLSD/HOW NE28 .... 51 F5
Ayton Av *ASHBK/HED/RY* SR2 .... 145 E5
Ayton Cl *WD/WHPE/BLK* NE5 .... 60 A3
Ayton Ct *BDLGTN* NE22 .... 6 C2
Ayton Rd *WASHS* NE38 .... 137 E2
Ayton St *BYK/HTN/WLK* NE6 .... 82 B3
Azalea Av *ASHBK/HED/RY* SR2 ...... 4 B6
Azalea Ter North
  ASHBK/HED/RY SR2 .... 4 B5
Azalea Ter South
  ASHBK/HED/RY SR2 .... 4 B6

B

Back Bridge St *SUND* SR1 .... 4 C2
Back Chapman St
  BYK/HTN/WLK NE6 .... 82 B1
Back Croft Rd *BLYTH* NE24 .... 11 D5 **2**
Back George St *ELS/FEN* NE4 .... 2 A6
Back Goldspink La *JES* NE2 .... 81 E1 **1**
Back Heaton Park Rd
  BYK/HTN/WLK NE6 .... 82 A2 **2**
Back La *BLAY* NE21 .... 76 A6
  CLS/BIR/GTL DH3 .... 167 F3
  HLS DH4 .... 140 A6
  MONK NE25 .... 40 A5
Back Lodge Ter *SUND* SR1 .... 5 H3
Back Maling St
  BYK/HTN/WLK NE6 .... 81 F3 **1**
Back Mitford St *ELS/FEN* NE4 .... 80 A5 **1**
Back New Bridge St *CNUT* NE1 ...... 3 G2
Back North Bridge St
  SWCK/CAS SR5 .... 126 C4
Back North Railway St
  SEA/MUR SR7 .... 176 C2
Back North Ter *SEA/MUR* SR7 .... 176 C2
Back Percy Gdns
  TYNE/NSHE NE30 .... 55 F4 **2**
Back Rw *WICK/BNPF* NE16 .... 95 F3
Back Ryhope St
  ASHBK/HED/RY SR2 .... 162 A1
Back Silver St *DHAM* DH1 .... 194 B4 **1**
Back South Railway St
  SEA/MUR SR7 .... 176 C3
Back Stephen St
  BYK/HTN/WLK NE6 .... 81 F2 **1**
Back St *BLAY* NE21 .... 94 A1 **1**
Back Walker Rd
  BYK/HTN/WLK NE6 .... 83 F4 **1**
Back Western HI *DHAM* DH1 .... 194 A3 **1**
Back Woodbine St *GATE* NE8 .... 98 C1
Backworth La *CRAM* NE23 .... 36 B2
Baden Crs *SWCK/CAS* SR5 .... 123 F1
Baden Powell St
  LWF/SPW/WRK NE9 .... 99 F3 **1**
Baden St *CLS/BIR/GTL* DH3 .... 153 E6
Badger Cl *SUNDSW* SR3 .... 160 C5
Badminton Cl *BOLCOL* NE35 ...... 104 C1 **1**
Baffin Ct *SUNDSW* SR3 .... 160 B2
Baildon Cl *WLSD/HOW* NE28 .... 67 E2 **1**
Bailey Ri *PLEE/EAS* SR8 .... 200 C6
Bailey Sq *SWCK/CAS* SR5 .... 105 F6 **1**
Bailey Wy *HLH* DH5 .... 186 A2
Bainbridge Av *HAR/WTLS* NE34 .... 87 E4
  SUNDSW SR3 .... 144 A3
Bainbridge Holme Cl
  SUNDSW SR3 .... 144 A3
Bainbridge Holme Rd
  SUNDSW SR3 .... 144 B3
Bainbridge St *DHAM* DH1 .... 196 C1
Bainford Av *BW/LEM/TK/HW* NE15 .. 77 F2
Baird Av *WLSD/HOW* NE28 .... 69 E4
Baird Cl *WASHN* NE37 .... 121 D2
Baird St *SWCK/CAS* SR5 .... 123 F1 **1**
Bakehouse La *DHAM* DH1 .... 194 C4
Baker Gdns *FELL* NE10 .... 102 A2
Baker Rd *CRAM* NE23 .... 12 C5
Baker St *HLH* DH5 .... 171 D1
  SWCK/CAS SR5 .... 123 F1
Bakewell Ter *BYK/HTN/WLK* NE6 ... 82 C4
Baldersdale Gdns *SUNDSW* SR3 .. 144 A4
Baldwin Av *BOL* NE36 .... 106 C3
  ELS/FEN NE4 .... 79 E1 **1**
Balfour Rd *BW/LEM/TK/HW* NE15 .. 77 F3
Balfour St *BLYTH* NE24 .... 10 C3
  GATE NE8 .... 98 C1 **2**
  HLH DH5 .... 171 D1
Balgonie Cottages *RYTON* NE40 .... 74 B3
Baliol Sq *DHAM* DH1 .... 204 C1 **1**
Balkwell Av *NSHW* NE29 .... 69 F1
Balkwell Gn *NSHW* NE29 .... 54 A6
Ballast HI *BLYTH* NE24 .... 11 E4 **1**
Ballast Hill Rd *NSHW* NE29 .... 70 C3
Ballater Cl *STLY/ANP* DH9 .... 149 D2
Balliol Av *LGB/KIL* NE12 .... 49 E3

Balliol Cl *PLEE/EAS* SR8.............. 208 A2
Balliol Gdns *LGB/HTN* NE7 .... 65 D1 **1**
Balmain Rd *GOS/KPK* NE3 .... 62 A2
Balmoral Av *GOS/KPK* NE3 .... 64 A2 **2**
  JRW NE32 .... 87 D5 **1**
Balmoral Cl *BDLGTN* NE22 .... 8 B2
Balmoral Ct *SWCK/CAS* SR5 ...... 123 F1 **2**
Balmoral Crs *HLH* DH5 .... 171 E3
Balmoral Dr *FELL* NE10 .... 100 B2
Balmoral Gdns *NSHW* NE29 .... 54 B5
Balmoral St *WLSD/HOW* NE28...... 67 D2
Balmoral Ter *ASHBK/HED/RY* SR2 .. 145 E4
  BYK/HTN/WLK NE6 .... 82 A1
  GOS/KPK NE3 .... 64 A2
  SUNDSW SR3 .... 159 E1
Balmoral Wy *FELL* NE10 .... 100 B3
Balroy Ct *LGB/KIL* NE12 .... 50 A4
Baltic Millennium Br *CNUT* NE1 ..... 3 G5
Baltic Rd *FELL* NE10 .... 82 C5
Baltimore Av *SWCK/CAS* SR5 ..... 105 D6
Baltimore Sq *SWCK/CAS* SR5 .... 123 E1
Bamborough Ct *CRAM* NE23 .... 34 B2 **1**
Bamborough Ter *TYNE/NSHE* NE30.. 54 C5
Bambro' St *ASHBK/HED/RY* SR2 ..... 5 F6 **1**
Bamburgh Av *SSH* NE33 .... 72 B5
Bamburgh Cl *BLYTH* NE24 .... 10 B5
  WASHS NE38 .... 137 F1
Bamburgh Dr *DUN/TMV* NE11...... 98 B4
Bamburgh Dr *FELL* NE10 .... 84 A6 **1**
  WLSD/HOW NE28 .... 68 B4
Bamburgh Gdns *SUNDSW* SR3 .. 144 A3 **1**
Bamburgh Gv *HAR/WTLS* NE34.... 73 D6
Bamburgh Rd *DHAM* DH1 .... 180 B5
  LGB/KIL NE12 .... 50 A4
  WD/WHPE/BLK NE5 .... 60 A3 **1**
Bampton Av *CLDN/WHIT/ROK* SR6... 108 B5
Banbury *WASHN* NE37 .... 121 D4
Banbury Gdns *WLSD/HOW* NE28 .. 67 F1 **1**
Banbury Rd *GOS/KPK* NE3 .... 46 B6
Banbury Ter *SSH* NE33 .... 71 F6
Banbury Wy *BLYTH* NE24 .... 16 C1
  NSHW NE29 .... 69 F2
Bancroft Ter *MLFD/PNYW* SR4 .... 125 E6
Banesley La *DUN/TMV* NE11 ...... 116 A3
Banff St *SWCK/CAS* SR5 .... 105 F6
Bank Av *WICK/BNPF* NE16 .... 95 F3
Bankdale Gdns *BLYTH* NE24 .... 9 F5
Bankhead Rd
  BW/LEM/TK/HW NE15 .... 58 B5 **1**
Bankhead Ter *HLS* DH4 .... 169 F1
Bank Rd *GATE* NE8 .... 3 G6
Banks Holt *CLSW/PEL* DH2 .... 152 B6 **1**
Bankside Cl *ASHBK/HED/RY* SR2 .. 162 A1
Bankside La *HAR/WTLS* NE34 .... 88 B3
Bankside Rd *BW/LEM/TK/HW* NE15.. 77 E3
Bankwell La *GATE* NE8 .... 3 F6
Bannister Dr *LGB/KIL* NE12 .... 50 B4
Bannockburn *LGB/KIL* NE12 .... 35 F6 **3**
Barbara St *ASHBK/HED/RY* SR2 .. 145 E3
Barbary Cl *CLSW/PEL* DH2 .... 152 A1
Barbary Dr *CLDN/WHIT/ROK* SR6 .. 127 E2
Barbondale Lonnen
  WD/WHPE/BLK NE5 .... 59 E5
Barbour Av *HAR/WTLS* NE34 .... 89 F1
Barclay Pl *WD/WHPE/BLK* NE5 .... 61 D5
Barclay St *SWCK/CAS* SR5 .... 126 C4 **1**
Barcusclose La *WICK/BNPF* NE16.. 112 B6
Bardolph Rd *NSHW* NE29 .... 53 F6
Bardon Cl *WD/WHPE/BLK* NE5 .... 60 B2 **1**
Bardon Crs *MONK* NE25 .... 25 E6 **1**
Bardsey Pl *LGB/KIL* NE12 .... 49 D6
Barehirst St *SSH* NE33 .... 88 A1
Barents Cl *WD/WHPE/BLK* NE5 .... 60 B4 **1**
Baret Rd *BYK/HTN/WLK* NE6 .... 66 A6
Barford Dr *CLSW/PEL* DH2 .... 165 F1
Baring St *SSH* NE33 .... 71 E2
Barker St *JES* NE2 .... 3 G1
Barking Crs *SWCK/CAS* SR5 .... 123 E1
Barking Sq *SWCK/CAS* SR5 .... 123 E1 **1**
Barkwood Rd *ROWG* NE39 .... 110 C2
Barlow Crs *BLAY* NE21 .... 92 B4 **1**
Barlow Fell Rd *BLAY* NE21 .... 92 B5
Barlowfield Cl *BLAY* NE21 .... 93 F2 **1**
Barlow La *BLAY* NE21 .... 92 C4
Barmoor La *RYTON* NE40 .... 74 A3
Barmouth Cl *WLSD/HOW* NE28 .... 67 F1 **2**
Barmouth Rd *NSHW* NE29 .... 69 E2
Barmouth Wy *NSHW* NE29 .... 69 F2
Barmston La *WASHN* NE37 .... 122 B6
  WASHS NE38 .... 140 A1
Barmston Rd *WASHS* NE38 .... 139 F2
Barmston Wy *WASHS* NE38 .... 121 E6
Barnard Cl *BDLGTN* NE22 .... 6 C3
  DHAM DH1 .... 180 C5
Barnard Crs *HEBB* NE31 .... 85 E2
Barnard Gv *JRW* NE32 .... 86 C4 **1**
Barnard St *BLYTH* NE24 .... 11 D5 **3**
  MLFD/PNYW SR4 .... 143 E1
Barnard Wynd *PLEE/EAS* SR8 .... 208 A5
Barnesbury Rd *ELS/FEN* NE4 .... 79 D3
Barnes Park Rd *MLFD/PNYW* SR4 .. 143 F2
Barnes Rd *SEA/MUR* SR7 .... 188 A1
  SSH NE33 .... 71 D6 **1**
Barnes Vw *MLFD/PNYW* SR4 ...... 143 E2

Barn HI *STLY/ANP* DH9 .... **148** A1
Barn Hollows *SEA/MUR* SR7 .... **190** B5
Barningham *WASHS* NE38 .... **139** F2
Barningham CI *SUNDSW* SR3................ **144** A4
Barns CI *JRW* NE32 .... **85** F4
Barnstaple CI *WLSD/HOW* NE28 ...... **67** F1 🔢
Barnstaple Rd *NSHW* NE29 .... **53** E4
The Barns *STLY/ANP* DH9 .... **131** D6
Barnton Rd *FELL* NE10 .... **101** D4
Barnwood CI *WLSD/HOW* NE28 ...... **67** E1 🔢
Baroness Dr *BW/LEM/TK/HW* NE15 .. **77** F1
Baron's Quay Rd *SWCK/CAS* SR5 .... **124** A4
Baronswood *GOS/KPK* NE3 .... **63** D2
Barrack Rd *ELS/FEN* NE4 .... **80** A1
Barrack St *SUND* SR1 .... **127** E4
Barras Av *BLYTH* NE24 .... **16** C1
  CRAM NE23 .... **35** D1
Barras Av West *BLYTH* NE24 .... **16** B2
Barras Br *CNUT* NE1 .... **2** D1
Barras Dr *SUNDSW* SR3 .... **144** A4
Barrasford CI *GOS/KPK* NE3 .... **62** C2
Barrasford Dr *DIN/WO* NE13 .... **33** E5
Barrasford Rd *CRAM* NE23 .... **22** B3 🔢
  DHAM DH1 .... **180** C6
Barrasford Av *WLSD/HOW* NE28 .... **69** E5 🔢
Barrass Av *CRAM* NE23................................ **36** A1
Barr CI *WLSD/HOW* NE28 .... **68** A1
Barrie Sq *SWCK/CAS* SR5 .... **126** A2
Barrington Av *TYNE/NSHE* NE30 ...... **54** B2
Barrington Ct *BDLGTN* NE22 .... **7** F4 🔢
Barrington Dr *WASHS* NE38 .... **138** C1
Barrington Pk *BDLGTN* NE22 .... **9** E1
Barrington Rd *BDLGTN* NE22 .... **8** B1
  STKFD/GP NE62 .... **7** E1
Barrington St *SSH* NE33 .... **71** E3 🔢
Barrington Ter *HLH* DH5 .... **171** F5 🔢
Barron St South *SWCK/CAS* SR5 .... **124** B3 🔢
Barrowburn PI *CRAM* NE23 .... **36** C1
Barrow St *SWCK/CAS* SR5 .... **105** F6 🔢
Barry St *DUN/TMV* NE11 .... **97** E1
  GATE NE8 .... **98** C3
Barsloan Gv *PLEE/EAS* SR8 .... **200** A6 🔢
Barton Ct *TYNE/NSHE* NE30 .... **55** D3
  WASHN NE37 .... **121** D2
  WLSD/HOW NE28 .... **67** F1 🔢
Barton Ct *CLDN/WHIT/ROK* SR6 .... **108** B5 🔢
Bartram Gdns *GATE* NE8 .... **99** D3 🔢
Bartram St *SWCK/CAS* SR5 .... **126** B1
Barwell CI *WLSD/HOW* NE28 .... **67** F1
Barwell Ct *LGB/HTN* NE7 .... **66** A3
Basildon Gdns *WLSD/HOW* NE28 ... **67** E1 🔢
Basil Wy *HAR/WTLS* NE34 .... **89** D5
Basingstoke PI *LGB/KIL* NE12 .... **49** E5
Basingstoke Rd *PLEE/EAS* SR8 .... **208** B1 🔢
Baslow Gdns *SUNDSW* SR3 .... **144** A3
Bassington Av *CRAM* NE23 .... **21** D1
Bassington CI *ELS/FEN* NE4 .... **80** A3 🔢
Bassington Dr *CRAM* NE23 .... **12** C6
Bassington La *CRAM* NE23 .... **12** C6
Bates La *BLAY* NE21 .... **77** E6
Bath CI *WLSD/HOW* NE28................. .... **68** A1
Bathgate CI *WLSD/HOW* NE28............ **68** A1
Bathgate Sq *SWCK/CAS* SR5 .... **123** E1 🔢
Bath La *BLYTH* NE24 .... **11** E5
  CNUT NE1 .... **2** B4
Bath Rd *FELL* NE10 .... **82** C6
  HEBB NE31 .... **85** D5 🔢
Bath St *BYK/HTN/WLK* NE6 .... **83** F3
Bath Ter *BLYTH* NE24 .... **11** E5
  GOS/KPK NE3 .... **63** F1
  TYNE/NSHE NE30 .... **55** D3
Batley St *SWCK/CAS* SR5 .... **123** E1 🔢
Battle Hill Dr *WLSD/HOW* NE28 ...... **68** D2
  WLSD/HOW NE28 .... **68** B1
Baugh CI *WASHN* NE37 .... **119** F6
Baulkham Hills *HLH* DH4 .... **157** D2
Bavington *FELL* NE10 .... **101** F5 🔢
Bavington Dr *WD/WHPE/BLK* NE5 ... **61** E5
Bavington Gdns *TYNE/NSHE* NE30... **54** C3
Bavington Rd *MONK* NE25 .... **24** C5
Bawtry Gv *NSHW* NE29 .... **70** A1
Baxter Av *ELS/FEN* NE4 .... **79** D2
Baxter Rd *SWCK/CAS* SR5 .... **105** E6
Baxter Sq *SWCK/CAS* SR5 .... **105** E6 🔢
Baybridge Rd
  WD/WHPE/BLK NE5 .... **60** A3 🔢
Baysdale *HLS* DH4 .... **139** D6 🔢
Bayswater Av *SWCK/CAS* SR5 .... **123** E1
Bayswater Rd *GATE* NE8 .... **100** A2 🔢
  JES NE2 .... **64** A4
Bayswater Sq *SWCK/CAS* SR5 .... **123** F1 🔢
Baytree Gdns *MONK* NE25....................... **54** A1
Baytree Ter *STLY/ANP* DH9 .... **151** D1
Baywood Gv *WLSD/HOW* NE28 .... **67** E1 🔢
Beach Av *WBAY* NE26 .... **40** C5
Beach Croft Av *TYNE/NSHE* NE30 ..... **55** D2
Beachcross Rd
  MLFD/PNYW SR4 .... **144** A1 🔢
Beach Gv *PLEE/EAS* SR8 .... **209** F2 🔢
Beach Rd *NSHW* NE29 .... **54** A5
  SSH NE33 .... **71** F4
  TYNE/NSHE NE30 .... **54** C4
Beach St *MLFD/PNYW* SR4 .... **126** A4
Beachville St *MLFD/PNYW* SR4 ..... **144** A1 🔢
Beachway *BLYTH* NE24 .... **17** E2

Beach Wy *TYNE/NSHE* NE30 .... **54** C3
Beacon Dr *CLDN/WHIT/ROK* SR6..... **127** E3
  DIN/WO NE13 .... **32** C5
Beacon Gld *HAR/WTLS* NE34 .... **90** B2
Beacon La *CRAM* NE23 .... **20** C2
Beacon Lough Rd
  LWF/SPW/WRK NE9 .... **99** F6
Beaconsfield Av
  LWF/SPW/WRK NE9 .... **99** F5
Beaconsfield CI *MONK* NE25 .... **39** F3
Beaconsfield Crs
  LWF/SPW/WRK NE9 .... **99** F5 🔢
Beaconsfield Rd
  LWF/SPW/WRK NE9 .... **99** E5
Beaconsfield St *BLYTH* NE24 .... **11** E4 🔢
  ELS/FEN NE4.. **79** F3
  STLY/ANP DH9 .... **148** B1 🔢
Beaconside *HAR/WTLS* NE34................. **90** B2
Beacon St *LWF/SPW/WRK* NE9 .... **99** E5
  SSH NE33 .... **71** E2
  TYNE/NSHE NE30 .... **55** D6
Beadling Gdns *ELS/FEN* NE4 .... **79** D2
Beadnell Av *NSHW* NE29 .... **69** F2
Beadnell CI *BLAY* NE21 .... **93** F2
Beadnell Gdns *SMOOR* NE27 .... **52** B1
Beadnell PI *JES* NE2 .... **3** G2
Beadnell Rd *BLYTH* NE24 .... **16** A1
Beadnell Wy *GOS/KPK* NE3 .... **46** C6 🔢
Beal CI *BLYTH* NE24 .... **10** B5
Beal Dr *LGB/KIL* NE12 .... **50** B4
Beal Gdns *WLSD/HOW* NE28................. **68** B1
Beal Rd *SMOOR* NE27 .... **52** B1
Beal Ter *BYK/HTN/WLK* NE6 .... **85** E4
Beal Wy *GOS/KPK* NE3............................. **63** D1
Beaminster Wy *GOS/KPK* NE3 .... **61** E1
  WD/WHPE/BLK NE5................................... **61** E1
Beamishburn Rd *STLY/ANP* DH9 ..... **131** F5
Beamish CI *WLSD/HOW* NE28 .... **67** E1 🔢
Beamish Gdns
  LWF/SPW/WRK NE9 .... **100** C6
Beamish Hills *STLY/ANP* DH9 .... **149** F1
Beamish St *STLY/ANP* DH9 .... **148** A1 🔢
Beamish Vw *CLSW/PEL* DH2 .... **151** D5
  STLY/ANP DH9 .... **149** D1
Beaney La *CLSW/PEL* DH2 .... **165** E4
Beanley Av *HEBB* NE31 .... **84** C4
Beanley Crs *TYNE/NSHE* NE30............. **55** E5
Beanley PI *LGB/HTN* NE7 .... **64** C3
Bearpark Colliery Rd
  BDN/LAN/SAC DH7 .... **192** A3
Beatrice Av *BLYTH* NE24 .... **16** A2 🔢
Beatrice Gdns *BOL* NE36 .... **106** C3 🔢
  HAR/WTLS NE34 .... **89** D2
Beatrice St *CLDN/WHIT/ROK* SR6 .... **127** D1
Beatrice Ter *HLS* DH4 .... **139** D5
Beattie St *HAR/WTLS* NE34 .... **88** A3 🔢
Beatty Av *JES* NE2 .... **64** A3
Beatty Rd *BDLGTN* NE22 .... **8** A4
Beaufort CI *HLS* DH4 .... **157** D3 🔢
  WD/WHPE/BLK NE5 .... **61** F3 🔢
Beaufort Gdns *WLSD/HOW* NE28 .... **67** E1 🔢
Beaufront CI *FELL* NE10 .... **102** A4 🔢
Beaufront Gdns *GATE* NE8 .... **100** A1 🔢
  WD/WHPE/BLK NE5 .... **61** E6
Beaufront Ter *JRW* NE32 .... **86** A5
  SSH NE33 .... **71** E6 🔢
Beauly *WASHS* NE38 .... **138** C3 🔢
Beaumaris Gdns *SUNDSW* SR3 .... **159** E1
Beaumaris Wy *WD/WHPE/BLK* NE5 .. **61** D2
Beaumont Dr *DHAM* DH1 .... **179** F5
Beaumont Crs *PLEE/EAS* SR8 .... **201** D5
Beaumont Dr *MONK* NE25........................ **39** E3
  WASHS NE38 .... **138** C2
Beaumont Mnr *BLYTH* NE24 .... **9** E5
Beaumont PI *PLEE/EAS* SR8 .... **209** D3 🔢
Beaumont St
  ASHBK/HED/RY SR2 .... **145** D2 🔢
  BLYTH NE24.. **10** C4
  ELS/FEN NE4 .... **79** E5
  NSHW NE29 .... **70** C1 🔢
  SEA/MUR SR7 .... **176** C4 🔢
  SWCK/CAS SR5 .... **125** F1
Beaumont Ter *GOS/KPK* NE3 .... **63** F1
  JRW NE32 .... **85** F3
  WD/WHPE/BLK NE5..................................... **60** B4
Beaver CI *DHAM* DH1 .... **180** D4
Bebdon Ct *BLYTH* NE24 .... **10** B6 🔢
Bebside Furnace Rd *BLYTH* NE24......... **8** E4
Bebside Rd *BLYTH* NE24 .... **8** B5
Beckenham Av *BOL* NE36 .... **106** C2
Beckenham CI *BOL* NE36 .... **107** D3 🔢
Beckenham Gdns
  WLSD/HOW NE28 .... **67** E2
Beckett St *GATE* NE8 .... **81** F4 🔢
Beckfoot CI *WD/WHPE/BLK* NE5 .... **61** D5
Beckford *WASHS* NE38 .... **139** F2
Beckford St *WLSD/HOW* NE28 .... **67** E1 🔢
Beck PI *PLEE/EAS* SR8............................. **208** C1
Beckside Gdns *WD/WHPE/BLK* NE5 .. **59** D5
Beckwith Rd *SUNDSW* SR3 .... **142** B6
Beda HI *BLAY* NE21 .... **76** B5
Bedale CI *DHAM* DH1 .... **196** C2
  WLSD/HOW NE28 .... **67** E1 🔢
Bedale Crs *SWCK/CAS* SR5 .... **123** F1
Bedale Dr *MONK* NE25 .... **54** B1

Bedale Gn *WD/WHPE/BLK* NE5 .... **61** F3
Bedale St *HLH* DH5 .... **185** F2
Bedburn *WASHS* NE38 .... **137** E5
Bede Av *DHAM* DH1 .... **195** F5
Bede Burn Rd *JRW* NE32 .... **86** A2 🔢
Bede Burn Vw *JRW* NE32....................... **86** A3
Bede CI *LGB/KIL* NE12............................... **51** D4
Bede Ct *CLS/BIR/GTL* DH3 .... **153** E5
  GATE NE8 .... **81** F6 🔢
Bede Crs *WASHS* NE38 .... **120** B6
  WLSD/HOW NE28 .... **67** F2
Bede St *CLDN/WHIT/ROK* SR6 .... **127** D2
  PLEE/EAS SR8 .... **201** E2
Bedesway *JRW* NE32 .... **86** A4
Bede Ter *BOL* NE36 .... **107** D3 🔢
  CLSW/PEL DH2 .... **153** D5
  JRW NE32 .... **86** B3 🔢
Bede Wk *HEBB* NE31 .... **85** E3
Bede Wy *DHAM* DH1 .... **180** A6 🔢
  PLEE/EAS SR8 .... **208** C2
Bedford Av *CLS/BIR/GTL* DH3 .... **136** C5
  SSH NE33 .... **71** E5
  WLSD/HOW NE28....................................... **66** C3
Bedford PI *SUNDSW* SR3 .... **143** F6 🔢
  WD/WHPE/BLK NE5................................... **59** E5 🔢
Bedford Rd *WLSD/HOW* NE28 .... **60** E1 🔢
Bedford St *NSHW* NE29 .... **70** C1 🔢
  NSHW NE29 .... **71** D1 🔢
  SUND SR1 .... **14** E3
Bedford Wy *NSHW* NE29 .... **70** C1
Bedlington Bank *BDLGTN* NE22 .... **7** F4
  CRAM NE23 .... **22** C3
  DIN/WO NE13 .... **31** D3
  GOS/KPK NE3 .... **46** B6
  HLS DH4 .... **170** C1
  WICK/BNPF NE16 .... **96** B2
Beechburn Wk *ELS/FEN* NE4 .... **79** F3 🔢
Beech CI *DHAM* DH1 .... **181** D4
  GOS/KPK NE3 .... **47** F3 🔢
Beech Crs *SEA/MUR* SR7 .... **176** B4
Beechcroft Av *BDN/LAN/SAC* DH7 .. **202** B5 🔢
  GOS/KPK NE3 .... **62** C3
Beechcroft CI *JRW* NE32 .... **86** C2 🔢
Beech Dr *DUN/TMV* NE11 .... **97** D1
Beecher St *BLYTH* NE24 .... **10** A3 🔢
Beechfield Gdns
  WLSD/HOW NE28....................................... **66** C3 🔢
Beechfield Rd *GOS/KPK* NE3 .... **63** D2
Beech Gv *BDN/LAN/SAC* DH7 .... **192** A5 🔢
  HAR/WTLS NE34 .... **89** E4
  LGB/KIL NE12 .... **49** F6
  LWF/SPW/WRK NE9 .... **119** E3
  WBAY NE26 .... **40** B5
  WLSD/HOW NE28 .... **67** D4
Beech Grove Rd *ELS/FEN* NE4 .... **79** F4
Beech Pk *BDN/LAN/SAC* DH7 .... **202** C5 🔢
Beech Rd *DHAM* DH1 .... **194** A1
  RDHAMSE DH6 .... **197** E4
Beech Sq *WASHS* NE38 .... **139** D2 🔢
Beech St *ELS/FEN* NE4 .... **79** D4
  GATE NE8 .... **100** A1
  JRW NE32 .... **85** F1
Beech Ter *BLAY* NE21 .... **94** B1 🔢
  STLY/ANP DH9 .... **149** D5
Beech Wy *LGB/KIL* NE12 .... **35** E6 🔢
Beechways *DHAM* DH1 .... **193** E3
Beechwood Av
  LWF/SPW/WRK NE9 .... **117** F1
  MONK NE25 .... **39** F6
  RYTON NE40 .... **74** B3
Beechwood CI *JRW* NE32 .... **86** C2 🔢
Beechwood Crs *SWCK/CAS* SR5 ...... **125** E2
Beechwood Gdns *DUN/TMV* NE11 ..... **98** A5
Beechwood PI *PONT/DH* NE20 .... **28** A3
Beechwoods *CLSW/PEL* DH2 .... **153** D3
Beechwood St
  ASHBK/HED/RY SR2 .... **144** A1
Beechwood Ter
  ASHBK/HED/RY SR2 .... **144** A1 🔢
  HLS DH4 .... **139** D5
Beeston Av *SWCK/CAS* SR5 .... **123** E1 🔢
Beetham Crs *WD/WHPE/BLK* NE5 ...... **60** C6
Beethoven St *SSH* NE33 .... **71** E4 🔢
Begonia CI *HEBB* NE31 .... **85** D5 🔢
Bek Rd *DHAM* DH1 .... **180** B6
Beldene Dr *MLFD/PNYW* SR4 .... **143** D2
Belford Av *SMOOR* NE27 .... **52** B1
Belford CI *ASHBK/HED/RY* SR2 .... **144** C3
  WLSD/HOW NE28 .... **67** E1 🔢
Belford Gdns *DUN/TMV* NE11 .... **97** F5 🔢
Belford Rd *ASHBK/HED/RY* SR2 .... **145** D3
Belford St *PLEE/EAS* SR8 .... **201** E6 🔢
Belford Ter *BYK/HTN/WLK* NE6 .... **83** D5
  TYNE/NSHE NE30 .... **54** C5
The Belfry *HLS* DH4 .... **156** C4
Belgrade Crs *SWCK/CAS* SR5 .... **105** E6
Belgrade Sq *SWCK/CAS* SR5 .... **123** E1 🔢
Belgrave Crs *BLYTH* NE24 .... **11** E5
Belgrave Pde *ELS/FEN* NE4 .... **80** A2
Belgrave Ter *FELL* NE10 .... **100** C3 🔢
  SSH NE33 .... **71** E3
Bellburn Ct *CRAM* NE23 .... **14** C6 🔢
Belle Gv West *JES* NE2 .... **80** A1 🔢

Bellerby Dr *CLSW/PEL* DH2 .... 135 D4 🔟
Belle St *STLY/ANP* DH9 .... 148 B1
Belle Vue Av *GOS/KPK* NE3 .... 63 F1
Belle Vue Bank *LWF/SPW/WRK* NE9.. 99 D5
Bellevue Crs *CRAM* NE23 .... 14 A4 🔟
Belle Vue Crs *SSH* NE33 .... 88 A2 🔟
Belle Vue Gv *LWF/SPW/WRK* NE9 .... 99 E5 🔟
Belle Vue Pk *ASHBK/HED/RY* SR2 .. 144 D2
Belle Vue Rd *ASHBK/HED/RY* SR2 ... 144 B2
Bellfield Av *GOS/KPK* NE3 .... 46 B6 🔟
Bellgreen Av *GOS/KPK* NE3 .... 47 F3
Bell Gv *LGB/KIL* NE12 .... 35 D6 🔟
Bell House Rd *SWCK/CAS* SR5 ...... 107 F5
Bellingham Cl *WLSD/HOW* NE28 ..... 67 F2 🔟
Bellingham Ct *GOS/KPK* NE3 .... 61 F1 🔟
Bellingham Dr *LGB/KIL* NE12........... 50 B5
Bellister Gv *WD/WHPE/BLK* NE5 ..... 61 E6
Bellister Pk *PLEE/EAS* SR8 .... 209 D4
Bellister Rd *NSHW* NE29 .... 53 F6 🔟
Bell Meadow *BDN/LAN/SAC* DH7 .... 202 C5
Belloc Av *HAR/WTLS* NE34 .... 88 A5
Bells Cl *BLYTH* NE24...................... 9 E4
  BW/LEM/TK/HW NE15............... 77 D3
Bell's Folly *DHAM* DH1 .... 204 C1
Bellshill Cl *WLSD/HOW* NE28 .... 52 A6
Bell's Pl *BDLGTN* NE22 .... 7 F4
Bell St *HEBB* NE31......................... 84 C2
  HLS DH4 .... 140 A6
  MLFD/PNYW SR4 .... 125 E6 🔟
  TYNE/NSHE NE30..................... 71 D1
  WASHS NE38 .... 139 E2 🔟
Belmont *FELL* NE10......................... 101 F5
Belmont Av *MONK* NE25 .... 39 F6
  SEA/MUR SR7 .... 190 A4
Belmont Cl *WLSD/HOW* NE28 .... 67 F1
Belmont Ri *HLH* DH5........................ 185 F3
Belmont Rd *MLFD/PNYW* SR4........ 143 E1
Belmont St *BYK/HTN/WLK* NE6 ...... 83 E5
Belmount Av *GOS/KPK* NE3 .... 47 F3
Belper Cl *WLSD/HOW* NE28 .... 67 E1 🔟
Belsay *WASHS* NE38 .... 137 E2
Belsay Av *DIN/WO* NE13 .... 32 C6 🔟
  HAR/WTLS NE34....................... 89 F1
  MONK NE25................................ 41 D6
Belsay Cl *WLSD/HOW* NE28 .... 67 E1 🔟
Belsay Ct *BLYTH* NE24 .... 10 B5 🔟
Belsay Gdns *DUN/TMV* NE11 .... 97 F5 🔟
  GOS/KPK NE3 .... 46 B4
  MLFD/PNYW SR4 .... 143 E1
Belsay Pl *ELS/FEN* NE4 .... 79 F2 🔟
Belsfield Gdns *JRW* NE32 .... 86 A4
Belsize Pl *BYK/HTN/WLK* NE6 .... 66 B6
Beltingham *WD/WHPE/BLK* NE5 ..... 60 A5 🔟
Belvedere *NSHW* NE29 .... 54 B5
Belvedere Av *MONK* NE25 .... 40 B6
Belvedere Gdns *LGB/KIL* NE12 .... 49 F6 🔟
Belvedere Pkwy *GOS/KPK* NE3 ...... 45 E6 🔟
Belvedere Rd *ASHBK/HED/RY* SR2 ... 4 B6
Belverdere Gdns *RDHAMSE* DH6 .... 206 A1
Bemersyde Dr *JES* NE2 .... 64 A3
Benbrake Av *NSHW* NE29 .... 54 A3
Bendigo Av *HAR/WTLS* NE34 .... 87 E5 🔟
Benedict Rd *CLDN/WHIT/ROK* SR6 .. 127 E2
Benevente St *SEA/MUR* SR7 .... 176 C4 🔟
Benfield Gv *WBAY* NE26 .... 26 A1
Benfield Rd *BYK/HTN/WLK* NE6 ...... 65 F4
Benjamin Rd *WLSD/HOW* NE28........ 68 C3
Benridge Bank *HLS* DH4................. 183 E2
Bensham Av *GATE* NE8 .... 98 C1
Bensham Ct *HAR/WTLS* NE34 .... 88 B3 🔟
Bensham Crs *GATE* NE8.................. 98 B1
Bensham Rd *GATE* NE8 .... 81 D6
Benson Rd *BYK/HTN/WLK* NE6 ...... 82 C2
Benson St *CLS/BIR/GTL* DH3 .... 153 E6
  STLY/ANP DH9 .... 148 A1
Bent House La *DHAM* DH1 .... 195 F6
Bentinck Rd *ELS/FEN* NE4 .... 79 E4
Benton Bank *BYK/HTN/WLK* NE6 .... 64 C5
  JES NE2 .... 64 C5
Benton Cl *LGB/HTN* NE7 .... 65 D1 🔟
Benton Hall Wk *LGB/HTN* NE7 .... 65 F4 🔟
Benton La *LGB/KIL* NE12 .... 49 D5
Benton Lodge Av *LGB/HTN* NE7 ..... 65 E1 🔟
Benton Park Rd *LGB/HTN* NE7 .... 64 B1
Benton Rd *HAR/WTLS* NE34............ 88 B6
  LGB/HTN NE7 .... 65 E1
  SMOOR NE27 .... 51 F2
Benton Wy *WLSD/HOW* NE28 .... 67 D5 🔟
Bents Park Rd *SSH* NE33 .... 72 A3
Benwell Dene Ter
  BW/LEM/TK/HW NE15............... 78 B3
Benwell Grange Av
  BW/LEM/TK/HW NE15............... 78 C3 🔟
Benwell Grange Rd
  BW/LEM/TK/HW NE15............... 78 B2
Benwell Grange Ter
  BW/LEM/TK/HW NE15............... 78 B3
Benwell Gv *ELS/FEN* NE4................ 79 D3
Benwell Hall Dr
  BW/LEM/TK/HW NE15............... 78 A2 🔟
Benwell Hill Gdns
  WD/WHPE/BLK NE5................... 78 B1 🔟
Benwell Hill Rd
  WD/WHPE/BLK NE5................... 78 A1

Benwell La
  BW/LEM/TK/HW NE15............... 78 A3 🔟
Benwell Village
  BW/LEM/TK/HW NE15............... 78 A2
Benwell Village Ms
  BW/LEM/TK/HW NE15............... 78 B2 🔟
Beresford Av *HEBB* NE31 .... 85 D5
Beresford Gdns *BYK/HTN/WLK* NE6.. 82 B3
Beresford Pk *ASHBK/HED/RY* SR2 .... 4 A5
  ASHBK/HED/RY SR2 .... 144 A1 🔟
Beresford Rd *TYNE/NSHE* NE30 ..... 54 C1
  WBAY NE26 .... 26 C3
Bergen Cl *NSHW* NE29 .... 69 D2
Bergen Sq *SWCK/CAS* SR5 .... 105 E6 🔟
Bergen St *SWCK/CAS* SR5............ 105 E6
Berkdale Rd *LWF/SPW/WRK* NE9 ... 117 D2
Berkeley Cl *BOLCOL* NE35 .... 105 D1
  LGB/KIL NE12 .... 36 A6
  SUNDSW SR3........................... 159 E1 🔟
Berkeley Sq *GOS/KPK* NE3 .... 47 D5 🔟
Berkely St *SSH* NE33 .... 71 F4 🔟
Berkhamstead Ct *FELL* NE10 .... 102 B3 🔟
Berkley Av *BLAY* NE21 .... 77 D6
Berkley Cl *WLSD/HOW* NE28 .... 67 F1
Berkley Rd *NSHW* NE29 .... 53 F6 🔟
Berkley St *BW/LEM/TK/HW* NE15 ... 58 B6 🔟
Berkley Wy *HEBB* NE31 .... 68 B6
Berkshire Cl *DHAM* DH1 .... 196 B3 🔟
  WD/WHPE/BLK NE5................... 60 B4
Berkshire Rd *PLEE/EAS* SR8 .... 200 B6
Bermondsey St *JES* NE2 .... 3 H2
Bernard St *BYK/HTN/WLK* NE6 ...... 83 F4
  HLS DH4 .... 170 C2
Berrington Dr *WD/WHPE/BLK* NE5 .. 61 D2
Berrishill Gv *MONK* NE25 .... 39 E4
Berry Cl *BYK/HTN/WLK* NE6........... 83 F3
  WLSD/HOW NE28 .... 67 E1 🔟🔟
Berryfield Cl *SUNDSW* SR3 .... 160 C3
Berry Hl *RYTON* NE40 .... 92 A1
Berryhill Cl *BLAY* NE21 .... 94 C1
Bertram Crs *BW/LEM/TK/HW* NE15 .. 78 B2
Bertram St *SSH* NE33 .... 71 E6
Berwick *WASHS* NE38 .... 137 E2
Berwick Av *SWCK/CAS* SR5 .... 105 E6
Berwick Cha *PLEE/EAS* SR8 .... 208 A5
Berwick Cl
  BW/LEM/TK/HW NE15............... 75 F1 🔟
Berwick Ct *PONT/DH* NE20 .... 28 B3 🔟
Berwick Dr *WLSD/HOW* NE28 .... 67 F1
Berwick Hill Rd *PONT/DH* NE20 ..... 28 B3
Berwick Sq *SWCK/CAS* SR5 .... 123 E1 🔟
Berwick Ter *NSHW* NE29 .... 69 F2
Besford Gv *SUND* SR1 .... 5 F3
Betjeman St *STLY/ANP* DH9 .... 148 C2
Betts Av *BW/LEM/TK/HW* NE15 ...... 78 A3
Beumaris *HLS* DH4 .... 155 F5
Bevan Av *ASHBK/HED/RY* SR2...... 162 A2
Bevan Gdns *FELL* NE10 .... 101 F2 🔟
Bevan Gv *DHAM* DH1 .... 196 A3
Bevan Sq *SEA/MUR* SR7 .... 174 B6
Beverley Cl *GOS/KPK* NE3 .... 47 D2 🔟
Beverley Crs *LWF/SPW/WRK* NE9 ... 99 D2 🔟
Beverley Dr *BLAY* NE21 .... 93 E2
  WICK/BNPF NE16 .... 96 B1
Beverley Gdns *CLS/BIR/GTL* DH3 .. 153 F6
  TYNE/NSHE NE30..................... 55 E1
Beverley Pk *MONK* NE25 .... 40 A6
Beverley Rd *WLSD/HOW* NE28 .... 68 B4
Beverley Rd *ASHBK/HED/RY* SR2 ... 145 E4
  LWF/SPW/WRK NE9 .... 99 F4
  MONK NE25............................... 40 B6
Beverley Ter *BYK/HTN/WLK* NE6 .... 83 F3 🔟
  TYNE/NSHE NE30..................... 55 E1
Beverley Wy *PLEE/EAS* SR8 .... 208 B1
Bevin Sq *RDHAMSE* DH6................ 188 A5
Beweshill Crs *BLAY* NE21 .... 93 F1
Beweshill La *BLAY* NE21 .... 75 F3 🔟
Bewick Cl *CLSW/PEL* DH2............. 165 F2
Bewick Crs *BW/LEM/TK/HW* NE15 .. 76 C1
Bewicke Rd *WLSD/HOW* NE28........ 68 C5
Bewicke St *WLSD/HOW* NE28 .... 69 D5
Bewick Pk *WLSD/HOW* NE28 .... 52 B6
Bewick Rd *GATE* NE8 .... 99 D1
Bewick St *CNUT* NE1 .... 2 B5 🔟
  SSH NE33 .... 71 E6
Bewley Gdns *WLSD/HOW* NE28 ..... 67 F1 🔟
Bewley Gv *PLEE/EAS* SR8............. 207 F5
Bexhill Rd *SWCK/CAS* SR5 .... 123 E1
Bexhill Sq *BLYTH* NE24 .... 17 D1 🔟
  SWCK/CAS SR5 .... 123 E1
Bexley Av *BW/LEM/TK/HW* NE15 ... 77 F2
Bexley Pl *WICK/BNPF* NE16 .... 95 F5
Bexley St *MLFD/PNYW* SR4 .... 125 E6
Bickington Ct *HLS* DH4 .... 157 E5 🔟
Biddick Hall Dr *HAR/WTLS* NE34 .... 88 A4
Biddick La *WASHS* NE38 .... 138 C3
Biddick Vw *WASHS* NE38 .... 139 D3
Biddick Vls *WASHS* NE38 .... 139 D3
Biddlestone Crs *NSHW* NE29 .... 69 F1 🔟
Biddlestone Rd *BYK/HTN/WLK* NE6.. 65 E5
Bideford Gdns *HAR/WTLS* NE34 ..... 72 C5 🔟
  JRW NE32 .... 86 C3
  LWF/SPW/WRK NE9 .... 117 E1
  WBAY NE26 .... 40 B4
Bideford Gv *WICK/BNPF* NE16 ...... 95 F5

Bideford Rd *GOS/KPK* NE3.............. 62 A2
Bideford St *ASHBK/HED/RY* SR2 ... 145 E4
Bigbury Cl *HLS* DH4...................... 157 E4 🔟
Bigges Gdns *WLSD/HOW* NE28 ...... 66 B2
Bilbrough Gdns *ELS/FEN* NE4 .... 78 C4
Billy Mill Av *NSHW* NE29 .... 54 A6
Billy Mill La *NSHW* NE29 .... 53 F5
Bilsdale *CLDN/WHIT/ROK* SR6 ..... 109 E3
Bilsdale Pl *LGB/KIL* NE12 .... 48 B6 🔟
Bilsmoor Av *LGB/HTN* NE7............. 65 D4
Bilton Hall Rd *JRW* NE32 .... 86 C2
Binchester St *HAR/WTLS* NE34 ..... 87 F4 🔟
Bingfield Gdns *WD/WHPE/BLK* NE5.. 61 E6
Bingley Cl *WLSD/HOW* NE28 .... 68 A1
Bingley St *SWCK/CAS* SR5 .... 123 E1
Bink Moss *WASHN* NE37 .... 119 F6
Binswood Av *WD/WHPE/BLK* NE5 ... 61 D3
Bircham Dr *BLAY* NE21................... 76 C6
Bircham St *STLY/ANP* DH9 .... 147 F3
Birch Av *CLDN/WHIT/ROK* SR6 ..... 109 E1
  FELL NE10 .... 101 F3
Birch Ct *SUNDSW* SR3 .... 160 A2
Birch Crs *WICK/BNPF* NE16 .... 111 E6
The Birches *STLY/ANP* DH9 .... 131 E6 🔟
  WICK/BNPF NE16 .... 114 B1
Birchfield *WICK/BNPF* NE16........... 96 A5 🔟
Birchfield Gdns
  BW/LEM/TK/HW NE15............... 77 D1
  LWF/SPW/WRK NE9 .... 117 F2
Birchfield Rd
  ASHBK/HED/RY SR2 .... 144 A1 🔟
Birchgate Cl *BLAY* NE21 .... 93 F1 🔟
Birch Gv *WLSD/HOW* NE28............. 67 F1 🔟
Birchgrove Av *DHAM* DH1 .... 196 A3 🔟
Birchington Av *SSH* NE33 .... 88 B1
Birch Rd *BLAY* NE21 .... 76 C6
Birch St *JRW* NE32......................... 85 F1
Birch Ter *BYK/HTN/WLK* NE6 .... 83 F3 🔟
Birchvale Av *WD/WHPE/BLK* NE5 ... 60 C4
Birchwood Av *DIN/WO* NE13 .... 33 D5
  LGB/HTN NE7 .... 65 E3
  WICK/BNPF NE16 .... 95 F5
Birchwood Cl *CRAM* NE23 .... 36 A1
  STLY/ANP DH9 .... 133 D6
Birdhill Pl *HAR/WTLS* NE34............ 88 B3
Birds Nest Rd *BYK/HTN/WLK* NE6.. 83 D4
Bird St *TYNE/NSHE* NE30 .... 55 E6 🔟
Birkdale *MONK* NE25 .... 39 F5
  SSH NE33 .... 72 A5
Birkdale Av *CLDN/WHIT/ROK* SR6 .. 109 D3
Birkdale Cl *LGB/HTN* NE7 .... 65 E2 🔟
  WLSD/HOW NE28 .... 67 D2 🔟
Birkdale Dr *HLS* DH4 .... 156 C4
Birkdale Gdns *DHAM* DH1 .... 196 C3
Birkheads La *DUN/TMV* NE11 .... 115 D6
Birkland La *WICK/BNPF* NE16 .... 114 C4
Birling Pl *WD/WHPE/BLK* NE5 .... 61 F4
Birnam Gv *JRW* NE32 .... 87 D6 🔟
Birnie Cl *ELS/FEN* NE4 .... 79 D4
Birrell Sq *SWCK/CAS* SR5 .... 105 E6 🔟
Birrell St *SWCK/CAS* SR5.............. 105 E6
Birtley Av *TYNE/NSHE* NE30 .... 55 F4 🔟
Birtley Cl *GOS/KPK* NE3 .... 62 C2
Birtley La *CLS/BIR/GTL* DH3 .... 136 B2 🔟
Birtwistle Av *HEBB* NE31 .... 84 C5 🔟
Biscop Ter *JRW* NE32 .... 86 A3
Bishop Crs *JRW* NE32 .... 69 E6
Bishopdale *HLS* DH4 .... 139 D6 🔟
  WLSD/HOW NE28 .... 66 B1
Bishopdale Av *BLYTH* NE24............. 9 F6
Bishop Morton Gv *SUND* SR1 .... 5 F4 🔟
Bishop Ramsay Ct
  HAR/WTLS NE34 .... 89 F2 🔟
Bishop Rock Cl *LGB/KIL* NE12 .... 48 C6
Bishop Rock Rd *LGB/KIL* NE12 ...... 48 C6 🔟
Bishop's Av *ELS/FEN* NE4 .... 79 F3 🔟
Bishops Cl *WLSD/HOW* NE28 .... 68 A4 🔟
Bishops Dr *RYTON* NE40................. 74 C5
Bishops Meadow *BDLGTN* NE22 ..... 7 D3 🔟
Bishop's Rd *ELS/FEN* NE4 .... 78 C4
Bishops Wy *DHAM* DH1 .... 180 A5
  SUNDSW SR3.......................... 160 B3
Bisley Dr *HAR/WTLS* NE34 .... 88 C1
Bittern Cl *WLSD/HOW* NE28............ 52 C6
Black Boy Rd *HLS* DH4 .... 169 D3
Blackburn Gn *FELL* NE10.............. 100 B3 🔟
Blackdown Cl *LGB/KIL* NE12 .... 48 C6 🔟
  PLEE/EAS SR8 .... 208 A3
Blackett Ct *CLS/BIR/GTL* DH3 ...... 154 C3
  CLS/BIR/GTL DH3 .... 155 E2
Blackett St *CNUT* NE1..................... 2 C3
  HEBB NE31 .... 68 B6
  STLY/ANP DH9 .... 146 A4
Blackfell Rd *WASHN* NE37 .... 119 E5
Blackfriars Wy *LGB/KIL* NE12 .... 48 C5
Blackheath Cl *WASHN* NE37 .... 120 B2 🔟
Blackheath Ct *WD/WHPE/BLK* NE5.. 61 D1
Blackhill Av *WLSD/HOW* NE28 .... 52 A5
Blackhill Crs *LWF/SPW/WRK* NE9 .. 100 C6
Blackhills Rd *PLEE/EAS* SR8 .... 201 F6
Blackhouse La *RYTON* NE40 .... 74 A3
Black La *BLAY* NE21........................ 75 F6
  LWF/SPW/WRK NE9 .... 118 A3
Black Rd *ASHBK/HED/RY* SR2 ...... 162 B1
  BDN/LAN/SAC DH7................... 204 A3

HEBB NE31 .... 85 E1
Blackrow La BW/LEM/TK/HW NE15... 56 C2
Blackstone Ct BLAY NE21 .... 75 F6
Blackthorn Dr WLSD/HOW NE28 ...... 67 E1
Blackthorn Pl ELS/FEN NE4 .... 80 A5 🔢
Blackthorn Wy HLS DH4 .... 156 C6
Blackwell Av BYK/HTN/WLK NE6 ...... 83 F2
Blackwood Rd SWCK/CAS SR5 ..... 105 F6 🔢
Bladen St JRW NE32 .... 85 F1
Blagdon Av HAR/WTLS NE34 .... 72 A6
Blagdon Cl BDLGTN NE22 .... 7 E4
Blagdon Crs CRAM NE23 .... 13 D6
Blagdon Dr BLYTH NE24 .... 16 B4
Blaidwood Dr DHAM DH1 .... 204 C3
Blair Cl RDHAMSE DH6 .... 197 E5 🔢
Blair Ct BDN/LAN/SAC DH7 .... 204 A3
Blake Av WICK/BNPF NE16 .... 96 A3
Blakelaw Rd WD/WHPE/BLK NE5 .. 61 D4 🔢
Blakemoor Pl
   WD/WHPE/BLK NE5 .... 61 E5 🔢
Blakes Cl STLY/ANP DH9 .... 148 C2
Blanche Gv PLEE/EAS SR8 .... 208 C3
Blanchland WASHS NE38 .... 139 D5
Blanchland
   BW/LEM/TK/HW NE15...................... 76 A1
   DHAM DH1 .... 181 D6
   DIN/WO NE13 .... 33 D4
Blanchland Dr WLSD/HOW NE28 ... 67 F2 🔢
Blanchland Dr MONK NE25 .... 25 E6
   SWCK/CAS SR5 .... 123 H1
Blanchland Ter TYNE/NSHE NE30..... 55 D5
Blandford Pl SEA/MUR SR7 .... 176 C3
Blandford Rd NSHW NE29 .... 53 F4
Blandford Sq CNUT NE1 .... 2 A5
Blandford St CNUT NE1 .... 2 A6
Blaxton Pl WICK/BNPF NE16 .... 95 E5
Blaydon Bank BLAY NE21 .... 76 A6
Blaydon Hwy BLAY NE21 .... 76 B5
Blaykeston Cl SEA/MUR SR7 .... 175 D1
Bleachfield FELL NE10 .... 101 E4 🔢
Bleasdale Crs HLS DH4 .... 157 D1
Blencathra WASHN NE37 .... 120 B5
Blenheim LGB/KIL NE12 .... 35 F6 🔢
Blenheim Dr BDLGTN NE22 .... 8 B1
Blenheim Pl DUN/TMV NE11 .... 97 D1
Blenheim St CNUT NE1 .... 2 A5
Blenkinsop Gv JRW NE32 .... 85 F5
Blenkinsopp Ct PLEE/EAS SR8 .... 208 A6 🔢
Blenkinsop St WLSD/HOW NE28 .... 66 C4
Blind La CLS/BIR/GTL DH3 .... 153 F2
   HLS DH4 .... 157 D5
   SUNDSW SR3 .... 143 F6
Blindy La HLH DH5 .... 186 B3
Bloomfield Dr HLH DH5 .... 184 C1
Bloomsbury Ct GOS/KPK NE3 ...... 63 D2 🔢
Blossom Gv HLS DH4 .... 157 D4
Blount St BYK/HTN/WLK NE6 .... 82 C2 🔢
Blucher Rd LGB/KIL NE12.................. 49 E3
   NSHW NE29 .... 70 B3
Bluebell Dene WD/WHPE/BLK NE5 ... 60 C1
Bluebell Wy HAR/WTLS NE34 .... 88 A3
Blueburn Dr LGB/KIL NE12................ 36 B6
Bluehouse Bank STLY/ANP DH9 ... 150 B5
Blue House Ct WASHN NE37 .... 120 A4
Blue House La
   CLDN/WHIT/ROK SR6 .... 107 E3
   WASHN NE37 .... 120 A4
Blue House Rd HEBB NE31 .... 84 C5
Blue Quarries Rd
   LWF/SPW/WRK NE9 .... 100 A4
Blyth Cl CRAM NE23 .... 34 B2
Blyth Ct BW/LEM/TK/HW NE15 ...... 76 B1 🔢
   HAR/WTLS NE34 .... 88 B3
Blyth Rd WBAY NE26 .... 27 D5
Blyth Sq SWCK/CAS SR5 .... 123 F1
Blyth St MONK NE25 .... 24 B4
   SWCK/CAS SR5 .... 123 F1
Blyton Av ASHBK/HED/RY SR2 .... 162 A1
   HAR/WTLS NE34 .... 87 E3
Bodlewell La SUND SR1 .... 5 F1 🔢
Bodley Ct GOS/KPK NE3 .... 61 F1 🔢
Bodmin Cl WLSD/HOW NE28 .... 68 A1
Bodmin Rd NSHW NE29 .... 53 E4 🔢
Bodmin Sq SWCK/CAS SR5 .... 123 F1 🔢
Bodmin Wy GOS/KPK NE3 .... 46 B6 🔢
Bognor St SWCK/CAS SR5 .... 105 E6
Bohemia Ter BLYTH NE24 .... 11 D6
Boker La BOL NE36 .... 106 A2
Bolam Av BLYTH NE24 .... 10 C5
   TYNE/NSHE NE30 .... 54 C6
Bolam Gdns WLSD/HOW NE28 ...... 69 D3
Bolam Gv TYNE/NSHE NE30.......... 54 C3
Bolam Rd LGB/KIL NE12 .... 49 F1 🔢
Bolam St BYK/HTN/WLK NE6........ 82 B3
   GATE NE8 .... 98 A2
Bolam Wy BYK/HTN/WLK NE6....... 82 B3
   MONK NE25 .... 24 B5
Bolbec Rd ELS/FEN NE4 .... 79 D1
Bolburn FELL NE10 .... 101 F3
Boldon Cl WLSD/HOW NE28............ 67 F1
Boldon Dr BOL NE36 .... 105 E3
Boldon Gdns LWF/SPW/WRK NE9 ... 118 B1
Boldon La CLDN/WHIT/ROK SR6 .... 107 D1
   HAR/WTLS NE34 .... 88 B4
Boldon North Br BOL NE36 .... 106 B2

Bolingbroke Rd NSHW NE29 .... 53 F6
Bolingbroke St BYK/HTN/WLK NE6 .. 81 F2
   SSH NE33 .... 71 F4 🔢
Bollihope Dr SUNDSW SR3 .... 144 A4
Bolton Cl DHAM DH1............................ 180 B5
Bonchester Cl BDLGTN NE22.......... 7 E2
Bond Cl SWCK/CAS SR5 .... 126 B3
Bondene Av FELL NE10 .... 101 D2 🔢
Bondene Av West FELL NE10 .... 100 C2
Bondene Wy CRAM NE23................... 14 A4
Bondfield Gdns FELL NE10 .... 101 F2
Bondicarr Pl WD/WHPE/BLK NE5 ... 61 F5 🔢
Bondicar Ter BLYTH NE24 .... 10 C5
Bonemill La CLS/BIR/GTL DH3 ...... 137 D6
   WASHS NE38 .... 138 B6
Bonington Wy
   WD/WHPE/BLK NE5 .... 61 D4 🔢
Bonner's Fld SWCK/CAS SR5 ...... 126 C4
Bonnivard Gdns CRAM NE23.......... 36 C1
Booth St FELL NE10 .... 100 C2
   MLFD/PNYW SR4 .... 125 F5
Bootle St SWCK/CAS SR5 .... 123 F1 🔢
Bordeaux Cl SUNDSW SR3 .... 160 A2 🔢
Border Rd WLSD/HOW NE28 .... 67 D5 🔢
Boreham Cl WLSD/HOW NE28 ...... 67 F1 🔢
Borodin Av SWCK/CAS SR5 .... 105 E6
Borough Rd HAR/WTLS NE34 .... 89 E3
   JRW NE32 .... 86 A2
   NSHW NE29 .... 70 C1
   SUND SR1 .... 5 H3
   SUND SR5 .... 5 F3 🔢
Borrowdale WICK/BNPF NE16 ...... 96 C3
Borrowdale Av BLYTH NE24 .... 9 F4
   BYK/HTN/WLK NE6 .... 83 E1
   CLDN/WHIT/ROK SR6 .... 108 B5
Borrowdale Cl BOL NE36 .... 106 B2 🔢
   DHAM DH1 .... 197 D2 🔢
Borrowdale Crs BLAY NE21.............. 94 A2
   HLS DH4 .... 139 F6
Borrowdale Dr DHAM DH1 .... 196 B2 🔢
Borrowdale Gdns
   LWF/SPW/WRK NE9 .... 118 A1
Borrowdale St HLH DH5.................. 185 F2
Boscombe Dr WLSD/HOW NE28 ... 67 E2 🔢
Boston Av LGB/HTN NE7 .... 65 D1
   WASHS NE38 .... 120 B6
Boston Cl WLSD/HOW NE28............ 67 F1
Boston Crs BOL NE36 .... 105 D6
   SWCK/CAS SR5 .... 105 D6
Boston St SWCK/CAS SR5.............. 105 D6
Boswell Av HAR/WTLS NE34 .... 88 A5
Bosworth LGB/KIL NE12.................... 35 F6
Bosworth Gdns BYK/HTN/WLK NE6.. 65 E4
Bothal St BYK/HTN/WLK NE6 .... 82 C2
Bottle Bank GATE NE8 .... 3 F6
Bottlehouse St BYK/HTN/WLK NE6 .. 82 B4
Bottle Works Rd SEA/MUR SR7 ..... 177 D3
Boulby Cl SUNDSW SR3 .... 161 E1 🔢
Boulmer Av CRAM NE23.................... 14 A4
Boulmer Cl GOS/KPK NE3 .... 46 B4 🔢
Boulmer Ct CLSW/PEL DH2 .... 153 E6
Boulmer Gdns DIN/WO NE13.......... 33 D4
Boulsworth Rd WASHN NE29 .... 54 A3
Boundary Gdns LGB/HTN NE7 .... 64 C3
Boundary St SWCK/CAS SR5 ...... 126 B2 🔢
Bourne Av ELS/FEN NE4 .... 79 D1
Bourne Ct STLY/ANP DH9 .... 148 C1
Bournemouth Dr SEA/MUR SR7 ... 175 E4 🔢
Bournemouth Gdns WBAY NE26 ...... 40 B4
   WD/WHPE/BLK NE5 .... 60 B3 🔢
Bournmoor Rd NSHW NE29 .... 69 E1 🔢
Bourn Lea HLS DH4.......................... 156 C3
Bourtree Cl WLSD/HOW NE28 .... 67 E2
Bowbank Cl SUNDSW SR3 .... 144 A3 🔢
Bowburn Av SWCK/CAS SR5 .... 124 B2 🔢
Bowburn Cl FELL NE10 .... 102 B3
Bower St CLDN/WHIT/ROK SR6 .... 108 C3 🔢
The Bower JRW NE32 .... 104 A2 🔢
Bowes Av SEA/MUR SR7 .... 175 D4
Bowes Cl WICK/BNPF NE16 .... 114 A2
Bowes Lea HLS DH4 .... 156 B4
Bowes Lyon Cl ROWG NE39 .... 110 C4 🔢
Bowes St BLYTH NE24 .... 10 C5
   GOS/KPK NE3 .... 64 A1 🔢
Bowfell Av WD/WHPE/BLK NE5 ...... 61 F3
Bowfell Cl WD/WHPE/BLK NE5 ...... 61 F3 🔢
Bowfield Av GOS/KPK NE3 .... 47 E3
Bow La DHAM DH1 .... 194 B5
Bowlynn Cl SUNDSW SR3 .... 160 A3 🔢
Bowman Dr CRAM NE23 .... 35 D2
Bowman St CLDN/WHIT/ROK SR6.. 109 E1
Bowmont Dr CRAM NE23 .... 14 C6 🔢
   STLY/ANP DH9 .... 130 B6
Bowness Av WLSD/HOW NE28 ...... 52 A6
Bowness Cl BOL NE36 .... 106 B3 🔢
   PLEE/EAS SR8 .... 209 D1 🔢
Bowness Pl LWF/SPW/WRK NE9...... 100 A6
Bowness Rd WD/WHPE/BLK NE5 ... 60 C5
   WICK/BNPF NE16 .... 96 C3 🔢
Bowness St SWCK/CAS SR5 .... 105 F6
Bowsden Ct GOS/KPK NE3 .... 64 A1 🔢
Bowsden Ter GOS/KPK NE3............ 64 A1
Boyd Crs WLSD/HOW NE28 .... 67 E4
Boyd Rd WLSD/HOW NE28.............. 67 E4
Boyd St BW/LEM/TK/HW NE15........ 58 A6

DHAM DH1 .... 194 C6
   JES NE2 .... 3 H2
Boyne Ct BDN/LAN/SAC DH7 ...... 203 F3 🔢
   BLYTH NE24 .... 11 D4 🔢
Brabourne St HAR/WTLS NE34 ...... 88 B2
Bracken Av WLSD/HOW NE28 .... 67 E1
Brackenbeds Cl CLSW/PEL DH2 ... 152 A1
Bracken Cl DIN/WO NE13.................. 30 C4
   STLY/ANP DH9 .... 147 F2
Brackendale Rd DHAM DH1 .... 196 C3
Brackendene Dr
   LWF/SPW/WRK NE9 .... 99 D5 🔢
Bracken Dr DUN/TMV NE11............ 97 E4
Bracken Field Rd DHAM DH1 .... 194 A1
Brackenfield Rd GOS/KPK NE3 ...... 63 D2
Bracken Hl PLEE/EAS SR8 .... 207 E3
Brackenridge WICK/BNPF NE16 .... 111 D6
Brackenside GOS/KPK NE3 .... 47 E3
Brackenwood Gv
   ASHBK/HED/RY SR2 .... 144 B4 🔢
Brackley WASHN NE37 .... 121 D3
Bracknell Cl SUNDSW SR3 .... 144 B6
Bracknell Gdns
   WD/WHPE/BLK NE5........................ 59 D5
Brack Ter FELL NE10 .... 84 A6 🔢
Bradbury Cl FELL NE10 .... 102 B3 🔢
   STLY/ANP DH9 .... 130 B6
Bradbury Ct MONK NE25.................. 24 C2
Bradford Av SWCK/CAS SR5 .... 105 F6
   WLSD/HOW NE28 .... 67 F1
Bradford Crs DHAM DH1 .... 195 E3
Bradley Av HAR/WTLS NE34 .... 89 F3
   HLH DH5 .... 171 D4
Bradley Cl CLSW/PEL DH2 .... 134 C4
Bradley Lodge Dr
   STLY/ANP DH9 .... 129 D6 🔢
Bradley Ter HLH DH5 .... 186 A3
Bradman Dr CLS/BIR/GTL DH3 ...... 154 A6
Bradman Sq SWCK/CAS SR5 .... 105 F6 🔢
Bradman St SWCK/CAS SR5 .... 105 F6
Bradshaw St SWCK/CAS SR5 .... 123 F1
Bradwell Rd GOS/KPK NE3 .... 62 A1
Bradwell Wy HLS DH4 .... 157 D4
Brady Sq WASHS NE38 .... 139 E2 🔢
Braebridge Pl GOS/KPK NE3 .... 62 B3 🔢
Braemar Cl FELL NE10 .... 84 A6 🔢
Braemar Dr HAR/WTLS NE34.......... 72 C6
Braemar Gdns SUNDSW SR3 ...... 144 A3 🔢
   SUNDSW SR3 .... 159 E2 🔢
Braeside ASHBK/HED/RY SR2 ...... 144 A2
   DUN/TMV NE11 .... 97 F4 🔢
Brahman Av NSHW NE29 .... 69 F2
Braintree Gdns GOS/KPK NE3 .... 62 B2
Braithwaite Rd PLEE/EAS SR8 ...... 209 E2
Bramble Dykes
   BW/LEM/TK/HW NE15 .... 78 A3 🔢
Bramley Cl MLFD/PNYW SR4 .... 141 F4
Bramley Ct LGB/HTN NE7 .... 66 A3
Brampton Av BYK/HTN/WLK NE6.... 83 E4
Brampton Ct PLEE/EAS SR8 .... 200 A3 🔢
Brampton Gdns
   BW/LEM/TK/HW NE15...................... 57 F4
   LWF/SPW/WRK NE9 .... 117 F1
   WLSD/HOW NE28 .... 68 C2
Brampton Pl NSHW NE29 .... 69 F1
Brampton Rd HAR/WTLS NE34 ...... 87 F3
Bramwell Rd ASHBK/HED/RY SR2 ... 5 F5
Brancepeth Av ELS/FEN NE4.......... 79 D4
   HLS DH4 .... 169 F1 🔢
Brancepeth Chare PLEE/EAS SR8.... 208 A5
Brancepeth Cl
   BW/LEM/TK/HW NE15.................... 59 E6
   DHAM DH1 .... 181 D6
Brancepeth Rd HEBB NE31 .... 68 B6
   WASHS NE38 .... 137 F2
Brancepeth Ter JRW NE32 .... 86 A5 🔢
Brancepeth Vw
   BDN/LAN/SAC DH7 .... 202 B5
Branch St BLAY NE21 .... 94 A1 🔢
Brancpeth Cl BDN/LAN/SAC DH7 ... 192 B5
Brand Av ELS/FEN NE4 .... 79 D1
Brandling Ct HAR/WTLS NE34 ...... 89 E4
Brandling La FELL NE10 .... 100 C1 🔢
Brandling Pk JES NE2...................... 63 F6
Brandling Pl FELL NE10 .... 100 C1 🔢
Brandling St CLDN/WHIT/ROK SR6 .. 127 D2
Brandling St South
   CLDN/WHIT/ROK SR6 .... 127 D3 🔢
Brandlings Wy PLEE/EAS SR8 ...... 208 C1
Brandon Av SMOOR NE27 .... 52 A1
Brandon Cl BLAY NE21 .... 93 F2 🔢
   BLYTH NE24 .... 10 A4
   HLS DH4 .... 170 C3 🔢
Brandon Gdns
   LWF/SPW/WRK NE9 .... 118 C1 🔢
Brandon Gv JES NE2 .... 81 F1 🔢
Brandon La BDN/LAN/SAC DH7 .... 203 F3
Brandon Rd GOS/KPK NE3 .... 46 B6 🔢
   NSHW NE29 .... 53 F6
Brandy La WASHN NE37 .... 120 A5
Brannen St NSHW NE29 .... 70 C1 🔢
Bransdale HLS DH4 .... 139 D6
Bransdale Av
   CLDN/WHIT/ROK SR6 .... 109 C3

Branston St *SWCK/CAS* SR5 .... 126 A2
Branton Av *HEBB* NE31 .... 84 C5
Brantwood *CLSW/PEL* DH2 .... 152 B5
Brantwood Av *WASHS* NE25 .... 39 F6
Branxton Crs *BYK/HTN/WLK* NE6 ...... 83 E3
Brass Thill *DHAM* DH1 .... 194 A5 **2**
Bray CI *WLSD/HOW* NE28 .... 67 F1
Braydon Dr *NSHW* NE29 .... 69 F3
Brayside *JRW* NE32 .... 104 C1
Breamish Dr *WASHS* NE38 .... 137 F6
Breamish St *CNUT* NE1 .... 3 H3
    JRW NE32 .... 85 F3
Brearley Wy *FELL* NE10 .... 100 B2 **1**
Breckenbeds Rd
    LWF/SPW/WRK NE9 .... 99 D6
Brecken Wy *BDN/LAN/SAC* DH7 .... 203 E4 **2**
Brecon CI *PLEE/EAS* SR8 .... 208 A3
    WD/WHPE/BLK NE5 .... 61 D2 **1**
Brecon PI *CLSW/PEL* DH2 .... 135 E6
Brecon Rd *DHAM* DH1 .... 181 D5
Bredon CI *WASHS* NE38 .... 138 A3
Brendale Av *WD/WHPE/BLK* NE5 .... 59 F3
Brendon PI *PLEE/EAS* SR8 .... 208 A1
Brenkley Av *SMOOR* NE27 .... 52 A2
Brenkley CI *DIN/WO* NE13 .... 31 D3 **1**
Brenkley Ct *DIN/WO* NE13 .... 33 E2 **1**
Brenkley Wy *DIN/WO* NE13 .... 33 D1
Brenlynn CI *SUNDSW* SR3 .... 160 A2
Brennan CI
    BW/LEM/TK/HW NE15 .... 78 A2 **3**
Brentford Av *SWCK/CAS* SR5 ...... 123 F1
Brentford Sq *SWCK/CAS* SR5 ...... 123 F1 **3**
Brentwood Av *JES* NE2 .... 63 F4
Brentwood CI *MONK* NE25 .... 38 A1
Brentwood Ct *STLY/ANP* DH9 ...... 149 E2
Brentwood Gdns *SUNDSW* SR3 .... 144 A3 **2**
    WICK/BNPF NE16 .... 96 A5
Brentwood Gv *WLSD/HOW* NE28 .... 67 F5 **1**
Brettanby Rd *FELL* NE10 .... 100 B3
Brett CI *LGB/HTN* NE7 .... 65 F5
Bretton Gdns *LGB/HTN* NE7 ...... 65 E4
Brewer's La *NSHW* NE29 .... 69 E3
Brewer Ter *ASHBK/HED/RY* SR2 ... 162 C2
Brewery Bank *WICK/BNPF* NE16 .... 95 F1 **1**
Brewery La *FELL* NE10 .... 100 C1
    PONT/DH NE20 .... 28 A4
    SSH NE33 .... 71 D4 **1**
    WICK/BNPF NE16 .... 95 F1 **2**
Brewhouse Bank
    TYNE/NSHE NE30 .... 55 E6 **3**
Briar Av *BDN/LAN/SAC* DH7 ...... 202 C5 **3**
    HLS DH4 .... 170 C2
    WBAY NE26 .... 40 B3
Briar CI *CLSW/PEL* DH2 .... 179 E1
    HLS DH4 .... 156 B4
    WLSD/HOW NE28 .... 67 E1 **1**
Briardale *BDLGTN* NE22 .... 7 D3
Briardale Rd *BLYTH* NE24 .... 9 F5
Briardene *DHAM* DH1 .... 194 A5
    WICK/BNPF NE16 .... 111 D6
Briardene CI *SUNDSW* SR3 ...... 159 E2
Briardene Crs *GOS/KPK* NE3 ...... 62 C3
Briardene Dr *FELL* NE10 .... 102 C3
Briar Edge *LGB/KIL* NE12 .... 49 F4
Briarfield Rd *GOS/KPK* NE3 ...... 63 D2
Briarhill *CLSW/PEL* DH2 .... 152 C5
Briar La *BW/LEM/TK/HW* NE15 .... 58 A5 **3**
    HLS DH4 .... 156 B4
Briar Lea *BDN/LAN/SAC* DH7 .... 178 A3
    HLS DH4 .... 156 B4
Briar PI *BW/LEM/TK/HW* NE15 .... 77 F3
Briar Rd *DHAM* DH1 .... 196 C2
    ROWG NE39 .... 110 C2 **1**
Briarside *WD/WHPE/BLK* NE5 ...... 60 C3
The Briars *SWCK/CAS* SR5 ...... 124 A3
Briarsyde CI *WICK/BNPF* NE16 .... 95 D5
Briarwood *CRAM* NE23 .... 35 D2 **1**
Briarwood Av *CLSW/PEL* DH2 .... 152 A5
    GOS/KPK NE3 .... 48 A6
Briarwood Crs *BYK/HTN/WLK* NE6.... 66 B5
Briarwood Rd *BLYTH* NE24 ...... 11 E6
The Briary *BW/LEM/TK/HW* NE15 .. 57 E4 **1**
Brick Garth *HLH* DH5 .... 186 A3
Brick Rw *ASHBK/HED/RY* SR2 .... 162 A1
Bridge Cottages *CRAM* NE23 .... 35 E2 **1**
Bridge Crs *SUND* SR1 .... 4 C1
Bridgemere Dr *DHAM* DH1 ...... 179 F6
Bridge Pk *GOS/KPK* NE3 .... 47 E4
Bridge Rd South *NSHW* NE29 .... 70 A2
Bridge St *BLAY* NE21 .... 76 A4
    BLYTH NE24 .... 11 E5
    DHAM DH1 .... 194 A4 **1**
    DIN/WO NE13 .... 33 D2
    GATE NE8 .... 5 J5
    STLY/ANP DH9 .... 147 F4
    SUND SR1 .... 4 C2
Bridgewater CI
    BW/LEM/TK/HW NE15 .... 76 B1 **2**
    WLSD/HOW NE28 .... 67 E2 **3**
Bridgewater Rd *WASHN* NE37 .... 121 D5
Bridle Pth *BOL* NE36 .... 106 B3
    SUNDSW SR3 .... 142 B6
The Bridle *SMOOR* NE27 .... 53 D2
Bridlington *WLSD/HOW* NE28 .... 67 F1 **7**

Bridlington Av
    LWF/SPW/WRK NE9 .... 117 E1
Bridport Rd *NSHW* NE29 .... 53 F3
Brier Dene Crs *WBAY* NE26 ...... 40 A2
Brierdene Rd *WBAY* NE26 ...... 40 B1
Brierfield Gv *MLFD/PNYW* SR4 .... 142 C2
Brierley Rd *BLYTH* NE24 .... 10 A5
Briermede Av *LWF/SPW/WRK* NE9.... 99 E6
Brieryside *WD/WHPE/BLK* NE5 .... 61 F4 **1**
Briery Vale Rd *ASHBK/HED/RY* SR2 .... 4 B6
Brigham Av *GOS/KPK* NE3 .... 62 A3
Brigham PI *SSH* NE33 .... 71 E3 **2**
Brightlea *CLS/BIR/GTL* DH3 ...... 137 D1
Brightman Rd *NSHW* NE29 ...... 54 B6
Brighton CI *WLSD/HOW* NE28 .... 68 A1
Brighton Gv *ELS/FEN* NE4 ...... 79 F2
    NSHW NE29 .... 54 B6
    WBAY NE26 .... 40 B3
Brighton Rd *GATE* NE8 .... 98 C2
Bright St *CLDN/WHIT/ROK* SR6 .... 127 D3
    SSH NE33 .... 71 F3
Brignall CI *CLS/BIR/GTL* DH3 .... 168 A4
Brignall Gdns
    BW/LEM/TK/HW NE15 .... 77 F1
Brignall Ri *SUNDSW* SR3 ...... 144 A4 **1**
Brindley Rd *PLEE/EAS* SR8 ...... 207 E2
    WASHN NE37 .... 121 D6
Brinkburn *CLSW/PEL* DH2 ...... 152 C5
    WASHS NE38 .... 139 D4
Brinkburn Av *BLYTH* NE24 ...... 11 E6
    CRAM NE23 .... 22 B2 **1**
    GATE NE8 .... 99 D2
    GOS/KPK NE3 .... 47 D6
    WICK/BNPF NE16 .... 95 F2 **1**
Brinkburn CI *BLAY* NE21 .... 95 F2
    BYK/HTN/WLK NE6 .... 82 A3
Brinkburn Crs *HLS* DH4 .... 157 E6
Brinkburn St *BYK/HTN/WLK* NE6 .. 82 A2 **3**
    HAR/WTLS NE34 .... 88 A2
    MLFD/PNYW SR4 .... 143 F1
    WLSD/HOW NE28 .... 69 E5
Brinkburn St South
    BYK/HTN/WLK NE6 .... 82 B3
Brisbane Av *HAR/WTLS* NE34 .... 87 E5
Brisbane St *SWCK/CAS* SR5 ...... 123 F1
Bristlecone *SUNDSW* SR3 ...... 160 A3 **1**
Bristol Av *WASHN* NE37 .... 120 A4
Bristol Dr *WLSD/HOW* NE28 ...... 67 F1
Bristol St *MONK* NE25 .... 24 B3
Bristol Ter *ELS/FEN* NE4 .... 79 F4 **1**
Britannia PI *ELS/FEN* NE4 .... 79 F5
Britannia Rd *SUNDSW* SR3 ...... 160 C1 **2**
Brixham Av *LWF/SPW/WRK* NE9.... 117 E1
Brixham CI *SEA/MUR* SR7 ...... 175 F4 **1**
Brixham Crs *JRW* NE32 .... 86 C3
Brixham Gdns *SUNDSW* SR3 .... 144 A4 **3**
Broad Chare *CNUT* NE1 .... 3 F4
Broadfield PI *HAR/WTLS* NE34 .... 88 C3 **1**
Broad Garth *CNUT* NE1 .... 3 F5
Broad Landing *SSH* NE33 .... 71 D3
Broadlands *CLDN/WHIT/ROK* SR6.... 107 F3
Broadlea *FELL* NE10 .... 102 A2 **2**
Broadmayne Av *MLFD/PNYW* SR4 .. 142 C2
Broadmayne Gdns
    MLFD/PNYW SR4 .... 142 C2 **1**
Broad Mdw *ASHBK/HED/RY* SR2.... 144 A1
Broadmeadows *SUNDSW* SR3 ...... 159 D2
    WASHS NE38 .... 139 D4
Broadmead Wy
    BW/LEM/TK/HW NE15 .... 77 F3
Broadoak *FELL* NE10 .... 102 A2 **3**
    FELL NE10 .... 102 A1 **1**
Broadpark *FELL* NE10 .... 102 A2
Broadsheath Ter *SWCK/CAS* SR5 .. 125 E3
Broadside *FELL* NE10 .... 102 A2
Broadstairs Ct *MLFD/PNYW* SR4.... 142 C2
Broadstone Gv
    WD/WHPE/BLK NE5 .... 59 E5
Broadwater *FELL* NE10 .... 102 A1
Broadway *BLYTH* NE24 .... 11 D6
    BW/LEM/TK/HW NE15............ 59 F6
    CLS/BIR/GTL DH3 .... 153 F3
    LWF/SPW/WRK NE9 .... 100 A3
    TYNE/NSHE NE30 .... 55 E5
    WICK/BNPF NE16 .... 95 E5
Broadway CI *MONK* NE25 .... 55 D1
Broadway Crs *BLYTH* NE24 ...... 11 D6 **1**
Broadway East *GOS/KPK* NE3 .... 47 E5
The Broadway *HLS* DH4 .... 171 D2
    MLFD/PNYW SR4 .... 142 B2
    TYNE/NSHE NE30 .... 55 D1
Broadway Vls
    BW/LEM/TK/HW NE15 .... 78 A3
Broadway West *GOS/KPK* NE3 .... 47 D5
Broadwell Ct *GOS/KPK* NE3 ...... 64 B2
Broadwood Rd
    BW/LEM/TK/HW NE15 .... 77 E1
Brockenhurst Dr
    MLFD/PNYW SR4 .... 141 F4
Brock Farm Ct *TYNE/NSHE* NE30.... 54 C6
Brockhampton CI *BOLCOL* NE35 .. 87 D6 **2**
Brock La *BDLGTN* NE22 .... 9 E1
Brockley Av *HAR/WTLS* NE34 .... 87 F4
Brockley St *SWCK/CAS* SR5 ...... 123 F1
Brockwell CI *BLAY* NE21 .... 93 F2 **1**

Brockwell Ct *BLYTH* NE24 ...... 16 B2 **1**
Brockwell Rd *WASHS* NE38 ...... 137 E1
Brodie CI *HAR/WTLS* NE34 ...... 88 B5 **1**
Brodrick CI *GOS/KPK* NE3 ...... 61 F1
Brodrick St *SSH* NE33 .... 71 F3 **1**
Brokenheugh
    WD/WHPE/BLK NE5 .... 60 B5 **1**
Bromford Rd *GOS/KPK* NE3 ...... 61 F1
Bromley Av *MONK* NE25 .... 54 A1
Bromley Gdns *BLYTH* NE24 ...... 17 D1
    WLSD/HOW NE28 .... 67 F1 **3**
Bromsgrove CI *WLSD/HOW* NE28 .. 68 A1 **1**
Bronte PI *STLY/ANP* DH9 ...... 149 D4
Bronte St *GATE* NE8 .... 100 A1 **3**
Brookbank CI *SUNDSW* SR3 ...... 160 B3
Brook Ct *BDLGTN* NE22 .... 7 F4 **2**
Brookdale *DHAM* DH1 .... 197 D3
Brooke Av *BOLCOL* NE35 ...... 106 A2
    WICK/BNPF NE16 .... 95 F2
Brooke St *SWCK/CAS* SR5 ...... 126 B4
Brookfield CS *WD/WHPE/BLK* NE5 .. 59 E5
Brookland Dr *LGB/KIL* NE12 ...... 50 A1
Brookland Rd *MLFD/PNYW* SR4 .. 125 E6 **3**
Brooklands Wy *BOLCOL* NE35 .... 104 C2
Brookside *BDN/LAN/SAC* DH7 .... 164 B6
    BDN/LAN/SAC DH7 .... 178 A4
    CRAM NE23 .... 34 C2
Brookside Av *BLYTH* NE24 ...... 10 A5
    DIN/WO NE13 .... 32 C5
Brookside Crs *WD/WHPE/BLK* NE5 .. 61 F5
Brookside Gdns
    ASHBK/HED/RY SR2 .... 144 B2 **2**
Brookside Wd *WASHS* NE38 ...... 138 C5
Brooksmead *WLSD/HOW* NE28.... 66 B2
Brook St *BYK/HTN/WLK* NE6 ...... 82 C3
    WBAY NE26 .... 41 D5
Brookvale Av *GOS/KPK* NE3 ...... 62 B2
Broom CI *STLY/ANP* DH9 ...... 149 D1
    WICK/BNPF NE16 .... 96 B4
Broom Ct *LWF/SPW/WRK* NE9 .... 119 E3
Broome CI *GOS/KPK* NE3 ...... 46 C6
Broome Rd *DHAM* DH1............ 196 C2
Broomfield *JRW* NE32 .... 104 B1
Broomfield Av *BYK/HTN/WLK* NE6.... 66 A5
    WLSD/HOW NE28 .... 67 E1
Broomfield Rd *GOS/KPK* NE3 ...... 63 D2
Broom Hall Dr *BDN/LAN/SAC* DH7 .. 192 A5
Broomhill Gdns
    WD/WHPE/BLK NE5 .... 61 F5 **2**
Broomhill Ter *HLH* DH5 .... 171 E5
Broom La *BDN/LAN/SAC* DH7 .... 192 A5
    WICK/BNPF NE16 .... 96 A5
Broomlea *NSHW* NE29 .... 53 D5
Broomlee Rd *LGB/KIL* NE12 ...... 49 F1
Broomley Wk *GOS/KPK* NE3 ...... 46 B5
Broomridge Av
    BW/LEM/TK/HW NE15 .... 78 C3
Broomshields Av *SWCK/CAS* SR5 .. 126 A1
Broomshields CI *SWCK/CAS* SR5 .. 126 A1
Broomside La *DHAM* DH1 ...... 196 C4
Broom Ter *WICK/BNPF* NE16 ...... 112 B6 **1**
Broomy Hill Rd
    BW/LEM/TK/HW NE15............ 77 F2
Brotherlee Rd *GOS/KPK* NE3 ...... 46 B5
Brougham Ct *PLEE/EAS* SR8 ...... 207 F5
Brougham St *SUND* SR1............ 4 B3
Brough Gdns *WLSD/HOW* NE28 .. 68 C2
Brough Park Wy
    BYK/HTN/WLK NE6 .... 82 C2
Brough St *BYK/HTN/WLK* NE6 ...... 82 B1
Broughton Rd *SSH* NE33 ...... 71 F4
Browbank *BDN/LAN/SAC* DH7 .... 178 C2
Browne Rd *CLDN/WHIT/ROK* SR6 .. 126 C1
Browney La *BDN/LAN/SAC* DH7 .. 203 F5
Browning CI *HAR/WTLS* NE34 .... 88 A6
    STLY/ANP DH9 .... 148 C1
Brownlow CI *LGB/HTN* NE7 ...... 66 A3
Brownlow Rd *HAR/WTLS* NE34.... 88 B2
Brownrigg Dr *CRAM* NE23 ...... 22 B3 **2**
Brownsea PI *LWF/SPW/WRK* NE9.... 99 F3
Browntop PI *HAR/WTLS* NE34 .... 88 B3
Broxburn CI *WLSD/HOW* NE28 .... 68 A1
Broxburn Ct *WD/WHPE/BLK* NE5 .. 61 E3 **2**
Broxholm Rd *BYK/HTN/WLK* NE6.... 65 D5
Bruce CI *HAR/WTLS* NE34............ 88 B4
    WD/WHPE/BLK NE5 .... 60 B4 **2**
Bruce Gdns *WD/WHPE/BLK* NE5.... 78 B1
Bruce Glasier Ter *RDHAMSE* DH6 .. 206 B3
Bruce Kirkup Rd *PLEE/EAS* SR8 .. 201 D6
Bruce PI *PLEE/EAS* SR8 .... 200 B6
Bruce St *BDN/LAN/SAC* DH7 .... 164 A4
Brundon Av *WBAY* NE26 .... 40 B3
Brunel Dr *CLDN/WHIT/ROK* SR6 .. 127 E3
Brunel St *ELS/FEN* NE4 .... 80 A5
    GATE NE8 .... 98 C2
Brunel Ter *ELS/FEN* NE4 .... 79 F5 **1**
Brunel Wk *ELS/FEN* NE4 .... 79 F5
Brunswick Gv *DIN/WO* NE13 ...... 32 C4 **1**
Brunswick Rd *SMOOR* NE27 ...... 52 B2
    SWCK/CAS SR5 .... 105 F6
Brunswick St *SSH* NE33 .... 71 E5
Brunton Av *BYK/HTN/WLK* NE6 .. 46 B6
    WLSD/HOW NE28 .... 69 D3
Brunton CI *SMOOR* NE27 .... 52 B2
Brunton Gv *GOS/KPK* NE3 ...... 46 B6 **4**

Brunton La DIN/WO NE13 .... 45 F2
DIN/WO NE13 .... 46 C2
GOS/KPK NE3 .... 45 E5
GOS/KPK NE3 .... 47 E3
GOS/KPK NE3 .... 61 E1
Brunton Rd DIN/WO NE13 .... 45 D5
Brunton St NSHW NE29 .... 69 F3
Brunton Ter MLFD/PNYW SR4 .... 125 F6 🛈
FELL NE10 .... 84 A6
Brussels Rd MLFD/PNYW SR4 .... 124 C5
WLSD/HOW NE28 .... 67 D5
Bryden Ct HAR/WTLS NE34 .... 88 C3 🛈
Bryers St CLDN/WHIT/ROK SR6 ... 109 E1
Buckingham SUNDSW SR3 .... 143 D6 🛈
Buckingham Cl
CLDN/WHIT/ROK SR6 .... 109 E1 🛈
Buckingham PI PLEE/EAS SR8........ 200 A6
Buckinghamshire Rd DHAM DH1 .. 196 B3
Buckingham St ELS/FEN NE4 .... 80 A3 🛈
Buckland Cl HLS DH4 .... 157 E6
WASHS NE38 .... 138 C3
Buckthorne Gv LGB/HTN NE7 ...... 65 E3
Buddle Cl ELS/FEN NE4 .... 78 C4
PLEE/EAS SR8 .... 200 C6
Buddle Ct ELS/FEN NE4 .... 79 D4
Buddle Rd ELS/FEN NE4 .... 78 C4
Buddle St WLSD/HOW NE28 .... 67 D6
Buddle Ter ASHBK/HED/RY SR2 ... 5 F6 🛈
Bude Gv NSHW NE29 .... 53 F3
Bude Sq SEA/MUR SR7 .... 174 C6
Budle Cl BLYTH NE24 .... 10 B5
Budleigh Rd GOS/KPK NE3 .... 62 B1
Budworth Av WBAY NE26 .... 26 C3
Bulfinch Dr WICK/BNPF NE16 ...... 95 F4
Bullion La CLSW/PEL DH2 .... 153 D5
Bulman's La NSHW NE29 .... 54 C4 🛈
Bulmer Rd HAR/WTLS NE34 .... 89 F1
The Bungalows STLY/ANP DH9 .... 130 B6
Bunyan Av HAR/WTLS NE34 .... 87 F5
Burdale Av WD/WHPE/BLK NE5 ... 60 C5
Burdon Av CRAM NE23 .... 21 E1
HLH DH5 .... 171 F2
Burdon Cl CLDN/WHIT/ROK SR6 .. 107 D1
Burdon Crs CLDN/WHIT/ROK SR6 . 107 D1
SEA/MUR SR7 .... 175 E1
Burdon Dr PLEE/EAS SR8.............. 207 D1
Burdon Gv SUNDSW SR3 .... 161 D1
Burdon La ASHBK/HED/RY SR2 ... 162 A2
SUNDSW SR3 .... 160 C4
Burdon Ldg WICK/BNPF NE16...... 114 B2
Burdon Pk WICK/BNPF NE16 ...... 114 B2
Burdon Pl PLEE/EAS SR8 .... 209 D2 🛈
Burdon Pln WICK/BNPF NE16 ...... 114 A5
Burdon Rd ASHBK/HED/RY SR2 .... 4 D5
CLDN/WHIT/ROK SR6 .... 107 D1
SUNDSW SR3 .... 161 D3
Burdon St NSHW NE29 .... 69 F3
Burdon Ter JES NE2 .... 63 F6
Burford Ct LGB/HTN NE7 .... 64 C2
Burford Gdns SUNDSW SR3 .... 144 A4
Burghley Rd FELL NE10 .... 100 B4
Burke St SWCK/CAS SR5 .... 123 F1 🛈
Burlawn Cl ASHBK/HED/RY SR2 .. 145 E6 🛈
Burleigh St SSH NE33 .... 71 F4
Burlington Cl ASHBK/HED/RY SR2 .. 5 G5 🛈
Burlington Ct WLSD/HOW NE28 .... 52 A5 🛈
Burlington Gdns
BYK/HTN/WLK NE6 .... 65 D6 🛈
Burnaby Dr RYTON NE40 .... 74 A4
Burnaby St MLFD/PNYW SR4 .... 143 F1 🛈
Burn Av LGB/KIL NE12 .... 49 F4
Burnbank Av MONK NE25 .... 39 D5
Burnbridge DIN/WO NE13 .... 33 D2
Burn Crook HLH DH5 .... 170 C4
Burnden Gv HLS DH4 .... 156 B3
Burnet Cl WLSD/HOW NE28........... 67 E1
Burney Vls GATE NE8 .... 99 F1
Burnfoot Wy GOS/KPK NE3........... 62 A3
Burn Gdns PLEE/EAS SR8 .... 200 B2
Burnhall Dr SEA/MUR SR7 .... 175 F1
Burnham Av BW/LEM/TK/HW NE15.. 75 F1
Burnham Gv BOL NE36................. 106 C3
Burnham St HAR/WTLS NE34 .... 88 B2 🛈
BYK/HTN/WLK NE6 .... 83 D4
Burn Heads Rd HEBB NE31 .... 84 C4
Burnhills La RYTON NE40 .... 92 A2
Burnhope Dr SWCK/CAS SR5 ...... 126 A1 🛈
Burnhope Rd WASHS NE38 .... 121 D6
Burnhope Wy PLEE/EAS SR8 .... 208 A2
Burnip Rd SEA/MUR SR7 .... 174 B6
Burn La HLH DH5 .... 185 F1
Burnlea Gdns CRAM NE23 .... 23 F6
Burnley St BLAY NE21 .... 76 B6 🛈
Burnmoor Gdns
LWF/SPW/WRK NE9..................... 118 C1
Burnopfield Gdns
BW/LEM/TK/HW NE15.................. 77 F2
Burnopfield Rd ROWG NE39 .... 111 E3
Burn Park Rd ASHBK/HED/RY SR2 .. 144 A1
HLS DH4 .... 170 B2
Burn Prom HLS DH4 .... 170 C2

Burn Rd BLAY NE21 .... 93 E1
Burns Av BLYTH NE24 .... 16 B1
BOLCOL NE35 .... 106 A2
Burns Av South HLH DH5............. 171 D3
Burns Cl HAR/WTLS NE34 .... 88 A5
HLS DH4 .... 183 F2
STLY/ANP DH9 .... 148 C2
WICK/BNPF NE16 .... 96 A5
Burns Crs WICK/BNPF NE16 .... 95 F2 🛈
Burnside BDLGTN NE22 .... 8 C1
BDN/LAN/SAC DH7 .... 178 A4
BOL NE36..................................... 107 D3
JRW NE32..................................... 86 B4
PLEE/EAS SR8 .... 208 B2
Burnside Av CRAM NE23 .... 35 D2
HLS DH4 .... 170 B1
PLEE/EAS SR8 .... 209 F2
Burnside Cl BLYTH NE24 .... 10 A4 🛈
WICK/BNPF NE16 .... 95 F6
Burnside Gdns GOS/KPK NE3 ...... 47 E5
ROWG NE39 .... 110 C3
TYNE/NSHE NE30 .... 55 D1
The Burnside CRAM NE23 .... 36 A1 🛈
Burnside Vw CRAM NE23 .... 36 A1 🛈
Burns St JRW NE32 .... 86 A1 2
Burn's Ter RDHAMSE DH6 .... 206 C3
Burnstones WD/WHPE/BLK NE5 ... 60 A5 🛈
Burnthouse Bank CLSW/PEL DH2 .. 152 B4
Burnthouse Cl BLAY NE21 .... 93 F2 🛈
Burnthouse La WICK/BNPF NE16... 95 F6
Burnt House Rd MONK NE25 .... 54 A1
Burntland Av SWCK/CAS SR5........ 125 E2
Burn Vw CRAM NE23 .... 35 D2 2
Burnville Rd MLFD/PNYW SR4 ..... 144 A1
Burnville Rd South
MLFD/PNYW SR4 .... 144 A1 2
Burradon Rd CRAM NE23................ 35 D4
Burrow St SSH NE33 .... 71 F3 🛈
Burscough Crs
CLDN/WHIT/ROK SR6 .... 126 C2 🛈
Burstow Av BYK/HTN/WLK NE6 .... 83 D5
Burt Av NSHW NE29 .... 70 A1
Burt Cl PLEE/EAS SR8 .... 200 C6
Burt Crs CRAM NE23 .... 35 D2 3
Burt Rd BDLGTN NE22 .... 9 D1 🛈
Burt St BLYTH NE24 .... 11 D4
Burwell Av WD/WHPE/BLK NE5 .... 60 B6
Burwood Cl BYK/HTN/WLK NE6 .... 83 F5 🛈
Burwood Rd BYK/HTN/WLK NE6 ... 83 E5
NSHW NE29 .... 53 E4
Bushblades La STLY/ANP DH9 ..... 146 B1
Buston Ter JES NE2 .... 64 B5
Busty Bank WICK/BNPF NE16 ...... 111 F4
Butcher's Bridge Rd JRW NE32 .... 86 A4
Bute Ct SUNDSW SR3 .... 160 B2
Buteland Rd BW/LEM/TK/HW NE15.. 77 F1
Bute St STLY/ANP DH9 .... 129 F4
Butsfield Gdns SUNDSW SR3 .... 144 A4 2
Buttermere CLDN/WHIT/ROK SR6 .. 107 F1
FELL NE10 .... 101 F2
PLEE/EAS SR8 .... 207 F5 🛈
Buttermere Av HLH DH5............... 186 B4
WICK/BNPF NE16 .... 96 B3
Buttermere Cl
WD/WHPE/BLK NE5 .... 61 D5 🛈
Buttermere Crs BLAY NE21 .... 94 A2 🛈
Buttermere Gdns
HAR/WTLS NE34 .... 89 D2 🛈
LWF/SPW/WRK NE9..................... 99 F5
Buttermere Rd TYNE/NSHE NE30.. 54 C2
Buttermere St
ASHBK/HED/RY SR2 .... 145 D4
Buttermere Wy BLYTH NE24 .... 10 A3 🛈
Buxton Cl JRW NE32 .... 86 B3
WLSD/HOW NE28 .... 67 F1 🛈
Buxton Gdns SUNDSW SR3 .... 144 A3
WD/WHPE/BLK NE5 .... 60 B5 🛈
Buxton Rd JRW NE32 .... 86 B3
Byers Ct SUNDSW SR3 .... 144 A6
Byer Sq HLH DH5 .... 171 F4
Byer St HLH DH5 .... 171 F4
The Byeways LGB/KIL NE12 .... 49 D6 🛈
Bygate Cl WD/WHPE/BLK NE5 ...... 62 A3
Bygate Rd MONK NE25 .... 40 A6
Byker Bank BYK/HTN/WLK NE6 ..... 81 F3
Byker Br CNUT NE1 .... 3 H2
Byker Buildings
BYK/HTN/WLK NE6 .... 81 F2 2
Byker Ter BYK/HTN/WLK NE6 .... 83 E2
Byland Cl HLS DH4 .... 157 E6 🛈
Byland Ct BDN/LAN/SAC DH7 ..... 192 A3 🛈
WASHS NE38 .... 138 B1
Byland Rd LGB/KIL NE12 .... 48 B6
Byony Toft ASHBK/HED/RY SR2 .. 162 C1
Byrness WD/WHPE/BLK NE5 .... 60 A5
Byrness Cl GOS/KPK NE3 .... 61 E2
Byron Av BLYTH NE24 .... 16 B1 🛈
BOLCOL NE35 .... 105 F2
CLSW/PEL DH2 .... 152 A5
HEBB NE31 .... 85 E2
Byron Cl CLSW/PEL DH2 .... 135 F5
Byron Rd SWCK/CAS SR5 .... 125 F2
Byron St JES NE2 .... 3 F1
SWCK/CAS SR5 .... 126 A3
Byron Ter RDHAMSE DH6 .... 206 C2

The By-way BW/LEM/TK/HW NE15 .. 57 F5
Bywell Av BW/LEM/TK/HW NE15 ... 77 D1
GOS/KPK NE3 .... 46 B4
HAR/WTLS NE34 .... 89 F1
SWCK/CAS SR5 .... 126 B1 🛈
Bywell Dr PLEE/EAS SR8 .... 208 B5
Bywell Gdns DUN/TMV NE11......... 97 F5
LWF/SPW/WRK NE9.................... 100 A4
Bywell Rd CLDN/WHIT/ROK SR6 .. 107 E2
Bywell St BYK/HTN/WLK NE6 .... 82 C3 🛈
Bywell Ter JRW NE32 .... 86 A5

C

Cadleston Ct CRAM NE23 .... 14 C6 3
Cadwell La PLEE/EAS SR8 .... 200 A2
Caernarvon Cl
WD/WHPE/BLK NE5 .... 61 D2 2
Caernarvon Dr SUNDSW SR3....... 159 E2
Caer Urfa Cl SSH NE33 .... 71 E2
Cairncross SWCK/CAS SR5........... 123 F3
Cairnglass Gn CRAM NE23 .... 14 C6 2
Cairngorm Av WASHS NE38 .... 137 F5
Cairnsmore Cl CRAM NE23............ 22 A4
Cairnsmore Dr WASHS NE38 .... 138 A3
Cairns Rd SEA/MUR SR7 .... 187 F1
SWCK/CAS SR5 .... 108 B6 🛈
Cairns Sq SWCK/CAS SR5 .... 108 B6 2
Cairns Wy GOS/KPK NE3 .... 46 B5
Cairo St ASHBK/HED/RY SR2 .... 145 D2
Caithness Rd SWCK/CAS SR5 ...... 123 E2
Caithness Sq SWCK/CAS SR5 ..... 123 E2 🛈
Calais Rd SWCK/CAS SR5 .... 123 E3 🛈
Caldbeck Av BYK/HTN/WLK NE6 .. 83 E5
Caldbeck Cl BYK/HTN/WLK NE6 ... 83 E5
Calderbourne Av
CLDN/WHIT/ROK SR6 .... 109 D6 🛈
Calderdale WLSD/HOW NE28 .... 66 B1
Calderdale Av BYK/HTN/WLK NE6 .. 83 E2
Calder Wk WICK/BNPF NE16 .... 113 F2
Calderwood Crs
LWF/SPW/WRK NE9..................... 117 F1
Caldew Ct HLH DH5....................... 186 A2
Caldew Crs WD/WHPE/BLK NE5 ... 60 C6
Caldwell Rd GOS/KPK NE3 .... 46 B4
Caledonian St HEBB NE31 .... 84 C1
Caledonia St BYK/HTN/WLK NE6 .. 83 F4 2
Calfclose La JRW NE32................... 86 B6
Calf Close Dr JRW NE32 .... 86 A6
Calf Close Wk JRW NE32 .... 86 A6 🛈
California BLAY NE21 .... 94 A1
Callaley Av WICK/BNPF NE16 .... 95 F4
Callaly Av CRAM NE23 .... 22 B2
Callaly Wy BYK/HTN/WLK NE6 ..... 82 C4 🛈
Callander CLSW/PEL DH2 .... 135 F4
Callerdale BLYTH NE24 .... 9 F5 🛈
Callerton LGB/KIL NE12 .... 35 F5 2
Callerton Av NSHW NE29 .... 53 E5
Callerton Ct PONT/DH NE20 .... 28 A6
Callerton La PONT/DH NE20 .... 28 A5
WD/WHPE/BLK NE5...................... 42 A4
Callerton Rd BW/LEM/TK/HW NE15.. 58 A4
Callerton Vw
WD/WHPE/BLK NE5 .... 59 D3 2
Calley Cl PLEE/EAS SR8 .... 208 B5 🛈
Callington Dr ASHBK/HED/RY SR2 .. 162 B1
Calvert Ter SEA/MUR SR7 .... 188 A1
Calvus Dr BW/LEM/TK/HW NE15 ... 56 B4 2
Camberley Cl SUNDSW SR3 .... 144 B6 🛈
Camberley Dr
BDN/LAN/SAC DH7 .... 202 B5 2
Camberley Rd WLSD/HOW NE28 .. 68 C2
Camberwell Cl DUN/TMV NE11...... 98 A4
Camberwell Wy SUNDSW SR3...... 159 F3
Cambo Av BDLGTN NE22 .... 8 B3
MONK NE25................................... 53 F1
Cambo Cl BLYTH NE24 .... 10 B5
GOS/KPK NE3 .... 63 F1 🛈
WLSD/HOW NE28 .... 51 F6
Cambo Dr CRAM NE23 .... 22 B3
Cambo Gn WD/WHPE/BLK NE5..... 61 E4
Cambo Pl TYNE/NSHE NE30.......... 54 C3
Camborne Gv GATE NE8................. 99 E1
Camborne Pl GATE NE8 .... 99 E1 2
Cambourne Av
CLDN/WHIT/ROK SR6 .... 109 D6 2
Cambria Gn MLFD/PNYW SR4 .... 123 F6 🛈
Cambrian St JRW NE32 .... 86 A1
Cambrian Wy WASHS NE38 .... 138 A3
Cambria St MLFD/PNYW SR4....... 123 F6
Cambridge Av HEBB NE31............. 85 E3
LGB/KIL NE12 .... 49 F4 3
WASHN NE37 .... 120 A4
WLSD/HOW NE28 .... 66 C3 2
Cambridge Dr CLS/BIR/GTL DH3 .. 167 F4
Cambridge Pl CLS/BIR/GTL DH3 .. 136 B5
Cambridge Rd PLEE/EAS SR8 ...... 200 B6
SUNDSW SR3 .... 160 C1
Cambridgeshire Dr DHAM DH1 .... 196 B4
Cambridge St ELS/FEN NE4 .... 80 A4 2
Camden St JES NE2 .... 3 F1
SWCK/CAS SR5 .... 125 F3 🛈
TYNE/NSHE NE30 .... 71 D1 2

Camelford Ct
 BW/LEM/TK/HW NE15 .... 59 E6 🔲
Camelot Cl *SEA/MUR* SR7 .... 176 B2 🔲
Cameron Cl *HAR/WTLS* NE34 ...... 88 B5 🔲
Camerton Pl *WLSD/HOW* NE28 ...... 52 A5
Camilla Rd *HAR/LEM/TK/HW* NE15 .... 56 B4
Camilla St *GATE* NE8 .... 99 E1 🔲
Campbell Park Rd *HEBB* NE31 ...... 85 D2
Campbell Pl *ELS/FEN* NE4 .... 79 F3
Campbell Rd *SWCK/CAS* SR5 ...... 123 E2
Campbell St *HEBB* NE31 .... 84 C1
Camperdown *WD/WHPE/BLK* NE5 .... 60 B5
Camperdown Av
 CLS/BIR/GTL DH3 .... 153 F3
Campion Dr *STLY/ANP* DH9 ...... 130 C6
Campion Gdns *FELL* NE10 .... 100 C5 🔲
Camp Rd *WLSD/HOW* NE28 ...... 67 D6
Campsie Crs *TYNE/NSHE* NE30 .... 54 C3
Camp Ter *NSHW* NE29 .... 54 C6
Campville *NSHW* NE29 .... 54 C6
Camsey Cl *LGB/KIL* NE12 .... 48 B6 🔲
Canberra Av *MONK* NE25 .... 53 F1
Canberra Dr *HAR/WTLS* NE34 .... 87 D4
Canberra Rd *MLFD/PNYW* SR4 .... 142 C2
Candelford Cl *LGB/HTN* NE7 ...... 65 F3 🔲
Candlish St *SSH* NE33 .... 71 F4
Candlish Ter *SEA/MUR* SR7 ...... 177 D4
Canning St *ELS/FEN* NE4 .... 78 C3
 HEBB NE31 .... 85 D3
Cannock *CLSW/PEL* DH2 .... 135 E4
 LGB/KIL NE12 .... 35 F6 🔲
Cannock Dr *LGB/HTN* NE7 .... 64 C2
Cannon St *GATE* NE8 .... 3 F6 🔲
Cann Rd *PLEE/EAS* SR8 .... 200 C6
Canonbie Sq *CRAM* NE23 .... 14 C6 🔲
Canon Cockin St
 ASHBK/HED/RY SR2 .... 145 D2
Canon Gv *JRW* NE32 .... 86 B1
Canonsfield Cl *SUNDSW* SR3 .... 160 B3
Canterbury Av *WLSD/HOW* NE28 .. 51 F6
Canterbury Rd *DHAM* DH1 .... 180 C4
 SWCK/CAS SR5 .... 123 F2
Canterbury St
 BYK/HTN/WLK NE6 .... 82 C2 🔲
 SSH NE33 .... 71 F6
Capetown Rd *SWCK/CAS* SR5 .... 123 E2 🔲
The Captains Rw *SSH* NE33 ...... 71 D6
Capulet Gv *HAR/WTLS* NE34 ...... 87 F3
Capulet Ter *ASHBK/HED/RY* SR2 .. 145 D2 🔲
Caradoc Cl *WASHS* NE38.......... 138 A3
Caragh Rd *CLSW/PEL* DH2 ...... 166 B1
Caraway Wk *HAR/WTLS* NE34 .... 89 D5
Carden Av *HAR/WTLS* NE34 ...... 90 A3 🔲
Cardiff Sq *SWCK/CAS* SR5 ...... 123 E3 🔲
Cardigan Gv *MONK* NE25 .... 54 C1
Cardigan Rd *SWCK/CAS* SR5 .... 123 E2
Cardigan Ter *BYK/HTN/WLK* NE6 .. 82 A1
Cardinal Cl *LGB/KIL* NE12 .... 48 C6 🔲
 WD/WHPE/BLK NE5.............. 59 D3
Cardinals Cl *SUNDSW* SR3 ...... 160 B3 🔲
Cardonnel St *NSHW* NE29 .... 70 C2
Cardwell St *CLDN/WHIT/ROK* SR6.. 127 D3
Careen Crs *SUNDSW* SR3 .... 159 D1
Carham Av *CRAM* NE23 .... 22 B2 🔲
Carham Cl *GOS/KPK* NE3 .... 47 F6
Carisbrooke *BDLGTN* NE22 ...... 7 E2
Caris St *GATE* NE8 .... 99 F2 🔲
Carlby Wy *CRAM* NE23 .... 13 E4
Carlcroft Pl *CRAM* NE23 .... 22 B3 🔲
Carley Hill Rd *SWCK/CAS* SR5.... 126 A1
Carley Rd *SWCK/CAS* SR5 ...... 126 A2
Carlingford Rd *CLSW/PEL* DH2 .. 166 A1
Carliol Sq *CNUT* NE1 .... 3 E3
Carliol St *CNUT* NE1 .... 3 E3
Carlisle Crs *HLS* DH4 .... 156 C1
Carlisle Rd *DHAM* DH1 .... 181 D5
Carlisle St *FELL* NE10............ 100 C1
Carlton Av *BLYTH* NE24 .... 18 B4
Carlton Cl *CLSW/PEL* DH2........ 135 D4
 GOS/KPK NE3 .... 62 C3 🔲
Carlton Crs *SUNDSW* SR3 ...... 159 E1
Carlton Gdns
 BW/LEM/TK/HW NE15 .... 77 D1 🔲
Carlton Rd *LGB/KIL* NE12 .... 49 F6
Carlton St *BLYTH* NE24 .... 11 E5 🔲
Carlton Ter *LWF/SPW/WRK* NE9 .. 99 D5
 NSHW NE29 .... 70 B1 🔲
Carlyle St *WLSD/HOW* NE28 ...... 68 C5 🔲
Carlyle Crs *WICK/BNPF* NE16...... 95 F2 🔲
Carlyle St *WLSD/HOW* NE28 ...... 68 C5 🔲
Carlyon St *ASHBK/HED/RY* SR2 .... 4 C6 🔲
Carmel Gv *CRAM* NE23 .... 13 F5 🔲
Carmel Rd *STLY/ANP* DH9 .... 147 F2
Carnaby Rd *BYK/HTN/WLK* NE6 .. 83 E4 🔲
Carnation Av *HLS* DH4 .... 155 F5
Carnegie Cl *HAR/WTLS* NE34 .... 88 B4 🔲
Carnegie St *ASHBK/HED/RY* SR2 .. 145 E4 🔲
Carnforth Cl *WLSD/HOW* NE28 .. 51 F5
Carnforth Gdns
 LWF/SPW/WRK NE9 .... 100 A6 🔲
 ROWG NE39 .... 111 D1 🔲
Carnforth Gn *GOS/KPK* NE3 .... 62 A2 🔲

Carnoustie *CLSW/PEL* DH2 ...... 135 E5
 HAR/WTLS NE34 .... 89 E5
 WASHN NE37.................... 120 B1
Carnoustie Cl *LGB/HTN* NE7 .... 65 E2 🔲
Carnoustie Dr *MONK* NE25........ 39 E5
Carnoustie Dr *HAR/WTLS* NE34 .. 89 E5 🔲
Carol Gdns *LGB/HTN* NE7 .... 65 D3
Caroline Gdns *WLSD/HOW* NE28.. 68 C3
Caroline St *ELS/FEN* NE4 .... 79 D4
 HLH DH5 .... 171 F6
 JRW NE32 .... 85 F1
 SEA/MUR SR7 .... 176 C3 🔲
Carol St *MLFD/PNYW* SR4 ...... 125 F5
Carolyn Cl *LGB/KIL* NE12 .... 49 E6 🔲
Carolyn Crs *WBAY* NE26 .... 40 A3
Carolyn Wy *WBAY* NE26 .... 40 A3
Carpenter St *SSH* NE33 .... 71 D4 🔲
Carr Av *BDN/LAN/SAC* DH7 ...... 203 D4
Carr Fld *PONT/DH* NE20 .... 28 B3
Carrfield Rd *GOS/KPK* NE3 ...... 62 B1 🔲
Carr Hill Rd *LWF/SPW/WRK* NE9 .. 99 F2 🔲
Carr House Dr *DHAM* DH1 ...... 180 B6
Carrhouse La *HLH* DH5 .... 173 D5
Carrick Dr *BLYTH* NE24 .... 16 C2
Carrigill Pl *LGB/KIL* NE12 .... 48 C6
Carrington Cl *CRAM* NE23........ 36 B1
Carrmere Rd *ASHBK/HED/RY* SR2.. 145 D5
Carrmyers *STLY/ANP* DH9 ...... 146 A2
Carrock Cl *PLEE/EAS* SR8 ...... 208 C5
Carrowmore Rd *CLSW/PEL* DH2.. 166 B3
Carrsdale *DHAM* DH1 .... 196 C1 🔲
Carr St *BLYTH* NE24.............. 16 B2
 HEBB NE31 .... 84 C1 🔲
Carrsway *DHAM* DH1 .... 196 C1 🔲
Carrsyde Cl *WICK/BNPF* NE16 .... 95 E5
Carsdale Rd *GOS/KPK* NE3........ 61 F1
Cartington Av *SMOOR* NE27 .... 52 A2
Cartington Cl *PLEE/EAS* SR8 .... 208 C5 🔲
Cartington Ct *GOS/KPK* NE3 .... 46 A5 🔲
Cartington Rd *DHAM* DH1 ...... 194 B1
 NSHW NE29 .... 70 A1
Cartington Ter *BYK/HTN/WLK* NE6.. 65 E5
Cartmel Ct *CLSW/PEL* DH2 ...... 152 C6
Cartmel Gv *GATE* NE8 .... 98 C3 🔲
Cartmel Pk *FELL* NE10 .... 101 F1 🔲
Cartwright Rd *SWCK/CAS* SR5.... 124 A3
Carville Rd *WLSD/HOW* NE28...... 67 D5
Carville St *FELL* NE10 .... 82 A6
Carvill Gdns *WLSD/HOW* NE28 .. 67 D6 🔲
Carvis Cl *DHAM* DH1 .... 202 C5
Carwarding Pl *WD/WHPE/BLK* NE5.. 61 E5
Caseton Cl *MONK* NE25 .... 39 E4
Caspian Cl *JRW* NE32 .... 86 B3 🔲
Caspian Rd *SWCK/CAS* SR5 .... 123 E3 🔲
Caspian Sq *SWCK/CAS* SR5 .... 123 E3
Castellian Rd *SWCK/CAS* SR5 .... 124 B3
Casterton Gv *WD/WHPE/BLK* NE5 .. 59 D5
Castle Chare *DHAM* DH1 ...... 194 B4 🔲
Castle Cl *CLS/BIR/GTL* DH5...... 153 F6
 GOS/KPK NE3 .... 61 F1 🔲
 HLH DH5 .... 186 A2
 WICK/BNPF NE16 .... 95 F3 🔲
Castledale Av *BLYTH* NE24........ 9 F6
Castledene Ct *GOS/KPK* NE3 .... 64 B2
Castle Dene Gv *HLS* DH4 .... 170 C2
Castleford Rd *SWCK/CAS* SR5 .. 123 E2
Castlegate Gdns *GATE* NE8 ...... 97 F1 🔲
Castlenook Pl
 BW/LEM/TK/HW NE15 .... 77 E1 🔲
Castlereagh Cl *SEA/MUR* SR7 .. 176 C3 🔲
Castlereagh Rd *SEA/MUR* SR7 .. 176 C3
Castlereagh St *SUNDSW* SR3...... 160 C1
Castlereigh Cl *HLS* DH4 .... 155 F5
Castle Riggs *CLSW/PEL* DH2 .... 153 D5
Castle Rd *WASHS* NE38 .... 137 F2
Castles Farm Rd *LGB/HTN* NE7 .. 64 A2
Castles Gn *LGB/KIL* NE12 .... 50 A1
Castleside Rd
 BW/LEM/TK/HW NE15.......... 77 F2
Castle Sq *SMOOR* NE27 .... 37 D6 🔲
Castle St *DIN/WO* NE13 .... 32 C6
 SUND SR1 .... 4 B2
Castle St South *SWCK/CAS* SR5 .. 124 B3 🔲
Castleton Cl *CRAM* NE23 .... 13 F5 🔲
 JES NE2 .... 64 B1 🔲
Castleton Gv *JES* NE2 .... 64 B4
Castleton Rd *JRW* NE32 .... 86 B3 🔲
Castletown Rd *SWCK/CAS* SR5 .. 124 B3
Castletown Wy *SWCK/CAS* SR5 .. 124 C2
Castle Vw *BDN/LAN/SAC* DH7 .. 192 B5 🔲
 CLS/BIR/GTL DH3 .... 153 E3
 SWCK/CAS SR5 .... 124 A3
Castleway *DIN/WO* NE13 .... 31 D4
Castlewood Cl *WD/WHPE/BLK* NE5.. 59 F4
Catchside Cl *WICK/BNPF* NE16 .. 95 F4
Catchwell Rd *STLY/ANP* DH9 .... 128 C6
Cateran Wy *CRAM* NE23.......... 22 B4
Caterhouse Rd *DHAM* DH1 .... 180 A6
Catharine St West
 MLFD/PNYW SR4 .... 125 F6 🔲
Cathedral Vw *BDN/LAN/SAC* DH7.. 178 C2 🔲
 HLS DH4 .... 157 F5
Catherine Cookson Ct *SSH* NE33 .. 72 A5 🔲
Catherine Rd *HLS* DH4 .... 157 F2
Catherine St *SSH* NE33 .... 71 F3 🔲

Catherine Ter *STLY/ANP* DH9 .... 131 E6 🔲
Catholic Rw *BDLGTN* NE22........ 7 D4
Cato Sq *SWCK/CAS* SR5 .... 125 F2
Cato St *SWCK/CAS* SR5 .... 125 F2 🔲
Catton Gv *WICK/BNPF* NE16 .... 114 A1
Catton Pl *WLSD/HOW* NE28 ...... 52 A6
Cauldwell Av *HAR/WTLS* NE34 .. 89 D1
 MONK NE25...................... 40 A6
Cauldwell Cl *MONK* NE25 .... 40 A6
Cauldwell La *MONK* NE25 .... 39 F6
Cauldwell Pl *HAR/WTLS* NE34 .. 89 D1
Cauldwell Vls *HAR/WTLS* NE34 .. 89 D1
Causeway *CLDN/WHIT/ROK* SR6 .. 126 C4 🔲
 LWF/SPW/WRK NE9 .... 100 A4
The Causeway
 BW/LEM/TK/HW NE15 .... 57 F5 🔲
 LWF/SPW/WRK NE9 .... 99 F2
Causey Bank *CNUT* NE1 .... 3 F4
Causey Dr *STLY/ANP* DH9........ 131 F6
Causey Rd *STLY/ANP* DH9 ...... 131 F4
Causey St *GOS/KPK* NE3 .... 63 C2
Cavalier Vw *HEBB* NE31 .... 84 C1
Cavalier Wy *SUNDSW* SR3 ...... 160 B1 🔲
Cavell Sq *PLEE/EAS* SR8 .... 200 C3
Cavendish Ct *BDN/LAN/SAC* DH7.. 202 C5
Cavendish Pl *JES* NE2 .... 64 B5
 SUNDSW SR3.................... 64 B5
Cavendish Rd *JES* NE2 .... 64 B5
Caversham Rd *WD/WHPE/BLK* NE5.. 59 D3
Cawnpore Sq *MLFD/PNYW* SR4 .. 125 D6
Caynham Cl *NSHW* NE29 .... 54 A4 🔲
Cayton Gv *WD/WHPE/BLK* NE5 .. 59 D4
Cecil Ct *NSHW* NE29 .... 70 C1
Cecil St *NSHW* NE29 .... 70 C1
Cedar Av *CLSW/PEL* DH2 .... 165 E6
Cedar Cl *BDLGTN* NE22 .... 7 E2
 DHAM DH1 .... 195 F3
Cedar Crs *DUN/TMV* NE11 ...... 97 E3
 LWF/SPW/WRK NE9 .... 99 E6
 SEA/MUR SR7 .... 176 B3
Cedar Dr *DHAM* DH1 .... 205 D3
Cedar Gv *CLDN/WHIT/ROK* SR6 .. 91 E6
 HAR/WTLS NE34 .... 89 E3
 RYTON NE40 .... 74 B3
 WLSD/HOW NE28 .... 67 E5
Cedar Rd *BLAY* NE21 .... 76 B6
 ELS/FEN NE4.................... 78 C1
Cedars Ct *ASHBK/HED/RY* SR2 .. 144 C2
Cedars Crs *SEA/MUR* SR7 ...... 188 C1
Cedars Gn *LWF/SPW/WRK* NE9 .. 117 F1
Cedars Pk *ASHBK/HED/RY* SR2 .. 145 D3
The Cedars *ASHBK/HED/RY* SR2.. 144 C2
 WICK/BNPF NE16 .... 96 A6
Cedartree Gdns *MONK* NE25...... 54 A1
Cedarway *FELL* NE10 .... 101 D5
Cedar Wy *LGB/KIL* NE12 .... 50 A4 🔲
Cedarwood Av
 BYK/HTN/WLK NE6 .... 66 C5 🔲
Cedarwood Gv
 ASHBK/HED/RY SR2............ 144 B4
Cedric Crs *ASHBK/HED/RY* SR2 .. 144 A2
Celadon Cl
 BW/LEM/TK/HW NE15 .... 59 E6 🔲
Celandine Cl *GOS/KPK* NE3 ...... 47 F5
Celandine Wy *FELL* NE10 ...... 100 C4
Celtic Cl *CLDN/WHIT/ROK* SR6 .. 107 D1
Celtic Crs *CLDN/WHIT/ROK* SR6 .. 107 D1 🔲
Cemetery Ap *HAR/WTLS* NE34 .. 72 A6
Cemetery Rd *GATE* NE8 .... 99 E1 🔲
 JRW NE32 .... 86 B3
 STLY/ANP DH9.................. 148 B1
Centenary Av *HAR/WTLS* NE34 .. 89 F2
Centenary Ct *ELS/FEN* NE4 ...... 79 D4 🔲
Central Av *BDN/LAN/SAC* DH7 .. 203 E5
 CLDN/WHIT/ROK SR6............ 109 D2
 HAR/WTLS NE34 .... 89 E2
 NSHW NE29 .... 70 A1
Central Gdns *HAR/WTLS* NE34 .. 89 E2 🔲
Centurian Wy *BDLGTN* NE22 .... 7 D2
Centurion Rd
 BW/LEM/TK/HW NE15.......... 60 A6
Centurion Wy
 BW/LEM/TK/HW NE15.......... 56 A4
 LWF/SPW/WRK NE9 .... 100 A4 🔲
Ceolfrid Ter *JRW* NE32 .... 86 B4
Chacombe *WASHS* NE38 .... 138 B3 🔲
Chadderton Dr
 WD/WHPE/BLK NE5.............. 59 D3
Chadwick St *WLSD/HOW* NE28 .. 67 D5 🔲
Chaffinch Wy *LGB/KIL* NE12 .... 35 E6
Chainbridge Rd *BLAY* NE21 ...... 76 C5
Chain Bridge Rd *BLAY* NE21 .... 77 E5
Chalfont Gv *MLFD/PNYW* SR4.... 141 E4
Chalfont Rd *BYK/HTN/WLK* NE6 .. 83 E4
Chalfont Wy *BDN/LAN/SAC* DH7 .. 203 E4 🔲
Chalford Rd *SWCK/CAS* SR5...... 126 A2
Chamberlain St *BLYTH* NE24 .... 11 E6 🔲
Chandler Cl *DHAM* DH1 .... 195 F5
Chandlers Ford *HLS* DH4 .... 139 E6 🔲
Chandlers Quay
 BYK/HTN/WLK NE6 .... 82 B4
Chandless St *GATE* NE8 .... 81 E5 🔲
Chandos *SUNDSW* SR3 .... 160 C4 🔲
Chandos St *GATE* NE8 .... 99 E2

Chandra Pl *WD/WHPE/BLK* NE5 .... **61** D4 🔟
Chantry Cl *SUNDSW* SR3.............. **160** A3
Chantry Dr *DIN/WO* NE13 .... **33** D3
Chapel Av *WICK/BNPF* NE16 ..... **112** A6 🔟
Chapel Cl *GOS/KPK* NE3 .... **47** F3 🔢
Chapel Ct *RDHAMSE* DH6 .... **197** F5
Chapel Hill Rd *PLEE/EAS* SR8 ...... **209** D1
Chapel House Dr
    WD/WHPE/BLK NE5 .... **59** E5
Chapel House Gv
    BW/LEM/TK/HW NE15............. **59** E5
Chapel Rd *JRW* NE32 .... **86** A1
Chapel Rw *HLS* DH4 .... **157** E3
Chapel St *HLH* DH5 .... **171** F6
    NSHW NE29............................... **70** A1
    STLY/ANP DH9 .... **129** F4
Chapel Vw *HLS* DH4 .... **183** E3
    ROWG NE39................................ **111** D1
Chaplin St *SEA/MUR* SR7 .... **176** C4
Chapman St
    CLDN/WHIT/ROK SR6 .... **109** D5 🔢
Chapter Rw *SSH* NE33 .... **71** E3
Charlaw Cl *BDN/LAN/SAC* DH7 ... **164** A6
Charlbury Cl *LWF/SPW/WRK* NE9 ... **119** E3
Charlcote Crs *BOL* NE36 .... **106** C3 🔢
Charles Av *GOS/KPK* NE3 .... **46** A6
    LGB/KIL NE12 .... **49** F4
Charles Baker Wk
    HAR/WTLS NE34 .... **90** A2 🔟
Charles Dr *CRAM* NE23 .... **35** D2
Charles St *BOLCOL* NE35.............. **105** E2
    CLDN/WHIT/ROK SR6................ **126** C4
    DIN/WO NE13 .... **32** C5 🔢
    GATE NE8................................... **81** E6
    SEA/MUR SR7 .... **176** C3
    STLY/ANP DH9 .... **148** A4
    SUND SR1 .... **5** E1 🔟
Charleswood *GOS/KPK* NE3 .... **47** F4 🔟
Charlotte Cl *ELS/FEN* NE4 .... **80** A5 🔢
Charlotte Sq *CNUT* NE1 .... **2** B4 🔟
Charlotte St *SSH* NE33 .... **71** E3
    STLY/ANP DH9 .... **148** A4
    TYNE/NSHE NE30 .... **71** D1
    WLSD/HOW NE28 .... **67** E4
Charlton Gv *CLDN/WHIT/ROK* SR6 ... **107** F2
Charlton Rd *SWCK/CAS* SR5 ...... **126** B1
Charlton St *BW/LEM/TK/HW* NE15... **76** C2
Charman St *SUND* SR1 .... **4** C2 🔟
Charminster Gdns
    BYK/HTN/WLK NE6 .... **65** E4
Charnwood *STLY/ANP* DH9 .... **131** D6 🔟
Charnwood Av *LGB/KIL* NE12 ...... **48** C6
Charter Dr *SUNDSW* SR3 .... **159** E1
Chasedale Crs *BLYTH* NE24 .... **9** F5
Chase Farm Dr *BLYTH* NE24 .... **9** E4
Chase Ms *BLYTH* NE24 .... **9** E5 🔟
The Chase *LGB/KIL* NE12 .... **48** C2
    NSHW NE29................................ **54** B6
    WASHS NE38 .... **137** E5
Chatham Ct *MONK* NE25 .... **37** F1
Chatham Rd *SWCK/CAS* SR5 ...... **123** F2
Chathill Cl *MONK* NE25 .... **39** E5
Chathill Ter *BYK/HTN/WLK* NE6 ... **83** E3
Chatsworth Crs
    MLFD/PNYW SR4 .... **143** F2 🔟
Chatsworth Gdns
    BYK/HTN/WLK NE6 .... **82** C4 🔢
    WD/WHPE/BLK NE5 .... **60** B3 🔢
Chatsworth Pl *WICK/BNPF* NE16 ... **95** F5
Chatsworth Rd *JRW* NE32 .... **86** B3 🔢
Chatsworth St *MLFD/PNYW* SR4 ... **143** F1
Chatsworth St South
    MLFD/PNYW SR4 .... **143** F2 🔟
Chatterton St *SWCK/CAS* SR5 ... **125** F2
Chatton Av *CRAM* NE23 .... **22** B3
    HAR/WTLS NE34 .... **73** D6
Chatton Cl *CLSW/PEL* DH2 .... **165** F1
Chatton St *WLSD/HOW* NE28 ...... **69** E5
Chatton Wynd *GOS/KPK* NE3 ...... **46** C5 🔢
Chaucer Av *HAR/WTLS* NE34 ...... **87** F5
Chaucer Cl *GATE* NE8 .... **81** F6
    STLY/ANP DH9 .... **148** C2
Chaucer Rd *WICK/BNPF* NE16 ..... **95** F2
Chaytor Gv *SUND* SR1 .... **5** F4
Chaytor St *JRW* NE32 .... **69** D6
Cheadle Av *CRAM* NE23 .... **13** F5 🔢
    WLSD/HOW NE28 .... **51** F6
Cheadle Rd *SWCK/CAS* SR5 ...... **123** F2
Cheam Cl *WICK/BNPF* NE16 .... **96** A5 🔢
Cheam Rd *SWCK/CAS* SR5 .... **123** F2
Cheeseburn Gdns
    WD/WHPE/BLK NE5 .... **61** E6
Cheldon Cl *MONK* NE25 .... **39** E4
Chelford Cl *WLSD/HOW* NE28 ..... **52** A5
Chelmsford Gv *JES* NE2 .... **81** F1
Chelmsford Rd *SWCK/CAS* SR5 ... **123** F2
Chelmsford Sq *SWCK/CAS* SR5 ... **123** F1 🔢
Chelsea Gdns *GATE* NE8 .... **100** A2
Chelsea Gv *ELS/FEN* NE4 .... **79** F3 🔢
Cheltenham Dr *BOLCOL* NE35....... **87** D6
Cheltenham Rd *SWCK/CAS* SR5 ... **123** F2 🔟
Cheltenham Sq *SWCK/CAS* SR5 ... **123** F2 🔟
Cheltenham Ter
    BYK/HTN/WLK NE6 .... **82** A1 🔟
Chelton Cl *DIN/WO* NE13 .... **33** D6 🔟

Chepstow Gdns *GATE* NE8 .... **98** C2 🔢
Chepstow Rd
    BW/LEM/TK/HW NE15................ **77** E2
Chepstow St *MLFD/PNYW* SR4 ... **126** A6 🔟
Cherry Banks *CLS/BIR/GTL* DH3 ... **153** F3
Cherry Blossom Wy *WASHN* NE37 ... **122** A4
Cherry Gv *LGB/KIL* NE12.............. **35** E6
Cherry Pk *BDN/LAN/SAC* DH7 ..... **202** C5
Cherrytree Cl *LGB/KIL* NE12........ **50** B2
Cherrytree Ct *BDLGTN* NE22 .... **8** C2 🔟
Cherry Tree Dr *BDLGTN* NE22 .... **7** E3
Cherrytree Dr *WICK/BNPF* NE16.... **96** B2
Cherrytree Gdns
    LWF/SPW/WRK NE9 .... **99** F6
    MONK NE25................................ **54** B1
Cherry Trees *BLYTH* NE24 .... **10** C6 🔟
Cherry Wy *HLS* DH4 .... **170** A1
Cherwell *WASHN* NE37 .... **121** E4
Cherwell Rd *PLEE/EAS* SR8 .... **208** A3
Chesham Gdns *WD/WHPE/BLK* NE5.. **59** D4
Cheshire Av *CLS/BIR/GTL* DH5 ... **158** B5
Cheshire Dr *DHAM* DH1 .... **196** B4
Cheshire Gdns *WLSD/HOW* NE28 ... **66** C3
Cheshire Gv *HAR/WTLS* NE34 ...... **90** A1
The Chesils *LGB/KIL* NE12 .... **64** C1
Chesmond Dr *BLAY* NE21............. **76** A5
Chessar Av *WD/WHPE/BLK* NE5 ... **61** D4
Chester Av *WLSD/HOW* NE28 ...... **68** B3
Chester Ct *LGB/KIL* NE12 .... **49** D6
Chesterfield Rd *ELS/FEN* NE4 .... **79** E4 🔢
Chester Gdns *HAR/WTLS* NE34 .... **89** D1
Chester Gv *BLYTH* NE24 .... **10** B6
    CRAM NE23 .... **36** A1
Chester Pl *GATE* NE8 .... **81** D6 🔟
    PLEE/EAS SR8 .... **200** A6
Chester Rd *CLS/BIR/GTL* DH3 ... **154** C4
    HLS DH4.................................... **155** F5
    MLFD/PNYW SR4 .... **141** D4
    MLFD/PNYW SR4 .... **143** D1
    STLY/ANP DH9 .... **148** C1
Chester Road East *STLY/ANP* DH9 ... **148** C1
Chesters Av *LGB/KIL* NE12 .... **48** C6
Chesters Pk *LWF/SPW/WRK* NE9 ... **99** E4 🔟
The Chesters *MONK* NE25 .... **39** F4
    WD/WHPE/BLK NE5.................. **59** E5
Chester St *HLS* DH4 .... **157** F6
    JES NE2 .... **81** E1
    MLFD/PNYW SR4 .... **125** F6
Chester St East
    MLFD/PNYW SR4 .... **126** A6 🔢
Chester St West
    MLFD/PNYW SR4 .... **125** F6 🔟
Chester Ter *SUND* SR1 .... **126** A6
Chester Ter North
    MLFD/PNYW SR4 .... **126** A6 🔢
Chesterton Rd *HAR/WTLS* NE34 ... **88** A4
Chesterwood Dr *WLSD/HOW* NE28 ... **66** C4
Chestnut Av *BLYTH* NE24.............. **10** C3
    MONK NE25................................ **38** A6
    WD/WHPE/BLK NE5.................. **62** A4
    WICK/BNPF NE16...................... **96** A5
Chestnut Cl *JRW* NE32 .... **104** C1
    LGB/KIL NE12 .... **35** D6 🔢
Chestnut Crs *SWCK/CAS* SR5 .... **125** E1
Chestnut Gdns *GATE* NE8............. **98** B2
Chestnut Gv *HAR/WTLS* NE34 ...... **89** E4
Chestnut St *WLSD/HOW* NE28 .... **67** E5 🔟
Cheswick Dr *GOS/KPK* NE3 .... **47** F6
Cheveley Wk *DHAM* DH1 .... **196** C3
Chevin Cl *BYK/HTN/WLK* NE6 ...... **66** C5
Chevington *FELL* NE10 .... **101** F4 🔟
Chevington Gdns
    WD/WHPE/BLK NE5 .... **61** F5 🔢
Chevington Gv *MONK* NE25 .... **39** F3
Cheviot Cl *WASHN* NE37.............. **119** F6
Cheviot Ct *SEA/MUR* SR7 .... **175** F2
Cheviot Gdns *DUN/TMV* NE11 ...... **97** F3 🔟
    SEA/MUR SR7 .... **175** F2
Cheviot Gra *CRAM* NE23............... **35** E4
Cheviot La *ASHBK/HED/RY* SR2.... **161** F1
Cheviot Pl *PLEE/EAS* SR8 .... **208** A2
Cheviot Rd *BLAY* NE21 .... **94** B1
    HAR/WTLS NE34 .... **72** C6
    JRW NE32 .... **85** E4 🔢
Cheviot St *MLFD/PNYW* SR4 ...... **125** E5
Cheviot Vw *CLSW/PEL* DH2 .... **165** F2
    DIN/WO NE13 .... **32** C4
The Cheyne *SUNDSW* SR3 .... **160** C3
Chichester Av *CRAM* NE23 .... **13** E6
Chichester Cl *GOS/KPK* NE3........ **45** E5
Chichester Gv *BDLGTN* NE22 .... **7** E2
Chichester Pl *SSH* NE33 .... **71** E6 🔢
Chichester Rd
    CLDN/WHIT/ROK SR6 .... **109** D5
    DHAM DH1 .... **180** C5
    SSH NE33 .... **71** F5 🔟
Chichester Rd East *SSH* NE33 ...... **71** F5
Chicken Rd *WLSD/HOW* NE28 ...... **66** A3
Chick's La *CLDN/WHIT/ROK* SR6 ... **109** D1
Chigwell Cl *HLS* DH4 .... **157** D1
Chilcrosse *FELL* NE10 .... **101** E3 🔟
Chilham Ct *NSHW* NE29 .... **53** D4
Chillingham Cl *BLYTH* NE24 .... **16** A1
Chillingham Dr *CLSW/PEL* DH2 .... **165** F2 🔟
    NSHW NE29 .... **69** F2 🔟

Chillingham Rd *BYK/HTN/WLK* NE6 ... **65** E5
    DHAM DH1 .... **180** C6
Chillingham Ter *JRW* NE32 .... **86** C4
Chilside Rd *FELL* NE10 .... **101** D2 🔢
Chiltern Cl *WASHS* NE38 .... **138** A3
Chiltern Dr *LGB/KIL* NE12 .... **49** D3
Chiltern Gdns *DUN/TMV* NE11 ...... **97** F3
Chiltern Rd *NSHW* NE29 .... **54** B2
Chilton Gdns *HLS* DH4 .... **169** F2 🔟
Chilton Garth *PLEE/EAS* SR8 ...... **209** D3
Chilton St *SWCK/CAS* SR5 .... **126** B3 🔟
China St *ASHBK/HED/RY* SR2...... **145** D2
Chingford Cl *HLS* DH4 .... **157** E1 🔟
Chipchase *WASHS* NE38 .... **137** E2
Chipchase Av *CRAM* NE23 .... **22** A3
Chipchase Cl *BDLGTN* NE22 .... **6** C3 🔟
Chipchase Ct *MONK* NE25 .... **24** B2
Chipchase Crs *WD/WHPE/BLK* NE5 ... **60** A3
Chipchase Ter *JRW* NE32 .... **86** A5
Chirton Av *HAR/WTLS* NE34 .... **90** B2
    NSHW NE29................................ **70** B1
Chirton Dene Quays *NSHW* NE29... **70** B4
Chirton Dene Wy *NSHW* NE29....... **70** B3
Chirton Gn *NSHW* NE29 .... **70** B3 🔢
Chirton Gv *HAR/WTLS* NE34 .... **90** B2
Chirton Hill Dr *NSHW* NE29 .... **53** E5
Chirton La *NSHW* NE29 .... **54** A6
Chirton West Vw *NSHW* NE29....... **70** B1
Chirton Wynd *BYK/HTN/WLK* NE6 ... **82** B3
Chislehurst Rd *HLS* DH4 .... **157** D1 🔟
Chiswick Gdns *GATE* NE8 .... **99** F2 🔟
Chiswick Rd *MONK* NE25 .... **24** C6
    SWCK/CAS SR5 .... **123** F2
Chollerford Av *MONK* NE25 .... **41** D6
    NSHW NE29................................ **53** E6
Chollerford Cl *GOS/KPK* NE3 .... **62** C2
Chollerford Ms *MONK* NE25 .... **25** E6
Chollerton Dr *BDLGTN* NE22 .... **7** F3
    LGB/KIL NE12 .... **50** C5
Choppington Rd *STKFD/GP* NE62... **7** E1
Chorley Pl *BYK/HTN/WLK* NE6...... **83** D3
Chowdene Bank *DUN/TMV* NE11.... **117** D2
    LWF/SPW/WRK NE9.................. **117** E1
Christal Ter *CLDN/WHIT/ROK* SR6 ... **126** C1
Christie Ter *BYK/HTN/WLK* NE6..... **83** E3
Christon Cl *GOS/KPK* NE3 .... **64** A1 🔢
Christon Rd *GOS/KPK* NE3 .... **63** E1
Christon Wy *FELL* NE10 .... **84** A6 🔢
Christopher Rd
    BYK/HTN/WLK NE6 .... **83** D1 🔟
Chudleigh Gdns
    WD/WHPE/BLK NE5 .... **59** D4
Church Av *GOS/KPK* NE3 .... **63** F1
Church Bank
    BW/LEM/TK/HW NE15 .... **75** E1 🔟
    JRW NE32 .... **86** C1
    STLY/ANP DH9 .... **148** B1
    SWCK/CAS SR5 .... **125** F3 🔢
    WLSD/HOW NE28 .... **67** F4
Church Chare *PONT/DH* NE20........ **28** B3
    WICK/BNPF NE16...................... **96** A3 🔟
Church Cl *BDLGTN* NE22 .... **7** E4 🔟
    DIN/WO NE13 .... **31** D3
    MONK NE25................................ **39** E6
    PLEE/EAS SR8 .... **209** D3
    SEA/MUR SR7 .... **176** B2
Church Ct *BDLGTN* NE22 .... **7** E4
    SEA/MUR SR7 .... **175** F2
Churchdown Cl *BOLCOL* NE35 ...... **87** D6 🔢
Church Dr *LWF/SPW/WRK* NE9 ..... **99** F4 🔢
Churcher Gdns *WLSD/HOW* NE28... **66** C2 🔟
Church Flatt *PONT/DH* NE20.......... **28** B3
Church Gn *SEA/MUR* SR7 .... **176** B2 🔢
Churchill Av *DHAM* DH1 .... **195** E4
    MONK NE25................................ **54** A1
    SWCK/CAS SR5 .... **125** F2 🔢
Churchill Gdns *JES* NE2 .... **64** C5 🔟
Churchill Sq *HLS* DH4 .... **170** A2 🔟
Churchill St *SUND* SR1 .... **5** E4
    WLSD/HOW NE28 .... **68** B2
Church La *BDLGTN* NE22 .... **7** F4
    CLDN/WHIT/ROK SR6................ **109** E2
    DHAM DH1 .... **194** C6 🔟
    GOS/KPK NE3 .... **63** F1
    LWF/SPW/WRK NE9 .... **100** A4 🔢
    SEA/MUR SR7 .... **188** A1
Church Pl *FELL* NE10 .... **100** C1
Church Ri *RYTON* NE40 .... **75** D3
    WICK/BNPF NE16...................... **96** A3
Church Rd
    BW/LEM/TK/HW NE15 .... **75** E1 🔢
    GOS/KPK NE3 .... **63** F1
    HLH DH5 .... **171** F4
    LWF/SPW/WRK NE9 .... **99** E6
    SMOOR NE27 .... **37** E5
Church St *BDN/LAN/SAC* DH7 ..... **178** A1
    BLAY NE21 .... **93** F1
    BYK/HTN/WLK NE6 .... **83** F4
    DHAM DH1 .... **194** C6
    DUN/TMV NE11 .... **97** F1
    GATE NE8 .... **3** F6
    HEBB NE31 .... **84** C1
    HLH DH5 .... **171** D2 🔟
    HLS DH4 .... **171** D2
    HLS DH4 .... **183** D2

Colliery Rd DUN/TMV NE11 .... 79 E6
Collin Av HAR/WTLS NE34 .... 90 A3
Collingwood Av WLSD/HOW NE28.. 67 D2
Collingwood Dr HLS DH4 .... 156 C2
Collingwood Gdns FELL NE10 .... 82 C6
Collingwood Rd MONK NE25 .... 38 C5 [1]
Collingwood St CNUT NE1 .... 2 D5
   HEBB NE31 .... 85 F2 [1]
   HLH DH5 .... 171 F4 [1]
   SSH NE33 .... 71 E6
   SWCK/CAS SR5 .... 126 A2 [4]
Collingwood Vw NSHW NE29 .... 70 B1
Collywell Bay Rd WBAY NE26 .... 26 C2
Collywell Ct WBAY NE26 .... 26 C2 [1]
Colman Av HAR/WTLS NE34 .... 87 F5
Colmbrook Cl GOS/KPK NE3 .... 45 F5
Colombo Rd SWCK/CAS SR5 .... 123 E5
Colston Ri PLEE/EAS SR8 .... 208 B1
Colston St ELS/FEN NE4 .... 78 C3
Colston Wy MONK NE25 .... 39 F3
Coltere Av BOL NE36 .... 107 D3
Colton Gdns LWF/SPW/WRK NE9 ... 117 F1
Coltpark WD/WHPE/BLK NE5 ..... 60 B5 [3]
Coltsfoot Gdns FELL NE10 .... 100 B5
Coltspool DUN/TMV NE11 .... 116 C6
Columba St SWCK/CAS SR5 ...... 126 A2 [3]
Columba Wk GOS/KPK NE3 .... 63 F1
Columbia Gra GOS/KPK NE3 ...... 62 A1 [2]
Columbia Ter BLYTH NE24 .... 11 D6 [2]
Colville Ct STLY/ANP DH9 .... 149 D2
Colwell Pl WD/WHPE/BLK NE5 .. 78 B1 [2]
Colwell Rd SMOOR NE27 .... 52 B2
Colwyne Pl WD/WHPE/BLK NE5 .... 61 D4
Combe Dr BW/LEM/TK/HW NE15 ... 76 A1
Comet Dr PLEE/EAS SR8 .... 200 B2 [1]
Comet Rw LGB/KIL NE12 .... 49 E2
Comet Sq SUNDSW SR3 .... 160 C1 [3]
Comical Cnr SSH NE33 .... 71 D2
Comma Ct DUN/TMV NE11 .... 98 A3
Commercial Rd
   ASHBK/HED/RY SR2 .... 145 E2
   BYK/HTN/WLK NE6 .... 82 B3
   GOS/KPK NE3 .... 64 A1 [3]
   JRW NE32 .... 69 E6 [1]
   SSH NE33 .... 71 D5
Commercial St BLAY NE21 .... 94 A1
Commissioners' Whf NSHW NE29... 70 B4
Compton Av HAR/WTLS NE34 .... 88 C1
Compton Rd NSHW NE29............... 70 B1
Concorde Wy JRW NE32 .... 86 A2
Condercum Ct
   BW/LEM/TK/HW NE15 .... 78 B3 [1]
Condercum Rd ELS/FEN NE4 .... 78 C3
Cone St SSH NE33 .... 71 D4
Congburn Bank
   BDN/LAN/SAC DH7 .... 164 A2
Conhope La BW/LEM/TK/HW NE15 .. 78 C3
Conifer Cl DHAM DH1 .... 195 F3 [2]
Coniscliffe Av GOS/KPK NE3 .... 62 B3
Coniscliffe Rd STLY/ANP DH9 ...... 147 F3
Conishead Ter RDHAMSE DH6 ...... 187 E4
Coniston CLS/BIR/GTL DH3 .... 136 C5
   FELL NE10 .... 101 F2
Coniston Av HEBB NE31............... 85 E3
   HLH DH5 .... 186 B4
   JES NE2 .... 64 A4 [1]
   SWCK/CAS SR5 .... 108 B6
   WICK/BNPF NE16 .... 96 C3 [2]
Coniston Crs BLAY NE21 .... 94 A2 [2]
Coniston Dr BDN/LAN/SAC DH7 ... 164 A6
   JRW NE32 .... 86 C5
Coniston Gdns
   LWF/SPW/WRK NE9 .... 100 A5
Coniston Pl LWF/SPW/WRK NE9 .. 100 A5 [1]
Coniston Rd BLYTH NE24 .... 9 E3
   TYNE/NSHE NE30 .... 54 B2
   WLSD/HOW NE28 .... 68 B2
Connaught Cl HLS DH4 .... 157 E5 [1]
Connaught Ter JRW NE32 .... 86 A2
Conningsby Cl GOS/KPK NE3 .... 47 F4
Conpott Rd DUN/TMV NE11 .... 97 F5
Constable Cl RYTON NE40 .... 74 B4
   STLY/ANP DH9 .... 148 B2
Constable Gdns HAR/WTLS NE34 .. 88 B5
Constance St CLSW/PEL DH2 .... 152 A1
Content St BLAY NE21 .... 94 B1
Conway Cl BDLGTN NE22 .... 6 C3
   RYTON NE40 .... 74 C5
Conway Dr LGB/HTN NE7 .... 64 C2
Conway Gdns SUNDSW SR3 .... 159 F1 [1][1]
   WLSD/HOW NE28 .... 66 C2
Conway Gv WBAY NE26 .... 26 A1
Conway Pl CLSW/PEL DH2 .... 135 E6
Conway Rd SWCK/CAS SR5 .... 123 E2
Conway Sq LWF/SPW/WRK NE9 .. 99 F2 [2]
   SWCK/CAS SR5 .... 123 E2 [3]
Conyers Av CLSW/PEL DH2 .... 153 D3
Conyers Gdns CLSW/PEL DH2 ...... 153 D3
Conyers Pl CLSW/PEL DH2............ 153 D3
Conyers Rd BYK/HTN/WLK NE6 .... 82 B2
   CLSW/PEL DH2 .... 153 D3

Cook Cl SSH NE33 .... 71 D6
Cook Crs SEA/MUR SR7 .... 188 A1
Cooke's Wd BDN/LAN/SAC DH7 ... 192 B6
Cook Gdns FELL NE10 .... 102 A2
Cookson Cl ELS/FEN NE4 .... 80 A3 [3]
Cookson's La CNUT NE1 .... 2 C6
Cookson St ELS/FEN NE4 .... 79 F3 [1]
Cookson Ter CLSW/PEL DH2 .... 153 D5
Cook Sq SWCK/CAS SR5 .... 123 F2 [3]
Cooks Wd WASHS NE38 .... 138 C3
Cook Wy PLEE/EAS SR8 .... 207 D1
Coomassie Rd BLYTH NE24 .... 11 D5
Coomside CRAM NE23 .... 22 B4 [2]
Co-operative Ter
   MLFD/PNYW SR4 .... 143 F1 [2]
   STLY/ANP DH9 .... 128 B6
Cooper Sq DHAM DH1 .... 195 E3
Cooper St CLDN/WHIT/ROK SR6 ... 127 D3 [2]
Copeland Ct DHAM DH1 .... 193 F6
Copland Ter JES NE2 .... 3 G2
Copley Av HAR/WTLS NE34 .... 88 R6
Copley Dr SUNDSW SR3 .... 144 A4
Copperas La
   BW/LEM/TK/HW NE15 .... 77 E1 [2]
Copperfield DHAM DH1 .... 204 C1 [1]
Coppergate Ct HEBB NE31 .... 85 E1
Coppice Wy JES NE2 .... 3 G1
Coppy La STLY/ANP DH9 .... 132 B3
   WICK/BNPF NE16 .... 132 A1
The Copse BLAY NE21.................. 77 F6
   WICK/BNPF NE16 .... 111 E6
Coquet WASHS NE38 .... 137 E5
Coquet Av BLYTH NE24 .... 17 D3 [3]
   GOS/KPK NE3 .... 47 D6
   HAR/WTLS NE34 .... 72 C6
   WBAY NE26 .... 40 C5
Coquetdale Av BYK/HTN/WLK NE6 .. 83 F2
Coquet Dr CLSW/PEL DH2 .... 135 D6
Coquet Gdns STLY/ANP DH9 ..... 148 A4 [1]
Coquet Gv BW/LEM/TK/HW NE15 .. 57 E5
Coquet St CNUT NE1 .... 3 H3 [1]
   CNUT NE1 .... 81 F2 [2]
   HEBB NE31 .... 84 C2 [1]
   JRW NE32 .... 85 F3
Coquet Ter BYK/HTN/WLK NE6 .... 65 D5
   CRAM NE23 .... 34 B2
Corbiere Cl SUNDSW SR3 .... 160 A2
Corbitt St GATE NE8 .... 98 B1
Corbridge Cl WLSD/HOW NE28 .... 52 A6
Corbridge Rd BYK/HTN/WLK NE6 .. 82 B2
Corbridge St BYK/HTN/WLK NE6 .. 82 A2
Corby Gdns BYK/HTN/WLK NE6 ... 83 E2
Corby Ga ASHBK/HED/RY SR2 ... 144 C2 [2]
Corby Gv PLEE/EAS SR8 .... 207 F5
Corby Hall Dr
   ASHBK/HED/RY SR2 .... 144 C2 [3]
Corchester Rd BDLGTN NE22 .... 7 D2
Corchester Wk LGB/HTN NE7 ...... 65 D2
Corinthian Sq SWCK/CAS SR5 ... 123 F2 [3]
Cork St SUND SR1 .... 5 E2
Cormorant Cl BLYTH NE24 .... 17 E2
Cornbank Cl SUNDSW SR3 .... 160 C3
Corndean WASHS NE38 .... 139 F2
Cornelia Ter SEA/MUR SR7 .... 176 B3
Cornel Rd LGB/HTN NE7 .... 65 D3
Corney St SSH NE33 .... 88 A1
The Cornfields HEBB NE31 .... 85 D2
Cornforth Cl FELL NE10............... 102 B4
Cornhill Av GOS/KPK NE3 .... 46 B5 [1]
Cornhill Crs NSHW NE29.............. 53 F5
Cornhill Rd CRAM NE23 .... 22 A2 [2]
   SWCK/CAS SR5 .... 126 A2 [3]
Corn Mill Dr HLH DH5 .... 170 C4
Cornmoor Gdns WICK/BNPF NE16.. 96 A5
Cornmoor Rd WICK/BNPF NE16 .... 96 A4
Cornthwaite Dr
   CLDN/WHIT/ROK SR6 .... 109 E2 [1]
Cornwallis Sq SSH NE33 .... 71 D5 [1]
Cornwallis St SSH NE33 .... 71 E3 [1]
Cornwall Rd HEBB NE31 .... 85 E5 [1]
Cornwell Ct LGB/HTN NE7 .... 64 B2 [1]
Cornwell Crs BDLGTN NE22 .... 8 A4 [1]
Coronation Av DHAM DH1 .... 196 C2 [2]
Coronation Gn HLH DH5 .... 186 C4 [1]
Coronation Rd WD/WHPE/BLK NE5.. 59 D3 [2]
   WICK/BNPF NE16 .... 114 A2 [1]
Coronation Sq RDHAMSE DH6 ... 188 A5 [1]
Coronation St CLS/BIR/GTL DH3.... 153 F6
   NSHW NE29 .... 70 C2 [1]
   SUND SR1 .... 5 E2 [1]
   WLSD/HOW NE28 .... 67 E4
Coronation Ter
   MLFD/PNYW SR4 .... 124 A6 [1]
Corporation Rd
   ASHBK/HED/RY SR2 .... 145 E2
Corporation St ELS/FEN NE4........ 2 A4
Corriedale Cl DHAM DH1 .... 180 B4 [1]
Corrofell Gdns FELL NE10 .... 83 D6
Corry Ct MLFD/PNYW SR4 .... 143 D2 [2]
Corsair WICK/BNPF NE16 .... 95 E4
Corsenside WD/WHPE/BLK NE5 .... 60 B5
Corstorphine Town SSH NE33 .... 71 D6
Cortina Av MLFD/PNYW SR4 .... 142 C2
Cossack Ter MLFD/PNYW SR4 ...... 125 D5
Cosserat Pl HEBB NE31 .... 84 C1 [1]

Cosser St BLYTH NE24 .... 16 A2 [2]
Coston Dr SSH NE33 .... 71 E3
Cosyn St BYK/HTN/WLK NE6 ..... 81 F3 [2]
Cotehill Rd WD/WHPE/BLK NE5 ... 61 D5 [2]
Cotemede FELL NE10 .... 101 F5
The Cotgarth FELL NE10 .... 101 D3 [1]
Cotherstone Ct SUNDSW SR3 ...... 144 A4
Cotherstone Rd DHAM DH1 .... 180 C6
Cotman Gdns HAR/WTLS NE34 .... 88 C6
Cotsford La PLEE/EAS SR8 .... 209 F2
Cotswold Av LGB/KIL NE12 ...... 49 D3 [1]
Cotswold Cl WASHS NE38 .... 138 A2
Cotswold Dr MONK NE25 .... 54 B1
Cotswold Gdns DUN/TMV NE11 ... 97 F3
   LGB/HTN NE7 .... 64 C3
Cotswold La BOLCOL NE35 .... 87 D6
Cotswold Pl PLEE/EAS SR8 .... 208 A1
Cotswold Rd NSHW NE29 .... 54 A2
   SWCK/CAS SR5 .... 123 F2
Cotswold Sq SWCK/CAS SR5 .... 123 F1 [3]
Cotswold St STLY/ANP DH9 .... 148 C3
Cottage La WD/WHPE/BLK NE5 .... 61 F5
Cottages Rd SEA/MUR SR7 .... 176 C4
Cottenham Chare ELS/FEN NE4 ... 80 A3 [4]
Cottenham St ELS/FEN NE4 ...... 80 A3 [3]
Cotterdale WLSD/HOW NE28 .... 66 B1 [1]
Cotter Riggs Pl
   WD/WHPE/BLK NE5 .... 59 D4
Cottersdale Gdns
   WD/WHPE/BLK NE5 .... 59 D3
Cottingham Cl PLEE/EAS SR8 ..... 208 A1
Cottingwood Gn BLYTH NE24 ...... 16 A3
Cottonwood SUNDSW SR3 .... 160 A3 [2]
Coulthards La GATE NE8 .... 81 F5
Coulthards Pl GATE NE8 .... 81 F4 [2]
Coulton Dr BOL NE36 .... 106 C3 [3]
Council Av HLS DH4 .... 157 D2 [1]
Counden Rd WD/WHPE/BLK NE5 .. 60 A3 [3]
Countess Av WBAY NE26 .... 40 C5
Countess Dr BW/LEM/TK/HW NE15.. 77 F1
Coupland Gv JRW NE32 .... 85 F5
Courtfield Rd BYK/HTN/WLK NE6... 66 B6
Court La DHAM DH1 .... 194 C5
Courtney Dr SUNDSW SR3 .... 143 E6
Court Rd BDLGTN NE22 .... 7 E3
The Court WICK/BNPF NE16 .... 96 B4
The Courtyard STLY/ANP DH9....... 130 B6
Cousin St SUND SR1 .... 5 F2
Coutts Rd BYK/HTN/WLK NE6 ..... 66 A6
Coventry Gdns ELS/FEN NE4......... 79 D4
   NSHW NE29 .... 70 A2 [1]
Coventry Rd DHAM DH1 .... 180 C5
Coverdale FELL NE10 .... 101 F4
   WLSD/HOW NE28 .... 66 B1
Coverdale Av BLYTH NE24 .... 9 F5 [2]
Coverley Rd SWCK/CAS SR5 .... 123 F1
The Covers LGB/KIL NE12 .... 50 A6
The Cove HLS DH4 .... 157 D2
Cowan Cl BLAY NE21 .... 75 F4
Cowan Av LGB/KIL NE12 .... 35 E6 [3]
Cowan Ter ASHBK/HED/RY SR2 .... 4 B4
Cowdray Rd SWCK/CAS SR5 .... 124 A2
Cowell Gv ROWG NE39 .... 110 B2
Cowell St PLEE/EAS SR8 .... 209 E1 [1]
Cowen Gdns LWF/SPW/WRK NE9... 117 F3
Cowen Rd BLAY NE21 .... 76 C5
Cowen St BYK/HTN/WLK NE6 .... 83 E2 [2]
Cowley Pl BLYTH NE24 .... 10 A4
Cowley Rd BLYTH NE24 .... 10 A3
Cowley St RDHAMSE DH6 .... 206 C2 [2]
Cowpen Hall Rd BLYTH NE24 .... 9 F4
Cowpen Rd BLYTH NE24 .... 9 F4
Coxfoot Cl HAR/WTLS NE34 ...... 88 B3 [3]
Coxgreen Rd HLS DH4 .... 139 F6
Coxlodge Rd GOS/KPK NE3 .... 62 C1
Coxlodge Ter GOS/KPK NE3 .... 62 C1
Coxon St ASHBK/HED/RY SR2 .... 5 E4
   FELL NE10 .... 84 A6
Cradock Av HEBB NE31 .... 84 C4 [1]
Craggyknowe WASHN NE37 .... 119 E6
Craghall Dene GOS/KPK NE3 ..... 64 A3 [3]
Craghall Dene Av JES NE2 .... 64 A2 [4]
Craghead La STLY/ANP DH9 .... 150 A5
Cragleas WICK/BNPF NE16 .... 129 F2
Cragside BDN/LAN/SAC DH7 .... 178 A4
   CLSW/PEL DH2 .... 163 C4
   CRAM NE23 .... 22 A4
   HAR/WTLS NE34 .... 90 A3
   LGB/HTN NE7 .... 65 D3
   WBAY NE26 .... 40 A3
Cragside Av NSHW NE29 .... 53 F4
Cragside Gdns DUN/TMV NE11 .... 97 F5
   LGB/KIL NE12 .... 36 B6
   WLSD/HOW NE28 .... 68 B3 [1]
Cragside Rd WASHN NE37 .... 119 F5
Cragston Av WD/WHPE/BLK NE5 .. 61 E3
Cragston Cl WD/WHPE/BLK NE5 .. 61 E4 [1]
Cragton Gdns BLYTH NE24 .... 10 A5 [1]
Craigavon Rd SWCK/CAS SR5 ...... 124 A3
Craig Crs CRAM NE23 .... 34 C2
Craighill HLS DH4 .... 156 C2 [1]
Craigmillar Av WD/WHPE/BLK NE5.. 61 E3
Craigmillar Cl WD/WHPE/BLK NE5 .. 61 D3
Craigmill Pk BLYTH NE24 .... 9 F4
Craigshaw Rd SWCK/CAS SR5 ... 123 E1 [1]

Craigwell Dr SUNDSW SR3 .... 160 C4
Craik Av HAR/WTLS NE34 .... 88 A3
Crake Wy WASHS NE38 .... 137 E4
Cramer St GATE NE8 .... 99 E1
Cramlington Rd SWCK/CAS NE3 ..... 123 E3
Cramlington Sq SWCK/CAS SR5 .. 123 E2 🔟
Cramlington Ter BLYTH NE24 .... 16 B2 🔟
Cramond Ct LWF/SPW/WRK NE9 ... 117 D1
Cramond Wy CRAM NE23 .... 22 A4
Cranberry Dr SWCK/CAS SR5 .... 123 F2
Cranberry Rd SWCK/CAS SR5 .... 123 F2
Cranberry Sq SWCK/CAS SR5 .... 123 F2 🔟
Cranbourne SUNDSW SR3 .... 159 E2
Cranbourne Gv
  TYNE/NSHE NE30 .... 55 D1 🔟
Cranbrook Av GOS/KPK NE3 .... 47 E5
Cranbrook Ct GOS/KPK NE3 .... 46 A5
Cranbrook Pl
  BW/LEM/TK/HW NE15 .... 78 A4 🔟
Cranbrook Rd
  BW/LEM/TK/HW NE15 .... 78 A4
Craneswater Av WBAY NE26 .... 40 B3
Cranfield Pl
  BW/LEM/TK/HW NE15 .... 76 B1 🔟
Cranford St HAR/WTLS NE34 .... 88 B2
Cranford Ter MLFD/PNYW SR4 ... 143 F1 🔟
Cranham Cl LGB/KIL NE12 .... 36 B6 🔟
Cranleigh Av DIN/WO NE13 .... 45 D5
Cranleigh Pl MONK NE25 .... 39 F3
Cranleigh Rd SWCK/CAS SR5 .... 123 F2
Cranshaw Pl CRAM NE23 .... 22 B5
Cranston Rd GOS/KPK NE3 .... 62 B1
Cranwell Dr DIN/WO NE13 .... 33 D4
Craster Av HAR/WTLS NE34 .... 73 E1
  LGB/KIL NE12 .... 50 B3
  SMOOR NE27 .... 52 A1
Craster Cl BLYTH NE24 .... 10 B5
  CLSW/PEL DH2 .... 165 E1
  MONK NE25 .... 39 F4
Craster Gdns WLSD/HOW NE28 ... 68 B3 🔟
Craster Rd NSHW NE29 .... 69 F1 🔟
Craster Sq GOS/KPK NE3 .... 46 C6
Craster Ter LGB/HTN NE7 .... 65 D4
Crawford Av PLEE/EAS SR8 .... 200 C1
Crawford Ct RDHAMSE DH6 .... 197 E5 🔟
Crawford Ct SUNDSW SR3 .... 160 B2 🔟
Crawford Pl MONK NE25 .... 40 A6
Crawford Pl BLYTH NE24 .... 10 C3
Crawford Ter BYK/HTN/WLK NE6 ... 85 F4
Crawhall Rd CNUT NE1 .... 3 H3
Crawlaw Rd PLEE/EAS SR8 .... 200 C1
Crawley Av HEBB NE31 .... 84 C5
Crawley Rd WLSD/HOW NE28 ... 96 B3 🔟
Crawley Rd WLSD/HOW NE28 .... 67 D5
Crawley Sq HEBB NE31 .... 84 C5
Craythorne Gdns
  BYK/HTN/WLK NE6 .... 65 E4
Creeverlea WASHS NE38 .... 138 B3
Creighton Av GOS/KPK NE3 .... 62 A3
Creland Wy WD/WHPE/BLK NE5 .. 61 E3 🔟
The Crescent BDN/LAN/SAC DH7 ... 178 A3
  BW/LEM/TK/HW NE15 .... 57 F4 🔟
  CLDN/WHIT/ROK SR6 .... 107 E2
  CLSW/PEL DH2 .... 153 D5
  CLSW/PEL DH2 .... 165 E1
  CRAM NE23 .... 36 B1
  DHAM DH1 .... 193 F3
  DIN/WO NE13 .... 45 D6
  HAR/WTLS NE34 .... 89 E4
  HLS DH4 .... 156 C3
  HLS DH4 .... 157 F4
  HLS DH4 .... 183 E2
  JRW NE32 .... 85 F4
  LGB/HTN NE7 .... 65 D1
  PLEE/EAS SR8 .... 201 D1
  RDHAMSE DH6 .... 197 E5
  ROWG NE39 .... 111 E2
  RYTON NE40 .... 74 C3
  STLY/ANP DH9 .... 130 C6
  SUNDSW SR3 .... 143 F5
  TYNE/NSHE NE30 .... 55 E4
  WICK/BNPF NE16 .... 96 B4
  WLSD/HOW NE28 .... 67 D3
Crescent Wy North LGB/KIL NE12 ... 50 A4
Crescent Wy South LGB/KIL NE12 ... 50 A4
Cressbourne Av
  CLDN/WHIT/ROK SR6 .... 109 D6 🔟
Cresswell Av LGB/KIL NF12 .... 50 A1
  NSHW NE29 .... 54 B5
  PLEE/EAS SR8 .... 209 F2
  WBAY NE26 .... 26 B2
Cresswell Cl BLAY NE21 .... 93 F2 🔟
  MONK NE25 .... 54 A1
Cresswell Dr BLYTH NE24 .... 16 A1
  GOS/KPK NE3 .... 46 A5
Cresswell Rd WLSD/HOW NE28 ...... 66 C5
Cresswell St BYK/HTN/WLK NE6 . 82 C2 🔟
  BYK/HTN/WLK NE6 .... 82 C3 🔟
The Crest BDLGTN NE22 .... 7 D3
  DIN/WO NE13 .... 31 D3
  WBAY NE26 .... 26 C4
Crichton Av CLS/BIR/GTL DH3 ...... 166 C1
Cricklewood Dr HLS DH4 .... 157 E2 🔟
  HLS DH4 .... 157 D1 🔟
Cricklewood Rd SWCK/CAS SR5 ... 123 E3
Criddle St GATE NE8 .... 81 F4

Crieff Gv JRW NE32 .... 86 C5
Crieff Sq SWCK/CAS SR5 .... 123 E2 🔟
Crigdon Hl WD/WHPE/BLK NE5 ...... 60 B5
Crighton WASHS NE38 .... 137 F1
Crimdon Gv HLS DH4 .... 170 B3 🔟
Cripps Av FELL NE10 .... 102 A2
Croft Av LGB/KIL NE12 .... 50 A5
  WLSD/HOW NE28 .... 67 E4 🔟
Croft Ct RYTON NE40 .... 74 C4
Croftdale Rd BLAY NE21 .... 76 A6
Crofter Cl CRAM NE23 .... 34 C1
Crofthead Dr CRAM NE23 .... 22 A4
Crofton St BLYTH NE24 .... 11 D5 🔟
  HAR/WTLS NE34 .... 88 B2
Crofton Wy BW/LEM/TK/HW NE15 .. 76 A1
Croft Rigg BDN/LAN/SAC DH7 ...... 202 C5
Croft Rd BLYTH NE24 .... 11 D5
Croftside Av CLDN/WHIT/ROK SR6 . 109 E2
Croft St CNUT NE1 .... 3 E3
Croftsway ELS/FEN NE4 .... 79 E4 🔟
Croft Ter JRW NE32 .... 86 A2
The Croft GOS/KPK NE3 .... 62 C2
  LGB/KIL NE12 .... 36 A6
Cromarty CLSW/PEL DH2 .... 135 E4
Cromarty St CLDN/WHIT/ROK SR6 . 126 C2
Cromdale Pl WD/WHPE/BLK NE5 ... 61 D5
Cromer Av LWF/SPW/WRK NE9 .... 117 D1
Cromer Gdns WBAY NE26 .... 40 C4
Crompton Rd BYK/HTN/WLK NE6 ... 65 D5
Cromwell Av BLAY NE21 .... 76 A6
Cromwell Ct BLAY NE21 .... 75 F4
Cromwell Rd FELL NE10 .... 84 A6
  WICK/BNPF NE16 .... 96 B2
Cromwell St GATE NE8 .... 99 F1
  MLFD/PNYW SR4 .... 125 F5
Cromwell Ter GATE NE8 .... 98 C1
Crondall St SSH NE33 .... 88 C1
Cronin Av HAR/WTLS NE34 .... 87 F4
Crookham Wy CRAM NE23 .... 22 B4
Cropthorne FELL NE10 .... 102 A4 🔟
Cross Av WLSD/HOW NE28 .... 66 B2
Crossbank Rd WD/WHPE/BLK NE5.. 61 F3
Crossbrook Rd
  WD/WHPE/BLK NE5 .... 61 F4 🔟
Crosby Ct ASHBK/HED/RY SR2 .... 5 G5
Crossfield Av CLDN/WHIT/ROK SR6 178 B2
Crossfield Pk FELL NE10 .... 100 B4
Crossfield Ter BYK/HTN/WLK NE6 . 83 F4 🔟
Crossgate DHAM DH1 .... 194 A5
  SSH NE33 .... 71 E4
Crossgate Moor Gdns DHAM 193 E4
Crossgate Peth DHAM DH1 .... 193 F5
Crosshill Rd BW/LEM/TK/HW NE15 78 A4
Cross Keys La LWF/SPW/WRK NE9 . 99 E5
Cross La BDN/LAN/SAC DH7 .... 164 B6
  DUN/TMV NE11 .... 78 C4
  DUN/TMV NE11 .... 115 F1
  WICK/BNPF NE16 .... 96 B2
Crosslaw WD/WHPE/BLK NE5 .... 60 B5
Crosslea Av SUNDSW SR3 .... 144 A3
Crossley Ter ELS/FEN NE4 .... 79 E2 🔟
  LGB/KIL NE12 .... 50 B3
Cross Morpeth St JES NE2 .... 63 D6 🔟
Cross Pde ELS/FEN NE4 .... 80 A4 🔟
Cross Pl SUND SR1 .... 5 E2 🔟
Cross Rigg Cl HLS DH4 .... 156 C1 🔟
Cross Rw GATE NE8 .... 100 A1
Cross St BYK/HTN/WLK NE6 .... 81 F3 🔟
  CNUT NE1 .... 2 B4
  GATE NE8 .... 99 E1 🔟
  HLS DH4 .... 169 F2 🔟
  HLS DH4 .... 170 C1 🔟
Cross Ter ROWG NE39 .... 110 C3 🔟
Cross Vale Rd ASHBK/HED/RY SR2 . 144 B2
Cross Villa Place No 4
  ELS/FEN NE4 .... 80 A3 🔟
Cross Villa Place No 5
  ELS/FEN NE4 .... 80 A3 🔟
Crossway HAR/WTLS NE34 .... 89 F3 🔟
  JES NE2 .... 64 A3
  LWF/SPW/WRK NE9 .... 99 F4
  TYNE/NSHE NE30 .... 55 E4
Crossways BOL NE36 .... 107 D3 🔟
  SUNDSW SR3 .... 160 B1
The Crossway
  BW/LEM/TK/HW NE15 .... 76 C1 🔟
The Cross Wy GOS/KPK NE3 .... 62 B2
Croudace Rw FELL NE10 .... 100 C2 🔟
Crow Bank WLSD/HOW NE28 .... 67 E4
Crow Hall La CRAM NE23 .... 21 E1
Crowhall La FELL NE10 .... 100 C2
Crow Hall Rd CRAM NE23 .... 13 E5
Crow La SUNDSW SR3 .... 159 D1
Crowley Av WICK/BNPF NE16 .... 96 B2 🔟
Crowley Gdns BLAY NE21 .... 76 B6
Crowley Rd WICK/BNPF NE16 .... 95 F1
Crown Rd SWCK/CAS SR5 .... 125 F4
Crown St BLYTH NE24 .... 11 E5 🔟
Crowther Rd WASHS NE38 .... 137 E1
Crowtree Rd SUND SR1 .... 4 B3
Crowtree Ter SUND SR1 .... 4 B3
Croydon Rd ELS/FEN NE4 .... 79 F2
Crozier St SWCK/CAS SR5 .... 126 B3 🔟

Crudwell Cl BOLCOL NE35 .... 87 D6 🔟
Crummock Av
  CLDN/WHIT/ROK SR6 .... 108 B6
Crummock Rd WD/WHPE/BLK NE5 .. 61 D6
Crumstone Ct LGB/KIL NE12 .... 36 A6
Cuba St ASHBK/HED/RY SR2 .... 145 D2
Cuillin Cl WASHS NE38 .... 138 A3
Culford Pl WLSD/HOW NE28 .... 52 A6
Cullercoats Rd SWCK/CAS SR5 ... 123 E3 🔟
Cullercoats St
  BYK/HTN/WLK NE6 .... 83 D3 🔟
Culloden Wk LGB/KIL NE12 .... 35 F6 🔟
Cumberland Av BDLGTN NE22 .... 7 D3 🔟
Cumberland Pl CLS/BIR/GTL DH3 . 136 C5
  HAR/WTLS NE34 .... 90 A1
Cumberland Rd NSHW NE29 .... 53 D5
  SUNDSW SR3 .... 143 F6
Cumberland St SUND SR1 .... 4 C1 🔟
  WLSD/HOW NE28 .... 67 E4
  WLSD/HOW NE28 .... 69 D5 🔟
Cumberland Wk LGB/HTN NE7 ..... 65 D2 🔟
Cumberland Wy WASHN NE37 ..... 120 C2 🔟
Cumbrian Av
  CLDN/WHIT/ROK SR6 .... 108 B5 🔟
Cumbrian Wy PLEE/EAS SR8 ...... 209 D2
Cumbria Pl STLY/ANP DH9 .... 148 C1
Cummings Av RDHAMSE DH6 ...... 197 E4
Cummings Sq BLYTH NE24 .... 11 D4 🔟
Cunningham Pl DHAM DH1 .... 195 E3 🔟
Curlew Cl LGB/KIL NE12 .... 48 C5 🔟
  RYTON NE40 .... 75 D4 🔟
  WASHS NE38 .... 137 F4
Curlew Rd JRW NE32 .... 69 E6
Curlew Wy BLYTH NE24 .... 17 D2
Curtis Rd ELS/FEN NE4 .... 79 E1
Curzon Rd WD/WHPE/BLK NE5 ... 61 D4 🔟
Curzon Rd West
  WLSD/HOW NE28 .... 67 D5 🔟
Curzon St GATE NE8 .... 98 C2
Cushat Cl BYK/HTN/WLK NE6 .... 82 B3
Cushy Cow La RYTON NE40 .... 74 C4
Cut Bank CNUT NE1 .... 81 F3
Cuthbert Av DHAM DH1 .... 195 F3
Cuthbert Cl DHAM DH1 .... 196 A5
Cuthbert Ct JRW NE32 .... 87 D2
Cuthbertson Cl
  CLDN/WHIT/ROK SR6 .... 109 D5 🔟
Cuthbert St GATE NE8 .... 98 C1 🔟
  WICK/BNPF NE16 .... 113 F3
Cygnet Cl WD/WHPE/BLK NE5 .... 59 F2
Cyncopa Wy WD/WHPE/BLK NE5 . 61 F4
Cypress Av ELS/FEN NE4 .... 79 D4
Cypress Ct BDN/LAN/SAC DH7 ... 203 D5 🔟
Cypress Crs BLYTH NE24 .... 11 D5
  DUN/TMV NE11 .... 97 E2
Cypress Dr BLYTH NE24 .... 11 D5
Cypress Gdns BLYTH NE24 .... 11 D5
Cypress Gv DHAM DH1 .... 195 E5
  RYTON NE40 .... 74 B2 🔟
Cypress Rd BLAY NE21 .... 76 B6
  LWF/SPW/WRK NE9 .... 118 C2 🔟
Cypress Sq SUNDSW SR3 .... 143 F6 🔟
Cyprus Gdns LWF/SPW/WRK NE9 . 99 F4 🔟

D

Dachet Rd MONK NE25 .... 39 F3
Dacre Rd CLDN/WHIT/ROK SR6 ..... 108 C6
Dacre St SSH NE33 .... 71 E6
Dahlia Ct MLFD/PNYW SR4 .... 126 A5
Dahlia Pl ELS/FEN NE4 .... 61 F6
Dainton Cl HLS DH4 .... 157 F4
Dairy La HLS DH4 .... 170 C2
Dalden Gv SEA/MUR SR7 .... 176 C3
Dalegarth WASHN NE37 .... 120 A6
Dalegarth Gv
  CLDN/WHIT/ROK SR6 .... 108 B3 🔟
Dale Rd MONK NE25 .... 39 F6
Daleside BDN/LAN/SAC DH7 .... 164 B6
Dale St BLYTH NE24 .... 11 D3
  SSH NE33 .... 71 F3
Dale Ter CLDN/WHIT/ROK SR6 ..... 127 D1
Dale Top MONK NE25 .... 38 A1
Dalla St MLFD/PNYW SR4 .... 123 F5 🔟
Dalmahoy WASHN NE37 .... 120 C1 🔟
Dalmatia Ter BLYTH NE24 .... 11 D6
Dalston Pl BLYTH NE24 .... 17 D2 🔟
Dalton Cl CRAM NE23 .... 22 A2 🔟
Dalton Ct WLSD/HOW NE28 .... 66 B1
Dalton Pl WD/WHPE/BLK NE5 .... 59 E3
Daltons La SSH NE33 .... 71 D4
Dalton St BYK/HTN/WLK NE6 ...... 82 A2 🔟
Dame Dorothy St
  CLDN/WHIT/ROK SR6 .... 126 C4
Dame Flora Robson Av
  HAR/WTLS NE34 .... 87 E4
Danby Cl SUNDSW SR3 .... 161 D2 🔟
  WASHS NE38 .... 137 E6
Danby Gdns BYK/HTN/WLK NE6 .. 65 F5 🔟
Danville Rd CLDN/WHIT/ROK SR6 . 109 D6
Daphne Crs SEA/MUR SR7 .... 176 B5
Darden Cl LGB/KIL NE12 .... 36 B6 🔟
Darden Lough WD/WHPE/BLK NE5 . 60 B5

Darien Av *CLDN/WHIT/ROK* SR6 ...... 108 C6
Darley Ct *CLSW/PEL* DH2 .... 165 F5
Darley Pl *BW/LEM/TK/HW* NE15.... 77 F3
Darlington Rd *DHAM* DH1 .... 193 F6
Darras Ct *SSH* NE33 .... 71 F5
Darras Dr *NSHW* NE29 .... 53 E5
Darrell St *DIN/WO* NE13 .... 32 C4
Dartford Rd *CLDN/WHIT/ROK* SR6 .. 108 C6
  SSH NE33...................................... 72 B4
Dartmouth Av
  LWF/SPW/WRK NE9 .... 117 E1
Dartmouth Ct *SEA/MUR* SR7 .... 175 F4 ②
Dart Rd *PLEE/EAS* SR8 .... 208 B3
Darvall Cl *MONK* NE25 .... 39 F3
Darwin Crs *GOS/KPK* NE3................. 62 B3
Darwin St *SWCK/CAS* SR5................ 125 E3
Daryl Cl *BLAY* NE21 .... 93 F1 ①
Daryl Wy *FELL* NE10 .... 102 C3 ①
Davenport Dr *GOS/KPK* NE3 .... 47 D3
David Gdns *CLDN/WHIT/ROK* NE3 .. 127 E1 ①
Davidson Rd *FELL* NE10 .... 84 A6
Davidson St *FELL* NE10 .... 100 C2 ②
David St *WLSD/HOW* NE28 .... 67 D5
Davison Av *SUNDSW* SR3 .... 161 D1
  WBAY NE26...................................... 40 B4
Davison Crs *SEA/MUR* SR7............. 174 A6
Davison St *BLYTH* NE24 .... 11 D4 ④
  BOLCOL NE35................................ 105 D1
  BW/LEM/TK/HW NE15.................... 58 A6
Davis Ter *PLEE/EAS* SR8 .... 200 C3
Davy Bank *WLSD/HOW* NE28 .... 67 F5
Davy Dr *PLEE/EAS* SR8 .... 199 E6
Dawdon Crs *SEA/MUR* SR7............. 176 C4
Dawlish Cl *SEA/MUR* SR7 .... 175 F4
Dawlish Gdns *LWF/SPW/WRK* NE9.. 117 E1
Dawlish Pl *WD/WHPE/BLK* NE5...... 59 E3
Dawson Ter *MLFD/PNYW* SR4 .... 123 F5
Daylesford Dr *LGB/HTN* NE7 .... 64 B2
Daylesford Rd *CRAM* NE23 .... 13 F4
Dayshield *WD/WHPE/BLK* NE5 .... 60 B5
Deacon Rd *WD/WHPE/BLK* NE5 .... 59 D4 ①
Deaconsfield Cl *SUNDSW* SR3 .... 160 B3 ③
Deal Cl *BLYTH* NE24 .... 17 D2
Dean Cl *PLEE/EAS* SR8 .... 209 E3
Deanery St *BDLGTN* NE22 .... 7 D3
Deanham Gdns
  WD/WHPE/BLK NE5...................... 61 E6
Dean Rd *SSH* NE33 .... 88 A1 ①
Deansfield Cl *SUNDSW* SR3 .... 160 B3 ④
Dean St *CNUT* NE1............................... 3 E4
  LWF/SPW/WRK NE9....................... 99 E5
Deans' Wk *DHAM* DH1 .... 195 E3
Dean Ter *SSH* NE33 .... 88 A1
  SWCK/CAS SR5 .... 125 E3
Dean View Dr *BLYTH* NE24 .... 10 A4
Dearham Gv *CRAM* NE23 .... 13 F4
Debdon Gdns *BYK/HTN/WLK* NE6.... 65 E5
Debdon Pl *CRAM* NE23 .... 22 A2 ③
Deckham Ter *GATE* NE8 .... 99 F2
Deepbrook Rd
  WD/WHPE/BLK NE5...................... 61 E5 ②
Deepdale *WLSD/HOW* NE28................ 66 B1
Deepdale Cl *WICK/BNPF* NE16.......... 96 B5
Deepdale Crs *WD/WHPE/BLK* NE5 .... 61 F4
Deepdale Gdns *LGB/KIL* NE12 .... 49 E1
Deepdale Rd *TYNE/NSHE* NE30........ 55 D2
Deepdale St *HLS* DH5 .... 185 F3
Deepdene Gv
  CLDN/WHIT/ROK SR6 .... 108 C5
Deepdene Rd
  CLDN/WHIT/ROK SR6 .... 108 C5
Deerbolt Pl *LGB/KIL* NE12 .... 49 E5 ①
Deer Bush *WD/WHPE/BLK* NE5 .... 60 B5
Deerness Hts *BDN/LAN/SAC* DH7 ... 203 D3
Dee Rd *HEBB* NE31 .... 85 E5 ②
Deer Park Wy *BLAY* NE21 .... 95 D1
Dees Av *WLSD/HOW* NE28................. 67 D3
Dee St *JRW* NE32 .... 86 B1 ①
Defender Ct *SWCK/CAS* SR5 .... 124 B4 ①
Defoe Av *HAR/WTLS* NE34 .... 88 A5
Deighton Wk
  WD/WHPE/BLK NE5...................... 60 B5 ③
Delacour Rd *BLAY* NE21 .... 76 B5
Delamere Ct *SUNDSW* SR3 .... 160 C2 ②
Delamere Crs *CRAM* NE23................. 13 F4
Delamere Rd *GOS/KPK* NE3.............. 62 B1
Delaval Av *NSHW* NE29 .... 54 A6
Delaval Ct *BDLGTN* NE22 .... 8 B2
  SSH NE33...................................... 71 F5
Delaval Crs *BLYTH* NE24 .... 16 B2 ③
Delavale Cl *PLEE/EAS* SR8 .... 209 E3 ①
Delaval Gdns
  BW/LEM/TK/HW NE15.................... 78 A4
Delaval Rd *BW/LEM/TK/HW* NE15 .... 78 A4
  LGB/KIL NE12 .... 49 F4
  WBAY NE26...................................... 41 E6
Delaval St *BLYTH* NE24 .... 16 A2
Delaval Ter *BLYTH* NE24 .... 10 C4
  GOS/KPK NE3 .... 62 C2 ①
Dellfield Dr *MLFD/PNYW* SR4 .... 141 F2 ①
The Dell *HLS* DH5 .... 157 F5
Delta Bank Rd *DUN/TMV* NE11........ 78 B5
Demesne Dr *BDLGTN* NE22 .... 7 F2
Dempsey Rd *DIN/WO* NE13 .... 33 D5 ①
Denbeigh Pl *LGB/KIL* NE12............... 49 E5

Denbigh Av *CLDN/WHIT/ROK* SR6.... 108 C6
  WLSD/HOW NE28 .... 68 C2
Denby Cl *CRAM* NE23 .... 13 F4
Dene Av *BW/LEM/TK/HW* NE15 ...... 76 C2
  DIN/WO NE13.................................. 32 C4
  GOS/KPK NE3 .... 64 A2
  HLH DH5....................................... 171 F2
  LGB/KIL NE12 .... 48 C2 ①
  PLEE/EAS SR8 .... 201 D1
  ROWG NE39................................... 110 C3
Denebank *MONK* NE25........................ 40 A5
Dene Bank Av *PLEE/EAS* SR8 .... 209 F2 ①
Dene Bank Vw *GOS/KPK* NE3......... 62 A3 ①
Dene Cl *LGB/HTN* NE7....................... 64 C4
  RYTON NE40.................................... 74 C3
Dene Ct *BDN/LAN/SAC* DH7 .... 178 A3
  CLS/BIR/GTL DH3 .... 118 B6
  WASHS NE38 .... 120 B6
Dene Crs *GOS/KPK* NE3 .... 64 A2
  ROWG NE39................................... 110 C3
  RYTON NE40.................................... 74 C3
  WBAY NE26...................................... 40 B4
  WLSD/HOW NE28 .... 67 F4
Dene Dr *DHAM* DH1 .... 196 C1
Deneford *LWF/SPW/WRK* NE9 .... 117 F3
Dene Gdns *FELL* NE10 .... 102 A1 ②
  HLH DH5....................................... 171 E3
Dene Gv *CRAM* NE23.......................... 23 F6
  GOS/KPK NE3 .... 64 A2
Deneholm *MONK* NE25 .... 40 A4
  WLSD/HOW NE28 .... 67 F3
Dene House Rd *SEA/MUR* SR7 ...... 176 B2
Dene La *CLDN/WHIT/ROK* SR6 ..... 108 C6 ③
Dene Pk *SWCK/CAS* SR5.................. 124 B2
Dene Rd *BLAY* NE21 .... 76 C5
  ROWG NE39................................... 110 C3
  SEA/MUR SR7 .... 176 A5
  SWCK/CAS SR5 .... 124 B3
  TYNE/NSHE NE30 .... 55 E4
Deneside *BDN/LAN/SAC* DH7 .... 164 B6
  BDN/LAN/SAC DH7 .... 178 A4 ①
  CRAM NE23 .... 23 F6
  DUN/TMV NE11 .... 97 E4
  WD/WHPE/BLK NE5 .... 60 B2
Deneside Av *LWF/SPW/WRK* NE9 .... 99 D5
Dene St *HLH* DH5.............................. 171 F4
  MLFD/PNYW SR4 .... 125 E5
  PLEE/EAS SR8 .... 209 F1
  SUNDSW SR3................................. 143 F5
Dene Ter *JRW* NE32........................... 85 F4
Dene Vw *BDLGTN* NE22 .... 8 B3
  GOS/KPK NE3 .... 64 A2
Dene Vw Crs *MLFD/PNYW* SR4 ..... 124 A6
Dene Vw East *BDLGTN* NE22 .... 8 B4
Dene Vw West *BDLGTN* NE22 .... 8 A4
Dene Vls *PLEE/EAS* SR8 .... 209 F2
  SEA/MUR SR7 .... 176 B2
Denewell Av *LGB/HTN* NE7 .... 64 C5
  LWF/SPW/WRK NE9....................... 99 E5
Denewood *LGB/KIL* NE12................... 50 A2
Denham Av *CLDN/WHIT/ROK* SR6.. 108 C6
Denham Dr *MONK* NE25..................... 24 C5
Denham Gv *BLAY* NE21 .... 93 E2
Denhill Pk *BW/LEM/TK/HW* NE15.... 78 C2
Denholm Av *CRAM* NE23 .... 13 F4 ②
Denmark Ct *BYK/HTN/WLK* NE6 ..... 82 B1 ①
  BYK/HTN/WLK NE6 .... 82 B2 ②
  GATE NE8 .... 81 E6 ①
Denshaw Cl *CRAM* NE23 .... 13 F4
Dentdale *HLS* DH4 .... 156 A1
Denton Av *BW/LEM/TK/HW* NE15 ... 76 C2
  NSHW NE29...................................... 53 E6
Denton Ga *WD/WHPE/BLK* NE5 ..... 60 C3 ②
Denton Gv *WD/WHPE/BLK* NE5 ..... 60 C3 ①
Denton Rd *BW/LEM/TK/HW* NE15 ... 77 E3
Denton Vw *BLAY* NE21 .... 76 A6
Dent St *BLYTH* NE24 .... 11 E6
  CLDN/WHIT/ROK SR6 .... 108 C6
Denver Gdns *BYK/HTN/WLK* NE6 ... 83 D3
Denway Gv *WBAY* NE26 .... 26 A1
Denwick Cl *CLSW/PEL* DH2............. 165 F2 ③
Denwick Ter *TYNE/NSHE* NE30 .... 55 D5
Depot Rd *BYK/HTN/WLK* NE6 .... 82 B1 ②
Deptford Rd *GATE* NE8...................... 81 F4
  MLFD/PNYW SR4 .... 126 A5
Deptford Ter *MLFD/PNYW* SR4 ..... 125 F4
Derby Crs *HEBB* NE31 .... 84 C3
Derby Gdns *WLSD/HOW* NE28 .... 66 C3 ③
Derby Rd *STLY/ANP* DH9.................. 148 A3
Derbyshire Dr *DHAM* DH1 .... 196 C4
Derby St *ASHBK/HED/RY* SR2 .... 4 A4
  ELS/FEN NE4.................................... 80 A2
  JRW NE32 .... 86 B1
  SSH NE33... 71 F4
Derby Ter *SSH* NE33 .... 71 F4
Dereham Ct *WBAY* NE26 .... 26 C3
Dereham Ct *WD/WHPE/BLK* NE5 .. 61 D2 ③
Dereham Rd *WBAY* NE26 .... 26 C4
Dereham Wy *NSHW* NE29................. 53 D4
Derry Av *CLDN/WHIT/ROK* SR6 ..... 109 D6
Derwent Av *DUN/TMV* NE11............. 98 C5

  HEBB NE31...................................... 85 D5 ③
  ROWG NE39................................... 111 D3
Derwent Cl *BDN/LAN/SAC* DH7 ..... 178 A1
  SEA/MUR SR7 .... 176 B2
Derwent Crs *WICK/BNPF* NE16 .... 95 F2
Derwentdale Gdns *LGB/HTN* NE7.... 65 D3
Derwent Gdns *WLSD/HOW* NE28 .... 68 C2
Derwenthaugh Rd *BLAY* NE21 .... 77 F6
Derwent Rd *PLEE/EAS* SR8 .... 209 D1
  TYNE/NSHE NE30 .... 55 D2
  WBAY NE26...................................... 26 A2
Derwent St *HLH* DH5 .... 186 A2
  SUND SR1 .... 14 F4
Derwent Vw *BLAY* NE21.................... 94 A1
Derwent Wk *WICK/BNPF* NE16 .... 94 C4
Derwentwater Rd *GATE* NE8 .... 98 B1
Derwent Wy *BLAY* NE21 .... 94 A1
  LGB/KIL NE12 .... 49 E1
Deuchar St *JES* NE2 .... 64 B6
Devon Crs *CLS/BIR/GTL* DH3 .... 118 A4
Devon Dr *SUNDSW* SR3 .... 143 F6
Devon Gdns *HAR/WTLS* NE34 .... 90 A1
Devonport *HLS* DH4 .... 157 E5
Devon Rd *HEBB* NE31........................ 85 E5
  NSHW NE29...................................... 53 F4
Devonshire Dr *LGB/KIL* NE12.......... 51 D3
  SMOOR NE27................................... 51 E3
Devonshire Gdns *WLSD/HOW* NE28.. 66 B3
Devonshire Pl *JES* NE2 .... 64 B5
Devonshire Rd *DHAM* DH1 .... 196 B4
Devonshire St *SSH* NE33 .... 88 A1
  SWCK/CAS SR5 .... 126 B5
Devonshire Ter *JES* NE2 .... 80 C1 ①
Devonworth Pl *BLYTH* NE24 .... 9 F5
Dewberry Cl *BLYTH* NE24 .... 16 B2
Dewley *CRAM* NE23 .... 22 A3
Dewley Pl *WD/WHPE/BLK* NE5 ..... 60 A2 ①
Dewley Rd *WD/WHPE/BLK* NE5 ..... 60 C5
Dewsgreen *CRAM* NE23 .... 22 A2
Dexter Wy *FELL* NE10........................ 100 B2
Deyncourt *DHAM* DH1 .... 204 C2 ①
Diamond Ct *GOS/KPK* NE3................ 61 E1
Diamond St *WLSD/HOW* NE28 ...... 67 D4 ③
Diana St *ELS/FEN* NE4 .... 80 A3
Dickens Av *HAR/WTLS* NE34 .... 88 A5
  WICK/BNPF NE16 .... 95 F2
Dickens St *HLS* DH4.......................... 170 C2
  SWCK/CAS SR5 .... 125 F3 ③
Dickens Wynd *DHAM* DH1 .... 204 C1
Didcot Av *NSHW* NE29 .... 70 A2 ②
Didcot Wy *BOL* NE36 .... 105 E3
  BOLCOL NE35................................ 105 E3
Dillon St *JRW* NE32 .... 85 F3
  SEA/MUR SR7 .... 176 C3
Dilston Av *MONK* NE25...................... 41 D6
Dilston Cl *PLEE/EAS* SR8 .... 208 B5
  SMOOR NE27................................... 52 B2
  WASHS NE38 .... 137 F2
Dilston Dr *WD/WHPE/BLK* NE5 ...... 60 A3
Dilston Gdns *MLFD/PNYW* SR4 ..... 143 E1 ①
Dilston Rd *DHAM* DH1 .... 180 C6 ①
  ELS/FEN NE4.................................... 79 F2
Dilston Ter *JRW* NE32........................ 86 A5
Dimbula Gdns *LGB/HTN* NE7 .... 65 F4
Dinsdale Av *WLSD/HOW* NE28.......... 67 E1
Dinsdale Dr *DHAM* DH1 .... 196 C2
Dinsdale Pl *JES* NE2.......................... 81 E1
Dinsdale Rd *CLDN/WHIT/ROK* SR6 .. 127 D2
  JES NE2 .... 81 E1
Dinsdale St *ASHBK/HED/RY* SR2 ... 162 B2
Dinting Cl *PLEE/EAS* SR8 .... 208 A3
Dipe La *BOL* NE36 .... 105 F4
Dipton Gdns *SUNDSW* SR3 .... 144 A4 ①
Dipton Gv *CRAM* NE23 .... 22 A2
Dipton Rd *MONK* NE25 .... 39 F3
Dipwood Rd *ROWG* NE39 .... 110 C3
Dipwood Wy *ROWG* NE39 .... 110 C4
Disraeli St *BLYTH* NE24 .... 10 C4
  HLS DH4... 170 A2
Dissington Pl *WD/WHPE/BLK* NE5 .. 61 E6
  WICK/BNPF NE16 .... 95 F5
Ditchburn Ter *MLFD/PNYW* SR4 .... 125 E4
Dixon Est *RDHAMSE* DH6 .... 206 B3
Dixon Estate Bungalows
  RDHAMSE DH6.............................. 206 B4
Dixon Pl *DUN/TMV* NE11 .... 97 E2 ②
Dixon Rd *HLH* DH5 .... 170 C4
Dixon's Sq *CLDN/WHIT/ROK* SR6 .. 126 C3 ②
Dixon St *GATE* NE8 .... 98 B1
  SSH NE33... 71 E5 ①
Dobson Cl *ELS/FEN* NE4 .... 80 A5 ①
Dobson Crs *BYK/HTN/WLK* NE6 ...... 82 B4
Dobson Ter *SEA/MUR* SR7 .... 188 B1 ①
Dockendale La *WICK/BNPF* NE16 ... 96 B3 ③
Dock Rd *NSHW* NE29 .... 70 C2
Dock Rd South *NSHW* NE29 .... 70 C2
Dock St *CLDN/WHIT/ROK* SR6 ...... 127 D4
Dockwray Cl *TYNE/NSHE* NE30 ..... 71 D1 ③
Dockwray Sq *TYNE/NSHE* NE30 ..... 71 D1
Doddfell Cl *WASHN* NE37 .... 119 F6
Doddington Cl
  BW/LEM/TK/HW NE15.................... 76 A1
Doddington Dr *CRAM* NE23............... 21 F2
Dolphin St *ELS/FEN* NE4 .... 78 C3
Dominies Cl *ROWG* NE39 .... 111 E1

Dominion Rd *BDN/LAN/SAC* DH7 ...... **203** D5
Donald Av *RDHAMSE* DH6 ...... **187** D4
Donald St *GOS/KPK* NE3 ...... **64** A1 ▣
Doncaster Rd *JES* NE2 ...... **81** E1
Doncrest Rd *WASHN* NE37 ...... **120** A3
Don Dixon Dr *JRW* NE32 ...... **104** A1 ▣
Don Gdns *BOL* NE36 ...... **105** E3
Donkin Rd *WASHN* NE37 ...... **119** E5
Donkin Ter *TYNE/NSHE* NE30 ...... **55** E5
Donnington Ct *SWCK/CAS* SR5 ...... **123** F3 ▣
Donnington St *GOS/KPK* NE3 ...... **64** B2
Donnini Pl *DHAM* DH1 ...... **195** E3
Donnison Gdns *SUND* SR1 ...... **5** F2 ▣
Donridge *WASHN* NE37 ...... **120** A3
Don Rd *JRW* NE32 ...... **86** C1
Don St *DUN/TMV* NE11 ...... **98** B6
Donvale Rd *WASHN* NE37 ...... **119** F3
Don Vw *BOL* NE36 ...... **105** E3
Dorcas Av *BW/LEM/TK/HW* NE15 ...... **78** B3
Dorchester Cl
  WD/WHPE/BLK NE5 ...... **59** D3 ▣
Dorchester Ct *MONK* NE25 ...... **24** B2
Dorchester Gdns
  LWF/SPW/WRK NE9 ...... **117** E2
Doreen Av *SEA/MUR* SR7 ...... **175** E4
Doric Rd *BDN/LAN/SAC* DH7 ...... **202** B1
Dorking Av *NSHW* NE29 ...... **70** A2
Dorking Cl *BLYTH* NE24 ...... **17** D2
Dorking Rd *CLDN/WHIT/ROK* SR6 ...... **108** C6
Dorlonco Vls *BDN/LAN/SAC* DH7 ...... **203** E5
Dormand Dr *PLEE/EAS* SR8 ...... **208** B5
Dornoch Crs *FELL* NE10 ...... **101** D4 ▣
Dorrington Rd *GOS/KPK* NE3 ...... **46** A6
Dorset Av *CLDN/WHIT/ROK* SR6 ...... **109** D6
  CLS/BIR/GTL DH3 ...... **136** B5
  HAR/WTLS NE34 ...... **90** A1
  HEBB NE31 ...... **85** E3
  WLSD/HOW NE28 ...... **66** C4
Dorset Gv *NSHW* NE29 ...... **53** F3
Dorset La *SUNDSW* SR3 ...... **161** D1
Dorset Rd *BW/LEM/TK/HW* NE15 ...... **77** E2
  GATE NE8 ...... **81** F4
Dorset St *HLH* DH5 ...... **186** B3
Double Rw *MONK* NE25 ...... **24** A3
Douglas Cl *HAR/WTLS* NE34 ...... **88** B4 ▣
Douglas Ct *STLY/ANP* DH9 ...... **146** A5
Douglas Gdns *DUN/TMV* NE11 ...... **97** F3
Douglas Rd *CLDN/WHIT/ROK* SR6 ...... **109** D6
Douglass St *WLSD/HOW* NE28 ...... **66** A6
Douglas St *ELS/FEN* NE4 ...... **80** A3 ▣
  HLS DH4 ...... **140** A6
Douglas Vls *DHAM* DH1 ...... **195** D4 ▣
Doulting Cl *LGB/KIL* NE12 ...... **49** D6 ▣
Dove Av *JRW* NE32 ...... **86** B5
Dovecote Cl *BDN/LAN/SAC* DH7 ...... **202** C4 ▣
Dovecote Cl *MONK* NE25 ...... **39** E4 ▣
Dovecote Rd *LGB/KIL* NE12 ...... **50** A5
Dovedale Av *BLYTH* NE24 ...... **9** F5
Dovedale Gdns *LGB/HTN* NE7 ...... **64** C3
  LWF/SPW/WRK NE9 ...... **99** F6
Dovedale Rd *CLDN/WHIT/ROK* SR6 ...... **108** B5
Dover Cl *BDLGTN* NE22 ...... **6** C3
  WD/WHPE/BLK NE5 ...... **59** E3
Dovercourt Rd *BYK/HTN/WLK* NE6 ...... **83** F4
Dowling Av *MONK* NE25 ...... **40** D6
Downe Cl *BLYTH* NE24 ...... **17** D2 ▣
Downend Rd *WD/WHPE/BLK* NE5 ...... **60** A3
Downfield *WASHN* NE37 ...... **120** C1 ▣
Downham *WD/WHPE/BLK* NE5 ...... **60** B5
Downhill La *BOL* NE36 ...... **105** D6 ▣
  WASHN NE37 ...... **104** C6
Downs La *HLH* DH5 ...... **172** A5
Downs Pit La *HLH* DH5 ...... **172** C5
Downswood *LGB/KIL* NE12 ...... **50** B1 ▣
Dowsey Rd *RDHAMSE* DH6 ...... **197** E4
Dowson Sq *SEA/MUR* SR7 ...... **187** F1
Doxford Av *HLH* DH5 ...... **171** E4
Doxford Dr *PLEE/EAS* SR8 ...... **207** E2
Doxford Gdns
  WD/WHPE/BLK NE5 ...... **61** F5 ▣
Doxford Park Wy *SUNDSW* SR3 ...... **160** A2 ▣
Doxford Pl *CRAM* NE23 ...... **22** A1 ▣
Doxford Ter *HLH* DH5 ...... **171** E4
Dragon La *DHAM* DH1 ...... **196** A4
Drake Cl *SSH* NE33 ...... **71** D6
Drayton Rd *CLDN/WHIT/ROK* SR6 ...... **108** C6
  GOS/KPK NE3 ...... **62** A2
The Drive *CLS/BIR/GTL* DH3 ...... **136** C5
  FELL NE10 ...... **101** D2
  GOS/KPK NE3 ...... **63** E3
  LGB/HTN NE7 ...... **65** D2
  LWF/SPW/WRK NE9 ...... **99** E4
  TYNE/NSHE NE30 ...... **55** F3
  WASHN NE37 ...... **120** B3
  WD/WHPE/BLK NE5 ...... **60** B6
  WICK/BNPF NE16 ...... **96** B4
  WLSD/HOW NE28 ...... **67** D4
Dronfield Cl *CLSW/PEL* DH2 ...... **165** E1
Drove Rd *BW/LEM/TK/HW* NE15 ...... **57** E3
Drummond Crs *HAR/WTLS* NE34 ...... **87** E3
Drummond Rd *GOS/KPK* NE3 ...... **62** B3
Drummond Ter *TYNE/NSHE* NE30 ...... **55** D5
Drumoyne Cl *SUNDSW* SR3 ...... **159** D2
Drumoyne Gdns *MONK* NE25 ...... **53** F1

Drum Rd *CLSW/PEL* DH2 ...... **153** D1
Drumsheugh Pl
  WD/WHPE/BLK NE5 ...... **61** D4
Druridge Av *CLDN/WHIT/ROK* SR6 ...... **108** C5
Druridge Crs *BLYTH* NE24 ...... **16** A1
  HAR/WTLS NE34 ...... **73** D6
Druridge Dr *BLYTH* NE24 ...... **16** A1
  WD/WHPE/BLK NE5 ...... **61** F5
Drury La *NSHW* NE29 ...... **55** E5
  SUND SR1 ...... **5** E2
Drybeck Ct *CRAM* NE23 ...... **14** C6
Drybeck Sq *SUNDSW* SR3 ...... **161** D2 ▣
Drybeck Wk *CRAM* NE23 ...... **14** C6 ▣
Dryborough St
  MLFD/PNYW SR4 ...... **126** A5 ▣
Dryburgh Cl *WASHS* NE38 ...... **138** B1
Dryburgh Cl *NSHW* NE29 ...... **54** A4
Dryburn Hl *DHAM* DH1 ...... **193** F2
Dryburn Rd *DHAM* DH1 ...... **193** F1
Dryden Cl *HAR/WTLS* NE34 ...... **88** A6
  STLY/ANP DH9 ...... **148** C2
Dryden Rd *LWF/SPW/WRK* NE9 ...... **99** E3
Dryden St *SWCK/CAS* SR5 ...... **125** F2
Drysdale Cl *DIN/WO* NE13 ...... **32** C4
Drysdale Crs *DIN/WO* NE13 ...... **32** C4
Dubmire Cottages *HLS* DH4 ...... **169** E2
Dubmire Ct *HLS* DH4 ...... **169** F2
Duchess Crs *JRW* NE32 ...... **86** A5
Duchess Crs East *JRW* NE32 ...... **86** A5 ▣
Duchess Dr *BW/LEM/TK/HW* NE15 ...... **77** F1
Duchess St *WBAY* NE26 ...... **40** C5
Duckpool La *WICK/BNPF* NE16 ...... **96** B2 ▣
Duddon Cl *PLEE/EAS* SR8 ...... **209** D2 ▣
Duddon Pl *LWF/SPW/WRK* NE9 ...... **100** A6
Dudley Av *CLDN/WHIT/ROK* SR6 ...... **108** C6 ▣
Dudley Dr *CRAM* NE23 ...... **34** C2
Dudley Gdns *SUNDSW* SR3 ...... **159** E2
Dudley La *CRAM* NE23 ...... **21** F3
  DIN/WO NE13 ...... **33** E2
Dugdale Rd *GOS/KPK* NE3 ...... **61** F1
Duke's Av *HEBB* NE31 ...... **84** C4
Dukes Dr *GOS/KPK* NE3 ...... **47** D3
Dukesfield *CRAM* NE23 ...... **22** A3 ▣
Dukes Meadow *DIN/WO* NE13 ...... **44** A4
Duke St *FELL* NE10 ...... **101** F1
  MLFD/PNYW SR4 ...... **125** F6 ▣
  SEA/MUR SR7 ...... **176** A2
  WBAY NE26 ...... **40** C5
Duke St North
  CLDN/WHIT/ROK SR6 ...... **126** C2
Dukesway *DUN/TMV* NE11 ...... **98** A5
Dulverston Cl
  WD/WHPE/BLK NE5 ...... **59** E3 ▣
Dulverton Av *SSH* NE33 ...... **88** C1
Dumfries Crs *JRW* NE32 ...... **87** D4
Dunbar Cl *WD/WHPE/BLK* NE5 ...... **59** E3
Dunbar St *MLFD/PNYW* SR4 ...... **143** E1
Dunblane Crs *WD/WHPE/BLK* NE5 ...... **60** B6
Dunblane Dr *BLYTH* NE24 ...... **17** D2
Dunblane Rd
  CLDN/WHIT/ROK SR6 ...... **109** D5
Dunbreck Gv *MLFD/PNYW* SR4 ...... **143** F2
Duncan St *BYK/HTN/WLK* NE6 ...... **83** F2
  GATE NE8 ...... **100** A1
  MLFD/PNYW SR4 ...... **125** E5
Duncombe Crs *STLY/ANP* DH9 ...... **131** E6
Duncow La *DHAM* DH1 ...... **194** B5 ▣
Dun Cow St *SUND* SR1 ...... **4** B2 ▣
Dundas St *CLDN/WHIT/ROK* SR6 ...... **126** C4 ▣
Dundas Wy *FELL* NE10 ...... **100** B2
Dundee Cl *WD/WHPE/BLK* NE5 ...... **59** E3
Dundrennan *WASHS* NE38 ...... **138** B3
Dunelm Dr *BOL* NE36 ...... **106** A3
  HLS DH4 ...... **170** B2
Dunelm Pl *RDHAMSE* DH6 ...... **206** C2 ▣
Dunelm Rd *HLH* DH5 ...... **171** E6
Dunelm St *SSH* NE33 ...... **71** F4 ▣
Dunelm Wk *PLEE/EAS* SR8 ...... **208** C1 ▣
Dunford Gdns
  WD/WHPE/BLK NE5 ...... **59** F2 ▣
Dunholm Cl *HLH* DH5 ...... **171** E4
Dunholme Cl *DHAM* DH1 ...... **194** A1
Dunholme Rd *ELS/FEN* NE4 ...... **79** E3
Dunira Cl *JES* NE2 ...... **64** B4 ▣
Dunkeld Cl *BLYTH* NE24 ...... **17** D2
Dunkirk Av *HLH* DH5 ...... **171** E3
Dunlin Cl *RYTON* NE40 ...... **75** D4 ▣
Dunlin Dr *BLYTH* NE24 ...... **17** D2
  WASHS NE38 ...... **137** E3
Dunlop Cl *LGB/HTN* NE7 ...... **65** E2 ▣
Dunlop Crs *HAR/WTLS* NE34 ...... **89** F2
Dunmoor Cl *GOS/KPK* NE3 ...... **62** C2 ▣
Dunmore Av *CLDN/WHIT/ROK* SR6 ...... **109** D5
Dunmorlie St *BYK/HTN/WLK* NE6 ...... **82** C2
Dunn St *SUNDSW* SR3 ...... **143** F5
Dunning St *SUND* SR1 ...... **4** B1
Dunnlynn Cl *SUNDSW* SR3 ...... **160** A2 ▣
Dunnock Dr *WASHS* NE38 ...... **137** E3
  WICK/BNPF NE16 ...... **113** F1
Dunn Rd *PLEE/EAS* SR8 ...... **208** C1
Dunn's Ter *JES* NE2 ...... **63** D6 ▣
Dunn St *ELS/FEN* NE4 ...... **80** A5
Dunnykirk Av *GOS/KPK* NE3 ...... **61** F1 ▣
Dunsdale Dr *CRAM* NE23 ...... **14** C6
Dunsdale Rd *MONK* NE25 ...... **25** D6

Dunsgreen *PONT/DH* NE20 ...... **28** A5
Dunsley Gdns *DIN/WO* NE13 ...... **31** D3
Dunsmuir Gv *GATE* NE8 ...... **99** D2
Dunstable Pl
  WD/WHPE/BLK NE5 ...... **59** D3 ▣
Dunstanburgh Cl *BDLGTN* NE22 ...... **6** C3
Dunstanburgh Cl *BDLGTN* NE22 ...... **6** C3 ▣
  BYK/HTN/WLK NE6 ...... **82** C3 ▣
  WASHS NE38 ...... **138** A2
Dunstanburgh Rd
  BYK/HTN/WLK NE6 ...... **82** C3
Dunstan Cl *CLSW/PEL* DH2 ...... **165** F1
Dunston Bank *DUN/TMV* NE11 ...... **97** D3
Dunston Pl *BLYTH* NE24 ...... **10** A5
Dunston Rd *DUN/TMV* NE11 ...... **97** E1
Dunvegan *CLS/BIR/GTL* DH3 ...... **137** D4
Dunvegan Av *CLSW/PEL* DH2 ...... **166** A1
Durant Rd *CNUT* NE1 ...... **3** E2
Durban St *BLYTH* NE24 ...... **10** C3
Durham Av *PLEE/EAS* SR8 ...... **201** E6
  WASHN NE37 ...... **120** A4
Durham Cl *BDLGTN* NE22 ...... **6** C3 ▣
Durham Dr *BOLCOL* NE35 ...... **104** A2
  JRW NE32 ...... **86** A6
Durham Gdns *BDN/LAN/SAC* DH7 ...... **178** A3
Durham Gv *JRW* NE32 ...... **85** F6
Durham La *PLEE/EAS* SR8 ...... **199** F3
  RDHAMSE DH6 ...... **198** A5
Durham Pl *CLS/BIR/GTL* DH3 ...... **136** B5
  GATE NE8 ...... **99** E1 ▣
Durham Rd *ASHBK/HED/RY* SR2 ...... **126** A6
  BDN/LAN/SAC DH7 ...... **178** B2
  CLS/BIR/GTL DH3 ...... **136** B1
  CLS/BIR/GTL DH3 ...... **166** B1
  CRAM NE23 ...... **14** B5
  GATE NE8 ...... **99** E1
  HLH DH5 ...... **158** B5
  HLS DH4 ...... **171** D2
  LWF/SPW/WRK NE9 ...... **99** E6
  LWF/SPW/WRK NE9 ...... **117** E3
  STLY/ANP DH9 ...... **146** C5
  SUNDSW SR3 ...... **143** F3
Durham St *ELS/FEN* NE4 ...... **79** E4
  FELL NE10 ...... **101** E1 ▣
  HLS DH4 ...... **169** F2
  SEA/MUR SR7 ...... **176** A2
  WLSD/HOW NE28 ...... **67** E4
Durham St West
  WLSD/HOW NE28 ...... **67** E4 ▣
Durham Ter *SUNDSW* SR3 ...... **143** F5
Durham Wy *PLEE/EAS* SR8 ...... **208** A5
Duxfield Rd *LGB/HTN* NE7 ...... **65** D3
Dwyer Crs *ASHBK/HED/RY* SR2 ...... **162** B2
Dyer Sq *SWCK/CAS* SR5 ...... **126** A2
Dykefield Av *GOS/KPK* NE3 ...... **46** A5
Dyke Heads La *RYTON* NE40 ...... **74** A6
Dykelands Rd
  CLDN/WHIT/ROK SR6 ...... **108** C6
Dykelands Wy *HAR/WTLS* NE34 ...... **87** E5
Dykenook Cl *WICK/BNPF* NE16 ...... **95** F6
Dykes Wy *FELL* NE10 ...... **100** C5
Dymock Ct *WD/WHPE/BLK* NE5 ...... **61** D1

E

Eaglescliffe Dr *LGB/HTN* NE7 ...... **65** F3
Eaglesdene *HLH* DH5 ...... **171** F6 ▣
Eagle St *DUN/TMV* NE11 ...... **98** A4
Ealing Dr *TYNE/NSHE* NE30 ...... **55** E3
Eardulph Av *CLS/BIR/GTL* DH3 ...... **153** F5
Earl Grey Wy *NSHW* NE29 ...... **70** B3
Earlington Ct *LGB/KIL* NE12 ...... **50** A3 ▣
Earl's Dr *BW/LEM/TK/HW* NE15 ...... **77** F1
  LWF/SPW/WRK NE9 ...... **99** E6
Earl's Gdns *BLYTH* NE24 ...... **10** B4 ▣
Earls Gn *HLH* DH5 ...... **184** C1
Earl St *MLFD/PNYW* SR4 ...... **126** A6
  SEA/MUR SR7 ...... **175** F2
Earlsway *DUN/TMV* NE11 ...... **98** B3
Earlswood Av *LWF/SPW/WRK* NE9 ...... **99** E6
Earlswood Gv *BLYTH* NE24 ...... **16** C3
Earnshaw Wy *MONK* NE25 ...... **39** F3
Earsdon Cl *WD/WHPE/BLK* NE5 ...... **60** C4
Earsdon Rd *GOS/KPK* NE3 ...... **62** B3
  HLH DH5 ...... **171** E2 ▣
  MONK NE25 ...... **39** F6
  SMOOR NE27 ...... **52** A1
Earsdon Vw *SMOOR* NE27 ...... **38** B6
Easby Cl *GOS/KPK* NE3 ...... **47** F4
Easby Rd *WASHS* NE38 ...... **138** C2
Easdale Av *GOS/KPK* NE3 ...... **47** E3
Easedale *WBAY* NE26 ...... **26** B2
Easedale Gdns *LWF/SPW/WRK* NE9 ...... **99** F6
Easington Av *CRAM* NE23 ...... **14** B4
  LWF/SPW/WRK NE9 ...... **118** B1
Easington Dr *PLEE/EAS* SR8 ...... **200** C1 ▣
  SWCK/CAS SR5 ...... **126** B4
Easington St North
  SWCK/CAS SR5 ...... **126** B4 ▣
East Acre *BLAY* NE21 ...... **76** C5
East Acres *DIN/WO* NE13 ...... **31** D2
East Av *HAR/WTLS* NE34 ...... **89** F2
  LGB/KIL NE12 ...... **49** F6

WASHS NE38 ... 138 B5
East Back Pde ASHBK/HED/RY SR2 .... 5 H5
East Bailey LGB/KIL NE12 ... 35 F6
LGB/KIL NE12 ... 49 F1
East Boldon Rd
CLDN/WHIT/ROK SR6 ... 107 E1 [1]
Eastbourne Av BYK/HTN/WLK NE6 .. 83 F1
GATE NE8 ... 99 D2
Eastbourne Gdns
BYK/HTN/WLK NE6 ... 83 F1
WBAY NE26 ... 40 B4
Eastbourne Gv SSH NE33 ... 71 F3 [3]
Eastcheap BYK/HTN/WLK NE6 ... 65 E5 [1]
East Cleft Rd
ASHBK/HED/RY SR2 ... 126 A6 [4]
Eastcliffe Av GOS/KPK NE3 ... 62 C3
East Cl HAR/WTLS NE34 ... 89 F2
Eastcombe Cl BOLCOL NE35 ... 87 D6 [5]
Eastcote Ter BYK/HTN/WLK NE6 .... 83 E5
East Crs BDLGTN NE22 ... 8 C2
East Cross St SUND SR1 ... 4 D1
Eastdene Rd SEA/MUR SR7 ... 175 E3
Eastdene Wy PLEE/EAS SR8 ... 209 E3
East Dr BLYTH NE24 ... 16 B2 [4]
CLDN/WHIT/ROK SR6 ... 107 D2
East End WBAY NE26 ... 27 D4
Eastern Av DUN/TMV NE11 ... 98 C6
Eastern Wy WD/WHPE/BLK NE5... 61 F4
Eastfield PLEE/EAS SR8 ... 209 F3
Eastfield Av BYK/HTN/WLK NE6 ... 66 C6
MONK NE25 ... 39 F6
Eastfield Rd HAR/WTLS NE34 ... 72 B6 [1]
LGB/KIL NE12 ... 49 E6
East Flds CLDN/WHIT/ROK SR6 ... 109 E2
Eastfield Ter MLFD/PNYW SR4 ... 143 F1
Eastfield Ter LGB/KIL NE12 ... 49 F6 [2]
East Forest Hall Rd LGB/KIL NE12 .. 50 A4 [3]
East Front JES NE2 ... 64 A6
Eastgarth WD/WHPE/BLK NE5 ... 60 C1
East Ga GATE NE8 ... 81 E5 [3]
Eastgate Gdns ELS/FEN NE4 ... 79 E4
East George Potts St SSH NE33 .... 71 F5 [2]
East George St TYNE/NSHE NE30 ... 55 E6
East Gra MONK NE25 ... 25 E6
SWCK/CAS SR5 ... 126 B1
East Grange Ct PLEE/EAS SR8 ... 200 A3 [5]
East Gn RDHAMSE DH6 ... 206 C2 [4]
East Gv MLFD/PNYW SR4 ... 142 A1
East Hill Rd GATE NE8 ... 100 A1
East Holborn SSH NE33 ... 71 D4
Eastlands BLAY NE21 ... 94 A1
LGB/HTN NE7 ... 64 C3
East Lea BLAY NE21 ... 94 B2
Eastlea Crs SEA/MUR SR7 ... 175 F3
Eastlea Rd SEA/MUR SR7 ... 175 E3
Eastleigh Cl BOLCOL NE35 ... 105 D2
East Moffett St SSH NE33 ... 71 F5 [3]
East Moor Rd MLFD/PNYW SR4 ... 125 E5
East Park Gdns BLAY NE21 ... 94 B1 [2]
East Park Rd LWF/SPW/WRK NE9 .. 99 E4
East Park Vw BLYTH NE24 ... 11 E5
East Percy St TYNE/NSHE NE30 ... 55 E6
East Riggs BDLGTN NE22 ... 7 E4
East Stevenson St SSH NE33 ... 71 F5 [4]
East Stoneycroft LGB/KIL NE12 .... 50 A2 [1]
East St CLDN/WHIT/ROK SR6 ... 109 E2
CLSW/PEL DH2 ... 150 C3
GATE NE8 ... 81 E5
RDHAMSE DH6 ... 206 C2
SSH NE33 ... 71 E3
STLY/ANP DH9 ... 149 D1
East Vw CLDN/WHIT/ROK SR6 ... 127 D1
HEBB NE31 ... 84 C4
PLEE/EAS SR8 ... 191 D6
SWCK/CAS SR5 ... 124 B3 [4]
East View Ter WICK/BNPF NE16 ... 96 A2 [1]
East Vines SUND SR1 ... 5 G1
Eastward Gn MONK NE25 ... 39 F6
Eastway HAR/WTLS NE34 ... 90 A3
Eastwood BDN/LAN/SAC DH7 ... 178 B2
Eastwood Av BLYTH NE24 ... 16 C3
Eastwood Cl CRAM NE23 ... 35 E5 [1]
Eastwood Gdns FELL NE10 ... 100 B1
GOS/KPK NE3 ... 62 B2
LWF/SPW/WRK NE9 ... 99 E6
Eastwood Pl CRAM NE23 ... 14 B4 [1]
Eaton Pl ELS/FEN NE4 ... 79 E3 [1]
Eavers Ct HAR/WTLS NE34 ... 88 B3 [2]
Ebba Wk GOS/KPK NE3 ... 63 F1 [1]
Ebchester Ct GOS/KPK NE3 ... 61 E1
Ebchester St HAR/WTLS NE34... 87 F3
Ebdon La CLDN/WHIT/ROK SR6... 108 C6
Ebor St BYK/HTN/WLK NE6 ... 65 E6
HAR/WTLS NE34 ... 87 F4
Eccleston Cl SMOOR NE27 ... 37 E6
Eccleston Rd SSH NE33 ... 72 A4
Ecgfrid Ter JRW NE32 ... 86 B3
Eddison Rd WASHS NE38 ... 139 E2
Eddleston Av GOS/KPK NE3 ... 62 C3
Eddrington Gv WD/WHPE/BLK NE5... 59 E3
Ede Av DUN/TMV NE11 ... 97 C2
HAR/WTLS NE34 ... 90 A2
Edenbridge Crs LGB/KIL NE12... 49 D5
Eden Cl WD/WHPE/BLK NE5 ... 59 E4

Edendale Av BLYTH NE24 ... 10 A4
BYK/HTN/WLK NE6 ... 83 F2
Edendale Ter GATE NE8 ... 99 E2
.... 209 E2 [2]
Edenfield STLY/ANP DH9 ... 150 C1
Edenhill Rd PLEE/EAS SR8 ... 209 D1
Eden House Rd MLFD/PNYW SR4... 144 A1
Eden La PLEE/EAS SR8 ... 200 C6
Eden Pl TYNE/NSHE NE30 ... 54 C3
Eden Rd DHAM DH1 ... 180 B6
Eden St PLEE/EAS SR8 ... 209 F1
WLSD/HOW NE28 ... 67 D5 [6]
Eden St West CLS/BIR/GTL DH3 ... 168 B2
SUND SR3 ... 4 A2
Eden Vw RDHAMSE DH6 ... 206 C2
Edgar St GOS/KPK NE3 ... 64 B1
Edgecote WASHN NE37 ... 121 E4
Edge Ct DHAM DH1 ... 195 E4
Edgefield Av GOS/KPK NE3 ... 62 B1
Edgefield Dr CRAM NE23 ... 14 B4
Edge Mt LGB/KIL NE12 ... 35 F6
Edgewood Av BDLGTN NE22 ... 8 B5 [2]
Edgeworth Cl BOLCOL NE35 ... 87 D6 [6]
Edgeworth Crs
CLDN/WHIT/ROK SR6 ... 126 C2 [2]
Edgmond Ct ASHBK/HED/RY SR2 ... 145 D6
Edgware Rd GATE NE8 ... 99 F2
Edhill Av HAR/WTLS NE34 ... 87 E3
Edinburgh Rd JRW NE32 ... 87 D4
Edington Gv TYNE/NSHE NE30 ... 54 C3
Edington Rd TYNE/NSHE NE30 ... 54 C3
Edison Gdns GATE NE8 ... 99 D3
Edison St SEA/MUR SR7 ... 188 B1
Edith Av BLAY NE21 ... 76 B6
Edith St ASHBK/HED/RY SR2 ... 145 D6 [3]
JRW NE32 ... 85 F1
SEA/MUR SR7 ... 177 D5
SWCK/CAS SR5 ... 126 B2 [2]
TYNE/NSHE NE30 ... 55 E4
Edlingham Cl GOS/KPK NE3 ... 64 B2
Edlingham Ct HLH DH5 ... 171 C2 [2]
Edlingham Rd DHAM DH1 ... 194 B1
Edmondsley La
BDN/LAN/SAC DH7 ... 164 A5
Edmund Pl LWF/SPW/WRK NE9 ... 99 E5 [5]
Edna Ter WD/WHPE/BLK NE5 ... 60 C3
Edward Av PLEE/EAS SR8 ... 209 E1
Edward Burdis St
SWCK/CAS SR5 ... 126 A2 [7]
Edward Cain Ct PLEE/EAS SR8 ... 209 F1 [1]
Edward Pl ELS/FEN NE4 ... 80 A3 [3]
Edward Rd BDLGTN NE22 ... 8 C2 [2]
CLS/BIR/GTL DH3 ... 136 A1
WLSD/HOW NE28 ... 68 B3
Edwardson Rd BDN/LAN/SAC DH7.. 203 F5
Edwards Rd WBAY NE26 ... 41 E6
Edward St BLYTH NE24 ... 10 C4
DHAM DH1 ... 195 E4
GOS/KPK NE3 ... 63 E1 [1]
HEBB NE31 ... 84 B1 [1]
HLH DH5 ... 171 F6
SEA/MUR SR7 ... 176 C4 [3]
STLY/ANP DH9 ... 149 E6
SUNDSW SR3 ... 160 C1
Edwin's Wk CNUT NE1 ... 2 C1
Edwin Gv WLSD/HOW NE28 ... 68 C3
Edwins Av LGB/KIL NE12 ... 50 A4
Edwin's Av South LGB/KIL NE12... 50 A4
Edwin St BYK/HTN/WLK NE6 ... 82 A2 [5]
HLH DH5 ... 171 D1
MLFD/PNYW SR4 ... 125 D5
Egerton Rd HAR/WTLS NE34 ... 88 B2
Egerton St ASHBK/HED/RY SR2 ... 5 E5
BW/LEM/TK/HW NE15 ... 78 B4
Eggleston Cl CLS/BIR/GTL DH3 ... 168 A3 [1]
DHAM DH1 ... 181 D6
Eggleston Dr SUNDSW SR3 ... 143 F4
Egham Rd WD/WHPE/BLK NE5... 59 E4
Eglesfield Rd SSH NE33 ... 71 E6
Eglinton St SWCK/CAS SR5... 126 B3
Eglinton St North SWCK/CAS SR5... 126 B3
Egremont Dr
LWF/SPW/WRK NE9 ... 100 A4 [3]
Egremont Gdns
LWF/SPW/WRK NE9 ... 99 F4 [6]
Egremont Gv PLEE/EAS SR8 ... 207 F5
Egremont Pl WBAY NE26 ... 41 D6
Eider Cl BLYTH NE24 ... 17 D3
Eighteenth Av BLYTH NE24 ... 16 B1 [2]
Eighth Av BLYTH NE24 ... 16 C1 [1]
BYK/HTN/WLK NE6 ... 65 E6
CLSW/PEL DH2 ... 153 D5
Eighth St PLEE/EAS SR8 ... 209 F1
Eighton Ter LWF/SPW/WRK NE9... 118 C1
Eishort Wy LGB/KIL NE12 ... 49 D6
Eland Cl GOS/KPK NE3 ... 61 F1
Eland Edge PONT/DH NE20... 28 B4
Eland La PONT/DH NE20 ... 28 B3
Elberfeld Ct JRW NE32 ... 86 A2
Elder Cl BDN/LAN/SAC DH7 ... 192 A5
Elder Gv HAR/WTLS NE34 ... 89 E4
LWF/SPW/WRK NE9 ... 99 E5 [5]
Elderwood Gdns DUN/TMV NE11... 98 A5
Eldon La CNUT NE1 ... 2 D3
Eldon Pl BW/LEM/TK/HW NE15 ... 76 C1

Eldon Rd BW/LEM/TK/HW NE15 ... 76 C1
Eldon St GATE NE8 ... 81 F5
MLFD/PNYW SR4 ... 125 F6
SSH NE33 ... 71 D5
WLSD/HOW NE28 ... 68 C4
Eleanor St SSH NE33 ... 71 F3
TYNE/NSHE NE30 ... 41 E6
Elemore La HLH DH5 ... 186 A4
RDHAMSE DH6 ... 185 D6
Elemore Vw RDHAMSE DH6 ... 187 D5
Elenbel Av BDLGTN NE22 ... 8 B3
Eleventh Av BLYTH NE24 ... 11 D6 [3]
Eleventh St PLEE/EAS SR8 ... 209 E1
Elford Cl MONK NE25 ... 39 F5
Elfordleigh HLS DH4 ... 157 E4 [2]
Elgar Av WD/WHPE/BLK NE5 ... 59 E4 [5]
Elgar Cl STLY/ANP DH9 ... 148 C3
Elgin Av SEA/MUR SR7 ... 175 E3
WLSD/HOW NE28 ... 68 B2
Elgin Cl NSHW NE29 ... 53 E4 [3]
Elgin Ct FELL NE10 ... 84 A6 [6]
Elgin Gdns BYK/HTN/WLK NE6 ... 83 E2
Elgin Gv STLY/ANP DH9 ... 149 D2
Elgin Rd LWF/SPW/WRK NE9... 100 A2
Elgin St JRW NE32 ... 87 D3
Elgy Rd GOS/KPK NE3 ... 63 D4
Elisabeth Av CLS/BIR/GTL DH3 ... 118 A6
Elizabeth Cl LGB/KIL NE12 ... 50 C4
Elizabeth Crs CRAM NE23 ... 34 C2
Elizabeth Diamond Gdns
SSH NE33 ... 71 D6 [2]
Elizabeth Dr LGB/KIL NE12 ... 50 C4
Elizabeth Rd WLSD/HOW NE28... 68 C3
Elizabeth St BYK/HTN/WLK NE6 ... 81 F2 [1]
HLH DH5 ... 171 D1
SEA/MUR SR7 ... 176 B3 [1]
SSH NE33 ... 71 F4 [6]
SWCK/CAS SR5 ... 124 A3 [3]
SWCK/CAS SR5 ... 126 B1 [2]
Ellam Av DHAM DH1 ... 193 F6
Ell-dene Crs FELL NE10 ... 101 D5
Ellerbeck Cl FELL NE10 ... 100 B2 [2]
Ellersmere Gdns
TYNE/NSHE NE30 ... 55 D2 [1]
Ellerton Wy CRAM NE23 ... 14 B4 [2]
FELL NE10 ... 100 B2
Ellesmere HLS DH4 ... 155 F5
Ellesmere Av BYK/HTN/WLK NE6 ... 83 D1
WD/WHPE/BLK NE5... 60 C4
Ellesmere Ct ASHBK/HED/RY SR2 ... 145 D5
Ellesmere Dr SEA/MUR SR7 ... 175 E3
Ellesmere Rd ELS/FEN NE4 ... 79 D3
Ellington Cl ASHBK/HED/RY SR2 .. 162 B3 [1]
BW/LEM/TK/HW NE15 ... 76 A1
Elliot Cl HLS DH4 ... 157 D1
Elliot Rd FELL NE10 ... 100 A1 [1]
Elliott Dr FELL NE10 ... 100 C2 [3]
Elliott Gdns WLSD/HOW NE28 ... 66 C2
Elliott Rd PLEE/EAS SR8 ... 208 C1
Elliott St BLYTH NE24 ... 16 A2
Elliott Ter ELS/FEN NE4 ... 79 F3 [5]
Ellison Pl CNUT NE1 ... 3 E2
JRW NE32 ... 69 D6
LWF/SPW/WRK NE9 ... 99 E6
Ellison Rd DUN/TMV NE11 ... 97 F2
PLEE/EAS SR8 ... 209 D1
Ellison St GATE NE8 ... 81 E5 [3]
HEBB NE31 ... 84 C2 [2]
JRW NE32 ... 86 A1 [1]
Ellis Rd SWCK/CAS SR5 ... 125 F1 [1]
Ellis Sq SWCK/CAS SR5 ... 126 A1
Elm Av BDN/LAN/SAC DH7 ... 203 D5
CLSW/PEL DH2 ... 151 E2
DIN/WO NE13 ... 31 D3
DUN/TMV NE11 ... 97 D3
HAR/WTLS NE34 ... 89 E4
WICK/BNPF NE16 ... 96 B2
Elm Cl CRAM NE23 ... 14 B4
Elm Ct WICK/BNPF NE16 ... 96 A5
Elm Crs CLSW/PEL DH2 ... 179 E1
Elm Croft Rd LGB/KIL NE12 ... 50 A5
Elm Dr BDLGTN NE22 ... 7 E5
CLDN/WHIT/ROK SR6 ... 109 F1
Elmfield Av DHAM DH1 ... 196 A3
Elmfield Cl SUNDSW SR3 ... 159 D2
Elmfield Gdns WLSD/HOW NE28.... 66 B2
Elmfield Gv GOS/KPK NE3 ... 63 D3
Elmfield Pk GOS/KPK NE3 ... 63 D3
Elmfield Rd
BW/LEM/TK/HW NE15 ... 58 A4 [2]
GOS/KPK NE3 ... 63 D3
HEBB NE31 ... 85 E5
Elmfield Ter HEBB NE31 ... 85 E4
Elm Gv BDN/LAN/SAC DH7 ... 192 A5
GOS/KPK NE3 ... 46 B5
HAR/WTLS NE34 ... 89 E4
LGB/KIL NE12 ... 49 F3
WICK/BNPF NE16 ... 111 E6
Elm Rd BLAY NE21 ... 76 C6
NSHW NE29 ... 53 D5
PONT/DH NE20 ... 28 C5
Elmsford Gv LGB/KIL NE12 ... 49 E6
Elmsleigh Gdns
CLDN/WHIT/ROK SR6 ... 89 F5
The Elms HLH DH5 ... 186 C3

Elm St *CLS/BIR/GTL* DH3 .... 153 E5
 DUN/TMV NE11 .... 98 A4
 JRW NE32 .... 85 F1
 STLY/ANP DH9 .... 147 F4
 WICK/BNPF NE16 .... 114 A2
Elm St West *WICK/BNPF* NE16 ...... 114 A2
Elmtree Ct *SEA/MUR* SR7 .... 176 B5
Elmtree Gdns *MONK* NE25 .... 54 A1
Elmtree Gv *GOS/KPK* NE3 .... 63 D2
Elm Trees *BLYTH* NE24 .... 10 C6 **2**
Elmway *CLSW/PEL* DH2 .... 152 C3
Elmwood Av *DIN/WO* NE13 .... 33 D5
 SWCK/CAS SR5 .... 125 E1
Elmwood Crs *BYK/HTN/WLK* NE6 .. 66 B5 **1**
Elmwood Dr *PONT/DH* NE20 .... 28 A3
Elmwood Gdns *DUN/TMV* NE11 ...... 98 A4
Elmwood Gv *WBAY* NE26 .... 40 C4
Elmwood Rd *MONK* NE25 .... 40 A6
Elmwood St
 ASHBK/HED/RY SR2 .... 144 A1 **3**
 HLS DH4 .... 169 D1
Elrick Cl *WD/WHPE/BLK* NE5 .... 59 E4 **3**
Elrington Gdns
 WD/WHPE/BLK NE5 .... 61 D6 **2**
Elsdon Av *MONK* NE25 .... 24 C5
Elsdonburn Rd *SUNDSW* SR3 ...... 160 A3 **3**
Elsdon Cl *BLYTH* NE24 .... 10 B5
 PLEE/EAS SR8 .... 208 B5
Elsdon Ct *WICK/BNPF* NE16 .... 95 F5
Elsdon Dr *LGB/KIL* NE12 .... 50 B4
Elsdon Gdns *DUN/TMV* NE11 .... 97 F2
Elsdon Pl *NSHW* NE29 .... 70 C2
Elsdon Rd *DHAM* DH1 .... 180 C6
 GOS/KPK NE3 .... 63 E1
 WICK/BNPF NE16 .... 95 F4
Elsdon St *NSHW* NE29 .... 70 C2 **3**
Elsdon Ter *NSHW* NE29 .... 69 F2
Elsing Cl *WD/WHPE/BLK* NE5 .... 61 D2
Elstob Pl *BYK/HTN/WLK* NE6 .... 83 D4
 SUNDSW SR3 .... 143 F4
Elston Cl *WD/WHPE/BLK* NE5 .... 59 E4 **7**
Elstree Ct *DIN/WO* NE13 .... 45 D5 **1**
Elstree Gdns *BLYTH* NE24 .... 16 C3 **1**
Elswick East Ter *ELS/FEN* NE4 .... 80 A4
Elswick Rd *ELS/FEN* NE4 .... 79 E4
Elswick Rw *ELS/FEN* NE4 .... 79 F3
Elswick St *ELS/FEN* NE4 .... 80 A3 **10**
Elswick Wy *HAR/WTLS* NE34 .... 87 F2
Elterwater Rd *CLSW/PEL* DH2 .... 166 A1
Elton St East *WLSD/HOW* NE28 .... 67 D5
Elton St West *WLSD/HOW* NE28 ...... 66 C5
Eltringham Cl *WLSD/HOW* NE28 .... 66 C4 **2**
Elvaston Rd *RYTON* NE40 .... 74 B2
Elvet Br *DHAM* DH1 .... 194 B5
Elvet Cl *DIN/WO* NE13 .... 33 D4 **2**
Elvet Ct *BYK/HTN/WLK* NE6 .... 82 B1
Elvet Crs *DHAM* DH1 .... 194 C5
Elvet Gn *CLSW/PEL* DH2 .... 153 E6
 HLH DH5 .... 185 F3 **1**
Elvet Hill Rd *DHAM* DH1 .... 205 H3
Elvington St *CLDN/WHIT/ROK* SR6 .. 127 D1
Elwin Cl *WBAY* NE26 .... 26 C3
Elwin Pl *CLSW/PEL* DH2 .... 152 A2
Elwin Ter *ASHBK/HED/RY* SR2 .... 4 A4
Elwyn Cl *WBAY* NE26 .... 26 C3
Ely Cl *LGB/KIL* NE12 .... 65 F2
Ely Rd *DHAM* DH1 .... 180 C4 **2**
Elysium La *GATE* NE8 .... 98 C1
Ely St *GATE* NE8 .... 99 D1 **1**
Embankment Rd *SEA/MUR* SR7 ...... 176 A1
 SEA/MUR SR7 .... 177 D3
Embassy Gdns I
 BW/LEM/TK/HW NE15 .... 78 A3
Emblehope *WASHN* NE38 .... 119 F6
Emblehope Dr *GOS/KPK* NE3 .... 62 C2
Embleton Av *GOS/KPK* NE3 .... 46 C5 **3**
 HAR/WTLS NE34 .... 73 D6
 WLSD/HOW NE28 .... 68 A1
Embleton Cl *DHAM* DH1 .... 180 C6 **2**
Embleton Crs *NSHW* NE29 .... 53 E4
Embleton Dr *BLYTH* NE24 .... 16 B1 **3**
Embleton Gdns
 WD/WHPE/BLK NE5 .... 61 F5 **3**
 NSHW NE29 .... 53 E4
Embleton Rd *FELL* NE10 .... 84 A6
 NSHW NE29 .... 53 E4
Embleton St *SEA/MUR* SR7 .... 176 C5 **3**
Emden Rd *GOS/KPK* NE3 .... 46 A6
Emily St *BYK/HTN/WLK* NE6 .... 83 D2
 GATE NE8 .... 100 A1 **3**
Emily St East *SEA/MUR* SR7 .... 176 C5 **7**
Emlyn Rd *HAR/WTLS* NE34 .... 88 B2
Emmbrook Cl *HLH* DH5 .... 170 C6 **1**
Emmerson Pl *SMOOR* NE27 .... 52 A1
Empress Rd *BYK/HTN/WLK* NE6 ...... 84 A4
Empress St *SWCK/CAS* SR5 .... 126 B3 **3**
Emsworth Rd *SWCK/CAS* SR5 .... 125 F1
Enderby Rd *MLFD/PNYW* SR4 .... 126 A5
Enfield Av *WICK/BNPF* NE16 .... 96 A1
Enfield Gdns *WICK/BNPF* NE16 ...... 96 A5
Enfield Rd *LWF/SPW/WRK* NE9 ...... 99 E5
 SEA/MUR SR7 .... 175 E3
Enfield St *MLFD/PNYW* SR4 .... 125 E5 **2**
Engine Inn Rd *WLSD/HOW* NE28 .... 68 B2
Engine La *LWF/SPW/WRK* NE9 .... 99 E6
Englemann Wy *SUNDSW* SR3 ...... 160 A4

Enid Av *CLDN/WHIT/ROK* SR6 ...... 126 C1
Enid St *DIN/WO* NE13 .... 32 C6 **2**
Ennerdale *ASHBK/HED/RY* SR2 ...... 144 B2
 CLS/BIR/GTL DH5 .... 136 C4
Ennerdale Cl *DHAM* DH1 .... 197 D2 **2**
 SEA/MUR SR7 .... 175 E3
Ennerdale Crs *BLAY* NE21 .... 94 A2 **3**
 HLS DH4 .... 139 F6 **1**
Ennerdale Gdns
 LWF/SPW/WRK NE9 .... 99 F5
 WLSD/HOW NE28 .... 68 C2 **2**
Ennerdale Rd *BLYTH* NE24 .... 9 E3
 BYK/HTN/WLK NE6 .... 83 E2
 TYNE/NSHE NE30 .... 54 C2
Ennerdale St *HLH* DH5 .... 185 D2
Enslin St *BYK/HTN/WLK* NE6 .... 83 E5
Epping Cl *SEA/MUR* SR7 .... 175 E4
Eppleton Hall Cl *SEA/MUR* SR7 .... 175 D2
Eppleton Rw *HLH* DH5 .... 172 A6 **1**
Epsom Cl *NSHW* NE29 .... 70 B2
Epsom Ct *GOS/KPK* NE3 .... 45 E5
Epsom Wy *BLYTH* NE24 .... 16 C3
Epworth *STLY/ANP* DH9 .... 130 B6
Equitable St *WLSD/HOW* NE28 ...... 67 D5 **2**
Erick St *CNUT* NE1 .... 3 E3 **1**
Erith Ter *MLFD/PNYW* SR4 .... 125 E6
Ernest Av *ASHBK/HED/RY* SR2 ...... 145 D2
 BOLCOL NE35 .... 105 F2
 CLSW/PEL DH2 .... 152 A1
Ernest Ter *STLY/ANP* DH9 .... 131 E6 **3**
Ernwill Av *SWCK/CAS* SR5 .... 124 A3
Errington Dr *STLY/ANP* DH9 .... 130 B6
Errington Ter *LGB/KIL* NE12 .... 50 A3 **3**
Errol Pl *CLS/BIR/GTL* DH3 .... 136 C4
Erskine Rd *SSH* NE33 .... 71 F4
Erskine Wy *SSH* NE33 .... 72 A4
Escallond Dr *SEA/MUR* SR7 .... 175 E4
Esdale *ASHBK/HED/RY* SR2 .... 162 A2
Esher Gdns *BLYTH* NE24 .... 16 C3
Eshmere Crs *WD/WHPE/BLK* NE5 .. 59 E4
Eshott Cl *GOS/KPK* NE3 .... 46 C6
 WD/WHPE/BLK NE5 .... 60 C5
Eskdale *CLS/BIR/GTL* DH3 .... 137 D5
 HLS DH4 .... 139 F6 **3**
Eskdale Av *BLYTH* NE24 .... 9 F4
 WLSD/HOW NE28 .... 67 F2
Eskdale Cl *SEA/MUR* SR7 .... 175 E3
Eskdale Ct *HAR/WTLS* NE34 .... 88 B2
Eskdale Dr *JRW* NE32 .... 86 C5
Eskdale Gdns *LWF/SPW/WRK* NE9 .. 99 F6
Eskdale Rd *CLDN/WHIT/ROK* SR6 .. 109 E4
Eskdale St *HAR/WTLS* NE34 .... 88 B3 **8**
 HLH DH5 .... 185 E2
Eskdale Ter *JES* NE2 .... 64 A4 **1**
 WBAY NE26 .... 41 E6
Eskdale Wk *PLEE/EAS* SR8 .... 209 D2 **4**
Esk St *LWF/SPW/WRK* NE9 .... 100 A3
Eslington Rd *JES* NE2 .... 81 D1 **2**
Eslington Ter *JES* NE2 .... 64 A6
Esmeralda Gdns *CRAM* NE23 .... 36 C1 **1**
Esplanade *WBAY* NE26 .... 41 D5
Espley Cl *LGB/KIL* NE12 .... 50 C4
Espley Ct *GOS/KPK* NE3 .... 46 A5 **3**
Essen Wy *SUNDSW* SR3 .... 144 A3
Essex Cl *ELS/FEN* NE4 .... 80 A5
Essex Crs *SEA/MUR* SR7 .... 175 E3
Essex Dr *WASHN* NE37 .... 120 C3 **1**
Essex Gdns *HAR/WTLS* NE34 .... 90 B1
 WLSD/HOW NE28 .... 68 A3
Essex Gv *SUNDSW* SR3 .... 143 F6
Essex Pl *PLEE/EAS* SR8 .... 200 B6
Essington Wy *PLEE/EAS* SR8 .... 200 B6
Esst Vw *HLH* DH5 .... 186 C3
Esther Sq *WASHS* NE38 .... 139 D2
Esthwaite Av *CLSW/PEL* DH2 .... 166 A1
Eston Ct *BLYTH* NE24 .... 10 A4
 WLSD/HOW NE28 .... 66 B1 **2**
Eston Gv *SWCK/CAS* SR5 .... 126 B1
Estuary Wy *MLFD/PNYW* SR4 .... 124 A5
Etal Av *MONK* NE25 .... 41 D6
 NSHW NE29 .... 69 F2
Etal Crs *JRW* NE32 .... 86 C4
 SMOOR NE27 .... 52 B1
Etal La *WD/WHPE/BLK* NE5 .... 60 C3
Etal Pl *GOS/KPK* NE3 .... 46 C5 **2**
Etal Rd *BLYTH* NE24 .... 16 A3 **1**
Etal Wy *WD/WHPE/BLK* NE5 .... 61 D2
Ethel Av *ASHBK/HED/RY* SR2 .... 162 C2
 BLAY NE21 .... 76 B3 **3**
Ethel St *CRAM* NE23 .... 34 C4
 ELS/FEN NE4 .... 78 C4
Ethel Ter *HAR/WTLS* NE34 .... 88 A3
 SWCK/CAS SR5 .... 124 A3
Etherley Cl *DHAM* DH1 .... 180 C5
Etherley Rd *BYK/HTN/WLK* NE6 ...... 82 C1
Etherstone Av *LGB/HTN* NE7 .... 65 E4
Eton Cl *CRAM* NE23 .... 14 B4 **3**
Eton Sq *HEBB* NE31 .... 85 E2
Ettrick Cl *LGB/KIL* NE12 .... 35 E6 **4**
Ettrick Gdns *GATE* NE8 .... 100 A2 **2**
 MLFD/PNYW SR4 .... 143 D2
Ettrick Gv *MLFD/PNYW* SR4 .... 143 E2
 SUNDSW SR3 .... 143 E3 **1**
Ettrick Rd *JRW* NE32 .... 85 F3
European Wy *MLFD/PNYW* SR4 ...... 124 C4

Euryalus Ct *SSH* NE33 .... 72 B5
Eustace Av *NSHW* NE29 .... 70 A1
Evanlade *FELL* NE10 .... 102 A4
Eva St *BW/LEM/TK/HW* NE15 .... 76 B2
Evelyn St *ASHBK/HED/RY* SR2 ...... 144 A1
Evenwood Gdns
 LWF/SPW/WRK NE9 .... 100 A5
Everard St *CRAM* NE23 .... 14 A3
Everest Gv *BOL* NE36 .... 106 A3 **3**
Eversleigh Pl
 BW/LEM/TK/HW NE15 .... 58 A4 **3**
Eversley Pl *WLSD/HOW* NE28 .... 68 B3 **3**
Everton Dr *SEA/MUR* SR7 .... 175 E3
Everton La *SWCK/CAS* SR5 .... 125 F1
Evesham Av *WBAY* NE26 .... 40 B4
Evesham Cl *BOLCOL* NE35 .... 105 E1
Evesham Garth *GOS/KPK* NE3 .... 62 A3
Evesham Rd *SEA/MUR* SR7 .... 175 E3
Evistones Gdns *BYK/HTN/WLK* NE6 .. 83 D5
Evistones Rd
 LWF/SPW/WRK NE9 .... 99 E4 **2**
Ewart Crs *HAR/WTLS* NE34 .... 87 D4
Ewbank Av *ELS/FEN* NE4 .... 79 D1
Ewehurst Crs *STLY/ANP* DH9 .... 129 D5
Ewehurst Pde *STLY/ANP* DH9 .... 129 D5
Ewehurst Rd *STLY/ANP* DH9 .... 129 D5
 WICK/BNPF NE16 .... 129 E4
Ewen Ct *NSHW* NE29 .... 53 D4
Ewesley *WASHS* NE38 .... 137 F6
Ewesley Cl *WD/WHPE/BLK* NE5 ...... 60 C4
Ewesley Gdns *DIN/WO* NE13 .... 33 D4
Ewesley Rd *MLFD/PNYW* SR4 .... 143 E1
Ewing Rd *MLFD/PNYW* SR4 .... 144 A1 **6**
Exebly Cl *GOS/KPK* NE3 .... 47 F4
Exeter Cl *CLS/BIR/GTL* DH3 .... 167 F4
Exeter Rd *WLSD/HOW* NE28 .... 66 C1
Exeter St *BYK/HTN/WLK* NE6 .... 83 F4
 GATE NE8 .... 99 D1
 MLFD/PNYW SR4 .... 143 E5
Exmouth Cl *SEA/MUR* SR7 .... 175 F4 **3**
Exmouth Rd *NSHW* NE29 .... 69 E1
Exmouth Sq *SWCK/CAS* SR5 .... 125 F1
Extension Rd *SUND* SR1 .... 5 H5
Eyemouth La *SWCK/CAS* SR5 .... 125 F1
Eyemouth Rd *NSHW* NE29 .... 69 E1 **2**
Eyre St *STLY/ANP* DH9 .... 147 F4

F

Faber Rd *SWCK/CAS* SR5 .... 125 F1
Factory Rd *BLAY* NE21 .... 76 C4
Fairbairn Rd *PLEE/EAS* SR8 .... 200 C6
Fairburn Av *HLH* DH5 .... 171 D4
 LGB/HTN NE7 .... 65 E2
Fairdale Av *LGB/HTN* NE7 .... 65 E2
Fairfield *CLSW/PEL* DH2 .... 151 F1
 LGB/KIL NE12 .... 48 B6
 STLY/ANP DH9 .... 146 B3
Fairfield Av *BLYTH* NE24 .... 16 C2
 WICK/BNPF NE16 .... 95 F5
Fairfield Cl *DUN/TMV* NE11 .... 97 E1 **1**
Fairfield Dr *CLDN/WHIT/ROK* SR6 .. 91 D6
 MONK NE25 .... 39 E6
 TYNE/NSHE NE30 .... 55 D2
Fairfield Gn *MONK* NE25 .... 39 E6
Fairfield Rd *JES* NE2 .... 63 F5
Fairfields *RYTON* NE40 .... 74 A4
Fair Gn *MONK* NE25 .... 39 E6
Fairgreen Cl *SUNDSW* SR3 .... 160 C3 **1**
Fairhaven Av *BYK/HTN/WLK* NE6 .... 83 F2
Fairhaven Av *BYK/HTN/WLK* NE6 .... 83 F2
Fairhill Cl *LGB/HTN* NE7 .... 65 E2
Fairholme Av *HAR/WTLS* NE34 .... 89 F2
Fairholme Rd *SUNDSW* SR3 .... 144 B3 **3**
Fairholm Rd *ELS/FEN* NE4 .... 79 D3
Fairlands East
 CLDN/WHIT/ROK SR6 .... 126 C2 **3**
Fairlands West *SWCK/CAS* SR5 ...... 126 C3
Fairlawn Gdns *MLFD/PNYW* SR4 .. 143 D2
Fairles St *SSH* NE33 .... 71 F2
Fairmead Wy *MLFD/PNYW* SR4 .... 141 F1
Fairmile Dr *SUNDSW* SR3 .... 160 C3
Fairmont Wy *LGB/HTN* NE7 .... 65 E2 **4**
Fairney Cl *PONT/DH* NE20 .... 28 B4
Fairney Edge *PONT/DH* NE20 .... 28 B4
Fairspring *WD/WHPE/BLK* NE5 .... 60 C4
Fairview Av *HAR/WTLS* NE34 .... 89 E1
Fairview Gn *LGB/HTN* NE7 .... 65 E2 **5**
Fairville Cl *DHAM* DH1 .... 14 A4
Fairville Crs *LGB/HTN* NE7 .... 65 E2
Fairway Cl *GOS/KPK* NE3 .... 47 D4
Fairways *MONK* NE25 .... 39 F5
 SUNDSW SR3 .... 161 D1 **3**
Fairways Av *LGB/HTN* NE7 .... 65 E1 **2**
The Fairways *BOL* NE36 .... 105 F3 **3**
 BOL NE36 .... 106 B3 **2**
 STLY/ANP DH9 .... 147 F6
The Fairway *BLAY* NE21 .... 75 F4
 GOS/KPK NE3 .... 47 D4
 WASHN NE37 .... 120 C1
Falconar's Ct *CNUT* NE1 .... 2 C3
Falconar St *JES* NE2 .... 3 F2

Falcon Pl *LGB/KIL* NE12 .... 48 C5
Falcon Wy *HAR/WTLS* NE34........... 88 A4
Faldonside *BYK/HTN/WLK* NE6 .... 65 F4 🔟
Falkirk *LGB/KIL* NE12 .... 35 F6 🔟
Falkland Av *GOS/KPK* NE3 .... 62 B3
  HEBB NE31................................ 85 D2
Falkland Rd *MLFD/PNYW* SR4 ...... 125 D6
Falla Park Crs *FELL* NE10 .... 100 B2
Falla Park Rd *FELL* NE10 .... 100 B2
Falloden Av *GOS/KPK* NE3 .... 46 B4
Fallodon Gdns
  WD/WHPE/BLK NE5 .... 61 F4 🔟
Fallodon Rd *NSHW* NE29 .... 69 F1
Fallowfeld *FELL* NE10 .... 101 F3
Fallowfield *WASHS* NE38 .... 139 D5
Fallowfield Av *GOS/KPK* NE3 .... 46 B6
Fallowfield Wy *WASHS* NE38....... 138 C4
Fallow Park Av *BLYTH* NE24 .... 10 B6 🔟
Fallow Rd *HAR/WTLS* NE34 .... 90 C2
Fallsway *DHAM* DH1 .... 196 C1
Falmouth Cl *SEA/MUR* SR7 .... 175 F4 🔟
Falmouth Dr *JRW* NE32 .... 86 C3
Falmouth Rd *BYK/HTN/WLK* NE6 .... 82 A1
  MLFD/PNYW SR4 .... 125 D5
  NSHW NE29............................. 53 F3
  NSHW NE29............................. 69 E1
Falmouth Sq *MLFD/PNYW* SR4 .... 125 D6
Falsgrave Pl *WICK/BNPF* NE16 ...... 95 E5
Falstaff Rd *NSHW* NE29 .... 53 F6
Falstone *FELL* NE10 .... 101 E5
  WASHS NE38........................... 139 D4
Falstone Av *BW/LEM/TK/HW* NE15 ... 60 A6
  HAR/WTLS NE34 .... 89 F2
Falstone Cl *LGB/KIL* NE12............. 50 C4
Falstone Dr *CLSW/PEL* DH2 .... 165 E1
Falstone Sq *GOS/KPK* NE3 .... 46 C6 🔟
Falston Rd *BLYTH* NE24 .... 16 B1
Faraday Cl *WASHS* NE38............. 140 A1
Faraday Gv *GATE* NE8................. 98 C3
  MLFD/PNYW SR4 .... 125 D6
Faraday Rd *PLEE/EAS* SR8 .... 201 D5
Faraday St *SEA/MUR* SR7 .... 188 D1 🔟
Fareham Gv *BOLCOL* NE35........... 104 C2
Farlam Av *TYNE/NSHE* NE30 .... 54 C3
Farlam Rd *WD/WHPE/BLK* NE5 .... 61 D6 🔟
Farleigh Ct *NSHW* NE29 .... 53 D4
Farm Cl *WASHN* NE37 .... 120 A3
  WICK/BNPF NE16 .... 114 A2
Farm Ct *BLAY* NE21 .... 77 E6
Farmer Crs *SEA/MUR* SR7 .... 188 A1
Farm Hill Rd *CLDN/WHIT/ROK* SR6 ... 89 F6
Farm Rd *DHAM* DH1 .... 205 F3
Farm St *SWCK/CAS* SR5 .... 126 A3
Farnborough Cl *CRAM* NE23........... 14 A6
Farnborough Dr *SUNDSW* SR3 ..... 144 A6
Farn Ct *DIN/WO* NE13................. 45 F4
Farndale *WLSD/HOW* NE28 .... 66 B1
Farndale Av *CLDN/WHIT/ROK* SR6 .. 109 E4
Farndale Cl *BLAY* NE21 .... 93 E2 🔟
  DIN/WO NE13 .... 31 D3 🔟
Farndale Rd *ELS/FEN* NE4 .... 79 C3
Farne Av *GOS/KPK* NE3 .... 46 C4
  HAR/WTLS NE34 .... 90 A1
Farne Rd *LGB/KIL* NE12 .... 50 A4
  SMOOR NE27 .... 52 B1
Farne Sq *MLFD/PNYW* SR4 .... 124 C5
Farne Ter *BYK/HTN/WLK* NE6 .... 83 D2
Farnham Cl *DHAM* DH1 .... 194 B1
Farnham Gv *BLYTH* NE24 .... 16 C2
Farnham Rd *DHAM* DH1 .... 180 B6
  HAR/WTLS NE34 .... 88 B2 🔟
Farnham St *BW/LEM/TK/HW* NE15 .. 76 C2
Farnley Hey Rd *DHAM* DH1 .... 193 F5 🔟
Farnley Mt *DHAM* DH1 .... 193 F5 🔟
Farnley Rdg *DHAM* DH1 .... 193 F5
Farnley Rd *BYK/HTN/WLK* NE6 .... 65 C5 🔟
Farnon Rd *GOS/KPK* NE3 .... 62 C1
Farquhar St *JES* NE2................. 64 B2
Farrier Cl *WASHS* NE38............. 139 D4
Farringdon Rd *TYNE/NSHE* NE30 ... 54 C2
Farringdon Rw *MLFD/PNYW* SR4 .. 126 A4
Farrington Av *SUNDSW* SR3 .... 142 B6
Farrow Dr *CLDN/WHIT/ROK* SR6 .. 109 D1
The Farthings *WASHN* NE37 .... 120 A2
Fatfield Pk *WASHS* NE38 .... 138 C5
Fatfield Rd *WASHS* NE38 .... 139 D2
Faversham Ct *GOS/KPK* NE3 .... 45 F5 🔟
Faversham Pl *CRAM* NE23 .... 14 A6
Fawcett St *SUND* SR1................. 4 C2
Fawcett Ter
  ASHBK/HED/RY SR2 .... 162 C2 🔟
Fawdon Cl *GOS/KPK* NE3 .... 46 A4
Fawdon La *GOS/KPK* NE3 .... 45 F5
Fawdon Park Rd *GOS/KPK* NE3 .... 46 A3 🔟
Fawdon Pl *NSHW* NE29 .... 53 E6
Fawley Cl *BOLCOL* NE35 .... 105 D1 🔟
Fawn Rd *MLFD/PNYW* SR4 .... 124 B6
Feather Bed La
  ASHBK/HED/RY SR2 .... 162 C2
Featherstone Gv *BDLGTN* NE22 ...... 6 C2
  JRW NE32................................ 85 F5
Featherstone Rd *DHAM* DH1 ...... 194 C1
Featherstone St
  CLDN/WHIT/ROK SR6 .... 127 E2

Federation Sq *SEA/MUR* SR7 ...... 188 B2
Federation Wy *DUN/TMV* NE11 ...... 97 D1 🔟
Feetham Av *LGB/KIL* NE12........... 50 B4
Felixstowe Dr *LGB/HTN* NE7 .... 65 E3
Fell Bank *CLS/BIR/GTL* DH3 .... 136 C2
Fell Cl *CLS/BIR/GTL* DH3 .... 137 D3
  WICK/BNPF NE16 .... 114 A2
Felldyke *FELL* NE10 .... 101 E5 🔟
Fellgate Av *JRW* NE32 .... 104 B1
Fellgate Gdns *FELL* NE10 .... 102 B2 🔟
Felling House Gdns *FELL* NE10 .... 82 C6 🔟
Felling Vw *BYK/HTN/WLK* NE6 ..... 83 E5
Fellmere Av *FELL* NE10................ 101 E2
Fell Rd *CLSW/PEL* DH2 .... 152 A5
  LWF/SPW/WRK NE9 .... 119 E3
  MLFD/PNYW SR4 .... 124 C5
Fellside *HAR/WTLS* NE34 .... 90 A3
Fellside Av *WICK/BNPF* NE16........ 114 A1
Fellside Ct *WICK/BNPF* NE16 .... 95 F3 🔟
Fellside Gdns *DHAM* DH1 .... 196 B2 🔟
Fellside Rd *WICK/BNPF* NE16 .... 95 E5
  WICK/BNPF NE16 .... 112 B5
The Fell Side *GOS/KPK* NE3 .... 62 B2
Fells Rd *DUN/TMV* NE11................ 98 C3
The Fell Wy *WD/WHPE/BLK* NE5 .. 59 F5 🔟
Felsham Sq *MLFD/PNYW* SR4 ..... 125 D6
Felstead Crs *MLFD/PNYW* SR4 .... 124 C5
Felstead Pl *BLYTH* NE24 .... 16 C2
Felstead Sq *MLFD/PNYW* SR4 ..... 124 C6
Felton Av *GOS/KPK* NE3 .... 46 C6
  HAR/WTLS NE34 .... 89 F2
  MONK NE25............................. 41 D6
Felton Cl *SMOOR* NE27............... 52 B1
Felton Crs *GATE* NE8.................. 99 D3
Felton Dr *LGB/KIL* NE12 .... 50 B3
Fencer Ct *GOS/KPK* NE3............. 47 E4
Fence Rd *CLS/BIR/GTL* DH3 .... 156 A2
Fenham Cha *ELS/FEN* NE4............ 61 F6
Fenham Hall Dr *ELS/FEN* NE4........ 61 F6
Fenham Rd *ELS/FEN* NE4 .... 79 E2 🔟
Fenkle St *CNUT* NE1 .... 2 B4
Fennel Gv *HAR/WTLS* NE34 .... 89 D5
Fenning Pl *BYK/HTN/WLK* NE6 .... 82 B4 🔟
Fenside Rd *ASHBK/HED/RY* SR2 .. 145 E6
Fenton Cl *CLSW/PEL* DH2............. 165 F1
Fenton Sq *MLFD/PNYW* SR4 ...... 124 C6 🔟
Fenton Well La *CLS/BIR/GTL* DH3 .. 167 D3
Fenwick Av *BLYTH* NE24 .... 16 C1 🔟
  HAR/WTLS NE34 .... 87 F3
Fenwick Cl *CLSW/PEL* DH2.......... 165 E1
  HLS DH4 .... 140 A6 🔟
Fenwick St *HLS* DH4 .... 140 A6
Ferens Cl *DHAM* DH1 .... 194 C3
Ferens Pk *DHAM* DH1 .... 194 C3
Ferguson Crs *DIN/WO* NE13 .... 32 C5
Ferguson's La
  BW/LEM/TK/HW NE15.............. 77 F2
Ferguson St *ASHBK/HED/RY* SR2 .. 5 H4
Fern Av *CLDN/WHIT/ROK* SR6 ...... 91 E6
  CRAM NE23............................. 14 A4
  GOS/KPK NE3 .... 46 C5 🔟
  JES NE2.................................. 64 A5
  NSHW NE29............................. 54 B6
  SWCK/CAS SR5 .... 125 F2
Fern Crs *SEA/MUR* SR7 .... 176 B6
Ferndale *DHAM* DH1 .... 196 C3
Ferndale Av *BOL* NE36 .... 106 C3
  GOS/KPK NE3 .... 47 F3
  WLSD/HOW NE28 .... 67 E4
Ferndale Cl *BLYTH* NE24 .... 9 F4 🔟
Ferndale Gv *BOL* NE36 .... 106 C3
Ferndale La *BOL* NE36 .... 106 C3
Ferndale Rd *HLS* DH4 .... 139 F6
Ferndale Ter *MLFD/PNYW* SR4 .... 125 D4
Ferndene Crs *MLFD/PNYW* SR4 .. 125 E6
Ferndene Gv *LGB/HTN* NE7 .... 65 D3
Fern Dene Rd *GATE* NE8............. 99 D2
Ferndown Ct *RYTON* NE40 .... 74 C4 🔟
Fern Dr *CLDN/WHIT/ROK* SR6 ..... 107 E1
  CRAM NE23............................. 34 C2
Fernhill Av *WICK/BNPF* NE16....... 95 F3
Fernlea Cl *WASHS* NE38 .... 139 D4
Fernley Vls *CRAM* NE23 .... 22 C2
Fern Rd *BDN/LAN/SAC* DH7 .... 178 C1
Fern St *MLFD/PNYW* SR4 .... 126 A5
Fernsway *SUNDSW* SR3 .... 144 A3 🔟
Fernville Av *WICK/BNPF* NE16...... 114 A2
Fernville Rd *GOS/KPK* NE3........... 63 D4
Fernville St *MLFD/PNYW* SR4 .... 144 A1 🔟
Fernwood Av *GOS/KPK* NE3 .... 47 F5
Fernwood Cl *SUNDSW* SR3 .... 160 C3 🔟
Fernwood Rd
  BW/LEM/TK/HW NE15.............. 76 C2
  JES NE2.................................. 64 A6
Ferrand Dr *HLS* DH4 .... 170 C2
Ferriby Cl *GOS/KPK* NE3 .... 47 F4 🔟
Ferrisdale Wy *GOS/KPK* NE3 .... 46 B5
Ferryboat La *SWCK/CAS* SR5....... 123 E4
Ferrydene Av *GOS/KPK* NE3 .... 62 B2
Ferry St *JRW* NE32 .... 69 D6
  SSH NE33 .... 71 D3
Festival Park Dr *DUN/TMV* NE11 .. 98 A3
Festival Wy *DUN/TMV* NE11 .... 97 F1
Field Cl *JES* NE2........................ 3 H2
Field Fare Ct *WICK/BNPF* NE16 ... 130 B1

Fieldhouse La *DHAM* DH1 .... 193 F3
Field House Rd *GATE* NE8 .... 99 D3
Fielding Ct *WD/WHPE/BLK* NE5 ... 60 C2 🔟
Fielding Pl *LWF/SPW/WRK* NE9 .. 100 A2 🔟
Field La *FELL* NE10 .... 101 E2
Fieldside *CLDN/WHIT/ROK* SR6 ... 109 D1
  CLSW/PEL DH2 .... 152 A1
  HLH DH5 .... 184 B1
Field Sq *MLFD/PNYW* SR4 .... 124 B6
Field St *FELL* NE10 .... 100 C1 🔟
  GOS/KPK NE3 .... 64 A1
Field Ter *JRW* NE32.................... 86 A3
Fieldway *BOLCOL* NE35............. 104 B2 🔟
  JRW NE32 .... 104 C1 🔟
Fife Av *JRW* NE32 .... 87 D5
Fife St *GATE* NE8...................... 99 F1
  SEA/MUR SR7 .... 188 C2
Fifteenth Av *BLYTH* NE24 .... 10 C6
Fifth Av *BYK/HTN/WLK* NE6 .... 82 B1 🔟
  DUN/TMV NE11 .... 98 C5
Fifth St *PLEE/EAS* SR8 .... 209 F1
Filby Dr *DHAM* DH1.................. 196 C1
Filey Cl *CRAM* NE23................... 14 A6
Filton Cl *CRAM* NE23.................. 14 A6
Finchale *WASHS* NE38............... 138 B5
Finchale Av *DHAM* DH1 .... 181 E4
Finchale Cl *ASHBK/HED/RY* SR2 ... 5 F5
  DUN/TMV NE11 .... 97 E4 🔟
  HLS DH4 .... 170 C2
Finchale Gdns
  BW/LEM/TK/HW NE15............. 57 F3
Finchale Rd *DHAM* DH1 .... 180 C4
  HEBB NE31............................. 85 D5
Finchale Ter *JRW* NE32.............. 86 B4
Finchale Vw *DHAM* DH1 .... 180 A5 🔟
  HLS DH4 .... 183 D2
Finchdale Cl *NSHW* NE29 .... 70 B2
Finchley Crs *BYK/HTN/WLK* NE6 ... 66 C6
Findon Av *BDN/LAN/SAC* DH7 .... 178 A3
Findon Gv *NSHW* NE29 .... 70 A2
Findon Hl *BDN/LAN/SAC* DH7 .... 178 B2
Finsbury Av *BYK/HTN/WLK* NE6 ... 83 D2
Finsbury St *SWCK/CAS* SR5 ...... 126 B3 🔟
Finsmere Av *WD/WHPE/BLK* NE5 . 61 D5 🔟
Finsmere Pl *WD/WHPE/BLK* NE5 .. 61 D5 🔟
Finstock Ct *LGB/HTN* NE7........... 64 B2
Fir Av *BDN/LAN/SAC* DH7 .... 203 D5
  DHAM DH1 .... 195 F5
Firbank Av *TYNE/NSHE* NE30 ...... 55 D2
Firbanks *JRW* NE32 .... 104 C1
Firfield Rd *WD/WHPE/BLK* NE5.... 61 F4
Fir Gv *HAR/WTLS* NE34 .... 89 E3
Fir Pk *BDN/LAN/SAC* DH7 .... 192 A4
First Av *BLYTH* NE24 .... 10 C5
  BYK/HTN/WLK NE6 .... 82 B1
  CLSW/PEL DH2 .... 136 A5
  DUN/TMV NE11 .... 98 B4
  NSHW NE29............................. 69 D2
The Firs *GOS/KPK* NE3 .... 63 D2 🔟
Fir St *JRW* NE32 .... 85 F1
First St *GATE* NE8 .... 98 C1
  PLEE/EAS SR8 .... 209 F1
Firth Sq *MLFD/PNYW* SR4 .... 124 C6
Firtree Av *BYK/HTN/WLK* NE6 ..... 66 C5
  LGB/KIL NE12 .... 49 E3
  WASHS NE38........................... 138 B5
Fir Tree Cl *DHAM* DH1 .... 195 F2 🔟
Firtree Crs *LGB/KIL* NE12 .... 49 E3
Firtree Gdns *MONK* NE25............. 54 B1
Firtree Rd *WICK/BNPF* NE16 .... 95 F4
Firtrees *CLSW/PEL* DH2 .... 153 D3
  FELL NE10 .... 101 D5
Firtrees Av *WLSD/HOW* NE28 ...... 69 D3
Firwood Gdns *DUN/TMV* NE11 ..... 98 A5
Fisher La *CRAM* NE23 .... 12 B6
  DIN/WO NE13 .... 20 A5
Fisher Rd *SMOOR* NE27 .... 37 D4
Fisher St *BYK/HTN/WLK* NE6 ...... 84 A1
  WLSD/HOW NE28 .... 84 A1
Fisherwell Rd *FELL* NE10 .... 83 F6
Fitzpatrick Pl *SSH* NE33 .... 72 A4 🔟
Fitzsimmons Av *WLSD/HOW* NE28 .. 67 D3
Flambard Rd *DHAM* DH1 .... 194 A1
Flassburn Rd *DHAM* DH1 .... 193 F3
Flass St *DHAM* DH1 .... 194 A4
Flaunden Cl *HAR/WTLS* NE34 ...... 90 A3 🔟
Flaxby Cl *GOS/KPK* NE3 .... 47 F4
Flax Sq *MLFD/PNYW* SR4 .... 124 B5 🔟
Fleet St *SUND* SR1..................... 5 H3
Fleming Gdns *FELL* NE10 .... 100 B3
Fleming Pl *PLEE/EAS* SR8 .... 208 C2 🔟
Fletcher Crs *HLS* DH4 .... 158 A2
Flexbury Gdns
  BW/LEM/TK/HW NE15............. 77 D1 🔟
  FELL NE10 .... 100 B2 🔟
  LWF/SPW/WRK NE9 .... 117 F2
Flint Hill Bank *STLY/ANP* DH9 .... 129 D5
Flodden *LGB/KIL* NE12 .... 35 F6
Flodden Cl *CLSW/PEL* DH2......... 165 E1
Flodden Rd *MLFD/PNYW* SR4 ..... 124 C6
Flodden St *BYK/HTN/WLK* NE6 .... 82 C3
Floral Dene *MLFD/PNYW* SR4 .... 123 F6
Flora St *BYK/HTN/WLK* NE6 .... 82 C3
Florence Av *LWF/SPW/WRK* NE9 .. 99 F4 🔟
Florence Crs *SWCK/CAS* SR5 ..... 125 E2

Florence St *BLAY* NE21 .... 94 A1
Florida St *MLFD/PNYW* SR4 .... 125 E4
Flotterton Gdns
  WD/WHPE/BLK NE5 .... 78 B1
The Fold *MONK* NE25 .... 40 A5
Folkestone Rd *HLS* DH4 .... 111 F5
Folldon Av
  CLDN/WHIT/ROK SR6 .... 126 C1 2
Follingsby Av *FELL* NE10 .... 103 D4
Follingsby Dr *FELL* NE10 .... 102 B3
Follingsby La *FELL* NE10 .... 103 D5
Follingsby Wy *FELL* NE10 .... 102 C4
Folly La *RYTON* NE40 .... 74 A6
Folly Ter *DHAM* DH1 .... 179 F5
The Folly *BOL* NE36 .... 105 F3
Fontaine Rd *SUND* SR1 .... 4 A1
Fontburn Ct *SWCK/CAS* SR5 .... 107 E6 1
Fontburn Pl *LGB/HTN* NE7 .... 64 C1
Fontburn Rd *MONK* NE25 .... 24 C5
Fontburn Ter *TYNE/NSHE* NE30 ..... 55 D6
Fonteyn Pl *CRAM* NE23 .... 14 A4
  STLY/ANP DH9 .... 149 D3
Fontwell Dr *GATE* NE8 .... 98 C3
Forbeck Rd *MLFD/PNYW* SR4 .... 124 C6
Forber Av *HAR/WTLS* NE34 .... 90 A2
Ford Av *MLFD/PNYW* SR4 .... 123 F6
  NSHW NE29 .... 69 F2
Ford Crs *JRW* NE32 .... 86 A5
  MLFD/PNYW SR4 .... 123 F6
  SMOOR NE27 .... 52 A1
Ford Dr *BLYTH* NE24 .... 10 B5
Fordenbridge Crs
  MLFD/PNYW SR4 .... 124 C6
Fordenbridge Rd
  MLFD/PNYW SR4 .... 124 C6 2
Fordenbridge Sq
  MLFD/PNYW SR4 .... 125 D6 1
Fordfield Rd *MLFD/PNYW* SR4 ..... 124 B6
Ford Gv *GOS/KPK* NE3 .... 47 F5
Fordhall Dr *MLFD/PNYW* SR4 ...... 125 D6 2
Fordham Rd *DHAM* DH1 .... 194 B1
  MLFD/PNYW SR4 .... 124 C5
Fordham Sq *MLFD/PNYW* SR4 ...... 125 D6
Fordland Pl *MLFD/PNYW* SR4 ...... 125 E6
Ford Ov *MLFD/PNYW* SR4 .... 124 A5
Ford Rd *DHAM* DH1 .... 180 C5
Ford St *BYK/HTN/WLK* NE6 .... 81 F3
  GATE NE8 .... 100 A1 6
Ford Ter *WLSD/HOW* NE28 .... 66 A4
Ford Vw *CRAM* NE23 .... 34 C1
Forest Av *LGB/KIL* NE12 .... 50 A4
Forest Dr *WASHS* NE38 .... 137 E6
Forest Hall Rd *LGB/KIL* NE12 ...... 50 A3
Fore St *JES* NE2 .... 64 C6
Forest Rd *BW/LEM/TK/HW* NE15 ... 78 A4
  MLFD/PNYW SR4 .... 124 C5
  SSH NE33 .... 71 E4
Forest Vw *BDN/LAN/SAC* DH7 .... 202 B5
Forest Wy *CRAM* NE23 .... 36 B1
Forfar St *SWCK/CAS* SR5 .... 126 C2
Forge La *CLS/BIR/GTL* DH3 .... 155 D5
Forge Rd *DUN/TMV* NE11 .... 97 F2
Forres Ct *STLY/ANP* DH9 .... 149 D2
Forres Pl *CRAM* NE23 .... 14 A6
Forrest Rd *WLSD/HOW* NE28 .... 66 C5 3
Forster Av *BDLGTN* NE22 .... 7 D3
  HAR/WTLS NE34 .... 89 D1 3
  RDHAMSE DH6 .... 197 E4
Forster St *BLYTH* NE24 .... 11 E5
  CLDN/WHIT/ROK SR6 .... 127 D5
Forsyth Rd *JES* NE2 .... 63 F5
Forth Banks *CNUT* NE1 .... 2 C6
Forth Ct *PLEE/EAS* SR8 .... 208 C3
Forth Ct *HAR/WTLS* NE34 .... 88 C5
Forth Pl *CNUT* NE1 .... 2 B5
Forth St *CNUT* NE1 .... 2 B6
Fortrose Av *SUNDSW* SR3 .... 143 F3
Fort St *SSH* NE33 .... 71 F2
Forum Ct *BDLGTN* NE22 .... 7 E3
The Forum *BW/LEM/TK/HW* NE15 ... 77 F1
Forum Wy *CRAM* NE23 .... 21 F2
Fossdyke *FELL* NE10 .... 101 E5 2
Fossefeld *FELL* NE10 .... 101 F3
Fosse Law *BW/LEM/TK/HW* NE15 ... 58 A5
Fosse Ter *LWF/SPW/WRK* NE9 ..... 100 A4 4
Fossway *BYK/HTN/WLK* NE6 .... 66 C6
Foster Ct *BYK/HTN/WLK* NE6 .... 84 A3
Foundry La *BYK/HTN/WLK* NE6 .... 81 F2
  JES NE2 .... 81 C2 3
Foundry Rd *SEA/MUR* SR7 .... 177 D3
Fountain Cl *BDLGTN* NE22 .... 7 E3 1
Fountain Gv *HAR/WTLS* NE34 .... 72 B6
Fountain Head Rd *WBAY* NE26 ..... 26 A2
Fountain La *BLAY* NE21 .... 76 A4
Fountain Rw *JES* NE2 .... 80 A1
Fountains Cl *DUN/TMV* NE11 .... 97 F4 2
  WASHS NE38 .... 138 C2
Fountains Crs *HEBB* NE31 .... 85 D5
  HLS DH4 .... 157 E6
Fouracres Rd *WD/WHPE/BLK* NE5 .. 62 A4
Four Lane Ends *HLH* DH5 .... 186 A2
Fourstones *WD/WHPE/BLK* NE5 ... 60 C4
Fourstones Cl *GOS/KPK* NE3 .... 61 F1
Fourstones Rd *MLFD/PNYW* SR4 .. 125 D5
Fourth Av *BLYTH* NE24 .... 10 C6 3

BYK/HTN/WLK NE6 .... 82 B1 4
CLSW/PEL DH2 .... 153 D5
DUN/TMV NE11 .... 98 B5
Fourth St *GATE* NE8 .... 98 C1 4
  PLEE/EAS SR8 .... 209 F1
Fowberry Crs *ELS/FEN* NE4 .... 79 D1
Fowberry Rd
  BW/LEM/TK/HW NE15 .... 77 E4
Fowler Cl *HLS* DH4 .... 157 E4 3
Fowler St *SSH* NE33 .... 71 E3
Fox & Hounds La
  BW/LEM/TK/HW NE15 .... 78 B2
Fox & Hounds Rd
  WD/WHPE/BLK NE5 .... 78 B1
Fox Av *HAR/WTLS* NE34 .... 87 E4
Foxcover La *SUNDSW* SR3 .... 159 D1
Foxcover Rd *MLFD/PNYW* SR4 .... 141 E4
Foxglove Ct *HAR/WTLS* NE34 ...... 87 F4
Foxhills Cl *WASHS* NE38 .... 139 D4
Foxhills Covert *WICK/BNPF* NE16 .. 95 D5
Foxhunters Rd *MONK* NE25 .... 54 B1
Foxlair Cl *SUNDSW* SR3 .... 160 C4
Fox Lea Wk *CRAM* NE23 .... 36 A1
Foxley *WASHN* NE37 .... 121 D4
Foxley Ct *LGB/KIL* NE12 .... 36 B6
Fox St *ASHBK/HED/RY* SR2 .... 144 A1
  SEA/MUR SR7 .... 176 C4
Foxton Av *GOS/KPK* NE3 .... 46 B5
  TYNE/NSHE NE30 .... 55 D1
Foxton Cl *NSHW* NE29 .... 70 A3
Foxton Hall *WASHN* NE37 .... 120 C1
Foxton Wy *FELL* NE10 .... 84 A6
Foyle St *SUND* SR1 .... 4 D3
Framlingham Ct *DHAM* DH1 .... 194 B4
Framwelgate Br *DHAM* DH1 .... 194 B5
Framwelgate Peth *DHAM* DH1 .... 194 A3
Framwelgate Waterside
  DHAM DH1 .... 194 B4
Frances St *BLAY* NE21 .... 75 F6
Francis St *CLDN/WHIT/ROK* SR6 .. 126 C2
Frankham St
  WD/WHPE/BLK NE5 .... 60 B4 3
Frankland Dr *MONK* NE25 .... 54 A1
Frankland La *DHAM* DH1 .... 194 B3
Frankland Rd *DHAM* DH1 .... 194 A1
Franklin St *HAR/WTLS* NE34 ...... 125 F5
  SSH NE33 .... 71 E3
Franklyn Av *WBAY* NE26 .... 26 A1
Franklyn Rd *PLEE/EAS* SR8 .... 208 A1
Frank Pl *NSHW* NE29 .... 54 C6 7
Frank St *DHAM* DH1 .... 195 F4
  SWCK/CAS SR5 .... 126 A2 8
  WLSD/HOW NE28 .... 67 D5
Fraser Cl *SSH* NE33 .... 71 D6
Freda St *SWCK/CAS* SR5 .... 125 E3
Frederick Gdns *HLS* DH4 .... 156 C1 2
Frederick Rd *SUND* SR1 .... 4 D2
Frederick St *MLFD/PNYW* SR4 .... 123 F6 2
  SEA/MUR SR7 .... 176 C3
  SSH NE33 .... 71 E6
  SUND SR1 .... 4 D3 1
Frederick Ter *RDHAMSE* DH6 ...... 187 E6
Freeman Rd *GOS/KPK* NE3 .... 64 B2
  LGB/HTN NE7 .... 64 B2
Freesia Gra *WASHS* NE38 .... 139 D3 1
Freezemoor Rd *HLS* DH4 .... 157 F2
Fremantle Rd *HAR/WTLS* NE34 ..... 90 A3
Frenchman's Wy *HAR/WTLS* NE34 .. 90 A1
French St *BLYTH* NE24 .... 11 D4 3
Frensham *WASHS* NE38 .... 139 F2 1
Frensham Wy
  BDN/LAN/SAC DH7 .... 203 E4 4
Frenton Cl *WD/WHPE/BLK* NE5 ... 59 E4 3
Friarage Av
  CLDN/WHIT/ROK SR6 .... 126 C3 1
Friar Rd *MLFD/PNYW* SR4 .... 124 C6
Friars Dene Rd *FELL* NE10 .... 82 B6
Friarsfield Cl *SUNDSW* SR3 .... 160 A3
Friarside Rd *BDN/LAN/SAC* DH7 .. 178 A4
Friarside Crs *ROWG* NE39 .... 110 C4
Friarside Rd *ELS/FEN* NE4 .... 62 A6
Friar Sq *MLFD/PNYW* SR4 .... 124 C6
Friars' Rw *DHAM* DH1 .... 195 E3
Friars St *CNUT* NE1 .... 2 B4
Friar St *RDHAMSE* DH6 .... 206 C2
Friars Wy *WD/WHPE/BLK* NE5 .... 61 E6 1
Friary Gdns *FELL* NE10 .... 100 B1
Frobisher Ct *SUNDSW* SR3 .... 160 B3
Frobisher St *HEBB* NE31 .... 85 E2
Frome Gdns *LWF/SPW/WRK* NE9 .. 117 C2
Frome Pl *CRAM* NE23 .... 14 A6
Frome Sq *MLFD/PNYW* SR4 .... 124 B6 1
Front Rd *MLFD/PNYW* SR4 .... 124 C6
Front St *BDN/LAN/SAC* DH7 .... 178 A1
  BDN/LAN/SAC DH7 .... 204 A2
  BLAY NE21 .... 94 A1
  BLYTH NE24 .... 8 C5
  BOL NE36 .... 106 B3
  BOLCOL NE35 .... 105 D1
  CLDN/WHIT/ROK SR6 .... 107 F1
  CLDN/WHIT/ROK SR6 .... 109 E2
  CLS/BIR/GTL DH3 .... 153 E5
  CLS/BIR/GTL DH3 .... 167 F3

CLSW/PEL DH2 .... 151 F1
CRAM NE23 .... 23 E6
CRAM NE23 .... 35 D1
CRAM NE23 .... 36 C1
DHAM DH1 .... 179 F6
DHAM DH1 .... 195 F5
DIN/WO NE13 .... 31 D3
DIN/WO NE13 .... 33 D1
HLH DH5 .... 171 F6
HLH DH5 .... 185 D3
HLS DH4 .... 157 F5
HLS DH4 .... 169 F2
LGB/HTN NE7 .... 65 E1
LGB/KIL NE12 .... 35 D5 2
MONK NE25 .... 38 C5
MONK NE25 .... 40 A6
NSHW NE29 .... 54 B4
NSHW NE29 .... 70 A1
RDHAMSE DH6 .... 183 F6
RDHAMSE DH6 .... 187 D4
RDHAMSE DH6 .... 197 F5
STLY/ANP DH9 .... 129 C5
STLY/ANP DH9 .... 130 C2
STLY/ANP DH9 .... 130 A4
STLY/ANP DH9 .... 148 A2
STLY/ANP DH9 .... 148 B1 3
STLY/ANP DH9 .... 148 C1
STLY/ANP DH9 .... 149 E5
TYNE/NSHE NE30 .... 55 F5
TYNE/NSHE NE30 .... 55 E1
WASHN NE37 .... 121 D4 1
WICK/BNPF NE16 .... 95 F3
WICK/BNPF NE16 .... 111 D6
WICK/BNPF NE16 .... 111 F6
WICK/BNPF NE16 .... 129 F2
Front St East *BDLGTN* NE22 .... 7 F4
Frosterley Cl *CLS/BIR/GTL* DH3 .. 168 A3
  DHAM DH1 .... 180 C6 3
  HLH DH5 .... 186 C3 1
Frosterley Gdns *SUNDSW* SR3 ... 144 A4 2
Frosterley Pl *ELS/FEN* NE4 .... 80 A2 4
Froude Av *HAR/WTLS* NE34 .... 88 A5
Fuchsia Pl *WD/WHPE/BLK* NE5 ... 61 F4 5
Fulbrook Rd *GOS/KPK* NE3 .... 62 B1
Fullerton Pl *LWF/SPW/WRK* NE9 .. 99 F2
Fulmar Dr *BLYTH* NE24 .... 17 D2
  WASHS NE38 .... 137 E3
Fulmar Wk *CLDN/WHIT/ROK* SR6 .. 91 E6
Fulwell Av *HAR/WTLS* NE34 .... 90 A1
Fulwell Gn *WD/WHPE/BLK* NE5 ... 61 D5 3
Fulwell Rd
  CLDN/WHIT/ROK SR6 .... 126 C5 3
  PLEE/EAS SR8 .... 209 E3
Furnace Bank *BDLGTN* NE22 .... 8 C3
Furness Ct *PLEE/EAS* SR8 .... 208 A2
Furrowfield *FELL* NE10 .... 100 B4 1
Furzefield Rd *GOS/KPK* NE3 .... 63 D2
Fylingdale Dr *SUNDSW* SR3 ...... 161 E1
Fyndoune Wy *BDN/LAN/SAC* DH7 .. 178 A4
Fynes Cl *PLEE/EAS* SR8 .... 200 C6
Fynway *BDN/LAN/SAC* DH7 .... 178 B2 1

G

The Gables *DIN/WO* NE13 .... 45 D6
Gainers Ter *WLSD/HOW* NE28 ...... 67 E6
Gainford *CLSW/PEL* DH2 .... 152 C5
Gainsborough Av *HAR/WTLS* NE34 .. 88 C5
  WASHS NE38 .... 139 D2
Gainsborough Cl *MONK* NE25 ...... 39 E5
Gainsborough Crs *HLS* DH4 .... 156 B3
  LWF/SPW/WRK NE9 .... 100 A3
Gainsborough Pl *CRAM* NE23 ...... 22 A5
Gainsborough Rd
  MLFD/PNYW SR4 .... 142 B4
  STLY/ANP DH9 .... 148 B3
Gainsbro Gv *ELS/FEN* NE4 .... 79 E2
Gairloch Dr *CLSW/PEL* DH2 .... 152 B1
  WASHS NE38 .... 137 F3
Gairloch Rd *MLFD/PNYW* SR4 .... 142 B3
Galashiels Gv *HLS* DH4 .... 157 D3 3
Galashiels Rd *MLFD/PNYW* SR4 .. 142 A3
Galashiels Sq *MLFD/PNYW* SR4 .. 142 B3 1
Gale St *STLY/ANP* DH9 .... 147 F3
Galfrid Cl *SEA/MUR* SR7 .... 175 E4 2
Gallalaw Ter *GOS/KPK* NE3 .... 64 B1 3
Galley's Gill Rd *SUND* SR1 .... 4 A2
Galloping Green Rd
  LWF/SPW/WRK NE9 .... 118 C2
Galloway Rd *PLEE/EAS* SR8 ...... 208 C1
Gallowgate *CNUT* NE1 .... 2 B3
Galsworthy Rd *HAR/WTLS* NE34 ... 87 F5
  MLFD/PNYW SR4 .... 142 B3
Galway Rd *MLFD/PNYW* SR4 ...... 142 A3 1
Gambia Rd *MLFD/PNYW* SR4 ..... 142 A4 1
Gambia Sq *MLFD/PNYW* SR4 ..... 142 A4 2
Ganton Av *CRAM* NE23 .... 22 A4
Ganton Cl *WASHN* NE37 .... 120 B2 3
Ganton Ct *HAR/WTLS* NE34 .... 89 E5 2
Garasdale Cl *BLYTH* NE24 .... 16 C2
Garden Cl *DIN/WO* NE13 .... 33 D1 1
Garden Cft *LGB/KIL* NE12 .... 50 A4
Garden Dr *HEBB* NE31 .... 84 C4 2

Gardener St *ELS/FEN* NE4 .... **79** F5 🔵
Garden La *SSH* NE33 .... **71** E4
Garden Pk *WLSD/HOW* NE28 ..... **68** B2 🔟
Garden Pl *HLS* DH4 .... **157** D1
  SUND SR1 .... **4** B2 🔵
The Gardens *CLSW/PEL* DH2 ...... **153** D5
  MONK NE25 .... **40** B6
Garden St *BLAY* NE21 .... **76** B5 🔵
  HLS DH4 .... **157** F5 🔵
Garden Ter *MONK* NE25 .... **38** C5
Gardiner Rd *MLFD/PNYW* SR4 .... **141** F3
Gardiner Sq *MLFD/PNYW* SR4 ... **142** A3 🔟
Gardner Pk *NSHW* NE29 .... **70** B1
Gardner Pl *NSHW* NE29 .... **70** C1 🟩
Garesfield Gdns *ROWG* NE39 ... **111** D1 🔵
Garesfield La *BLAY* NE21 .... **93** E3
Gareston Cl *BLYTH* NE24 .... **10** A5
Garfield St *MLFD/PNYW* SR4 .... **125** E5 🟩
Garforth Cl *CRAM* NE23 .... **21** F4
Garleigh Cl *LGB/KIL* NE12 .... **50** B1 🟩
Garner Cl *WD/WHPE/BLK* NE5.... **59** F3
Garnet St *MLFD/PNYW* SR4 ...... **125** E5
Garrick Cl *NSHW* NE29 .... **53** E5
Garrick St *SSH* NE33 .... **71** E6
Garrigill *WASHS* NE38 .... **139** E5
Garron St *SEA/MUR* SR7 .... **176** C4
Garsdale Av *WASHN* NE37 .... **120** A4
Garsdale Rd *WBAY* NE26 .... **40** A1
Garside Av *CLS/BIR/GTL* DH3 ... **136** B1
Garside Gv *PLEE/EAS* SR8 .... **200** A6
Garsin Cl *HLTN* NE7 .... **66** A3
Garth Cornfield *PLEE/EAS* SR8 . **209** E3
Garth Crs *BLAY* NE21 .... **94** A1
  HAR/WTLS NE34 .... **72** C5
Garth Farm Rd *BLAY* NE21 .... **94** A1
Garthfield Crs *WD/WHPE/BLK* NE5 .. **60** C4
Garth Heads *CNUT* NE1 .... **3** G4
Garth Six *LGB/KIL* NE12 .... **49** E1
Garth Sixteen *LGB/KIL* NE12 .... **35** E6 🟩
The Garth *GOS/KPK* NE3 .... **62** B2
  WD/WHPE/BLK NE5 .... **60** A5 🔟
Garth Thirteen *LGB/KIL* NE12 ... **35** D6 🔵
Garth Thirty Three *LGB/KIL* NE12 .. **49** F1
Garth Thirty Two *LGB/KIL* NE12 .. **50** A1
Garth Twelve *LGB/KIL* NE12 ...... **35** E6 🟢
Garth Twenty *LGB/KIL* NE12 ..... **50** A1
Garth Twenty Five *LGB/KIL* NE12 .. **50** B1 🔟
Garth Twenty Four
  LGB/KIL NE12 .... **50** B1 🟩
Garth Twenty Seven *LGB/KIL* NE12 .. **50** B1
Garth Twenty Two *LGB/KIL* NE12 .. **50** A1
Gartland Rd *MLFD/PNYW* SR4.... **141** F3
Garvey Vls *LWF/SPW/WRK* NE9 .. **100** B4
Garwood St *SSH* NE33 .... **71** D6
Gas House La *HLS* DH4 .... **170** C1
Gaskell Av *HAR/WTLS* NE34 .... **88** A5
Gas La *BLAY* NE21 .... **76** B4
Gas Works Bridge Rd
  DUN/TMV NE11 .... **97** F1
Gas Works Rd *SEA/MUR* SR7 .... **177** D4
Gatacre St *BLYTH* NE24 .... **11** D4 🟫
Gateley Av *BLYTH* NE24 .... **16** C2
Gatesgarth *LWF/SPW/WRK* NE9 .. **99** F5
Gatesgarth Gv
  CLDN/WHIT/ROK SR6 .... **108** B5 🟩
Gateshead Hwy *GATE* NE8 .... **81** E6
Gateshead Rd *WICK/BNPF* NE16 .. **114** B1
Gatwick Rd *MLFD/PNYW* SR4 .... **142** A3
Gaughan Cl *BYK/HTN/WLK* NE6 .. **83** E5 🔟
Gayhurst Crs *SUNDSW* SR3 ...... **160** C2
Gayton Rd *WASHN* NE37 .... **121** D3
Geddes Rd *MLFD/PNYW* SR4 ..... **142** A3
Gelt Crs *HLH* DH5 .... **186** A2 🔟
General Graham St
  MLFD/PNYW SR4 .... **143** E1 🟩
General Havelock Rd
  MLFD/PNYW SR4 .... **125** D6
The General's Wd *WASHS* NE38 .. **138** B6
Geneva Rd *MLFD/PNYW* SR4 .... **142** A3 🟩
Genister Pl *ELS/FEN* NE4 .... **61** F6 🔟
Geoffrey Av *DHAM* DH1 .... **193** F6
Geoffrey St *CLDN/WHIT/ROK* SR6 .. **109** E1
Geoffrey Ter *STLY/ANP* DH9 ..... **147** F3
George Pit La *CLS/BIR/GTL* DH3 .. **168** B4
George Rd *BDLGTN* NE22 .... **8** C2 🟩
  WLSD/HOW NE28 .... **67** D6
George Scott St *SSH* NE33 .... **71** F2 🔟
George Smith Gdns *FELL* NE10 .. **82** C6 🟩
Georges Rd *ELS/FEN* NE4 .... **79** E5
George Stephenson Wy
  NSHW NE29 .... **70** B3
George St *ASHBK/HED/RY* SR2 .. **162** C2
  BLAY NE21 .... **76** C5 🔟
  BLYTH NE24 .... **11** D6 🟫
  CLS/BIR/GTL DH3 .... **136** A2
  CLS/BIR/GTL DH3 .... **153** F6
  DHAM DH1 .... **193** F5
  ELS/FEN NE4 .... **2** A6
  FELL NE10 .... **101** E1 🟩
  GOS/KPK NE3 .... **62** C1 🟩
  HLH DH5 .... **171** F5
  RDHAMSE DH6 .... **197** E5
  SEA/MUR SR7 .... **176** B3
  SEA/MUR SR7 .... **188** B2
  TYNE/NSHE NE30 .... **55** D6

  WD/WHPE/BLK NE5 .... **58** B4
Wick *WICK/BNPF* NE16 .... **95** F3 🟩
  WLSD/HOW NE28 .... **69** D5
George St North
  CLDN/WHIT/ROK SR6 .... **126** C4 🟩
George Ct *LGB/KIL* NE12 .... **49** D3
  MLFD/PNYW SR4 .... **143** F2 🟩
Gerald St *ELS/FEN* NE4 .... **78** C4
  HAR/WTLS NE34 .... **88** B5
Gerrard Cl *CRAM* NE23 .... **22** A4
  WBAY NE26 .... **40** A1
Gerrard Rd *MLFD/PNYW* SR4 .... **142** A3 🟩
  WBAY NE26 .... **40** A1
Gertrude St *HLS* DH4 .... **157** F6 🔟
Ghyll Field Rd *DHAM* DH1 .... **194** A1
Gibside *CLSW/PEL* DH2 .... **152** C5
Gibside Cl *STLY/ANP* DH9 .... **149** D1
Gibside Ct *DUN/TMV* NE11 ...... **97** E4 🟩
Gibside Gdns
  BW/LEM/TK/HW NE15............... **78** A2
Gibside Vw *BLAY* NE21 .... **94** A2
Gibside Wy *WICK/BNPF* NE16 .... **78** A6
Gibson Ct *BOLCOL* NE35 .... **105** E2 🔟
Gibson St *CNUT* NE1 .... **3** H3
  WLSD/HOW NE28 .... **68** A2
Gifford Sq *MLFD/PNYW* SR4 .... **142** B2
Gilbert Rd *MLFD/PNYW* SR4 .... **142** A3
  PLEE/EAS SR8 .... **208** D1
Gilbert St *SSH* NE33 .... **71** E6 🟩
Gilderdale *HLS* DH4 .... **139** D6
Gilderdale Wy *CRAM* NE23 ...... **21** F5 🔟
  CRAM NE23 .... **22** A5 🔟
Gilesgate *DHAM* DH1 .... **194** C4
Gilesgate Ct *DHAM* DH1 .... **194** C4 🔟
Gilesgate Rd *HLH* DH5 .... **186** A2
Gilhurst Gra *SUND* SR1 .... **126** A6 🟩
Gillas La *HLH* DH5 .... **171** F3
Gillas La East *HLH* DH5 .... **171** E3
Gillas La West *HLH* DH5 .... **171** D4
Gillies St *BYK/HTN/WLK* NE6 .... **82** C2
Gillingham Rd *MLFD/PNYW* SR4 .. **142** B3
Gill Rd *SUND* SR1 .... **4** B1
Gill Side Gv *CLDN/WHIT/ROK* SR6 .. **127** D2
Gill St *ELS/FEN* NE4 .... **79** D3
Gilmore Cl *WD/WHPE/BLK* NE5... **59** F3
Gilpin St *HLS* DH4 .... **170** C2
Gilsland Av *WLSD/HOW* NE28 .... **68** B3
Gilsland Gv *CRAM* NE23 .... **14** A5 🔟
Gilsland St *MLFD/PNYW* SR4 ... **125** F5 🔟
Gilwell Wy *GOS/KPK* NE3 .... **47** D3
Girtin Rd *HAR/WTLS* NE34 .... **88** C6
Girton Cl *PLEE/EAS* SR8 .... **208** A3
Girvan Cl *STLY/ANP* DH9............ **149** D2
Gishford Wy *WD/WHPE/BLK* NE5 .. **61** D4
Givens St *CLDN/WHIT/ROK* SR6 .. **127** D2
Gladeley Wy *WICK/BNPF* NE16 .. **113** F2
The Glade *JRW* NE32 .... **104** A1
  WD/WHPE/BLK NE5 .... **58** C4
Gladstonbury Pl *LGB/KIL* NE12 ... **49** E6
Gladstone Pl *JES* NE2 .... **81** D1 🔵
Gladstone St *BLYTH* NE24 .... **10** C4
  BW/LEM/TK/HW NE15 .... **76** B2 🔟
  CLDN/WHIT/ROK SR6 .... **126** C3
  HEBB NE31 .... **85** E2
  HLS DH4 .... **170** A2
  STLY/ANP DH9 .... **147** F3
  STLY/ANP DH9 .... **149** F1
  WLSD/HOW NE28 .... **69** D5 🟩
Gladstone Ter *JES* NE2 .... **81** D1 🟩
Gladstone Ter West *GATE* NE8 .... **99** D1
Gladwyn Rd *MLFD/PNYW* SR4 .. **142** A4 🟩
Glaholm Rd *ASHBK/HED/RY* SR2 ... **5** G4
Glaisdale Dr *CLDN/WHIT/ROK* SR6 .. **109** D4
Glaisdale Rd *LGB/HTN* NE7 .... **64** C1 🔟
Glamis Av *GOS/KPK* NE3 .... **47** E2
  MLFD/PNYW SR4 .... **142** B2
Glamis Ct *HAR/WTLS* NE34 .... **89** E5
Glamis Crs *ROWG* NE39 .... **93** F6
Glamis Vls *CLS/BIR/GTL* DH3 ... **118** B6
Glanmore Rd *MLFD/PNYW* SR4 .. **142** A3 🟩
Glantlees *WD/WHPE/BLK* NE5.... **60** C4
Glanton Av *MONK* NE25 .... **24** B5
Glanton Cl *CLSW/PEL* DH2 ...... **152** C6
Glanton Rd *NSHW* NE29 .... **53** F5
Glanton Sq *MLFD/PNYW* SR4 ... **142** B3 🟩
Glanton Wynd *GOS/KPK* NE3 .... **47** D5
Glanville Cl *DUN/TMV* NE11....... **98** A3
Glanville Rd *SUNDSW* SR3 .... **159** F3
Glasbury Av *MLFD/PNYW* SR4 .. **142** B2 🔟
Glasgow Rd *JRW* NE32 .... **87** D5
Glasshouse St *BYK/HTN/WLK* NE6 .. **82** B5
Glastonbury *WASHS* NE38 ...... **138** C2 🔟
Glastonbury Gv *JES* NE2 .... **64** B4
Gleaston Ct *PLEE/EAS* SR8........ **208** A5
Glebe Av *LGB/KIL* NE12 .... **49** F5
  WICK/BNPF NE16 .... **96** A3
Glebe Cl *WD/WHPE/BLK* NE5 ..... **59** F3 🟩
Glebe Crs *LGB/KIL* NE12 .... **49** F3
  WASHS NE38 .... **121** D6
Glebe Ms *BDLGTN* NE22 .... **7** E3 🟩
Glebe Ri *WICK/BNPF* NE16 .... **95** F3
Glebe Rd *BDLGTN* NE22 .... **7** E3
  LGB/KIL NE12 .... **49** F3
Glebeside *BDN/LAN/SAC* DH7 .. **178** A4
Glebe St *ELS/FEN* NE4 .... **78** C2

Glebe Ter *LGB/KIL* NE12 .... **49** F3
  PLEE/EAS SR8 .... **200** B2
Glebe Vls *LGB/KIL* NE12 .... **49** E3
Glenallen Gdns *TYNE/NSHE* NE30.. **55** E3
Glen Barr *CLSW/PEL* DH2 .... **153** D4
Glenbrooke Ter
  LWF/SPW/WRK NE9..................... **99** E6
Glenburn Cl *WASHS* NE38 .... **137** E5
Glencarron Cl *WASHN* NE38 ..... **137** F2
Glen Cl *ROWG* NE39 .... **111** D1
Glencoe *LGB/KIL* NE12 .... **35** F6
Glencoe Av *CLSW/PEL* DH2 ...... **153** D4
  CRAM NE23 .... **22** A5
Glencoe Rd *MLFD/PNYW* SR4 ... **142** A4
Glencourse *BOL* NE36 .... **107** D3
Glendale Av *BLYTH* NE24 .... **9** D4
  GOS/KPK NE3 .... **62** C2
  NSHW NE29 .... **54** A6
  WBAY NE26 .... **40** C3
  WICK/BNPF NE16 .... **95** F4
  WLSD/HOW NE28 .... **67** D2 🟩
Glendale Cl *BLAY* NE21 .... **93** E2
  SUNDSW SR3 .... **159** E2
  WD/WHPE/BLK NE5 .... **59** F2
Glendale Gdns
  LWF/SPW/WRK NE9..................... **100** A5
Glendale Gv *NSHW* NE29 .... **54** B6 🔟
Glendale Rd *SMOOR* NE27 .... **52** C1
Glendale Ter *BYK/HTN/WLK* NE6 .. **82** B2 🟩
Glendford Pl *BLYTH* NE24 .... **16** C2
Glendower Av *NSHW* NE29 .... **53** F6 🟩
Glendyn Cl *LGB/HTN* NE7 .... **64** C5
Gleneagle Cl *WD/WHPE/BLK* NE5 .. **59** F3
Gleneagles *SSH* NE33 .... **72** A5 🟩
Gleneagles Cl *LGB/HTN* NE12 ... **65** E1 🟩
Gleneagles Dr *WASHN* NE37 .... **120** A2
Gleneagles Rd
  LWF/SPW/WRK NE9..................... **117** D1
  MLFD/PNYW SR4 .... **142** B3 🟩
Gleneagles Sq *MLFD/PNYW* SR4 .. **142** A4 🔟
Glenesk Gdns
  ASHBK/HED/RY SR2 .... **144** B4 🟩
Glenesk Rd *ASHBK/HED/RY* SR2 .. **144** B3
Glenfield Av *CRAM* NE23 .... **14** A5
Glenfield Rd *LGB/KIL* NE12........ **49** A5
Glengarvan Cl *WASHS* NE38 ..... **137** F3
Glenhurst Dr *WD/WHPE/BLK* NE5 .. **59** F3
  WICK/BNPF NE16 .... **89** E2
Glenhurst Gv *HAR/WTLS* NE34 .. **89** E2
Glenhurst Rd *PLEE/EAS* SR8 .... **200** C2
Glenleigh Dr *MLFD/PNYW* SR4 .. **142** B3
Glen Luce Dr *ASHBK/HED/RY* SR2 .. **145** E4
Glenluce Dr *CRAM* NE23 .... **21** F5
Glenmoor *HEBB* NE31 .... **84** C1
Glenmore Av *CLSW/PEL* DH2.... **153** D4
Glenmuir Av *CRAM* NE23 .... **21** F5 🟩
Glenorrin Cl *WASHS* NE38 .... **137** F3
Glen Pth *ASHBK/HED/RY* SR2 .. **144** C3
Glenridge Av *BYK/HTN/WLK* NE6 .. **65** D5
Glenroy Gdns *CLSW/PEL* DH2 .. **153** D4
Glenshiel Cl *WASHS* NE38 .... **137** F3
Glen St *HEBB* NE31 .... **84** C3
Glen Ter *CLSW/PEL* DH2 .... **153** C4
The Glen *ASHBK/HED/RY* SR2 .. **144** C3 🔟
Glenthorn Rd *JES* NE2 .... **64** A4
Glenuce *CLS/BIR/GTL* DH3 ...... **137** D3
Gloria Av *MONK* NE25 .... **24** C2
Gloucester Av
  CLDN/WHIT/ROK SR6 .... **109** D6
Gloucester Cl *CLS/BIR/GTL* DH3 .. **167** F4
Gloucester Pl *HAR/WTLS* NE34 .. **89** F3 🟩
  PLEE/EAS SR8 .... **208** A1
Gloucester Rd *ELS/FEN* NE4 ...... **79** F3
  NSHW NE29 .... **53** D5
Gloucestershire Dr *DHAM* DH1 .. **196** B3
Gloucester Ter *ELS/FEN* NE4 ...... **79** F4 🟩
Gloucester Wy *ELS/FEN* NE4...... **80** A4 🟩
Glover Rd *MLFD/PNYW* SR4 ...... **142** A4
  WASHN NE37 .... **121** E4
Glynfellis *FELL* NE10 .... **101** E6
Glynwood Cl *CRAM* NE23 .... **14** A5 🟩
Glynwood Gdns
  LWF/SPW/WRK NE9..................... **99** F5
Goathland Av *LGB/KIL* NE12 ...... **49** E5
Goathland Cl *SUNDSW* SR3 ...... **161** E1
Goathland Dr *SUNDSW* SR3 ..... **161** D1
Godfrey Rd *MLFD/PNYW* SR4 ... **141** F3
Goldcrest Rd *WASHS* NE38........ **137** E3
Goldlynn Dr *SUNDSW* SR3 .... **159** F2
Goldsmith Rd *MLFD/PNYW* SR4 .. **142** A4
Goldspink La *JES* NE2 .... **81** F1 🟩
Golf Course Rd *HLS* DH4 .... **156** B4
Gompertz Gdns *SSH* NE33 .... **71** D6
Goodrich Cl *HLS* DH4 .... **157** E3 🟩
Good St *STLY/ANP* DH9 .... **131** D6
Goodwood *LGB/KIL* NE12 .... **50** B1 🟩
Goodwood Av *GATE* NE8 .... **98** B2 🔟
Goodwood Cl
  WD/WHPE/BLK NE5 .... **59** F3
Goodwood Rd
  MLFD/PNYW SR4 .... **141** F3 🔟
Goole Rd *MLFD/PNYW* SR4 .... **142** B3
Gordon Av *GOS/KPK* NE3 .... **63** E2 🔟
  SWCK/CAS SR5 .... **123** F4
Gordon Dr *BOL* NE36 .... **106** C3

Gordon Rd HAR/WTLS NE34 .... **88** B2
MLFD/PNYW SR4 .... **141** F4
Gordon Sq BYK/HTN/WLK NE6 .... **82** A3
WBAY NE26 .... **41** E6
Gordon St GATE NE8 .... **80** C6
SSH NE33 .... **71** E6
Gordon Ter SWCK/CAS SR5 .... **125** F2
Gorleston Wy SUNDSW SR3 ...... **160** B4
Gorse Av HAR/WTLS NE34 .... **89** C3
Gorsedale Gv DHAM DH1 .... **196** C3 🔟
Gorsedene Rd WBAY NE26 .... **40** B1
Gorse Rd ASHBK/HED/RY NE3 .... **4** C6
Gort Pl DHAM DH1 .... **195** E3
Goschen St BLYTH NE24 .... **10** C4 🔟
BLYTH NE24 .... **11** D3 🔟
GATE NE8 .... **98** C2 🔟
SWCK/CAS SR5 .... **125** F2
Gosforth Av HAR/WTLS NE34 .... **88** B5
Gosforth Park Wy LGB/KIL NE12 .... **48** B5
Gosforth St JES NE2 .... **3** G1
Gosforth Ter FELL NE10 .... **101** E1
Gosport Wy BLYTH NE24 .... **16** C2
Gossington WASHS NE38 .... **139** F1
Goswick Av LGB/HTN NE7 .... **65** D4
Goswick Dr GOS/KPK NE3 .... **46** B4
Goundry Av ASHBK/HED/RY SR2 .. **162** C2
Gowanburn CRAM NE23 .... **21** F5 🔟
WASHS NE38 .... **139** D4
Gowan Ter JES NE2 .... **64** B5
Gower Rd SWCK/CAS SR5 .... **125** F2
Gower St BYK/HTN/WLK NE6 .... **83** F4
Gower Wk FELL NE10 .... **100** B2
Gowland Av ELS/FEN NE4 .... **79** D1
Gracefield Cl WD/WHPE/BLK NE5 .. **59** F3 🔟
Grace Gdns WLSD/HOW NE28 ...... **66** C2
Grace St BYK/HTN/WLK NE6 .... **82** B2
DUN/TMV NE11 .... **97** E2
Grafton Rd WBAY NE26 .... **41** E6
Grafton St BYK/HTN/WLK NE6 ...... **82** A2 🔟
MLFD/PNYW SR4 .... **125** F5
Graham Av WICK/BNPF NE16 .... **95** F2
Graham Ct BDN/LAN/SAC DH7 .... **178** B1 🔟
Graham Park Rd GOS/KPK NE3 ..... **63** E3
Grahamsley St GATE NE8 .... **81** E6
Graham St SSH NE33 .... **71** F4 🔟
The Graham Wy SEA/MUR SR7 .... **175** F4
Grainger Park Rd ELS/FEN NE4 ..... **79** E4
Grainger St CNUT NE1 .... **2** C4
Grampian Av PLEE/EAS SR8 .... **208** A3
Grampian Gv BOL NE36 .... **106** A3 🔟
Grampian Pl LGB/KIL NE12 .... **49** D3 🔟
Granby Cl SUNDSW SR3 .... **144** A4
WICK/BNPF NE16 .... **114** A1
Grand Pde TYNE/NSHE NE30 .... **55** F4
Grandstand Rd JES NE2 .... **62** B6
Grange Av BDLGTN NE22 .... **8** C1
HLS DH4 .... **169** F1
LGB/KIL NE12 .... **50** A6
PLEE/EAS SR8 .... **200** A3
SMOOR NE27 .... **38** B6
Grange Cl BLYTH NE24 .... **16** C2
MONK NE25 .... **39** F6
PLEE/EAS SR8 .... **200** B6
TYNE/NSHE NE30 .... **55** D2 🔟
WLSD/HOW NE28 .... **67** E4
Grange Crs FELL NE10 .... **101** F5
RYTON NE40 .... **74** B4
Grange Dr RYTON NE40 .... **74** B4
Grange Est DUN/TMV NE11 .... **116** B6
Grange Farm Dr WICK/BNPF NE16 .. **95** F5
Grange La WICK/BNPF NE16 .... **95** F5
Grange Lonnen RYTON NE40 .... **74** A3
Grangemere Cl
ASHBK/HED/RY SR2 .... **145** E4
Grange Nook WICK/BNPF NE16 ..... **95** F5
Grange Pk MONK NE25 .... **53** E1
Grange Park Av BDLGTN NE22 .... **8** C1
SWCK/CAS SR5 .... **126** B3
Grange Pl JRW NE32 .... **86** A1
Grange Rd BW/LEM/TK/HW NE15 .. **58** A6
DHAM DH1 .... **196** B2
ELS/FEN NE4 .... **78** C2
FELL NE10 .... **101** F3
GOS/KPK NE3 .... **47** E5
JRW NE32 .... **86** A1
PONT/DH NE20 .... **28** A3
RYTON NE40 .... **74** B3
STLY/ANP DH9 .... **147** F2
SWCK/CAS SR5 .... **123** F5
Grange Rd West JRW NE32 .... **85** F1
Grange St CLSW/PEL DH2 .... **152** A2
Grange St South
ASHBK/HED/RY SR2 .... **145** C4
Grange Ter BOL NE36 .... **105** C3 🔟
LWF/SPW/WRK NE9 .... **99** F2 🔟
SWCK/CAS SR5 .... **126** A2
The Grange STLY/ANP DH9 .... **130** B6
Grange Vw HLH DH5 .... **170** C5
HLS DH4 .... **157** F5
RYTON NE40 .... **74** B4
SWCK/CAS SR5 .... **126** B1
Grange Vls WLSD/HOW NE28 .... **67** E4
Grantham Dr LWF/SPW/WRK NE9 .... **99** D6
Grantham Pl CRAM NE23 .... **21** F4 🔟

Grantham Rd
CLDN/WHIT/ROK SR6 .... **127** D2
JES NE2 .... **81** E1
Grantham St BLYTH NE24 .... **11** E6
Grants Crs SEA/MUR SR7 .... **176** C3
Grant St JRW NE32 .... **85** F1
PLEE/EAS SR8 .... **209** F1 🔟
Granville Av LGB/KIL NE12 .... **50** A3
WBAY NE26 .... **26** C3
Granville Crs LGB/KIL NE12 .... **50** A6
Granville Dr HLS DH4 .... **157** E3
LGB/KIL NE12 .... **50** A4
WD/WHPE/BLK NE5 .... **59** F3
Granville Gdns JES NE2 .... **64** C6 🔟
Granville Rd GOS/KPK NE3 .... **47** E5
JES NE2 .... **64** A6
PLEE/EAS SR8 .... **209** E3
Granville St GATE NE8 .... **99** F1 🔟
MLFD/PNYW SR4 .... **126** A5
Grape La DHAM DH1 .... **194** B5 🔟
Grasmere CLDN/WHIT/ROK SR6 .. **107** F1
Grasmere Av BYK/HTN/WLK NE6 ... **83** D3
FELL NE10 .... **101** E2
HLH DH5 .... **186** D4
JRW NE32 .... **86** C5
Grasmere Ct LGB/KIL NE12 .... **49** E1 🔟
Grasmere Crs BLAY NE21 .... **94** A2 🔟
SWCK/CAS SR5 .... **126** B1
WBAY NE26 .... **40** B1
Grasmere Gdns HAR/WTLS NE34 ... **89** D2 🔟
HEBB NE31 .... **85** E3
PLEE/EAS SR8 .... **209** D1
WICK/BNPF NE16 .... **96** B3
WLSD/HOW NE28 .... **66** C5
Grasmere Pl GOS/KPK NE3 .... **47** D5
Grasmere Rd CLSW/PEL DH2 .... **166** A1
HEBB NE31 .... **85** E3
PLEE/EAS SR8 .... **209** D1
WICK/BNPF NE16 .... **96** B3
WLSD/HOW NE28 .... **66** C5
Grasmere St GATE NE8 .... **99** D1 🔟
Grasmere St West GATE NE8 .... **99** D1 🔟
Grasmere Ter RDHAMSE DH6 ...... **188** A5 🔟
SEA/MUR SR7 .... **188** D1
Grasmoor Pl
BW/LEM/TK/HW NE15 .... **76** A1 🔟
Grassdale DHAM DH1 .... **196** C3
Grassholme Mdw SUNDSW SR3 ... **144** A4
Grassholm Pl LGB/KIL NE12 .... **48** C5
Grassington Dr CRAM NE23 .... **21** F4
Grasslees WASHS NE38 .... **137** E6
Grasswell Dr WD/WHPE/BLK NE5 .. **61** F3
Gravel Wks HLH DH5 .... **171** D1
Gravesend Rd MLFD/PNYW SR4 .. **142** A4 🔟
Gravesend Sq MLFD/PNYW SR4 .. **142** B4 🔟
Gray Av DHAM DH1 .... **193** F1
DIN/WO NE13 .... **33** E3
RDHAMSE DH6 .... **197** E4
SEA/MUR SR7 .... **188** B1
Grayling Ct SUNDSW SR3 .... **159** E3 🔟
Gray Rd ASHBK/HED/RY SR2 .... **5** H5
Grays Ter BOLCOL NE35 .... **105** D3 🔟
Graystones FELL NE10 .... **102** A3
Gray St BLYTH NE24 .... **11** D3
Graythwaite CLSW/PEL DH2 .... **152** B5
Greathead St SSH NE33 .... **88** A1 🔟
Great Lime Rd DIN/WO NE13 .... **34** C5
LGB/KIL NE12 .... **48** B1
Great North Forest Trail
HAR/WTLS NE34 .... **90** C1
Great North Rd GOS/KPK NE3 .... **47** E5
JES NE2 .... **63** F6
Grebe Cl BLYTH NE24 .... **17** D1
Greely Rd WD/WHPE/BLK NE5 .... **60** B4
Greenacres CLSW/PEL DH2 .... **151** F1
Green Av HLS DH4 .... **157** F4 🔟
Greenbank BLAY NE21 .... **76** B6
JRW NE32 .... **86** A1
Greenbank Dr MLFD/PNYW SR4 .. **141** F1
Greenbourne Gdns FELL NE10 ..... **100** B3 🔟
Green Cl TYNE/NSHE NE30 .... **55** D3
Green Crs CRAM NE23 .... **34** B2 🔟
Greencroft RDHAMSE DH6 .... **188** A5
Greencroft Av BYK/HTN/WLK NE6 .. **66** C6
Greendale Cl BLYTH NE24 .... **9** F4 🔟
Greendale Gdns HLH DH5 .... **185** E2
Greenfield Av WD/WHPE/BLK NE5 .. **60** C4
Greenfield Rd DIN/WO NE13 .... **47** D2
GOS/KPK NE3 .... **47** D3
Greenfinch Cl WASHS NE38 .... **137** E3
Greenford DUN/TMV NE11 .... **116** C6
Greenford La DUN/TMV NE11 .... **117** D5
Greenford Rd BYK/HTN/WLK NE6 .. **83** E5
Greenhaugh LGB/KIL NE12 .... **49** D3
Greenhead WASHS NE38 .... **137** E2
Greenhills LGB/KIL NE12 .... **35** F5
Greenhill Vw WD/WHPE/BLK NE5 .. **62** A4
Green Hill Wk HAR/WTLS NE34 ...... **90** B3
Greenholme Ct CRAM NE23 .... **14** A2 🔟
Greenhow Cl
ASHBK/HED/RY SR2 .... **162** B3 🔟
Greenlands STLY/ANP DH9 .... **117** F4 🔟
Greenlands Ct MONK NE25 .... **24** C4
Green La BOL NE36 .... **106** C4
DHAM DH1 .... **195** E4
DIN/WO NE13 .... **44** B4
FELL NE10 .... **82** C6
HAR/WTLS NE34 .... **88** A4
LGB/KIL NE12 .... **50** A1 🔟

SEA/MUR SR7 .... **173** D4
Greenlaw WD/WHPE/BLK NE5 .... **60** A6
Greenlaw Rd CRAM NE23 .... **21** F5
Green Lea BDN/LAN/SAC DH7 ...... **178** A3
Greenlea NSHW NE29 .... **53** D3
Greenlea Cl MLFD/PNYW SR4 ...... **142** B3
Greenlee Dr LGB/HTN NE7 .... **65** F3
Green Pk WLSD/HOW NE28 .... **66** A3
Green's Bank STLY/ANP DH9 .... **150** C1
Greenrigg Gdns SUNDSW SR3 ..... **144** A3 🔟
Greenshields Rd MLFD/PNYW SR4 . **142** A4
Greenside Av PLEE/EAS SR8 .... **209** E1
WLSD/HOW NE28 .... **68** B3
Greenside Crs
BW/LEM/TK/HW NE15 .... **77** F1
Green's Pl SSH NE33 .... **71** E2
Green St SEA/MUR SR7 .... **176** C3
SUND SR1 .... **4** C2
Green Ter SUND SR1 .... **4** B3
The Green BW/LEM/TK/HW NE15 .. **58** B5
GOS/KPK NE3 .... **62** B3
HLH DH5 .... **171** E1
MONK NE25 .... **40** A4
PLEE/EAS SR8 .... **207** F4
PONT/DH NE20 .... **28** B2
SWCK/CAS SR5 .... **125** F3
Greenway ELS/FEN NE4 .... **61** F6
WD/WHPE/BLK NE5 .... **59** E2
The Greenway
MLFD/PNYW SR4 .... **142** B2 🔟
Greenwell Cl BLAY NE21 .... **93** F1 🔟
Greenwich Pl GATE NE8 .... **81** F4
Greenwood LGB/KIL NE12 .... **50** B1 🔟
Greenwood Av BDLGTN NE22 .... **8** C1 🔟
BYK/HTN/WLK NE6 .... **66** C5 🔟
HLS DH4 .... **170** B2
Greenwood Gdns
DUN/TMV NE11 .... **97** F5 🔟
FELL NE10 .... **82** C6 🔟
Greenwood Rd MLFD/PNYW SR4 .. **142** A3
Greetlands Rd
ASHBK/HED/RY SR2 .... **144** B3
Gregson St BDN/LAN/SAC DH7 .... **178** B1
Gregson Ter SEA/MUR SR7 .... **175** E1
Grenada Cl WBAY NE26 .... **40** B2 🔟
Grenada Dr WBAY NE26 .... **40** B2
Grenada Pl WBAY NE26 .... **40** B2 🔟
Grenfell Sq MLFD/PNYW SR4 ...... **142** A4 🔟
Grenville Dr GOS/KPK NE3 .... **47** D3
Grenville Wy WBAY NE26 .... **40** A3
Gresford St SSH NE33 .... **88** B2
Gresham Cl CRAM NE23 .... **22** A4
Gresley Pl PLEE/EAS SR8 .... **207** F2
Greta Gdns SSH NE33 .... **71** F6
Greta Ter MLFD/PNYW SR4 .... **143** F1
Gretna Dr HAR/WTLS NE34 .... **87** E6 🔟
Gretna Rd BW/LEM/TK/HW NE15 ... **78** A1
Gretton Pl LGB/HTN NE7 .... **64** C3 🔟
Grey Av CRAM NE23 .... **21** F5
Greybourne Gdns
ASHBK/HED/RY SR2 .... **144** B4 🔟
Greyfriars La LGB/KIL NE12 .... **48** C6 🔟
Greystead Cl WD/WHPE/BLK NE5 .. **59** F3
Greystead Rd MONK NE25 .... **39** D5
Greystoke Av ASHBK/HED/RY SR2 . **144** B4
JES NE2 .... **81** F1
WICK/BNPF NE16 .... **96** A4
Greystoke Gdns
ASHBK/HED/RY SR2 .... **144** B3 🔟
JES NE2 .... **64** C6
LWF/SPW/WRK NE9 .... **118** A2
WICK/BNPF NE16 .... **96** A5
Greystoke Pk GOS/KPK NE3 .... **47** E4
Greystoke Wk WICK/BNPF NE16 ... **96** A4 🔟
Grey St CNUT NE1 .... **2** D3
DIN/WO NE13 .... **32** C4 🔟
HLS DH4 .... **170** C1
TYNE/NSHE NE30 .... **55** D6
WLSD/HOW NE28 .... **67** E4
Greywood Av ELS/FEN NE4 .... **79** D1
Grieves' Rw CRAM NE23 .... **34** C2
Grieve St BLYTH NE24 .... **10** C3 🔟
Grimsby St BLYTH NE24 .... **11** D6
Grindon Av MLFD/PNYW SR4 ...... **142** A1 🔟
Grindon Cl CRAM NE23 .... **21** F5
MONK NE25 .... **54** A2
Grindon Ct MLFD/PNYW SR4 ...... **142** B3 🔟
Grindon Gdns MLFD/PNYW SR4 .. **142** B3
Grindon La MLFD/PNYW SR4 ...... **142** A1
SUNDSW SR3 .... **143** D4 🔟
Grindon Pk MLFD/PNYW SR4 ...... **142** B3 🔟
Grindon Ter MLFD/PNYW SR4 ...... **143** F1
Grinstead Cl HAR/WTLS NE34 .... **89** E1 🔟
Grinstead Wy DHAM DH1 .... **196** C1
Grisedale Gdns LWF/SPW/WRK NE9 . **99** F6
Grisedale Rd PLEE/EAS SR8 .... **209** D2 🔟
Grizedale WASHN NE37 .... **120** A6
Grizedale Ct CLDN/WHIT/ROK SR6 . **108** B4
Grosvenor Av JES NE2 .... **64** B5
WICK/BNPF NE16 .... **96** A2
Grosvenor Cl CRAM NE23 .... **21** F5 🔟
Grosvenor Ct
WD/WHPE/BLK NE5 .... **59** F3 🔟
Grosvenor Crs HEBB NE31 .... **85** E5

Grosvenor Dr
  CLDN/WHIT/ROK SR6 .... **107** D1
  HAR/WTLS NE34 .... **72** B6
  MONK NE25 .... **40** C6
Grosvenor Gdns *HAR/WTLS* NE34 ... **89** E2 ⓶
  JES NE2 .... **64** C6 ⓵
  WLSD/HOW NE28 .... **68** C3
Grosvenor Pl *JES* NE2 .... **64** B5
  NSHW NE29 .... **54** C6
Grosvenor Rd *HAR/WTLS* NE34 .... **72** A6
  JES NE2 .... **64** B5
Grosvenor St *SWCK/CAS* SR5 .... **125** E2
Grosvenor Wy *WD/WHPE/BLK* NE5 .. **59** F4
Grotto Gdns *HAR/WTLS* NE34 .... **90** C2
Grotto Rd *HAR/WTLS* NE34 .... **90** C2
Grove Av *GOS/KPK* NE3 .... **63** F2 ⓵
Grove Ct *RDHAMSE* DH6 .... **206** B3
Grove Rd *BDN/LAN/SAC* DH7 .... **203** D6
  BW/LEM/TK/HW NE15 .... **58** C5
  LWF/SPW/WRK NE9 .... **99** F4
Grove St *DHAM* DH1 .... **194** A6
The Grove *ASHBK/HED/RY* SR2 ..... **144** C2
  ASHBK/HED/RY SR2 .... **162** B1
  DHAM DH1 .... **193** F3
  GOS/KPK NE3 .... **63** F2
  HLH DH5 .... **171** D4
  JES NE2 .... **64** B4 ⓷
  JES NE2 .... **64** B5 ⓵
  JRW NE32 .... **104** A1
  LGB/KIL NE12 .... **49** F6
  MONK NE25 .... **40** B6
  PLEE/EAS SR8 .... **199** F2
  ROWG NE39 .... **111** E3
  SWCK/CAS SR5 .... **124** A3 ⓸
  WD/WHPE/BLK NE5 .... **59** F5
  WICK/BNPF NE16 .... **96** B4
Guardians Ct *PONT/DH* NE20 .... **28** B3 ⓶
Guelder Rd *LGB/HTN* NE7 .... **65** E3
Guernsey Rd *MLFD/PNYW* SR4 ...... **142** A4
Guernsey Sq *MLFD/PNYW* SR4 ..... **142** A4
Guildford Pl *BYK/HTN/WLK* NE6 ..... **82** A1
Guildford St *ASHBK/HED/RY* SR2 .. **145** D2
Guillemot Cl *BLYTH* NE24 .... **17** D1 ⓵
Guisborough Dr *NSHW* NE29......... **53** D4
Guisborough St *MLFD/PNYW* SR4 .. **143** E1
Gullane *WASHN* NE37 .... **120** C1
Gullane Cl *FELL* NE10 .... **84** B6
  STLY/ANP DH9 .... **149** D2
Gunnerston Gv *GOS/KPK* NE3 .... **61** F1 ⓹
Gunnerton Cl *CRAM* NE23 .... **22** A4
Gunnerton Pl *NSHW* NE29 .... **53** F6 ⓸
Gunn St *DUN/TMV* NE11 .... **97** E2
Gut Rd *WLSD/HOW* NE28 .... **68** B4
Guyzance Av *GOS/KPK* NE3 .... **46** C6

H

Hackworth Rd *PLEE/EAS* SR8 .... **199** E5
Hackworth Wy *NSHW* NE29 .... **70** B3 ⓵
Haddington Rd *MONK* NE25 .... **39** E3
Haddon Cl *MONK* NE25 .... **39** D5
Haddon Gn *MONK* NE25 .... **39** D5
Haddricksmill Rd *GOS/KPK* NE3 ..... **64** C6
Hadleigh Rd *MLFD/PNYW* SR4 ...... **142** C1
Hadrian Av *CLS/BIR/GTL* DH3 .... **153** F3
Hadrian Gdns *NE21* **94** C1
Hadrian Pl *BW/LEM/TK/HW* NE15 .. **57** F4
  LWF/SPW/WRK NE9 .... **100** A3 ⓷
Hadrian Rd *BLYTH* NE24 .... **16** B3
  ELS/FEN NE4 .... **79** D2
  JRW NE32 .... **86** C5
  WLSD/HOW NE28 .... **67** E5
Hadrians Ct *DUN/TMV* NE11 .... **98** C6
Hadrian St *MLFD/PNYW* SR4 .... **125** F5
Hadstone Pl *WD/WHPE/BLK* NE5 .. **61** E5 ⓹
Haggerston Cl
  WD/WHPE/BLK NE5 .... **61** D2 ⓸
Haggerston Ct
  WD/WHPE/BLK NE5 .... **61** D2 ⓹
Haggerston Crs
  WD/WHPE/BLK NE5 .... **61** D2
Haggerstone Dr *SWCK/CAS* SR5 .. **123** F4 ⓵
Haggerston Ter *JRW* NE32 .... **87** D4
Haggie Av *WLSD/HOW* NE28 .... **67** F5 ⓵
Haig Av *MONK* NE25 .... **40** B6
Haig Crs *BW/LEM/TK/HW* NE15 ..... **77** F3
  DHAM DH1 .... **195** F5
Haig Rd *BDLGTN* NE22 .... **8** A4
Hailsham Av *LGB/KIL* NE12 .... **49** E5
Haininghead *WASHS* NE38 .... **139** D4
Hainingwood Ter *FELL* NE10 .... **84** A6 ⓷
Haldane Ter *JES* NE2 .... **64** A6
Hale Ri *PLEE/EAS* SR8 .... **208** C2
Halewood Av *GOS/KPK* NE3 .... **62** A2
Half Fields Rd *BLAY* NE21 .... **94** A1
Half Moon La *GATE* NE8 .... **3** F6 ⓶
  GATE NE8 .... **81** D5 ⓵
Halfway House La
  ASHBK/HED/RY SR2 .... **145** F3
Halidon Rd *ASHBK/HED/RY* SR2 .. **144** C5
Halidon Sq *ASHBK/HED/RY* SR2 .. **144** C5 ⓵

Halifax Pl *DUN/TMV* NE11 .... **97** D1 ⓶
Halifax Rd *DUN/TMV* NE11 .... **97** D1
Halkirk Wy *CRAM* NE23 .... **13** F5
Hallam Rd *PLEE/EAS* SR8 .... **208** C1 ⓷
Hall Cl *HLS* DH4 .... **183** F2
  SEA/MUR SR7 .... **174** C2
Hall Dr *LGB/KIL* NE12 .... **35** E5 ⓷
Halleyslike Ct *LGB/HTN* NE7 .... **65** F3 ⓶
Hall Farm Rd *SUNDSW* SR3 .... **160** B3
Hallfield Cl *SUNDSW* SR3 .... **160** C3
Hallfield Dr *PLEE/EAS* SR8 .... **199** F3
Hall Gdns *BOL* NE36 .... **105** F3
  FELL NE10 .... **100** C3
Hallgarth Rd *BLAY* NE21 .... **76** A6
Hallgarth St *DHAM* DH1 .... **194** C6
  RDHAMSE DH6 .... **197** E4
The Hallgarth *DHAM* DH1 .... **194** C6
Hall Gn *BLYTH* NE24 .... **10** A5
Halling Cl *BYK/HTN/WLK* NE6 .... **83** F4 ⓹
Hallington Dr *MONK* NE25................ **24** C5
Halliwell St *HLS* DH4 .... **170** C1
Hall La *HLH* DH5 .... **171** D3
  HLS DH4 .... **183** F2
Hallow Dr *BW/LEM/TK/HW* NE15 .. **57** F5
Hall Pk *BLAY* NE21 .... **75** F4
Hall Rd *HEBB* NE31 .... **85** D3
  WASHN NE37 .... **121** D4 ⓷
Hallside Rd *BLYTH* NE24 .... **10** A1
Hall Ter *FELL* NE10 .... **84** A6 ⓻
Hall Vw *CLDN/WHIT/ROK* SR6 ...... **109** E2
Hall Wks *PLEE/EAS* SR8 .... **199** F3
Halstead Sq *MLFD/PNYW* SR4 ...... **142** C1
Halterburn Cl *GOS/KPK* NE3 .... **63** D2
Halton Rd *DHAM* DH1 .... **194** C1 ⓵
Hamar Cl *NSHW* NE29 .... **69** E2
Hambard Wy *WASHS* NE38 .... **138** C2
Hambledon Av *TYNE/NSHE* NE30 . **54** C1
Hambledon Cl *BOLCOL* NE35 .... **105** D2 ⓵
Hambledon Gdns *LGB/HTN* NE7 .... **64** C3
Hambledon Pl *PLEE/EAS* SR8 ...... **207** F3 ⓵
Hambledon St *BLYTH* NE24 .... **10** C4 ⓷
Hambledon Dr *SEA/MUR* SR7 ...... **176** A2 ⓶
Hambledon Rd *WASHS* NE38 .... **138** A3
Hamilton Ct *RDHAMSE* DH6 .... **206** B2 ⓵
Hamilton Crs *ELS/FEN* NE4 .... **80** A2 ⓶
  NSHW NE29 .... **53** E4
Hamilton Dr *WBAY* NE26 .... **40** E2
Hamilton St *PLEE/EAS* SR8 .... **209** E1 ⓶
  BOL NE36 .... **105** F3 ⓹
Hammer Square Bank
  STLY/ANP DH9 .... **133** E5
Hampden Rd
  CLDN/WHIT/ROK SR6 .... **127** D2
Hampden St *SSH* NE33 .... **71** E6 ⓸
Hampshire Ct *ELS/FEN* NE4 .... **79** F6
Hampshire Pl *WASHN* NE37 .... **120** C3 ⓶
Hampshire Rd *DHAM* DH1 .... **196** B3
Hampshire Wy *HAR/WTLS* NE34 ... **90** B1 ⓵
Hampstead Cl *BLYTH* NE24 .... **16** B3
Hampstead Rd *ELS/FEN* NE4 .... **79** D3
  MLFD/PNYW SR4 .... **142** C2
Hampstead Sq
  MLFD/PNYW SR4 .... **142** B2 ⓷
Hampton Cl *CRAM* NE23 .... **22** C1 ⓵
Hampton Ct *CLS/BIR/GTL* DH3 ..... **153** F1
Hampton Dr *FELL* NE10 .... **100** B2
Hampton Rd *TYNE/NSHE* NE30 ...... **54** C2
Hamsterley Cl *CLS/BIR/GTL* DH3 .. **168** A3 ⓶
Hamsterley Ct *SUNDSW* SR3 .... **160** C3 ⓷
Hamsterley Crs
  BW/LEM/TK/HW NE15 .... **76** A1 ⓷
  DHAM DH1 .... **180** C6
  LWF/SPW/WRK NE9 .... **118** B1
Hamsterley Dr *LGB/KIL* NE12 .... **35** E6
Hamsterley Gdns *STLY/ANP* DH9 .. **146** B3
Hanby Gdns *SUNDSW* SR3 .... **143** F3 ⓹
Hancock St *CNUT* NE1 .... **80** C1
Handel St *MLFD/PNYW* SR4 .... **125** F5 ⓶
  SSH NE33 .... **71** F4 ⓷
Handley St *PLEE/EAS* SR8 .... **209** E1 ⓷
Handy Dr *DUN/TMV* NE11 .... **78** C6
Hangmans La *HLH* DH5 .... **160** A5
Hanlon Ct *JRW* NE32 .... **85** E1
Hannington St
  BYK/HTN/WLK NE6 .... **81** F2 ⓶
Hannington St *BYK/HTN/WLK* NE6 . **81** F2
Hanover Ct *CRAM* NE23 .... **35** D1 ⓵
Hanover Dr *BLAY* NE21 .... **93** F1
Hanover Pl *CRAM* NE23 .... **13** F4 ⓷
  MLFD/PNYW SR4 .... **126** A4
Hanover St *CNUT* NE1 .... **2** D6
Harbottle Av *GOS/KPK* NE3 .... **46** C6
  SMOOR NE27 .... **52** B2
Harbottle Ct *BYK/HTN/WLK* NE6 .... **82** B4
Harbottle Crs *JRW* NE32 .... **86** A6
Harbour Dr *SSH* NE33 .... **71** F1
The Harbour *HLS* DH4 .... **157** D2 ⓶
Harbour Vw *CLDN/WHIT/ROK* SR6 . **127** E3
  SSH NE33 .... **71** E1
Harbour Wk *SEA/MUR* SR7 .... **176** B2
Harcourt Rd
  ASHBK/HED/RY SR2 .... **144** C5 ⓶
Harcourt St *LWF/SPW/WRK* NE9 ... **99** F5 ⓶

Hardgate Rd
  ASHBK/HED/RY SR2 .... **145** D5 ⓵
Hardie Av *WICK/BNPF* NE16 .... **95** F2
Hardie Dr *BOL* NE36 .... **105** F3
Hardwick Ct *GATE* NE8 .... **99** F1 ⓵
Hardwick Pl *GOS/KPK* NE3 .... **62** C3 ⓶
Hardwick St *PLEE/EAS* SR8 .... **209** F2
Hardyards Ct *HAR/WTLS* NE34 .... **88** B3 ⓹
Hardy Av *HAR/WTLS* NE34 .... **88** A5
Hardy Gv *WLSD/HOW* NE28 .... **66** C1 ⓵
Hardy Sq *SWCK/CAS* SR5 .... **125** E2
Hardy St *SEA/MUR* SR7 .... **176** C3 ⓼
Harebell Rd *LWF/SPW/WRK* NE9 .. **100** B6
Harehills Av *WD/WHPE/BLK* NE5 ... **61** F3
Harelaw Gv *WD/WHPE/BLK* NE5 ... **59** F5 ⓸
Hareside *CRAM* NE23 .... **21** F3
Harewood Cl *WICK/BNPF* NE16...... **95** F6
Harewood Dr *BDLGTN* NE22 .... **8** B2
Harewood Gdns *SUNDSW* SR3 .... **143** F3 ⓸
Harewood Rd *GOS/KPK* NE3 .... **47** E6
Hareydene *WD/WHPE/BLK* NE5 ..... **60** B1
Hargill Dr *WASHS* NE38 .... **137** F5
Hargrave Ct *BLYTH* NE24 .... **10** B6 ⓷
Harland Wy *WASHS* NE38 .... **138** C1
Harle Cl *WD/WHPE/BLK* NE5 .... **60** A5 ⓹
Harle Rd *SMOOR* NE27 .... **37** F6
Harleston Wy *FELL* NE10 .... **101** D4
Harle St *WLSD/HOW* NE28 .... **67** D4 ⓸
Harley Ter *GOS/KPK* NE3 .... **63** F1
Harlow Av *GOS/KPK* NE3 .... **46** B5
  SMOOR NE27 .... **51** F1
Harlow Green La
  LWF/SPW/WRK NE9 .... **117** F2
Harlow Pl *LGB/HTN* NE7 .... **65** D3
Harlow St *MLFD/PNYW* SR4 .... **126** A6 ⓸
Harnham Av *NSHW* NE29 .... **69** E1
Harnham Gdns
  WD/WHPE/BLK NE5 .... **61** E6
Harnham Gv *CRAM* NE23 .... **21** F3
Harold St *JRW* NE32 .... **86** B1
Harperley Dr *SUNDSW* SR3 .... **144** A4
Harperley La *STLY/ANP* DH9 .... **129** F5
Harperley Rd *STLY/ANP* DH9 .... **146** B3
Harper St *BLYTH* NE24 .... **10** C5
Harras Bank *CLS/BIR/GTL* DH3 .... **136** B3
Harriet St *BLAY* NE21 .... **76** B6
  BYK/HTN/WLK NE6 .... **82** C2 ⓷
Harrington St *WLSD/HOW* NE28 ..... **67** D4 ⓹
Harriot Dr *LGB/KIL* NE12 .... **48** C2
Harrison Cl *PLEE/EAS* SR8 .... **209** D3
Harrison Gdns *GATE* NE8 .... **98** C3 ⓶
Harrison Garth *RDHAMSE* DH6 ..... **197** E4 ⓵
Harrison Pl *JES* NE2 .... **81** D1 ⓹
Harrison Rd *WLSD/HOW* NE28 .... **68** C3
Harrogate Ter *SEA/MUR* SR7 .... **188** B1 ⓹
Harrogate St *ASHBK/HED/RY* SR2 ... **5** E5
Harrow Gdns *DIN/WO* NE13 .... **33** E5
Harrow Sq *MLFD/PNYW* SR4 .... **142** C1
Hartburn Cl *FELL* NE10 .... **101** F5
Hartburn Dr *WD/WHPE/BLK* NE5 ... **59** F3
Hartburn Pl *ELS/FEN* NE4 .... **79** D1
Hartburn Rd *TYNE/NSHE* NE30 ...... **54** B3
Hartburn Wk *GOS/KPK* NE3 .... **61** F1
Hartford Bank *CRAM* NE23 .... **12** B2
Hartford Br *BDLGTN* NE22 .... **12** B2
Hartford Crs *BDLGTN* NE22 .... **7** D4
Hartford Crs *BDLGTN* NE22 .... **12** B1
Hartford Rd *BDLGTN* NE22 .... **6** C6
  GOS/KPK NE3 .... **47** F5
  HAR/WTLS NE34 .... **87** F3
  MLFD/PNYW SR4 .... **142** C1
Hartford St *BYK/HTN/WLK* NE6 ...... **65** E6 ⓶
Hartforth Crs *FELL* NE10 .... **102** A1 ⓷
Harthope Av *SWCK/CAS* SR5 .... **124** B1 ⓵
Harthope Cl *WASHS* NE38 .... **137** E6
Harthope Dr *NSHW* NE29 .... **70** A3
Hartington Rd *TYNE/NSHE* NE30 ... **54** C3
Hartington St
  CLDN/WHIT/ROK SR6 .... **127** D2
  ELS/FEN NE4 .... **79** F3
  GATE NE8 .... **99** E1
Hartington Ter *SSH* NE33 .... **71** F6
Hartland Dr *CLS/BIR/GTL* DH3 ...... **136** C4
Hartlands *BDLGTN* NE22 .... **7** D4
Harleigh Pl *BLYTH* NE24 .... **1U** A5 ⓶
Hartley Av *WBAY* NE26 .... **40** A5
Hartleyburn Av *HEBB* NE31 .... **84** C5
Hartley La *MONK* NE25 .... **39** D4
Hartley St *MONK* NE25 .... **24** B5
  SUND SR1 .... **5** G1
Hartley Ter *BLYTH* NE24 .... **16** B2 ⓷
Hartoft Cl *HLS* DH4 .... **157** F5 ⓶
Harton Gv *HAR/WTLS* NE34 .... **89** D1
Harton House Rd *HAR/WTLS* NE34.. **89** E1
Harton House Rd East
  HAR/WTLS NE34 .... **89** E1
Harton La *HAR/WTLS* NE34 .... **88** B3
Harton Ri *HAR/WTLS* NE34 .... **89** E1
Hartside *BW/LEM/TK/HW* NE15 ...... **76** B1
  CLS/BIR/GTL DH3 .... **136** C5
Hartside Crs *BLAY* NE21 .... **13** F4 ⓸
  CRAM NE23 .... **21** F6
  SMOOR NE27 .... **37** F6

Hartside Gdns *HLH* DH5 .... 186 B3
  JES NE2 .... 64 B5 2
Hartside Pl *CLDN/WHIT/ROK* NE3 .... 47 E3 1
Hartside Vw *DHAM* DH1 .... 179 F5
Hart Sq *MLFD/PNYW* SR4 .... 142 C1
Harvard Rd *GOS/KPK* NE3 .... 62 A1 3
Harvest Cl *SUNDSW* SR3 .... 160 B3 3
Harvey Cl *PLEE/EAS* SR8 .... 208 C1
  WASHS NE38 .... 137 E1
Harvey Combe *LGB/KIL* NE12 .... 49 D1
Harvey Crs *FELL* NE10 .... 102 A2 4
Harwick St *STLY/ANP* DH9 .... 149 E2
Harwood Cl *CRAM* NE23 .... 21 F3
  WASHS NE38 .... 137 F5 1
Harwood Dr *LGB/KIL* NE12 .... 50 B1
Hascombe Cl *MONK* NE25 .... 39 F4
Haslemere Dr *SUNDSW* SR3 .... 143 F3 5
Hassop Wy *BDLGTN* NE22 .... 7 E2
Hastings Av *DHAM* DH1 .... 204 C1
  GOS/KPK NE3 .... 45 F5
  LGB/KIL NE12 .... 49 F5 3
  WBAY NE26 .... 26 A1 1
Hastings Ct *BDLGTN* NE22 .... 8 B2
Hastings Dr *TYNE/NSHE* NE30 .... 55 E4
Hastings Gdns *MONK* NE25 .... 24 C2
Hastings St *ASHBK/HED/RY* SR2 ...... 145 D2
  CRAM NE23 .... 22 B3
Hastings Ter *ASHBK/HED/RY* SR2 .... 145 D2
  CRAM NE23 .... 14 C4
  MONK NE25 .... 24 C1
Haswell Cl *FELL* NE10 .... 102 C3
Haswell Gdns *TYNE/NSHE* NE30 ...... 54 C6
Hatfield Av *HEBB* NE31 .... 85 E2
Hatfield Cl *DHAM* DH1 .... 179 F6
Hatfield Dr *CRAM* NE23 .... 23 E6
Hatfield Gdns *MONK* NE25 .... 39 D6
  SUNDSW SR3 .... 143 F3 6
Hathaway Gdns *SUNDSW* SR3 .... 143 F3 4
Hatherton Av *TYNE/NSHE* NE30 ...... 55 D1
Hatherty La *BLYTH* NE24 .... 14 C3
Haugh La *RYTON* NE40 .... 75 D2
Haughton Crs *MLFD/PNYW* NE32 .... 86 A6 2
  WD/WHPE/BLK NE5 .... 60 A5
Haughton Ter *BLYTH* NE24 .... 11 D5
Hautmont Rd *HEBB* NE31 .... 85 E4
Hauxley *LGB/KIL* NE12 .... 35 F5 3
Hauxley Dr *CLSW/PEL* DH2 .... 165 E2 3
  CRAM NE23 .... 13 F4
  GOS/KPK NE3 .... 46 A5
Hauxley Gdns
  WD/WHPE/BLK NE5 .... 61 F4 6
Havanna *LGB/KIL* NE12 .... 35 F5 4
Havannah Crs *DIN/WO* NE13 .... 31 D4 1
Havannah Rd *WASHN* NE37 .... 120 A5
Havant Gdns *DIN/WO* NE13 .... 33 D3
Havelock Cl *GATE* NE8 .... 81 D6 4
Havelock Crs *BDLGTN* NE22 .... 9 E1 1
Havelock Rd *SMOOR* NE27 .... 51 F1
Havelock St *SSH* NE33 .... 71 E2 6
  SUND SR1 .... 5 F1
Havelock Ter
  ASHBK/HED/RY SR2 .... 144 A1 8
  GATE NE8 .... 81 D6
  JRW NE32 .... 86 A3
Haven Ct *BLYTH* NE24 .... 10 B6 5
  DHAM DH1 .... 180 B4 2
The Haven *HLS* DH4 .... 157 D2 3
  NSHW NE29 .... 70 C2
Havercroft *FELL* NE10 .... 102 A3
Haverley Dr *SEA/MUR* SR7 .... 175 D2
Haversham Pk *SWCK/CAS* SR5 .... 108 B5
Haversham Rd *LGB/HTN* NE7 .... 64 C1
Hawarden Crs *MLFD/PNYW* SR4 .... 143 F1
Hawes Av *CLSW/PEL* DH2 .... 166 B3
Hawes Ct *CLDN/WHIT/ROK* SR6 .... 108 B5
Hawes Rd *PLEE/EAS* SR8 .... 208 C1
Haweswater Cl *HAR/WTLS* NE34 .... 88 C2 1
Hawick Ct *STLY/ANP* DH9 .... 149 D2
Hawick Crs *BYK/HTN/WLK* NE6 ...... 82 A4
Hawkey's La *NSHW* NE29 .... 54 B6
Hawkhill Cl *CLSW/PEL* DH2 .... 165 F2
Hawkhurst *WASHS* NE38 .... 139 D4 1
Hawkins Cl *SUNDSW* SR3 .... 160 B2 2
Hawksbury *WICK/BNPF* NE16 .... 95 F3 3
Hawkshead Ct *DIN/WO* NE13 .... 45 F5 2
Hawkwell Pl
  LWF/SPW/WRK NE9 .... 100 A5
Hawksley *WD/WHPE/BLK* NE5 .... 60 B4
Hawks Rd *GATE* NE8 .... 3 H6
Hawks St *GATE* NE8 .... 81 F4 5
Hawthorn Av *DIN/WO* NE13 .... 32 C5
  SUNDSW SR3 .... 144 A6
Hawthorn Cl *CLSW/PEL* DH2 .... 179 E1
  WICK/BNPF NE16 .... 96 A6
Hawthorn Cottages
  RDHAMSE DH6 .... 188 A5
Hawthorn Crs *DHAM* DH1 .... 195 F3
Hawthorn Dr *DUN/TMV* NE11 .... 97 E2
  JRW NE32 .... 86 C6
Hawthorne Av *HAR/WTLS* NE34 ...... 89 E4
  HEBB NE31 .... 85 E2

Hawthorne Cl *SEA/MUR* SR7 .... 188 C2
Hawthorne Rd *BLYTH* NE24 .... 11 E5 4
Hawthorne Ter *RDHAMSE* DH6 ...... 206 B2
Hawthorn Gdns *GOS/KPK* NE3 .... 62 B2
  NSHW NE29 .... 54 B5 1
  WBAY NE26 .... 40 B5
Hawthorn Pk
  BDN/LAN/SAC DH7 .... 203 D4 2
Hawthorn Pl *ELS/FEN* NE4 .... 80 A4 4
  LGB/KIL NE12 .... 35 E6 7
Hawthorn Rd *BLAY* NE21 .... 76 B6
  DHAM DH1 .... 196 C1
  GOS/KPK NE3 .... 63 E2
Hawthorn Rd West *GOS/KPK* NE3 .. 63 E2
The Hawthorns *BOL* NE36 .... 106 C3
Hawthorn St *JRW* NE32 .... 85 F1 6
  MLFD/PNYW SR4 .... 125 F6
  PLEE/EAS SR8 .... 200 C1
Hawthorn Ter
  CLDN/WHIT/ROK SR6 .... 109 D4 1
  DHAM DH1 .... 194 A5
  ELS/FEN NE4 .... 79 F4 3
  WD/WHPE/BLK NE5 .... 58 C4
Hawthorn Vls *CRAM* NE23 .... 22 B2
Haydock Dr *FELL* NE10 .... 102 A3
Haydon *WASHN* NE38 .... 139 D5
Haydon Pl *WD/WHPE/BLK* NE5 .... 60 C6
Haydon Sq *MLFD/PNYW* SR4 .... 142 C1
Hayes Wk *DIN/WO* NE13 .... 33 D4
Hayfield La *WICK/BNPF* NE16 .... 96 A4
Hayhole Rd *NSHW* NE29 .... 70 A4
Hayleazes Rd
  BW/LEM/TK/HW NE15 .... 77 E1
The Haynyng *FELL* NE10 .... 101 D3 2
The Hayricks *STLY/ANP* DH9 .... 130 C2
Hay St *SWCK/CAS* SR5 .... 126 B4
Hayton Av *HAR/WTLS* NE34 .... 89 F3
Hayton Cl *CRAM* NE23 .... 22 B1
Hayton Rd *TYNE/NSHE* NE30 .... 54 B3
Hazard La *HLH* DH5 .... 185 D1
Hazel Av *BDN/LAN/SAC* DH7 .... 202 C5
  NSHW NE29 .... 54 B5
  SUNDSW SR3 .... 144 A6 1
Hazeldene *MONK* NE25 .... 39 F5
Hazeldene Av *GOS/KPK* NE3 .... 61 E2
Hazeldene Ct *TYNE/NSHE* NE30 ...... 55 E5
Hazeley Gv *GOS/KPK* NE3 .... 61 F1
Hazeley Wy *GOS/KPK* NE3 .... 61 F1 6
Hazel Gv *CLSW/PEL* DH2 .... 152 C3
Hazelgrove *FELL* NE10 .... 102 A3
Hazel Gv *HAR/WTLS* NE34 .... 89 E4
  LGB/KIL NE12 .... 49 D2
Hazel Leigh *CLS/BIR/GTL* DH3 ...... 167 F3
Hazelmere Av *BDLGTN* NE22 .... 7 D3
Hazelmere Crs *CRAM* NE23 .... 14 B6
Hazelmere Dene *CRAM* NE23 .... 36 A1 2
Hazelmoor *HEBB* NE31 .... 84 C1 5
Hazel Rd *BLAY* NE21 .... 76 C6
  GATE NE8 .... 98 B2
Hazel St *JRW* NE32 .... 85 F1
Hazel Ter *RDHAMSE* DH6 .... 206 B2
  STLY/ANP DH9 .... 149 D5
Hazelwood *LGB/KIL* NE12 .... 50 B1 3
Hazelwood Av *JES* NE2 .... 64 A4
  SWCK/CAS SR5 .... 125 D2
Hazelwood Cl *LWF/SPW/WRK* NE9 .. 118 C2
Hazelwood Ter *WLSD/HOW* NE28 .... 68 C4
Hazledene Ter *MLFD/PNYW* SR4 .. 125 E6 4
Hazlitt Av *HAR/WTLS* NE34 .... 88 A5
Hazlitt Pl *CRAM* NE23 .... 36 C1 2
Headlam St *BYK/HTN/WLK* NE6 ...... 82 B2 4
Headlam Vw *WLSD/HOW* NE28 .... 68 C4
Healey Dr *SUNDSW* SR3 .... 144 A4
Heartsbourne Dr
  HAR/WTLS NE34 .... 89 E5 3
Heath Cl *DUN/TMV* NE11 .... 98 A3
  PLEE/EAS SR8 .... 209 D3
Heath Crs *BW/LEM/TK/HW* NE15 .... 77 F4
Heathdale Gdns *LGB/HTN* NE7 .... 65 D3
Heather Cl *CLDN/WHIT/ROK* SR6 .. 89 F6 4
Heatherdale Crs *DHAM* DH1 .... 196 C3
Heather Dr *HLH* DH5 .... 171 F5
Heather Gv *FELL* NE10 .... 102 A3
Heather Lea *STLY/ANP* DH9 .... 129 D4 1
Heatherlea Gdns *SUNDSW* SR3 .... 144 A3 7
Heather Pl *ELS/FEN* NE4 .... 62 A4
Heatherslaw Rd
  WD/WHPE/BLK NE5 .... 61 E6
Heather Wy *STLY/ANP* DH9 .... 147 F2
Heatherwell Gn *FELL* NE10 .... 100 B3 3
Heathery La *GOS/KPK* NE3 .... 48 A5
Heathfield *ASHBK/HED/RY* SR2 .... 144 B4
Heathfield Crs *WD/WHPE/BLK* NE5 .. 61 F3
Heathfield Pl *GOS/KPK* NE3 .... 47 E3 5
Heathfield Rd *LWF/SPW/WRK* NE9 .. 99 E4
Heath Gra *HLH* DH5 .... 171 F4
Heathmeads *CLSW/PEL* DH2 .... 151 E2
Heath Sq *MLFD/PNYW* SR4 .... 143 D1
Heathway *JRW* NE32 .... 86 B6
  SEA/MUR SR7 .... 176 B5
Heathwell Gdns
  WICK/BNPF NE16 .... 96 A2 2
Heathwell Rd
  BW/LEM/TK/HW NE15 .... 77 E1
Heathwood Av *WICK/BNPF* NE16 .. 95 F3 6

Heaton Gdns *HAR/WTLS* NE34 .... 88 B6
Heaton Gv *BYK/HTN/WLK* NE6 .... 82 A1
Heaton Hall Rd *BYK/HTN/WLK* NE6 .. 82 A1
Heaton Park Rd
  BYK/HTN/WLK NE6 .... 81 F1
Heaton Park Vw
  BYK/HTN/WLK NE6 .... 82 A1
Heaton Pl *BYK/HTN/WLK* NE6 .... 82 A1 2
Heaton Rd *BYK/HTN/WLK* NE6 .... 65 D5
Heaton Ter *BYK/HTN/WLK* NE6 .... 81 F2
  NSHW NE29 .... 54 A6
Heaviside Pl *DHAM* DH1 .... 195 D4
Heber St *ELS/FEN* NE4 .... 2 A3
Hebron Wy *CRAM* NE23 .... 21 F3
Hector St *SMOOR* NE27 .... 38 B6
Heddon Banks
  BW/LEM/TK/HW NE15 .... 56 A5
Heddon Cl *GOS/KPK* NE3 .... 46 C6 3
Heddon Vw *BLAY* NE21 .... 76 A6
Heddon Wy *HAR/WTLS* NE34 .... 88 A2
Hedge Cl *DUN/TMV* NE11 .... 98 A3
Hedgefield Gv *BLYTH* NE24 .... 16 B3
Hedgefield Vw *CRAM* NE23 .... 34 C1
Hedgehope Rd
  WD/WHPE/BLK NE5 .... 60 C2
Hedgelea *RYTON* NE40 .... 74 A3
Hedgelea Rd *HLH* DH5 .... 184 B1
Hedgeley Rd *HEBB* NE31 .... 85 D2
  NSHW NE29 .... 53 F5 1
  WD/WHPE/BLK NE5 .... 60 A6 2
Hedgeley Vw *BYK/HTN/WLK* NE6 .. 83 E2 3
Hedley La *ASHBK/HED/RY* SR2 ...... 114 B6
Hedley Pl *WLSD/HOW* NE28 .... 67 D5 3
Hedley Rd *MONK* NE25 .... 25 D6
  NSHW NE29 .... 70 B3
Hedley St *GATE* NE8 .... 98 C2
  GOS/KPK NE3 .... 63 E1
  SSH NE33 .... 71 E2 1
Hedley Ter *ASHBK/HED/RY* SR2 .. 162 C2 2
  GOS/KPK NE3 .... 47 E6
Hedworth Av *HAR/WTLS* NE34 ...... 87 F4 2
Hedworth La *BOLCOL* NE35 .... 104 C1
  JRW NE32 .... 86 C6
Hedworth Ter *SUND* SR1 .... 5 F3
Heighley St *BW/LEM/TK/HW* NE15 .. 77 E3
Helen St *BLAY* NE21 .... 75 F6
  CLDN/WHIT/ROK SR6 .... 109 D6
Helford Rd *PLEE/EAS* SR8 .... 208 B4
Helmdon *WASHN* NE37 .... 121 D4
Helmsdale Av *FELL* NE10 .... 100 C1 4
Helmsdale Rd *MLFD/PNYW* SR4 .... 142 C1
Helmsley Cl *HLS* DH4 .... 156 C2
Helmsley Ct *SWCK/CAS* SR5 .... 125 D1
Helmsley Dr *WLSD/HOW* NE28 ...... 68 B4
Helmsley Rd *DHAM* DH1 .... 180 B5 1
  JES NE2 .... 81 E1
Helston Ct
  BW/LEM/TK/HW NE15 .... 76 A1 4
Helvellyn Av *WASHS* NE38 .... 137 F3
Helvellyn Rd *ASHBK/HED/RY* SR2 .. 144 C4
Hemingston Cl
  ASHBK/HED/RY SR2 .... 162 B2 2
Hemmel Cts *BDN/LAN/SAC* DH7 .. 203 E3 3
Hemming St
  ASHBK/HED/RY SR2 .... 145 E4 2
Hemsley Rd *HAR/WTLS* NE34 .... 72 B5
Henderson Av *WICK/BNPF* NE16 .... 95 F2 3
Henderson Gdns *FELL* NE10 .... 102 A3
Henderson Rd *HAR/WTLS* NE34 .... 87 E3
  MLFD/PNYW SR4 .... 143 E1
  WLSD/HOW NE28 .... 67 D3 1
Hendersyde Cl
  WD/WHPE/BLK NE5 .... 61 D3 1
Hendon Burn Av
  ASHBK/HED/RY SR2 .... 5 F6
Hendon Cl *NSHW* NE29 .... 70 C3 2
Hendon Gdns *JRW* NE32 .... 86 C6
Hendon Rd *LWF/SPW/WRK* NE9 .... 100 A2
  SUND SR1 .... 5 F2
Hendon Rd East *SUND* SR1 .... 5 H3
Hendon St *SUND* SR1 .... 5 G4
Hendon Valley Rd
  ASHBK/HED/RY SR2 .... 5 E6
Henley Av *CLSW/PEL* DH2 .... 152 A5
Henley Cl *CRAM* NE23 .... 22 C1
Henley Gdns *WLSD/HOW* NE28 ...... 69 D2
Henley Rd *MLFD/PNYW* SR4 .... 142 C1
  TYNE/NSHE NE30 .... 55 D3
Henley Wy *BOLCOL* NE35 .... 105 D2
Henlow Rd
  BW/LEM/TK/HW NE15 .... 76 B1 6
Henry Nelson St *SSH* NE33 .... 71 F2
Henry Sq *JES* NE2 .... 3 G2 1
Henry St *GOS/KPK* NE3 .... 63 E1
  HLH DH5 .... 171 F4
  HLH DH5 .... 171 D1
  NSHW NE29 .... 70 C1
  SEA/MUR SR7 .... 176 C2 1
  SSH NE33 .... 71 F2 2
Henry St East *ASHBK/HED/RY* SR2 .... 5 G4
Hensby Ct *WD/WHPE/BLK* NE5 .... 61 D2 2
Henshaw Gv *MONK* NE25 .... 25 E6
Henshaw Pl *WD/WHPE/BLK* NE5 .... 77 F1
Henshelwood Ter *JES* NE2 .... 64 A5 1
Henson Cl *WASHS* NE38 .... 138 C3

Hepburn Gdns *FELL* NE10 .... **100** B1
Hepburn Gv *SWCK/CAS* SR5 ...... **123** E3 6
Hepple Ct *BLYTH* NE24 .... **10** B6 6
Hepple Wy *GOS/KPK* NE3 .... **46** C6 6
Hepscott Dr *MONK* NE25 .... **39** F4
Hepscott Ter *HAR/WTLS* NE34 .... **88** C1
Herbert St *GATE* NE8 .... **99** F1
Herbert Ter *SEA/MUR* SR7 .... **176** C3
Herd Cl *BLAY* NE21 .... **93** F1 6
Herd House La *BLAY* NE21 .... **75** E6
Herdinghill *WASHN* NE37 .... **119** E6
Herdlaw *CRAM* NE23 .... **21** F2
Hereford Ct
  ASHBK/HED/RY SR2 .... **144** C5 6
  DIN/WO NE13 .... **45** F4
Hereford Rd *ASHBK/HED/RY* SR2 .. **144** C5
Herefordshire Dr *DHAM* DH1 .... **196** B3
Hereford Sq
  ASHBK/HED/RY SR2 .... **144** C5 6
Hermiston *MONK* NE25 .... **40** A3
Heron Cl *BLYTH* NE24 .... **17** D3
  WASHS NE38 .... **137** F4
Heron Dr *SSH* NE33 .... **71** E2
Heron Pl *LGB/KIL* NE12 .... **48** C5 6
Herrick St *WD/WHPE/BLK* NE5 .... **60** C3
Herring Gull Cl *BLYTH* NE24 .... **17** D3
Herrington Rd *HLS* DH4 .... **158** B2
  SUNDSW SR3 .... **159** D1
Hersham Cl *DIN/WO* NE13 .... **45** F4 2
  DIN/WO NE13 .... **45** E4 1
  GOS/KPK NE3 .... **45** F5
Hertford *LWF/SPW/WRK* NE9 .... **117** E2
Hertford Av *HAR/WTLS* NE34 .... **90** A1
Hertford Cl *MONK* NE25 .... **39** E4
Hertford Crs *HLH* DH5 .... **171** E6
Hertford Gv *CRAM* NE23 .... **22** B1
Herton Cl *PLEE/EAS* SR8 .... **208** B1
Hesket Ct *GOS/KPK* NE3 .... **46** A5 5
Hesleden Rd *RHTLP* TS27 .... **209** F6
Hesleyside Dr *WD/WHPE/BLK* NE5 .. **61** D6
Hesleyside Rd *MONK* NE25 .... **39** D5
Hester Av *MONK* NE25 .... **24** C2
Hetton Rd *HLH* DH5 .... **171** D3
Heugh Hi *LWF/SPW/WRK* NE9 ..... **119** F2
Hewitson Ter *FELL* NE10 .... **100** B3
Hewitt Av *ASHBK/HED/RY* SR2 ..... **145** D6
Hewley Crs *BW/LEM/TK/HW* NE15... **57** F5
Hextol Gdns
  BW/LEM/TK/HW NE15 .... **77** E1 3
Heybrook Av *NSHW* NE29 .... **54** B4
Heyburn Gdns
  BW/LEM/TK/HW NE15............ **78** C3
Hibernian Rd *JRW* NE32 .... **86** A1 8
Hibernia Rd *BYK/HTN/WLK* NE6 .... **83** F4 5
Hickling Ct *WD/WHPE/BLK* NE5 ..... **61** D2
Hickstead Cl *WLSD/HOW* NE28 ... **52** A5 2
Hickstead Gv *CRAM* NE23 .... **22** C1
Hiddleston Av *LGB/HTN* NE7 .... **65** D1
Higgins Ter *SUNDSW* SR3 .... **161** D1
Higham Pl *CNUT* NE1 .... **3** E2 1
High Back Cl *JRW* NE32 .... **85** F4
High Barnes Ter
  MLFD/PNYW SR4 .... **143** F1 6
High Br *CNUT* NE1 .... **2** D4
  MONK NE25 .... **40** A5 1
Highbury Av *LWF/SPW/WRK* NE9 .. **119** F2
Highbury Cl *LWF/SPW/WRK* NE9 ... **119** F2
Highbury Pl *NSHW* NE29 .... **70** B1
High Carr Cl *DHAM* DH1 .... **134** A1
High Chare *CLS/BIR/GTL* DH3 ...... **153** E5
Highcliffe Gdns *GATE* NE8 .... **99** F2 6
High Cft *CLDN/WHIT/ROK* SR6..... **109** E1
  WASHN NE37 .... **120** A3
High Croft Cl *HEBB* NE31 .... **84** C4 5
Highcroft Dr
  CLDN/WHIT/ROK SR6 .... **109** D1 1
Highcross Rd *TYNE/NSHE* NE30 .... **54** C1
High Dene *LGB/HTN* NE7 .... **64** C5
Highfield *BDN/LAN/SAC* DH7 .... **178** B1
  WICK/BNPF NE16 .... **84** A1
Highfield Cl *WD/WHPE/BLK* NE5 ... **60** B3 8
Highfield Ct *FELL* NE10 .... **101** D3 5
Highfield Crs *CLS/BIR/GTL* DH3 ... **153** E3
Highfield Dr *HAR/WTLS* NE34 .... **72** B6
  HLS DH4 .... **170** A2
Highfield Gra *HLS* DH4 .... **170** A3 1
Highfield Pl *DIN/WO* NE13 .... **32** C5 4
Highfield Ri *CLS/BIR/GTL* DH3 ..... **153** E3

Highfield Rd *GATE* NE8 .... **99** F1
  HAR/WTLS NE34 .... **72** B6
  HLS DH4 .... **156** C2
  ROWG NE39 .... **110** B3
  WD/WHPE/BLK NE5 .... **60** B4
Highfield Ter *BYK/HTN/WLK* NE6 ... **83** F4 7
High Flatworth *NSHW* NE29 .... **69** F2
Highgate Gdns *JRW* NE32 .... **86** C6 1
Highgreen Cha *MLFD/PNYW* SR4 .. **142** C1
The High Ga *GOS/KPK* NE3............. **62** A2
Highgreen Cha *WICK/BNPF* NE16 ... **95** F6
High Gv *RYTON* NE40 .... **74** C4
Highgrove *WD/WHPE/BLK* NE5 ...... **59** F4
Highheath *WASHN* NE37 .... **119** F6 1
High Heworth La *FELL* NE10 .... **101** E2
High Horse Cl *ROWG* NE39 .... **93** F6
High Horse Close Wd *ROWG* NE39 .. **93** F6
High House Gdns *FELL* NE10 .... **101** D1 1
Highland Rd *WD/WHPE/BLK* NE5 ... **61** F3
High La *HLS* DH4 .... **158** B4
High Lane Rw *HEBB* NE31 .... **68** B6
High La *FELL* NE10........................ **101** E3
High Laws *GOS/KPK* NE3 .... **64** B2
High Level Br *CNUT* NE1 .... **3** E5
High Meadow *HAR/WTLS* NE34...... **72** B6
High Mdw *BDN/LAN/SAC* DH7 ...... **202** C3
High Moor Pl *HAR/WTLS* NE34 ...... **88** B3 10
High Pasture *WASHS* NE38 .... **139** D5 1
High Rdg *DIN/WO* NE13 .... **33** D5 2
The High Rd *HAR/WTLS* NE34 .... **89** E2
High Rw *BW/LEM/TK/HW* NE15 ...... **76** B2
High Sandgrove
  CLDN/WHIT/ROK SR6 .... **107** F1
Highside Dr *SUNDSW* SR3 .... **143** F3
Highstead Av *CRAM* NE23 .... **13** F5
High St *BDN/LAN/SAC* DH7 .... **204** A3
  BLYTH NE24 .... **10** C5 1
  BW/LEM/TK/HW NE15............. **75** E1
  DHAM DH1 .... **196** B2
  FELL NE10 .... **100** C2
  GATE NE8 .... **3** F6
  GOS/KPK NE3 .... **63** E1
  HLH DH5 .... **186** B3
  JRW NE32 .... **86** B1
  MLFD/PNYW SR4 .... **123** F6
  RDHAMSE DH6 .... **184** A6
  STLY/ANP DH9 .... **148** B1
High St East *SUND* SR1 .... **5** F1
  WLSD/HOW NE28 .... **67** E5
High Street South Back
  BDN/LAN/SAC DH7 .... **204** A3
High St West *BYK/HTN/WLK* NE6 ... **66** C5
  SUND SR1 .... **4** C2
High Swinburne Pl
  ELS/FEN NE4 .... **80** A3 11
Hightree Cl *SUNDSW* SR3 .... **160** B3 6
  SUNDSW SR3 .... **160** C3 3
High Vw *WLSD/HOW* NE28.............. **67** D3
High Vw North *WLSD/HOW* NE28.... **67** D2
Highwell La *WD/WHPE/BLK* NE5 .... **60** A5 6
High West St *GATE* NE8 .... **81** D5 7
Highwood Rd
  BW/LEM/TK/HW NE15............. **77** E1
High Wood Vw *DHAM* DH1 .... **194** C6
Highworth Dr *LGB/HTN* NE7 .... **66** A3 8
  LWF/SPW/WRK NE9 .... **119** E2
Hilda Av *DHAM* DH1 .... **195** F5
Hilda Cl *DHAM* DH1 .... **196** A5
Hilda Pk *CLSW/PEL* DH2 .... **153** D3
Hilda St *CLDN/WHIT/ROK* SR6 .... **126** C1 6
  GATE NE8.................................... **98** C1
Hilden Gdns *LGB/HTN* NE7............. **65** E4
Hillary Av *LGB/KIL* NE12 .... **50** A4
Hillary Pl *WD/WHPE/BLK* NE5 .... **60** C3 6
Hill Av *CRAM* NE23.......................... **23** F6
Hill Crs *SEA/MUR* SR7 .... **177** D5
  SEA/MUR SR7 .... **188** B1
Hill Crest *BDN/LAN/SAC* DH7 ...... **178** B2
  WICK/BNPF NE16 .... **112** A6
Hillcrest *DHAM* DH1 .... **194** C4
  HAR/WTLS NE34 .... **90** A4
  JRW NE32 .... **86** B6
  MONK NE25................................ **40** A5
  SUNDSW SR3 .... **159** D1
Hill Crest *DUN/TMV* NE11............... **97** D3
Hill Crest Gdns *JES* NE2 .... **64** A7 8
Hillcroft *LWF/SPW/WRK* NE9 .... **99** F4
Hill Dyke *LWF/SPW/WRK* NE9 ...... **118** B2
Hillfield *MONK* NE25 .... **39** F5
Hillfield Gdns *SUNDSW* SR3 .... **144** A3
Hillfield St *GATE* NE8 .... **81** D6
Hillgate *GATE* NE8 .... **3** F6
Hill Head Dr *WD/WHPE/BLK* NE5 ... **59** F5
Hillhead Gdns *DUN/TMV* NE11 ...... **97** F4 8
Hillhead La *WICK/BNPF* NE16 ...... **112** C3
Hillhead Pkwy *WD/WHPE/BLK* NE5 .. **59** E4
Hill Head Rd *WD/WHPE/BLK* NE5 ... **59** F4
Hillheads Rd *MONK* NE25 .... **54** B1
Hillhead Wy *WD/WHPE/BLK* NE5 ... **60** A3
Hill House Rd
  BW/LEM/TK/HW NE15............. **57** D4
Hillingdon Gv *MLFD/PNYW* SR4 ... **141** F4
Hill La *HLS* DH4 .... **140** B5
Hillmeads *CLSW/PEL* DH2 .... **165** E6
Hill Park Rd *JRW* NE32 .... **86** B3

Hill Ri *WASHS* NE38 .... **121** D6
Hillrise Crs *SEA/MUR* SR7 .... **174** C2
Hillsden Rd *MONK* NE25 .... **39** F3
Hillside *BDN/LAN/SAC* DH7 .... **178** A3
  BLAY NE21 .... **76** A6
  BOL NE36 .... **105** F3 6
  CLS/BIR/GTL DH3 .... **136** C2
  CLS/BIR/GTL DH3 .... **153** E4
  DUN/TMV NE11 .... **97** D3
  HAR/WTLS NE34 .... **90** A4
  SUNDSW SR3 .... **144** B3
Hillside Av *BW/LEM/TK/HW* NE15... **77** C1
Hillside Cl *ROWG* NE39 .... **111** D1 3
Hillside Crs *BW/LEM/TK/HW* NE15 .. **77** F4
Hillside Dr *CLDN/WHIT/ROK* SR6 .. **109** D1
Hillside Gdns *STLY/ANP* DH9 .... **131** F6
  SUNDSW SR3 .... **144** B3 5
Hillside Pl *LWF/SPW/WRK* NE9 ...... **99** F4
Hillside Wy *HLS* DH4 .... **171** D1
Hillsleigh Rd *WD/WHPE/BLK* NE5 .. **61** F3
Hill St *JRW* NE32 .... **85** F1
  SEA/MUR SR7 .... **176** C4
  SSH NE33 .... **71** F3
  SUNDSW SR3 .... **160** C1
Hillsview Av *GOS/KPK* NE3 .... **62** B1 5
Hill Ter *HLS* DH4 .... **158** A2 1
Hillthorne Cl *WASHS* NE38 .... **139** E2 5
Hill Top *BLAY* NE21 .... **94** A1
  CLS/BIR/GTL DH3 .... **136** C2
  STLY/ANP DH9 .... **149** D1
Hill Top Av *LWF/SPW/WRK* NE9...... **99** F5
Hill Top Gdns *LWF/SPW/WRK* NE9 .. **99** F5
Hilltop Gdns *SUNDSW* SR3 .... **161** E1 3
Hillview *SUNDSW* SR3 .... **159** D1
Hillview Crs *HLS* DH4 .... **157** F5 9
Hill View Gdns *SUNDSW* SR3 .... **144** A3
Hillview Gv *HLS* DH4 .... **157** F5 6
Hill View Rd *ASHBK/HED/RY* SR2 .. **145** D4
Hillview Rd *HLS* DH4 .... **157** F5 5
Hill View Sq *ASHBK/HED/RY* SR2 .. **144** C4
Hilton Av *WD/WHPE/BLK* NE5 .... **61** D4
Hilton Cl *CRAM* NE23 .... **13** F4
Hilton Dr *PLEE/EAS* SR8 .... **208** C3
Hindley Gdns *ELS/FEN* NE4 .... **78** C1
Hindmarch Dr *BOL* NE36 .... **105** F3
Hind St *SUND* SR1 .... **4** A3 11
Hinkley Cl *SUNDSW* SR3 .... **160** C2
Hipsburn Dr *SUNDSW* SR3 .... **143** F3
Hiram Dr *BOL* NE36 .... **106** C3
Histon Wy *WD/WHPE/BLK* NE5 ...... **61** D3
Hither Gn *JRW* NE32 .... **86** C6 2
Hobart Av *WD/WHPE/BLK* NE5 ...... **60** D4
Hobart Rd *WD/WHPE/BLK* NE5 ...... **60** B3
Hobart Av *HAR/WTLS* NE34 .... **87** E4
Hodgkin Park Crs
  BW/LEM/TK/HW NE15............. **78** B3
Hodgkin Park Rd
  BW/LEM/TK/HW NE15............. **78** B3
Hodgson's Rd *BLYTH* NE24 .... **10** C4
Hodkin Gdns *LWF/SPW/WRK* NE9 .. **100** A4
Hogarth Dr *WASHS* NE38 .... **139** D3
Hogarth Rd *HAR/WTLS* NE34 .... **88** B5
Holbein Rd *HAR/WTLS* NE34 .... **88** B5
Holborn Pl *WD/WHPE/BLK* NE5 .... **60** A5 12
Holborn Rd *MLFD/PNYW* SR4 ...... **142** C2
Holborn Sq *MLFD/PNYW* SR4 ...... **142** C2 9
Holburn Cl *RYTON* NE40 .... **74** C3 11
Holburn Ct *BDN/LAN/SAC* DH7 ... **192** A5 13
  RYTON NE40 .... **74** C3 2
Holburn Gdns *RYTON* NE40 .... **75** D3
Holburn La *RYTON* NE40 .... **74** C3
Holburn Ter *RYTON* NE40 .... **75** D3
Holburn Wk *RYTON* NE40 .... **75** D3
Holburn Wy *RYTON* NE40 .... **74** C3
Holden Pl *WD/WHPE/BLK* NE5 ...... **61** F4 7
Holder House La *HAR/WTLS* NE34 .. **89** D5
Holderness Rd *BYK/HTN/WLK* NE6.. **65** D5
  WLSD/HOW NE28 .... **68** C3
Hole La *WICK/BNPF* NE16............... **95** F5
Holeyn Rd *BW/LEM/TK/HW* NE15 .. **57** E5 1
Holland Dr *JES* NE2 .... **80** A1
Holland Pk *WLSD/HOW* NE28 .... **66** A3
Holland Park Dr *JRW* NE32 .... **86** C6
Hollinghill Rd *MONK* NE25 .... **25** D6
Hollings Crs *WLSD/HOW* NE28 ...... **67** D2 8
Hollingside La *DHAM* DH1 .... **205** E2
Hollington Av *LGB/KIL* NE12 .... **49** D6
Hollinhill *ROWG* NE39 .... **95** H6
Hollinhill La *ROWG* NE39 .... **93** E6
Hollinside Cl *WICK/BNPF* NE16 ..... **95** F5
Hollinside Gdns
  BW/LEM/TK/HW NE15............. **78** A2
Hollinside Rd *MLFD/PNYW* SR4.... **142** C2
  WICK/BNPF NE16 .... **78** A6
Hollinside Sq *MLFD/PNYW* SR4 ... **142** B1
Hollinside Ter *ROWG* NE39 .... **110** C2 3
Hollowdene *HLH* DH5 .... **185** F1
Holly Av *BLAY* NE21 .... **94** B4
  CLDN/WHIT/ROK SR6 .... **109** E2
  DUN/TMV NE11 .... **97** E3
  GOS/KPK NE3 .... **46** B6
  HAR/WTLS NE34 .... **89** F3
  HLH DH5 .... **171** D2
  JES NE2 .... **64** A5
  LGB/KIL NE12 .... **49** F3
  MONK NE25................................ **39** D5

RYTON NE40 .... **74** B2
SUNDSW SR3................ **144** A6
WBAY NE26 .... **40** C5
WLSD/HOW NE28 .... **67** E5
Holly Av West JES NE2 .... **64** A5
Hollybush Rd FELL NE10 .... **100** B2
Hollycarrside Rd
  ASHBK/HED/RY SR2........ **145** D6
Holly Crs BDN/LAN/SAC DH7 .... **178** B2
Hollydene DUN/TMV NE11 .... **116** C6
  ROWG NE39................ **111** E2
Holly Hvn HLH DH5 .... **170** C6
Holly Hl FELL NE10 .... **100** C2
Holly Hill Gdns STLY/ANP DH9 .... **148** B4
Holly Hill Gdns East
  STLY/ANP DH9 .... **148** C4
Holly Hill Gdns West
  STLY/ANP DH9 .... **148** B4
Hollymount Sq BDLGTN NE22 .... **7** F4
Holly Pk BDN/LAN/SAC DH7 .... **203** D4
Holly Rd WD FELL NE10 .... **100** C2
Holly Rd NSHW NE29 .... **54** B5
The Hollys CLS/BIR/GTL DH3 .... **118** A5
Holly St DHAM DH1 .... **194** A5
  JRW NE32................. **85** F1
Hollywell Ct BDN/LAN/SAC DH7 .... **192** A5
Hollywell Gv DIN/WO NE13 .... **44** B4
Hollywell Rd NSHW NE29.... **53** F6
Hollywood Av GOS/KPK NE3 .... **47** E6
  SWCK/CAS SR5 .... **125** E2
Hollywood Crs GOS/KPK NE3 .... **47** F6
Hollywood Gdns DUN/TMV NE11 .. **98** A5
  WICK/BNPF NE16.......... **96** A3
Holme Gdns SUNDSW SR3 .... **144** A3
  WLSD/HOW NE28 .... **68** C4
Holme Ri WICK/BNPF NE16 .... **96** A3
Holmesdale Rd
  WD/WHPE/BLK NE5 .... **61** F5
Holmeside SUND SR1 .... **4** C3
Holmewood Dr ROWG NE39 .... **110** C4
Holmfield Av HAR/WTLS NE34 .... **89** D1
Holm Gn MONK NE25 .... **39** F6
Holmhill La CLS/BIR/GTL DH3 .... **166** B3
  PLEE/EAS SR8 .... **200** C1
Holmland BW/LEM/TK/HW NE15 .... **78** B4
Holmlands MONK NE25 ...... **40** A3
Holmlands Pk North
  ASHBK/HED/RY SR2........ **144** B2
Holmlands Pk South
  ASHBK/HED/RY SR2........ **144** B2
Holmside Av DUN/TMV NE11 .... **97** F2
Holmwood Av MONK NE25 .... **39** F6
Holmwood Gv JES NE2 ..... **63** F4
Holyfields SMOOR NE27 .... **51** F2
Holylake Sq MLFD/PNYW SR4 .... **142** C1
Holyoake Gdns
  CLS/BIR/GTL DH3 .... **136** B2
  LWF/SPW/WRK NE9 .... **99** E2
Holyoake St CLSW/PEL DH2 .... **151** E2
Holystone Av GOS/KPK NE3 .... **47** D6
  MONK NE25............... **41** D6
Holystone Cl BLYTH NE24 .... **16** B1
  HLS DH4 .... **157** D6
Holystone Crs LGB/HTN NE7 .... **64** C3
Holystone Dr SMOOR NE27 .... **51** E2
Holystone Gdns NSHW NE29.... **53** F5
Holystone St HEBB NE31 .... **84** C2
Holywell Av BYK/HTN/WLK NE6 .... **83** D5
  MONK NE25............... **25** E6
  WBAY NE26 .... **40** A4
Holywell Cl ELS/FEN NE4 .... **80** A2
  MONK NE25............... **25** E6
Holywell Dene Rd MONK NE25.... **38** B1
Home Av LWF/SPW/WRK NE9 .... **99** E6
Home Pk WLSD/HOW NE28 .... **66** A3
Homestall Cl HAR/WTLS NE34 .... **88** C3
Honeycomb Cl SUNDSW SR3 .... **160** B3
Honeysuckle Av HAR/WTLS NE34.... **88** A4
Honeysuckle Cl SUNDSW SR3 .... **160** C3
Honister Av JES NE2 ...... **64** A3
Honister Cl
  BW/LEM/TK/HW NE15 ...... **76** C1
Honister Dr SWCK/CAS SR5 .... **126** B1
Honister Pl BW/LEM/TK/HW NE15 .... **76** C1
Honister Rd TYNE/NSHE NE30 .... **55** F2
Honister Wy BLYTH NE24.... **16** B3
Honiton Cl HLS DH4 .... **157** E4
Honiton Ct WD/WHPE/BLK NE5 .... **45** D6
Honiton Wy NSHW NE29 .... **53** D4
Hood Cl SWCK/CAS SR5 .... **126** B3
Hood St CNUT NE1 .... **2** D3
  WICK/BNPF NE16.......... **95** F1
Hooper Ter RDHAMSE DH6 .... **208** B2
Hopedene FELL NE10 .... **101** F5
Hope Shield WASHS NE38 .... **137** E5
Hope St HAR/WTLS NE34 .... **88** A3
  JRW NE32................. **86** B1
  RDHAMSE DH6 .... **197** E5
  SUND SR1 .... **4** A3
Hopgarth Gdns CLS/BIR/GTL DH3.... **153** F4
Hopkins Ct MLFD/PNYW SR4.... **125** E5
Hopper Pl GATE NE8 .... **81** E5
Hopper Rd FELL NE10....... **100** B3
Hopper St GATE NE8 .... **81** E5

NSHW NE29................. **70** B1
WLSD/HOW NE28 .... **67** D4
Horatio St CLDN/WHIT/ROK SR6 .... **127** D3
  CNUT NE1 .... **81** F3
Hornbeam Pl ELS/FEN NE4 .... **80** A5
Horncliffe Gdns
  WICK/BNPF NE16 .... **96** B3
Horncliffe Pl
  BW/LEM/TK/HW NE15...... **57** D4
Hornsea Cl DIN/WO NE13 .... **33** D5
Hornsey Ter HLH DH5 ...... **186** A3
Horse Crofts BLAY NE21 .... **76** B5
Horsham Gdns SUNDSW SR3 .... **143** F5
Horsham Gv NSHW NE29..... **70** A2
Horsley Av SMOOR NE27 .... **52** B2
Horsley Ct GOS/KPK NE3 .... **46** A6
  MONK NE25............... **25** E6
Horsley Gdns DUN/TMV NE11.... **97** F2
  MONK NE25............... **25** E6
Horsley Gv SUNDSW SR3 .... **143** F3
Horsley Hill Rd SSH NE33.... **72** A5
Horsley Hill Sq HAR/WTLS NE34 .... **90** A1
Horsley Rd LGB/HTN NE7.... **65** D5
  WASHS NE38 .... **121** F6
Horsley Ter BYK/HTN/WLK NE6 .... **83** E1
Horsley V HAR/WTLS NE34.... **89** C1
Horton Av BDLGTN NE22 .... **7** E4
  HAR/WTLS NE34 .... **88** C5
  SMOOR NE27.............. **52** B2
Horton Crs DIN/WO NE13 .... **31** D5
Hortondale Gv BLYTH NE24.... **10** A5
Horton Dr CRAM NE23 ...... **13** F5
Horton Pl BLYTH NE24 ..... **16** A2
Horton Rd BLYTH NE24..... **8** B6
Horwood Av WD/WHPE/BLK NE5.... **59** F4
Hospital Dr HEBB NE31 .... **84** C4
Hospital La BW/LEM/TK/HW NE15 .... **76** A1
Hotch Pudding Pl
  WD/WHPE/BLK NE5 ...... **60** B6
Hotspur Av BDLGTN NE22 .... **7** E4
  HAR/WTLS NE34 .... **89** D1
  MONK NE25............... **40** C6
Hotspur Rd WLSD/HOW NE28 .... **66** C1
Hotspur St BYK/HTN/WLK NE6 .... **81** F1
  TYNE/NSHE NE30 .... **55** F4
Houghton Av TYNE/NSHE NE30 .... **55** D1
  WD/WHPE/BLK NE5 ...... **61** F3
Houghton Cut HLH DH5 .... **171** D1
Houghton Rd HLH DH5 ..... **171** E4
  HLS DH4 .... **157** F5
Houghton St MLFD/PNYW SR4 .... **125** F6
Houlskye Cl SUNDSW SR3 .... **161** E1
Houndelee Pl
  WD/WHPE/BLK NE5 ...... **61** E5
Hounslow Gdns JRW NE32 .... **86** C6
House Ter WASHN NE37 .... **120** C4
Houston St ELS/FEN NE4 .... **80** A4
Houxty Rd MONK NE25 ..... **39** D5
Hovingham La PLEE/EAS SR8 .... **209** D3
Hovingham Gdns SUNDSW SR3 .... **143** F5
Howardian Cl WASHS NE38 .... **138** A3
Howard St CNUT NE1 .... **3** H3
  FELL NE10 .... **100** A1
  GATE NE8 .... **100** A1
  JRW NE32................. **86** B2
  SWCK/CAS SR5 .... **126** C3
  TYNE/NSHE NE30 .... **55** D6
Howarth St MLFD/PNYW SR4 .... **125** F6
Howat Av WD/WHPE/BLK NE5 .... **62** A5
Howdene Rd
  BW/LEM/TK/HW NE15...... **77** E2
Howdon La WLSD/HOW NE28 .... **68** C3
Howdon Rd NSHW NE29 ..... **70** C2
  WLSD/HOW NE28 .... **69** E4
Howe Sq MLFD/PNYW SR4 .... **142** B1
Howe St GATE NE8 .... **100** A1
  HEBB NE31 .... **85** F2
Howick Av GOS/KPK NE3 .... **46** C5
Howletch La PLEE/EAS SR8 .... **208** B2
Howlett Hall Rd
  BW/LEM/TK/HW NE15...... **77** E2
Howley Av SWCK/CAS SR5 .... **124** B2
Hownam Cl GOS/KPK NE3 .... **62** C2
Hoy Crs SEA/MUR SR7 ...... **175** E1
Hoylake Av LGB/HTN NE7 .... **65** E1
Hoyle Av ELS/FEN NE4 ..... **79** D2
Hoyle Fold SUNDSW SR3 .... **160** C4
Hubert St BOLCOL NE35 .... **105** E2
Huddleston Ri
  CLDN/WHIT/ROK SR6 ..... **127** D4
Huddleston Rd BYK/HTN/WLK NE6 .... **82** C1
Hudson Av BDLGTN NE22.... **8** A3
Hudson Rd SUND SR1 ...... **5** E3
Hudson St GATE NE8 .... **81** D5
  HAR/WTLS NE34 .... **88** A2
  TYNE/NSHE NE30 .... **55** E6
Hudspeth Crs DHAM DH1 .... **179** F5
Hugh St CLDN/WHIT/ROK SR6 .... **127** D1
  WASHS NE38 .... **139** E2
  WLSD/HOW NE28 .... **67** D5
Hull St ELS/FEN NE4 ...... **79** E4
Hulme Ct PLEE/EAS SR8 .... **208** B3
Hulne Av TYNE/NSHE NE30 .... **55** E5
Humber Gdns GATE NE8 .... **100** A1
Humber Hl STLY/ANP DH9 .... **148** C3
Humbert St JRW NE32 ...... **86** A2

Hume St BYK/HTN/WLK NE6 .... **81** F3
  MLFD/PNYW SR4 .... **125** F5
Humford Gn BLYTH NE24.... **9** E5
Humford Wy BDLGTN NE22.... **7** F5
Humsford Gv CRAM NE23 .... **14** B6
Humshaugh Cl LGB/KIL NE12 .... **50** C4
Humshaugh Rd NSHW NE29 .... **53** E6
Hunstanton Ct
  LWF/SPW/WRK NE9 .... **117** D1
Huntcliffe Av
  CLDN/WHIT/ROK SR6 ..... **109** D4
Huntcliffe Gdns BYK/HTN/WLK NE6.. **65** E5
Hunter Av BLYTH NE24.... **11** E6
Hunter Cl BOL NE36 ...... **106** C4
Hunter Rd PLEE/EAS SR8 .... **207** F3
Hunters Cl NSHW NE29..... **69** F3
Hunters Ct WLSD/HOW NE28 .... **67** E4
Hunters Hall Rd
  MLFD/PNYW SR4 .... **144** A1
Hunters Ldg WLSD/HOW NE28 .... **67** D4
Hunter's Moor Cl JES NE2 .... **62** C6
Hunter's Pl JES NE2 ..... **63** D6
Hunter's Rd GOS/KPK NE3 .... **64** B1
  JES NE2 .... **79** F1
Hunter St HLS DH4 .... **156** C3
  SSH NE33................ **71** F5
Hunter Ter ASHBK/HED/RY SR2 .... **145** D3
Huntingdon Cl DIN/WO NE13 .... **45** E4
Huntingdon Gdns
  SUNDSW SR3 .... **143** F3
Huntingdon Pl TYNE/NSHE NE30 .... **55** F5
Huntingdon Rd PLEE/EAS SR8 .... **200** B6
Huntingdonshire Dr DHAM DH1 .. **196** C3
Huntington Dr CRAM NE23 .... **22** B1
Hunt Lea WICK/BNPF NE16 .... **95** D5
Huntley Av SEA/MUR SR7 .... **188** A1
Huntley Crs BLAY NE21 .... **93** F2
Huntley Sq MLFD/PNYW SR4 .... **142** C1
Huntly Rd MONK NE25 ..... **39** E3
Hurst Ter BYK/HTN/WLK NE6 .... **83** D2
Hurstwood Rd MLFD/PNYW SR4 .... **143** F2
Hurworth Av HAR/WTLS NE34 .... **89** F2
Hurworth Pl JRW NE32 .... **86** A2
Hustledown Gdns
  STLY/ANP DH9 .... **148** B4
Hustledown Rd STLY/ANP DH9.... **148** A4
Hutton Cl HLS DH4 .... **170** B2
  WASHS NE38 .... **137** E1
Hutton St BOLCOL NE35 .... **105** D1
  MLFD/PNYW SR4 .... **144** A1
Hutton Ter JES NE2 ...... **81** E1
  LWF/SPW/WRK NE9 .... **99** E6
Huxley Crs GATE NE8 ...... **98** C3
Hyacinth Ct MLFD/PNYW SR4 .... **126** A5
Hyde Pk WLSD/HOW NE28.... **66** B3
Hydepark St GATE NE8 .... **98** C2
Hyde St ASHBK/HED/RY SR2 .... **145** E2
  SSH NE33................ **71** F4
Hyde Ter GOS/KPK NE3 .... **63** F1
Hylton Av HAR/WTLS NE34 .... **90** A2
Hylton Bank MLFD/PNYW SR4 .... **124** A6
Hylton Castle Rd SWCK/CAS SR5 .... **124** A3
Hylton Cl BDLGTN NE22 .... **6** C3
Hylton Gra SWCK/CAS SR5 .... **123** E5
Hylton La BOL NE36 ...... **105** F4
  SWCK/CAS SR5 .... **123** F1
Hylton Park Rd SWCK/CAS SR5 .... **125** D3
Hylton Rd DHAM DH1 .... **180** B6
  JRW NE32................. **86** A4
  MLFD/PNYW SR4 .... **125** D6
  MLFD/PNYW SR4 .... **126** A5
Hylton St GATE NE8 .... **100** A1
  HLS DH4 .... **157** F6
  MLFD/PNYW SR4 .... **125** F6
  NSHW NE29 .... **70** C2
Hylton Wk MLFD/PNYW SR4 .... **141** F1
  MLFD/PNYW SR4 .... **142** A1
Hymers Av HAR/WTLS NE34 .... **87** E4
Hyperion Av HAR/WTLS NE34 .... **87** F3

I

Ilchester St SEA/MUR SR7 .... **176** C4
Ilderton Pl WD/WHPE/BLK NE5 .... **60** A6
Ilex St DUN/TMV NE11 ..... **98** B4
Ilford Av CRAM NE23 ...... **13** F5
Ilford Pl GATE NE8........ **99** F2
Ilford Rd JES NE2 .... **63** F3
  WLSD/HOW NE28 .... **68** B3
Ilfracombe Av ELS/FEN NE4 .... **79** D3
Ilminster Ct GOS/KPK NE3 .... **45** E6
Imeary Gv SSH NE33 .... **71** F5
Imeary St SSH NE33 .... **71** F5
Inchberry Cl ELS/FEN NE4 .... **79** D4
Inchbury Cl ELS/FEN NE4 .... **79** D4
Inchcliffe Crs WD/WHPE/BLK NE5 .... **61** E4
Indigo St DUN/TMV NE11.... **98** B4
Industrial Rd WASHN NE37 .... **121** D5
Industrial St CLSW/PEL DH2 .... **151** E2
Industry Rd BYK/HTN/WLK NE6 .... **65** F4
Ingham Gra SSH NE33 ..... **72** A5
Ingham Gv CRAM NE23 ..... **13** F5
Ingleby Ter MLFD/PNYW SR4 .... **143** F1

Ingleby Wy *BLYTH* NE24...................... 16 C3
Inglemere Pl
  BW/LEM/TK/HW NE15............. 77 F2 **1**
Ingleside *WICK/BNPF* NE16................ 95 E4
Ingleside Rd *NSHW* NE29................... 54 B5
Ingleton Dr *BW/LEM/TK/HW* NE15... 57 D4
Ingleton Gdns *BLYTH* NE24................ 16 B3
Inglewood Cl *BLYTH* NE24.................... 9 E5
Inglewood Pl *GOS/KPK* NE3.............. 47 E3 **2**
Ingoe Av *GOS/KPK* NE3...................... 46 B5 **2**
Ingoe Cl *BLYTH* NE24........................ 10 B5
Ingoe St *BW/LEM/TK/HW* NE15....... 76 B2
  WLSD/HOW NE28............................ 69 E4
Ingoldsby Ct *MLFD/PNYW* SR4 ...... 143 D2 **3**
Ingram Av *GOS/KPK* NE3.................. 46 B4 **3**
Ingram Cl *CLSW/PEL* DH2................ 135 F1
  WLSD/HOW NE28............................ 68 B1 **1**
Ingram Dr *BLYTH* NE24..................... 10 A5
  WD/WHPE/BLK NE5......................... 59 F2
Ingram Ter *BYK/HTN/WLK* NE6...... 83 F2 **1**
Inkerman Rd *WASHN* NE37................ 120 C3
Inkerman St *SWCK/CAS* SR5............ 125 F3
Inleborough Dr *RYTON* NE40............. 74 C4
Innesmoor *HEBB* NE31...................... 84 C1
Inskip Ter *GATE* NE8.......................... 99 E2
Institute Ter West *CLSW/PEL* DH2 .. 135 E6
Inverness Rd *JRW* NE32..................... 87 D5
Inverness St *CLDN/WHIT/ROK* SR6.. 126 C2
Invincible Dr *ELS/FEN* NE4................ 79 F5
Iolanthe Crs *BYK/HTN/WLK* NE6...... 83 D1
Iolanthe Ter *SSH* NE33...................... 72 A4
Iona Pl *BYK/HTN/WLK* NE6............. 83 F2 **2**
Iona Rd *FELL* NE10.......................... 100 A3
  JRW NE32.. 87 D5
Irene Av *ASHBK/HED/RY* SR2......... 145 E5
Iris Crs *CLSW/PEL* DH2................... 135 E4
Iris Pl *ELS/FEN* NE4........................... 78 C1
Iris St *DUN/TMV* NE11....................... 98 B4
Iroko St *DUN/TMV* NE11.................... 98 B4
Ironside St *HLH* DH5........................ 171 D1
Irthing Av *BYK/HTN/WLK* NE6.......... 82 C4
Irton St *GOS/KPK* NE3....................... 63 E1
Irwin Av *WLSD/HOW* NE28................ 67 D3
Isabella Cl *ELS/FEN* NE4.................. 79 D5 **1**
Isabella Rd *BLYTH* NE24.................... 10 B6
Isabella Wk
  BW/LEM/TK/HW NE15............... 57 F5 **4**
Isis Rd *PLEE/EAS* SR8...................... 208 B3
Ivanhoe *MONK* NE25.......................... 40 A5
Ivanhoe Vw *LWF/SPW/WRK* NE9 .... 118 A2
Iveagh Cl *ELS/FEN* NE4..................... 78 C4
Iveson St *BDN/LAN/SAC* DH7.......... 178 A1
Iveston Ter *STLY/ANP* DH9............... 148 B1
Ivor St *ASHBK/HED/RY* SR2........... 145 F4
Ivy Av *RYTON* NE40.......................... 74 B2 **3**
  SEA/MUR SR7............................... 176 A3
Ivy Cl *ELS/FEN* NE4.......................... 80 A5
Ivy La *LWF/SPW/WRK* NE9............. 117 F1
Ivymount Rd *BYK/HTN/WLK* NE6...... 65 D5
Ivy Rd *BYK/HTN/WLK* NE6............... 66 B6
  GOS/KPK NE3................................. 62 A1
  LGB/KIL NE12................................ 50 A4
Ivy St *DUN/TMV* NE11....................... 98 B4
Ivyway *CLSW/PEL* DH2.................... 152 A1
Ixia St *DUN/TMV* NE11..................... 98 B4

J

Jackson Av *PONT/DH* NE20............... 28 B3
Jackson St *BYK/HTN/WLK* NE6 ...... 83 E2 **4**
  GATE NE8....................................... 81 E5
  MLFD/PNYW SR4........................... 143 F1
  TYNE/NSHE NE30.......................... 55 D6
Jackson St West *TYNE/NSHE* NE30 .. 55 D6
Jack's Ter *HAR/WTLS* NE34............... 88 B3
Jacques St *MLFD/PNYW* SR4 .... 125 E5 **3**
Jacques Ter *CLSW/PEL* DH2............ 153 D5
Jade Cl *BW/LEM/TK/HW* NE15......... 59 E6
James Armitage St
  SWCK/CAS SR5........................... 126 A2 **9**
James Mather St *SSH* NE33............... 71 F2
James St *ELS/FEN* NE4..................... 79 E4
  PLEE/EAS SR8.............................. 200 C1
  SEA/MUR SR7............................... 176 A2
  SWCK/CAS SR5............................ 125 F2 **8**
  WD/WHPE/BLK NE5....................... 60 B4 **4**
  WICK/BNPF NE16........................... 95 F5 **2**
James Ter *HLH* DH5........................ 186 A4
  HLS DH4.. 169 F2
  SUNDSW SR3............................... 161 D1
  WLSD/HOW NE28............................ 67 D5 **9**
James Williams St *SUND* SR1............. 5 F4
Jane Eyre Ter *GATE* NE8................ 100 A1 **8**
Jane St *BYK/HTN/WLK* NE6.............. 82 B2 **5**
Jane Ter *BYK/HTN/WLK* NE6............ 83 F3
Janet St *BYK/HTN/WLK* NE6............ 82 B3 **1**
Janus Cl *WD/WHPE/BLK* NE5........... 59 E2 **2**
Jarrow Rd *HAR/WTLS* NE34.............. 87 F2
  JRW NE32....................................... 87 E2
Jarvis Rd *PLEE/EAS* SR8................ 200 C6
Jasmin Av *WD/WHPE/BLK* NE5......... 59 E2
Jasmine Cl *BYK/HTN/WLK* NE6........ 66 A5

Jasmine Ct *MLFD/PNYW* SR4 .... 126 A5 **7**
Jasmine Crs *SEA/MUR* SR7............ 176 B5
Jasper Av *RYTON* NE40..................... 92 A1
Jedburgh Cl *GATE* NE8..................... 99 E1 **3**
  NSHW NE29.................................. 54 A4
  WD/WHPE/BLK NE5....................... 59 E2
Jedburgh Gdns
  BW/LEM/TK/HW NE15............... 78 A2
Jedburgh Rd *HLS* DH4.................... 157 D2 **4**
Jedmoor *HEBB* NE31........................ 84 C1
Jefferson Pl *ELS/FEN* NE4................ 80 A2 **7**
Jellicoe Rd *BYK/HTN/WLK* NE6........ 83 D5 **1**
Jenifer Gv *LGB/HTN* NE7.................. 64 C3
Jenison Av *BW/LEM/TK/HW* NE15... 78 B3
Jennifer Av *SWCK/CAS* SR5............ 124 A3 **5**
Jervis St *HEBB* NE31........................ 85 E2
Jesmond Dene Rd *JES* NE2............... 63 F4
Jesmond Gdns *JES* NE2................. 64 B5 **3**
Jesmond Pk East *LGB/HTN* NE7....... 65 D4
Jesmond Pk West *LGB/HTN* NE7...... 65 D5 **1**
Jesmond Rd *JES* NE2........................ 64 C6 **3**
Jesmond Ter *WBAY* NE26.................. 40 C6
Jesmond V *BYK/HTN/WLK* NE6........ 81 F1
Jesmond Vale La
  BYK/HTN/WLK NE6...................... 65 D6
Jessel St *LWF/SPW/WRK* NE9......... 99 E6
Joan Av *ASHBK/HED/RY* SR2......... 145 E5
Joannah St *SWCK/CAS* SR5........... 126 B1 **3**
Joan St *ELS/FEN* NE4........................ 78 C4
Jobling Av *BLAY* NE21........................ 75 F6
Joel Ter *FELL* NE10........................... 84 A6
John Av *RYTON* NE40......................... 92 A1
John Brown Ct *BDLGTN* NE22............ 7 E3 **3**
John Candlish Rd
  MLFD/PNYW SR4......................... 125 F5
John Clay St *SSH* NE33................... 71 F5 **6**
John Dobson St *CNUT* NE1................ 2 D1
John Reid Rd *HAR/WTLS* NE34......... 87 E4
Johnson Cl *PLEE/EAS* SR8............ 200 C6
Johnson St
  BW/LEM/TK/HW NE15............... 76 B2 **2**
  DUN/TMV NE11.............................. 97 E1
  GATE NE8....................................... 98 A1
  SSH NE33....................................... 88 B1
Johnston Av *HEBB* NE31.................. 84 C5
John St *BDN/LAN/SAC* DH7............ 178 B1
  BLYTH NE24................................. 10 A4
  DHAM DH1................................... 16 A4
  FELL NE10.................................. 101 E1 **3**
  GATE NE8.................................... 100 A1
  GOS/KPK NE3............................... 62 C1
  HLH DH5..................................... 171 E2
  HLH DH5..................................... 185 F1
  HLH DH5..................................... 186 A1 **1**
  HLS DH4...................................... 169 F2
  MLFD/PNYW SR4......................... 123 F5 **2**
  MONK NE25................................... 38 C5
  PLEE/EAS SR8............................ 201 D1
  STLY/ANP DH9.............................. 147 F4
  STLY/ANP DH9............................. 149 E6
  STLY/ANP DH9............................. 149 F1
  SUND SR1..................................... 4 D2 **1**
  TYNE/NSHE NE30.......................... 41 E6
  WLSD/HOW NE28........................... 67 D4
John Taylor Ct *SWCK/CAS* SR5...... 125 F1 **2**
John Williamson St *SSH* NE33.......... 88 A1
John Wilson Ct *PLEE/EAS* SR8 ..... 209 F1 **3**
Joicey Gdns *STLY/ANP* DH9............ 148 B1 **5**
Joicey Rd *LWF/SPW/WRK* NE9........ 99 E4
Joicey St *FELL* NE10....................... 101 F1
Jolliffe St *CLS/BIR/GTL* DH3........... 166 C1
Jonadab Rd *FELL* NE10.................... 83 F6
Jonadab St *FELL* NE10.................... 101 F1
Jones St *CLS/BIR/GTL* DH3............. 136 A2
Jonquil Cl *WD/WHPE/BLK* NE5........ 59 E2 **3**
Joseph Cl *ELS/FEN* NE4................... 79 D4
Joseph St *STLY/ANP* DH9.............. 148 A3 **1**
Jowett Sq *SWCK/CAS* SR5............. 125 F2 **3**
Joyce Ter *SWCK/CAS* SR5............. 124 A3 **3**
Jubilee Av *LWF/SPW/WRK* NE9....... 118 B3
Jubilee Ct *BDN/LAN/SAC* DH7........ 164 A3
Jubilee Crs *GOS/KPK* NE3................ 46 C6
Jubilee Pl *RDHAMSE* DH6............... 206 B1 **1**
Jubilee Rd *BLYTH* NE24.................... 11 D6
  CNUT NE1...................................... 3 C3
  GOS/KPK NE3................................ 62 B2
Jubilee Sq *HLH* DH5....................... 186 B3 **1**
Jubilee Ter *WICK/BNPF* NE16........... 95 F1 **1**
Jude Pl *PLEE/EAS* SR8.................... 200 B6 **1**
  PLEE/EAS SR8.............................. 200 C6 **1**
Julian Av *BYK/HTN/WLK* NE6........... 66 A6
  SSH NE33...................................... 71 F2
Julian Rd *FELL* NE10...................... 102 C2
Julian St *SSH* NE33.......................... 71 F2
Juliet Av *NSHW* NE29....................... 53 F6 **5**
Julius Caesar St *SWCK/CAS* SR5 ... 125 F2 **3**
June Av *BLAY* NE21.......................... 94 B4
Juniper Cl *BLYTH* NE24.................... 16 B2
  GOS/KPK NE3................................ 47 F3 **4**
Jupiter Ct *PLEE/EAS* SR8............... 200 B2 **1**
Jutland Av *HEBB* NE31..................... 85 D3
Jutland Ter *STLY/ANP* DH9............ 130 C6

K

Kalmia St *DUN/TMV* NE11................. 98 B5
Kane Gdns *FELL* NE10..................... 100 B4
Katrine Cl *CLSW/PEL* DH2.............. 153 D6
Katrine Ct *SUNDSW* SR3................ 160 C3 **4**
Kayll Rd *MLFD/PNYW* SR4.............. 125 E6
Kay St *STLY/ANP* DH9..................... 148 B1
Kearsley Cl *MONK* NE25................... 24 C5 **2**
Kearton Av *WD/WHPE/BLK* NE5...... 59 E3
Keats Av *BLYTH* NE24...................... 16 B1 **4**
  BOLCOL NE35................................ 106 A2
  SWCK/CAS SR5........................... 125 F2 **7**
Keats Cl *STLY/ANP* DH9................. 148 C2
Keats Rd *BW/LEM/TK/HW* NE15...... 75 F2
Keebledale Av
  BYK/HTN/WLK NE6....................... 83 E1 **1**
Keelman's La *MLFD/PNYW* SR4...... 124 A5
Keelman's Rd *MLFD/PNYW* SR4..... 124 A5
Keir Hardie Av *FELL* NE10............... 101 F2
  STLY/ANP DH9.............................. 148 B4
Keir Hardie St *HLS* DH4.................. 170 A2
Keir Hardie Wy *SWCK/CAS* SR5..... 126 A3
Keith Cl *ELS/FEN* NE4..................... 79 D4
Keldane Gdns *ELS/FEN* NE4............ 79 D3
Kelfield Gv *CRAM* NE23.................... 14 A4 **3**
Kellfield Av *LWF/SPW/WRK* NE9..... 99 F4
Kellfield Rd *LWF/SPW/WRK* NE9..... 99 F5
Kell Rd *PLEE/EAS* SR8................... 209 E2 **2**
Kells La *LWF/SPW/WRK* NE9........... 99 E6
Kellsway *FELL* NE10....................... 101 E5 **3**
Kell's Wy *ROWG* NE39.................... 111 D3
Kelly Rd *HEBB* NE31....................... 85 D5
Kelsey Wy *CRAM* NE23.................... 14 A4
Kelso Cl *WD/WHPE/BLK* NE5.......... 59 E2 **2**
Kelso Dr *NSHW* NE29....................... 54 A4
Kelso Gdns *BW/LEM/TK/HW* NE15 ... 78 A2
  WLSD/HOW NE28............................ 68 C2
Kelso Gv *HLS* DH4......................... 156 C2 **2**
Kelson Wy *WD/WHPE/BLK* NE5...... 59 E2 **3**
Kelso Pl *GATE* NE8.......................... 98 A1
Kelston Wy *WD/WHPE/BLK* NE5...... 61 E4
Kelvin Gv *CLDN/WHIT/ROK* SR6 .. 107 D1 **2**
  CLDN/WHIT/ROK SR6................... 127 D2
  GATE NE8....................................... 98 C2
  HAR/WTLS NE34............................. 72 B5
  JES NE2... 81 E1
  NSHW NE29.................................. 53 E5
Kemble Cl *CRAM* NE23..................... 14 A4 **4**
Kemp Rd *PLEE/EAS* SR8................ 208 B1
Kempton Gdns *GATE* NE8................ 98 B3 **1**
Kendal Av *BLYTH* NE24.................... 10 C6 **3**
  TYNE/NSHE NE30.......................... 55 D2
Kendal Cl *PLEE/EAS* SR8............... 207 F5
Kendal Crs *LWF/SPW/WRK* NE9 .... 100 A3
Kendal Dr *BOL* NE36....................... 106 B3
  CRAM NE23................................... 14 B6
Kendale Wk *WD/WHPE/BLK* NE5 .. 60 A3 **4**
Kendal Gdns *WLSD/HOW* NE28....... 68 C1
Kenilworth *LGB/KIL* NE12................. 35 F6
Kenilworth Rd *ELS/FEN* NE4............ 79 F4 **4**
  MONK NE25................................... 40 B6
Kenilworth Sq *SWCK/CAS* SR5...... 106 B6
Kenilworth Vw
  LWF/SPW/WRK NE9..................... 117 F2
Kenley Rd *WD/WHPE/BLK* NE5........ 60 C6
Kenmoor Wy *WD/WHPE/BLK* NE5.... 59 E3
Kenmore Crs *RYTON* NE40............... 74 A4
Kennersdene *TYNE/NSHE* NE30...... 55 E4
Kennet Av *JRW* NE32....................... 86 B5
Kennington Gv *BYK/HTN/WLK* NE6 .. 83 D3
Kenny Pl *DHAM* DH1...................... 195 E3
Kensington Av *GOS/KPK* NE3.......... 47 E5
Kensington Gdns
  TYNE/NSHE NE30.......................... 55 D6 **2**
  WLSD/HOW NE28............................ 66 A3
Kensington Gv *TYNE/NSHE* NE30 .. 55 D5 **1**
Kensington Ter *JES* NE2.................. 80 C1
Kent Av *DUN/TMV* NE11................... 97 F2 **1**
  HEBB NE31.................................... 84 C3
  WLSD/HOW NE28............................ 68 B4
Kentchester Rd *SWCK/CAS* SR5..... 106 A6
Kent Gdns *HLH* DH5...................... 171 E6
Kentmere Av *BYK/HTN/WLK* NE6..... 83 E2
  CLDN/WHIT/ROK SR6.................. 108 B5
Kentmere Cl *CRAM* NE23................. 23 F6
Kentmere Pl *PLEE/EAS* SR8.......... 209 D2 **2**
Kenton Av *GOS/KPK* NE3................. 62 C3
Kenton Ct *SSH* NE33........................ 71 F5
Kenton Crs *GOS/KPK* NE3................ 62 B2
Kenton Gv *CLDN/WHIT/ROK* SR6 .. 126 C3
Kenton La *GOS/KPK* NE3................. 61 F2
  WD/WHPE/BLK NE5....................... 62 A2
Kenton Rd *GOS/KPK* NE3................. 62 C1
  NSHW NE29.................................. 53 E5
Kent Pl *HAR/WTLS* NE34.................. 89 E2
Kent St *JRW* NE32........................... 85 F2
Kentucky Rd *SWCK/CAS* SR5......... 105 F6
Kenya Rd *SWCK/CAS* SR5.............. 106 A6
Kepier Ct *DHAM* DH1...................... 194 C4

Kepier Gdns *MLFD/PNYW* SR4 ...... 123 F6 5
Keppel St *SSH* NE33 .... 71 E3
Kerry Cl *BLYTH* NE24 .... 11 D4 7
Kerryhill Dr *DHAM* DH1 .... 180 B4 3
Keston Dr *CRAM* NE23 .... 14 A4
Kestrel Cl *WASHS* NE38 .... 137 F4
Kestrel Ms *WICK/BNPF* NE16 ... 95 F3 6
Kestrel Pl *LGB/KIL* NE12 .... 49 D5
Kestrel St *DUN/TMV* NE11 .... 98 B4
Kestrel Wy *HAR/WTLS* NE34 ..... 88 A4
    NSHW NE29........................ 70 C3
Keswick Av *CLDN/WHIT/ROK* SR6 ... 108 B6
Keswick Dr *TYNE/NSHE* NE30 ..... 55 D2
Keswick Gdns *WLSD/HOW* NE28 ... 68 C3
Keswick Gv *WD/WHPE/BLK* NE5 .... 60 C6
Keswick Rd *PLEE/EAS* SR8 ...... 209 D2
    STLY/ANP DH9 .... 147 F4
Keswick St *GATE* NE8 .... 99 D1
Keswic Ter *RDHAMSE* DH6 ...... 187 D4
Kettering Pl *CRAM* NE23 .... 14 B6 1
Kettlewell Ter *TYNE/NSHE* NE30.... 55 D6
Ketton Cl *LGB/KIL* NE12 .... 49 D6 4
Kew Gdns *WBAY* NE26 .... 40 B4
Keyes Gdns *JES* NE2 .... 64 A3
Kibblesworth Bank
    DUN/TMV NE11 .... 116 A6
Kidd Av *RDHAMSE* DH6.............. 197 E5
Kidderminster Dr
    WD/WHPE/BLK NE5 .... 59 E3 2
Kidderminster Rd *SWCK/CAS* SR5... 124 A1
Kidlandlee Gn
    WD/WHPE/BLK NE5 .... 60 C2 3
Kidlandlee Pl *WD/WHPE/BLK* NE5 ... 60 C2
Kielder Av *CRAM* NE23 .... 20 C2
Kielder Cl *BLYTH* NE24 .... 16 A1
    LGB/KIL NE12 .... 35 E6 8
    WD/WHPE/BLK NE5 .... 60 C2 4
Kielder Gdns *JRW* NE32 .... 85 F5
Kielder Pl *MONK* NE25 .... 39 D5
Kielder Rd *BW/LEM/TK/HW* NE15.... 76 A1
    MONK NE25....................... 39 D5
Kielder Ter *TYNE/NSHE* NE30 ..... 55 D6 5
Kielder Wy *GOS/KPK* NE3 .... 47 D5 2
Kier Hardie Av *STLY/ANP* DH9 ... 148 B3
Kilburn Dr *PLEE/EAS* SR8 .... 201 E5
Kilburne Cl *LGB/HTN* NE7 .... 66 A3 3
Kilburn Gdns *NSHW* NE29 .... 69 F3
Kildale *HLS* DH4 .... 139 D6 3
Kilkenny Cl *WD/WHPE/BLK* NE5 .... 59 E2 8
Killingworth Av *SMOOR* NE27...... 36 C6
Killingworth Dr *LGB/KIL* NE12...... 49 D2
    SUNDSW SR3 .... 142 C2
Killingworth La *LGB/KIL* NE12 ...... 50 C1
Killingworth Pl *CNUT* NE1 .... 2 C2
Killingworth Rd *GOS/KPK* NE3 ..... 64 B1
    LGB/KIL NE12 .... 50 A3
Killingworth Wy *CRAM* NE23 .... 36 A5
    LGB/KIL NE12 .... 34 C6
Kiln Ri *WICK/BNPF* NE16............ 95 F6
Kilnshaw Pl *GOS/KPK* NE3 .... 47 F3 3
Kimberley *WASHS* NE38 .... 139 F1
Kimberley Av *NSHW* NE29 .... 54 A6
Kimberley Gdns *JES* NE2 .... 64 C6 4
Kimberley St *BLYTH* NE24 .... 10 C4
    MLFD/PNYW SR4 .... 125 E6 5
Kingarth Av *CLDN/WHIT/ROK* SR6 ... 109 D5
Kingdom Pl *NSHW* NE29 .... 70 C3 3
King Edward Pl *GATE* NE8 ...... 100 A1 9
King Edward Rd
    BYK/HTN/WLK NE6 .... 65 D5
    MLFD/PNYW SR4 .... 124 A6 3
    RYTON NE40 .... 75 D4
    SEA/MUR SR7 .... 176 C4
    TYNE/NSHE NE30 .... 55 E5
King Edward St *GATE* NE8 .... 100 A1
Kingfisher Rd *LGB/KIL* NE12 .... 48 C5
Kingfisher Wy *BLYTH* NE24 .... 17 D2
    WLSD/HOW NE28 .... 52 C6
King George Av *DUN/TMV* NE11.... 97 E3
King George Rd *GOS/KPK* NE3 .... 46 A6
    HAR/WTLS NE34................. 89 D1
Kingham Ct *LGB/HTN* NE7 .... 64 B2 2
King John St *BYK/HTN/WLK* NE6 .... 65 D6
King John Ter *BYK/HTN/WLK* NE6 .... 65 D6
Kings Av *CLDN/WHIT/ROK* SR6 ... 109 D5
    HEBB NE31 .... 85 E3
Kingsbridge *LGB/KIL* NE12 .... 48 B5 1
Kings Cl *GATE* NE8 .... 100 A1 10
Kingsdale Av *BLYTH* NE24 .... 9 F5
Kingsdale Rd *LGB/KIL* NE12 .... 48 B5
King's Dr *WBAY* NE26 .... 40 C5
King's Gdns *BLYTH* NE24 .... 10 B4
Kings Gv *DHAM* DH1 .... 204 C1 3
Kingsland *JES* NE2 .... 64 A6 8
King's La *CLSW/PEL* DH2 .... 151 F1
Kingsley Av *GOS/KPK* NE3 .... 47 F3
    HAR/WTLS NE34................. 87 F5
    MONK NE25....................... 40 B6
Kingsley St *SWCK/CAS* SR5 ...... 125 F3 2
Kingsley Pl *DUN/TMV* NE11 .... 97 E1 2
    WICK/BNPF NE16 .... 96 A2
    WLSD/HOW NE28 .... 68 B3 4
Kingsley Ter *ELS/FEN* NE4 .... 9 A2
Kingsmere *CLS/BIR/GTL* DH3...... 153 E1

Kingsmere Gdns
    BYK/HTN/WLK NE6 .... 83 F4 8
King's Pl *MLFD/PNYW* SR4 ...... 125 F5
King's Rd *BDLGTN* NE22 .... 8 C2
    CNUT NE1........................... 2 C1
    LGB/KIL NE12 .... 49 E3
    WBAY NE26 .... 40 B4
Kings Rd North *WLSD/HOW* NE28 ... 67 D2
Kings Rd South *WLSD/HOW* NE28 ... 67 D3
The King's Rd *SWCK/CAS* SR5 ... 125 F2
King's Ter *MLFD/PNYW* SR4........ 125 E5
Kingston Av *BYK/HTN/WLK* NE6 .... 82 C3
Kingston Cl *WBAY* NE26 .... 40 B2
Kingston Dr *WBAY* NE26 .... 40 B3
Kingston Park Av *GOS/KPK* NE3 ... 45 E6
Kingston Park Rd *DIN/WO* NE13 .... 45 F4
    GOS/KPK NE3 .... 46 B5
Kingston Rd *GATE* NE8 .... 99 F2
Kingston Ter *CLDN/WHIT/ROK* SR6.. 126 C2
King St *BLYTH* NE24 .... 11 D4
    CLDN/WHIT/ROK SR6 .... 108 C6
    CLS/BIR/GTL DH3 .... 136 A2
    CNUT NE1........................... 3 F5
    FELL NE10 .... 101 F1
    GATE NE8 .... 98 B2
    RDHAMSE DH6.................. 197 E5
    RDHAMSE DH6.................. 206 C2
    SSH NE33 .... 71 E3
    SUND SR1 .... 4 C2
    TYNE/NSHE NE30 .... 55 D6
Kingsway *BLYTH* NE24 .... 11 D6 9
    ELS/FEN NE4 .... 62 A6
    HLH DH5 .... 171 E2
    PONT/DH NE20.................... 28 A4
    SSH NE33 .... 72 B4
    TYNE/NSHE NE30 .... 55 E4
    WICK/BNPF NE16 .... 113 F1
Kingsway Av *GOS/KPK* NE3 .... 47 E5
Kingsway North *DUN/TMV* NE11.... 98 A4
Kingsway Rd *SWCK/CAS* SR5 ..... 105 F6
Kingsway South *DUN/TMV* NE11 ... 98 C6
Kingswood Av *JES* NE2 .... 63 F3 2
Kingswood Cl *BOLCOL* NE35 ..... 105 D1
Kingswood Gv *MLFD/PNYW* SR4 ... 141 E4
Kingswood Rd *CRAM* NE23 .... 14 B6
King Ter *STLY/ANP* DH9 .... 147 F3
Kinlett *WASHS* NE38 .... 139 F1 2
Kinley Rd *DHAM* DH1 .... 196 C1
Kinloch Ct *CLSW/PEL* DH2 ...... 166 A1
Kinloss Sq *CRAM* NE23 .... 14 B6 2
Kinnaird Av *BW/LEM/TK/HW* NE5 ... 77 F2
Kinross Ct *FELL* NE10 .... 84 A6
Kinross Dr *GOS/KPK* NE3 .... 62 A1
    STLY/ANP DH9 .... 149 D2
Kinver Dr *WD/WHPE/BLK* NE5 ..... 59 E3
Kiphill Ct *STLY/ANP* DH9 .... 131 F6
Kipling Av *BOLCOL* NE35 .... 106 A2
    HEBB NE31 .... 85 E2
    WICK/BNPF NE16 .... 96 A2
Kipling Ct *STLY/ANP* DH9 .... 148 C2
Kipling St *WICK/BNPF* NE16 ...... 96 A2 3
Kipling St *SWCK/CAS* SR5 ...... 125 F3 5
Kira Dr *DHAM* DH1 .... 180 B4
Kirby Av *DHAM* DH1 .... 193 F1
Kirby Cl *HAR/WTLS* NE34 .... 87 E4
Kirkbride Pl *CRAM* NE23 .... 14 B6 3
Kirkdale Gn *ELS/FEN* NE4 .... 80 A4 6
Kirkdale St *HLH* DH5 .... 185 E2
Kirkham Av *GOS/KPK* NE3 .... 45 E5 1
Kirkham Rd *DHAM* DH1 .... 180 C6
Kirkheaton Pl *WD/WHPE/BLK* NE5... 61 E6
Kirkland Hl *PLEE/EAS* SR8 .... 208 C1
Kirklands *CRAM* NE23 .... 35 E5
Kirkland Wk *SMOOR* NE27.......... 52 A1
Kirklea Rd *HLH* DH5 .... 171 E2
Kirkleatham Gdns
    BYK/HTN/WLK NE6 .... 65 F4 4
Kirkley Av *HAR/WTLS* NE34 .... 89 F2
Kirkley Cl *GOS/KPK* NE3 .... 47 E5
Kirkley Dr *PONT/DH* NE20 .... 28 A3
Kirkley Rd *SMOOR* NE27............ 52 B2
Kirklinton Rd *TYNE/NSHE* NE30 .... 54 C2
Kirkside *HLS* DH4 .... 158 A2
Kirkston Av *BW/LEM/TK/HW* NE15 ... 76 C1
Kirkstone *CLS/BIR/GTL* DH3....... 136 C4
Kirkstone Av *JRW* NE32 .... 86 C5
    PLEE/EAS SR8 .... 209 D2
    SWCK/CAS SR5 .... 126 B1
    TYNE/NSHE NE30 .... 54 C2
Kirkstone Cl *HLH* DH5 .... 171 E2
Kirkstone Dr *DHAM* DH1 .... 196 B1
Kirkstone Gdns *LGB/HTN* NE7 .... 64 C3 2
Kirkstone Rd *FELL* NE10........... 101 E1
Kirk Vw *HLS* DH4 .... 157 F5 6
Kirkwall Cl *SWCK/CAS* SR5 ...... 123 F5
Kirkwood *CRAM* NE23 .... 35 E5
Kirkwood Av *MLFD/PNYW* SR4 ... 141 F4
Kirkwood Cl *CRAM* NE23 .... 23 F6
Kirkwood Dr *GOS/KPK* NE3 ...... 62 B1 6
Kirkwood Gdns *FELL* NE10 ...... 102 A2
Kirton Av *ELS/FEN* NE4 .... 79 D2
Kirton Wy *CRAM* NE23 .... 14 B6
Kismet St *SWCK/CAS* SR5 ...... 125 F2
Kitchener Rd *CLDN/WHIT/ROK* SR6 .. 91 D4

Kitchener St *LWF/SPW/WRK* NE9 ... 99 F2 5
    MLFD/PNYW SR4 .... 143 E2
Kitchener Ter *ASHBK/HED/RY* SR2.. 145 E4
    JRW NE32 .... 86 A3
    TYNE/NSHE NE30 .... 55 E5
Kitching Rd *PLEE/EAS* SR8........ 199 F5
Kittiwake Cl *BLYTH* NE24 .... 17 D3
    NSHW NE29....................... 52 C5
Kittiwake Dr *WASHS* NE38 ...... 137 E3
Kittiwake St *DUN/TMV* NE11 ...... 98 B5
Kitty Brewster Rd *BLYTH* NE24..... 9 E4
Knaresborough Cl *BLYTH* NE24..... 6 C2
Knaresborough Rd *SEA/MUR* SR7 .. 188 B1
Knaresdale *CLS/BIR/GTL* DH3 .... 136 C5
Knarsdale Av *NSHW* NE29 .... 53 F6
Knarsdale Pl *WD/WHPE/BLK* NE5.. 60 A5 8
Kneller Cl *STLY/ANP* DH9 .... 148 B2
Knightsbridge *GOS/KPK* NE3 ..... 47 E6
    SUNDSW SR3 .... 143 D6 2
Knightside Gdns *DUN/TMV* NE11 ... 97 E4 4
Knivestone Ct *LGB/KIL* NE12 ...... 36 A6
Knobbyends La *BLAY* NE21 .... 93 E2
Knoll Ri *DUN/TMV* NE11 .... 97 E3
Knollside Cl *SUNDSW* SR3........ 160 B3
Knott Pl *BW/LEM/TK/HW* NE15 ..... 77 F3
Knoulberry *WASHN* NE37.......... 119 F6
Knoulberry Rd *WASHN* NE37...... 119 F6
Knowledge Hl *BLAY* NE21 .... 94 A1
Knowle Pl *LGB/KIL* NE12 .... 65 D1
Knowsley Ct
    WD/WHPE/BLK NE5 .... 61 D1 9
Knox Cl *BDLGTN* NE22 .... 8 C2 4
Knox Rd *BDLGTN* NE22 .... 8 A4
Knox Sq *SWCK/CAS* SR5 .... 125 F1
Kristin Av *JRW* NE32................. 86 B4
Kyffin Vw *HAR/WTLS* NE34 .... 90 A3
Kyle Cl *ELS/FEN* NE4 .... 80 A4
Kyle Rd *GATE* NE8 .... 98 B2
Kyloe Av *MONK* NE25 .... 24 C6
Kyloe Cl *GOS/KPK* NE3 .... 46 A5
Kyloe Pl *WD/WHPE/BLK* NE5 ...... 60 C3
Kyloe Vls *WD/WHPE/BLK* NE5 .... 60 C3 5
Kyo Heugh Rd *STLY/ANP* DH9 ... 146 C2
Kyo La *STLY/ANP* DH9 .... 147 D3
Kyo Rd *STLY/ANP* DH9 .... 146 B3

L

Laburnam Pk
    BDN/LAN/SAC DH7 .... 202 C5 1
Laburnam Rd
    CLDN/WHIT/ROK SR6 .... 126 C1 3
Laburnum Av *BLYTH* NE24.......... 10 C4
    BYK/HTN/WLK NE6 .... 66 B6
    DHAM DH1 .... 194 A5
    FELL NE10 .... 101 F3
    WLSD/HOW NE28 .... 67 D2
Laburnum Ct *LGB/KIL* NE12 .... 35 E6 6
Laburnum Crs *DUN/TMV* NE11 ... 116 B6
    SEA/MUR SR7 .... 176 B6 4
Laburnum Gdns *JRW* NE32 .... 85 F4
Laburnum Gv
    CLDN/WHIT/ROK SR6 .... 107 F1
    HAR/WTLS NE34................. 89 E3
    SWCK/CAS SR5 .... 123 F4
    WICK/BNPF NE16 .... 95 F3 9
    WICK/BNPF NE16 .... 114 A1
Laburnum Rd *BLAY* NE21 .... 76 B6
    CLDN/WHIT/ROK SR6 .... 126 C1 6
Lacebark *SUNDSW* SR3............ 160 A4
Ladock Cl *ASHBK/HED/RY* SR2 ... 145 F6 1
Lady Anne Rd *RDHAMSE* DH6 ... 197 E4
Ladybank *WD/WHPE/BLK* NE5 ..... 59 D3
Ladyhaugh Dr *WICK/BNPF* NE16 .. 95 F6 1
Ladykirk Rd *ELS/FEN* NE4 .... 79 D3
Ladykirk Wy *CRAM* NE23 .... 21 D2 1
Ladysmith Ct *STLY/ANP* DH9 ..... 148 C3
Ladysmith St *SSH* NE33 .... 71 F4
Lady's Piece La *RDHAMSE* DH6 .. 183 F6
Lady's Wk *SSH* NE33 .... 71 E2
Ladywell Rd *BLAY* NE21 .... 96 C1
Ladywood Pk *HLS* DH4 .... 139 E6 2
Laet St *NSHW* NE29.................. 71 D1
Laindon Av *CLDN/WHIT/ROK* SR6 .. 108 C6
Laing Gv *WLSD/HOW* NE28 .... 68 C3
Laith Rd *GOS/KPK* NE3 .... 62 A1
Lake Ap *BLAY* NE21 .... 95 E1 1
Lake Av *HAR/WTLS* NE34 .... 90 B2
Lake Ct *SUNDSW* SR3.............. 160 C1 2
Lakeland Dr *PLEE/EAS* SR8 ...... 209 D1
Lake Rd *HLH* DH5.................... 171 D2
Lakeside *BLAY* NE21 .... 95 E1
    HAR/WTLS NE34................. 90 C2
Lake Vw *HEBB* NE31 .... 84 C4
Lambden Cl *NSHW* NE29 .... 70 A3
Lambert Rd *WASHN* NE37......... 119 E5
Lambeth Pl *GATE* NE8 .... 99 F2 8
Lambley Av *TYNE/NSHE* NE30 .... 55 D2
Lambley Cl *WICK/BNPF* NE16 ... 113 F2
Lambley Crs *HEBB* NE31 .... 84 C5
Lambourn Av *LGB/KIL* NE12 .... 49 E5
    NSHW NE29....................... 69 F2
Lambourne Cl *HLS* DH4 .... 156 A5

Lambourne Rd
ASHBK/HED/RY SR2 .... **144** B3
Lamb St BYK/HTN/WLK NE6 .... **83** F3 **2**
Lambton Av WLSD/HOW NE28 ...... **96** B2
Lambton Cl PLEE/EAS SR8 .... **208** B5
SUNDSW SR3 .... **159** E1 **3**
WASHS NE38 .... **137** D6
Lambton Dr HLH DH5 .... **185** F2
Lambton Rd HEBB NE31 .... **85** E1 **2**
JES NE2 .... **64** A6
Lambton St DHAM DH1 .... **194** A4 **2**
GATE NE8 .... **81** D5
SUND SR1 .... **4** D1
Lambton Ter JRW NE32 .... **86** B5
Lampeter Cl WD/WHPE/BLK NE5 .. **61** D2 **7**
Lamport St HEBB NE31 .... **84** B1 **2**
Lampton Ct BDLGTN NE22 .... **8** B2 **1**
Lanark Cl NSHW NE29 .... **53** E4
Lanark Dr JRW NE32 .... **87** D5
Lancashire Dr DHAM DH1 .... **196** C3
Lancaster Ct GOS/KPK NE3 ...... **45** F5 **3**
Lancaster Dr WLSD/HOW NE28 .... **51** F5
Lancaster Rd DUN/TMV NE11 ...... **97** D1
Lancaster St ELS/FEN NE4 .... **80** A3 **12**
Lancaster Ter CLS/BIR/GTL DH3 .. **153** F6
Lancastrian Rd CRAM NE23 .... **21** F3
Lancefield Av BYK/HTN/WLK NE6.. **83** E4
Lanchester Av
LWF/SPW/WRK NE9 .... **118** C1
Lanchester Cl FELL NE10 .... **102** B4 **1**
Lanchester Gn BDLGTN NE22 ...... **7** E2 **1**
Lanchester Pk WASHS NE38 .... **139** D4 **2**
Lancing Ct GOS/KPK NE3 .... **45** E5
Landseer Cl STLY/ANP DH9 .... **148** B2
Landseer Gdns HAR/WTLS NE34 ... **88** C6
LWF/SPW/WRK NE9 .... **100** A2 **1**
Lane Cnr HAR/WTLS NE34 .... **88** B3
Lanercost WASHS NE38 .... **138** B1
Lanercost Av BLAY NE21 .... **76** A6 **1**
Lanercost Dr WD/WHPE/BLK NE5 .. **61** D6
Lanercost Gdns
BW/LEM/TK/HW NE15 .... **57** F3
FELL NE10 .... **100** B4 **2**
Lanercost Rd NSHW NE29 .... **70** A1
Langdale MONK NE25 .... **40** A5
Langdale Cl LGB/KIL NE12 .... **48** C6
Langdale Crs DHAM DH1 .... **196** B1
Langdale Dr CRAM NE23 .... **21** D2
Langdale Gdns
BYK/HTN/WLK NE6 .... **83** F2 **5**
WLSD/HOW NE28 .... **68** C2
Langdale Pl PLEE/EAS SR8 .... **209** D2 **7**
Langdale Rd DHAM DH1 .... **139** F6
LWF/SPW/WRK NE9 .... **99** F5
Langdale St HLH DH5 .... **185** E2
Langdale Wy BOL NE36 .... **106** B3
Langdon Cl NSHW NE29 .... **54** B3 **6**
Langford Dr BOLCOL NE35 .... **87** D6
Langham Av NSHW NE29 .... **53** E4
Langham Rd
BW/LEM/TK/HW NE15 .... **77** E3 **1**
Langholm Rd BOL NE36 .... **106** C2
GOS/KPK NE3 .... **47** E5 **1**
Langhurst ASHBK/HED/RY SR2 ... **145** D6
Langleeford Rd
WD/WHPE/BLK NE5 .... **60** C3
Langley Av BLYTH NE24 .... **10** A4
FELL NE10 .... **102** A4
MONK NE25 .... **53** F1
SMOOR NE27 .... **52** C2
Langley Cl WASHS NE38 .... **138** A2
Langley Crs BDN/LAN/SAC DH7 ... **203** F3
Langley Rd BYK/HTN/WLK NE6 .... **83** E2
DHAM DH1 .... **180** B6
NSHW NE29 .... **53** F6
SUNDSW SR3 .... **144** A4
WD/WHPE/BLK NE5 .... **60** B6
Langley St HLS DH4 .... **157** F2
Langley Ter JRW NE32 .... **86** A5
Langport Rd
ASHBK/HED/RY SR2 .... **144** C3 **2**
Langton Cl MLFD/PNYW SR4 .... **126** A6 **7**
Langton Dr CRAM NE23 .... **14** B4
Langton St GATE NE0 .... **00** F1 **1**
Langton Ter LGB/HTN NE7 .... **65** D4 **1**
Lanivet Cl ASHBK/HED/RY SR2 ... **145** E6
Lansbury Cl CLS/BIR/GTL DH3 ... **118** A6
Lansbury Ct CLS/BIR/GTL DH3 ... **118** A6
SEA/MUR SR7 .... **188** B1 **1**
Lansbury Gdns FELL NE10 .... **101** F2
Lansbury Rd WICK/BNPF NE16 .... **96** B4
Lansbury Wy SWCK/CAS SR5 ...... **124** C3
Lansdowne ASHBK/HED/RY SR2 ... **162** A1
Lansdowne Gdns JES NE2 .... **64** C6
Lansdowne Rd LGB/KIL NE12 ...... **49** F4
Lansdowne St MLFD/PNYW SR4 .. **126** A5 **3**
Lansdowne Ter NSHW NE29 .... **54** B6
Lansdowne Ter West NSHW NE29 .. **54** A6
Lanthwaite Rd LWF/SPW/WRK NE9.. **99** F5
Lanton St HLS DH4 .... **157** F2
Lapford Dr CRAM NE23 .... **14** B5
Lapwing Cl BLYTH NE24 .... **17** D2 **2**
WASHS NE38 .... **137** E3
Lapwing Ct WICK/BNPF NE16 ..... **130** B1

L'arbre Crs WICK/BNPF NE16....... **95** E3
Larch Av CLDN/WHIT/ROK SR6 ..... **109** F1
HAR/WTLS NE34 .... **89** F3
HLS DH4 .... **170** C1
Larch Cl LWF/SPW/WRK NE9 .... **118** C2
Larches Rd DHAM DH1 .... **193** F3 **1**
The Larches WICK/BNPF NE16 ..... **112** A5 **1**
Larch Rd BLAY NE21 .... **76** C5
Larch Ter STLY/ANP DH9 .... **129** F5
Larchwood WASHS NE38 .... **138** A5
Larchwood Av BYK/HTN/WLK NE6.. **66** A6
DIN/WO NE13 .... **33** E5
GOS/KPK NE3 .... **46** B5 **8**
Larchwood Gv
ASHBK/HED/RY SR2 .... **144** B4 **0**
Larkfield Crs HLS DH4 .... **156** C3 **11**
Larkfield Rd ASHBK/HED/RY SR2 ... **144** B3
Lark Rise CI LGB/HTN NE7 .... **65** F3 **5**
Larkspur Cl STLY/ANP DH9.......... **130** C6
Larkspur Rd WICK/BNPF NE16 .... **95** F4
Larkspur Ter JES NE2 .... **64** A5
Larne Crs LWF/SPW/WRK NE9...... **99** F5
Larriston Pl CRAM NE23 .... **21** E2 **1**
Lartington Cl CLS/BIR/GTL DH3 ... **168** A4 **1**
Lartington Gdns GOS/KPK NE3 ..... **64** B1 **0**
Larwood Cl CLS/BIR/GTL DH3 ...... **167** D1
Larwood Ct STLY/ANP DH9 .... **146** A5
Lascelles Av HAR/WTLS NE34 ...... **89** D3
Laski Gdns FELL NE10 .... **102** A2
Latimer St TYNE/NSHE NE30 .... **55** F4
Lauderdale Av WLSD/HOW NE28 ... **67** D2
Launceston Cl DIN/WO NE13........ **45** F4
Launceston Dr SUNDSW SR3 ...... **159** F1
Laura St SUND SR1 .... **4** D4
Laurel Av DHAM DH1 .... **195** F4
GOS/KPK NE3 .... **46** C6
LGB/KIL NE12 .... **50** C3
SEA/MUR SR7 .... **176** A3
Laurel Ct CLSW/PEL DH2 .... **153** D3
Laurel Crs BYK/HTN/WLK NE6 ..... **66** B5
STLY/ANP DH9 .... **151** D1
Laurel Gv ASHBK/HED/RY SR2...... **144** B4
Laurel Rd BLAY NE21 .... **76** C6
Laurel St BW/LEM/TK/HW NE15 ... **57** F3
WLSD/HOW NE28 .... **67** E5
Laurelwood Gdns DUN/TMV NE11 .. **98** A5
Lauren Ct PLEE/EAS SR8 .... **200** B2
Laurens Ct WASHN NE37 .... **120** C4 **1**
Lavender Gdns BDN/LAN/SAC DH7.. **178** C1
JES NE2 .... **63** F5
Lavender Gv SWCK/CAS SR5 .... **123** F3
Lavender La HAR/WTLS NE34 ...... **88** A3
Lavender Rd WICK/BNPF NE16 .... **95** F4
Laverock Hall Rd BLYTH NE24...... **15** F3
Laverock Pl BLYTH NE24 .... **16** A3 **1**
GOS/KPK NE3 .... **61** F1 **7**
Lavington Rd HAR/WTLS NE34 ..... **72** A6
Lawe Rd SSH NE33 .... **71** F2
Lawmill Wy WD/WHPE/BLK NE5 ... **61** D4 **7**
Lawn Dr BOL NE36 .... **105** E4
The Lawns HLH DH5 .... **186** B3
Lawnswood HLH DH5 .... **171** E3
Lawrence Av BLAY NE21 .... **76** B5
HAR/WTLS NE34 .... **88** C2
Lawrence Ct BLAY NE21 .... **76** B5 **0**
Lawrence St SUND SR1 .... **5** F5
Lawson Av JRW NE32 .... **86** B4
Lawson Crs CLDN/WHIT/ROK SR6 .. **108** C6
Lawson St NSHW NE29 .... **70** C2
WLSD/HOW NE28 .... **67** E5
Lawson Ter DHAM DH1 .... **194** A5
ELS/FEN NE4 .... **79** D4 **2**
HLH DH5 .... **186** A3
Laws St CLDN/WHIT/ROK SR6 ..... **108** C6
Laxford Ct SUNDSW SR3 .... **160** C3
Laybourn Gdns HAR/WTLS NE34 .. **87** F4 **1**
Layburn Gdns
BW/LEM/TK/HW NE15 .... **60** A6 **4**
Layburn Pl PLEE/EAS SR8 .... **208** A1
Layfield Rd GOS/KPK NE3 .... **47** E3
Laygate SSH NE33 .... **71** E6 **3**
Laygate St SSH NE33 .... **71** E5
Laygate St SSH NE33 .... **71** D5
Lea Av JRW NE32 .... **86** B6
Leabank BW/LEM/TK/HW NE15 ..... **59** F6
Leafield Crs HAR/WTLS NE34...... **72** C6
Lea Gn CLS/BIR/GTL DH3 .... **137** D5
Leagreen Ct GOS/KPK NE3 .... **62** C1 **5**
Leaholme Crs BLYTH NE24 .... **10** B6
Lea La PLEE/EAS SR8 .... **190** A6
Lealholm Rd LGB/HTN NE7 .... **64** C1 **2**
Leam Gdns FELL NE10 .... **102** B2
Leamington St MLFD/PNYW SR4 ... **126** A6
Leam La FELL NE10 .... **101** F5
JRW NE32 .... **86** C4
JRW NE32 .... **103** F1
LWF/SPW/WRK NE9 .... **101** E6
Leamside FELL NE10 .... **101** E4
JRW NE32 .... **86** B4
Leander Av CLS/BIR/GTL DH3 ...... **153** F1
Leander Dr BOLCOL NE35 .... **105** D2
Leaplish WASHS NE38 .... **139** E4
Lea Riggs HLS DH4 .... **183** F2 **1**
The Leas HLS DH4 .... **157** F5

Leazes Ct DHAM DH1 .... **194** C4
Leazes Crs CNUT NE1 .... **2** B2
Leazes La CNUT NE1 .... **2** C2
DHAM DH1 .... **194** C4
Leazes Park Rd CNUT NE1 .... **2** B2
Leazes Pkwy
BW/LEM/TK/HW NE15 .... **57** E5
Leazes Pl DHAM DH1 .... **194** C4
Leazes Ri PLEE/EAS SR8 .... **209** E2
Leazes Rd DHAM DH1 .... **194** C4
Leazes Ter CNUT NE1 .... **2** B1
The Leazes HAR/WTLS NE34 .... **89** E2
SUND SR1 .... **126** A6 **3**
Leazes Vw ROWG NE39 .... **110** C2
Lecondale FELL NE10 .... **101** E5
Ledbury Rd ASHBK/HED/RY SR2... **144** C3
Leechmere Rd
ASHBK/HED/RY SR2 .... **144** B4
Leechmere Wy
ASHBK/HED/RY SR2 .... **145** D6
Lee Cl WASHS NE38 .... **140** A1
Leeds Ct CLDN/WHIT/ROK SR6 .... **126** C2 **1**
Leeholme HLH DH5 .... **171** E3
Leeholme Ct STLY/ANP DH9 .... **146** C5 **1**
Leeming Gdns
LWF/SPW/WRK NE9 .... **100** A4
Leesfield Dr BDN/LAN/SAC DH7 ... **203** E5
Leesfield Gdns BDN/LAN/SAC DH7.. **203** D5
Leesfield Rd BDN/LAN/SAC DH7 .. **203** E5 **1**
Lees St STLY/ANP DH9 .... **148** B1
Lee St CLDN/WHIT/ROK SR6........ **108** C6
SWCK/CAS SR5 .... **126** A3 **1**
Legg Av BDLGTN NE22 .... **9** D1
Legges Dr DIN/WO NE13 .... **18** C2
Legion Gv BW/LEM/TK/HW NE15 .. **77** E1 **1**
Legion Rd BW/LEM/TK/HW NE15 .. **77** E1 **5**
Leicester Cl WLSD/HOW NE28 ..... **66** C1
Leicestershire Dr DHAM DH1 ...... **196** C3 **3**
Leicester St BYK/HTN/WLK NE6 ... **83** D3
Leighton Rd ASHBK/HED/RY SR2 .. **144** C4
Leighton St BYK/HTN/WLK NE6 .... **81** F2 **7**
SSH NE33 .... **72** A4
Leith Ct HAR/WTLS NE34 .... **88** B3
Leith Gdns STLY/ANP DH9 .... **130** C5
Lemington Gdns
WD/WHPE/BLK NE5 .... **78** B1
Lemington Rd
BW/LEM/TK/HW NE15 .... **75** F1
Lemon St SSH NE33 .... **88** A2
Lena Av MONK NE25 .... **40** A6
Lenin Ter STLY/ANP DH9............. **148** C3
Leominster Rd
ASHBK/HED/RY SR2 .... **144** C4
Leopold St JRW NE32 .... **86** A2 **1**
Lesbury Av SMOOR NE27 .... **52** A1
WLSD/HOW NE28 .... **68** B3
Lesbury Cha GOS/KPK NE3 .... **47** D6
Lesbury Cl CLSW/PEL DH2 .... **165** E1
Lesbury Rd BYK/HTN/WLK NE6 .... **65** D5
Lesbury St BW/LEM/TK/HW NE15 .. **76** C2
WLSD/HOW NE28 .... **69** E5 **3**
Leslie Av HEBB NE31 .... **85** D3
Leslie Cl RYTON NE40 .... **75** D4
Leslie Crs GOS/KPK NE3 .... **63** C5 **3**
Letch Av SEA/MUR SR7 .... **189** F4
Leven Av CLSW/PEL DH2 .... **166** A1
Levisham Cl SUNDSW SR3 .... **161** E1 **5**
Lewis Crs ASHBK/HED/RY SR2..... **5** C1
Lewis Dr ELS/FEN NE4 .... **79** E2
Lexington Ct BDN/LAN/SAC DH7 .. **202** C5
Leybourne Av LGB/KIL NE12 .... **49** F3
Leyburn Cl CLSW/PEL DH2 .... **134** C5
HLS DH4 .... **170** B1
Leyburn Dr LGB/HTN NE7 .... **64** C3
Leyburn Gv HLS DH4 .... **170** B1
Leyburn Pl CLS/BIR/GTL DH3 ...... **118** A6
Leyfield Cl SUNDSW SR3 .... **161** D3 **1**
Leyton Pl GATE NE8 .... **100** A2 **5**
Liburn Cl BOL NE36 .... **106** A2
Lichfield Av BYK/HTN/WLK NE6 .... **83** D4
Lichfield Cl CLS/BIR/GTL DH3 ..... **167** F4 **2**
GOS/KPK NE3 .... **45** F5
Lichfield Rd SWCK/CAS SR5 .... **125** F1
Lidcombe Cl SUNDSW SR3 .... **161** D1
Liddell Cl CLDN/WHIT/ROK SR6 .... **126** C4 **5**
NSHW NE29 .... **71** D1
Liddell Ter GATE NE8 .... **98** C2
Liddle Av RDHAMSE DH6 .... **197** E4 **2**
Liddle Cl PLEE/EAS SR8 .... **200** A6
Liddle Rd ELS/FEN NE4 .... **79** F3
Lieven St DIN/WO NE13 .... **32** C5 **1**
Liffey Rd HEBB NE31 .... **85** E5
Lightbourne Rd
BYK/HTN/WLK NE6 .... **83** F2
Lightwood Av
BW/LEM/TK/HW NE15 .... **77** F4 **1**
Lilac Av BDN/LAN/SAC DH7 .... **178** B1
BLYTH NE24................................ **10** C4
CLDN/WHIT/ROK SR6 .... **91** E5
DHAM DH1 .... **194** A1
HAR/WTLS NE34 .... **89** E3
LGB/KIL NE12 .... **50** B4
SUNDSW SR3 .... **144** A6
Lilac Cl WD/WHPE/BLK NE5 .... **59** D2 **8**
Lilac Gdns LWF/SPW/WRK NE9 .... **99** E4

WICK/BNPF NE16 .... 95 F4
Lilac Gv CLSW/PEL DH2........ 152 C3
Lilac Pk BDN/LAN/SAC DH7 .... 192 A5
Lilac Rd BYK/HTN/WLK NE6 ..... 66 C5
Lilac Sq HLS DH4 .... 156 A5
Lilac St MLFD/PNYW SR4 .... 123 F6
Lilac Ter RDHAMSE DH6 .... 206 B2
Lilburn Cl CLSW/PEL DH2 ...... 165 F2
Lilburn Gdns GOS/KPK NE3 ..... 64 B2
Lilburn Pl SWCK/CAS SR5 ..... 125 F3
Lilburn Rd SMOOR NE27......... 52 A2
Lilburn St NSHW NE29 .... 70 B1
Lilian Av ASHBK/HED/RY SR2.... 145 D6
WLSD/HOW NE28 .... 66 C5
Lilley Gv SWCK/CAS SR5 .... 124 A3
Lily Av BDLGTN NE22 .... 8 A4
JES NE2 .... 64 A5
Lily Bank WLSD/HOW NE28 ...... 67 D4
Lily Crs CLDN/WHIT/ROK SR6.... 91 E5
JES NE2 .... 64 A5
Lily Gdns STLY/ANP DH9........ 129 D6
Lily St MLFD/PNYW SR4 .... 126 A5
Lily Ter WD/WHPE/BLK NE5 ..... 60 C3
Lilywhite Ter HLH DH5 .... 186 A2
Lime Av HLS DH4 .... 170 B2
Limecragg Av DHAM DH1 .... 196 A3
Limecroft JRW NE32 .... 104 B1
Lime Gv RYTON NE40 .... 74 B3
Limekiln Rd WLSD/HOW NE28.... 67 F4
Lime Pk BDN/LAN/SAC DH7 ..... 203 D4
The Limes HLS DH4 .... 140 A6
Lime St BLAY NE21 .... 94 C1
CNUT NE1 .... 81 F3
MLFD/PNYW SR4 .... 126 A5
Limetrees Gdns
LWF/SPW/WRK NE9 .... 99 E3
Limewood Ct JES NE2 .... 63 D6
Limewood Gv DIN/WO NE13 ...... 33 D5
Linacre Cl DIN/WO NE13........ 45 D6
Linbridge Dr WD/WHPE/BLK NE5 .. 60 A5
Linburn WASHS NE38 .... 137 F5
Lincoln Av SUNDSW SR3 .... 143 F6
WLSD/HOW NE28 .... 66 C3
Lincoln Gn GOS/KPK NE3 .... 47 D3
Lincoln Rd CRAM NE23 .... 14 B5
DHAM DH1 .... 180 C5
HAR/WTLS NE34 .... 90 A1
Lincolnshire Cl DHAM DH1...... 196 B3
Lincoln St GATE NE8 .... 99 D1
MLFD/PNYW SR4 .... 125 E5
Lindale Av WICK/BNPF NE16 .... 95 F5
Lindale Rd ELS/FEN NE4........ 62 A6
Lindean Pl CRAM NE23 .... 21 E2
Linden Av ELS/FEN NE4 .... 78 C1
GOS/KPK NE3 .... 63 E2
Linden Gdns
ASHBK/HED/RY SR2 .... 144 B3
Linden Gv DUN/TMV NE11....... 97 E2
HLS DH4 .... 170 C2
Linden Pk BDN/LAN/SAC DH7 ... 203 D4
Linden Rd ASHBK/HED/RY SR2 .. 144 B3
BLAY NE21 .... 76 C6
GOS/KPK NE3 .... 63 E2
LGB/KIL NE12 .... 49 F5
MONK NE25 .... 24 A5
Lindfield Av WD/WHPE/BLK NE5 .. 61 D5
Lindisfarne PLEE/EAS SR8 ..... 208 B4
WASHS NE38 .... 138 B2
Lindisfarne Av CLS/BIR/GTL DH3 .. 153 F5
Lindisfarne Cl HLS DH4 .... 170 A1
JES NE2 .... 64 B3
WD/WHPE/BLK NE5 .... 60 B5
Lindisfarne Ct JRW NE32 ...... 87 E2
Lindisfarne Dr GATE NE8...... 81 E5
Lindisfarne Pl WLSD/HOW NE28 .. 67 F3
Lindisfarne Recess JRW NE32 .. 86 C4
Lindisfarne Rd DHAM DH1 ..... 194 C1
HEBB NE31 .... 85 D5
JES NE2 .... 64 B4
Lindisfarne Ter TYNE/NSHE NE30.. 54 C5
Lindom Av CLS/BIR/GTL DH3 ... 153 F5
Lindon Rd STLY/ANP DH9....... 148 A3
Lindrick Ct FELL NE10 .... 102 B3
Lindsay Av BLYTH NE24 .... 10 B4
Lindsay Cl ASHBK/HED/RY SR2 .. 5 E5
Lindsay Rd ASHBK/HED/RY SR2 .. 5 F5
Lindsay St HLH DH5 .... 172 A4
Lindsey Cl CRAM NE23 .... 21 D2
Lindum Rd LWF/SPW/WRK NE9 .. 99 E2
Lingdale DHAM DH1 .... 196 C3
Lingdale Av CLDN/WHIT/ROK SR6.. 109 D4
Lingey Gdns FELL NE10 .... 102 B2
Lingey La FELL NE10 .... 102 A3
Lingholme CLSW/PEL DH2 ...... 152 C4
Lingmell WASHS NE37 .... 120 A6
Lingshaw FELL NE10 .... 102 A3
Linhope Av GOS/KPK NE3 ...... 46 B5
Linhope Rd WD/WHPE/BLK NE5 .. 60 B4
Link Av BDLGTN NE22 ....
Link Rd WD/WHPE/BLK NE5 ..... 62 A4
Links Av TYNE/NSHE NE30 ...... 55 E2
WBAY NE26 .... 40 B3
Links Gn GOS/KPK NE3 .... 47 F6
Links Rd BLYTH NE24 .... 17 E3
TYNE/NSHE NE30 .... 55 E2

The Links DHAM DH1 .... 196 C2
WBAY NE26 .... 26 B2
Links Vw BLYTH NE24 .... 16 B2
Linkway JRW NE32 .... 104 C1
Linley Hl WICK/BNPF NE16..... 95 D6
Linnel Dr BW/LEM/TK/HW NE15 .. 77 D1
Linnet Gv SWCK/CAS SR5 ...... 124 B3
Linskell ASHBK/HED/RY SR2 ... 145 D6
Linskill Pl TYNE/NSHE NE30 ... 55 D5
Linskill St TYNE/NSHE NE30 ... 71 D1
Linskill Ter TYNE/NSHE NE30... 55 D6
Lintfort CLS/BIR/GTL DH3 ..... 153 F1
Linthorpe Rd GOS/KPK NE3..... 47 E5
TYNE/NSHE NE30 .... 55 D3
Linton Rd LWF/SPW/WRK NE9 .. 117 E1
WBAY NE26 .... 40 A1
Lintzford Gdns
BW/LEM/TK/HW NE15 .... 77 D2
ROWG NE39 .... 110 C4
Lintzford La ROWG NE39 ...... 110 A4
Lintz Green La ROWG NE39 .... 110 A5
Lintz St WICK/BNPF NE16 ..... 128 C2
Linum Pl ELS/FEN NE4 .... 62 A6
Linwood Pl GOS/KPK NE3 ...... 47 E3
Lisa Av MLFD/PNYW SR4 .... 141 F1
Lisburn Ter MLFD/PNYW SR4 .. 125 F1
Lisle Gv WLSD/HOW NE28 ...... 68 C3
Lisle Rd HAR/WTLS NE34 ...... 89 E1
Lisle St WLSD/HOW NE28 ...... 67 D4
Lismore Av SSH NE33 .... 88 C1
Lismore Pl BW/LEM/TK/HW NE15.. 78 B2
Lister Av DUN/TMV NE11 ...... 97 E1
Lister Cl HLH DH5............ 170 C4
Lister Rd PLEE/EAS SR8 ...... 199 F6
Litchfield Cl BLAY NE21 ...... 94 A1
Litchfield Rd DHAM DH1 ...... 180 C4
Little Bedford St NSHW NE29 .. 71 D1
Littlebridge Ct DHAM DH1 .... 179 F5
Littleburn HLS DH4 .... 157 E6
Littleburn La BDN/LAN/SAC DH7.. 204 A3
Littleburn Rd BDN/LAN/SAC DH7 .. 204 A4
Littledene LWF/SPW/WRK NE9 .. 99 E3
Little Eden PLEE/EAS SR8 ..... 208 C1
Little Villiers St SUND SR1 .... 4 D2
Little Wy BW/LEM/TK/HW NE15 .. 78 A4
Littondale WLSD/HOW NE28 ... 66 B2
Livingstone Rd SUND SR1...... 4 A2
Livingstone St SSH NE33 ..... 71 F2
Lizard La CLDN/WHIT/ROK SR6 .. 91 D6
HAR/WTLS NE34 .... 90 C2
Lloyd Av HLH DH5 .... 170 B6
Lobban Av HEBB NE31 .... 84 C5
Lobelia Av FELL NE10 .... 82 A6
Lobelia Cl WD/WHPE/BLK NE5 .. 59 E3
Lobley Gdns DUN/TMV NE11.... 97 F4
Lobley Hill Rd DUN/TMV NE11 .. 97 F4
Lobleyhill Rd WICK/BNPF NE16.. 112 C4
Lochcraig Pl CRAM NE23 ...... 21 E2
Lochmaben Ter SWCK/CAS SR5.. 126 C2
Lockerbie Rd CRAM NE23 ..... 21 E2
Lockhaugh Rd ROWG NE39..... 111 E1
Locksley Cl NSHW NE29 ...... 53 D3
Locomotion Wy LGB/KIL NE12 .. 35 D5
NSHW NE29 .... 70 C3
Lodgeside Meadow SUNDSW SR3 .. 161 D3
The Lodges
LWF/SPW/WRK NE9 .... 117 D1
Lodore Gv JRW NE32 .... 86 C5
Lodore Rd JES NE2 .... 63 F5
Logan Rd BYK/HTN/WLK NE6 ... 66 B5
Logan St HLH DH5 .... 185 F1
Lola St DIN/WO NE13 .... 32 B5
Lombard Dr CLS/BIR/GTL DH3 .. 153 E1
Lombard St SUND SR1 .... 5 F2
Lomond Ct SUNDSW SR3 .... 160 C2
Lomond Pl CLSW/PEL DH2 ..... 166 A1
London Av WASHN NE37 ...... 120 A3
Londonderry Av DHAM DH1 ... 195 F5
Londonderry St SEA/MUR SR7 .. 177 D5
SUNDSW SR3 .... 160 C1
Londonderry Ter SUNDSW SR3 .. 161 D1
Longacre HLS DH4 .... 170 B2
WASHS NE38 .... 139 D2
Long Acres DHAM DH1 .... 195 D3
Long Bank CLS/BIR/GTL DH3 ... 118 B5
LWF/SPW/WRK NE9 .... 116 B4
Longborough Ct LGB/HTN NE7 .. 64 C2
Long Brun Dr CLSW/PEL DH2 .. 152 B6
Long Dl CLSW/PEL DH2 .... 152 B6
Longdean Cl HEBB NE31 ...... 84 B3
Longdean Pk CLS/BIR/GTL DH3 .. 153 E2
Longfield Rd CLDN/WHIT/ROK SR6.. 126 C1
Longfield Ter BYK/HTN/WLK NE6.. 83 E4
Long Gair BLAY NE21 .... 93 F2
Long Garth DHAM DH1 .... 194 B5
Longhirst FELL NE10 .... 101 F3
LGB/KIL NE12 .... 36 B6
WD/WHPE/BLK NE5 .... 60 B4
Longhirst Dr DIN/WO NE13 .... 33 D5
Longlands Dr HLH DH5 .... 171 D3
Longley St ELS/FEN NE4 ...... 79 F2
Longmeadows SUNDSW SR3 ... 159 E2
Longnewton St SEA/MUR SR7 .. 176 C5
Longniddry WASHN NE37 ..... 120 B1

Longniddry Ct
LWF/SPW/WRK NE9 .... 117 D1
Longridge Av LGB/HTN NE7 .... 65 F3
WASHS NE38 .... 137 F4
Longridge Dr WBAY NE26 ..... 40 A3
Long Ridge Rd RYTON NE40 ... 74 B6
Longridge Sq
ASHBK/HED/RY SR2 .... 144 C4
Longridge Wy CRAM NE23 .... 21 E2
STKFD/GP NE62 .... 7 F1
Longrigg FELL NE10 .... 101 E3
Long Rigg WICK/BNPF NE16 ... 95 F1
Longrigg Rd WICK/BNPF NE16.. 95 F1
Long Rw SSH NE33 .... 71 D3
Longsdale Av BLYTH NE24 .... 9 D4
Longshank La CLS/BIR/GTL DH3 .. 117 F6
Longston Av TYNE/NSHE NE30 .. 55 F1
Longstone Ct LGB/KIL NE12 ... 36 A6
Longstone Sq WD/WHPE/BLK NE5.. 59 F5
Longwood Cl WICK/BNPF NE16 .. 114 A1
Lonnen Av ELS/FEN NE4 ...... 78 C1
Lonnen Dr WICK/BNPF NE16 ... 95 F2
The Lonnen HAR/WTLS NE34... 90 A4
Lonsdale CLS/BIR/GTL DH3 .... 137 D5
Lonsdale Av CLDN/WHIT/ROK SR6.. 109 D4
Lonsdale Gdns WLSD/HOW NE28 .. 68 C2
Lonsdale Rd CLDN/WHIT/ROK SR6.. 127 D2
Lonsdale Ter JES NE2 .... 64 A4
Loraine Ter
BW/LEM/TK/HW NE15 .... 76 B2
Lord Byrons Wk SEA/MUR SR7 .. 175 E1
Lordenshaw WD/WHPE/BLK NE5 .. 60 B4
Lord Nelson St HAR/WTLS NE34.. 88 A2
Lord St SEA/MUR SR7 .... 176 C4
SSH NE33 .... 72 A5
SUNDSW SR3 .... 161 D1
Lorimers Cl PLEE/EAS SR8 .... 208 A4
Lorne St HLH DH5 .... 186 A4
Lorne Ter ASHBK/HED/RY SR2... 4 B6
Lorrain Rd HAR/WTLS NE34 ... 88 C6
Lorton Av TYNE/NSHE NE30 ... 54 C2
Lorton Rd LWF/SPW/WRK NE9 .. 99 F6
Losh Ter BYK/HTN/WLK NE6 ... 83 E3
Lossiemouth Rd NSHW NE29 .. 69 D1
Lothian Ct WD/WHPE/BLK NE5.. 61 D3
Lotus Cl WD/WHPE/BLK NE5.... 59 D3
Lotus Pl ELS/FEN NE4 .... 78 C1
Loudon St HAR/WTLS NE34 .... 88 B3
Loughborough Av
ASHBK/HED/RY SR2 .... 144 B3
Loughrigg Av CRAM NE23 ..... 21 D2
Louie Ter LWF/SPW/WRK NE9 .. 99 F5
Louis Av CLDN/WHIT/ROK SR6.. 126 C1
Loup St BLAY NE21 .... 76 B5
Lovaine Av MONK NE25 ...... 40 C6
NSHW NE29 .... 70 C1
Lovaine Pl NSHW NE29........ 70 C1
Lovaine Pl West NSHW NE29 .. 70 B1
Lovaine Rw TYNE/NSHE NE30 .. 55 E1
Lovaine St BW/LEM/TK/HW NE15 .. 58 A6
CLSW/PEL DH2 .... 151 E2
Lovaine Ter NSHW NE29 ...... 54 C6
Love Av CRAM NE23 .... 35 D3
Loveless Gdns FELL NE10 ..... 102 A3
Lowbiggin WD/WHPE/BLK NE5 .. 44 A6
Low Chare CLS/BIR/GTL DH3 .. 153 F5
Lowdham Av NSHW NE29 ..... 70 A2
Low Downs Rd HLH DH5 ...... 171 F4
Lower Dundas St
CLDN/WHIT/ROK SR6 .... 126 C4
Lower Rudyerd St NSHW NE29 .. 71 D1
Lowerson Av HLS DH4 .... 156 C3
Lowery La STLY/ANP DH9 ..... 149 F6
Lowe's Barn Bank DHAM DH1 .. 204 B1
Lowes Ct DHAM DH1 .... 193 F6
Lowes Fall DHAM DH1 .... 193 F6
Lowes Ri DHAM DH1 .... 204 C1
Loweswater Av HLH DH5 ..... 186 B4
Loweswater Cl BLYTH NE24 ... 9 E3
Loweswater Rd
WD/WHPE/BLK NE5 .... 61 D5
Loweswood Cl LGB/HTN NE7 .. 64 C5
Lowes Wynd DHAM DH1 ...... 193 F6
Lowfield Ter BYK/HTN/WLK NE6.. 83 E4
Low Flatts Rd CLSW/PEL DH2 .. 153 D2
Low Friar St CNUT NE1 .... 2 C4
Lowgate BW/LEM/TK/HW NE15 .. 57 F5
Low Gosforth Ct GOS/KPK NE3 .. 47 F3
Low Haugh PONT/DH NE20..... 28 B3
Low Heyworth La FELL NE10 .. 101 E1
Lowhills Rd PLEE/EAS SR8 .... 200 A6
Lowland Cl SUNDSW SR3 ..... 160 C3
Lowland Rd BDN/LAN/SAC DH7 .. 203 D4
Low La HAR/WTLS NE34 .... 88 B4
Low Meadow
CLDN/WHIT/ROK SR6 .... 107 F1
Lownds Ter BYK/HTN/WLK NE6 .. 83 F2
Low Quay BLYTH NE24 .... 11 E5
Lowrey's La LWF/SPW/WRK NE9 .. 99 E5
Low Rw PLEE/EAS SR8 .... 200 A2
Lowry Gdns HAR/WTLS NE34 .. 88 C6
Lowry Rd CLDN/WHIT/ROK SR6 .. 109 D5
Low Station Rd HLS DH4 ...... 183 D2
Low St SUND SR1............ 5 F1
Lowther Cl PLEE/EAS SR8 ..... 208 C1

Lowther Ct *PLEE/EAS* SR8 .... 208 A6
Lowthian Crs *BYK/HTN/WLK* NE6 .... 83 D3
Low West Av *ROWG* NE39 .... 110 B3
Lucknow St *SUND* SR1 .... 5 C1
Lucock St *HAR/WTLS* NE34 ...... 88 A3 🖪
Ludlow Av *NSHW* NE29 .... 54 A4
Ludlow Ct *GOS/KPK* NE3 .... 46 A5 🖪
Ludlow Dr *MONK* NE25 .... 39 D6
Ludlow Rd *ASHBK/HED/RY* SR2 .... 144 C4
Luffness Dr *HAR/WTLS* NE34 .... 89 E5
Luke Crs *SEA/MUR* SR7 .... 188 A1
Luke's La *HEBB* NE31 .... 85 E6
Lulsgate *SWCK/CAS* SR5 .... 123 F3
Lulworth Av *JRW* NE32 .... 86 C3
Lulworth Ct *SUNDSW* SR3 .... 159 E1 🖪
Lulworth Gdns
  ASHBK/HED/RY SR2 .... 144 B3 🖪
  WICK/BNPF NE16 .... 96 A1
Lumley Av *HAR/WTLS* NE34 .... 90 A2
Lumley Cl *WASHS* NE38 .... 138 A1
Lumley Ct *BDLGTN* NE22 .... 0 D2 🖪
  SUNDSW SR3 .... 159 E1 🖪
Lumley Dr *PLEE/EAS* SR8 .... 208 C5
Lumley Gdns *GATE* NE8 .... 100 A1
Lumley New Rd *CLS/BIR/GTL* DH3 .. 154 B6
  HLS DH4 .... 168 C1
Lumley Rd *DHAM* DH1 .... 180 B5
Lumley St *HLS* DH4 .... 157 F6
  MLFD/PNYW SR4 .... 125 F6
Lumley Ter *CLS/BIR/GTL* DH3 ...... 153 F6
  JRW NE32 .... 86 A5
Lumsden Sq *SEA/MUR* SR7 .... 188 A1 🖪
Lund Av *DHAM* DH1 .... 179 F6
Lunedale Av *CLDN/WHIT/ROK* SR6 . 108 B5
Lunedale Dr *CLS/BIR/GTL* DH3 .... 168 A4 🖪
Lunesdale St *HLH* DH5 .... 185 F2
Lupin Cl *WD/WHPE/BLK* NE5 .... 59 E2 🖪
Luss Av *JRW* NE32 .... 87 D5
Lutterworth Cl *LGB/KIL* NE12 ...... 49 D6 🖪
Lutterworth Dr *LGB/KIL* NE12 ...... 48 C6
Lutterworth Rd
  ASHBK/HED/RY SR2 .... 144 B3
  LGB/KIL NE12 .... 65 D1 🖪
Luxembourg Rd *MLFD/PNYW* SR4 .. 124 C5
Lydbury Cl *CRAM* NE23 .... 14 B5 🖪
Lydcott *WASHS* NE38 .... 140 A2
Lydford Ct *HLS* DH4 .... 157 E5 🖪
  WD/WHPE/BLK NE5 .... 45 E6
Lydford Wy *CLS/BIR/GTL* DH3 ...... 136 C3
Lyncroft Rd *NSHW* NE29 .... 54 A6
Lyndale *CRAM* NE23 .... 14 B5
Lyndhurst Av *CLS/BIR/GTL* DH3 .... 153 E2
  JES NE2 .... 63 F4
  LWF/SPW/WRK NE9 .... 99 E6
Lyndhurst Cl *BLAY* NE21 .... 93 F2 🖪
Lyndhurst Crs *LWF/SPW/WRK* NE9 .. 99 F6
Lyndhurst Dr *DHAM* DH1 .... 193 F5 🖪
  LWF/SPW/WRK NE9 .... 99 F6
Lyndhurst Gdns *JES* NE2 .... 63 F4 🖪
Lyndhurst Gv *LWF/SPW/WRK* NE9 .. 99 F6
Lyndhurst Rd *LGB/KIL* NE12 .... 49 F5
  STLY/ANP DH9 .... 147 F2 🖪
Lyndhurst St *NSHS* NE33 .... 71 F4 🖪
Lyndhurst Ter *MLFD/PNYW* SR4 .. 125 D4 🖪
Lyndon Cl *BOL* NE36 .... 106 A3
Lyndon Dr *BOL* NE36 .... 106 A3
Lyndon Gv *BOL* NE36 .... 106 A3
Lyndon Wk *BLYTH* NE24 .... 9 E4
Lyne Cl *CLSW/PEL* DH2 .... 135 E6
Lyne's Dr *BDN/LAN/SAC* DH7 .... 203 F3 🖪
Lynfield *WBAY* NE26 .... 40 A2
Lynfield Ct *WD/WHPE/BLK* NE5 .... 61 D3 🖪
Lynfield Pl *WD/WHPE/BLK* NE5 .... 61 D3 🖪
Lynford Gdns
  ASHBK/HED/RY SR2 .... 144 B3 🖪
Lynholm Gv *LGB/KIL* NE12 .... 49 F4 🖪
Lynmouth Pl *LGB/HTN* NE7 .... 65 D3 🖪
Lynmouth Rd *NSHW* NE29 .... 69 E1 🖪
Lynndale Av *BLYTH* NE24 .... 9 F5
Lynnholme Gdns
  LWF/SPW/WRK NE9 .... 99 F2 🖪
Lynn Rd *NSHW* NE29 .... 53 F5 🖪
  WLSD/HOW NE28 .... 66 C5
Lynn St *BLYTH* NE24 .... 10 C5
Lynnwood Av *ELS/FEN* NE4 ...... 79 F1 🖪
Lynthorpe *ASHBK/HED/RY* SR2 .... 145 E6
Lyn-thorpe Gv
  CLDN/WHIT/ROK SR6 .... 127 D1
Lynton Av *JRW* NE32 .... 87 D3
Lynton Ct *HLS* DH4 .... 157 E5
Lynton Pl *WD/WHPE/BLK* NE5 .... 61 D3
Lynton Wy *WD/WHPE/BLK* NE5 .... 61 D3
Lynwood Av *BLAY* NE21 .... 76 B5 🖪
  MLFD/PNYW SR4 .... 141 F4
Lyons Av *HLH* DH5 .... 186 A2
Lyons La *HLH* DH5 .... 186 B3
Lyon St *HEBB* NE31 .... 84 C2
Lyric Cl *NSHW* NE29 .... 53 D4
Lysdon Av *MONK* NE25 .... 24 C2
Lyster Cl *SEA/MUR* SR7 .... 175 D1
Lytham Cl *CRAM* NE23 .... 21 D2 🖪
  WASHN NE37 .... 120 B3 🖪
  WLSD/HOW NE28 .... 52 A5
Lytham Dr *MONK* NE25 .... 39 F5
Lytham Gra *HLS* DH4 .... 156 C4

Lytham Pl *BYK/HTN/WLK* NE6 ...... 83 D3
Lythe Wy *LGB/KIL* NE12 .... 49 E6

M

Mabel St *BLAY* NE21 .... 76 B5
Macadam St *GATE* NE8 .... 98 C3
Maclynn Cl *SUNDSW* SR3 .... 160 A2
Macmerry Cl *SWCK/CAS* SR5 .... 123 E4 🖪
Macmillan Gdns *FELL* NE10 ...... 101 F2 🖪
Maddison St *BLYTH* NE24 .... 11 D4
Maddox Rd *LGB/KIL* NE12 .... 49 F6
Madeira Av *WBAY* NE26 .... 40 B3
Madeira Cl *WD/WHPE/BLK* NE5 .... 59 E2
Madeira Ter *SSH* NE33 .... 71 F5
Madras St *HAR/WTLS* NE34 .... 87 F4
Mafeking Pl *NSHW* NE29 .... 53 D3
Mafeking St *BYK/HTN/WLK* NE6 .. 83 C3 🖪
  LWF/SPW/WRK NE9 .... 99 F2 🖪
  MLFD/PNYW SR4 .... 125 E6
Magdalene Av *DHAM* DH1 .... 196 B2
Magdalene Hts *DHAM* DH1 ...... 195 D4 🖪
Magdalene St *DHAM* DH1 .... 195 D4 🖪
Magdalene Pl *MLFD/PNYW* SR4 .. 125 E5
Magenta Crs *WD/WHPE/BLK* NE5.. 59 E2
Maglona St *SEA/MUR* SR7 .... 176 C5
Maiden Law *HLS* DH4 .... 169 F3 🖪
Maiden St *ELS/FEN* NE4 .... 80 A5 🖪
Maidstone Cl *SUNDSW* SR3 ...... 159 F2 🖪
Main Crs *WLSD/HOW* NE28 .... 66 B2
Main Rd *DIN/WO* NE13 .... 31 D3
  DIN/WO NE13 .... 45 D5
  RYTON NE40 .... 74 A3
Mainsforth Ter West
  ASHBK/HED/RY SR2 .... 145 D2
Mains Park Rd *CLS/BIR/GTL* DH3 .. 153 F6
Mainstone Cl *CRAM* NE23 ...... 21 F2 🖪
Main St *PONT/DH* NE20 .... 28 A4
Main St North *CRAM* NE23.......... 36 A2
Makendon St *HEBB* NE31 .... 85 D1
Malaburn Wy *SWCK/CAS* SR5 .. 125 F3 🖪
Malaga Cl *WD/WHPE/BLK* NE5 .... 59 D2
Malaya Dr *BYK/HTN/WLK* NE6 .... 83 F3
Malcolm St *BYK/HTN/WLK* NE6 .. 81 F2
  SEA/MUR SR7 .... 176 C4 🖪
Malden Cl *CRAM* NE23 .... 21 E2
Maling Pk *MLFD/PNYW* SR4 ...... 124 A5 🖪
Malings Cl *SUND* SR1 .... 5 G3
Maling St *BYK/HTN/WLK* NE6 .... 81 F3 🖪
Mallard Cl *WASHS* NE38 .... 137 E2
Mallard Wy *BLYTH* NE24 .... 17 E3
  WLSD/HOW NE28 .... 52 C6
Mallowburn Crs *GOS/KPK* NE3 .... 61 E2
Malmo Cl *NSHW* NE29 .... 69 D1
Malone Gdns *CLS/BIR/GTL* DH3.. 118 C6
Maltby Cl *WASHS* NE38 .... 138 C2
Malton Cl *BLYTH* NE24 .... 10 A5 🖪
  BW/LEM/TK/HW NE15 .... 77 D2 🖪
Malton Crs *NSHW* NE29 .... 70 A2
Malton Gdns *WLSD/HOW* NE28.... 67 D3
Malvern Cl *BW/LEM/TK/HW* NE15 .. 76 A1
Malvern Crs *SEA/MUR* SR7........ 175 F1
Malvern Gdns
  CLDN/WHIT/ROK SR6 .... 127 D1
  DUN/TMV NE11 .... 97 F4 🖪
  DUN/TMV NE11 .... 97 F3 🖪
Malvern Rd *NSHW* NE29 .... 54 A4
  WBAY NE26 .... 26 C3
  WLSD/HOW NE28 .... 68 B3
Malvern St *SSH* NE33 .... 88 B1
Malvern Ter *STLY/ANP* DH9 ...... 148 C3
Malvins Close Rd *BLYTH* NE24...... 10 B5
Malvins Rd *BLYTH* NE24 .... 10 A4
Mandale Crs *TYNE/NSHE* NE30 .. 54 C1
Mandarin Cl *WD/WHPE/BLK* NE5 .. 59 D2
Mandela Cl *STLY/ANP* DH9 .... 147 F3
Mandela Wy *DUN/TMV* NE11 ...... 97 B8
Mandeville *WASHN* NE37 .... 121 D4
Manet Gdns *HAR/WTLS* NE34 .... 88 C4
Mangrove Cl *WD/WHPE/BLK* NE5.. 59 D2
Manila St *ASHBK/HED/RY* SR2 .... 145 D2
Manisty Ter *PLEE/EAS* SR8.......... 200 B7
Mann Crs *SEA/MUR* SR7 .... 174 C6 🖪
Manningford Cl *CRAM* NE23 .... 21 F3 🖪
Manningford Dr *SUNDSW* SR3 .... 160 A3
Manor Av *LGB/HTN* NE7 .... 65 E1
Manor Chare *CNUT* NE1 .... 3 F4
Manor Cl *GOS/KPK* NE3 .... 63 F1 🖪
Manor Dr *LGB/HTN* NE7 .... 65 E1
  STLY/ANP DH9 .... 146 B3
Manorfields *LGB/KIL* NE12.......... 49 F6
Manor Gdns *FELL* NE10 .... 102 B2
  LGB/HTN NE7 .... 65 E1 🖪
Manor Gv *BW/LEM/TK/HW* NE15 .. 75 E1
  HLS DH4 .... 158 B1
  LGB/HTN NE7 .... 65 E1
Manor Hall Cl *SEA/MUR* SR7 ...... 175 D2
Manor House Rd *JES* NE2 .... 64 B5
Manor Pl *LGB/HTN* NE7 .... 65 E1
Manor Rd *LGB/HTN* NE7 .... 65 E2
  STLY/ANP DH9 .... 148 B1 🖪
  TYNE/NSHE NE30 .... 55 F4

Manor Ter *BLAY* NE21 .... 94 B3
Manor Vw *WASHN* NE37 .... 120 C4
Manor Vw East *WASHN* NE37 .... 121 D4
Manor Wk *LGB/HTN* NE7 .... 65 E1 🖪
Manor Wy *PLEE/EAS* SR8 .... 209 D3
Manorway *TYNE/NSHE* NE30 ...... 55 F4 🖪
Mansell Crs *PLEE/EAS* SR8 ...... 209 D1
Mansell Pl *GOS/KPK* NE3 .... 62 A3
Mansfield Ct *BOL* NE36............ 105 F3 🖪
Mansfield Crs
  CLDN/WHIT/ROK SR6 .... 127 D1
Mansfield Pl *ELS/FEN* NE4 ...... 80 A3 🖪🖪
Mansfield St *ELS/FEN* NE4 .... 80 A3
Manston Cl *SUNDSW* SR3 .... 159 F3
Manx Sq *SWCK/CAS* SR5 .... 126 A1
Maple Av *DHAM* DH1 .... 195 F4
  DUN/TMV NE11 .... 97 F3
  MONK NE25 .... 54 B1
  SUNDSW SR3 .... 144 B3
Maplebeck Cl *SUNDSW* SR3 .... 159 F3 🖪
Maple Cl *BW/LEM/TK/HW* NE15 .. 77 D2 🖪
Maple Ct *BDN/LAN/SAC* DH7 .... 202 B5
  MONK NE25 .... 24 C2 🖪
Maple Crs *BLYTH* NE24 .... 9 E4
  SEA/MUR SR7 .... 176 A6
Mapledene Rd *GOS/KPK* NE3 .... 46 B6
Maple Gv *CLDN/WHIT/ROK* SR6.. 109 E1
  FELL NE10 .... 101 D2 🖪
  GATE NE8 .... 99 D3
  HAR/WTLS NE34 .... 89 E3
Maple Pk *BDN/LAN/SAC* DH7 .... 192 A5
Maple Rd *BLAY* NE21 .... 76 B6
Maple Rw *WICK/BNPF* NE16 ...... 78 A6
Maple St *ELS/FEN* NE4 .... 80 A4
  JRW NE32 .... 85 F1
  STLY/ANP DH9 .... 147 F4
Maple Ter *HLS* DH4 .... 156 C3
Maplewood *CLSW/PEL* DH2 ...... 153 D4
Maplewood Av *SWCK/CAS* SR5 .. 125 E1
Maplewood St *HLS* DH4 .... 169 D1
Mapperley Dr
  BW/LEM/TK/HW NE15............ 77 D1
Marblet Ct *DUN/TMV* NE11 ...... 98 A3 🖪
Marbury Cl *SUNDSW* SR3 .... 159 F2 🖪
March Rd *CRAM* NE23 .... 35 D3 🖪
Marcia Av *CLDN/WHIT/ROK* SR6 .. 126 C1 🖪
Marconi Wy *WICK/BNPF* NE16 .... 96 A1
Marcross Cl *WD/WHPE/BLK* NE5 .. 59 D2 🖪
Marcross Dr *SUNDSW* SR3 ...... 159 F3
Mardale *WASHN* NE37 .... 120 A5
Mardale Gdns *LWF/SPW/WRK* NE9.. 117 F1
Mardale Rd *WD/WHPE/BLK* NE5.. 61 D5
Mardale St *HLH* DH5 .... 185 F2
Marden Av *TYNE/NSHE* NE30 .... 55 E1
Marden Ct *WBAY* NE26 .... 26 A1 🖪
Marden Crs *WBAY* NE26 .... 41 E6
Marden Rd South *MONK* NE25 .... 40 C6
Marden Ter *TYNE/NSHE* NE30 .... 55 E1
Mareburn Crs *FELL* NE10 .... 101 D2
Maree Cl *SUNDSW* SR3 .... 160 A3
Margaret Alice St
  MLFD/PNYW SR4 .... 125 D5 🖪
Margaret Dr *LGB/KIL* NE12 ...... 50 C4 🖪
Margaret Gv *HAR/WTLS* NE34 .... 87 F3 🖪
Margaret Rd *WBAY* NE26 .... 41 E6
Margaret St *ASHBK/HED/RY* SR2 .. 145 E4
  SEA/MUR SR7 .... 176 C4
Margaret Ter *ROWG* NE39 .... 110 B3
Margery La *DHAM* DH1 .... 194 A6
Marguerite Ct *MLFD/PNYW* SR4 .. 126 A5 🖪
Marian Ct *GATE* NE8 .... 98 C1 🖪
Marian Dr *FELL* NE10 .... 84 A6
Marian Wy *HAR/WTLS* NE34 ...... 89 E5
Maria St *ELS/FEN* NE4 .... 79 D4
  SEA/MUR SR7 .... 176 C3
  SUNDSW SR3...................... 160 C1
Marie Curie Dr *ELS/FEN* NE4 .... 79 E4 🖪
Marigold Av *FELL* NE10 .... 82 A6
Marigold Ct *MLFD/PNYW* SR4 .... 126 A5 🖪🖪
Marigold Crs *HLS* DH4 .... 156 A5
Marigold Wk *HAR/WTLS* NE34 .... 88 A3
Marina Av *CLDN/WHIT/ROK* SR6 .. 108 B6
Marina Ct *CLDN/WHIT/ROK* SR6 .. 126 C1 🖪
Marina Dr *MONK* NE25 .... 39 E6
  SSH NE33 .... 72 A3
Marina Gv *CLDN/WHIT/ROK* SR6 .. 126 C1 🖪
Marina Ter *CLDN/WHIT/ROK* SR6 .. 109 E1 🖪
Marina Veiw *WLSD/HOW* NE28 .... 68 B4
Marina Vw *HEBB* NE31 .... 84 C2
Marina Wy *SSH* NE33 .... 72 A4
Marine Av *WBAY* NE26 .... 40 C4 🖪
Marine Dr *ASHBK/HED/RY* SR2 .... 145 E6
  HEBB NE31 .... 85 F5
  JRW NE32 .... 85 F6
Marine Gdns *WBAY* NE26 .... 40 C5
Mariners' La *TYNE/NSHE* NE30 .... 55 E5
Marine Ter *BLYTH* NE24 .... 10 C5
Marine Wk *CLDN/WHIT/ROK* SR6 .. 127 E2
Marion St *ASHBK/HED/RY* SR2 .... 145 D2
Maritime Crs *PLEE/EAS* SR8........ 201 E4
Maritime St *SUND* SR1 .... 4 C3 🖪
Marius Av *BW/LEM/TK/HW* NE15 .. 56 B4
Marville East *ASHBK/HED/RY* SR2.. 162 C3

Mariville West
ASHBK/HED/RY SR2 .... 162 C3
Markby Cl *SUNDSW SR3* .... 160 A3 ◪
Market La *CNUT NE1*.................... 2 D4
WICK/BNPF NE16 .... 95 F1
WICK/BNPF NE16 .... 96 C2
Market Pl *HLH DH5* 171 E2
Market Sq *JRW NE32* .... 86 A1 ◪
Market St *CNUT NE1* 2 D3
CRAM NE23............................ 34 C2
HLH DH5 .... 172 A6
Market Wy *DUN/TMV NE11* 98 C4
Markham Av *CLDN/WHIT/ROK SR6* .. 109 F2
Markham St
ASHBK/HED/RY SR2 .... 145 E4 ◪
Markington Dr
ASHBK/HED/RY SR2 .... 162 B2
Markle Gv *HLH DH5*.................. 170 C5
Mark Ri *HLH DH5* 171 F5
Mark's La *HLS DH4* 169 E6
Marlboro Av *WICK/BNPF NE16* ... 96 A2
Marlborough Ap *GOS/KPK NE3* ... 47 E3 ◪
Marlborough Av *GOS/KPK NE3* 47 D6
Marlborough Ct *GOS/KPK NE3* 45 F5
HLH DH5 .... 171 D4 ◪
Marlborough Rd
MLFD/PNYW SR4 .... 141 E3
WASHN NE37 .... 121 D3
Marlborough St North *SSH NE33* .. 71 F6 ◪
Marlborough St South *SSH NE33* .. 71 F6
Marleen Av *BYK/HTN/WLK NE6* 65 E6
Marleen Ct *BYK/HTN/WLK NE6* .... 65 E6 ◪
Marley Crs *SWCK/CAS SR5* 125 E1
Marlfield Ct *WD/WHPE/BLK NE5* .. 61 D3 ◪
Marlow Dr *SUNDSW SR3* 159 F3
Marlowe Gdns *GATE NE8* .... 99 E1 ◪
Marlowe Pl *HLH DH5* 171 D3
Marlow Pl *LGB/KIL NE12* 49 E6
Marlow St *BLAY NE24* 10 C5
Marmion Rd *BYK/HTN/WLK NE6* .. 66 B6
Marmion Ter *MONK NE25* 40 B5
Marne St *HLS DH4* 157 D2
Marondale Av *BYK/HTN/WLK NE6* .. 83 E1
Marquis Av *WD/WHPE/BLK NE5* ... 59 E1
Marr Rd *HEBB NE31* 85 E3
Marsden Av *CLDN/WHIT/ROK SR6* .. 91 E4
Marsden Cl *HLH DH4* 170 B2
Marsden Gv
LWF/SPW/WRK NE9 .... 118 C2 ◪
Marsden La *HAR/WTLS NE34* 90 A1
WD/WHPE/BLK NE5 .... 60 C3
Marsden Rd *CLDN/WHIT/ROK SR6* .. 107 E2
HAR/WTLS NE34 .... 89 E1
Marshall St *CLDN/WHIT/ROK SR6* . 108 C6
Marshall Wallis Rd *SSH NE33*..... 71 E6
Marsham Ct *BW/LEM/TK/HW NE15* .. 77 D1
CLDN/WHIT/ROK SR6 .... 89 F6
Marsham Rd
WD/WHPE/BLK NE5 .... 60 A3 ◪
Marsh Ct *DUN/TMV NE11* 98 A3
Marske Ter *BYK/HTN/WLK NE6* ... 83 D2
Marston *LGB/KIL NE12* .... 35 F6 ◪
Martello Gdns *LGB/HTN NE7* 65 F4
Martin Ct *WASHS NE38* 137 E4
Martindale Av
CLDN/WHIT/ROK SR6 .... 108 B5
Martindale Pk *HLH DH5* 171 D3
Martin Rd *WLSD/HOW NE28* 68 B4
Marwell Dr *WASHN NE37* .... 121 D2 ◪
Marwood Gv *PLEE/EAS SR8*...... 208 B5
Mary Agnes St *GOS/KPK NE3* .... 62 C1 ◪
Mary Av *CLS/BIR/GTL DH3* 118 A6
Maryhill Cl *ELS/FEN NE4* .... 79 D4 ◪
Mary's Pl *BYK/HTN/WLK NE6*...... 84 A2
Mary St *BLAY NE24* 75 F6
BLAY NE21 .... 76 B5
SEA/MUR SR7 .... 177 D3 ◪
SUND SR1 .... 4 B4 ◪
SUNDSW SR3 .... 143 F6
Mary Ter *WD/WHPE/BLK NE5* 60 C4
Masefield Av *WICK/BNPF NE16* ... 96 A5 ◪
Masefield Cl *STLY/ANP DH9* 149 D1
Masefield Dr *HAR/WTLS NE34* 87 F6
Mason Rd *WLSD/HOW NE28* 66 C2
Mason St *BYK/HTN/WLK NE6* ..... 82 B3 ◪
Mast La *TYNE/NSHE NE30* 55 D1
Matamba Ter *MLFD/PNYW SR4* .. 126 A6
Matanzas St *ASHBK/HED/RY SR2* .. 145 D3
Matfen Av *SMOOR NE27* 52 B1
Matfen Cl *BLYTH NE24* 10 B5
BW/LEM/TK/HW NE15 .... 77 D2 ◪
Matfen Dr *SUNDSW SR3* .... 159 F2 ◪
Matfen Gdns *WLSD/HOW NE28* .. 68 B1
Matfen Pl *ELS/FEN NE4* 79 E1
GOS/KPK NE3 .... 46 C6 ◪
Mather Rd *ELS/FEN NE4* .... 80 A4 ◪
Matlock Gdns
WD/WHPE/BLK NE5 .... 60 B3 ◪
Matlock Rd *JRW NE32* .... 86 B3 ◪
Matlock St *SUND SR1* 4 C1
Matterdale Rd *PLEE/EAS SR8* 209 E2
Matthew Bank *JES NE2* 64 A3
Matthew Rd *BLYTH NE24* 17 E1
Matthew St *BYK/HTN/WLK NE6* ... 82 A2 ◪
Maudlin Pl *WD/WHPE/BLK NE5* ... 61 F5 ◪

Maudlin St *HLH DH5* 172 A4
Mauds La *SUND SR1* 5 F2
Maud St *BW/LEM/TK/HW NE15* .. 76 B2 ◪
CLDN/WHIT/ROK SR6 .... 109 D6
Maughan St *BLYTH NE24* 11 E5
Maureen Ter *SEA/MUR SR7* 176 B3
Maurice Rd *WLSD/HOW NE28* .... 67 D6 ◪
Mautland St *HLS DH4* .... 171 D1 ◪
Mavin St *DHAM DH1* 194 C6
Maxton Cl *SUNDSW SR3* .... 159 F3 ◪
Maxwell *SSH NE33* 71 E4
Maxwell St *GATE NE8* .... 98 C3 ◪
MLFD/PNYW SR4 .... 125 E5 ◪
SSH NE33 .... 71 E4
May Av *BLAY NE21* 94 B3
RYTON NE40 .... 74 B2 ◪
Maydown Cl *SWCK/CAS SR5* .... 123 E4 ◪
Mayfair Gdns *GATE NE8* .... 99 F2 ◪
HAR/WTLS NE34 .... 89 D1
PONT/DH NE20 .... 28 B4
Mayfair Rd *JES NE2* .... 63 F4 ◪
Mayfield *WICK/BNPF NE16* .... 96 A5 ◪
Mayfield Av *BW/LEM/TK/HW NE15* .. 58 A5
CRAM NE23 .... 22 B2
Mayfield Ct *CLDN/WHIT/ROK SR6* .. 126 C1 ◪
Mayfield Dr
CLDN/WHIT/ROK SR6 .... 108 A2 ◪
Mayfield Gdns
BW/LEM/TK/HW NE15 .... 58 A5 ◪
JRW NE32 .... 85 F2
WLSD/HOW NE28 .... 66 B3 ◪
Mayfield Gv *MLFD/PNYW SR4* ... 141 F4
Mayfield Pl *DIN/WO NE13* 32 C5
Mayfield Rd *GOS/KPK NE3* 63 D2
MLFD/PNYW SR4 .... 125 E6
Mayfield Ter *WD/WHPE/BLK NE5* .. 62 A5 ◪
May Gv *CLDN/WHIT/ROK SR6* 91 E5
May Lea *BDN/LAN/SAC DH7* 178 A3
Maynard's Rw *DHAM DH1* 195 E4
Mayo Dr *SUNDSW SR3* .... 160 A3 ◪
Mayoral Wy *DUN/TMV NE11* 116 C2
Mayorswell Cl *DHAM DH1* .... 194 C4 ◪
Mayorswell Fld *DHAM DH1* ...... 194 C4 ◪
Mayorswell St *DHAM DH1* .... 194 C4 ◪
Maypole Cl *SWCK/CAS SR5* ...... 126 A3 ◪
May St *BLAY NE21* 94 A1
CLS/BIR/GTL DH3 .... 136 B1
DHAM DH1 .... 194 A5
MLFD/PNYW SR4 .... 126 A5
SSH NE33 .... 71 F7 ◪
Mayswood Rd
CLDN/WHIT/ROK SR6 .... 126 C1
Maythorne Dr *RDHAMSE DH6* ... 188 A6
Maywood Cl *GOS/KPK NE3* 62 A2
Mcanany Av *HAR/WTLS NE34* 88 C3
Mcclaren Wy *HLS DH4* 158 B1
Mccracken Cl *GOS/KPK NE3* 47 E4
Mccracken Dr *DIN/WO NE13* 33 E3
Mcewan Gdns *ELS/FEN NE4* ..... 79 E3 ◪
Mcintyre Rd *HEBB NE31* .... 85 E1 ◪
Mckendrick Vls
WD/WHPE/BLK NE5 .... 61 F5
Mcnally Pl *DHAM DH1* .... 195 E4 ◪
Mcnamara Rd *WLSD/HOW NE28* .. 68 A3
Meacham Wy *WICK/BNPF NE16* ... 95 F5
Mead Av *LGB/KIL NE12* 50 A4
Mead Crs *LGB/KIL NE12* 50 A4
Meadowbrook Dr *FELL NE10* ... 102 B3 ◪
Meadow Cl *BLAY NE21* 93 E1
CRAM NE23 .... 23 E6 ◪
HLH DH5 .... 171 E5 ◪
LGB/KIL NE12 .... 49 D6 ◪
RYTON NE40 .... 74 C3
Meadow Ct *BDLGTN NE22* 7 D3
PONT/DH NE20 .... 28 A5
Meadowdale Crs *BDLGTN NE22* ... 6 C3
WD/WHPE/BLK NE5 .... 61 F3
Meadow Dr *CLSW/PEL DH2* 152 B6
DIN/WO NE13 .... 33 E2
SUNDSW SR3 .... 159 D3
Meadowfield *MONK NE25* 39 F5
PONT/DH NE20 .... 28 A5
Meadowfield Av *GOS/KPK NE3* ... 46 C6
Meadowfield Dr
CLDN/WHIT/ROK SR6 .... 107 F1
Meadowfield Gdns
BYK/HTN/WLK NE6 .... 66 C5 ◪
Meadowfield Rd *GOS/KPK NE3* ... 63 D2 ◪
Meadowfield Wy *STLY/ANP DH9* .. 130 B6
Meadow Gdns *SUNDSW SR3* .... 144 A3 ◪
Meadow Gra *HLS DH4* 156 A6
Meadow Gv *MLFD/PNYW SR4* 141 F1
Meadow La *DUN/TMV NE11* ...... 97 E1 ◪
Meadow Laws *HAR/WTLS NE34* .. 89 F4
Meadow Ri *WD/WHPE/BLK NE5* ... 61 D2
Meadow Rd *BW/LEM/TK/HW NE15* .. 76 C1
MONK NE25 .... 39 F6
WBAY NE26 .... 26 A2
WLSD/HOW NE28 .... 68 B5 ◪
Meadowside *ASHBK/HED/RY SR2* .. 144 A2
Meadows La *HLS DH4* 170 A6
The Meadows *GOS/KPK NE3* 46 B6
HLS DH4.............................. 155 F5
HLS DH4 .... 183 F1
RYTON NE40 .... 74 C3

Meadow St *HLH DH5* 170 B6
Meadow V *ASHBK/HED/RY SR2* .. 144 B2
Meadow Vw *MONK NE25*............ 24 C2
STLY/ANP DH9 .... 129 D5 ◪
SUNDSW SR3....................... 159 D3
Meadow Well Wy *NSHW NE29* .... 70 A2 ◪
Mead Wk *BYK/HTN/WLK NE6* 83 E2
Mead Wy *LGB/KIL NE12* 50 B4
Meadway Dr *LGB/KIL NE12* 50 B5
Means Dr *CRAM NE23*.............. 35 D5
Medburn Av *TYNE/NSHE NE30* ... 55 E2
Medburn Rd *BW/LEM/TK/HW NE15*.. 76 A1
MONK NE25.......................... 40 B6
Medham Cl *FELL NE10* .... 101 D4 ◪
Medina Cl *SUNDSW SR3* .... 160 A3 ◪
Medomsley Gdns
LWF/SPW/WRK NE9 .... 101 D6 ◪
Medomsly St *MLFD/PNYW SR4* .. 125 F5
Medway *JRW NE32* 86 B6
Medway Av *HEBB NE31* 85 D5
Medway Cl *PLEE/EAS SR8* 208 B4
Medway Crs *GATE NE8* 100 A2
Medway Gdns *MLFD/PNYW SR4* .. 142 C2 ◪
TYNE/NSHE NE30 .... 54 C5 ◪
Medway Pl *CRAM NE23* 14 B5
Megstone Av *CRAM NE23* 21 F3
Megstone Ct *LGB/KIL NE12* 36 A6
Melbeck Dr *CLSW/PEL DH2* 135 D4
Melbourne Crs *MONK NE25* 54 A1
Melbourne Gdns *HAR/WTLS NE34* .. 87 E5
Melbourne Pl *MLFD/PNYW SR4* .. 143 D2
Melbourne St *CNUT NE1* 3 F4
Melbury *MONK NE25* 39 E4
Melbury Ct
CLDN/WHIT/ROK SR6 .... 126 C1 ◪
Melbury Rd *LGB/HTN NE7* 64 C5
Melbury St *SEA/MUR SR7* 176 C5
Meldon Av *GOS/KPK NE3* .... 46 B5 ◪
HAR/WTLS NE34 .... 89 D2
RDHAMSE DH6 .... 197 F5
Meldon Gdns *DUN/TMV NE11* ... 97 F5
Meldon Rd *MLFD/PNYW SR4* .... 125 E5 ◪
Meldon St *WLSD/HOW NE28* 69 E5
Meldon Ter *BYK/HTN/WLK NE6* ... 65 D6
Meldon Wy *BLAY NE21* 93 E2
STLY/ANP DH9 .... 147 D4
Melgarve Dr *SUNDSW SR3* 160 A3
Melkington Ct
WD/WHPE/BLK NE5 .... 61 D3 ◪
Melkridge Pl *CRAM NE23* 21 E3
Mellendean Cl
WD/WHPE/BLK NE5 .... 61 D3 ◪
Melling Rd *CRAM NE23*............. 21 E2
Melmerby Cl *GOS/KPK NE3* 47 F5
Melness Rd *DIN/WO NE13* 32 C5
Melrose *WASHS NE38* 138 C3
Melrose Av *BDLGTN NE22* 8 B1
HEBB NE31 .... 85 D5
SEA/MUR SR7 .... 187 F2
SMOOR NE27 .... 37 E5
TYNE/NSHE NE30 .... 54 C2
Melrose Cl *BW/LEM/TK/HW NE15*.. 77 D2
GOS/KPK NE3 .... 47 D2 ◪
Melrose Ct *BDLGTN NE22* 8 C2
Melrose Crs *SEA/MUR SR7* 175 E2
Melrose Gdns
CLDN/WHIT/ROK SR6 .... 127 D1
WLSD/HOW NE28 .... 68 C2
Melrose Gv *JRW NE32* .... 87 D4 ◪
Meisonby Cl *SUNDSW SR3* ...... 159 F2 ◪
Meltham Ct *WD/WHPE/BLK NE5* .. 59 D4 ◪
Meltham Dr *SUNDSW SR3* .... 160 A3 ◪
Melton Av *BYK/HTN/WLK NE6* .... 83 E3 ◪
Melton Crs *WBAY NE26* 26 C4
Melton Dr *MONK NE25* 24 C2
Melvaig Cl *SUNDSW SR3* 160 A3
Melville Av *BLYTH NE24* 16 C1
Melville Gdns *MONK NE25* 39 E6
Melville Gv *LGB/HTN NE7* 64 C3
Melville St *CLS/BIR/GTL DH3* 153 E6
Melvin Pl *WD/WHPE/BLK NE5* ... 61 D4
Melvyn Gdns
CLDN/WHIT/ROK SR6 .... 127 D1
Membury Cl *SUNDSW SR3* .... 160 A3 ◪
Memorial Av *PLEE/EAS SR8* 201 D1
Mendip Av *CLSW/PEL DH2* 153 D6
Mendip Cl *PLEE/EAS SR8* 208 A2
Mendip Dr *WASHS NE38* 138 A3
Mendip Gdns *DUN/TMV NE11* ... 98 A4 ◪
Mendip Ter *STLY/ANP DH9* 148 C3
Mendip Wy *LGB/KIL NE12* .... 48 B6 ◪
Menvill Pl *SUND SR1* 5 F3
Mercantile Rd *HLS DH4* 170 B3
Merchants Whf
BYK/HTN/WLK NE6 .... 82 B4 ◪
Mercia Wy *BW/LEM/TK/HW NE15* .. 77 D3
Mere Dr *DHAM DH1* 180 A5
Mere Knolls Rd
CLDN/WHIT/ROK SR6 .... 109 D6
Meresyde *FELL NE10* 101 F3
Merevale Cl *WASHN NE37* 121 D2
Meridan Wy *LGB/HTN NE7* 65 F3
Merlay Dr *DIN/WO NE13* .... 31 D4 ◪
Merle Ter *MLFD/PNYW SR4* ...... 125 E4 ◪
Merlin Cl *SEA/MUR SR7* 176 B2

Merlin Crs *WLSD/HOW* NE28 .... 68 B3
Merlin Dr *CLS/BIR/GTL* DH3 .... 153 F1
Merlin Pl *LGB/KIL* NE12 .... 48 C5
Merlin Wy *SMOOR* NE27 .... 52 C3 **5**
Merrington Cl *SUNDSW* SR3 .... 159 F2 **5**
Merrion Cl *SUNDSW* SR3 .... 159 F2 **6**
Merryfield Gdns
  CLDN/WHIT/ROK SR6 .... 127 D1 **5**
Mersey Pl *GATE* NE8 .... 100 A1
Mersey Rd *GATE* NE8 .... 100 A2
  HEBB NE31 .... 85 D5
Merton Ct *ELS/FEN* NE4 .... 78 C4
Merton Rd *BYK/HTN/WLK* NE6 .... 83 E4
  PONT/DH NE20 .... 28 A4 **1**
Merton Sq *BLYTH* NE24 .... 11 D4 **5**
Metcalfe Crs *SEA/MUR* SR7 .... 188 A1
Methuen St
  LWF/SPW/WRK NE9 .... 99 F2 **10**
Methven Wy *CRAM* NE23 .... 14 B4
The Mews *BLAY* NE21 .... 77 D6
  HLS DH4 .... 169 T3 **2**
  SUNDSW SR3 .... 159 D1
  TYNE/NSHE NE30 .... 54 C6
Michaelgate *BYK/HTN/WLK* NE6 .... 82 B2 **6**
Mickle Cl *WASHN* NE37 .... 119 F6
Mickleton Cl *CLS/BIR/GTL* DH3 .... 168 A3
Mickleton Gdns *SUNDSW* SR3 .... 144 A4 **5**
Middle Cl *WASHS* NE38 .... 138 A5
Middle Dr *WD/WHPE/BLK* NE5 .... 59 F4
Middle Dr *WD/WHPE/BLK* NE13 .... 44 B3
Middle Engine La *SMOOR* NE27 .... 52 C5
  WLSD/HOW NE28 .... 68 B1
Middlefield *CLSW/PEL* DH2 .... 152 A1
Middlegarth *WD/WHPE/BLK* NE5 .... 61 F4 **12**
Middle Ga *WD/WHPE/BLK* NE5 .... 59 F5
Middle Gn *MONK* NE25 .... 39 E6
Middleham Cl *CLSW/PEL* DH2 .... 135 D5
Middleham Ct *SWCK/CAS* SR5 .... 125 D1
Middleham Rd *DHAM* DH1 .... 180 C5
Middles Rd *STLY/ANP* DH9 .... 148 C5
Middle St *BYK/HTN/WLK* NE6 .... 83 F2
  SUND SR1 .... 4 B2 **5**
  TYNE/NSHE NE30 .... 55 F5
Middle St East *BYK/HTN/WLK* NE6 .... 83 F2
Middleton Cl *ELS/FEN* NE4 .... 79 D2
  ROWG NE39 .... 111 E3 **1**
Middleton Cl *SEA/MUR* SR7 .... 175 D1
Middleton St *BLYTH* NE24 .... 11 D5
Middlewood Pk *ELS/FEN* NE4 .... 62 A6
Midfield Dr *CLDN/WHIT/ROK* SR6 .... 127 D2
Midgley Dr *SUNDSW* SR3 .... 160 A3
Midhill Cl *BDN/LAN/SAC* DH7 .... 203 D3
Midhurst Av *HAR/WTLS* NE34 .... 72 B6
Midhurst Cl *SUNDSW* SR3 .... 159 F2
Midhurst Rd *LGB/KIL* NE12 .... 49 F5
Midmoor Rd *MLFD/PNYW* SR4 .... 125 D5
Midsomer Cl *SUNDSW* SR3 .... 159 F3 **5**
Midway *BYK/HTN/WLK* NE6 .... 83 F2
Milbanke Cl *CLSW/PEL* DH2 .... 135 F5
Milbank Ter *RDHAMSE* DH6 .... 206 B2
Milburn Dr *BW/LEM/TK/HW* NE15 .... 78 A2
Mildmay Rd *JES* NE2 .... 63 F4 **4**
Milecastle Ct *WD/WHPE/BLK* NE5 .... 59 F4
Mile End Rd *SSH* NE33 .... 71 E2
Milfield Av *SMOOR* NE27 .... 52 B1
  WLSD/HOW NE28 .... 67 E2
Milford Gdns *GOS/KPK* NE3 .... 47 D3
Milford Rd *BW/LEM/TK/HW* NE15 .... 78 B3
Military Rd *TYNE/NSHE* NE30 .... 55 D4
Milk Market *CNUT* NE1 .... 3 G4
Millais Gdns *HAR/WTLS* NE34 .... 88 B3
Mill Bank *SWCK/CAS* SR5 .... 108 B6
Millbank Pl *BDLGTN* NE22 .... 8 A4
Millbank Rd *BDLGTN* NE22 .... 8 A3
  BYK/HTN/WLK NE6 .... 83 F4
Millbeck Gv *HLH* DH5 .... 170 C4 **1**
Millbrook *NSHW* NE29 .... 70 A1 **1**
Millbrook Rd *CRAM* NE23 .... 14 B5
Millburngate *DHAM* DH1 .... 194 B4 **5**
Millburn St *MLFD/PNYW* SR4 .... 126 A5 **11**
Mill Cl *NSHW* NE29 .... 70 A1 **2**
Mill Ct *HLS* DH4 .... 156 A6
Mill Crs *HEBB* NE31 .... 84 B6
Milldale *SEA/MUR* SR7 .... 175 E2
Milldale Av *BLYTH* NE24 .... 9 F5 **3**
Mill Dam *SSH* NE33 .... 71 D4
Milldene Av *TYNE/NSHE* NE30 .... 55 E4
Mill Dene Vw *SEA/MUR* SR7 .... 86 A3
Mill Dyke Cl *MONK* NE25 .... 39 E4
Millenium Wy *SWCK/CAS* SR5 .... 126 B4
Miller Gdns *CLSW/PEL* DH2 .... 151 F4
Miller's La *WICK/BNPF* NE16 .... 96 A1
Millers Rd *BYK/HTN/WLK* NE6 .... 82 B1
Miller St *GATE* NE8 .... 98 C2 **4**
Miller Ter *SUNDSW* SR3 .... 143 F6
Millfield *BDLGTN* NE22 .... 26 C3
  WBAY NE26 .... 26 C3
Millfield Av *GOS/KPK* NE3 .... 62 A3
Millfield Cl
  BW/LEM/TK/HW NE15 .... 58 B6 **2**
  CLSW/PEL DH2 .... 165 F1
Millfield Ct *BDLGTN* NE22 .... 7 F4
Millfield East *BDLGTN* NE22 .... 7 F4
Millfield Gdns *BLYTH* NE24 .... 10 C3 **3**
  FELL NE10 .... 100 B3 **4**
  TYNE/NSHE NE30 .... 55 E4

Millfield Gv *TYNE/NSHE* NE30 .... 55 E4
Millfield La *BW/LEM/TK/HW* NE15 .... 58 B6
Millfield North *BDLGTN* NE22 .... 7 F4
Millfield Rd *WICK/BNPF* NE16 .... 96 A4
Millfield South *BDLGTN* NE22 .... 7 F5
Millfield West *BDLGTN* NE22 .... 7 F4
Millford *FELL* NE10 .... 101 F5
Mill Gv *HAR/WTLS* NE34 .... 90 A4
  TYNE/NSHE NE30 .... 55 E4
Millgrove Vw *GOS/KPK* NE3 .... 62 B3 **5**
Mill Hl *HLH* DH5 .... 170 C4
Mill Hill Gdns *SR8* 199 F6
Mill Hill Rd *SUNDSW* SR3 .... 160 B2
  WD/WHPE/BLK NE5 .... 60 B6
Mill La *BLAY* NE21 .... 94 A3
  BW/LEM/TK/HW NE15 .... 56 B3
  CLDN/WHIT/ROK SR6 .... 91 E5
  CLSW/PEL DH2 .... 166 A6
  CRAM NE23 .... 35 E1
  DHAM DH1 .... 195 F3
  ELS/FEN NE4 .... 79 F4
  HEBB NE31 .... 84 C6
  NSHW NE29 .... 71 D2
  RDHAMSE DH6 .... 197 E5
  STLY/ANP DH9 .... 134 C4
Millne Ct *BDLGTN* NE22 .... 7 E3
Millom Ct *PLEE/EAS* SR8 .... 207 F5
Millom Pl *LWF/SPW/WRK* NE9 .... 100 A5
Mill Pit *HLS* DH4 .... 157 D2 **5**
Mill Ri *GOS/KPK* NE3 .... 64 A2
Mill Rd *BDN/LAN/SAC* DH7 .... 204 A3
  GATE NE8 .... 3 H6
  SEA/MUR SR7 .... 175 E2
Mills Gdns *WLSD/HOW* NE28 .... 67 D3
Mill St *MLFD/PNYW* SR4 .... 126 A5
Millthorp Cl *ASHBK/HED/RY* SR2 .... 145 F5 **5**
Mill Vw *BOL* NE36 .... 105 F3
  FELL NE10 .... 100 B3
Mill View Av *CLDN/WHIT/ROK* SR6 .... 126 C3
Millview Dr *TYNE/NSHE* NE30 .... 55 E4
Millway *LWF/SPW/WRK* NE9 .... 99 F3
  WBAY NE26 .... 26 C6
Milner Crs *BLAY* NE21 .... 93 F1 **7**
Milner St *SSH* NE33 .... 72 A4
Milne Wy *GOS/KPK* NE3 .... 46 B6 **5**
Milrig Cl *SUNDSW* SR3 .... 160 A3 **9**
Milsted Cl *SUNDSW* SR3 .... 159 F3 **4**
Milsted Ct *WD/WHPE/BLK* NE5 .... 59 D4 **4**
Milton Av *HEBB* NE31 .... 85 D2
  HLH DH5 .... 171 E3
Milton Cl *JES* NE2 .... 81 E1
  SEA/MUR SR7 .... 176 A3
  STLY/ANP DH9 .... 149 D2
Milton Gv *NSHW* NE29 .... 54 B6 **5**
  RDHAMSE DH6 .... 206 C2
Milton La *PLEE/EAS* SR8 .... 200 B2
Milton Pl *JES* NE2 .... 81 E1
  LWF/SPW/WRK NE9 .... 119 D3
  NSHW NE29 .... 54 B6 **5**
Milton Rd *WICK/BNPF* NE16 .... 96 A2
Milton St *JRW* NE32 .... 69 D6 **1**
  MLFD/PNYW SR4 .... 125 F5
  SSH NE33 .... 71 F5
Milton Ter *NSHW* NE29 .... 54 B6
Milvain Av *ELS/FEN* NE4 .... 79 D2
Milvain Cl *GATE* NE8 .... 99 E1 **3**
Milvain St *GATE* NE8 .... 99 E1 **9**
Milverton Ct *GOS/KPK* NE3 .... 45 E6
Mimosa Dr *HEBB* NE31 .... 85 D5
Mimosa Pl *ELS/FEN* NE4 .... 61 F6
Mindrum Ter *BYK/HTN/WLK* NE6 .... 83 E4
  NSHW NE29 .... 69 F2
Mindrum Wy *MONK* NE25 .... 24 C5
Minehead Gdns *SUNDSW* SR3 .... 143 F6 **5**
Minerva Cl *WD/WHPE/BLK* NE5 .... 59 E2
Mingarry Cl *HLH* DH5 .... 170 B6 **1**
Minorca Cl *SUND* SR1 .... 5 F5
Minorca Pl *GOS/KPK* NE3 .... 62 B3
Minskip Cl *SUNDSW* SR3 .... 159 F3 **5**
Minster Gv *WD/WHPE/BLK* NE5 .... 59 D3
Minster Pde *JRW* NE32 .... 86 B3 **7**
Minting Pl *CRAM* NE23 .... 21 E2
Minton Ct *NSHW* NE29 .... 70 B2
Minton La *NSHW* NE29 .... 70 B2
Minton Sq *MLFD/PNYW* SR4 .... 125 D5 **7**
Mirk La *GATE* NE8 .... 3 F6
Mirlaw Rd *CRAM* NE23 .... 21 E3 **1**
Mistletoe Rd *JES* NE2 .... 64 A5
Mistletoe St *DHAM* DH1 .... 194 A5
Mitcham Crs *LGB/HTN* NE7 .... 65 D3
Mitchell Av *JES* NE2 .... 64 A4
  MONK NE25 .... 39 F6
Mitchell Cl *PLEE/EAS* SR8 .... 200 A6 **2**
Mitchell Gdns *HAR/WTLS* NE34 .... 88 B3 **6**
Mitchell St *BYK/HTN/WLK* NE6 .... 84 A3 **5**
  DHAM DH1 .... 144 A4 **3**
  STLY/ANP DH9 .... 147 F4
Mitford Av *BLYTH* NE24 .... 10 B6 **7**
  MONK NE25 .... 24 B5
Mitford Cl *WASHS* NE38 .... 138 A2
Mitford Ct *PLEE/EAS* SR8 .... 208 C4 **1**
Mitford Dr *RDHAMSE* DH6 .... 197 F4
  WD/WHPE/BLK NE5 .... 60 A3 **5**
Mitford Gdns *DUN/TMV* NE11 .... 97 F5
  WLSD/HOW NE28 .... 68 B1

Mitford Pl *GOS/KPK* NE3 .... 46 C6 **8**
Mitford Rd *HAR/WTLS* NE34 .... 89 D2
Mitford St *CLDN/WHIT/ROK* SR6 .... 109 D6
  WLSD/HOW NE28 .... 69 E4 **1**
Mitford Ter *JRW* NE32 .... 86 A6
Mitford Wy *DIN/WO* NE13 .... 31 D4
Mithras Gdns
  BW/LEM/TK/HW NE15 .... 56 A4
Mitre Pl *SSH* NE33 .... 71 D6
Moat Gdns *FELL* NE10 .... 102 B2
Modder St *BYK/HTN/WLK* NE6 .... 83 E5
Moffat Av *JRW* NE32 .... 87 D4
Moffat Cl *NSHW* NE29 .... 53 F4
Moine Gdns *CLDN/WHIT/ROK* SR6 .... 127 D1
Molineux St *BYK/HTN/WLK* NE6 .... 82 A2 **8**
Monarch Rd *ELS/FEN* NE4 .... 79 F5
Monarch Wy *SUNDSW* SR3 .... 159 E3
Mona St *STLY/ANP* DH9 .... 148 B1 **8**
Moncreiff Ter *PLEE/EAS* SR8 .... 200 B2
Monday Crs *ELS/FEN* NE4 .... 80 A2 **3**
Monday Pl *ELS/FEN* NE4 .... 80 A2 **5**
Money Slack *DHAM* DH1 .... 205 D3
Monkchester Rd
  BYK/HTN/WLK NE6 .... 83 D3
Monk Ct *PLEE/EAS* SR8 .... 208 A5
Monkdale Av *BLYTH* NE24 .... 9 F6
Monkhouse Av *TYNE/NSHE* NE30 .... 54 C3
Monkridge *WBAY* NE26 .... 40 A3
  WD/WHPE/BLK NE5 .... 59 D4
Monkridge Gdns *DUN/TMV* NE11 .... 97 E3
Monks Av *MONK* NE25 .... 53 F1
Monks' Crs *DHAM* DH1 .... 195 E5
Monkseaton Dr *MONK* NE25 .... 39 E5
Monkseaton Rd *MONK* NE25 .... 39 D5
Monksfeld *FELL* NE10 .... 101 D3
Monksfield Cl *SUNDSW* SR3 .... 160 B3 **5**
Monkside Cl *WASHS* NE38 .... 137 F4
Monks Park Wy *LGB/KIL* NE12 .... 48 C6
Monks Rd *MONK* NE25 .... 53 E1
Monkstone Av *TYNE/NSHE* NE30 .... 55 E4 **1**
Monkstone Cl *TYNE/NSHE* NE30 .... 55 E4 **2**
Monkstone Crs *TYNE/NSHE* NE30 .... 55 E4 **3**
Monk St *CLDN/WHIT/ROK* SR6 .... 126 C3 **9**
Monksway *JRW* NE32 .... 87 D2
Monks Wy *TYNE/NSHE* NE30 .... 55 E3
Monks Wd *NSHW* NE29 .... 54 A4
Monkswood Sq *SUNDSW* SR3 .... 161 D2 **4**
Monkton *FELL* NE10 .... 101 E4
Monkton Av *HAR/WTLS* NE34 .... 87 E4
Monkton La *HEBB* NE31 .... 85 D6
  JRW NE32 .... 85 E4
Monkton Rd *JRW* NE32 .... 86 A1 **7**
Monkton Ter *JRW* NE32 .... 86 A1 **8**
Monmouth Gdns *WLSD/HOW* NE28 .... 68 C2
Monroe Pl *WD/WHPE/BLK* NE5 .... 61 F4 **6**
Mons Av *HEBB* NE31 .... 85 D3
Montagu Av *GOS/KPK* NE3 .... 62 C4
Montagu Ct *GOS/KPK* NE3 .... 62 C4
Montague St
  BW/LEM/TK/HW NE15 .... 76 C2
  CLDN/WHIT/ROK SR6 .... 126 C1 **10**
Monterey *SUNDSW* SR3 .... 160 A3 **10**
  WASHN NE37 .... 120 C3
Montfalcon Cl *PLEE/EAS* SR8 .... 208 B2 **1**
Montford Cl *SUNDSW* SR3 .... 159 F3 **5**
Montgomery Rd *DHAM* DH1 .... 195 E3
Montpellier Pl *GOS/KPK* NE3 .... 62 B3 **4**
Montpellier Ter
  ASHBK/HED/RY SR2 .... 145 D2
Montrose Cl *MONK* NE25 .... 24 C2
Montrose Crs *LWF/SPW/WRK* NE9 .... 100 A3
Montrose Dr *FELL* NE10 .... 102 B3
Montrose Gdns *SUNDSW* SR3 .... 143 F3
Monument Vw *HLS* DH4 .... 139 F6
Moor Cl *NSHW* NE29 .... 53 E4
Moor Ct *CLDN/WHIT/ROK* SR6 .... 109 D2
Moor Crs *DHAM* DH1 .... 195 F3
  GOS/KPK NE3 .... 63 E3
Moorcroft Cl
  BW/LEM/TK/HW NE15 .... 76 C1
Moorcroft Rd
  BW/LEM/TK/HW NE15 .... 77 D1
Moordale Av *BLYTH* NE24 .... 9 F6 **1**
Moore Av *HAR/WTLS* NE34 .... 89 D2
Moore Crs South *HLH* DH6 .... 171 D3
Moor Edge Rd *BDN/LAN/SAC* DH7 .... 203 D5
Moor Edge Rd *SMOOR* NE27 .... 38 A6
Moore St *GATE* NE8 .... 99 F1
  STLY/ANP DH9 .... 148 A2 **2**
Moorfield *JES* NE2 .... 63 F3
Moorfield Gdns
  CLDN/WHIT/ROK SR6 .... 107 F3 **1**
Moorfoot Av *CLSW/PEL* DH2 .... 153 E6
Moorfoot Gdns *DUN/TMV* NE11 .... 97 F3
Moorhead *WD/WHPE/BLK* NE5 .... 62 A5
Moorhill Dun/TMV NE11 .... 116 B6
Moorhouse Cl *HAR/WTLS* NE34 .... 88 C3 **4**
Moorhouses Rd *NSHW* NE29 .... 53 E5 **5**
The Moorings
  BYK/HTN/WLK NE6 .... 82 B4 **5**
Moorland Av *BDLGTN* NE22 .... 9 D1
Moorland Ct *BDLGTN* NE22 .... 9 D1 **2**
Moorland Crs *BDLGTN* NE22 .... 9 D1 **3**
  BYK/HTN/WLK NE6 .... 83 D1
Moorland Dr *BDLGTN* NE22 .... 9 D2

Moorlands *JRW* NE32 .... 104 C1
The Moorlands *STLY/ANP* DH9 .. 129 D5 🔢
Moorland Vis *BDLGTN* NE22 .... 9 C1
Moorland Wy *CRAM* NE23 .... 13 D5
Moor La *BOL* NE36 .... 107 D2
   CLDN/WHIT/ROK SR6 .... 108 B2
   HAR/WTLS NE34 .... 89 D2
   WD/WHPE/BLK NE5 .... 61 F2
Moor La East *HAR/WTLS* NE34 ...... 89 F2
Moormill La *DUN/TMV* NE11 .... 117 D6
Moor Park Ct *NSHW* NE29 .... 53 E5
Moor Park Rd *NSHW* NE29 .... 53 D5
Moor Pl *GOS/KPK* NE3 .... 63 E3
Moor Rd North *GOS/KPK* NE3 ...... 63 F3
Moor Rd South *JES* NE2 .... 63 F3
Moorsburn Dr *HLS* DH4 .... 170 B1
Moors Cl *HLS* DH4 .... 170 A2
Moorsfield *HLS* DH4 .... 170 A2
Moorside *WASHN* NE37 .... 120 A5
Moorside North *ELS/FEN* NE4 ...... 62 A5
Moorside Rd *SUNDSW* SR3 .... 159 F3
Moorside South *ELS/FEN* NE4 ...... 79 E1
Moorsley Rd *HLH* DH5 .... 184 B4
   HLH DH5 .... 185 E2
Moor St *SUND* SR1 .... 5 F2
Moor Ter *SUND* SR1 .... 5 G3
Morvale La *WD/WHPE/BLK* NE5 .... 62 A4
Moorview Crs *WD/WHPE/BLK* NE5 .. 62 A4
Moorway *WASHN* NE37 .... 120 A6
Moorway Dr *BW/LEM/TK/HW* NE15.. 77 D1
Moralee Cl *LGB/HTN* NE7 .... 65 F3
Moran St *CLDN/WHIT/ROK* SR6 .. 108 C6 🔢
Moray Cl *CLS/BIR/GTL* DH3 .... 136 C5
   PLEE/EAS SR8 .... 208 B3
Moray St *CLDN/WHIT/ROK* SR6 .. 126 C2
Morcott Gdns *NSHW* NE29 .... 70 B2 🔢
Morden St *CNUT* NE1 .... 2 C1
Mordey Cl *ASHBK/HED/RY* SR2 ..... 5 F3
Moreland Ct
   CLDN/WHIT/ROK SR6 .... 126 C2 🔢
Morgan St *SWCK/CAS* SR5 .... 126 A2
Morgans Wy *BLAY* NE21 .... 75 F6
Morland Av *WASHS* NE38 .... 139 D3
Morland Gdns
   LWF/SPW/WRK NE9 .... 100 A3 🔢
Morley Hill Rd
   WD/WHPE/BLK NE5 .... 60 B6 🔢
Morley Ter *HLS* DH4 .... 169 F2
Morningside *BDN/LAN/SAC* DH7.. 164 B2
   WASHS NE38 .... 137 D6
Mornington Av *GOS/KPK* NE3 ...... 62 B3
Morpeth Av *DIN/WO* NE13 .... 33 E3
   HAR/WTLS NE34 .... 89 D1
   JRW NE32 .... 86 A5 🔢
Morpeth Cl *WASHS* NE38 .... 137 E2
Morpeth Dr *SUNDSW* SR3 .... 159 F2
Morpeth St *JES* NE2 .... 63 D6
   PLEE/EAS SR8 .... 201 E6
Morpeth Ter *NSHW* NE29 .... 69 F2
Morris Av *HAR/WTLS* NE34 .... 88 A5
Morris Crs *BOLCOL* NE35 .... 105 F2
Morris Gdns *FELL* NE10 .... 102 A2
Morrison St *GATE* NE8 .... 80 B6
Morris Rd *WICK/BNPF* NE16 .... 96 A2
Morris St *CLS/BIR/GTL* DH3 .... 136 A2
Morston Dr *BW/LEM/TK/HW* NE15... 77 D2
Mortimer Av *NSHW* NE29 .... 53 F6 🔢
   WD/WHPE/BLK NE5 .... 60 C3
Mortimer Cha *CRAM* NE23 .... 14 A5 🔢
Mortimer Rd *HAR/WTLS* NE34 ...... 89 D1
   SSH NE33 .... 71 F6
Mortimer St *MLFD/PNYW* SR4.... 125 E5
Morton Cl *WASHS* NE38 .... 138 C2 🔢
Morton Sq *PLEE/EAS* SR8 .... 208 B1
Morton St *BYK/HTN/WLK* NE6 ...... 82 C2
   SSH NE33 .... 71 E2 🔢
Morval Cl *SUNDSW* SR3 .... 159 F3
Morven Dr *FELL* NE10 .... 102 A1
Morwick Cl *CRAM* NE23 .... 21 E3
Morwick Pl *WD/WHPE/BLK* NE5 .. 61 F5 🔢
Morwick Rd *NSHW* NE29 .... 53 F4
Mosley St *CNUT* NE1 .... 3 F4
Moss Bank *LWF/SPW/WRK* NE9 .. 118 A1
Moss Cl *BW/LEM/TK/HW* NE15 .... 59 E6 🔢
Mossdale *DHAM* DH1 .... 196 C2
Moss Side *WLF/SPW/WRK* NE9 ... 118 A1
Mossway *CLSW/PEL* DH2 .... 151 F1
Moulton Pl *WD/WHPE/BLK* NE5 ... 61 E4
Mountbatten Av *HEBB* NE31 .... 85 D4
Mount Cl *LGB/KIL* NE12 .... 35 F6
   MLFD/PNYW SR4 .... 124 A6
   MONK NE25 .... 53 F1
Mountfield Gdns *GOS/KPK* NE3 ... 62 B2
Mountford Rd *MONK* NE25 .... 24 C1
Mount Gv *DUN/TMV* NE11 .... 97 E3
   MLFD/PNYW SR4 .... 143 F2
Mount La *LWF/SPW/WRK* NE9 ... 119 D4
Mount Pleasant *BLAY* NE21 .... 94 A1 🔢
   CLS/BIR/GTL DH3 .... 136 B3
   HLH DH5 .... 171 E2
   STLY/ANP DH9 .... 129 D5 🔢
   SWCK/CAS SR5 .... 125 F3 🔢

Mount Pleasant Ct
   BW/LEM/TK/HW NE15 .... 57 F4 🔢
Mount Rd *CLS/BIR/GTL* DH3 ...... 136 C1
   LWF/SPW/WRK NE9 .... 119 D4
   MLFD/PNYW SR4 .... 143 E2
Mountside Gdns *DUN/TMV* NE11 .. 97 E3
Mount Stewart St *SEA/MUR* SR7 .. 176 C5
Mount Ter *SSH* NE33 .... 71 E4 🔢
The Mount *BW/LEM/TK/HW* NE15 .. 57 E4
   RYTON NE40 .... 74 B3
Mount Vw *WICK/BNPF* NE16 .... 96 A2
Mourne Gdns *DUN/TMV* NE11.... 97 F4
Moutter Cl *PLEE/EAS* SR8............ 201 D6
Mowbray Cl *ASHBK/HED/RY* SR2 ... 4 D6
Mowbray Rd *ASHBK/HED/RY* SR2 ... 5 E6
   LGB/KIL NE12 .... 49 F4
   NSHW NE29 .... 53 F6
   SSH NE33 .... 72 A5
Mowbray St *BYK/HTN/WLK* NE6 .. 81 F2
   DHAM DH1 .... 194 A4
Mozart St *SSH* NE33 .... 71 F4
Muirfield *MONK* NE25 .... 39 F5
   SSH NE33 .... 72 B5
Muirfield Dr *FELL* NE10 .... 100 C4
   WASHN NE37 .... 120 B2
Muirfield Rd *LGB/HTN* NE7 .... 65 E1
Mulben Cl *ELS/FEN* NE4 .... 79 D4 🔢
Mulberry Pl *ELS/FEN* NE4 .... 80 A5 🔢
Mulberry St *FELL* NE10 .... 100 C4
Mulcaster Gdns
   WLSD/HOW NE28 .... 66 C3 🔢
Mulgrave Dr *CLDN/WHIT/ROK* SR6.. 127 D4
Mulgrave Ter *GATE* NE8 .... 81 D5
Mullen Dr *RYTON* NE40 .... 74 B4
Mullen Gdns *WLSD/HOW* NE28 .. 66 C2
Mullen Rd *WLSD/HOW* NE28 ...... 66 C2
Mull Gv *JRW* NE32 .... 87 D5 🔢
Muncaster Ms *PLEE/EAS* SR8 ..... 207 F5
Mundella Ter *BYK/HTN/WLK* NE6 .. 82 A1
Mundell St *STLY/ANP* DH9 .... 147 F4
Mundle Av *BLAY* NE21 .... 94 B4
Mundles La *BOL* NE36 .... 106 B3
Munslow Rd *SUNDSW* SR3 .... 142 D6 🔢
Muriel St *STLY/ANP* DH9 .... 148 A5
Murphy Gv *ASHBK/HED/RY* SR2 .. 162 A1 🔢
Murray Av *HLS* DH4 .... 169 F1 🔢
Murrayfield *CRAM* NE23 .... 23 E6 🔢
Murrayfield Dr *BDN/LAN/SAC* DH7.. 202 C5
Murrayfield Rd
   WD/WHPE/BLK NE5 .... 61 F3 🔢
Murrayfields *SMOOR* NE27 .... 51 F3
Murray Rd *DUN/TMV* NE11 .... 97 F3 🔢
Murray Rd *CLSW/PEL* DH2 .... 153 D5
   WLSD/HOW NE28 .... 68 B3
Murray St *BLAY* NE21 .... 76 B5
   PLEE/EAS SR8 .... 209 F2
Murton La *HLH* DH5 .... 186 C3
   NSHW NE29 .... 52 C3
Murton St *SUND* SR1 .... 5 E4
Muscott Gv
   BW/LEM/TK/HW NE15 .... 77 F2 🔢
Musgrave Rd *LWF/SPW/WRK* NE9 ... 99 E4
Musgrave Ter
   BYK/HTN/WLK NE6 .... 83 D2 🔢
Muswell Hl *BW/LEM/TK/HW* NE15... 77 F3
Mutual St *WLSD/HOW* NE28 .... 67 D4
Mylord Crs *LGB/KIL* NE12 .... 35 D5
Myrella Crs *ASHBK/HED/RY* SR2 .. 144 B4
Myreside Pl *LGB/KIL* NE12 .... 49 D5 🔢
Myrtle Av *CLDN/WHIT/ROK* SR6 .. 109 E1
   DUN/TMV NE11 .... 97 E3
Myrtle Crs *LGB/KIL* NE12 .... 49 F3
Myrtle Gv *HAR/WTLS* NE34 .... 89 E4 🔢
   JES NE2 .... 64 A4
   LWF/SPW/WRK NE9 .... 99 E6
   SUNDSW SR3 .... 161 D1
   WLSD/HOW NE28 .... 67 F5
Myrtle Rd *BLAY* NE21 .... 94 B1 🔢
Myrtles *CLSW/PEL* DH2 .... 153 D3

N

Nafferton Pl *WD/WHPE/BLK* NE5... 61 E6
Nailsworth Cl *BOLCOL* NE35 ...... 87 D6 🔢
Nairn Cl *CLS/BIR/GTL* DH3 .... 136 C4
   WASHN NE37 .... 120 B2
Nairn Rd *CRAM* NE23 .... 22 A1
Nairn St *JRW* NE32 .... 87 D5
Naisbitt Av *PLEE/EAS* SR8 .... 201 D6
Nansen Cl *WD/WHPE/BLK* NE5 .... 60 B4 🔢
Napier Rd *SEA/MUR* SR7 .... 175 F2
   WICK/BNPF NE16 .... 95 F1 🔢
Napier St *HAR/WTLS* NE34 .... 88 A2
   JES NE2 .... 3 G1
   JRW NE32 .... 86 A1 🔢
Napier Wy *BLAY* NE21 .... 77 D6 🔢
Narvik Wy *NSHW* NE29 .... 69 D1
Nash Av *HAR/WTLS* NE34 .... 88 C5
Naters St *WBAY* NE26 .... 41 E6
Natley Av *BOL* NE36 .... 107 D3
Navenby Cl *GOS/KPK* NE3 .... 47 F4 🔢
Naworth Av *TYNE/NSHE* NE30 .... 54 C3
Naworth Ct *PLEE/EAS* SR8.......... 208 A5

Naworth Dr *WD/WHPE/BLK* NE5 ... 60 A3
Naworth Ter *JRW* NE32 .... 86 C4
Nawton Av *SWCK/CAS* SR5 .... 126 B2
Nayland Rd *CRAM* NE23 .... 21 F1
Naylor Av *BLAY* NE21 .... 94 B4
Naylor Pl *WBAY* NE26 .... 26 A1
Neale St *CLDN/WHIT/ROK* SR6.... 126 C1
Nearlane Cl *DIN/WO* NE13 .... 33 E2 🔢
Neasdon Crs *TYNE/NSHE* NE30 ... 55 D3
Neasham Rd *SEA/MUR* SR7 .... 175 F1
Nedderton Cl
   WD/WHPE/BLK NE5 .... 59 D2 🔢
Needham Pl *CRAM* NE23 .... 22 A1
Neill Dr *WICK/BNPF* NE16 .... 114 A2
Neilson Rd *FELL* NE10 .... 82 A6
Neil St *HLH* DH5 .... 186 B3
Nelson Av *CRAM* NE23 .... 13 D6
   GOS/KPK NE3 .... 62 C1 🔢
   SSH NE33 .... 72 A3
Nelson Cl *PLEE/EAS* SR8 .... 209 F1 🔢
Nelson Crs *NSHW* NE29 .... 69 F3 🔢
Nelson Dr *CRAM* NE23 .... 13 D6
Nelson Rd *BYK/HTN/WLK* NE6 .... 84 A4
   CRAM NE23 .... 13 D5
   MONK NE25 .... 39 D5
Nelson St *ASHBK/HED/RY* SR2 .. 162 B1 🔢
   CLS/BIR/GTL DH3 .... 153 E6
   CNUT NE1 .... 2 C3
   DUN/TMV NE11 .... 97 E1 🔢
   GATE NE8 .... 81 E5 🔢
   HLH DH5 .... 185 F1 🔢
   SEA/MUR SR7 .... 176 A2
   SSH NE33 .... 71 E3 🔢
   WASHS NE38 .... 139 D2
Nelson Ter *NSHW* NE29 .... 69 F3
Nelson Wy *CRAM* NE23 .... 12 C4
Nenthead Cl *CLS/BIR/GTL* DH3 .. 168 A3
Neptune Rd *BW/LEM/TK/HW* NE15 ... 76 C2
   WLSD/HOW NE28 .... 67 D6
Nesbit Rd *PLEE/EAS* SR8 .... 209 D3
Nesburn Rd *MLFD/PNYW* SR4 ... 143 F2
Nesham Pl *HLH* DH5 .... 171 D2
Ness Ct *BLAY* NE21 .... 75 F6
Nest Rd *FELL* NE10 .... 82 C6
Netherburn Rd *SWCK/CAS* SR5 .. 126 B2
Netherby Dr *WD/WHPE/BLK* NE5 .. 61 E6
Netherdale *BDLGTN* NE22 .... 6 C3 🔢
Nether Farm Rd *FELL* NE10 .... 101 E1
Nether Riggs *BDLGTN* NE22 .... 7 E4 🔢
Netherton Av *NSHW* NE29 .... 53 F5
Netherton Cl *CLSW/PEL* DH2 ..... 152 B6
Netherton Gdns *DIN/WO* NE13 ... 33 D4 🔢
Netherton Gv *NSHW* NE29 .... 53 F5 🔢
Netherton La *BDLGTN* NE22 .... 6 B2
   BDLGTN NE22 .... 7 D3 🔢
Nettleham Rd *SWCK/CAS* SR5 ... 126 B2
Nettles La *SUNDSW* SR3 .... 161 D2
Neville Dene *DHAM* DH1 .... 193 E5
Neville Rd *BW/LEM/TK/HW* NE15 .. 76 C1
   MLFD/PNYW SR4 .... 125 E5
   PLEE/EAS SR8 .... 208 B1
Neville's Cross Bank *DHAM* DH1 .. 193 F6 🔢
Neville's Cross Rd *HEBB* NE31.... 85 E3
Neville Sq *DHAM* DH1 .... 204 C1 🔢
Neville St *CNUT* NE1 .... 2 B5
   DHAM DH1 .... 194 B5
Nevinson Av *HAR/WTLS* NE34 ..... 88 C5
Nevis Cl *WBAY* NE26 .... 39 F2
Nevis Gv *BOL* NE36 .... 106 A3
Newacres Rd *STLY/ANP* DH9 ..... 148 A6
Newark Cl *PLEE/EAS* SR8 .... 208 B1
Newark Crs *SEA/MUR* SR7 .... 175 F2
Newark Dr *CLDN/WHIT/ROK* SR6 .. 109 E2
Newarth Cl *BW/LEM/TK/HW* NE15... 76 C1
Newbiggin La
   WD/WHPE/BLK NE5 .... 60 B3 🔢
Newbold Av *SWCK/CAS* SR5........ 126 B2
Newbold St *BYK/HTN/WLK* NE6 .. 82 C3
Newbottle La *HLS* DH4 .... 169 E3
Newbottle St *HLS* DH4 .... 157 F6
Newbridge Av *SWCK/CAS* SR5 ... 126 B2 🔢
Newbridge Bank
   CLS/BIR/GTL DH3 .... 154 A3
Newbridge Banks *CLSW/PEL* DH2 .. 150 C4
New Bridge St *CNUT* NE1 .... 3 F2
New Bridge St West *CNUT* NE1 .... 3 F2 🔢
Newbrough Crs *JES* NE2 .... 64 A4 🔢
Newburgh Av *MONK* NE25 .... 24 B6
Newburn Av *SWCK/CAS* SR5 ...... 126 B2
Newburn Bridge Rd *BLAY* NE21 ... 75 D2
Newburn Ct *SSH* NE33 .... 71 F5 🔢
Newburn Crs *HLS* DH4 .... 170 C1
Newburn Rd
   BW/LEM/TK/HW NE15................ 58 A5
   STLY/ANP DH9 .... 131 F6
Newbury *LGB/KIL* NE12 .... 35 F6
Newbury Av *GATE* NE8 .... 98 C2
Newbury Cl *BW/LEM/TK/HW* NE15 .. 76 C1
Newbury St *SSH* NE33 .... 88 C1 🔢
   SWCK/CAS SR5 .... 126 B1
Newby Pl *LWF/SPW/WRK* NE9 ... 100 A6
Newcastle Av *PLEE/EAS* SR8 ...... 201 E6
Newcastle Bank *CLS/BIR/GTL* DH3 .. 118 A5
Newcastle Rd *BLYTH* NE24 .... 16 B2

BOL NE36.. 103 F3
CLS/BIR/GTL DH3 .... 118 B6 🔟
CLS/BIR/GTL DH3 .... 153 E3
DHAM DH1 .... 193 F6 🔟
HAR/WTLS NE34 .... 87 E3
SWCK/CAS SR5 .... 107 F5
Newcastle St *NSHW* NE29 .... 70 C1 🔟
New Dr *SEA/MUR* SR7 .... 176 A1
New Durham Rd
  ASHBK/HED/RY SR2 .... 126 A6
New Elvet *DHAM* DH1 .... 194 C5
New Front *STLY/ANP* DH9 .... 146 B4
New Front St *STLY/ANP* DH9 .... 130 C5
New George St *SSH* NE33 .... 71 E6
New Grange Ter *CLSW/PEL* DH2 .... 151 F4
New Green St *SSH* NE33 .... 71 E5 🔟
Newham Av *DIN/WO* NE13 .... 32 C6
Newhaven Av *SWCK/CAS* SR5 .... 126 B2
Newington Ct *SWCK/CAS* SR5 .... 126 B2
Newington Rd *BYK/HTN/WLK* NE6.... 81 F2
  JES NE2 .... 81 F2
Newland Ct *HAR/WTLS* NE34 .... 88 B3 🔟🔟
Newlands Av *BLYTH* NE24 .... 16 C1 🔟
  GOS/KPK NE3 .... 47 E3
  MONK NE25...................................... 53 F1
  SUNDSW SR3 .... 144 A3
Newlands PI *BLYTH* NE24 .... 16 C1 🔟
  DHAM DH1 .... 196 B2
  JES NE2 .... 63 F3
Newlands Rd East
  SEA/MUR SR7 .... 176 A2 🔟
Newlands Rd West *SEA/MUR* SR7 .. 175 F1
Newlyn Crs *NSHW* NE29 .... 70 A1
Newlyn Dr *CRAM* NE23 .... 14 A6
  JRW NE32 .... 86 C2
Newlyn Rd *GOS/KPK* NE3 .... 62 A1
Newman Ter *GATE* NE8 .... 99 F2 🔟🔟
Newmarch St *JRW* NE32 .... 85 F1
New Mills *ELS/FEN* NE4 .... 80 A2
Newminster Cl *HLS* DH4 .... 157 D6
Newport Gv *SUNDSW* SR3 .... 143 F6 🔟
New Quay *NSHW* NE29 .... 71 D2
Newquay Gdns
  LWF/SPW/WRK NE9 .... 117 E2
Newriggs *WASHS* NE38 .... 139 D4
New Rd *BOLCOL* NE35....................... 105 F2
  DUN/TMV NE11 .... 98 A4
  FELL NE10 .... 102 B5
  STLY/ANP DH9 .... 150 B1
  WICK/BNPF NE16 .... 111 F5
Newsham Cl *WD/WHPE/BLK* NE5 .. 59 D2 🔟
Newsham Rd *BLYTH* NE24 .... 16 B1
Newstead Ct *WASHS* NE38 .... 138 B1 🔟
Newstead Rd *HLS* DH4 .... 157 E6
Newsteads Cl *MONK* NE25 .... 39 F5 🔟
Newsteads Dr *MONK* NE25 .... 39 E5
Newstead Sq *SUNDSW* SR3 .... 160 C2 🔟
New Strangford Rd *SEA/MUR* SR7.. 176 B3
New St *DHAM* DH1 .... 194 A5
  MLFD/PNYW SR4 .... 123 F6 🔟
Newton Av *TYNE/NSHE* NE30 .... 55 D1
  WLSD/HOW NE28 .... 68 B3
Newton Cl *BW/LEM/TK/HW* NE15 .. 77 D1
Newton Dr *DHAM* DH1 .... 194 A1
Newton Gv *HAR/WTLS* NE34 .... 87 F3 🔟
Newton PI *LGB/HTN* NE7 .... 65 D4
Newton Rd *LGB/HTN* NE7 .... 64 C4
Newton St *DUN/TMV* NE11 .... 97 E1 🔟
  GATE NE8 .... 98 C2 🔟
New York Rd *NSHW* NE29 .... 53 D3
  SMOOR NE27 .... 52 A2
New York Wy *SMOOR* NE27 .... 52 C4
Nicholas Av *SWCK/CAS* SR6..... 109 E2
Nicholas St *HLH* DH5......................... 172 A5
Nicholson Ter *LGB/KIL* NE12 .... 50 A3
Nichol St *ELS/FEN* NE4 .... 78 C3
Nickleby Chare *DHAM* DH1 .... 205 D1
Nidderdale Av *HLH* DH5 .... 185 E2
Nidderdale Cl *BLYTH* NE24 .... 9 F4
Nidsdale Av *BYK/HTN/WLK* NE6 .... 83 F1
Nightingale Cl *WASHN* NE4 .... 141 F2
Nightingale PI *STLY/ANP* DH9 ...... 149 D3
Nile Cl *BW/LEM/TK/HW* NE15 .... 77 E4
Nile St *NSHW* NE29 .... 70 C1 🔟
  SSH NE33 .... 71 H4
  SUND SR1 .... 5 E2
Nilverton Av *ASHBK/HED/RY* SR2 .. 144 C3
Nimbus Ct *SUNDSW* SR3 .... 160 C2 🔟
Nine Lands *HLS* DH4 .... 170 B2
Ninth Av *BLYTH* NE24 .... 10 C6
  BYK/HTN/WLK NE6 .... 65 E6
  CLSW/PEL DH2 .... 151 E2
Ninth St *PLEE/EAS* SR8 .... 209 F1 🔟
Nissan Wy *WASHN* NE37 .... 122 A5
Nixon St *GATE* NE8 .... 81 F4
Nixon Ter *BLYTH* NE24 .... 11 E6 🔟
Noble's Bank Rd
  ASHBK/HED/RY SR2 .... 5 G5 🔟
Noble St *ASHBK/HED/RY* SR2 .... 5 G6
  ELS/FEN NE4 .... 78 C5 🔟
  FELL NE10 .... 100 C1 🔟
  PLEE/EAS SR8 .... 200 C1
Noble Ter *ASHBK/HED/RY* SR2 ..... 5 G6 🔟
Noel Av *BLAY* NE21 .... 94 B4

Noel St *STLY/ANP* DH9 .... 148 C1
Noel Ter *BLAY* NE21 .... 94 C3
Noirmont Wy *SUNDSW* SR3 .... 160 A2
Nookside *MLFD/PNYW* SR4 .... 142 C2
Nookside Ct *MLFD/PNYW* SR4 .. 142 B2 🔟
The Nook *NSHW* NE29 .... 70 B1
Nora St *HAR/WTLS* NE34 .... 88 B3
  MLFD/PNYW SR4 .... 143 E2
Norbury Gv *BYK/HTN/WLK* NE6 .... 82 C3
Nordale Wy *BLYTH* NE24 .... 9 F4
Norfolk Av *CLS/BIR/GTL* DH3 .... 136 B5
  SUNDSW SR3 .... 143 E6
Norfolk Cl *SEA/MUR* SR7 .... 175 F1
Norfolk Dr *WASHN* NE37 .... 120 C2
Norfolk Gdns *WLSD/HOW* NE28 ...... 68 A2
Norfolk Rd *GATE* NE8 .... 81 F4
  HAR/WTLS NE34 .... 90 B1
Norfolk St *SUND* SR1 .... 4 D2
  TYNE/NSHE NE30 .... 55 D6
Norfolk Wk *PLEE/EAS* SR8 .... 200 B6 🔟
Norfolk Wy
  BW/LEM/TK/HW NE15 .... 77 D2 🔟
Norham Av North *HAR/WTLS* NE34 .. 72 C6
Norham Av North *HAR/WTLS* NE34 .. 72 C6
Norham Av South *HAR/WTLS* NE34 .. 72 C6
Norham Cl *BLYTH* NE24 .... 10 B5
  DIN/WO NE13 .... 32 C5 🔟
Norham Dr *PLEE/EAS* SR8 .... 208 B5 🔟
  WD/WHPE/BLK NE5 .... 60 A3 🔟
Norham PI *JES* NE2 .... 64 A5 🔟
Norham Rd *DHAM* DH1 .... 180 B5
  GOS/KPK NE3 .... 47 D6
  MONK NE25.. 40 B5
  NSHW NE29 .... 53 E6 🔟
  NSHW NE29 .... 69 E1 🔟
Norham Rd North *NSHW* NE29 ..... 53 D4
Norham Ter *JRW* NE32 .... 86 A4
Norhurst *WICK/BNPF* NE16 .... 95 D5
Norland Rd *BW/LEM/TK/HW* NE15.. 77 E3
Norley Av *SWCK/CAS* SR5 .... 126 B2
Norma Crs *WBAY* NE26 .... 41 F6
Norman Av *SUNDSW* SR3 .... 161 D1
Normanby Cl *SEA/MUR* SR7 .... 175 F1
Normanby Crs *HLH* DH5 .... 171 F2
Normand Rd *ROWG* NE39 .... 111 D3
Norman Ter *WLSD/HOW* NE28 .... 69 D4
Normanton Ter *ELS/FEN* NE4 .... 79 F3
Normount Rd *ELS/FEN* NE4............. 79 D3
Northampton Rd *PLEE/EAS* SR8..... 200 B6
Northamptonshire Dr
  DHAM DH1 .... 196 C3 🔟
North Ap *CLSW/PEL* DH2 .... 153 D4
North Av *GOS/KPK* NE3 .... 63 D2
  HAR/WTLS NE34 .... 89 D2
  LGB/KIL NE12 .... 49 F6
  PLEE/EAS SR8 .... 209 E1 🔟
  WD/WHPE/BLK NE5 .... 60 B4
North Bailey *DHAM* DH1 .... 194 B5
Northbourne Rd *HEBB* NE31 .... 85 F2
Northbourne St *ELS/FEN* NE4......... 79 E4
  GATE NE8 .... 99 E2
North Brancepeth Cl
  BDN/LAN/SAC DH7 .... 204 A2 🔟
North Bridge St
  CLDN/WHIT/ROK SR6 .... 126 C4 🔟
  SWCK/CAS SR5 .... 126 C4
North Burns *CLS/BIR/GTL* DH3 ..... 153 E4
North Cl *BYK/HTN/WLK* NE6 .... 82 B1
  HAR/WTLS NE34 .... 89 D2
  RYTON NE40 .... 74 B3
Northcote *WICK/BNPF* NE16 .... 95 F5
Northcote Av *SUND* SR1 .... 5 E4
  WD/WHPE/BLK NE5 .... 59 E5
Northcote St *ELS/FEN* NE4 .... 79 F3
  SSH NE33 .... 71 F6
North Crs *PLEE/EAS* SR8................ 200 B3
  WASHS NE38 .... 138 B5 🔟
North Cft *LGB/KIL* NE12 .... 50 A5
North Cross St *GOS/KPK* NE3 .... 63 E1
Northdene *CLS/BIR/GTL* DH3 ...... 118 B6
Northdene Av *SEA/MUR* SR7........ 176 C2
North Dr *CLDN/WHIT/ROK* SR6 .... 107 D1
  CLS/BIR/GTL DH3 .... 153 F1
  HEBB NE31 .... 84 B3
North Durham St *SUND* SR1 .... 5 F2
North Emb *BDN/LAN/SAC* DH7 .. 202 C5 🔟
  DHAM DH1 .... 194 A3 🔟
Northern Wy *SWCK/CAS* SR5 .... 125 F2
North Farm Av *MLFD/PNYW* SR4 .. 142 A4
North Farm Rd *HEBB* NE31 .... 84 C3
Northfield Cl *WICK/BNPF* NE16....... 95 E5
Northfield Dr *LGB/KIL* NE12 .... 49 D2
  MLFD/PNYW SR4 .... 142 A4 🔟
Northfield Gdns *HAR/WTLS* NE34 .. 72 B6
Northfield Rd *GOS/KPK* NE3 .... 63 D2
  SSH NE33 .... 72 B5
Northgate *LGB/KIL* NE12 .... 35 F6
North Gra *PONT/DH* NE20 .... 28 A2
North Gv *CLDN/WHIT/ROK* SR6 .. 127 D1
  RYTON NE40 .... 74 C3
North Guards
  CLDN/WHIT/ROK SR6 .... 109 D2
North Hall Rd *MLFD/PNYW* SR4 .. 142 C2
North Hvn *SEA/MUR* SR7 .... 176 A2
North Hylton Rd *SWCK/CAS* SR5.. 124 C2

North Jesmond Av *JES* NE2 .... 64 A4 🔟
North King St *TYNE/NSHE* NE30 .... 55 D6
Northlands *BLAY* NE21 .... 94 A1 🔟
North La *BOL* NE36 .... 106 B3
  HLH DH5 .... 172 C5
Northlea *BW/LEM/TK/HW* NE15 .. 60 A6 🔟
Northlea Rd *SEA/MUR* SR7 .... 175 F2
North Mason Ldg *DIN/WO* NE13.... 30 C3
North Milburn St
  MLFD/PNYW SR4 .... 126 A5
North Moor Ct *SUNDSW* SR3 ...... 143 D5
North Moor La *SUNDSW* SR3 ...... 143 D5
Northmoor Rd *BYK/HTN/WLK* NE6.. 66 A4
North Moor Rd *SUNDSW* SR3 ...... 143 D5
Northolt Av *CRAM* NE23................... 22 A1
North Pde *WBAY* NE26 .... 41 D5
North Railway St *SEA/MUR* SR7 .. 176 C3 🔟
Northside PI *MONK* NE25 .... 25 D6
North St *BLAY* NE21 .... 75 F6
  CLDN/WHIT/ROK SR6 .... 107 F1
  CNUT NE1 .... 2 D1
  HLH DH5 .... 170 C5
  HLH DH4 .... 157 F4
  JRW NE32 .... 86 A1
  SSH NE33 .... 71 E3
  SUNDSW SR3 .... 143 F6
  SWCK/CAS SR5 .... 126 B3 🔟
North Ter *SEA/MUR* SR7.................. 176 C2
  SUNDSW SR3 .... 143 F6 🔟
  WLSD/HOW NE28 .... 68 A4
Northumberland Av *BDLGTN* NE22.. 7 D3
  GOS/KPK NE3 .... 62 C2
  LGB/KIL NE12 .... 49 F5
Northumberland Dock Rd
  WLSD/HOW NE28 .... 69 E5
Northumberland Gdns *JES* NE2 .... 64 C3 🔟
  WD/WHPE/BLK NE5 .... 59 D3
Northumberland PI
  PLEE/EAS SR8 .... 200 A6 🔟
Northumberland Rd
  BW/LEM/TK/HW NE15 .... 76 B2 🔟
  CNUT NE1 .... 3 E1
  RYTON NE40 .... 74 B2
Northumberland Sq
  TYNE/NSHE NE30 .... 54 C6 🔟
Northumberland St *CNUT* NE1 .... 2 D2
  GATE NE8 .... 98 B1 🔟
  PLEE/EAS SR8 .... 201 E6
  TYNE/NSHE NE30 .... 55 E6
  WLSD/HOW NE28 .... 67 E4
Northumberland Ter
  TYNE/NSHE NE30 .... 55 F5 🔟
Northumberland Vls
  WLSD/HOW NE28 .... 68 A4
Northumberland Wy
  WASHN NE37 .... 120 C2
  WASHS NE38 .... 139 D3
Northumbrian Rd *CRAM* NE23 .... 14 B6
Northumbrian Wy *LGB/KIL* NE12 .. 49 E2
  NSHW NE29 .... 70 C3
Northumbria PI *STLY/ANP* DH9..... 148 C1
North Vw *BYK/HTN/WLK* NE6 .... 82 A2
  CLDN/WHIT/ROK SR6 .... 126 C1
  DIN/WO NE13 .... 44 A3
  HAR/WTLS NE34 .... 72 B6 🔟
  HLH DH5 .... 186 C3
  JRW NE32 .... 85 F2
  LGB/KIL NE12 .... 49 F4 🔟
  SWCK/CAS SR5 .... 124 B3
  WBAY NE26 .... 41 E6
  WICK/BNPF NE16 .... 95 F3
  WLSD/HOW NE28 .... 67 E4
North Walbottle Rd
  WD/WHPE/BLK NE5 .... 58 C4
Northway *BW/LEM/TK/HW* NE15.... 57 F3
  LWF/SPW/WRK NE9 .... 100 A3
Northwood Ct *SWCK/CAS* SR5 ... 126 B2 🔟
Northwood Rd *SEA/MUR* SR7 .... 176 A2
Norton Av *SEA/MUR* SR7 .... 175 F1
Norton Cl *CLSW/PEL* DH2 .... 165 E1
Norton Rd *SWCK/CAS* SR5 .... 125 F1
Norton Wy *BW/LEM/TK/HW* NE15.. 77 D2
Norway Av *MLFD/PNYW* SR4 .... 143 D2
Norwich Av *DIN/WO* NE13 .... 33 D5 🔟
Norwich Cl *CLS/BIR/GTL* DH3 ...... 167 F3
Norwich Rd *DHAM* DH1 .... 180 C5
Norwood Av *BYK/HTN/WLK* NE6 .... 65 D5
  GOS/KPK NE3 .... 47 E2
Norwood Rd
  BW/LEM/TK/HW NE15 .... 59 F6
  DUN/TMV NE11 .... 98 A3

Nottingham Pl PLEE/EAS SR8 .... 200 A6
Nottinghamshire Rd DHAM DH1 ... 196 B3
Nuneaton Wy WD/WHPE/BLK NE5 ... 59 D2
Nuns La CNUT NE1 .... 2 C4
  GATE NE8 .... 81 E5 **5**
Nuns Moor Crs ELS/FEN NE4.......... 79 D1
Nuns Moor Rd ELS/FEN NE4.......... 79 D1
Nuns' Rw DHAM DH1 .... 195 E3
Nun St CNUT NE1........................ 2 C3
Nunwick Gdns NSHW NE29 .... 53 E6 **5**
Nunwick Wy LGB/HTN NE7 .... 65 F3
Nursery La SUNDSW SR3................ 143 F4
Nursery Gdns PLEE/EAS SR8 .... 199 F1
Nursery La CLDN/WHIT/ROK SR6 ... 107 F1
  FELL NE10 .... 100 B3
Nursery Rd SUNDSW SR3 .... 143 F4
Nutley Pl BW/LEM/TK/HW NE15...... 77 F3
Nye Dene SWCK/CAS SR5 .... 124 C3

O

Oakapple Cl BDLGTN NE22.............. 7 E3
Oak Av DHAM DH1 .... 195 F5
  DIN/WO NE13 .... 31 E3
  DUN/TMV NE11 .... 97 E3
  HAR/WTLS NE34 .... 89 F3
Oak Crs CLDN/WHIT/ROK SR6 .... 109 F1
  CLSW/PEL DH2 .... 179 F1
Oakdale BDLGTN NE22.................. 6 A4
Oakdale Cl BW/LEM/TK/HW NE15 ... 76 C2
Oakenshaw BW/LEM/TK/HW NE15 .. 76 C2
Oakerside Dr PLEE/EAS SR8 .... 208 B4
Oakes Pl ELS/FEN NE4 .... 80 A3
Oakeys Rd STLY/ANP DH9 .... 131 E5
Oakfield Av WICK/BNPF NE16 .... 96 A4
Oakfield Cl SUNDSW SR3 .... 159 E2
  WICK/BNPF NE16 .... 96 A4
Oakfield Dr LGB/KIL NE12 .... 50 B1
  WICK/BNPF NE16 .... 96 A4 **2**
Oakfield Gdns
  BW/LEM/TK/HW NE15................ 78 C3
  WLSD/HOW NE28 .... 66 B3 **2**
Oakfield Gra DIN/WO NE13 .... 31 D3
Oakfield North RYTON NE40 .... 74 A3 **1**
Oakfield Rd DUN/TMV NE11 .... 97 F4
  GOS/KPK NE3 .... 63 D3
  WICK/BNPF NE16 .... 95 E5
Oakfields WICK/BNPF NE16 .... 112 A5
Oakfield Ter GOS/KPK NE3............ 63 D2
Oakfield Wy CRAM NE23 .... 36 B1
Oakgreen Flats
  BDN/LAN/SAC DH7 .... 203 D4
Oak Gv WLSD/HOW NE28 .... 67 F4
Oakham Av WICK/BNPF NE16 .... 95 E4
Oakham Dr DHAM DH1................ 196 C1
Oakham Gdns NSHW NE29 .... 70 A2
Oakhurst Dr GOS/KPK NE3 .... 62 C4
Oakhurst Ter LGB/KIL NE12 .... 49 F6 **3**
Oakland Rd JES NE2 .... 66 A5 **2**
  MONK NE25............................. 39 F6
Oaklands GOS/KPK NE3 .... 63 E3
  WICK/BNPF NE16 .... 96 A2
Oaklands Crs SWCK/CAS SR5 .... 125 F2
Oaklands Ter MLFD/PNYW SR4 ...... 143 F1 **2**
Oak Lea BDN/LAN/SAC DH7 .... 178 A3
Oaklea CLSW/PEL DH2 .... 152 C4
Oakleigh Gdns
  CLDN/WHIT/ROK SR6 .... 89 F6 **2**
Oakley Cl CRAM NE23 .... 35 D2
Oakley Dr CRAM NE23 .... 22 B1
Oakmere Cl HLS DH4 .... 157 D2 **6**
Oakridge WICK/BNPF NE16 .... 95 E4
Oak Rd NSHW NE29..................... 52 C5
  PLEE/EAS SR8 .... 200 C3
The Oaks RYTON NE40 .... 92 A1 **1**
Oak St HLS DH4 .... 169 D1
  JRW NE32 .... 85 F1
  SUND SR1 .... 5 H3
Oak Ter CLSW/PEL DH2 .... 151 E1
  SEA/MUR SR7 .... 188 B1
  STLY/ANP DH9 .... 149 D5
Oaktree Av WLSD/HOW NE28 .... 66 C5
Oaktree Gdns MONK NE25............ 54 A1
Oakwellgate GATE NE8 .... 3 C6
Oakwood FELL NE10.................... 101 D5
  HEBB NE31 .... 84 B1
  RDHAMSE DH6 .... 188 A6
Oakwood Av DIN/WO NE13........... 33 E5
  LWF/SPW/WRK NE9................ 117 F1
Oakwood Gdns DUN/TMV NE11 .... 98 A5
Oakwood Pl WD/WHPE/BLK NE5 ... 61 E5 **3**
Oakwood St
  ASHBK/HED/RY SR2 .... 144 A1 **1**
Oates St MLFD/PNYW SR4 .... 125 F6
Oatlands Rd MLFD/PNYW SR4 ...... 143 D2 **2**
Oatlands Wy DHAM DH1 .... 180 B4
Oban Av WLSD/HOW NE28............ 68 B2
Oban St FELL NE10 .... 100 B3
  JRW NE32 .... 87 D5
Obelisk La DHAM DH1................. 194 A4
Ocean Rd ASHBK/HED/RY SR2 ...... 145 F4
  SSH NE33 .... 71 E3
Ocean Vw ASHBK/HED/RY SR2 ...... 162 B1

WBAY NE26 .... 41 D5 **1**
Ochiltree Ct WBAY NE26 .... 26 C2
Octavia Cl BDLGTN NE22.............. 7 D2
Octavia Ct WLSD/HOW NE28 .... 68 A2
Octavian Wy DUN/TMV NE11 ...... 116 B1
Offerton Cl MLFD/PNYW SR4 .... 123 E6
Offerton La MLFD/PNYW SR4 .... 123 E6
  MLFD/PNYW SR4 .... 141 E3
Offerton St MLFD/PNYW SR4 .... 125 F6
Office Pl HLH DH5 .... 185 F1
Office St PLEE/EAS SR8 .... 201 E2
Ogden St MLFD/PNYW SR4 .... 125 F6
Ogle Av DIN/WO NE13 .... 32 C6 **1**
Ogle Dr BLYTH NE24 .... 10 B6
Ogle Gv JRW NE32..................... 85 F5
O'hanlon Crs WLSD/HOW NE28..... 66 C2
Oil Mill Rd BYK/HTN/WLK NE6 ..... 84 A1
Okehampton Dr HLS DH4 .... 157 E4
Okehampton Sq SWCK/CAS SR5 ... 125 F1 **1**
Old Coronation St SSH NE33 .... 71 E4 **2**
Old Course Rd
  CLDN/WHIT/ROK SR6 .... 107 F2 **1**
Old Durham Rd
  LWF/SPW/WRK NE9................ 100 A5
Old Elvet DHAM DH1 .... 194 C5
Old Farm Ct WICK/BNPF NE16 ..... 114 A2 **1**
Oldfield Rd BYK/HTN/WLK NE6 ..... 83 E5
Old Fold Rd FELL NE10 .... 82 A6
  GATE NE8 .... 100 A1 **11**
Old Mill La CLS/BIR/GTL DH3 .... 167 E4
Old Mill Rd ASHBK/HED/RY SR2 .... 5 H5
  SWCK/CAS SR5 .... 125 F1
Oldstead Gdns MLFD/PNYW SR4 .. 143 D2
Old Well La BLAY NE21 .... 94 A1
Olive Gdns LWF/SPW/WRK NE9 .... 99 F4
Olive Pl ELS/FEN NE4 .... 78 C1
Oliver Pl DHAM DH1 .... 204 C1
Oliver St BW/LEM/TK/HW NE15 .... 78 A3
  SEA/MUR SR7 .... 176 A2
  STLY/ANP DH9 .... 148 A4 **3**
Olive St CLSW/PEL DH2................ 165 D1
  SSH NE33 .... 88 A2 **1**
  SUND SR1 .... 15 G2
Ollerton Dr BW/LEM/TK/HW NE15.. 57 D4
Ollerton Gdns FELL NE10 .... 100 B3
Olney Cl CRAM NE23.................. 22 C1
O'neil Dr PLEE/EAS SR8 .... 208 C3
Ongar Wy LGB/KIL NE12.............. 49 D5
Onslow Gdns LWF/SPW/WRK NE9 .. 99 E5
Onslow St MLFD/PNYW SR4 .... 125 D5 **3**
Orange Gv CRAM NE23................ 35 D1
  WICK/BNPF NE16 .... 96 B3
Orb Ct ELS/FEN NE4 .... 78 C1
Orchard Av ROWG NE39.............. 110 C3
Orchard Cl HAR/WTLS NE34......... 88 A3
  LGB/KIL NE12 .... 50 B2
  ROWG NE39.......................... 110 C4
  STLY/ANP DH9 .... 150 C2
Orchard Ct RYTON NE40.............. 74 B3
Orchard Dene ROWG NE39 .... 110 C3
Orchard Dr DHAM DH1 .... 195 D3
Orchard Gdns
  CLDN/WHIT/ROK SR6 .... 109 D2
  CLS/BIR/GTL DH3 .... 166 B1
  LWF/SPW/WRK NE9 .... 99 F6
  WLSD/HOW NE28 .... 66 C3
Orchard-leigh
  BW/LEM/TK/HW NE15............. 76 C2
Orchard Pk CLS/BIR/GTL DH3 ...... 136 B2
Orchard Pl JES NE2.................... 64 B5
Orchard Priory DHAM DH1 .... 194 A5
Orchard Rd ROWG NE39.............. 110 C3
  WICK/BNPF NE16 .... 96 B3
The Orchards BLYTH NE24 .... 10 A4
Orchard St CLS/BIR/GTL DH3........ 136 B2
  CLSW/PEL DH2 .... 152 A1
  CNUT NE1 .... 2 D5
  MLFD/PNYW SR4 .... 125 E5
Orchard Ter CLS/BIR/GTL DH3....... 166 B1
The Orchard
  BW/LEM/TK/HW NE15 .... 76 C2 **1**
  DHAM DH1 .... 180 A4
  WICK/BNPF NE16 .... 96 B3 **1**
Orde Av WLSD/HOW NE28 .... 68 A3
Ordley Cl BW/LEM/TK/HW NE15.... 77 D2
Ord St ELS/FEN NE4 .... 80 B5 **1**
Oriel Cl CLDN/WHIT/ROK SR6 ...... 126 C3 **3**
Orkney Dr ASHBK/HED/RY SR2 ..... 144 C6
Orlando Rd NSHW NE29............... 53 F6
Ormesby Rd
  CLDN/WHIT/ROK SR6 .... 126 C1 **12**
Ormiscraig BW/LEM/TK/HW NE15.. 76 C2
Ormiston BW/LEM/TK/HW NE15 .... 77 D2
Ormonde Av
  BW/LEM/TK/HW NE15.............. 77 F2
Ormonde St JRW NE32................ 86 A1
  MLFD/PNYW SR4 .... 143 E1
Ormskirk Cl BW/LEM/TK/HW NE15 .. 76 C2
Ormskirk Gv CRAM NE23 .... 22 B1 **1**
Ormston St CRAM NE23 .... 14 A3
Orpen Av HAR/WTLS NE34 .... 88 B5
Orpington Av BYK/HTN/WLK NE6... 83 D1
Orpington Rd CRAM NE23 .... 22 B1
Orr Av SUNDSW SR3................... 161 D2
Orton Cl ELS/FEN NE4 .... 79 D4 **3**

Orwell Cl HAR/WTLS NE34 .... 88 A6
  PLEE/EAS SR8 .... 208 A4
Orwell Gdns STLY/ANP DH9 .... 148 A4
Osbaldeston Gdns GOS/KPK NE3 .. 63 D3
Osborne Av JES NE2 .... 64 A6
  SSH NE33 .... 71 F5
Osborne Cl BDLGTN NE22............ 8 B2
Osborne Gdns NSHW NE29 .... 54 C5 **2**
  WBAY NE26 .... 40 B5
Osborne Rd JES NE2 .... 64 A6
  SWCK/CAS SR5 .... 125 F2
Osborne St CLDN/WHIT/ROK SR6 .. 126 C2
  SSH NE33 .... 72 A5
Osborne Ter JES NE2 .... 81 D1 **6**
Oslo Cl NSHW NE29 .... 69 D2
Osman Cl ASHBK/HED/RY SR2...... 5 E5
Osprey Dr BLYTH NE24 .... 17 D2
  NSHW NE29 .... 52 C6
Osprey Wy HAR/WTLS NE34 .... 87 F4
Oswald Cl DHAM DH1 .... 195 F5
Oswald Ct DHAM DH1................. 194 C6
Oswald Rd HLH DH5 .... 145 D5
Oswald St MLFD/PNYW SR4 .... 125 F5 **3**
Oswald Ter ASHBK/HED/RY SR2 .... 145 E4
  GATE NE8 .... 98 C1 **6**
  PLEE/EAS SR8 .... 200 C1 **2**
Oswald Ter South SWCK/CAS SR5.. 124 B3
Oswald Wk GOS/KPK NE3 .... 64 A1
Oswestry Pl CRAM NE23 .... 22 B1
Oswin Av LGB/KIL NE12............... 50 A4
Oswin Ct LGB/KIL NE12............... 50 A3
Oswin Ter NSHW NE29 .... 69 F1
Otley Cl CRAM NE23 .... 22 C1
Otterburn Av MONK NE25............ 39 D6
Otterburn Cl LGB/KIL NE12 .... 50 B4
Otterburn Crs HLS DH4 .... 170 B1
Otterburn Gdns DUN/TMV NE11 ... 97 F3 **4**
  HAR/WTLS NE34 .... 89 D2
  LWF/SPW/WRK NE9................ 99 D6
  WICK/BNPF NE16 .... 96 A3
Otterburn Gv BLYTH NE24 .... 10 A6
Otterburn Rd NSHW NE29 .... 54 B5
Otterburn Ter JES NE2................. 64 A5
Ottercap Cl BW/LEM/TK/HW NE15.. 76 C2
Otterington WASHS NE38 .... 139 F2
Ottershaw BW/LEM/TK/HW NE15 .. 77 D2
Otto Ter ASHBK/HED/RY SR2........ 144 A1
Ottovale Crs BLAY NE21............... 93 F1
Ottringham Cl
  BW/LEM/TK/HW NE15............. 76 C2
Oulton Cl CRAM NE23 .... 22 C1
Ousby Ct DIN/WO NE13 .... 45 F5 **4**
Ouseburn Cl
  ASHBK/HED/RY SR2 .... 145 E6 **2**
Ouseburn Rd BYK/HTN/WLK NE6 .. 65 D5
  CNUT NE1 .... 81 F2 **5**
Ouselaw DUN/TMV NE11 .... 116 C6
Ouse St CNUT NE1 .... 81 F3
Ouslaw La DUN/TMV NE11 .... 116 A6
Ousterley Ter STLY/ANP DH9........ 149 D6
Ouston Cl FELL NE10.................. 102 B3
Ouston La CLSW/PEL DH2 .... 152 B1
Ouston St BW/LEM/TK/HW NE15 .. 77 E3
Outram St HLH DH5 .... 171 D1
Oval Park Vw FELL NE10 .... 100 C3 **2**
The Oval BDLGTN NE22............... 16 A3
  BLYTH NE24......................... 16 A3
  BYK/HTN/WLK NE6 .... 83 D5
  CLSW/PEL DH2 .... 135 E4
  CLSW/PEL DH2 .... 166 A3
  DIN/WO NE13 .... 44 B4
  HLS DH4 .... 170 B2
  LGB/KIL NE12 .... 49 F6
Overdene BW/LEM/TK/HW NE15 ... 77 F1 **1**
  SEA/MUR SR7 .... 175 E5 **1**
Overfield Rd GOS/KPK NE3 .... 62 B1
Overton Cl BW/LEM/TK/HW NE15 .. 76 C2
Overton Rd NSHW NE29 .... 54 A4 **2**
Ovingham Cl WASHS NE38 .... 139 E1
Ovingham Gdns DIN/WO NE13 ..... 33 D4 **4**
Ovington Gv WD/WHPE/BLK NE5... 61 E6
Owen Brannigan Dr CRAM NE23 ... 35 D2 **2**
Owen Dr BOL NE36 .... 106 A2
Owengate DHAM DH1 .... 194 B5 **3**
Owen St HAR/WTLS NE34............. 88 A3
Owlet Cl BLAY NE21 .... 93 F1 **1**
Oxbridge St ASHBK/HED/RY SR2 ... 145 E4
Oxclose Rd WASHS NE38 .... 139 D2
Oxford Av CRAM NE23 .... 22 B1
  SSH NE33 .... 71 F6 **5**
  WASHN NE37 .... 120 A4
  WLSD/HOW NE28 .... 66 C3
Oxford Cl SUNDSW SR3 .... 143 E6
Oxford Crs HEBB NE31 .... 85 E2
Oxford Pl CLS/BIR/GTL DH3 .... 136 B5
Oxfordshire Dr DHAM DH1 .... 196 B3 **2**
Oxford Sq MLFD/PNYW SR4 .... 125 D5
Oxford St BLYTH NE24 .... 11 E5 **5**
  CNUT NE1 .... 3 E2
  MLFD/PNYW SR4 .... 125 D5
  SEA/MUR SR7 .... 175 F3
  SSH NE33 .... 71 F6
  TYNE/NSHE NE30 .... 55 F5
  WBAY NE26 .... 41 D5
Oxnam Crs JES NE2.................... 80 A1

Oxted Cl CRAM NE23...... 22 C1
Oxted Pl BYK/HTN/WLK NE6 ...... 83 D5
Oyston St SSH NE33...... 71 E4
Ozanam Cl CRAM NE23 ...... 35 D3

P

Pacific Hall SEA/MUR SR7 ...... 175 D2 [5]
Packham Rd MLFD/PNYW SR4 ...... 142 B1
Paddock Cl
  CLDN/WHIT/ROK SR6 ...... 107 D1 [5]
  HLS DH4...... 156 B3
Paddock HI PONT/DH NE20...... 28 B3
Paddock La SUNDSW SR3...... 161 E1
The Paddock BLYTH NE24 ...... 10 B5
  BW/LEM/TK/HW NE15...... 58 B5
  CRAM NE23...... 22 C2
  DIN/WO NE13 ...... 44 B4
  FELL NE10 ...... 101 E4
  HLS DH4...... 158 B1
  STLY/ANP DH9 ...... 130 B6
Pader Cl DIN/WO NE13 ...... 33 D5 [3]
Padgate Rd MLFD/PNYW SR4 ...... 142 D1
Padstow Cl ASHBK/HED/RY SR2 .. 145 E6 [5]
Padstow Rd NSHW NE29 ...... 70 A2
Page Av HAR/WTLS NE34...... 89 D1
Page St HEBB NE31 ...... 85 E1 [4]
Paignton Av ELS/FEN NE4 ...... 79 D3
  MONK NE25...... 39 F6
Paignton Sq SUNDSW SR3 ...... 143 D4 [2]
Paisley Sq SUNDSW SR3 ...... 143 D4 [3]
Palace Rd BDLGTN NE22 ...... 8 C2
Palace St ELS/FEN NE4 ...... 80 A4 [3]
Palermo St MLFD/PNYW SR4 ...... 125 E4
Paley St SUND SR1 ...... 4 A2 [2]
Palgrave Rd MLFD/PNYW SR4 ...... 142 B1
Palgrove Sq MLFD/PNYW SR4 ...... 142 B1
Pallinsburn Ct
  WD/WHPE/BLK NE5 ...... 61 D3 [7]
Pallion New Rd MLFD/PNYW SR4... 125 E4
Pallion Pk MLFD/PNYW SR4 ...... 125 E4
Pallion Rd MLFD/PNYW SR4 ...... 125 E6
Pallion Subway
  MLFD/PNYW SR4 ...... 125 E4 [2]
Palm Av ELS/FEN NE4...... 78 C1 [5]
  HAR/WTLS NE34 ...... 89 F3
Palmer Crs HEBB NE31...... 85 E2
Palmer Rd PLEE/EAS SR8 ...... 207 F3
  STLY/ANP DH9 ...... 129 D5
Palmers Garth DHAM DH1 ...... 194 C5
Palmers Gn LGB/KIL NE12 ...... 50 B3
Palmer's Hill Rd
  CLDN/WHIT/ROK SR6...... 126 C4
Palmerston Av BYK/HTN/WLK NE6 .. 83 F1
Palmerston Rd MLFD/PNYW SR4 ... 142 A3
Palmer St JRW NE32 ...... 85 F1 [4]
  STLY/ANP DH9 ...... 147 F3 [1]
Palm Lea BDN/LAN/SAC DH7 ...... 202 C4 [2]
Palmstead Rd MLFD/PNYW SR4 ...... 142 B1
Palmstead Sq MLFD/PNYW SR4 ...... 142 B1
Palm Ter STLY/ANP DH9 ...... 149 D5
Pancras Rd SUNDSW SR3 ...... 143 D4
Pandon CNUT NE1 ...... 3 F4
Pandon Bank CNUT NE1 ...... 3 F3
Pangbourne Cl
  BW/LEM/TK/HW NE15 ...... 59 E6
Pankhurst Gdns FELL NE10 ...... 101 F2
Pankhurst Pl STLY/ANP DH9 ...... 149 D3 [1]
Pann La SUND SR1 ...... 4 C2
Panns Bank SUND SR1 ...... 4 D1
The Parade ASHBK/HED/RY SR2... 5 H4
  BYK/HTN/WLK NE6 ...... 83 F3
  CLSW/PEL DH2 ...... 151 E2
Paradise Crs PLEE/EAS SR8 ...... 200 C2
Paradise La PLEE/EAS SR8 ...... 200 C2
Paradise Rw CRAM NE23 ...... 22 A2 [1]
Park Av BDLGTN NE22 ...... 9 D1
  BLAY NE21 ...... 76 B6
  CLDN/WHIT/ROK SR6 ...... 127 D1
  GOS/KPK NE3 ...... 46 B5
  HAR/WTLS NE34 ...... 89 C4
  SMOOR NE27 ...... 52 B1
  SUNDSW SR3 ...... 161 D1
  TYNE/NSHE NE30 ...... 55 E5
  WBAY NE26 ...... 40 C5
  WLSD/HOW NE28 ...... 67 D4
Park Chare WASHS NE38 ...... 139 D1 [1]
Park Cl ELS/FEN NE4 ...... 79 F4 [3]
  STLY/ANP DH9 ...... 146 C5
Park Crs SMOOR NE27 ...... 52 B1
  TYNE/NSHE NE30 ...... 55 D6
Park Crs East TYNE/NSHE NE30 ...... 55 E5
Parkdale Ri WICK/BNPF NE16 ...... 95 E3
Park Dr BLYTH NE24 ...... 16 A2
  GOS/KPK NE3 ...... 47 E3
  LGB/KIL NE12 ...... 50 A4
  WICK/BNPF NE16 ...... 96 B3
Parker Av GOS/KPK NE3 ...... 63 D3
Park Farm Vls BLYTH NE24 ...... 16 B4
Park Fld RYTON NE40 ...... 74 B3
Park Field Ter WBAY NE26 ...... 26 B2
Park Gdns WBAY NE26 ...... 40 C5

Park Ga CLDN/WHIT/ROK SR6 ...... 127 D1
Parkgate La BLAY NE21 ...... 94 A2
Park Gv SMOOR NE27 ...... 52 B1
  WASHN NE37 ...... 120 C3
Parkham Cl CRAM NE23 ...... 14 A5 [3]
Parkhead STLY/ANP DH9 ...... 146 A6
Parkhead Gdns BLAY NE21 ...... 94 A2
Park Head Rd LGB/HTN NE7 ...... 64 C4
Parkhouse Av SWCK/CAS SR5 ...... 124 A4
Park House Cl RDHAMSE DH6 ...... 197 E4 [5]
Park House Rd DHAM DH1 ...... 204 C1
Parkhurst Rd MLFD/PNYW SR4 ...... 142 A2
Parkin Gdns FELL NE10 ...... 101 D3 [5]
Parkland BLAY NE21 ...... 75 F4
  LGB/KIL NE12 ...... 49 F6
Parkland Av BLAY NE21 ...... 94 A2
Parkland Ct SEA/MUR SR7 ...... 176 A2
Parklands Ct FELL NE10 ...... 102 B1
Parklands Wy FELL NE10 ...... 102 B1
Parkland Ter SEA/MUR SR7 ...... 176 A2
Park La BLAY NE21 ...... 94 A2
  GATE NE8...... 81 F5
  PLEE/EAS SR8 ...... 209 F1
  SEA/MUR SR7 ...... 188 A1
  SMOOR NE27 ...... 52 B1
  SUND SR1 ...... 4 C4
Park Lea SUNDSW SR3 ...... 159 D2
Park Lea Rd CLDN/WHIT/ROK SR6 .. 127 D1
Parkmore Rd MLFD/PNYW SR4 ...... 141 F3 [3]
Park Pde CLDN/WHIT/ROK SR6 ...... 127 D2
  WBAY NE26 ...... 40 C5
Park Pl CLS/BIR/GTL DH3 ...... 153 F3
Park Ri BW/LEM/TK/HW NE15 ...... 76 B1
Park Rd ASHBK/HED/RY SR2 ...... 4 C5
  BDLGTN NE22 ...... 7 F3
  BW/LEM/TK/HW NE15 ...... 58 B6
  ELS/FEN NE4 ...... 79 F4
  FELL NE10 ...... 82 B6
  GATE NE8 ...... 82 A6
  HEBB NE31 ...... 85 F2 [5]
  JRW NE32 ...... 85 F2 [8]
  MONK NE25 ...... 24 B5
  PLEE/EAS SR8 ...... 201 E6
  ROWG NE39 ...... 110 C2 [3]
  SMOOR NE27 ...... 52 B1
  STLY/ANP DH9 ...... 147 F3
  WBAY NE26 ...... 40 C4
  WLSD/HOW NE28 ...... 67 D4
Park Road Central
  CLS/BIR/GTL DH3 ...... 153 F5
Park Rd North CLS/BIR/GTL DH3 ... 153 E3
Park Rd South CLS/BIR/GTL DH3 ... 153 F6
Park Rw FELL NE10 ...... 100 C2 [5]
  SWCK/CAS SR5 ...... 125 F5 [5]
Parkshiel HAR/WTLS NE34 ...... 89 E4
Parkside BDLGTN NE22 ...... 9 D1
  BDN/LAN/SAC DH7 ...... 178 B1
  BW/LEM/TK/HW NE15 ...... 58 A5
  DUN/TMV NE11 ...... 97 E2
  HEBB NE31 ...... 84 B4
  STLY/ANP DH9 ...... 130 B5
  TYNE/NSHE NE30 ...... 55 F3
  WLSD/HOW NE28 ...... 67 F3 [2]
Parkside Av BLAY NE21 ...... 94 A1
  LGB/HTN NE7 ...... 65 D1
Parkside Crs SEA/MUR SR7 ...... 176 B5
  TYNE/NSHE NE30 ...... 55 F4
The Parks CLS/BIR/GTL DH3 ...... 167 D1
Parkstone Cl MLFD/PNYW SR4 ...... 141 F4
Park St SEA/MUR SR7 ...... 176 C4
Park St South SWCK/CAS SR5 ...... 124 B5 [6]
Park Ter BDLGTN NE22 ...... 8 B1
  DUN/TMV NE11 ...... 97 D2
  JES NE2 ...... 80 C1
  PLEE/EAS SR8 ...... 209 F2
  SWCK/CAS SR5 ...... 125 E2
  TYNE/NSHE NE30 ...... 55 E5
  WICK/BNPF NE16 ...... 95 F1
  WLSD/HOW NE28 ...... 67 D4
Park Vw BLAY NE21 ...... 94 B2
  BLYTH NE24...... 11 E5
  BYK/HTN/WLK NE6 ...... 83 F3 [3]
  CLSW/PEL DH2 ...... 165 E6
  HLH DH5 ...... 185 F1
  JRW NE32 ...... 86 A4
  LGB/KIL NE12 ...... 49 F4 [3]
  MONK NE25...... 24 C5
  PLEE/EAS SR8 ...... 40 C5
  WLSD/HOW NE28 ...... 67 D4
Parkway WASHS NE38 ...... 138 C1
  WICK/BNPF NE16 ...... 95 D5
Parmeter St STLY/ANP DH9 ...... 148 A4 [4]
Parmontley St
  BW/LEM/TK/HW NE15 ...... 77 E3 [2]
Parnell St HLS DH4 ...... 170 A2
Parry Dr CLDN/WHIT/ROK SR6 ...... 109 D1
Parson's Av BYK/HTN/WLK NE6 ...... 83 E3
Parsons Rd PLEE/EAS SR8 ...... 200 C5
  WASHN NE37 ...... 120 A5
Partick Rd MLFD/PNYW SR4 ...... 142 A2
Partick Sq MLFD/PNYW SR4 ...... 142 B2 [5]
Partridge Cl WASHS NE38 ...... 137 E3
Passfield Wy PLEE/EAS SR8 ...... 207 F4
Pasteur Rd RDHAMSE DH6 ...... 187 E5 [1]
Paston Rd MONK NE25...... 24 C6

The Pastures BLYTH NE24 ...... 16 C2
Pathside JRW NE32 ...... 86 A6
Patience Av DIN/WO NE13 ...... 33 E2
Patina Cl BW/LEM/TK/HW NE15 .... 59 E6 [5]
Paton Rd SUNDSW SR3...... 143 E4
Paton Sq SUNDSW SR3 ...... 143 E4
Patrick Crs RDHAMSE DH6...... 187 F2
Patterdale Cl BOL NE36 ...... 106 B3 [5]
  DHAM DH1 ...... 197 D2 [3]
Patterdale Gdns LGB/HTN NE7 ...... 65 D3
Patterdale Gv SWCK/CAS SR5 ...... 108 B6 [5]
Patterdale Rd BLYTH NE24 ...... 9 F4
Patterdale St HLH DH5 ...... 185 F2
Patterdale Ter GATE NE8 ...... 99 E2 [3]
Patterson St BLAY NE21 ...... 77 D4
Pattinson Gdns FELL NE10 ...... 82 B6
  LWF/SPW/WRK NE9 ...... 100 A3
Pattinson Rd WASHS NE38 ...... 122 A6
Pauline Av
  CLDN/WHIT/ROK SR6 ...... 126 C1 [13]
Pauline Gdns
  BW/LEM/TK/HW NE15 ...... 77 F1
Pauls Gn HLH DH5 ...... 171 F4
Paulsway JRW NE32 ...... 87 D2
Paxford Cl LGB/HTN NE7 ...... 64 B1
Paxton Ter MLFD/PNYW SR4 ...... 125 F5 [9]
Peacock Ct DUN/TMV NE11 ...... 98 A3
Peacock St West
  MLFD/PNYW SR4 ...... 125 E6
Pea Flatts La CLS/BIR/GTL DH3... 168 B3
Peareth Gv CLDN/WHIT/ROK SR6 .. 127 D1
Peareth Hall Rd
  LWF/SPW/WRK NE9 ...... 119 E3
  WASHN NE37 ...... 120 A2
Peareth Rd CLDN/WHIT/ROK SR6... 109 D6
Pear Lea BDN/LAN/SAC DH7 ...... 202 C4
Pearl Rd SUNDSW SR3 ...... 143 E4
Pearson Pl JRW NE32 ...... 69 E6 [2]
  TYNE/NSHE NE30 ...... 55 D6
Pearson St SSH NE33 ...... 71 F2
  STLY/ANP DH9 ...... 131 E6 [4]
Peart Cl RDHAMSE DH6 ...... 197 F5 [2]
Peartree Gdns BYK/HTN/WLK NE6... 66 B5
Peary Cl WD/WHPE/BLK NE5...... 60 B4
Pease Av BW/LEM/TK/HW NE15 .... 78 B2
Peasemoor Rd MLFD/PNYW SR4 ... 142 A1
Pease Rd PLEE/EAS SR8 ...... 199 F6 [1]
Pecket Cl BLYTH NE24 ...... 15 F1
Peebles Cl NSHW NE29 ...... 53 D4
Peebles Rd SUNDSW SR3 ...... 143 D4
Peel Av DHAM DH1 ...... 196 A3
Peel La CNUT NE1 ...... 2 B5
Peggy's Wicket STLY/ANP DH9 ...... 133 E6
Pegwood Rd MLFD/PNYW SR4 ...... 142 B1 [1]
Pelaw Av CLSW/PEL DH2 ...... 153 D3
  STLY/ANP DH9 ...... 131 F6
Pelaw Bank CLS/BIR/GTL DH3 ...... 153 E4
Pelaw Crs CLSW/PEL DH2 ...... 153 D3
Pelaw Grange Ct
  CLS/BIR/GTL DH3 ...... 136 B6
Pelaw Leazes La DHAM DH1 ...... 194 C4 [5]
Pelaw Pl CLSW/PEL DH2...... 153 E3
Pelaw Rd CLSW/PEL DH2 ...... 153 D3
Pelaw Sq CLSW/PEL DH2 ...... 153 D3
  MLFD/PNYW SR4 ...... 124 B5 [2]
Pelaw Wy FELL NE10 ...... 101 F2
Peldon Cl LGB/HTN NE7 ...... 64 B1
Pelham Ct GOS/KPK NE3 ...... 46 A5 [2]
Peltondale Av BLYTH NE24 ...... 9 F6
Pelton Fell Rd CLSW/PEL DH2 ...... 152 C4
Pelton La CLSW/PEL DH2 ...... 151 E1
Pelton Ms CLSW/PEL DH2 ...... 151 E2
Pelton Rd MLFD/PNYW SR4 ...... 142 B2 [6]
Pemberton Bank HLH DH5 ...... 186 A3
Pemberton Cl SWCK/CAS SR5 ...... 126 A3 [5]
Pemberton Gdns SUNDSW SR3 .. 144 A3 [5]
Pemberton St HLH DH5 ...... 171 F6 [5]
Pembroke Av CLS/BIR/GTL DH3 ... 136 C5
  SUNDSW SR3 ...... 160 C2
Pembroke Gdns WLSD/HOW NE28... 68 C2
Pembroke Ter SSH NE33 ...... 88 B1 [2]
Pembrooke Av BW/LEM/TK/HW NE6 .. 66 A6
Pendeford WASHS NE38 ...... 139 F2
Pendle Cl WASHS NE38 ...... 138 A3
Pendleton Dr CRAM NE23 ...... 13 F5
Pendower Wy
  BW/LEM/TK/HW NE15...... 78 B2
Penfold Cl LGB/HTN NE7 ...... 65 E2 [3]
Penhale Dr ASHBK/HED/RY SR2 ... 162 B1
Penhill Cl CLSW/PEL DH2 ...... 135 D5
Penistone Rd MLFD/PNYW SR4 ...... 141 F2
Penman Pl NSHW NE29 ...... 70 C2 [5]
Penman Sq MLFD/PNYW SR4 ...... 142 A2 [1]
Penman St NSHW NE29 ...... 70 C2
Pennant Sq MLFD/PNYW SR4 ...... 124 B6 [2]
Pennine Dr PLEE/EAS SR8 ...... 208 A2
Pennine Gdns DUN/TMV NE11 ...... 97 F3
  STLY/ANP DH9 ...... 148 C3
Pennine Gv BOL NE36...... 106 A3
Pennine Wy LGB/KIL NE12...... 48 C6
Penn Sq MLFD/PNYW SR4 ...... 124 B6
Penn St ELS/FEN NE4 ...... 80 A5
Pennycross Rd MLFD/PNYW SR4 ... 141 F2
Pennycross Sq MLFD/PNYW SR4 ... 141 F2 [2]
Pennyfine Cl NSHW NE29 ...... 54 C4 [3]

Pennyfine Rd *WICK/BNPF* NE16 ...... 114 B1
Pennygate Sq *MLFD/PNYW* SR4 .. 141 F1 🔳
Pennygreen Sq
  MLFD/PNYW SR4 .... 141 F1 🔳
Pennymore Sq
  MLFD/PNYW SR4 .... 141 F2 🔳
Pennywell Rd *MLFD/PNYW* SR4 ...... 142 B2
Penrith Av *TYNE/NSHE* NE30............. 54 C2
Penrith Gdns *LWF/SPW/WRK* NE9 .. 100 A1
Penrith Rd *HEBB* NE31.......................... 85 E4
  SWCK/CAS SR5 .... 108 B6
Penryn Av *SEA/MUR* SR7................... 188 C1
Penryn Wy *BDN/LAN/SAC* DH7 ...... 203 E4
Pensford Ct *GOS/KPK* NE3 .... 61 E1 🔳
Penshaw Gn *WD/WHPE/BLK* NE5..... 61 F3
Penshaw La *HLS* DH4........................... 140 A6
Penshaw Vw *BDN/LAN/SAC* DH7 ..... 178 C2
  FELL NE10 .... 102 B2
  HEBB NE31.. 84 C4 🔳
  JRW NE32 .... 86 A4 🔳
Penshaw Wy *CLS/BIR/GTL* DH3....... 137 D2
Pensher St *MLFD/PNYW* SR4............ 125 F6
Pensher St East *FELL* NE10 .... 100 B1
Pentland Cl *CRAM* NE23 .... 14 A5 🔳
  NSHW NE29 .... 54 B3 🔳
  PLEE/EAS SR8 .... 207 F3
  WASHS NE38 .... 138 A3
Pentland Gdns *DUN/TMV* NE11 ... 97 F5 🔳
Pentland Gv *LGB/KIL* NE12 .... 49 D3
Pentlands Ter *STLY/ANP* DH9 .... 148 C3
Pentridge Cl *CRAM* NE23 .... 22 B1
Penwood Rd *MLFD/PNYW* SR4 ...... 142 B1
Penyghent Wy *WASHN* NE37 .... 119 F6
Penzance Bungs *SEA/MUR* SR7 ..... 174 C6
Penzance Rd *MLFD/PNYW* SR4 ...... 142 A2
Percival St *MLFD/PNYW* SR4 .... 125 E5 🔳
Percy Av *WBAY* NE26 .... 40 B5
Percy Ct *NSHW* NE29 .... 69 F3
Percy Crs *NSHW* NE29 .... 69 F3
Percy Gdns *DUN/TMV* NE11 .... 97 F3
  LGB/KIL NE12 .... 49 F4 🔳
  MONK NE25.. 40 C6
Percy La *DHAM* DH1............................ 193 F5
Percy Pk *TYNE/NSHE* NE30 .... 55 F4
Percy Park Rd *TYNE/NSHE* NE30 ... 55 F4
Percy Rd *WBAY* NE26 .... 41 D5
Percy Scott St *HAR/WTLS* NE34 ..... 88 B5
Percy St *BLYTH* NE24 .... 11 E5 🔳
  BW/LEM/TK/HW NE15 .... 76 B2 🔳
  CNUT NE1 .... 2 C
  CRAM NE23 .... 22 B3
  HLH DH5 .... 172 A6
  JRW NE32 .... 86 B1
  LGB/KIL NE12 .... 49 F4 🔳
  SSH NE33 .... 71 F4 🔟
  TYNE/NSHE NE30 .... 55 F5 🔳
  WLSD/HOW NE28 .... 67 E4
Percy St South *BLYTH* NE24 .... 11 E5 🔳
Percy Ter *ASHBK/HED/RY* SR2...... 145 D2
  DHAM DH1 .... 193 F5
  MONK NE25.. 40 A5
Percy Ter South
  ASHBK/HED/RY SR2........................ 145 D3
Percy Wy *BW/LEM/TK/HW* NE15 .... 58 C5
Peregrine Pl *LGB/KIL* NE12 .... 48 C5
Perivale Rd *MLFD/PNYW* SR4 .... 142 A2
Perrycrofts *SUNDSW* SR3 .... 160 C4 🔳
Perry St *GATE* NE8 .... 99 E2 🔳
Perth Av *JRW* NE32.............................. 86 C3
Perth Cl *NSHW* NE29 .... 53 E4 🔳
  WLSD/HOW NE28 .... 68 B2 🔳
Perth Ct *SUNDSW* SR3 .... 143 D5
Perth Gdns *WLSD/HOW* NE28 .... 68 B2 🔳
Perth Rd *SUNDSW* SR3 .... 143 D5
Perth Sq *SUNDSW* SR3 .... 143 E4 🔳
Pesspool La *RDHAMSE* DH6............ 198 A2
Peterborough Rd *DHAM* DH1 .... 181 D6
Peter's Bank *STLY/ANP* DH9 .... 146 C1
Petersfield Rd *MLFD/PNYW* SR4..... 142 A2
Petersham Rd *MLFD/PNYW* SR4.... 124 B6
Petherton Ct *GOS/KPK* NE3............. 45 E6
Peth Gn *HLH* DH5 .... 186 A3 🔳
Peth La *RYTON* NE40........................... 74 C2
Petrel Cl *SSH* NE33............................. 71 E2 🔳
Petrel Wy *BLYTH* NE24 .... 17 E2
Petterill *WASHS* NE38 .... 137 F5
Petwell Crs *PLEE/EAS* SR8 .... 200 B2
Petwell La *PLEE/EAS* SR8 .... 200 C1
Pevensey Cl *NSHW* NE29 .... 54 B3 🔳
Philadelphia La *HLS* DH4 .... 157 E3
Philiphaugh *WLSD/HOW* NE28 ...... 67 D6 🔳
Philip Pl *ELS/FEN* NE4 .... 79 F2 🔳
Philipson St *BYK/HTN/WLK* NE6 ..... 83 E2
Philip Sq *SUNDSW* SR3 .... 143 D4
Phillips Av *WICK/BNPF* NE16 .... 95 F2 🔳
Phoenix Cha *NSHW* NE29.................. 53 D4
Phoenix Rd *MLFD/PNYW* SR4 .... 124 B6
  WASHS NE38 .... 119 D6
Phoenix Wy *HLS* DH4 .... 170 B3
Piccadilly *SUNDSW* SR3 .... 143 D6 🔳
Picherwell *FELL* NE10 .... 100 C3 🔳
Pickard Cl *PLEE/EAS* SR8 .... 209 D1
Pickard St *MLFD/PNYW* SR4 .... 125 E5 🔳
Pickering Rd *MLFD/PNYW* SR4 ...... 141 F3

Pickering Sq *MLFD/PNYW* SR4 ...... 142 A2
Pickhurst Rd *MLFD/PNYW* SR4 ...... 142 A3
Pickhurst Sq *MLFD/PNYW* SR4 ... 142 A3 🔳
Picktree La *CLS/BIR/GTL* DH3 .... 153 F4
  WASHS NE38 .... 137 D6
Picktree Ldg *CLS/BIR/GTL* DH3 ..... 136 C6
Pickwick Ct *DHAM* DH1 .... 205 D1 🔳
Pier Pde *SSH* NE33............................. 72 A2
Pier Vw *CLDN/WHIT/ROK* SR6 .... 127 F2
Pikestone Cl *WASHS* NE38 .... 137 F3
Pilgrim Cl *SWCK/CAS* SR5 .... 126 B3
Pilgrim St *CNUT* NE1 .... 3 F5 🔳
Pilgrims' Wy *DHAM* DH1 .... 195 E3
Pilgrimsway *JRW* NE32 .... 87 D2
  LWF/SPW/WRK NE9 .... 99 F3
Pilton Rd *WD/WHPE/BLK* NE5......... 60 B3
Pimlico *DHAM* DH1 .... 194 B6
Pimlico Rd *HLH* DH5 .... 186 A3
  MLFD/PNYW SR4 .... 142 A2
Pine Av *DHAM* DH1 .... 195 F5
  DIN/WO NE13 .... 31 E3
  GOS/KPK NE3 .... 46 B5
  HAR/WTLS NE34 .... 89 F3
Pinedale Dr *RDHAMSE* DH6 .... 187 E5
Pine Lea *BDN/LAN/SAC* DH7 .... 202 C4
Pine Pk *BDN/LAN/SAC* DH7 .... 192 A5
Pine Rd *BLAY* NE21............................. 76 B6 🔳
The Pines *RYTON* NE40....................... 92 A1
Pine St *CLS/BIR/GTL* DH3 .... 136 B1
  CLSW/PEL DH2 .... 150 C3
  JRW NE32 .... 85 F2
  MLFD/PNYW SR4 .... 125 E5 🔳
  STLY/ANP DH9 .... 147 F4
Pinesway *SUNDSW* SR3 .... 144 A3
Pinetree Gdns *MONK* NE25 .... 54 A1
Pinetree Wy *WICK/BNPF* NE16 ...... 78 A6
Pinewood *HEBB* NE31 .... 84 B1 🔳
Pinewood Av *CRAM* NE23 .... 14 A5 🔳
  DIN/WO NE13 .... 33 E5
  GOS/KPK NE3 .... 33 E5
  WASHS NE38 .... 138 B5
Pinewood Cl *BYK/HTN/WLK* NE6 ... 66 A6
  DIN/WO NE13 .... 45 D6
Pinewood Gdns *DUN/TMV* NE11 ... 97 F5
Pinewood Rd *SWCK/CAS* SR5 .... 125 E2
Pinewood Sq *SWCK/CAS* SR5 .... 125 E2 🔳
Pinewood St *HLS* DH4 .... 169 D1
Pinewood Vis *HAR/WTLS* NE34 ...... 89 F2 🔳
Pink La *CNUT* NE1 .... 2 C5 🔳
Pinner Rd *BYK/HTN/WLK* NE6........ 83 D4
Pinner Rd *MLFD/PNYW* SR4 .... 142 B1 🔳
Pipershaw *WASHN* NE37 .... 119 E6
Pipe Track La *ELS/FEN* NE4 .... 78 C4
Pipewellgate *GATE* NE8 .... 80 C5
Pitcairn Rd *MLFD/PNYW* SR4 .... 142 B1
Pithouse La *HLS* DH4 .... 183 D1
Pit La *DHAM* DH1 .... 180 B6
Pittington La *DHAM* DH1 .... 197 D1
Pittington Rd *HLH* DH5 .... 183 F4
Pitt St *ELS/FEN* NE4 .... 80 A2
Plains Rd *SUNDSW* SR3................... 143 E4
Plaistow Sq *MLFD/PNYW* SR4 ...... 124 B6 🔳
Plaistow Wy *CRAM* NE23 .... 14 A5 🔳
Planesway *FELL* NE10 .... 101 D5 🔳
Planet Pl *LGB/KIL* NE12 .... 49 E2
Planetree Av *ELS/FEN* NE4 .... 61 F6
Plane Tree Ct *SUNDSW* SR3 .... 160 A2 🔳
Plantation Av *WICK/BNPF* NE16 ..... 95 F2
Plantation Gv *FELL* NE10 .... 84 A6
Plantation Rd *MLFD/PNYW* SR4 .... 125 D5
Plantation Sq *MLFD/PNYW* SR4 ... 125 D5 🔳
Plantation St *WLSD/HOW* NE28 ...... 67 D6 🔳
The Plantation *LWF/SPW/WRK* NE9... 99 F3
Plantation Vw *STLY/ANP* DH9 .... 150 B2
Plantation Wk *RDHAMSE* DH6 .... 187 E5
Plawsworth Gdns
  LWF/SPW/WRK NE9 .... 118 B1
Plawsworth Rd
  BDN/LAN/SAC DH7 .... 178 B1
Plenmeller Pl *WICK/BNPF* NE16 ..... 113 F1
Plessey Av *BLYTH* NE24 .... 11 D6
Plessey Crs *MONK* NE25.................... 41 D6
Plessey Gdns *NSHW* NE29 .... 69 F1 🔳
Plessey Rd *BLYTH* NE24 .... 11 E4 🔳
  BLYTH NE24 .... 16 E1
Plessey Ter *LGB/HTN* NE7 .... 65 D4
Plough Rd *SUNDSW* SR3 .... 160 B3
Plover Cl *BLYTH* NE24 .... 17 D2
Plover Dr *WICK/BNPF* NE16 .... 130 B1
Plunkett Rd *STLY/ANP* DH9 .... 129 D5
Plunkett Ter *CLSW/PEL* DH2 .... 151 F4
Plymouth Cl *SEA/MUR* SR7 .... 175 E4 🔳
Plymouth Sq *SUNDSW* SR3 .... 143 D4 🔳
Point Pleasant Ter
  WLSD/HOW NE28 .... 68 A4
Polden Cl *PLEE/EAS* SR8.................. 207 F3
Polden Crs *NSHW* NE29 .... 54 A2
Polebrook Rd *MLFD/PNYW* SR4 .. 124 B6 🔳
Pollard St *SSH* NE33 .... 71 F2
Polmuir Rd *SUNDSW* SR3 .... 143 D4
Polmuir Sq *SUNDSW* SR3 .... 143 D4 🔳
Polpero Cl *CLS/BIR/GTL* DH3 .... 136 C3
Polperro Cl *ASHBK/HED/RY* SR2 ... 162 B1
Polton Sq *MLFD/PNYW* SR4............ 124 B6
Polwarth Crs *GOS/KPK* NE3.............. 47 E4

Polwarth Dr *GOS/KPK* NE3 .... 47 E3
Polwarth Rd *GOS/KPK* NE3 .... 47 E3
Polworth Sq *SUNDSW* SR3 .... 143 E4 🔳
Ponefract Rd
  MLFD/PNYW SR4 .... 142 A3 🔳
Ponteland Cl *NSHW* NE29 .... 53 E5 🔳
  WASHS NE38 .... 137 E2
Ponteland Rd
  BW/LEM/TK/HW NE15..................... 57 F2
  DIN/WO NE13 .... 44 C5
  ELS/FEN NE4 .... 62 B5
  PONT/DH NE20 .... 28 C4
  WD/WHPE/BLK NE5.......................... 45 D6
  WD/WHPE/BLK NE5.......................... 62 A5
Ponthaugh *ROWG* NE39.................. 111 E1
Pontop Sq *MLFD/PNYW* SR4 .... 124 B6 🔳
Pontop St *HLH* DH5............................ 170 B6
Pontop Vw *ROWG* NE39.................... 110 C2
Pont Vw *PONT/DH* NE20 .... 28 B3
Poole Cl *CRAM* NE23.......................... 22 B1
Poole Rd *MLFD/PNYW* SR4 .... 124 B6 🔳
Pooley Cl *WD/WHPE/BLK* NE5........ 61 D5
Pooley Rd *WD/WHPE/BLK* NE5....... 61 D5
Poplar Av *BLYTH* NE21...................... 10 C3
  BYK/HTN/WLK NE6 .... 66 B5 🔳
  DIN/WO NE13 .... 31 E3
Poplar Crs *CLS/BIR/GTL* DH3 .... 136 A1
  DUN/TMV NE11 .... 97 E3
  GATE NE8 .... 81 D6 🔳
Poplar Dr *CLDN/WHIT/ROK* SR6 .... 109 E1
  DHAM DH1 .... 195 F3
Poplar Gv *ASHBK/HED/RY* SR2 .... 145 D6
  BDLGTN NE22 .... 8 A3
  HAR/WTLS NE34 .... 89 E3
Poplar Lea *BDN/LAN/SAC* DH7 .... 202 C4
Poplar Rd *BLAY* NE21 .... 94 B1 🔳
  DHAM DH1 .... 196 C2 🔳
The Poplars *GOS/KPK* NE3............... 63 E3
  HLH DH5 .... 186 B3
  SWCK/CAS SR5 .... 125 E2 🔳
Poplar St *CLS/BIR/GTL* DH3 .... 153 E5
  STLY/ANP DH9 .... 147 F4
Popplewell Gdns
  LWF/SPW/WRK NE9 .... 99 F6
Popplewell Ter *NSHW* NE29 .... 54 C4 🔳
The Populars *HLS* DH4 .... 140 A6
Porchester Dr *CRAM* NE23 .... 22 B1
Porlock Ct *CRAM* NE23 .... 13 F5
Porlock Rd *JRW* NE32......................... 86 C3
Portadown Rd
  MLFD/PNYW SR4 .... 142 A3 🔳
Portberry St *SSH* NE33....................... 71 D6
Portberry Wy *SSH* NE33..................... 71 D5
Portchester Gv *BOLCOL* NE35......... 105 D2
Portchester Rd *MLFD/PNYW* SR4 .. 142 B2
Portchester Sq *MLFD/PNYW* SR4 .. 142 B2
Porter Ter *SEA/MUR* SR7.................. 188 B1
Porthcawl Dr *WASHN* NE37 .... 120 B2
Portland Av *SEA/MUR* SR7 .... 175 F3
Portland Gdns *CRAM* NE23 .... 22 B1
  LWF/SPW/WRK NE9 .... 117 E2
  TYNE/NSHE NE30 .... 54 C5
Portland Ms *JES* NE2 .... 81 E1 🔳
Portland Rd *BW/LEM/TK/HW* NE15... 58 A4
  JES NE2 .... 81 E1
  SUNDSW SR3 .... 143 E4
Portland Sq *SUNDSW* SR3 .... 143 E3 🔳
Portland St *BLYTH* NE24.................... 10 C3
  ELS/FEN NE4 .... 79 F4 🔳
  ELS/FEN NE4 .... 80 A4 🔳
  FELL NE10 .... 101 F1 🔳
Portland Ter *JES* NE2 .... 81 D1 🔳
Portman Pl *BYK/HTN/WLK* NE6 .... 83 D5 🔳
Portman Sq *MLFD/PNYW* SR4 ...... 142 B1
Portmeads Rd *CLS/BIR/GTL* DH3 .. 136 C2
Portobello La
  CLDN/WHIT/ROK SR6 .... 126 C3
Portree Sq *SUNDSW* SR3 .... 143 D5
Portrush Cl *WASHN* NE37 .... 120 B2 🔳
Portrush Rd *MLFD/PNYW* SR4 ...... 124 B6
Portrush Wy *LGB/HTN* NE7 .... 65 C1
Portside Rd *MLFD/PNYW* SR4 .... 142 A1
Portsmouth Rd *MLFD/PNYW* SR4 .. 142 A1
  NSHW NE29 .... 69 E1
Portsmouth Sq *MLFD/PNYW* SR4 .. 142 A2
Portugal Pl *WLSD/HOW* NE28 ...... 67 D5 🔟
Post Office La *NSHW* NE29 .... 54 C3 🔳
Post Office St *BLYTH* NE24 .... 11 E4 🔳
Potterhouse La *DHAM* DH1............. 179 E4
Potter Pl *STLY/ANP* DH9 .... 149 D5
Potters Bank *DHAM* DH1 .... 205 D1
Potters Cl *DHAM* DH1 .... 204 C1
Potter Sq *SUNDSW* SR3 .... 143 D4
Potter St *JRW* NE32 .... 85 F1
  WLSD/HOW NE28 .... 68 A4
Pottersway *LWF/SPW/WRK* NE9 ... 99 F4
Pottery Bank *BYK/HTN/WLK* NE6... 83 E5
Pottery La *CNUT* NE1 .... 80 B5
  MLFD/PNYW SR4 .... 123 F5 🔳
Pottery Rd *SWCK/CAS* SR5.............. 125 F3
Pottery Yd *HLS* DH4 .... 171 D2 🔳
Potto St *RDHAMSE* DH6 .... 206 C2 🔳
Potts St *BYK/HTN/WLK* NE6............. 82 B2
Powburn Cl *CLSW/PEL* DH2............ 165 F1
Powburn Gdns *ELS/FEN* NE4 .... 62 A6

Powis Rd *SUNDSW* SR3.......................... **143** E4
Powis Sq *SUNDSW* SR3 .... **143** E4 [5]
Poynings Cl *WD/WHPE/BLK* NE5 .... **61** E1
Praetorian Dr *WLSD/HOW* NE28 ...... **67** D6 [5]
Prebends Fld *DHAM* DH1..................... **195** E6
Prefect Pl *LWF/SPW/WRK* NE9 .... **99** F3 [2]
Premier Rd *SUNDSW* SR3...................... **143** D4
Prendwick Av *HEBB* NE31................... **84** C5
Prendwick Ct *CLSW/PEL* DH2 .... **165** F2
Prengarth Av
  CLDN/WHIT/ROK SR6..................... **126** C1
Prensgarth Wy *HAR/WTLS* NE34 ...... **87** E5 [2]
Prescot Rd *MLFD/PNYW* SR4............ **124** B6
Press La *SUND* SR1 .... **4** D2
Prestbury Av *CRAM* NE23 .... **13** F5
Prestbury Rd *MLFD/PNYW* SR4 .... **141** F2
Prestdale Av *BLYTH* NE24 .... **9** F5
Presthope Rd *MLFD/PNYW* SR4 .... **141** F2
Prestmede *FELL* NE10.......................... **101** D3 [6]
Preston Av *TYNE/NSHE* NE30 .... **54** C5
Preston North Rd *NSHW* NE29 .... **54** B3
Preston Pk *NSHW* NE29....................... **54** C5
Preston Rd *ASHBK/HED/RY* SR2 ...... **145** C2
Preston Wd *TYNE/NSHE* NE30 .... **54** C3
Prestwick *FELL* NE10........................... **101** D3 [7]
Prestwick Av *NSHW* NE29 .... **53** E5
Prestwick Cl *WASHN* NE37 .... **120** B3 [5]
Prestwick Dr *FELL* NE10...................... **102** B3
Prestwick Gdns *GOS/KPK* NE3 .... **62** B2
Prestwick Rd *MLFD/PNYW* SR4........ **124** B6
Pretoria St *SUNDSW* SR3 .... **143** D4 [3]
Pretoria St
  BW/LEM/TK/HW NE15 .... **77** F2 [4]
Price St *HEBB* NE31 .... **84** B1 [4]
Priestfield Cl *SUNDSW* SR3................. **160** B3
Priestley Ct *HAR/WTLS* NE34............. **87** F5
Priestley Gdns *FELL* NE10 .... **102** A2 [5]
Priestly Crs *MLFD/PNYW* SR4 .... **126** A4 [1]
Priestman Ct *MLFD/PNYW* SR4 .... **124** C6 [3]
Primate Rd *SUNDSW* SR3.................... **143** D4
Primrose Av *HAR/WTLS* NE34 .... **88** A3 [4]
Primrose Cl *CRAM* NE23 .... **34** C2
Primrose Crs
  CLDN/WHIT/ROK SR6..................... **126** C1
  HLS DH4....................................... **156** A5
Primrose Gdns *WLSD/HOW* NE28 ...... **66** C2 [2]
Primrose Hl *LWF/SPW/WRK* NE9 ...... **99** F3 [3]
Primrose Prec
  CLDN/WHIT/ROK SR6..................... **126** C1 [14]
Primrose St *MLFD/PNYW* SR4 .... **123** F6 [5]
Primrose Ter *CLS/BIR/GTL* DH3........ **136** C2
  JRW NE32 .... **86** B4
Prince Albert Ter *JES* NE2 .... **3** G2 [2]
Prince Consort La *HEBB* NE31 .... **84** C2
Prince Consort Rd *GATE* NE8 .... **81** D6
  HEBB NE31 .... **84** B2
  JRW NE32 .... **86** B2
Prince Consort Wy *NSHW* NE29 ...... **70** C3
Prince Edward Gv *HAR/WTLS* NE34.. **90** B2
Prince Edward Rd *HAR/WTLS* NE34.. **89** E3
Prince Edward Rd East
  HAR/WTLS NE34 .... **90** B2
Prince George Av
  CLDN/WHIT/ROK SR6..................... **108** C6 [6]
Prince of Wales Cl
  HAR/WTLS NE34 .... **89** D3 [1]
Prince Philip Cl
  BW/LEM/TK/HW NE15.................... **78** B3
Prince Rd *WLSD/HOW* NE28 .... **67** D3
Princes Av *CLDN/WHIT/ROK* SR6..... **109** D5
  GOS/KPK NE3 .... **47** D6
Princes Cl *GOS/KPK* NE3.................... **47** D6
Prince's Gdns *BLYTH* NE24 .... **10** B4
  CLDN/WHIT/ROK SR6..................... **109** D5 [2]
Prince's Meadow *GOS/KPK* NE3 ...... **62** C1
Princes Pk *DUN/TMV* NE11 .... **98** A5
Prince Rd *GOS/KPK* NE3..................... **47** D3
Princess Dr *GATE* NE8 .... **97** F2
Princess Louise Rd *BLYTH* NE24 .... **10** C5
Princess Rd *SEA/MUR* SR7................ **176** B3
Princess St *ASHBK/HED/RY* SR2 ...... **4** B5
  FELL NE10...................................... **101** F1 [5]
  WICK/BNPF NE16 .... **114** A2
  TYNE/NSHE NE30 .... **55** D5
Prince St *SUND* SR1.............................. **4** C2 [2]
Princesway *DUN/TMV* NE11 .... **98** A4
Princetown Ter *SUNDSW* SR3 .... **143** D4
Princeway *TYNE/NSHE* NE30 .... **55** F4
Pringle Cl *BDN/LAN/SAC* DH7 .... **202** A1
Pringle Gv *BDN/LAN/SAC* DH7 .... **202** B1
Pringle Pl *BDN/LAN/SAC* DH7 .... **202** B1
Prinn Pl *WICK/BNPF* NE16 .... **114** A2
Priors Cl *DHAM* DH1 .... **193** F4
Prior's Ter *TYNE/NSHE* NE30 .... **55** F5
Priors Wy *WLSD/HOW* NE28 .... **68** A4
Priory Av *MONK* NE25 .... **40** B6
Priory Ct *BDN/LAN/SAC* DH7 .... **178** B2
Priory Gra *BLYTH* NE24 .... **10** B4
Priory Grn *MLFD/PNYW* SR4 .... **143** E1
Priory Pl *BYK/HTN/WLK* NE6 .... **82** B3 [3]
  DIN/WO NE13 .... **32** C5 [6]
Priory Rd *DHAM* DH1.......................... **194** A1
  JRW NE32 .... **69** E6 [3]

Priory Wy *WD/WHPE/BLK* NE5 .... **60** B2
Proctor Sq *SUNDSW* SR3 .... **143** F4
Proctor St *BYK/HTN/WLK* NE6 .... **83** F3 [4]
Promenade *ASHBK/HED/RY* SR2 .... **145** F3
  SEA/MUR SR7 .... **176** C2
  SSH NE33.. **72** B3
  WBAY NE26 .... **40** C4
Prospect Av *MONK* NE25 .... **24** B5
  WLSD/HOW NE28 .... **67** D3
Prospect Av North
  WLSD/HOW NE28 .... **67** D2
Prospect Crs *HLH* DH5 .... **186** B4
Prospect Gdns *BOL* NE36.................. **105** F3
Prospect Pl *ELS/FEN* NE4................... **79** F3
Prospect Rw *SUND* SR1 .... **5** G1
Prospect Ter *TYNE/NSHE* NE30......... **55** E6
Prospect Vw *HLS* DH4 .... **183** E2
Providence Pl *FELL* NE10................... **100** C1 [5]
Providence Rw *DHAM* DH1 .... **194** C4
Provident St *CLSW/PEL* DH2 .... **151** E2
Provost Gdns *ELS/FEN* NE4 .... **78** C4 [1]
Prudhoe Gv *JRW* NE32........................ **85** F5
Prudhoe St *MLFD/PNYW* SR4 ...... **125** E5 [10]
  NSHW NE29.................................... **70** C2
Prudhoe Ter *TYNE/NSHE* NE30 .... **55** F4 [5]
Pudding Chare *CNUT* NE1 .... **2** D5
Purbeck Gdns *CRAM* NE23................. **22** B1
Purbeck Rd *LGB/KIL* NE12 .... **49** D6
Purley *WASHS* NE38 .... **139** F2 [2]
Purley Cl *WLSD/HOW* NE28 .... **68** D1
Purley Gdns *GOS/KPK* NE3................. **62** B2
Purley Rd *SUNDSW* SR3 .... **143** D4
Purley Sq *SUNDSW* SR3 .... **143** D4
Putney Sq *MLFD/PNYW* SR4 .... **142** A2
Pykerley Rd *MONK* NE25 .... **40** A5

Q

The Quadrant *NSHW* NE29 .... **70** A1
  SUND SR1.. **5** C1
Quality Rw *BYK/HTN/WLK* NE6 .... **82** A3
Quality Row Rd
  WICK/BNPF NE16 .... **95** F1 [7]
Quantock Cl *LGB/KIL* NE12 .... **48** C6 [5]
  NSHW NE29.................................... **54** B2 [1]
Quantock Pl *PLEE/EAS* SR8 .... **207** F2
Quarry Bank *ELS/FEN* NE4 .... **80** A3 [14]
Quarryfield Rd *GATE* NE8................... **3** H6
Quarryheads La *DHAM* DH1............... **194** A6
Quarry House La *DHAM* DH1............. **193** E5
  HLH DH5 .... **170** C6
Quarry La *HAR/WTLS* NE34 .... **89** F3
  HAR/WTLS NE34 .... **90** C2 [1]
Quarry Rd *BW/LEM/TK/HW* NE15 .. **76** B2 [7]
  HEBB NE31 .... **85** D3
  STLY/ANP DH9 .... **148** B1
  SUNDSW SR3 .... **161** D1 [3]
Quarry Rw *FELL* NE10 .... **100** C1 [7]
Quarry St *SUNDSW* SR3.................... **160** C1
Quay Rd *BLYTH* NE24 .... **11** E4 [3]
Quayside *BLYTH* NE24 .... **11** E4 [6]
  BYK/HTN/WLK NE6 .... **82** A4
  CNUT NE1 .... **3** F5
The Quay *HLH* DH5.............................. **185** F1
Quay Vw *WLSD/HOW* NE28 .... **68** B4
Queen Alexandra Rd
  ASHBK/HED/RY SR2 .... **145** D4
  NSHW NE29.................................... **54** B5
  SEA/MUR SR7 .... **176** C4
  SUNDSW SR3 .... **144** A3
Queen Alexandra Rd West
  NSHW NE29.................................... **54** A5
Queen Elizabeth Av
  LWF/SPW/WRK NE9 .... **100** A5
Queen Elizabeth Dr *HLH* DH5 .... **186** C4
Queens Av *CLDN/WHIT/ROK* SR6 .... **109** D5
Queensberry St
  MLFD/PNYW SR4 .... **126** A5 [13]
Queensbridge *LGB/KIL* NE12 .... **48** B5 [2]
Queensbury Dr
  WD/WHPE/BLK NE5....................... **59** D4
Queensbury Rd *SEA/MUR* SR7 .... **175** F3
Queen's Cl *BW/LEM/TK/HW* NE15 ... **30** C1 [5]
  GATE NE8 .... **98** B1 [2]
  GOS/KPK NE3 .... **47** E2 [1]
Queen's Crs *HEBB* NE31 .... **84** C4
  MLFD/PNYW SR4 .... **143** F1
  WLSD/HOW NE28 .... **66** C3
Queen's Dr *WBAY* NE26 .... **40** C5
  WICK/BNPF NE16 .... **96** A5
Queen's Gdns *BLYTH* NE24 .... **10** B4
Queens Gv *DHAM* DH1....................... **204** C1
Queensland Av *HAR/WTLS* NE34...... **87** D4
Queens La *CNUT* NE1......................... **2** D5 [2]
Queensmere *CLS/BIR/GTL* DH3 ...... **153** E1
Queen's Rd *BDLGTN* NE22 .... **8** C2
  BW/LEM/TK/HW NE15.................... **58** C5
  CRAM NE23 .... **35** D1
  JES NE2.. **56** A3
  SWCK/CAS SR5 .... **126** A3 [8]
  WBAY NE26 .... **26** C2
  WBAY NE26 .... **40** B4

  WD/WHPE/BLK NE5 .... **60** C4
Queen's Ter *JES* NE2 .... **64** B5
  WLSD/HOW NE28 .... **67** D4
Queen St *ASHBK/HED/RY* SR2 .... **145** E6
  CLSW/PEL DH2 .... **150** C3
  CNUT NE1 .... **3** F5
  GATE NE8 .... **98** B2 [8]
  HLH DH5 .... **171** F5
  SEA/MUR SR7 .... **176** B5
  SSH NE33.. **71** E3
  SUND SR1 .... **4** B1 [1]
  TYNE/NSHE NE30 .... **55** D6
Queen St East *SUND* SR1 .... **5** F2 [2]
Queensway *ELS/FEN* NE4 .... **61** F6
  GOS/KPK NE3 .... **47** D3
  HLH DH5 .... **171** E2 [5]
  TYNE/NSHE NE30 .... **55** D6
Queensway North *DUN/TMV* NE11 .. **98** B3
Queen Victoria Rd *CNUT* NE1 .... **2** C1
Queen Victoria St *FELL* NE10 .... **101** E1
Quentin Av *GOS/KPK* NE3 .... **61** F1
Quinn Cl *PLEE/EAS* SR8 .... **208** C3
Quilton Cl *WD/WHPE/BLK* NE5........ **61** D2

R

Rabbit Banks Rd *GATE* NE8 .... **80** C5
Raby Av *PLEE/EAS* SR8 .... **201** D3
Raby Cl *HLS* DH4 .... **169** F1 [5]
Raby Dr *SUNDSW* SR3 .... **159** E3
Raby Gdns *JRW* NE32 .... **86** A4
Raby Rd *DHAM* DH1 .... **180** B5
  WASHS NE38 .... **137** F1
Raby St *BYK/HTN/WLK* NE6 .... **82** B2
  GATE NE8 .... **99** E2
  MLFD/PNYW SR4 .... **128** A6
Raby Wy *BYK/HTN/WLK* NE6 .... **82** B2
Rachel Cl *ASHBK/HED/RY* SR2 .... **161** E1
Rackly Wy *CLDN/WHIT/ROK* SR6..... **109** E2
Radcliffe Pl *WD/WHPE/BLK* NE5 .. **61** F4 [10]
Radcliffe Rd *SWCK/CAS* SR5 .... **125** D2
Radcliffe St *CLS/BIR/GTL* DH3 .... **136** B3
Radlett Rd *SWCK/CAS* SR5 .... **124** C2
Radnor Gdns *WLSD/HOW* NE28 .... **68** C3
Radnor St *CNUT* NE1........................... **3** F1
Radstock Av *BYK/HTN/WLK* NE6 .... **82** C3
Rae Av *WLSD/HOW* NE28 .... **67** D2
Raeburn Av *WASHS* NE38.................. **139** D3
Raeburn Gdns
  LWF/SPW/WRK NE9 .... **100** A3
Raeburn Rd *HAR/WTLS* NE34 .... **88** C6
  SWCK/CAS SR5 .... **124** B1 [2]
Raglan *WASHS* NE38 .... **137** F1
Raglan Av *ASHBK/HED/RY* SR2 .... **145** D3
Raglan Pl *WICK/BNPF* NE16.............. **112** A6
Railway Cl *DHAM* DH1 .... **197** D5
Railway Rw *SUND* SR1 .... **128** A6
Railway St *DUN/TMV* NE11 .... **79** E6
  ELS/FEN NE4 .... **80** A5
  HEBB NE31 .... **85** E1
  HLH DH5 .... **171** F6 [4]
  JRW NE32 .... **85** F1
  STLY/ANP DH9 .... **146** C5
  STLY/ANP DH9 .... **149** E6
  SUND SR1 .... **5** G3 [1]
Railway Ter *ELS/FEN* NE4 .... **80** A5
  NSHW NE29.................................... **70** C1 [9]
Raine Gv *SUND* SR1............................. **5** F4
Rainford Av *ASHBK/HED/RY* SR2 .... **145** D4
Rainhill Cl *WASHN* NE37 .... **121** D3
Rainhill Rd *WASHN* NE37 .... **121** D3
Rainton Cl *FELL* NE10 .... **102** B4 [2]
Rainton Gv *HLH* DH5 .... **171** D4 [2]
Rainton St *HLS* DH4 .... **140** A6
  MLFD/PNYW SR4 .... **125** F6
  SEA/MUR SR7 .... **176** C4
Rainton Vw *HLS* DH4.......................... **183** E2
Rake La *NSHW* NE29 .... **53** E3
Raleigh Cl *SSH* NE33 .... **71** D6
Raleigh Rd *SWCK/CAS* SR5 .... **124** C2
Raleigh Sq *SWCK/CAS* SR5 .... **124** C2
Ralph Av *ASHBK/HED/RY* SR2 .... **145** DC
Ralph St *HEBB* NE31 .... **85** E1
Ramilies *ASHBK/HED/RY* SR2 .... **161** F2
Ramilies Rd *SWCK/CAS* SR5............. **124** B1
The Ramparts
  BW/LEM/TK/HW NE15.................... **60** A6
Ramsay St *BLAY* NE21 .... **94** A1 [5]
Ramsey Cl *DHAM* DH1 .... **195** F4 [1]
  PLEE/EAS SR8 .... **200** C6
Ramsey St *CLS/BIR/GTL* DH3 .... **153** E6
Ramsgate Rd *SWCK/CAS* SR5 .... **125** D1
Ramside Vw *DHAM* DH1 .... **196** C1 [9]
Randolph St *JRW* NE32 .... **86** B3
Rangoon Rd *SWCK/CAS* SR5 .... **124** B1 [3]
Ranmere Rd *BW/LEM/TK/HW* NE15.. **77** F3
Rannoch Av *CRAM* NE23.................... **22** A1
Rannoch Av *CLSW/PEL* DH2 .... **166** A1
Rannoch Cl *FELL* NE10....................... **102** B2
Rannoch Rd *SWCK/CAS* SR5 .... **124** B1
Ranson Crs *HAR/WTLS* NE34 .... **87** E5 [1]
Ranson St *MLFD/PNYW* SR4 .... **143** F2

Raphael Av *HAR/WTLS* NE34 .... 88 B5
Rathmore Gdns *TYNE/NSHE* NE30 .... 54 C4
Ratho Ct *FELL* NE10 .... 101 D4
Ravenburn Gdns
  BW/LEM/TK/HW NE15 .... 77 E2 **1**
Ravenna Rd *SWCK/CAS* SR5 .... 124 A1
Ravensbourne Av *BOL* NE36 .... 106 C2
Ravenscar Ct *WICK/BNPF* NE16 .... 95 D5 **3**
Ravenscourt Rd *SWCK/CAS* SR5 .... 124 B2
Ravenshill Rd *WD/WHPE/BLK* NE5 .... 59 F5
Ravenside Rd *ELS/FEN* NE4 .... 62 A6
Ravenstone *WASHN* NE37 .... 120 A5
Ravenswood Cl *LGB/KIL* NE12 .... 50 A4
Ravenswood Gdns
  LWF/SPW/WRK NE9 .... 117 E1
Ravenswood Rd
  BYK/HTN/WLK NE6 .... 65 E5
  SWCK/CAS SR5 .... 124 B1
Ravenswood Sq *SWCK/CAS* SR5 .... 124 B1
Ravensworth St *MLFD/PNYW* SR4 .... 126 A5
Ravensworth Av *HLS* DH4 .... 169 E1
Ravensworth Cl *WLSD/HOW* NE28 .... 68 B4
Ravensworth Ct *DUN/TMV* NE11 ... 97 F1 **5**
  RDHAMSE DH6 .... 187 C5
Ravensworth Rd
  CLS/BIR/GTL DH3 .... 136 A1
  DUN/TMV NE11 .... 97 F2
Ravensworth St *WLSD/HOW* NE28... 68 B4
Ravensworth Ter *DHAM* DH1 ... 194 C4 **6**
  DUN/TMV NE11 .... 97 F2
  ELS/FEN NE4 .... 80 A3 **13**
  JRW NE32 .... 86 A5 **4**
  SSH NE33 .... 88 B1
Rawdon Rd *SWCK/CAS* SR5 .... 125 D1
Rawling Rd *GATE* NE8 .... 99 D3
Rawlston Wy *WD/WHPE/BLK* NE5 .. 61 E3
Rawmarsh Rd *SWCK/CAS* SR5 .... 124 B1 **4**
Raydale *SWCK/CAS* SR5 .... 125 D1 **1**
Raydale Av *WASHN* NE37 .... 120 A4
Raylees Gdns *DUN/TMV* NE11 ... 97 F3 **6**
Rayleigh Dr *DIN/WO* NE13 .... 33 D3
Rayleigh Gv *GATE* NE8 .... 98 C3
Raynham Cl *CRAM* NE23 .... 21 E5
Readhead Av *SSH* NE33 .... 72 A5
Readhead Dr *BYK/HTN/WLK* NE6 .... 83 E4
Readhead Rd *HAR/WTLS* NE34 .... 72 A6
Reading Rd *HAR/WTLS* NE34 .... 88 C1
  SWCK/CAS SR5 .... 124 B1
Reading Sq *SWCK/CAS* SR5 .... 124 B1
Rea Pl *GOS/KPK* NE3 .... 62 C1 **6**
Reasby Gdns *RYTON* NE40 .... 74 A3
Reavley Av *BDLGTN* NE22 .... 9 D1
Reay Crs *BOLCOL* NE35 .... 106 A2
Reay Gdns *WD/WHPE/BLK* NE5 .... 60 C4
Reay St *FELL* NE10 .... 84 A6
Rectory Bank *BOL* NE36 .... 105 F3 **5**
Rectory Ct *WICK/BNPF* NE16............. 96 A1
Rectory Dr *JES* NE2 .... 64 A2
Rectory Gn *BOL* NE36 .... 105 E3 **1**
Rectory Gv *GOS/KPK* NE3 .... 63 F1
Rectory La *BLAY* NE21 .... 94 A1
  WICK/BNPF NE16 .... 96 A4
Rectory Pl *GATE* NE8 .... 98 C1
Rectory Rd *FELL* NE10 .... 100 B3
  GATE NE8 .... 99 D1
  GOS/KPK NE3 .... 63 F2
  HLH DH5 .... 185 F1 **2**
Rectory Rd East *FELL* NE10 .... 100 C3
Red Admiral Ct *DUN/TMV* NE11 ... 98 A3 **2**
Red Barnes *CNUT* NE1 .... 3 H3
Red Berry Wy *HAR/WTLS* NE34 .... 88 A6
Redburn Cl *HLS* DH4 .... 170 B2 **1**
Redburn Rd *WD/WHPE/BLK* NE5 ..... 60 B2
Redcar Rd *BYK/HTN/WLK* NE6 .... 65 F5
  SWCK/CAS SR5 .... 125 D2
  WLSD/HOW NE28 .... 68 C3
Redcar Sq *SWCK/CAS* SR5 .... 125 D2 **1**
Redcliffe Wy *WD/WHPE/BLK* NE5 .... 61 D3
Redditch Sq *SWCK/CAS* SR5 .... 124 C1 **1**
Rede Av *HEBB* NE31 .... 85 D2 **2**
Redemarsh *FELL* NE10 .... 101 F4 **2**
Redesdale Av *BLAY* NE21 .... 93 E2
  GOS/KPK NE3 .... 62 C1
Redesdale Cl *LGB/KIL* NE12 .... 49 E4 **3**
Redesdale Gdns *DUN/TMV* NE11 ..... 97 E3
Redesdale Gv *NSHW* NE29 .... 53 E6
Redesdale Pl *BLYTH* NE24 .... 10 A5 **4**
  NSHW NE29 .... 53 E6
  SWCK/CAS SR5 .... 124 B1
Rede St *DUN/TMV* NE11 .... 98 B5
  JRW NE32 .... 85 F3 **1**
Redewater Gdns
  WICK/BNPF NE16 .... 95 F4 **1**
Redewater Rd *ELS/FEN* NE4 .... 62 A6
Red Firs *BDN/LAN/SAC* DH7 .... 203 D4
Redford Pl *LGB/KIL* NE12 .... 35 E5 **4**
Red Hall Dr *LGB/HTN* NE7 .... 65 F3
Redheugh Bridge Rd
  ELS/FEN NE4 .... 80 B5 **2**
Redheugh Rd *MONK* NE25.................... 39 D5
Redhill *CLDN/WHIT/ROK* SR6 .... 109 D2

Redhill Dr *WICK/BNPF* NE16 .... 95 D6 **1**
Redhill Rd *SWCK/CAS* SR5 .... 124 C1
Redhills La *DHAM* DH1 .... 193 F4
Redhills Wy *HLH* DH5 .... 185 F2
Redhouse Cl *BDN/LAN/SAC* DH7 .... 178 C2
Red House Dr *MONK* NE25 .... 39 E4
Red House Farm *BDLGTN* NE22 .... 6 B4
Red House Rd *HEBB* NE31 .... 85 E2
Redland Av *GOS/KPK* NE3 .... 45 F6
Red Lion La *WASHN* NE37 .... 120 B2
Redmires Cl *CLSW/PEL* DH2 .... 135 D5
Redmond Rd *SWCK/CAS* SR5 .... 125 D1
Redmond Sq *SWCK/CAS* SR5 .... 125 D1
Rednam Pl *WD/WHPE/BLK* NE5 .... 61 D4
Redruth Gdns
  LWF/SPW/WRK NE9 .... 117 E2
Redruth Sq *SWCK/CAS* SR5 .... 124 C1 **2**
Redshank Cl *WASHS* NE38 .... 137 E4
Redshank Dr *BLYTH* NE24 .... 17 D2 **3**
Red Wk *LGB/HTN* NE7........................... 64 C1
Redwell Ct *HAR/WTLS* NE34 .... 90 B1 **7**
Redwell La *HAR/WTLS* NE34 .... 90 C1
Redwing Cl *WASHS* NE38 .... 137 E3
Redwood Cl *BDN/LAN/SAC* DH7 ..... 203 D4
Redwood Cl *HLH* DH5 .... 35 E6 **10**
  GATE/KIL NE12 .... 35 E5
Reed Av *LGB/KIL* NE12 .... 35 E5
Reedham Ct *WD/WHPE/BLK* NE5 .. 61 D2 **8**
Reedling Ct *SWCK/CAS* SR5 .... 106 B6 **1**
Reedside *RYTON* NE40 .... 74 C3
Reedsmouth Pl
  WD/WHPE/BLK NE5 .... 61 D6
Reed St *SSH* NE33 .... 71 D6
  TYNE/NSHE NE30 .... 55 D6
Reedswood Crs *CRAM* NE23 .... 22 C3
Reestones Pl *GOS/KPK* NE3 .... 61 F1
Reeth Rd *SWCK/CAS* SR5 .... 124 C2
Reeth Sq *SWCK/CAS* SR5 .... 124 C2
Reeth Wy *BW/LEM/TK/HW* NE15 ..... 57 E5
Regal Rd *MLFD/PNYW* SR4 .... 125 F5
Regency Ct *SEA/MUR* SR7 .... 176 C3
Regency Dr *SUNDSW* SR3 .... 144 A6
  WICK/BNPF NE16 .... 95 E4
Regency Gdns *NSHW* NE29 .... 54 A6
Regent Av *GOS/KPK* NE3 .... 63 D1
Regent Dr *WICK/BNPF* NE16 .... 95 E6
Regent Farm Rd *GOS/KPK* NE3........... 46 C6
Regent Rd *ASHBK/HED/RY* SR2 .... 162 C5
  GOS/KPK NE3 .... 63 E1
  JRW NE32 .... 86 B2
  WLSD/HOW NE28 .... 66 C3 **5**
Regents Ct *WLSD/HOW* NE28 .... 66 A2
Regents Dr *TYNE/NSHE* NE30 .... 55 E4
Regents Pk *WLSD/HOW* NE28 .... 66 A3
Regent St *BLYTH* NE24 .... 11 D4
  HLH DH5 .... 171 F5
Regent Ter *ASHBK/HED/RY* SR2 ..... 14 C5 **4**
  NSHW NE29 .... 54 A5
Reginald St *BOLCOL* NE35 .... 105 C2
  GATE NE8.. 100 A1
  MLFD/PNYW SR4 .... 125 E5 **11**
Regina Sq *SWCK/CAS* SR5 .... 124 C1 **3**
Reid Av *WLSD/HOW* NE28 .... 67 D3
Reid Park Cl *JES* NE2 .... 64 B4 **4**
Reid Park Rd *JES* NE2 .... 64 B4
Reid's La *CRAM* NE23 .... 36 A1
Reigate Sq *CRAM* NE23 .... 22 A1
Rekendyke La *SSH* NE33 .... 71 D5
Reiley Ct *BDN/LAN/SAC* DH7 .... 192 A5 **1**
Relly Pth *DHAM* DH1 .... 193 F6
Relton Av *BYK/HTN/WLK* NE6 .... 82 C4
Relton Cl *HLS* DH4 .... 169 F3
Relton Ter *CLS/BIR/GTL* DH3 .... 153 E6
  MONK NE25 .... 40 A5
Rembrandt Av *HAR/WTLS* NE34 .... 88 B6
Remus Cl *DIN/WO* NE13 .... 33 D5 **8**
Rendel St *DUN/TMV* NE11 .... 97 F3
Rendle Rd *BYK/HTN/WLK* NE6........... 84 A4
Renforth St *DUN/TMV* NE11 .... 97 E2
Renfrew Cl *NSHW* NE29 .... 53 E4
Renfrew Rd *SWCK/CAS* SR5 .... 124 C1
Rennie Rd *SWCK/CAS* SR5 .... 124 A1
Rennie Sq *SWCK/CAS* SR5 .... 124 A1 **1**
Rennington *FELL* NE10 .... 101 E5
Rennington Av *TYNE/NSHE* NE30.... 55 E3
Rennington Pl
  WD/WHPE/BLK NE5 .... 61 F5 **5**
Renny's La *DHAM* DH1 .... 195 F4
Renny St *DHAM* DH1 .... 195 D4 **4**
Renoir Gdns *HAR/WTLS* NE34 .... 88 C6
Renwick Av *GOS/KPK* NE3 .... 46 A6
Renwick Rd *BLYTH* NE24 .... 10 C5
Renwick St *BYK/HTN/WLK* NE6.......... 82 C2
Resida Cl *BW/LEM/TK/HW* NE15 ...... 59 E6 **5**
Retford Rd *SWCK/CAS* SR5 .... 124 C1
Retford Sq *SWCK/CAS* SR5 .... 124 C1
The Retreat
  ASHBK/HED/RY SR2 .... 126 A6 **9**
Revell Ter *WD/WHPE/BLK* NE5 ...... 62 A5 **3**
Revelstoke Rd *SWCK/CAS* SR5........... 124 A1
Revesby St *SSH* NE33 .... 88 B2 **5**
Reynolds Av *HAR/WTLS* NE34 .... 88 C5
  LGB/KIL NE12 .... 49 D2
  WASHS NE38 .... 139 D2
Reynolds Cl *STLY/ANP* DH9 .... 148 B2

Rheims Ct *MLFD/PNYW* SR4 .... 124 C5
Rheydt Av *WLSD/HOW* NE28 .... 66 B4
Rhodesia Rd *SWCK/CAS* SR5 .... 124 C1
Rhodes St *BYK/HTN/WLK* NE6........... 83 F3
Rhondda Rd *SWCK/CAS* SR5 .... 124 A1
Rhuddlan Ct *WD/WHPE/BLK* NE5 .. 61 D2 **8**
Rhyl Sq *SWCK/CAS* SR5 .... 125 D1
Ribbledale Gdns *LGB/HTN* NE7 ..... 65 D3 **2**
Ribble Rd *SWCK/CAS* SR5 .... 124 B2 **3**
Ribblesdale *HLS* DH4 .... 157 F3
  WLSD/HOW NE28 .... 66 B2 **1**
Ribblesdale Av *BLYTH* NE24 .... 9 F4 **4**
Richard Av *MLFD/PNYW* SR4 .... 143 F2
Richard Browell Rd
  BW/LEM/TK/HW NE15 .... 57 F5
Richardson Av *HAR/WTLS* NE34 .... 87 E4 **1**
Richardson Rd *JES* NE2 .... 80 A1
Richardson St
  BYK/HTN/WLK NE6 .... 65 E6 **4**
  WLSD/HOW NE28 .... 67 F4
Richardson Ter
  ASHBK/HED/RY SR2 .... 162 C2
  HLH DH5 .... 185 F1
Richard St *BLYTH* NE24 .... 11 D5
Richmond Av *ASHBK/HED/RY* SR2 .... 161 E1
Richmond Av *FELL* NE10 .... 102 B1
  WASHS NE38 .... 120 C6
  WICK/BNPF NE16 .... 96 A1
Richmond Cl *BDLGTN* NE22 .... 7 D2
Richmond Ct *GATE* NE8 .... 99 E1 **10**
Richmond Gdns *WLSD/HOW* NE28 ... 68 A3
Richmond Gv *NSHW* NE29 .... 70 A1
Richmond Ms *GOS/KPK* NE3 .... 63 D5 **1**
Richmond Pk *WLSD/HOW* NE28 ..... 66 B3 **5**
Richmond Rd *DHAM* DH1................... 180 C5
  HAR/WTLS NE34 .... 88 B2
Richmond St *SWCK/CAS* SR5 .... 126 B4
Richmond Ter *WBAY* NE26 .... 40 B3
Richmond Wy *CRAM* NE23 .... 21 F5 **5**
Rickgarth *FELL* NE10 .... 101 E5
Rickleton Av *CLS/BIR/GTL* DH3 .... 153 F3
Rickleton Wy *WASHS* NE38 .... 137 E5
Riddell Av *BW/LEM/TK/HW* NE15.... 78 B3
Riddings Rd *SWCK/CAS* SR5 .... 124 C1
Riddings Sq *SWCK/CAS* SR5 .... 124 C1 **4**
Ridgely Dr *PONT* DH NE20................... 28 C4
Ridge Ter *BDLGTN* NE22 .... 7 D3
The Ridge *RYTON* NE40 .... 74 B4
Ridgeway *ASHBK/HED/RY* SR2 .... 161 E2
  ELS/FEN NE4 .... 62 A6
  FELL NE10 .... 102 A4
Ridge Wy *MONK* NE25 .... 38 A1
Ridgeway Crs *SUNDSW* SR3.............. 144 A3
The Ridge *GOS/KPK* NE3 .... 62 B2
The Ridgeway *HAR/WTLS* NE34 .... 89 E5
Ridgewood Crs *GOS/KPK* NE3 .... 64 B1
Ridgewood Gdns *GOS/KPK* NE3 .... 64 A1 **6**
Ridgewood Vls *GOS/KPK* NE3 .... 64 A1 **7**
Riding Hill Rd *STLY/ANP* DH9 .... 146 B3
Riding La *DUN/TMV* NE11 .... 134 A2
Riding Lea *BLAY* NE21.......................... 93 F1
The Ridings *MONK* NE25 .... 39 E4
The Riding *GOS/KPK* NE3 .... 62 A3
Ridley Av *ASHBK/HED/RY* SR2......... 162 B1
  BLYTH NE24 .... 11 E5
  WLSD/HOW NE28 .... 68 C2
Ridley Cl *GOS/KPK* NE3 .... 46 B4
Ridley Gdns *WICK/BNPF* NE16 .... 95 F1 **2**
Ridley Gv *HAR/WTLS* NE34 .... 89 F1
Ridley Pl *CNUT* NE1................................ 2 D1
Ridley St *BLYTH* NE24 .... 11 E4 **7**
  GATE NE8 .... 98 C2 **6**
  STLY/ANP DH9 .... 148 B1
  SWCK/CAS SR5 .... 126 A2 **10**
Ridley Ter *ASHBK/HED/RY* SR2 .... 5 G6
Ridsdale Av *WD/WHPE/BLK* NE5 ...... 59 F5
Ridsdale Cl *MONK* NE25 .... 24 B5
  WLSD/HOW NE28 .... 67 E2
Ridsdale Ct *GATE* NE8 .... 98 C1 **7**
Rievaulx *WASHS* NE38 .... 138 B3
Riga Sq *SWCK/CAS* SR5 .... 124 B1
The Riggs *HLH* DH5 .... 171 E2
Rignall *WASHS* NE38 .... 139 F1
Riley St *JRW* NE32 .... 85 F1
Ringmore Ct
  ASHBK/HED/RY SR2 .... 144 B4 **8**
Ringway *SWCK/CAS* SR5 .... 123 F4
Ringwood Dr *CRAM* NE23 .... 22 A1 **1**
Ringwood Gn *LGB/KIL* NE12 .... 49 E5 **3**
Ringwood Rd *SWCK/CAS* SR5 .... 124 C1
Ringwood Sq *SWCK/CAS* SR5 .... 124 C1 **5**
Rink St *BLYTH* NE24 .... 11 E4
Ripley Av *NSHW* NE29 .... 70 A2
Ripley Cl *BDLGTN* NE22........................ 6 C2
Ripley Dr *CRAM* NE23 .... 21 E5
Ripley Ter *BYK/HTN/WLK* NE6 .... 83 D2
Ripon Cl *CRAM* NE23 .... 21 E5
Ripon Gdns *JES* NE2 .... 4 C3
  WLSD/HOW NE28 .... 68 A3
Ripon Rd *DHAM* DH1 .... 180 C4 **3**
Ripon St *CLDN/WHIT/ROK* SR6 .... 127 D3
  GATE NE8 .... 99 D1
Ripon Ter *SEA/MUR* SR7 .... 188 B1
The Rise *BLAY* NE21 .... 75 F4

GOS/KPK NE3	62 A2
WBAY NE26	26 C3
Rishton Sq SWCK/CAS SR5	124 B1 9
Ritson Cl NSHW NE29	54 A5
Ritson St CLDN/WHIT/ROK SR6	109 D6
STLY/ANP DH9	148 A2 11
Riverbank Rd SWCK/CAS SR5	124 C2
Riverdale SWCK/CAS SR5	124 A4
River Dr SSH NE33	74 B2
River La RYTON NE40	71 E2
Rivermead Wy WASHS NE38	139 D5 9
Riverside Wy	
BW/LEM/TK/HW NE15	76 A2
Riverside PONT/DH NE20	28 A4
Riverside Ct DUN/TMV NE11	97 F1 4
SSH NE33	71 D4 3
Riverside Pk MLFD/PNYW SR4	124 A5
Riverside Rd SWCK/CAS SR5	125 D2
Riverside Wy BLAY NE21	77 F5
ROWG	110 C4
WICK/BNPF NE16	77 F5
River Vw BLAY NE21	76 A6
TYNE/NSHE NE30	55 E6
River View Cl BDLGTN NE22	8 C3
Roachburn Rd WD/WHPE/BLK NE5	60 A4
Robert Owen Gdns FELL NE10	100 B3
Robertson Rd SWCK/CAS SR5	124 A1
Robertson Sq SWCK/CAS SR5	124 A2 2
Robert Sq SEA/MUR SR7	177 D4
Roberts St BW/LEM/TK/HW NE15	77 F4
Roberts Ter JRW NE32	86 A3
Robert St MLFD/PNYW SR4	177 D4 1
SEA/MUR SR7	177 D4 1
SSH NE33	71 F5
SUNDSW SR3	161 D1
Robert Ter STLY/ANP DH9	131 E6 5
Robert Westall Wy NSHW NE29	70 C3
Robin Ct HLH DH5	184 B1
Robin Gv SWCK/CAS SR5	124 B3 6
Robin La HLH DH5	184 A2
Robinson Gdns	
CLDN/WHIT/ROK SR6	109 E1 3
WLSD/HOW NE28	68 C1
Robinson St BYK/HTN/WLK NE6	82 B2 7
SSH NE33	71 F5 9
Robinson Ter ASHBK/HED/RY SR2	145 E2
SUNDSW SR3	161 D1
Robsheugh Pl WD/WHPE/BLK NE5	61 D6
Robson Av PLEE/EAS SR8	208 C1
Robson Pl ASHBK/HED/RY SR2	162 C2
Robson St BYK/HTN/WLK NE6	81 F2
LWF/SPW/WRK NE9	99 E5
Rochdale Rd SWCK/CAS SR5	124 C1
Rochdale St HLH DH5	185 F2
WLSD/HOW NE28	66 C5 9
Roche Ct WASHS NE38	138 B2
Rochester Gdns DUN/TMV NE11	97 F2
Rochester Rd DHAM DH1	180 C5
Rochester St BYK/HTN/WLK NE6	83 F3
Rochford Gv CRAM NE23	21 E6
Rochford Rd SWCK/CAS SR5	124 B1 8
Rockcliffe SSH NE33	72 B5
Rockcliffe Gdns	
BW/LEM/TK/HW NE15	77 E1 7
Rockcliffe St WBAY NE26	41 E5
Rockcliffe Wy	
LWF/SPW/WRK NE9	118 B2
Rocket Wy LGB/KIL NE12	50 B4
Rock Gv LWF/SPW/WRK NE9	99 E5 3
Rockhope WASHS NE38	137 E6
Rockingham Rd SWCK/CAS SR5	124 B1
Rockingham Sq SWCK/CAS SR5	124 B1 7
Rock Lodge Rd	
CLDN/WHIT/ROK SR6	127 D1
Rockmore Rd BLAY NE21	94 B1
Rock Ter JES NE2	3 G1
Rockville CLDN/WHIT/ROK SR6	109 D6 6
Rodin Av HAR/WTLS NE34	88 D5
Rodney Cl ASHBK/HED/RY SR2	161 E2 1
TYNE/NSHE NE30	55 F5
Rodney St BYK/HTN/WLK NE6	82 A3
Rodney Wy WBAY NE26	39 F3
Rodsley Av GATE NE8	99 D2
Roeburn Wy GOS/KPK NE3	62 B3
Roedean Rd SWCK/CAS SR5	125 D1
Roehedge FELL NE10	102 A4 4
Rogers Cl PLEE/EAS SR8	209 F2 2
Rogerson Ter WD/WHPE/BLK NE5	60 A3
Roger St BYK/HTN/WLK NE6	82 A2
Rokeby Av BW/LEM/TK/HW NE15	76 C2
Rokeby Dr GOS/KPK NE3	62 B2
Rokeby Sq DHAM DH1	204 C1 14
Rokeby St BW/LEM/TK/HW NE15	76 C2
MLFD/PNYW SR4	124 A6
Rokeby Ter BYK/HTN/WLK NE6	65 E5 3
Rokeby Vw LWF/SPW/WRK NE9	117 F3
Roker Av CLDN/WHIT/ROK SR6	126 C4
MONK NE25	54 A1
Roker Baths Rd	
CLDN/WHIT/ROK SR6	127 D2
Rokerby Av WICK/BNPF NE16	96 B4
Roker Park Rd	
CLDN/WHIT/ROK SR6	127 D2

Roker Park Ter	
CLDN/WHIT/ROK SR6	127 E2
Roker Ter CLDN/WHIT/ROK SR6	127 E1
Roland Rd WLSD/HOW NE28	68 A4
Rollesby Ct WD/WHPE/BLK NE5	61 D2 10
Rolling Mill Rd JRW NE32	68 C6
Romaldskirk Cl	
MLFD/PNYW SR4	142 A1 3
Roman Av BYK/HTN/WLK NE6	83 D1
CLS/BIR/GTL DH3	153 F5
Roman Rd SSH NE33	71 F2
Roman Rd North SSH NE33	71 E2 4
The Roman Wy	
WD/WHPE/BLK NE5	59 F5
Romford Cl CRAM NE23	21 F5 6
Romford Pl LWF/SPW/WRK NE9	99 F3
Romford St MLFD/PNYW SR4	125 E6 6
Romilly St SSH NE33	71 F4
Romley Gv FELL NE10	102 C3 2
Romney Av ASHBK/HED/RY SR2	145 D3 1
HAR/WTLS NE34	88 C5 1
WASHS NE38	139 D2
Romney Cl HLS DH4	157 E3
Romney Dr DHAM DH1	196 C1
Romney Gdns	
LWF/SPW/WRK NE9	100 A3
Romsey Cl CRAM NE23	22 A1
Romsey Dr BOLCOL NE35	105 D1 4
Romsey Gv BW/LEM/TK/HW NE15	59 E6
Ronald Dr BW/LEM/TK/HW NE15	77 F2
Ronald Gdns HEBB NE31	84 C4
Ronaldsay Cl	
ASHBK/HED/RY SR2	145 D6 1
Ronald Sq	
CLDN/WHIT/ROK SR6	126 C1 15
Rookery Cl BLYTH NE24	10 A5
Rookery La WICK/BNPF NE16	95 D6 2
Rookswood Gdns ROWG NE39	111 D1
Rookwood Dr DIN/WO NE13	33 E2
Rookwood Rd WD/WHPE/BLK NE5	60 C6
Roosevelt Rd DHAM DH1	195 E3
Ropery La CLS/BIR/GTL DH3	153 F6
CLS/BIR/GTL DH3	154 C6
HEBB NE31	84 C2 3
WLSD/HOW NE28	68 A4
Ropery Rd GATE NE8	98 A1
MLFD/PNYW SR4	125 F4
The Ropery BYK/HTN/WLK NE6	82 C4
Ropery Wk SEA/MUR SR7	177 D4 2
Rosalie Ter ASHBK/HED/RY SR2	145 D2
Rosalind Av BDLGTN NE22	7 F4
Rosamond Pl BLYTH NE24	11 E5 7
Rosa St SSH NE33	71 F4
Rose Av HLS DH4	169 E1
STLY/ANP DH9	147 F3
WICK/BNPF NE16	96 A3
Rosebank Cl	
ASHBK/HED/RY SR2	145 D6 2
Rosebay Rd BDN/LAN/SAC DH7	204 A4
Roseberry Gra LGB/KIL NE12	50 C3 1
Roseberry St STLY/ANP DH9	149 F1
Roseberry Vls CLSW/PEL DH2	151 E3
Rosebery Av BLYTH NE24	10 C5 2
GATE NE8	99 F2 12
NSHW NE29	54 B4
SSH NE33	72 A5
Rosebery Crs JES NE2	64 C6
Rosebery Pl JES NE2	64 C6
Rosebery St SWCK/CAS SR5	126 C3 7
Roseby Rd PLEE/EAS SR8	209 E1
Rose Ct PLEE/EAS SR8	209 F2 3
Rose Crs BDN/LAN/SAC DH7	178 C1 4
CLDN/WHIT/ROK SR6	91 E6
Rosedale BDLGTN NE22	7 D3
WLSD/HOW NE28	66 B2
Rosedale Av CLDN/WHIT/ROK SR6	109 D4
Rosedale Ct WD/WHPE/BLK NE5	59 F5
Rosedale Crs HLS DH4	157 E6 3
Rosedale Rd DHAM DH1	196 C2
Rosedale St HLH DH5	185 D3
SUND SR1	126 A6
Rosedale Ter	
CLDN/WHIT/ROK SR6	109 D6
JES NE2	81 E1
PLEE/EAS SR8	209 E1
TYNE/NSHE NE30	55 D6 7
Roseden Ct LGB/KIL NE12	49 E5 4
Rosedene Vls CRAM NE23	22 C2
Rose Gdns WLSD/HOW NE28	67 D2
Rosegill WLSD/HOW NE28	67 D1
Rosehill WLSD/HOW NE28	68 A4
Rosehill Rd WLSD/HOW NE28	68 B4
Rose Hill Wy WD/WHPE/BLK NE5	61 E5
Rose Lea BDN/LAN/SAC DH7	178 A3
Roselea Av ASHBK/HED/RY SR2	162 B1
Rosemary La PLEE/EAS SR8	200 A2
Rosemary Rd SWCK/CAS SR5	124 C1
Rosemary Ter BLYTH NE24	11 E6
Rosemount DHAM DH1	180 C4
MLFD/PNYW SR4	141 F1
WD/WHPE/BLK NE5	60 B4
Rosemount Cl WASHN NE37	120 B2 8
Rosemount Ct BOL NE36	106 A3 3
Rosemount Wy LGB/HTN NE7	65 E1 6
MONK NE25	39 E5

Rose St GATE NE8	80 B6
HEBB NE31	84 C3
MLFD/PNYW SR4	126 A5
Rose St West HLS DH4	140 A6
Rose Ter WD/WHPE/BLK NE5	62 A5
Roseville St MLFD/PNYW SR4	144 A1 11
Rosewell Pl WICK/BNPF NE16	95 F6
Rosewood Av LGB/KIL NE12	50 B1 10
Rosewood Av GOS/KPK NE3	45 D6
Rosewood Crs BYK/HTN/WLK NE6	66 B5
WBAY NE26	26 C4
Rosewood Gdns GOS/KPK NE3	62 B2
LWF/SPW/WRK NE9	100 B4
Rosewood Sq MLFD/PNYW SR4	141 F4 1
Rosewood Ter WLSD/HOW NE28	68 C4 2
Roseworth Av GOS/KPK NE3	63 E2 3
Roseworth Crs GOS/KPK NE3	63 E3
Roslin Pk BDLGTN NE22	8 B3
Roslin Wy CRAM NE23	21 F5 7
Ross CLSW/PEL DH2	135 F4
Ross Av DUN/TMV NE11	97 E1
Rosse Cl WASHN NE37	120 A4
Rossendale Pl LGB/KIL NE12	48 B5 5
Ross Gv CRAM NE23	21 E1
Ross Lea HLS DH4	156 C4
Rosslyn Av ASHBK/HED/RY SR2	162 B3
GOS/KPK NE3	62 A1
Rosslyn St MLFD/PNYW SR4	125 F6
Ross St SWCK/CAS SR5	126 E3 7
Ross Wy GOS/KPK NE3	46 B3
WBAY NE26	40 A3
Rosyth Rd SWCK/CAS SR5	125 D1
Rosyth Sq SWCK/CAS SR5	125 D1
Rotary Wy BLYTH NE24	17 E2
NSHW NE29	70 A3
Rothay Pl WD/WHPE/BLK NE5	61 E4 2
Rothbury ASHBK/HED/RY SR2	161 F2
Rothbury Av BLYTH NE24	10 A6
FELL NE10	101 F1
GOS/KPK NE3	47 D6
JRW NE32	85 E2
PLEE/EAS SR8	201 E6
Rothbury Cl CLSW/PEL DH2	165 F1
LGB/KIL NE12	35 E6 11
Rothbury Gdns DUN/TMV NE11	97 F5
WLSD/HOW NE28	68 B3
Rothbury Rd DHAM DH1	180 B5
SWCK/CAS SR5	124 C1
Rothbury Ter BYK/HTN/WLK NE6	65 D6
NSHW NE29	69 E2
Rotherfield Cl CRAM NE23	22 A1
Rotherfield Gdns	
LWF/SPW/WRK NE9	117 F2 1
Rotherfield Rd SWCK/CAS SR5	124 B1
Rotherfield Sq SWCK/CAS SR5	124 B1 5
Rotherham Cl HLH DH5	170 C4 2
Rotherham Rd SWCK/CAS SR5	124 B1
Rothley WASHS NE38	139 E4
Rothley Av WD/WHPE/BLK NE5	78 B1
Rothley Cl GOS/KPK NE3	63 F1 5
Rothley Ct SWCK/CAS SR5	107 E6 2
Rothley Gdns TYNE/NSHE NE30	54 C2
Rothley Gv MONK NE25	24 B5 2
Rothley Wy WBAY NE26	40 A3
Rothsay CLSW/PEL DH2	135 E5
Rothwell Rd GOS/KPK NE3	63 E1
SWCK/CAS SR5	124 B1
Roundhill Av WD/WHPE/BLK NE5	61 E4 2
The Roundway LGB/KIL NE12	49 D5 3
Rowan Av WASHS NE38	138 B5
Rowanberry Rd LGB/KIL NE12	49 D6
Rowan Cl BDLGTN NE22	7 E2
MLFD/PNYW SR4	142 A1
Rowan Ct BLYTH NE24	10 C6 5
Rowan Dr DHAM DH1	181 D4
GOS/KPK NE3	46 A6
HLH DH5	171 E6
PONT/DH NE20	28 A3
Rowan Lea BDN/LAN/SAC DH7	203 D4
Rowan Tree Av DHAM DH1	195 F2
Rowantree Rd BYK/HTN/WLK NE6	66 C5
Rowanwood Gdns DUN/TMV NE11	77 F5
Rowell Cl SUNDSW SR3	161 E2
Rowes Ms BYK/HTN/WLK NE6	82 B4 4
Rowland Sq SEA/MUR SR7	188 A1
Rowley Cl BDN/LAN/SAC DH7	202 A1
Rowley Dr BDN/LAN/SAC DH7	192 A5
Rowley St BLYTH NE24	11 E5
Rowntree Wy NSHW NE29	70 C3
Rowsley Rd JRW NE32	86 B3 5
Roxburgh Cl BLAY NE21	93 F2
Roxburgh Pl BYK/HTN/WLK NE6	82 A1 3
Roxburgh St CLDN/WHIT/ROK SR6	126 C2
Roxburgh Ter WBAY NE26	40 C5
Roxby Gdns NSHW NE29	70 A1
Royal Crs ELS/FEN NE4	62 A6
Royal Rd STLY/ANP DH9	148 A1
The Royalty	
ASHBK/HED/RY SR2	126 A6 10
Roydon Av ASHBK/HED/RY SR2	145 D3 2
Royle St ASHBK/HED/RY SR2	145 E4
Royston Ter BYK/HTN/WLK NE6	83 F4 2
Ruabon Cl CRAM NE23	21 F5
Rubens Av HAR/WTLS NE34	88 C5

Ruby St HLS DH4 .... 157 F6
Rudby Cl GOS/KPK NE3 .... 47 F4
Rudchester Pl WD/WHPE/BLK NE5 .. 61 E6
Rudyard Av
  ASHBK/HED/RY SR2 .... 145 D3 [3]
Rudyerd St NSHW NE29 .... 70 C1 [10]
Rugby Gdns LWF/SPW/WRK NE8 .. 118 C1
Ruislip Pl CRAM NE23 .... 21 E5
Ruislip Rd MLFD/PNYW SR4.... 141 F1
Runcorn ASHBK/HED/RY SR2 .. 161 E1
Runcorn Rd SWCK/CAS SR5 .... 124 B1
Runhead Est RYTON NE40 .... 74 C3
Runnymede
  ASHBK/HED/RY SR2 .... 161 F1 [1]
Runnymede Rd SWCK/CAS SR5.. 124 C1
  WICK/BNPF NE16 .... 95 F4
Runnymede Wy GOS/KPK NE3 .. 62 A2 [2]
  SWCK/CAS SR5 .... 124 C1
Runswick Av LGB/KIL NE12 ...... 48 B6
Runswick Cl SUNDSW SR3 ...... 161 E1
Rupert Sq SWCK/CAS SR5........ 125 D1
Rupert St CLDN/WHIT/ROK SR6 .. 109 E1
Rushall Pl LGB/KIL NE12 .... 49 D6
Rushey Gill BDN/LAN/SAC DH7 .. 202 C4 [3]
Rushford ASHBK/HED/RY SR2.... 161 F1
Rushie Av BW/LEM/TK/HW NE6 .. 78 B3
Rushley Crs BLAY NE21 .... 76 B5
Rushsyde Cl WICK/BNPF NE16 .... 95 D5
Rushton Av
  ASHBK/HED/RY SR2 .... 145 D3 [4]
Rushyrig WASHN NE37 .... 119 F6
Ruskin Av CLSW/PEL DH2 ...... 152 A5
  DUN/TMV NE11 .... 97 E4
  HLH DH5 .... 186 B4
  LGB/KIL NE12 .... 49 E5 [1]
Ruskin Cl WLSD/HOW DH9........ 149 D2
Ruskin Crs HAR/WTLS NE34 ...... 88 A5
Ruskin Dr BOLCOL NE35 .... 105 F2
  LGB/HTN NE7 .... 66 A4
Ruskin Rd CLS/BIR/GTL DH3 .. 136 D2 [5]
  LWF/SPW/WRK NE8 .... 100 A3
  WICK/BNPF NE16 .... 95 F2
Russell Av HAR/WTLS NE34 ...... 89 F2
Russell Sq DIN/WO NE13 .... 33 E2
Russell St JRW NE32 .... 86 B1
  NSHW NE29........ 70 C1
  SSH NE33 .... 71 E5 [6]
  SUND SR1 .... 5 E1
Russell Ter BDLGTN NE22........ 7 E4
  JES NE2 .... 3 G2 [3]
Ruswarp Dr SUNDSW SR3 ...... 161 D2
Rutherford Av SEA/MUR SR7 .... 175 E2
Rutherford Rd SWCK/CAS SR5 .. 124 A1
  WASHN NE37 .... 121 D3
Rutherford Sq SWCK/CAS SR5.... 124 A1
Rutherford St BLYTH NE24 ...... 11 D6 [5]
  CNUT NE1 .... 2 B4 [2]
  WLSD/HOW NE28 .... 69 D3
Rutherglen Rd SWCK/CAS SR5 .. 125 D1
  SUNDSW SR3........ 160 B1
Rutland Av BYK/HTN/WLK NE6 .. 83 F1
  SUNDSW SR3........ 160 B1
Rutland Pl NSHW NE29 .... 54 A6 [1]
  WASHN NE37 .... 120 C2 [2]
Rutland Rd HEBB NE31 .... 85 E5
  WLSD/HOW NE28 .... 66 C5
Rutland Sq CLS/BIR/GTL DH3 .. 136 A1
Rutland St HAR/WTLS NE34 ...... 88 A2 [2]
  MLFD/PNYW SR4 .... 125 E5
Ryal Cl BLYTH NE24 .... 10 A5
  MONK NE25........ 24 C5
Ryal Ter BYK/HTN/WLK NE6........ 83 E3
Rydal FELL NE10 .... 101 F2 [2]
Rydal Av HLH DH5........ 186 B4
  STLY/ANP DH9 .... 147 F4
  TYNE/NSHE NE30 .... 54 C2
Rydal Cl BDN/LAN/SAC DH7 .... 178 A1
  BOL NE36........ 106 B2
  LGB/KIL NE12 .... 50 B1
Rydal Crs BLAY NE21........ 94 A2
  PLEE/EAS SR8 .... 209 D2
Rydal Gdns HAR/WTLS NE34 .... 89 D2
Rydal Mt PLEE/EAS SR8 .... 200 C2
  SWCK/CAS SR5........ 123 F4
  SWCK/CAS SR5........ 126 B1
Rydal Rd BW/LEM/TK/HW NE6 .. 59 F6
  CLSW/PEL DH2 .... 166 A1
  GOS/KPK NE3........ 63 F1
Rydal St GATE NE8........ 99 D1
Ryde Pl CRAM NE23........ 22 A1
Rye Cl BW/LEM/TK/HW NE6 .. 58 A5 [3]
Ryedale CLDN/WHIT/ROK SR6.... 109 E3
  DHAM DH1 .... 196 C3
  WLSD/HOW NE28........ 66 B1
Rye Hi ELS/FEN NE4........ 80 A4
Ryehill Vw HLH DH5 .... 170 B6
Ryelands Wy DHAM DH1 .... 180 B4
Ryemount Rd ASHBK/HED/RY SR2.. 161 F1
Rye View Rd ASHBK/HED/RY SR2.. 145 E6
Ryhope Gdns LWF/SPW/WRK NE9 .. 118 C1
Ryhope Rd ASHBK/HED/RY SR2 .. 145 E5
Ryhope St ASHBK/HED/RY SR2 .. 162 A1
  HLH DH5........ 171 E2
Rymers Cl PLEE/EAS SR8 .... 199 F3
Ryton Ct SSH NE33........ 71 F5
Ryton Crs SEA/MUR SR7 .... 175 F3

STLY/ANP DH9 .... 131 E6 [6]
Ryton Hall Dr RYTON NE40 .... 74 B2 [5]
Ryton Ter BYK/HTN/WLK NE6 ...... 83 E4

S

Sackville Rd BYK/HTN/WLK NE6 ...... 65 E5
  SUNDSW SR3........ 143 D3
Sacriston Av SUNDSW SR3 .. 143 E3 [3]
Saddleback WASHN NE37 .... 120 A4
Saddler St DHAM DH1 .... 194 B4
Saffron Pl BYK/HTN/WLK NE6 .. 83 F3 [5]
Sage Cl BW/LEM/TK/HW NE15 .. 59 E6 [7]
St Aidan's Av ASHBK/HED/RY SR2 .. 145 E5
  DHAM DH1 .... 193 F1
  LGB/KIL NE12 .... 51 E3
St Aidan's Cl NSHW NE29 ...... 53 F4 [1]
St Aidan's Crs DHAM DH1 ...... 193 F4
  STLY/ANP DH9 .... 146 B5
St Aidan's Rd SSH NE33........ 71 F2
  WLSD/HOW NE28 .... 66 C5 [5]
St Aidan's St GATE NE8 .... 98 C1 [6]
St Aidan's Ter HLS DH4........ 158 A2
St Alban's Cl CLS/BIR/GTL DH3 .. 168 A3
St Alban's Crs BYK/HTN/WLK NE6 .. 65 F4
St Alban's St ASHBK/HED/RY SR2 .. 145 D3
St Alban's Ter GATE NE8 .... 99 E1 [11]
St Albans Vw SMOOR NE27 ...... 52 A2
St Aldwyn Rd SEA/MUR SR7 .... 176 A2
St Aloysius Vw HEBB NE31 ...... 84 C2
St Andrews HLS DH4........ 170 A2
St Andrews Av WASHN NE37 .... 120 A4
St Andrew's Dr
  LWF/SPW/WRK NE9 .... 117 D1
St Andrew's Rd STLY/ANP DH9 .. 131 E5
St Andrew's Cl CNUT NE1 .... 2 B3
  HEBB NE31 .... 84 B1 [5]
St Andrew's Ter
  CLDN/WHIT/ROK SR6 .... 127 D2 [5]
St Ann's Cl CNUT NE1........ 81 F3
St Ann's St CNUT NE1 .... 3 H4
St Anselm Crs NSHW NE29........ 53 E5
St Anselm Rd NSHW NE29........ 53 E5
St Anthony's Rd
  BYK/HTN/WLK NE6 .... 83 D4
St Asaph Cl BYK/HTN/WLK NE7 .. 65 F2
St Aubyn's Wy STLY/ANP DH9 .. 149 D1 [1]
St Austell Cl WD/WHPE/BLK NE5 .. 61 E2 [1]
St Austell Gdns
  LWF/SPW/WRK NE9 .... 117 E2
St Barnabas HLS DH4........ 155 F5
St Barnabas Wy
  ASHBK/HED/RY SR2 .... 5 G6
St Bede's Cl DHAM DH1 .... 193 F5
St Bede's Dr GATE NE8 .... 81 E6 [2]
St Bedes Pl BLYTH NE24 .... 16 A2
St Bedes Rd BLYTH NE24 .... 16 A2 [2]
St Bedes Wy BDN/LAN/SAC DH7 .. 204 A3 [1]
St Brandon's Gv
  BDN/LAN/SAC DH7 .... 202 C4
St Buryan Crs WD/WHPE/BLK NE5.. 61 E2
St Catherine's Ct SWCK/CAS SR5 .. 124 C3
St Chad's Crs SUNDSW SR3 ...... 159 D1 [1]
St Chad's Rd SUNDSW SR3 ...... 159 D1
St Chad's Vis BOL NE36........ 106 C3 [6]
St Christopher's Rd SUNDSW SR3 .. 143 F4
Saint Ct SUNDSW SR3 .... 160 C3
St Cuthbert Av CLS/BIR/GTL DH3 .. 153 F5
St Cuthberts Av DHAM DH1 .... 193 F1
  HAR/WTLS NE34 .... 72 C6
St Cuthberts Cl BLYTH NE24 .... 11 E5 [8]
St Cuthberts Dr
  BDN/LAN/SAC DH7 .... 178 A1
  FELL NE10 .... 101 E3
St Cuthberts Pk WICK/BNPF NE16 .. 113 F4
St Cuthbert's Pl GATE NE8 ...... 98 C1 [9]
St Cuthbert's Rd GATE NE8 ...... 80 C6
  HLS DH4 .... 157 F5 [7]
  PLEE/EAS SR8 .... 208 C3 [1]
  WD/WHPE/BLK NE5........ 78 A1
  WICK/BNPF NE16 .... 113 F5
  WLSD/HOW NE28........ 67 F3
St Cuthbert's Ter
  MLFD/PNYW SR4 .... 126 A5 [18]
St Cuthberts Wk
  BDN/LAN/SAC DH7 .... 204 A3
St Cuthberts Wy BLAY NE21 .... 76 C5
  RDHAMSE DH6 .... 197 E5
St David's Wy WBAY NE26........ 40 B2
St Edmund's Ct GATE NE8 ...... 99 F1 [3]
St Edmund's Dr FELL NE10 ...... 101 E3
St Edmund's Rd GATE NE8 ...... 99 E1 [12]
St Gabriel's Av BYK/HTN/WLK NE6 .. 65 D5
  MLFD/PNYW SR4 .... 125 E6
St George's Av SSH NE33........ 72 A6
St George's Cl JES NE2........ 64 A4
St Georges Crs MONK NE25........ 40 B6
  NSHW NE29........ 70 B1
St George's Est WASHS NE38 .. 138 B6 [11]
St George's Pl
  BW/LEM/TK/HW NE15 .... 77 D3 [1]
St George's Rd
  BW/LEM/TK/HW NE15 .... 77 D3 [2]

TYNE/NSHE NE30 .... 55 D1
St George's Ter BOL NE36 ...... 106 C3
  BW/LEM/TK/HW NE15 .... 77 D3 [3]
  CLDN/WHIT/ROK SR6 .... 127 E2
  JES NE2........ 64 A4
St George's Wy
  ASHBK/HED/RY SR2 .... 4 C5 [1]
St Giles Cl DHAM DH1 .... 195 E4
St Godric's Cl DHAM DH1 ...... 180 B5
St Godric's Dr HLS DH4........ 183 F2
St Helen's Crs
  LWF/SPW/WRK NE9 .... 99 D5 [3]
St Heliers Wy STLY/ANP DH9 .. 149 D1
St Hilda's Av WLSD/HOW NE28 .. 68 A3 [2]
St Hilda St SSH NE33........ 71 E4
St Hilds Ct DHAM DH1 .... 195 F4
St Hild's La DHAM DH1 .... 195 D4 [3]
St Ignatius Cl ASHBK/HED/RY SR2 .. 5 F5 [3]
St Ives Wy WD/WHPE/BLK NE5.... 61 E2
St James Ct GATE NE8 .... 100 A1 [12]
St James' Crs
  BW/LEM/TK/HW NE15 .... 78 C4 [2]
St James' Rd
  BW/LEM/TK/HW NE15........ 78 C3
  GATE NE8 .... 81 F6
St James Sq GATE NE8 .... 81 F6
St James' St CNUT NE1........ 2 B2
  GOS/KPK NE3 .... 63 F1
St James' Ter NSHW NE29 ...... 69 F3
St John's Av HEBB NE31........ 84 C3
St John's Cl WBAY NE26 .... 40 B2 [3]
St John's Crs BDLGTN NE22 ...... 8 C1
St John's Gn NSHW NE29 ...... 69 F3
St John's Pl BDLGTN NE22 ...... 8 C1
  CLS/BIR/GTL DH3 .... 136 B2
  FELL NE10 .... 100 C2
  WBAY NE26........ 40 B2 [4]
St John's Rd BDLGTN NE22 ...... 8 C2
  BDN/LAN/SAC DH7 .... 204 A4
  DHAM DH1 .... 193 F5
  ELS/FEN NE4........ 79 D4
St John's St NSHW NE29 .... 69 F3
St John's Ter BOL NE36........ 107 D3
  JRW NE32 .... 86 A1 [9]
  NSHW NE29........ 69 F3
St John St CNUT NE1 .... 2 C4
St Johns V MLFD/PNYW SR4 .. 141 F2 [3]
St John's Wk NSHW NE29 ...... 69 F3 [3]
St Joseph's Cl DHAM DH1 ...... 195 F4
St Joseph's Ct HEBB NE31 ...... 84 C3 [2]
St Joseph's Wy JRW NE32 ...... 104 A1 [1]
St Jude's Ter SSH NE33........ 71 E5
St Julien Gdns LGB/HTN NE7 .. 65 F3 [5]
  WLSD/HOW NE28 .... 69 D3 [8]
St Lawrence Rd BYK/HTN/WLK NE6.. 82 A4
St Lawrence Sq BYK/HTN/WLK NE6.. 82 A3
St Leonard St ASHBK/HED/RY SR2 .. 145 D2
St Lucia Cl ASHBK/HED/RY SR2 .. 5 E6 [2]
  WBAY NE26........ 40 A2
St Luke's Rd MLFD/PNYW SR4 .. 124 B5 [5]
St Luke's St NSHW NE29 .... 69 F3
St Luke's Ter MLFD/PNYW SR4 .. 125 D1
St Margaret's Av SWCK/CAS SR5 .. 123 F3
St Margaret's Ct DHAM DH1 .. 194 A5 [3]
St Margaret's Dr STLY/ANP DH9 .. 130 B3
St Margaret's Rd
  BW/LEM/TK/HW NE15........ 78 A4
St Margarets Av LGB/KIL NE12 .. 49 F6 [6]
St Mark's Cl BYK/HTN/WLK NE6 .. 82 B1
St Mark's Rd MLFD/PNYW SR4 .. 126 A6
St Mark's Rd North
  MLFD/PNYW SR4 .... 125 F5
St Mark's St MLFD/PNYW SR4 .. 126 A6 [11]
St Mark's Ter MLFD/PNYW SR4 .. 126 A6 [13]
St Martin's Cl WBAY NE26........ 40 A3
St Mary's Av HAR/WTLS NE34 .. 89 C2
  WBAY NE26........ 40 B3
St Marys Cl CLSW/PEL DH2 .... 153 D6
  PLEE/EAS SR8 .... 199 F3 [1]
St Mary's Dr BLYTH NE24 ...... 16 A1
  HLS DH4 .... 183 F2 [2]
  RDHAMSE DH6 .... 197 E5
St Mary's Pl
  BW/LEM/TK/HW NE15 .... 58 A4 [4]
  CNUT NE1 .... 2 D1
St Mary's Rd DHAM DH1 .... 196 B2
St Mary's Ter BOL NE36........ 106 C3
St Mary's Vw SUND SR1........ 4 E2
St Mary's Wynd WBAY NE26 .... 27 D4
St Matthews Vw SUNDSW SR3 .. 160 C1 [4]
St Michaels HLS DH4........ 170 A2
St Michael's Av MONK NE25 .... 25 D2
  SSH NE33........ 71 F5
St Michael's Av North SSH NE33.... 71 F5
St Michael's Rd BYK/HTN/WLK NE6 .. 82 A3
St Michaels Wy SUND SR1 ...... 4 A2
  WICK/BNPF NE16 .... 96 A1
St Monica Gv DHAM DH1 ...... 193 F5
St Nicholas Av GOS/KPK NE3 .. 63 E2 [4]
  SUNDSW SR3........ 144 A3
St Nicholas' Church Yd CNUT NE1 .. 2 D4 [11]
St Nicholas Dr DHAM DH1 ...... 193 E2
St Nicholas Rd BOL NE36........ 105 F3 [8]
St Nicholas' St CNUT NE1........ 2 D4

St Nicholas Ter *PLEE/EAS* SR8 ...... **200** C2 **1**
St Omers Rd *DUN/TMV* NE11 .... **79** E6
St Oswald Av *BYK/HTN/WLK* NE6 ...... **83** D1
St Oswald's Dr *DHAM* DH1 .... **204** C3
St Oswald's Gn *BYK/HTN/WLK* NE6 .. **83** D1
St Oswald's Rd *HEBB* NE31 .... **85** E1
 WLSD/HOW NE28 .... **67** F2
St Oswin's Pl *TYNE/NSHE* NE30....... **55** F5
St Oswin's St *SSH* NE33 .... **88** C1
St Pauls Dr *HLS* DH4 .... **139** D6
St Paul's Gdns *MONK* NE25 .... **40** C6
St Paul's Rd *JRW* NE32 .... **86** D1
St Peter's Av *HAR/WTLS* NE34........ **89** D2
St Peter's Quayside East
 BYK/HTN/WLK NE6 .... **82** C4 **5**
St Peter's Quayside West
 BYK/HTN/WLK NE6 .... **82** B5 **1**
St Peter's Rd *HAR/WTLS* NE34 .... **82** B4
 WLSD/HOW NE28 .... **67** F2
St Peters' Wy
 CLDN/WHIT/ROK SR6 .... **127** D4
St Peter's Whf
 BYK/HTN/WLK NE6 .... **82** B4 **5**
St Philips Cl *ELS/FEN* NE4 .... **80** A3 **16**
St Philips Wy *ELS/FEN* NE4 .... **80** A3 **17**
St Ronan's Dr *WBAY* NE26 .... **26** A1
St Ronan's Rd *MONK* NE25 .... **40** B6
St Ronans Vw
 LWF/SPW/WRK NE9 .... **117** F2
St Simon St *HAR/WTLS* NE34 .... **87** F4
St Stephen's Cl *MONK* NE25 .... **24** A5 **1**
St Stephen's Wy *NSHW* NE29 .... **69** F4
St Stevens Cl *HLS* DH4 .... **139** D6 **4**
St Thomas Cl *PLEE/EAS* SR8 .... **199** F3 **2**
St Thomas' Crs *CNUT* NE1 .... **2** C1
St Thomas' St *CNUT* NE1 .... **2** C1
 LWF/SPW/WRK NE9 .... **99** F5 **4**
 SUND SR1 .... **4** D2
St Vincent Ct *GATE* NE8 .... **99** F1 **4**
St Vincents Cl
 BW/LEM/TK/HW NE15 .... **60** A6 **3**
St Vincent's Pl *WBAY* NE26 .... **40** B2 **3**
St Vincent St *ASHBK/HED/RY* SR2 .... **5** E5
 GATE NE8 .... **99** F1
 SSH NE33 .... **72** A5
St Vincent's Wy *WBAY* NE26 .... **40** B2 **6**
Salcombe Av *JRW* NE32 .... **86** C3
Salcombe Cl *SEA/MUR* SR7 .... **175** F4 **3**
Salcombe Gdns
 LWF/SPW/WRK NE9 .... **117** E2
Salem Hl *ASHBK/HED/RY* SR2 .... **5** E6
Salem Rd *ASHBK/HED/RY* SR2 .... **5** E5
Salem St *ASHBK/HED/RY* SR2 .... **5** E5
 JRW NE32 .... **86** B1
 SSH NE33 .... **71** E3 **7**
Salem St South *ASHBK/HED/RY* SR2 .. **5** E6
Salem Ter *ASHBK/HED/RY* SR2 ...... **5** E5 **1**
Salisbury Av *NSHW* NE29 .... **54** B5
Salisbury Cl *CLS/BIR/GTL* DH3 ...... **167** F4
 CRAM NE23 .... **21** D2
Salisbury Gdns *JES* NE2 .... **64** C6
Salisbury Pl *SSH* NE33 .... **72** A3
Salisbury Rd *DHAM* DH1 .... **181** D5
Salisbury St *ASHBK/HED/RY* SR2 ...... **4** D4
 FELL NE10 .... **101** F1 **3**
 SSH NE33 .... **71** F4 **11**
 STLY/ANP DH9 .... **147** F3
Salkeld Gdns *LWF/SPW/WRK* NE9.... **99** F2
Salkeld Rd *LWF/SPW/WRK* NE9........ **99** F4
Salmon St *SSH* NE33 .... **71** F2
Saltburn Gdns *WLSD/HOW* NE28 .... **69** D3 **3**
Saltburn Rd *SUNDSW* SR3 .... **143** D3
Saltburn Sq *SUNDSW* SR3 .... **143** D3
Salterfen La *ASHBK/HED/RY* SR2 .... **145** F6
Salters Cl *GOS/KPK* NE3 .... **48** A6
Salter's La *HLH* DH5 .... **160** A6
 HLH DH5 .... **187** D1
 LGB/KIL NE12 .... **48** B6
 RDHAMSE DH6 .... **187** D6
 RDHAMSE DH6 .... **206** B5
 SEA/MUR SR7 .... **173** E4
Salters' Rd *GOS/KPK* NE3 .... **62** C2
Saltmeadows Rd *GATE* NE8 .... **82** A5
Saltwell Rd *GATE* NE8 .... **98** C3
Saltwell Rd South
 LWF/SPW/WRK NE9 .... **99** D4
Saltwell St *GATE* NE8 .... **98** C2
Saltwell Vw *LWF/SPW/WRK* NE9 .... **99** D3
Samson Cl *LGB/KIL* NE12 .... **49** D2
Sancroft Dr *HLH* DH5 .... **171** D3
Sandalwood *HAR/WTLS* NE34 .... **88** C5 **2**
Sandalwood Sq *MLFD/PNYW* SR4 .. **141** F4
Sanderling Cl *RYTON* NE40 .... **75** D4 **3**
Sanderson Rd *JES* NE2 .... **64** A4
Sanderson St *ELS/FEN* NE4 .... **79** E5
Sandfield Rd *TYNE/NSHE* NE30....... **55** D1
Sandford Av *CRAM* NE23 .... **32** A5
Sandford Ms *DIN/WO* NE13.............. **32** B5
Sandgate *CNUT* NE1 .... **3** C4
 STLY/ANP DH9 .... **147** D4
Sandgrove
 CLDN/WHIT/ROK SR6 .... **107** F1 **2**
Sandholm Cl *WLSD/HOW* NE28 ...... **68** B1 **2**
Sandhurst Av *TYNE/NSHE* NE30 ...... **55** D2

Sandmere Pl
 BW/LEM/TK/HW NE15 .... **77** F3 **3**
Sandmere Rd
 ASHBK/HED/RY SR2 .... **145** D5 **2**
Sandoe Gdns
 BW/LEM/TK/HW NE15...................... **78** A3
Sandon Cl *SMOOR* NE27 .... **37** E5
Sandown *MONK* NE25 .... **39** E5
Sandown Cl *SMOOR* NE27 .... **37** F1
Sandown Gdns *GATE* NE8 .... **98** B3
 SUNDSW SR3 .... **143** E6 **1**
 WLSD/HOW NE28 .... **68** B2
Sandpiper Cl *BLYTH* NE24 .... **17** D2
 RYTON NE40 .... **74** C4 **2**
Sand Point Rd
 CLDN/WHIT/ROK SR6 .... **127** D3
Sandray Cl *CLS/BIR/GTL* DH3.......... **136** C5
Sandringham Av *LGB/KIL* NE12 ...... **49** E6
Sandringham Dr *BLYTH* NE24 .... **16** C3
 MONK NE25 .... **39** D6
 STLY/ANP DH9 .... **146** B3 **1**
 WICK/BNPF NE16 .... **95** F3 **10**
Sandringham Gdns *NSHW* NE29...... **54** C5
Sandringham Rd
 CLDN/WHIT/ROK SR6 .... **126** C2
 GOS/KPK NE3 .... **64** A2
 WD/WHPE/BLK NE5 .... **60** A6 **7**
Sandringham Ter
 CLDN/WHIT/ROK SR6 .... **127** D2
Sandsay Cl *ASHBK/HED/RY* SR2 .... **144** C6
Sands Rd *WICK/BNPF* NE16 .... **95** F1
Sandstone Cl *HAR/WTLS* NE34 .... **87** E5
Sandwell Dr *HLS* DH4 .... **139** E6
Sandwich Rd *NSHW* NE29 .... **54** B3
Sandwich St *BYK/HTN/WLK* NE6 .... **83** E5 **3**
Sandy Chare *CLDN/WHIT/ROK* SR6.. **109** D2
Sandy Crs *BYK/HTN/WLK* NE6 .... **83** D4
Sandyford *CLSW/PEL* DH2 .... **151** F1
Sandyford Rd *CNUT* NE1 .... **3** E1
 JES NE2 .... **81** D1 **7**
Sandy La *DIN/WO* NE13 .... **31** F4
 GOS/KPK NE3 .... **34** A6
 LWF/SPW/WRK NE9 .... **118** C3
Sandypath La *WICK/BNPF* NE16 .... **111** F5 **1**
Sans St South *SUND* SR1 .... **5** E3 **1**
Sargent Av *HAR/WTLS* NE34 .... **88** C6
Satley Gdns *SUNDSW* SR3 .... **144** A4
Saturn Cl *PLEE/EAS* SR8 .... **200** B2 **3**
Saturn St *SEA/MUR* SR7 .... **175** F3
Saunton Ct *HLS* DH4 .... **157** E5 **3**
Saville St *SSH* NE33 .... **71** F3 **4**
 TYNE/NSHE NE30 .... **71** D1
Saville St West *NSHW* NE29 .... **70** C1 **10**
Savory Rd *WLSD/HOW* NE28 .... **68** B3
Sawmill La *BDN/LAN/SAC* DH7 ...... **202** C4
Saxilby Dr *GOS/KPK* NE3 .... **47** F4
Saxon Cl *CLDN/WHIT/ROK* SR6 .... **107** D1 **4**
Saxon Crs *SUNDSW* SR3 .... **143** E5
Saxondale Rd *GOS/KPK* NE3 .... **62** A1
Saxon Dr *TYNE/NSHE* NE30 .... **55** E3
Saxon Wy *JRW* NE32 .... **69** E6
Saxton Gv *LGB/HTN* NE7 .... **64** C2
Scafell Cl *CLS/BIR/GTL* DH3 .... **136** C4
Scafell Ct *PLEE/EAS* SR8 .... **209** D2
Scafell Dr *WD/WHPE/BLK* NE5 .... **61** F3
Scafell Gdns *DUN/TMV* NE11.......... **97** F4
Scalby Cl *GOS/KPK* NE3 .... **47** F4 **3**
Scarborough Ct
 BYK/HTN/WLK NE6 .... **82** C2 **3**
Scarborough Rd
 BYK/HTN/WLK NE6 .... **82** C2
 SUNDSW SR3.................................. **143** E6
Scardale Wy *DHAM* DH1 .... **197** D2
Sceptre Pl *ELS/FEN* NE4 .... **79** F3 **6**
Sceptre St *ELS/FEN* NE4 .... **79** F3
Schalksmuhle Rd *BDLGTN* NE22 ...... **7** E3
Schiller St *SWCK/CAS* SR5 .... **126** A2 **11**
School Ap *HAR/WTLS* NE34 .... **88** F2
School Av *DUN/TMV* NE11................ **97** E2
School Cl *FELL* NE10 .... **100** C4
Schoolhouse La *WICK/BNPF* NE16 .. **113** D5
School La *STLY/ANP* DH9 .... **147** F3 **9**
 WICK/BNPF NE16 .... **96** A3
School Loaning *HAR/WTLS* NE34 .... **88** A3 **5**
School Rd *BDLGTN* NE22 .... **8** C1
 HLH DH5 .... **170** B6
School St *CLS/BIR/GTL* DH3 .... **136** B2
 HEBB NE31 .... **85** D1
 PLEE/EAS SR8 .... **201** D2
 SEA/MUR SR7 .... **176** C5 **2**
 WICK/BNPF NE16 .... **95** F3
School Ter *STLY/ANP* DH9 .... **147** F3
School Vw *HLH* DH4 .... **186** C4
 HLS DH4 .... **185** E3 **1**
Scorer's La *CLS/BIR/GTL* DH3......... **168** A2
Scorer St *NSHW* NE29 .... **70** B1
Scotland Head *BLAY* NE21 .... **95** F3
Scotland St *ASHBK/HED/RY* SR2 .... **162** C2
Scotswood Rd
 BW/LEM/TK/HW NE15...................... **76** C3
 CNUT NE1 .... **2** A6
 ELS/FEN NE4 .... **78** C5
Scotswood Vw *WICK/BNPF* NE16.... **78** B6
Scott Av *CRAM* NE23........................ **13** E6
Scott Ct *CLS/BIR/GTL* DH3 .... **167** F3

Scott's Ter *HLH* DH5 .... **171** F6
Scott St *CRAM* NE23 .... **14** A3
 STLY/ANP DH9 .... **148** A2
Scripton Gill *BDN/LAN/SAC* DH7 .... **202** C4
Scripton Gill Rd
 BDN/LAN/SAC DH7 .... **202** B5
Scripton La *BDN/LAN/SAC* DH7 .... **202** C6
Scrogg Rd *BYK/HTN/WLK* NE6 .... **83** D1
Scruton Av *SUNDSW* SR3 .... **143** E4
Seaburn Dr *HLS* DH4 .... **170** B2
Seaburn Gdns
 CLDN/WHIT/ROK SR6 .... **109** D6
 LWF/SPW/WRK NE9 .... **118** C1
Seaburn Gv *WBAY* NE26 .... **26** B2
Seaburn Hl
 CLDN/WHIT/ROK SR6 .... **109** D6 **7**
Seaburn Ter
 CLDN/WHIT/ROK SR6 .... **109** E6 **1**
Seaburn Vw *MONK* NE25 .... **24** C2
Seacombe Av *TYNE/NSHE* NE30...... **55** D1
Seafield Rd *BLYTH* NE24 .... **17** D1 **7**
Seafields *CLDN/WHIT/ROK* SR6 .... **109** D5
Seafield Ter *SSH* NE33 .... **71** F3
 TYNE/NSHE NE30 .... **55** F4
Seaforth Rd *SUNDSW* SR3 .... **143** F3
Seaforth St *BLYTH* NE24 .... **11** D4 **1**
Seaham Gdns *LWF/SPW/WRK* NE9.. **118** B2
Seaham Rd *HLH* DH5 .... **171** E2
Seaham St *SEA/MUR* SR7 .... **177** D5 **3**
 SUNDSW SR3.................................. **143** F3
Sea La *CLDN/WHIT/ROK* SR6 .... **109** D6
Sea Rd *CLDN/WHIT/ROK* SR6 .... **108** C6
 SSH NE33 .... **71** F3
Seascale Pl *LWF/SPW/WRK* NE9 .... **100** A6
Seaside La *PLEE/EAS* SR8.............. **200** B2 **1**
Seaton Av *BLYTH* NE24.................... **16** B2
 HLH DH5 .... **171** F2
Seaton Cl *FELL* NE10 .... **102** A4 **5**
Seaton Crs *MONK* NE25 .... **25** E6
 MONK NE25 .... **40** A5
 SEA/MUR SR7 .... **175** D1
Seaton Cft *CRAM* NE23 .... **35** E2 **2**
Seaton Gv *SEA/MUR* SR7 .... **174** C2
Seaton La *SEA/MUR* SR7 .... **175** D1
Seaton Pk *SEA/MUR* SR7 .... **175** E2
Seaton Pl *BYK/HTN/WLK* NE6 .... **83** D5
 DIN/WO NE13.................................... **32** C4
Seaton Rd *SMOOR* NE27 .... **38** C6
 SUNDSW SR3.................................. **142** C3
Seatonville Crs *MONK* NE25 .... **54** A1
Seatonville Rd *MONK* NE25 .... **54** A1
Sea Vw *ASHBK/HED/RY* SR2 .... **162** C2
 PLEE/EAS SR8 .... **200** A3
Sea View Gdns
 CLDN/WHIT/ROK SR6 .... **127** D1
 PLEE/EAS SR8 .... **201** F6
Sea View Pk *CLDN/WHIT/ROK* SR6 . **108** C2
 CRAM NE23 .... **22** C2
Sea View Rd *ASHBK/HED/RY* SR2 .. **145** D4
Sea View Rd West
 ASHBK/HED/RY SR2 .... **145** D4
Sea View St *ASHBK/HED/RY* SR2 .. **145** E4
Sea View Wk *SEA/MUR* SR7 .... **175** D6
Sea Wy *SSH* NE33 .... **72** A3
Second Av *BLYTH* NE24 .... **10** C6 **3**
 BYK/HTN/WLK NE6 .... **82** B3
 CLSW/PEL DH2 .... **136** A6
 CLSW/PEL DH2 .... **153** D6
 DUN/TMV NE11 .... **98** B4
 NSHW NE29...................................... **69** D2
Second St *GATE* NE8 .... **98** C1
Sedgeletch Rd *HLS* DH4 .... **169** F1
Sedgemoor *LGB/KIL* NE12 .... **35** F6
Sedgemoor Av
 BW/LEM/TK/HW NE15...................... **77** F4
Sedgewick Pl *GATE* NE8 .... **99** D1 **3**
Sedley Rd *WLSD/HOW* NE28 .... **67** D5
Sedling Rd *WASHS* NE38.............. **138** A4
Sefton Av *BYK/HTN/WLK* NE6 .... **65** D5
Sefton Ct *CRAM* NE23 .... **14** B5
Sefton Sq *SUNDSW* SR3 .... **143** D3
Selborne Gdns *JES* NE2 .... **64** C6
Selbourne Cl *CRAM* NE23 .... **21** D3 **5**
Selbourne St *SSH* NE33 .... **71** F4 **12**
Selby Cl *CRAM* NE23 .... **14** A5
Selby Gdns *BYK/HTN/WLK* NE6 ...... **66** B6
 WLSD/HOW NE28 .... **67** D3
Selby Sq *SUNDSW* SR3 .... **143** D3
Selkirk Crs *CLS/BIR/GTL* DH3 .... **136** A4
Selkirk Gv *CRAM* NE23 .... **14** B5
Selkirk Sq *SUNDSW* SR3 .... **142** C3 **1**
Selkirk St *JRW* NE32 .... **87** D5
Selkirk Wy *NSHW* NE29 .... **53** E4
Selsdon Av *MLFD/PNYW* SR4 .... **141** F4 **2**
Selsey Ct *FELL* NE10 .... **101** D4
Selwood Ct *HAR/WTLS* NE34 .... **89** E5 **1**
Selwyn Av *MONK* NE25 .... **53** F1
Serlby Cl *WASHN* NE37 .... **120** B3
Seton Av *HAR/WTLS* NE34 .... **87** E4
Setting Stones *WASHS* NE38 .... **137** F6
Sevenoaks Dr *MLFD/PNYW* SR4 .... **141** F3
Seventh Av *BLYTH* NE24 .... **10** C6
 BYK/HTN/WLK NE6 .... **82** B1

CLSW/PEL DH2 ...... 153 D5
Seventh St PLEE/EAS SR8 ...... 209 F1
Severn Av HEBB NE31 ...... 85 D5
Severn Cl PLEE/EAS SR8 ...... 208 B4
Severn Dr JRW NE32 ...... 86 B6
Severus Rd ELS/FEN NE4 ...... 79 D1
Seymour Cl DUN/TMV NE11 ...... 97 F1 [5]
Seymour Sq SUNDSW SR3 ...... 143 D3 [1]
Seymour St DUN/TMV NE11 ...... 97 F1
  NSHW NE29 ...... 70 C2
Seymour Ter HLH DH5 ...... 186 A3
Shadforth Cl PLEE/EAS SR8 ...... 207 F4
Shadon Wy CLS/BIR/GTL DH3 ...... 137 D2
Shaftesbury Av
  ASHBK/HED/RY SR2 ...... 162 A1
  HAR/WTLS NE34 ...... 87 D3
  JRW NE32 ...... 86 C2
  WBAY NE26 ...... 40 B3
Shaftesbury Crs SUNDSW SR3 ...... 143 E3
  TYNE/NSHE NE30 ...... 54 C1
Shaftesbury Gv BYK/HTN/WLK NE6 ...... 82 A1
Shaftoe Rd SUNDSW SR3 ...... 143 D4
Shaftoe Sq SUNDSW SR3 ...... 142 C4 [1]
Shaftoe Wy DIN/WO NE13 ...... 30 C3
  WLSD/HOW NE28 ...... 68 A3
Shaftsbury Dr BDN/LAN/SAC DH7 ...... 202 C6
Shakespeare Av HEBB NE31 ...... 85 D2
Shakespeare St HLH DH5 ...... 171 D3
  JRW NE32 ...... 69 D6 [2]
  SEA/MUR SR7 ...... 176 C3 [10]
  SSH NE33 ...... 71 F5 [10]
  SWCK/CAS SR5 ...... 125 F1
  WLSD/HOW NE28 ...... 68 B4
Shakespeare Ter
  ASHBK/HED/RY SR2 ...... 4 A5
  PLEE/EAS SR8 ...... 200 B2
Shakespere Ter CLSW/PEL DH2 ...... 152 A5
Shalcombe Cl SUNDSW SR3 ...... 160 C2
Shallcross ASHBK/HED/RY SR2 ...... 144 A2
Shalstone WASHN NE37 ...... 121 E3 [1]
Shamrock Cl
  BW/LEM/TK/HW NE15 ...... 59 E6
Shandon Wy GOS/KPK NE3 ...... 62 A1 [2]
Shanklin Pl CRAM NE23 ...... 21 D2 [4]
Shannon Cl SWCK/CAS SR5 ...... 123 F5 [2]
Shap Cl WASHS NE38 ...... 138 C3
Shap La WD/WHPE/BLK NE5 ...... 60 C5
Shap Rd TYNE/NSHE NE30 ...... 54 C2
Sharnford Cl SMOOR NE27 ...... 37 F5
Sharon Cl LGB/KIL NE12 ...... 49 D2
Sharp Crs DHAM DH1 ...... 195 F3
Sharpendon St HEBB NE31 ...... 85 D1 [1]
Sharpley Dr SEA/MUR SR7 ...... 175 D2
Shaw Av HAR/WTLS NE34 ...... 88 A4
Shawdon Cl
  WD/WHPE/BLK NE5 ...... 61 D2 [11]
Shaw Gdns FELL NE10 ...... 102 A2 [8]
Shaw St SEA/MUR SR7 ...... 176 C3 [11]
Shaw Wood Cl DHAM DH1 ...... 193 F3
Shearlegs Rd GATE NE8 ...... 81 F5
Shearwater CLDN/WHIT/ROK SR6 ...... 91 E5
Shearwater Av LGB/KIL NE12 ...... 48 C5
Shearwater Cl
  WD/WHPE/BLK NE5 ...... 61 D2 [12]
Shearwater Wy BLYTH NE24 ...... 17 E2
Sheelin Av LGB/KIL NE12 ...... 48 C5
Sheen Cl WD/WHPE/BLK NE5 ...... 61 D1
Sheen Ct WD/WHPE/BLK NE5 ...... 61 D1
Sheepfolds North
  SWCK/CAS SR5 ...... 126 C4 [3]
Sheepfolds Rd SWCK/CAS SR5 ...... 126 C4 [5]
Sheep Hl WICK/BNPF NE16 ...... 112 A6
Sheldon Gv CRAM NE23 ...... 14 A5
  GOS/KPK NE3 ...... 62 B4
Sheldon Rd HAR/WTLS NE34 ...... 72 B5
Sheldon St JRW NE32 ...... 86 A1
Shelford Gdns
  BW/LEM/TK/HW NE15 ...... 77 D1 [3]
Shelley Av BOLCOL NE35 ...... 105 F2
  HAR/WTLS NE34 ...... 90 A3
  HLH DH5 ...... 186 C4 [2]
  LWF/SPW/WRK NE9 ...... 119 D3
Shelley Ct CLSW/PEL DH2 ...... 152 A5
Shelley Dr GATE NE8 ...... 81 F6
Shelley Gdns CLSW/PEL DH2 ...... 152 B5
Shelley Rd BW/LEM/TK/HW NE15 ...... 75 E1
Shelley St SEA/MUR SR7 ...... 176 C3
Shepherd St MLFD/PNYW SR4 ...... 125 F5 [2]
Shepherds Wy BOL NE36 ...... 105 F3 [7]
Shepherd Wy WASHS NE38 ...... 139 D4
Sheppard Ter SWCK/CAS SR5 ...... 124 A3 [7]
Sheppey Ct SUNDSW SR3 ...... 160 C2 [3]
Shepton Cottages
  WICK/BNPF NE16 ...... 114 B1
Sheraton Cl FELL NE10 ...... 101 F5
Sheraton St JES NE2 ...... 63 D6
Sherborne Av NSHW NE29 ...... 53 F4 [2]
Sherburn Gra North JRW NE32 ...... 85 F5 [2]
Sherburn Gra South JRW NE32 ...... 85 F4 [1]
Sherburn Gn ROWG NE39 ...... 111 E1
Sherburn Gv FELL DH4 ...... 170 D1
Sherburn Park Dr ROWG NE39 ...... 111 E1
Sherburn Rd DHAM DH1 ...... 195 F4 [2]

Sherburn Wy FELL NE10 ...... 102 A4
Sherfield Dr LGB/HTN NE7 ...... 65 F4
Sheridan Gn WASHS NE38 ...... 137 F5
Sheridan Rd HAR/WTLS NE34 ...... 87 F5
Sheridan St MLFD/PNYW SR4 ...... 125 E5
Sheriffs Cl FELL NE10 ...... 100 A2
Sheriff's Moor Av HLH DH5 ...... 186 B4
Sheringham Av NSHW NE29 ...... 53 F5
Sheringham Cl SUNDSW SR3 ...... 160 C4 [4]
Sheringham Dr CRAM NE23 ...... 21 D2
Sheringham Gdns
  BW/LEM/TK/HW NE15 ...... 57 D4
Sherringham Av GOS/KPK NE3 ...... 62 A1
Sherwood Cl SMOOR NE27 ...... 53 D2
  WASHS NE38 ...... 138 C1 [1]
Sherwood Ct SUNDSW SR3 ...... 160 C2 [9]
Sherwood Pl GOS/KPK NE3 ...... 47 E2
Sherwood Vw WLSD/HOW NE28 ...... 66 C2
Shetland Ct SUNDSW SR3 ...... 160 C2 [10]
Shibdon Bank BLAY NE21 ...... 76 C5
Shibdon Crs BLAY NE21 ...... 76 C6 [1]
Shibdon Park Vw BLAY NE21 ...... 76 C6 [2]
Shibdon Rd BLAY NE21 ...... 76 B5
Shibdon Wy BLAY NE21 ...... 77 E6
Shield Av WICK/BNPF NE16 ...... 96 A1 [2]
Shieldfield La JES NE2 ...... 3 G2
Shield Rd CLDN/WHIT/ROK SR6 ...... 108 B5
Shieldrow La STLY/ANP DH9 ...... 146 C5
Shields Rd BDLGTN NE22 ...... 12 A1
  BYK/HTN/WLK NE6 ...... 82 A2
  CLDN/WHIT/ROK SR6 ...... 108 A4
  CLS/BIR/GTL DH3 ...... 153 F3
  FELL NE10 ...... 101 F1
  HAR/WTLS NE34 ...... 89 F5
  MONK NE25 ...... 54 B2
Shields Rd West
  BYK/HTN/WLK NE6 ...... 81 F2 [9]
Shield St JES NE2 ...... 3 G1
Shiel Gdns CRAM NE23 ...... 21 D2
Shillaw Pl CRAM NE23 ...... 35 D5 [3]
Shilmore Rd GOS/KPK NE3 ...... 62 B1 [7]
Shilton Cl HAR/WTLS NE34 ...... 90 A3
Shincliffe Av SWCK/CAS SR5 ...... 124 B2 [4]
Shincliffe Gdns
  LWF/SPW/WRK NE9 ...... 118 B1
Shinwell Ter WLSD/HOW NE28 ...... 188 A1
Shipcote La GATE NE8 ...... 99 E2
Shipcote Ter GATE NE8 ...... 99 E2
Shipley Av ELS/FEN NE4 ...... 79 D2
Shipley St GATE NE8 ...... 99 E1 [13]
Shipley Rd TYNE/NSHE NE30 ...... 55 E5
Shipley St BW/LEM/TK/HW NE15 ...... 76 B2
Shipton Cl BOLCOL NE35 ...... 105 D1
Shire Cha DHAM DH1 ...... 180 C4 [4]
Shirley Gdns SUNDSW SR3 ...... 144 A3
Shirwood Av WICK/BNPF NE16 ...... 95 F5
Shop Spouts BLAY NE21 ...... 76 B5 [7]
Shoreham Sq SUNDSW SR3 ...... 143 D3 [2]
Shorestone Av TYNE/NSHE NE30 ...... 55 D1
Shore St CLDN/WHIT/ROK SR6 ...... 126 C3 [8]
Short Gv SEA/MUR SR7 ...... 187 F1
Shortridge St SSH NE33 ...... 71 F3 [9]
Shortridge Ter JES NE2 ...... 64 B5
Shot Factory La CNUT NE1 ...... 80 B5
Shotley Av SWCK/CAS SR5 ...... 124 B2 [5]
Shotley Gdns LWF/SPW/WRK NE9 ...... 99 F3
Shotton Av BLYTH NE24 ...... 11 D6
Shotton Bank PLEE/EAS SR8 ...... 207 E5
Shotton La CRAM NE23 ...... 12 B4
  PLEE/EAS SR8 ...... 207 F4
  RDHAMSE DH6 ...... 206 D2
  RDHAMSE DH6 ...... 207 E3
Shotton Rd PLEE/EAS SR8 ...... 207 D1
  PLEE/EAS SR8 ...... 209 E1
Shotton Wy FELL NE10 ...... 103 D4
Shrewsbury Cl LGB/KIL NE12 ...... 65 F2
  PLEE/EAS SR8 ...... 208 A3
Shrewsbury Crs SUNDSW SR3 ...... 143 E3
Shrewsbury Dr SMOOR NE27 ...... 37 E5
Shrewsbury St DUN/TMV NE11 ...... 97 E2
  SEA/MUR SR7 ...... 176 C5
Shrewsbury Ter SSH NE33 ...... 88 B1 [3]
Shrigley Gdns GOS/KPK NE3 ...... 62 B1
Shropshire Dr DHAM DH1 ...... 196 B4
Shunner Cl WASHN NE37 ...... 119 F6
Sibthorpe St NSHW NE29 ...... 71 D1 [3]
Side CNUT NE1 ...... 3 E5
Side Cliff Rd CLDN/WHIT/ROK SR6 ...... 126 C1
Sidegate DHAM DH1 ...... 194 B4
Sidlaw Av CLSW/PEL DH2 ...... 152 C6
  NSHW NE29 ...... 54 B3
Sidmouth Cl HLS DH4 ...... 157 E4 [5]
  SEA/MUR SR7 ...... 175 E4
Sidmouth Rd LWF/SPW/WRK NE9 ...... 117 F1
  NSHW NE29 ...... 53 E6
Sidney Gv ELS/FEN NE4 ...... 79 F2
  GATE NE8 ...... 98 C1 [10]
Sidney St BLYTH NE24 ...... 10 C5
  BOLCOL NE35 ...... 105 E2
  NSHW NE29 ...... 70 C1
Sidney Ter STLY/ANP DH9 ...... 130 C6
Silkey's La NSHW NE29 ...... 70 B1
Silksworth Cl SUNDSW SR3 ...... 143 E6 [2]
Silksworth Gdns
  LWF/SPW/WRK NE9 ...... 118 B2

Silksworth Hall Dr SUNDSW SR3 ...... 160 B2
Silksworth La
  ASHBK/HED/RY SR2 ...... 144 A2 [2]
  SUNDSW SR3 ...... 143 E6
Silksworth Rd SUNDSW SR3 ...... 159 E1
Silksworth Rw SUND SR1 ...... 4 A2 [3]
Silksworth Ter SUNDSW SR3 ...... 160 C1 [2]
Silksworth Wy SUNDSW SR3 ...... 159 F2
Silkwood Cl CRAM NE23 ...... 14 A5
Silloth Av WD/WHPE/BLK NE5 ...... 60 C5
Silloth Dr WASHN NE37 ...... 120 B2
Silloth Pl TYNE/NSHE NE30 ...... 55 D2
Silloth Rd SUNDSW SR3 ...... 142 C4 [2]
Silver Cts BDN/LAN/SAC DH7 ...... 203 D4
Silverdale SUNDSW SR3 ...... 160 C4
Silverdale Av FELL NE10 ...... 102 C3
Silverdale Dr BLAY NE21 ...... 93 E1
Silverdale Rd CRAM NE23 ...... 14 A5
Silverdale Ter GATE NE8 ...... 99 E2 [3]
Silverdale Wy HAR/WTLS NE34 ...... 87 E5
  WICK/BNPF NE16 ...... 95 E6
Silver Fox Wy SMOOR NE27 ...... 52 B4
Silverhill Dr WD/WHPE/BLK NE5 ...... 77 F1
The Silverlink North SMOOR NE27 ...... 52 A3
The Silverlink SMOOR NE27 ...... 52 C5
Silver Lonnen WD/WHPE/BLK NE5 ...... 61 D6
Silvermere Dr RYTON NE40 ...... 74 C4
Silverstone LGB/KIL NE12 ...... 50 A1
Silverstone Rd WASHN NE37 ...... 121 D4
Silver St DHAM DH1 ...... 194 B5
  TYNE/NSHE NE30 ...... 55 F5 [3]
Silverwood Gdns DUN/TMV NE11 ...... 98 A5
Simonburn Av ELS/FEN NE4 ...... 62 A6
  NSHW NE29 ...... 53 E6
Simon Pl DIN/WO NE13 ...... 32 C5 [7]
Simonside Av WLSD/HOW NE28 ...... 68 B2
Simonside Rd BLAY NE21 ...... 94 B1 [5]
  SUNDSW SR3 ...... 142 C3
Simonside Ter BYK/HTN/WLK NE6 ...... 65 D6
Simonside Vw JRW NE32 ...... 86 B4
Simonside Wy LGB/KIL NE12 ...... 36 B6
Simpson St BLYTH NE24 ...... 11 D4 [10]
  MLFD/PNYW SR4 ...... 126 A4
  NSHW NE29 ...... 70 A1
  TYNE/NSHE NE30 ...... 41 E6 [7]
Simpson Ter JES NE2 ...... 3 G2
Sinclair Dr CLS/BIR/GTL DH3 ...... 136 C6
Sinclair Gdns MONK NE25 ...... 24 C5
Sinderby Cl GOS/KPK NE3 ...... 47 F4
Six-mile Br DIN/WO NE13 ...... 33 E2
Sixth Av BLYTH NE24 ...... 10 C6
  BYK/HTN/WLK NE6 ...... 82 B1
Sixth St PLEE/EAS SR8 ...... 209 F1
Skaylock Dr WASHS NE38 ...... 137 F3
Skelder Av LGB/KIL NE12 ...... 49 D6
Skelton Ct GOS/KPK NE3 ...... 46 A4
Skerne Cl PLEE/EAS SR8 ...... 208 B4
Skiddaw Cl PLEE/EAS SR8 ...... 209 D2
Skiddaw Dr
  CLDN/WHIT/ROK SR6 ...... 108 B5 [3]
Skiddaw Pl LWF/SPW/WRK NE9 ...... 100 A6
Skinnerburn Rd ELS/FEN NE4 ...... 80 A6
Skipton Cl BDLGTN NE22 ...... 6 C2
  CRAM NE23 ...... 14 B5 [3]
Skirlaw Cl WASHS NE38 ...... 138 C2
Ski Vw SUNDSW SR3 ...... 143 E6
Skye Ct SUNDSW SR3 ...... 160 B2
Skye Gv JRW NE32 ...... 87 D6 [3]
Slaidburn Rd STLY/ANP DH9 ...... 148 B1 [7]
Slake Rd JRW NE32 ...... 69 F5
Slaley WASHS NE38 ...... 139 D5
Slaley Cl FELL NE10 ...... 102 B3
Slaley Ct BDLGTN NE22 ...... 7 F3
  SUNDSW SR3 ...... 160 C2
Slatyford La WD/WHPE/BLK NE5 ...... 60 D6
Sledmere Cl PLEE/EAS SR8 ...... 200 C6 [2]
Sleekburn Av BDLGTN NE22 ...... 8 C1 [2]
Slingley Cl SEA/MUR SR7 ...... 175 D2 [2]
Slingsby Gdns LGB/HTN NE7 ...... 65 F3
Smailes La ROWG NE39 ...... 110 B2 [1]
Smailes St STLY/ANP DH9 ...... 148 A3
Smeaton Ct WLSD/HOW NE28 ...... 68 C5 [5]
Smeaton St WLSD/HOW NE28 ...... 68 C5 [3]
Smillie Cl PLEE/EAS SR8 ...... 208 C1
Smithburn Rd FELL NE10 ...... 100 C3
Smith Cl RDHAMSE DH6 ...... 197 D5
Smithfield DHAM DH1 ...... 180 A4
Smith Gv ASHBK/HED/RY SR2 ...... 162 A2
Smith St ASHBK/HED/RY SR2 ...... 162 B2
  SSH NE33 ...... 71 D6
Smith Ter GATE NE8 ...... 98 A1
Smithyford LWF/SPW/WRK NE9 ...... 117 F3
Smithy La DUN/TMV NE11 ...... 117 D3
Smithy St SSH NE33 ...... 71 E3 [3]
Smyrna Pl SUND SR1 ...... 5 F3
Snipes Dene ROWG NE39 ...... 111 D1
Snowdon Gdns DUN/TMV NE11 ...... 97 F4 [3]
Snowdon Gv BOL NE36 ...... 106 A3 [5]
Soane Gdns HAR/WTLS NE34 ...... 88 C3
Softley Pl BW/LEM/TK/HW NE15 ...... 77 E1
Solingen Est BLYTH NE24 ...... 17 E1
Solway Av TYNE/NSHE NE30 ...... 54 C2
Solway Rd HEBB NE31 ...... 85 D4
Solway Sq SUNDSW SR3 ...... 143 D3

Somersby Dr GOS/KPK NE3 62 A1
Somerset Gdns
WLSD/HOW NE28 66 C3 6
Somerset Gv NSHW NE29 53 F4 3
Somerset Pl ELS/FEN NE4 79 F3
Somerset Rd HEBB NE31 85 E5 3
SUNDSW SR3 142 C3
Somerset Sq SUNDSW SR3 142 C3 2
Somerset St SUNDSW SR3 143 F5 1
Somerton Ct GOS/KPK NE3 45 E6
Sophia St SEA/MUR SR7 176 C3
Sophy St SWCK/CAS SR5 126 A2 12
Sorley St MLFD/PNYW SR4 125 F6
Sorrel Gdns HAR/WTLS NE34 89 D5
Soulby Ct DIN/WO NE13 45 F4
Sourmilk Hill La
LWF/SPW/WRK NE9 99 F4
Souter Rd GOS/KPK NE3 62 C1 7
South Ap CLSW/PEL DH2 153 E6
South Av HAR/WTLS NE34 89 E3
South Bailey DHAM DH1 194 B6
South Bend GOS/KPK NE3 47 D3
South Bents Av
CLDN/WHIT/ROK SR6 109 D4
South Benwell Rd
BW/LEM/TK/HW NE15 78 B4
Southburn Cl HLS DH4 170 B2 2
South Burns CLS/BIR/GTL DH3 153 E4
South Cl HAR/WTLS NE34 89 E3
HLH DH5 186 C4
RYTON NE40 74 B4
Southcote WICK/BNPF NE16 95 F5
South Crs BOLCOL NE35 105 E2
SEA/MUR SR7 177 D3
WASHS NE38 138 A6
South Cft LGB/KIL NE12 50 A5
Southcroft WASHS NE38 138 C5
South Dene HAR/WTLS NE34 88 A3
South Dr CLDN/WHIT/ROK SR6 107 E1 2
DIN/WO NE13 19 D2
DIN/WO NE13 44 B4
HEBB NE31 84 B4
South Eldon St SSH NE33 88 A1
Southend Av BLYTH NE24 10 B6
Southend Rd LWF/SPW/WRK NE9 100 A5
SUNDSW SR3 143 D4
Southern Rd BYK/HTN/WLK NE6 83 E4
Southern Wy RYTON NE40 74 B4 1
Southey St SSH NE33 71 F6 6
Southfield CLSW/PEL DH2 152 A1
Southfield Gdns WICK/BNPF NE16 96 B3
Southfield Rd HAR/WTLS NE34 72 B6
LGB/KIL NE12 49 E6
WICK/BNPF NE16 96 B4
Southfields CRAM NE23 34 C2 1
Southfield Ter
BYK/HTN/WLK NE6 83 F4 10
Southfield Wy DHAM DH1 193 F2
Southfork BW/LEM/TK/HW NE15 59 E6
South Frederick St SSH NE33 88 A1 3
Southgate LGB/KIL NE12 49 F2
South Grange Pk SEA/MUR SR7 162 B6
South Gv RYTON NE40 74 C4
South Hetton Rd HLH DH5 186 C4
South Hill Rd GATE NE8 98 B1
Southhill Rd HAR/WTLS NE34 89 F2
Southlands JRW NE32 104 C1
LGB/HTN NE7 64 C4
TYNE/NSHE NE30 55 D4
South La BOL NE36 106 B3
South Lea BDN/LAN/SAC DH7 178 A4
South Market St HLH DH5 172 A6
Southmayne Rd
MLFD/PNYW SR4 142 C2 4
Southmead Av WD/WHPE/BLK NE5 61 D5
South Mdw STLY/ANP DH9 128 C6
Southmoor Rd BYK/HTN/WLK NE6 83 D1
South Moor Rd STLY/ANP DH9 148 A4
South Nelson Rd CRAM NE23 13 D6
South Newsham Rd BLYTH NE24 16 B3
South Pde FELL NE10 84 A6
WBAY NE26 41 D5
South Preston Gv NSHW NE29 70 C1 11
South Railway St SEA/MUR SR7 176 C3
South Rdg GOS/KPK NE3 47 D4
South Riggs BDLGTN NE22 7 E4
South Rd DHAM DH1 205 E2
South Rw GATE NE8 82 A4 1
South Shore Rd GATE NE8 3 H5
South Side PLEE/EAS SR8 200 A3
South St CLSW/PEL DH2 153 D4
CNUT NE1 2 C6
DHAM DH1 194 B5
GATE NE8 99 E1 14
GOS/KPK NE3 62 C1 8
HLH DH5 170 B6 2
HLS DH4 157 F5
SMOOR NE27 38 B6
SUND SR1 4 C2
South Ter DHAM DH1 193 F1
PLEE/EAS SR8 209 E1
SEA/MUR SR7 177 D3 3
SWCK/CAS SR5 126 A3 7
WLSD/HOW NE28 68 A4
South Vw BDN/LAN/SAC DH7 203 E5
BLYTH NE24 16 B2
CLDN/WHIT/ROK SR6 126 C1
CLS/BIR/GTL DH3 136 C2
HLH DH5 186 C5
JRW NE32 85 F2
SEA/MUR SR7 175 E5
STLY/ANP DH9 130 A4
WASHS NE38 139 D5
WD/WHPE/BLK NE5 60 A6
South View Rd MLFD/PNYW SR4 141 F1
South View Ter HLS DH4 170 A2
WICK/BNPF NE16 96 A2
South Vw West BYK/HTN/WLK NE6 81 F2
Southward WBAY NE26 26 C3
Southward Cl WBAY NE26 26 C3 1
Southward Wy MONK NE25 38 A1
Southway BW/LEM/TK/HW NE15 77 D1
LWF/SPW/WRK NE9 100 A4
PLEE/EAS SR8 208 B3
Southwick Rd SWCK/CAS SR5 126 C4 10
SWCK/CAS SR5 126 C3 9
Southwold Gdns SUNDSW SR3 143 E6 3
Southwold Pl CRAM NE23 21 D2 5
South Woodbine St SSH NE33 71 F4
Southwood Gdns GOS/KPK NE3 62 B2
Sovereign Pl ELS/FEN NE4 79 F4
Spalding Cl LGB/HTN NE7 65 E2 7
Sparkwell Cl HLS DH4 157 F4 2
Spartylea WASHS NE38 139 E5 1
Spa Well Cl BLAY NE21 94 A2
Spa Well Dr SWCK/CAS SR5 124 B2
Spelter Works Rd
ASHBK/HED/RY SR2 145 E3
Spencer Cl STLY/ANP DH9 149 D2
Spencer Ct BLYTH NE24 10 A3
Spencer Gv WICK/BNPF NE16 96 A2 4
Spencer Rd BLYTH NE24 10 A3
Spencers Bank WICK/BNPF NE16 95 F1 9
Spencer St BYK/HTN/WLK NE6 65 E6
NSHW NE29 70 C1 12
Spence Ter NSHW NE29 70 B1
Spenfield Rd WD/WHPE/BLK NE5 61 F3 4
Spenser St JRW NE32 69 D6 3
Spen St STLY/ANP DH9 148 A3
Spinneyside Gdns DUN/TMV NE11 97 E3
The Spinney CRAM NE23 35 E2
PLEE/EAS SR8 199 F2
WASHS NE38 138 C4
Spire Hollin PLEE/EAS SR8 208 B2
Spire Rd WASHN NE37 121 E5
Spires La BYK/HTN/WLK NE6 82 B2
Spital Ter GOS/KPK NE3 63 E1
Split Crow Rd GATE NE8 99 F2
Spohr Ter SSH NE33 71 F5
Spoor St DUN/TMV NE11 97 E1
Spout La WASHN NE37 120 C5
WASHS NE38 120 C6
Springbank Rd
BYK/HTN/WLK NE6 81 F1 4
JES NE2 81 F1
SUNDSW SR3 142 C3
Springbank Sq SUNDSW SR3 142 C3 3
Springfield NSHW NE29 54 C6 10
Springfield Av
LWF/SPW/WRK NE9 118 B3
Springfield Crs SEA/MUR SR7 176 B4
Springfield Gdns
CLS/BIR/GTL DH3 153 E3
WLSD/HOW NE28 66 B3
Springfield Gv MONK NE25 54 A1
Springfield Pk DHAM DH1 193 F3
Springfield Pl LWF/SPW/WRK NE9 99 F4
Springfield Rd BLAY NE21 76 A6
HLS DH4 157 F5 8
WD/WHPE/BLK NE5 61 E5 6
Spring Garden Cl SUND SR1 5 F2 3
Spring Garden La ELS/FEN NE4 80 A2 10
Springhill Gdns
BW/LEM/TK/HW NE15 78 C2
Spring Pk BDLGTN NE22 7 F4
Springside BDN/LAN/SAC DH7 178 B1
The Springs CLS/BIR/GTL DH3 136 C3
Springsyde Cl WICK/BNPF NE16 95 D5 4
Spring Ter NSHW NE29 54 C6 11
Springwell Av BYK/HTN/WLK NE6 83 D4
DHAM DH1 193 F3
JRW NE32 86 B2
LWF/SPW/WRK NE9 118 B2 1
Springwell Rd DHAM DH1 193 F3
JRW NE32 86 A3
LWF/SPW/WRK NE9 118 C1
MLFD/PNYW SR4 142 C3
Springwood HEBB NE31 84 B1
Squires Gdns FELL NE10 100 C3
Stack Garth BDN/LAN/SAC DH7 203 E3
Stadium Wy SWCK/CAS SR5 126 B4 2
Stafford Gv ASHBK/HED/RY SR2 162 A2 1
SWCK/CAS SR5 126 A2
Stafford Pl PLEE/EAS SR8 208 A1
Staffordshire Dr DHAM DH1 196 C3
Staffords La
CLDN/WHIT/ROK SR6 109 E2 2
Stafford St SUND SR1 127 E4 1
Stagshaw LGB/KIL NE12 35 E5 5
Staindrop FELL NE10 101 F5
Staindrop Rd DHAM DH1 180 C6
Staines Rd BYK/HTN/WLK NE6 82 C4
Stainmore Dr CLS/BIR/GTL DH3 168 A4
Stainton Dr FELL NE10 100 C2 6
Stainton Gv CLDN/WHIT/ROK SR6 108 B5
Stainton St East SSH NE33 71 F5 11
Stainton Wy PLEE/EAS SR8 208 B2
Staithes Av LGB/KIL NE12 49 E6
Staithes Rd WASHS NE38 139 F3
Staithes St BYK/HTN/WLK NE6 84 A2
Staith La BLAY NE21 75 F4
Staiths Rd DUN/TMV NE11 79 F6 1
Stalks Rd DIN/WO NE13 33 D4
Stamford Av MONK NE25 25 D6
SUNDSW SR3 143 E3
Stamfordham Av NSHW NE29 69 F1
Stamfordham Cl
WLSD/HOW NE28 66 C4 3
Stamfordham Ms
WD/WHPE/BLK NE5 61 F5 9
Stamfordham Rd
WD/WHPE/BLK NE5 42 B6
Stampley Cl BLAY NE21 93 F2 6
Stamps La SUND SR1 5 G1
Standfield Gdns FELL NE10 102 B2 2
Standish St STLY/ANP DH9 147 F3
Stanelaw Wy STLY/ANP DH9 131 E5
Staneway FELL NE10 101 D6
Stanfield Ct LGB/HTN NE7 66 A3 4
Stanhope WASHS NE38 137 E1
Stanhope Cl BDN/LAN/SAC DH7 203 E4 5
DHAM DH1 180 C5
HLS DH4 170 C3
Stanhope Pde SSH NE33 71 F6 7
Stanhope Rd
CLDN/WHIT/ROK SR6 109 D6
HAR/WTLS NE34 88 A2
JRW NE32 86 C3
SSH NE33 88 C1
Stanhope St ELS/FEN NE4 79 F2
SSH NE33 71 E3
Stanley Cl RDHAMSE DH6 197 E5
Stanley Gdns LWF/SPW/WRK NE9 118 B2
Stanley Gv BDLGTN NE22 8 A3
LGB/HTN NE7 64 C3
Stanley St BLYTH NE24 11 E4
HAR/WTLS NE34 88 A3
JRW NE32 86 B1
NSHW NE29 70 C1 13
SEA/MUR SR7 176 A2
SWCK/CAS SR5 124 A3 8
WLSD/HOW NE28 68 B3
Stanley St West NSHW NE29 70 C1
Stanmore Rd BYK/HTN/WLK NE6 65 E5
Stannington Av BYK/HTN/WLK NE6 82 A1
Stannington Gdns
ASHBK/HED/RY SR2 144 B4 6
Stannington Gv
ASHBK/HED/RY SR2 144 B4
BYK/HTN/WLK NE6 82 A1 4
Stannington Pl
BYK/HTN/WLK NE6 82 A1 5
PONT/DH NE20 28 A2
Stannington Rd NSHW NE29 69 E1
Stannington St BLYTH NE24 11 E5
Stansfield St CLDN/WHIT/ROK SR6 127 D3
Stanstead Cl SWCK/CAS SR5 123 F4 2
Stanton Av BLYTH NE24 16 A1
HAR/WTLS NE34 89 D1
Stanton Cl FELL NE10 102 C3
Stanton Rd SMOOR NE27 52 A2
TYNE/NSHE NE30 54 B3
Stanton St ELS/FEN NE4 79 F2
Stanway Dr LGB/HTN NE7 64 C3
Stanwick St TYNE/NSHE NE30 55 F4 6
Stapeley Vw GOS/KPK NE3 61 F1
Staple Rd JRW NE32 69 D6
Stapylton Dr ASHBK/HED/RY SR2 144 A2
Starbeck Av JES NE2 81 E1 3
Starbeck Ms JES NE2 81 E1 4
Stardale Av BLYTH NE24 9 F6
Stargate La RYTON NE40 75 D4
Starlight Crs MONK NE25 24 B5 3
Startforth Cl CLS/BIR/GTL DH3 168 A3 4
Station Ap BOL NE36 107 D3
DHAM DH1 194 A4
LGB/KIL NE12 49 F6 6
SSH NE33 71 E3 9
Station Av BDN/LAN/SAC DH7 203 E4
HLH DH5 185 F1
Station Bank DHAM DH1 194 B4 4
RYTON NE40 74 B2
Station Crs SEA/MUR SR7 176 A2
Station Est East SEA/MUR SR7 187 F1
Station Est North SEA/MUR SR7 187 F1
Station Est South SEA/MUR SR7 187 F1
Station Field Rd STLY/ANP DH9 131 E5
Station La CLS/BIR/GTL DH3 136 A2
CLSW/PEL DH2 151 F2
DHAM DH1 195 D4
Station Rd ASHBK/HED/RY SR2 162 C2
BDLGTN NE22 8 B2
BDN/LAN/SAC DH7 203 E4
BOLCOL NE35 87 D6
BW/LEM/TK/HW NE15 56 B4

BW/LEM/TK/HW NE15...................... 75 E1
CLS/BIR/GTL DH3 .... 153 E5
CLSW/PEL DH2 .... 153 E5
CRAM NE23 .... 21 F1
CRAM NE23 .... 22 A1 2
CRAM NE23 .... 34 B2
CRAM NE23 .... 36 B1
DIN/WO NE13 .... 45 D6
FELL NE10 .... 84 A6
GOS/KPK NE3 .... 64 A1
HEBB NE31 .... 84 C2
HLH DH5 .... 185 F1
HLS DH4 .... 139 E6
HLS DH4 .... 156 C2 8
HLS DH4 .... 170 C1
HLS DH4 .... 183 E3
LGB/KIL NE12 .... 35 D6
LGB/KIL NE12 .... 49 F6
LGB/KIL NE12 .... 49 D1
LWF/SPW/WRK NE9 .... 99 D6
NSHW NE33.................................. 69 F2
PLEE/EAS SR8 .... 201 E3
RDHAMSE DH6 .... 183 F5
RDHAMSE DH6 .... 206 A1
ROWG NE39................................. 111 E3
SEA/MUR SR7 .... 175 E3
SEA/MUR SR7 .... 187 F1
SMOOR NE27 .... 51 F1
SSH NE33................................... 71 E4
STLY/ANP DH9 .... 133 D6
STLY/ANP DH9 .... 146 B5
STLY/ANP DH9 .... 148 B1
SWCK/CAS SR5 .... 108 D6
TYNE/NSHE NE30............................ 55 E1
WASHS NE38 .... 139 D1
WASHS NE38 .... 139 D5
WBAY NE26 .... 41 D6
WLSD/HOW NE28 .... 66 C4
WLSD/HOW NE28 .... 66 B3
WLSD/HOW NE28 .... 67 E5
WLSD/HOW NE28 .... 68 C5
Station Rd North LGB/KIL NE12 ...... 49 F4 8
Station St BLYTH NE24 .... 11 D4
        SUND SR1 .... 4 C2
Station Ter TYNE/NSHE NE30............ 55 F5
Station Vw HLH DH5........................ 185 F1
Staveley Rd CLDN/WHIT/ROK NE6 .. 108 D5
        PLEE/EAS SR8 .... 209 D2
Stavordale St SEA/MUR SR7 .... 176 C4 6
Stavordale St West
        SEA/MUR SR7 .... 176 C5 9
Stavordale Ter
        LWF/SPW/WRK NE9 .... 99 F5 3
Staward Av MONK NE25 .... 24 C6
Staward Ter BYK/HTN/WLK NE6 ...... 83 E4 2
Staynebrigg FELL NE10 .... 101 F4 5
Stead La BDLGTN NE22 .... 8 A3
Stead St WLSD/HOW NE28.................. 68 C3
Stedham Cl WASHN NE37 .... 121 D2
Steep Hl SUNDSW SR3 .... 142 A6
Stella Bank BLAY NE21 .... 75 E3
Stella Hall BLAY NE21 .... 75 E4
Stella La BLAY NE21 .... 75 E4
Stella Rd BLAY NE21 .... 75 E4
Stephenson Cl HLH DH5.................. 172 A6 2
Stephenson Rd BYK/HTN/WLK NE6 .. 65 D5
        PLEE/EAS SR8 .... 200 B5
        WASHN NE37 .... 121 D2
Stephenson St GATE NE8 .... 98 C2 7
        SEA/MUR SR7 .... 188 B1 9
        TYNE/NSHE NE30..................... 55 F5 4
Stephenson Ter FELL NE10 .... 100 C3
Stephenson Wy BLAY NE21 .... 94 A2
Stephens Rd SEA/MUR SR7 .... 188 A1
Stephen St BLYTH NE24 .... 11 D4
        BYK/HTN/WLK NE6 .... 81 F2
Stepney La CNUT NE1........................ 3 G3
Stepney Rd JES NE2 .... 3 H1
Sterling St MLFD/PNYW SR4 .... 125 F6
Steward Crs HAR/WTLS NE34 .... 90 A1
Stewart Av ASHBK/HED/RY SR2 ...... 162 A2
Stewart Dr BOL NE36 .... 106 A3 7
Stewart St MLFD/PNYW SR4 .... 125 F6
        PLEE/EAS SR8 .... 200 C1
        SEA/MUR SR7 .... 177 D4
        SUNDSW SR3........................... 160 C1
Stileford HLS DH4 .... 101 F3
Stirling Av JRW NE32 .... 87 D4
        ROWG NE39.......................... 111 D3
Stirling Cl WASHS NE38.................. 139 E2
Stirling Dr BDLGTN NE22 .... 8 B2
        NSHW NE33............................ 53 E4
Stirling La ROWG NE39 .... 111 D3
Stobart St BDN/LAN/SAC DH7 .... 164 A3 1
        SWCK/CAS SR5 .... 126 B4
Stockholm Cl NSHW NE29 .... 69 D1
Stockley Av SWCK/CAS SR5 .... 124 B2 5
Stockley Ct BDN/LAN/SAC DH7 ...... 192 B5
Stocksfield Av WD/WHPE/BLK NE5 .. 78 B3
Stockton Rd ASHBK/HED/RY SR2 ...... 4 B5
        ASHBK/HED/RY SR2 .... 162 B3
        DHAM DH1 .... 194 C6
        NSHW NE29 .... 70 B3 2
        PLEE/EAS SR8 .... 199 F4

        SEA/MUR SR7 .... 162 B6
        SEA/MUR SR7 .... 189 F4
        SUND SR1 .... 4 B4 2
Stockton St SEA/MUR SR7 .... 176 A2
Stockwell Gn BYK/HTN/WLK NE6 ...... 66 B6
Stoddart St HAR/WTLS NE34 .... 88 B2 2
        JES NE2 .... 3 H1
Stoker Av HAR/WTLS NE34 .... 87 E4
Stokesley Gv LGB/HTN NE7 .... 64 C3
Stone Cellar Rd WASHN NE37 .... 120 A2
Stonechat Pl LGB/KIL NE12 .... 48 C5
Stonecroft Gdns LGB/HTN NE7 ...... 65 F3
Stonefold Cl WD/WHPE/BLK NE5 .. 61 D3 3
Stoneleigh Av LGB/KIL NE12 .... 48 C5
Stoneleigh Cl HLS DH4 .... 170 B1 1
Stone Rw CLSW/PEL DH2 .... 150 C3
Stonesdale HLS DH4 .... 139 D6
Stone St FELL NE10 .... 100 B4
Stoneygate La FELL NE10 .... 83 D6
Stoneyhurst Av
        BW/LEM/TK/HW NE15 .... 78 A3 3
Stoneyhurst Rd GOS/KPK NE3 ...... 64 A2
Stoney La LWF/SPW/WRK NE9 ...... 119 E3
        SWCK/CAS SR5 .... 125 F3 10
Stoneylea Rd WD/WHPE/BLK NE5 .. 66 B6
Stony La STLY/ANP DH9 .... 133 F6
Store St BW/LEM/TK/HW NE15 ...... 76 B2 3
Storey La BLAY NE21 .... 75 F4 1
Stormont St NSHW NE29 .... 70 B1
Stotfold Cl SEA/MUR SR7 .... 175 D2
Stothard St JRW NE32 .... 86 B1
Stotts Rd BYK/HTN/WLK NE6 .... 66 C6
Stowell St CNUT NE1........................ 2 B4
The Stow LGB/KIL NE12 .... 64 C1
Straker St JRW NE32...................... 86 C2
Straker Ter HAR/WTLS NE34 .... 88 A3
The Strand SUNDSW SR3 .... 143 D6 6
Strangford Rd SEA/MUR SR7 .... 176 A3
Strangways St SEA/MUR SR7 .... 176 C4 7
Stranton Ter CLDN/WHIT/ROK SR6.. 126 C2
Stratfield St MLFD/PNYW SR4 ...... 125 D5 9
Stratford Av ASHBK/HED/RY SR2 ... 145 D3
Stratford Cl CRAM NE23................. 21 D1
        LGB/KIL NE12 .... 50 A1
Stratford Gdns
        LWF/SPW/WRK NE9 .... 99 E4 3
Stratford Gv West
        BYK/HTN/WLK NE6 .... 81 F1
Stratford Rd BYK/HTN/WLK NE6 .... 81 F1
Strathearn Wy ROWG NE39 .... 111 D3 1
Strathmore Av ROWG NE39 .... 111 D3 1
Strathmore Cl STLY/ANP DH9 .... 149 D1
Strathmore Crs ELS/FEN NE4 .... 79 D3
Strathmore Rd GOS/KPK NE3 .... 47 E5
        LWF/SPW/WRK NE9 .... 100 A3
        ROWG NE39.......................... 110 C3
        SUNDSW SR3 .... 143 D4
Strathmore Sq SUNDSW SR3 .... 143 D4 7
Stratton Cl ASHBK/HED/RY SR2 ..... 145 F6
Stratus Ct SUNDSW SR3 .... 160 C2
Strawberry Gdns WLSD/HOW NE28.. 66 C2
Strawberry La CNUT NE1................. 2 B2
Strawberry Pl CNUT NE1................. 2 B3
Street Gate Pk WICK/BNPF NE16 ... 114 B1
Stretton Cl HLS DH4 .... 169 F3 9
Stretton Wy SMOOR NE27 .... 37 E5
Stridingedge WASHN NE37 .... 119 F6
Stuart Ct GOS/KPK NE3 .... 45 D6
Stuart Gdns BW/LEM/TK/HW NE15 .. 57 E4
Stubbs Av WICK/BNPF NE16 .... 95 F2 5
Studdon Wk GOS/KPK NE3 .... 61 F1
Studley Gdns
        LWF/SPW/WRK NE9 .... 99 E5 5
        MONK NE25............................ 40 C6
Studley Ter ELS/FEN NE4................ 79 E1
Studley Vls LGB/KIL NE12 .... 50 A5 1
Sturdee Gdns JES NE2 .... 64 A3
Styford Gdns
        BW/LEM/TK/HW NE15 .... 77 D1 4
Success Rd HLS DH4 .... 157 D3
Sudbury Wy CRAM NE23................. 21 D1
Suddick St SWCK/CAS SR5 .... 126 A3 3
Suez St TYNE/NSHE NE30 .... 55 D6 4
Suffolk Gdns HAR/WTLS NE34......... 90 B1
        WLSD/HOW NE28 .... 68 A2
Suffolk Pl CLS/BIR/GTL DH3........... 136 C5
        GATE NE8 .... 81 F4
Suffolk Rd HEBB NE31 .... 85 E5
Suffolk St ASHBK/HED/RY SR2 .... 5 F6
        JRW NE32 .... 86 A2
Suffolk Wk PLEE/EAS SR8 .... 200 B6 3
Suffolk Wy DHAM DH1 .... 180 C4 3
Sugley Dr BW/LEM/TK/HW NE15 .... 76 C2
Sugley St BW/LEM/TK/HW NE15 .... 76 C2
Sulgrave Rd WASHN NE37 .... 121 E3
Sullivan Wk HEBB NE31 .... 85 D3
Summerfield STLY/ANP DH9 .... 150 C2
Summerfield Rd
        LWF/SPW/WRK NE9 .... 99 E3
Summerhill BLAY NE21 .... 76 A5
        JRW NE32 .... 104 C1
        SUNDSW SR3.......................... 159 D1
Summerhill Av HAR/WTLS NE34 ...... 47 F5
Summerhill Rd HAR/WTLS NE34 ..... 89 E1
Summerhill St ELS/FEN NE4 .... 80 A4

Summerhill Ter CNUT NE1................. 2 A5
Summerhouse Farm HLH DH5 ...... 170 C5 1
Summerson St HLH DH5 .... 172 A6
Summerson Wy BDLGTN NE22 .... 8 C2
Summer St FELL NE10 .... 100 C1
Summerville DHAM DH1 .... 194 A5
Sunbury Av JES NE2 .... 64 A4
Sunderland Av PLEE/EAS SR8 .... 201 E6
Sunderland Hwy WASHS NE38 ...... 119 E6
Sunderland Rd BOL NE36 .... 107 D3
        CLDN/WHIT/ROK SR6 .... 108 A2
        DHAM DH1 .... 195 E4
        FELL NE10 .... 101 E2
        FELL NE10 .... 102 C2 1
        GATE NE8............................... 81 E6
        HAR/WTLS NE34 .... 89 D1
        HLS DH4 .... 158 A5
        PLEE/EAS SR8 .... 200 A2
        SEA/MUR SR7 .... 190 A6
        SSH NE33.............................. 71 F6
        SWCK/CAS SR5 .... 125 F2
Sunderland St CNUT NE1................. 2 A5
        HLH DH5 .... 171 D1
        HLS DH4 .... 171 D3
Sundew Rd LWF/SPW/WRK NE9...... 100 B5
Sundridge Dr FELL NE10 .... 102 B3
Sunholme Dr WLSD/HOW NE28 ..... 66 C1
Sunlea Av TYNE/NSHE NE30 .... 55 E2
Sunnidale WICK/BNPF NE16 .... 95 D5
Sunnilaws HAR/WTLS NE34 .... 89 F4
Sunningdale SSH NE33 .... 72 A5 5
Sunningdale Av
        BYK/HTN/WLK NE6 .... 83 F2 4
        WLSD/HOW NE28 .... 67 E4 3
Sunningdale Cl FELL NE10............. 100 C3
Sunningdale Dr WASHN NE37 .... 120 B2 7
Sunningdale Rd SUNDSW SR3....... 142 C3
Sunrise HAR/WTLS NE34................ 89 F4
Sunside WLFD/PNYW SR4 .... 123 F6
        NSHW NE29 .... 69 F1
Sunniside Ct WICK/BNPF NE16 ..... 114 A2
Sunniside Dr HAR/WTLS NE34 .... 89 F4
Sunniside Gdns
        BW/LEM/TK/HW NE15 .... 78 A2 4
Sunniside La CLDN/WHIT/ROK SR6... 90 A6
Sunniside Rd WICK/BNPF NE16...... 96 A5
Sunniside Ter CLDN/WHIT/ROK SR6 .. 89 F6
Sunnybank Av
        BW/LEM/TK/HW NE15................ 78 C3
Sunny Blunts PLEE/EAS SR8 .... 208 B4
Sunnybrow SUNDSW SR3 .... 143 E6
Sunnycrest Av BYK/HTN/WLK NE6... 83 E2
Sunny Ter STLY/ANP DH9 .... 148 A1
Sunnyway WD/WHPE/BLK NE5 ...... 61 E4
Surrey Av WD/WHPE/BLK NE5 .... 60 C2
Surrey Pl ELS/FEN NE4................... 79 E3
Surrey Rd HEBB NE31.................... 85 E5
        NSHW NE29 .... 53 F6 7
Surrey St JRW NE32 .... 85 F2
Surtees Dr DHAM DH1.................. 193 F4
Surtees Rd PLEE/EAS SR8 .... 209 D2
Sussex Gdns WLSD/HOW NE28 ...... 68 A3
Sussex Pl WASHN NE37 .... 120 C3 3
Sussex St BLYTH NE24 .... 11 E4 8
        JRW NE32 .... 85 F2 2
Sutherland Av ELS/FEN NE4 .... 79 D1
Sutherland Ct HAR/WTLS NE34 ..... 88 C6 1
Sutherland Gra HLS DH4 .... 157 F2 1
Sutherland St
        CLDN/WHIT/ROK SR6 .... 126 C2
        GATE NE8 .... 99 E1 15
        SEA/MUR SR7 .... 176 A2
Sutton Cl HLS DH4 .... 156 C2
Sutton Ct WLSD/HOW NE28............ 66 B1
Sutton St BYK/HTN/WLK NE6 .... 66 A6
        DHAM DH1 .... 194 A4 1
Sutton Wy HAR/WTLS NE34............ 90 A3
Swainby Cl GOS/KPK NE3............... 47 F4
Swaledale CLDN/WHIT/ROK SR6 ... 109 E3
        WLSD/HOW NE28 .... 66 B1 3
Swaledale Av BLYTH NE24............... 9 F5
Swaledale Cl HLH DH5 .... 185 D3
Swaledale Crs HLS DH4 .... 139 F6
Swaledale Gdns LGB/HTN NE7 .... 65 E3
        MLFD/PNYW SR4 .... 143 E1 3
The Swallows WLSD/HOW NE28 ..... 52 A5
Swallow Tail Ct HAR/WTLS NE34 .... 88 A4 1
Swallow Tail Dr DUN/TMV NE11 .... 98 A3
Swalwell Bank WICK/BNPF NE16 .... 95 F1
Swan Av WLSD/HOW NE28............. 67 F3 3
Swan Dr DUN/TMV NE11 .... 97 F1 6
Swan Rd BYK/HTN/WLK NE6 .... 84 A4
        PLEE/EAS SR8 .... 207 E3
        WASHS NE38 .... 139 E3
Swan St GATE NE8 .... 81 E5 7
        STLY/ANP DH9 .... 146 A3
        SWCK/CAS SR5 .... 126 B3
Swanton Cl WD/WHPE/BLK NE5 ..... 61 D2
Swards Rd FELL NE10 .... 101 D3
Swarland Av LGB/HTN NE7 .... 65 D1
Swarland Rd MONK NE25 .... 24 C6
Swarth Cl WASHN NE37 .... 119 F6
Sweetbriar Wy BLYTH NE24 .... 16 B2
Sweethope Av BLYTH NE24 .... 10 C4 3
Swiftden Dr MLFD/PNYW SR4........ 141 F2

Swinbourne Gdns *WBAY* NE26 .... **40** B4
Swinbourne Ter *JRW* NE32 .... **86** A5
Swinburne Pl *GATE* NE8 .... **81** D5 ⑤
Swinburne St *GATE* NE8 .... **81** D5
  JRW NE32 .... **87** D2
Swinburn Rd *MONK* NE25 .... **24** C6
Swindale Dr *LGB/KIL* NE12 .... **49** E1
Swindon Rd *SUNDSW* SR3 .... **143** D3 ③
Swindon St *HEBB* NE31 .... **84** C2
Swindon Ter *BYK/IITN/WLK* NF6 ... **65** D5 ③
Swing Br *CNUT* NE1 .... **3** L5
Swinhoe Gdns *DIN/WO* NE13 .... **33** D3
Swinhope *WASHS* NE38 .... **137** F6
Swinley Gdns
  BW/LEM/TK/HW NE15......... **77** E2
Swinside Dr *DHAM* DH1 .... **196** B2
The Swirle *CNUT* NE1 .... **3** H4 ①
Sycamore Av *BLYTH* NE24 .... **10** C3
  DIN/WO NE13 .... **31** E3
  HAR/WTLS NE34 .... **89** E4
  MONK NE25 .... **40** B6
Sycamore Cl *JES* NE2 .... **64** B4 ⑤
Sycamore Dr *SWCK/CAS* SR5 .... **126** A1
Sycamore Gv *FELL* NE10 .... **101** D2
  LWF/SPW/WRK NE9 .... **119** E3
Sycamore Rd *BLAY* NE21 .... **76** B6
  CLDN/WHIT/ROK SR6 .... **109** C1
  CLSW/PEL DH2 .... **179** E1
The Sycamores
  ASHBK/HED/RY SR2 .... **145** D3
  WICK/BNPF NE16 .... **130** B1
Sycamore St
  BW/LEM/TK/HW NE15......... **57** F3
  WLSD/HOW NE28 .... **67** E5 ②
Sydenham Ter *MLFD/PNYW* SR4 ... **143** F1
  SSH NE33 .... **71** F3 ⑥
Sydney Gdns *HAR/WTLS* NE34 .... **87** E5
Sydney Gv *WLSD/HOW* NE28 .... **66** C1
Sydney St *HLS* DH4 .... **156** A6
  STLY/ANP DH9 .... **150** C1
Syke Rd *WICK/BNPF* NE16 .... **111** E6
Sylvia Ter *STLY/ANP* DH9 .... **131** E6
Symington Gdns *SUNDSW* SR3 ... **143** E6 ④
Syon St *TYNE/NSHE* NE30 .... **55** F4
Syron *WICK/BNPF* NE16 .... **95** E4
Syston Cl *HLS* DH4 .... **169** F3

Taberna Cl *BW/LEM/TK/HW* NE15 ... **56** A4
Tadcaster Rd *SUNDSW* SR3 .... **142** B5
Tadema Rd *SSH* NE33 .... **72** B4
Talbot Cl *WASHS* NE38 .... **138** C2
Talbot Gn *WD/WHPE/BLK* NE5 .... **60** B6
Talbot Pl *SEA/MUR* SR7 .... **176** C3
Talbot Rd *CLDN/WHIT/ROK* SR6 ... **127** D1
  HAR/WTLS NE34 .... **88** B2
Talgarth *WASHS* NE38 .... **140** A1
Talisman Cl *RDHAMSE* DH6 .... **197** E5
Talley Ct *WASHS* NE38 .... **138** B1
Tamar Cl *NSHW* NE29 .... **53** E4
  PLEE/EAS SR8 .... **208** B3
Tamar St *HLH* DH5 .... **186** B4
Tamerton Dr *CLS/BIR/GTL* DH3 ... **136** C4
Tamerton St *MLFD/PNYW* SR4 ... **125** E6 ⑦
Tamworth Rd *ELS/FEN* NE4......... **79** F2
Tamworth Sq *SUNDSW* SR3 .... **142** B5 ①
Tanfield Gdns *HAR/WTLS* NE34 ... **90** A2
Tanfield Pl *LWF/SPW/WRK* NE9......... **118** B2
Tanfield Rd *BW/LEM/TK/HW* NE15 ... **77** F2
  LWF/SPW/WRK NE9 .... **118** B2
  SUNDSW SR3 .... **142** C5
Tangier St *MLFD/PNYW* SR4 .... **125** D5 ⑧
Tangmere Cl *CRAM* NE23 .... **22** B1
Tankerville Pl *JES* NE2 .... **64** A3 ④
Tankerville Ter *JES* NE2 .... **64** A6
Tanmeads *CLSW/PEL* DH2 .... **165** E6
Tanners' Bank *TYNE/NSHE* NE30 ... **55** E6
Tantobie Rd *BW/LEM/TK/HW* NE15 ... **77** F2
Tarlton Crs *FELL* NE10 .... **100** B2 ⑤
Tarn Cl *PLEE/EAS* SR8 .... **209** D2 ③
Tarn Dr *ASHBK/HED/RY* SR2 .... **145** E6
Tarragon Wy *HAR/WTLS* NE34 .... **88** C5
Tarrington Cl *WLSD/HOW* NE28 ... **68** B1 ③
Tarset Rd *MONK* NE25 .... **39** D5
Tarset St *CNUT* NE1 .... **81** F3
Tasmania Rd *HAR/WTLS* NE34......... **87** E5
Tasman Rd *SUNDSW* SR3 .... **142** B6
Tate St *BLYTH* NE24 .... **11** E4 ⑨
Tatham St *SUND* SR1 .... **5** E3
Tatham Street Back *SUND* SR1......... **5** E3
Tattershall *ASHBK/HED/RY* SR2 ... **144** A2
Taunton Av *JRW* NE32 .... **87** D3
  NSHW NE29 .... **53** F4 ④
Taunton Cl *WLSD/HOW* NE28 .... **68** B1
Taunton Pl *CRAM* NE23 .... **14** A6
Taunton Rd *SUNDSW* SR3 .... **142** C5
Tavistock Cl *HLS* DH4 .... **157** E5 ④
Tavistock Pl *JRW* NE32 .... **86** C3
  SUND SR1 .... **4** D3
Tavistock Rd *JES* NE2 .... **64** A4

Tavistock Sq *SUNDSW* SR3......... **143** F6
Taylor Av *BDN/LAN/SAC* DH7 ... **192** A3
  DIN/WO NE13 .... **33** E4
  ROWG NE39 .... **111** E3
Taylor Gdns *WBAY* NE26......... **26** C2
Taylor St *BLYTH* NE24 .... **9** F4
  SSH NE33 .... **88** A1
  STLY/ANP DH9 .... **146** A3
Taynton Gv *CRAM* NE23 .... **23** E6 ③
Tay Rd *SUNDSW* SR3 .... **142** B4
Tay St *HLH* DH5 .... **186** B4
Teal Av *BLYTH* NE24 .... **17** E2
Teal Cl *WASHS* NE38......... **137** E3
Team St *GATE* NE8 .... **98** A1
Teasdale St *ASHBK/HED/RY* SR2 ... **5** G6 ②
Tebay Dr *WD/WHPE/BLK* NE5......... **60** B6
Teddington Cl *DIN/WO* NE13 .... **45** D5
Teddington Sq *SUNDSW* SR3 ... **142** B4 ②
Tedham Rd *BW/LEM/TK/HW* NE15 ... **76** B1
Tees Cl *PLEE/EAS* SR8 .... **208** B4
Tees Ct *HAR/WTLS* NE34 .... **88** B2
Tees Crs *STLY/ANP* DH9 .... **148** B3
Teesdale Av *HLS* DH4 .... **139** F6
Teesdale Gdns *LGB/HTN* NE7 .... **65** D3
Teesdale Gv *LGB/KIL* NE12 .... **49** E4 ⑨
Teesdale Pl *BLYTH* NE24 .... **9** E4
Tees Rd *HEBB* NE31......... **85** D5
Tees St *HLH* DH5 .... **186** C4 ③
  PLEE/EAS SR8 .... **209** F1
  SEA/MUR SR7 .... **176** C2
Teign Cl *PLEE/EAS* SR8 .... **208** B3
Teindland Cl *ELS/FEN* NE4 .... **79** D4
Tel-el-kebir Rd
  ASHBK/HED/RY SR2 .... **145** D2
Telford Cl *SMOOR* NE27 .... **37** E5
Telford Ct *WLSD/HOW* NE28 .... **69** E4
Telford Rd *SUNDSW* SR3 .... **142** C4
Telford St *GATE* NE8 .... **98** C3
  WLSD/HOW NE28 .... **69** E4
Tempest Rd *SEA/MUR* SR7......... **176** C3
Tempest St *BLAY* NE21 .... **75** F4 ②
  SUNDSW SR3 .... **160** C1 ③
Temple Gn *GATE* NE8 .... **98** B2 ③
  HAR/WTLS NE34 .... **89** D3
Temple Park Rd *HAR/WTLS* NE34 ... **88** C2
Temple St *CNUT* NE1 .... **2** B5
  FELL NE10 .... **100** C1
  SSH NE33 .... **88** A1
Temple St West *SSH* NE33 .... **71** D6 ③
Temple Town *SSH* NE33 .... **71** D6
Tenbury Crs *LGB/KIL* NE12 .... **49** E5
  NSHW NE29 .... **54** A3
Tenby Rd *SUNDSW* SR3 .... **142** B6 ②
Tenby Sq *CRAM* NE23 .... **14** B6 ②
Ten Flds *HLH* DH5 .... **185** E1
Tennant St *HAR/WTLS* NE34 .... **87** F4
Tennyson Av *BOLCOL* NE35......... **106** A2
  HEBB NE31 .... **85** E2 ①
Tennyson Crs *WICK/BNPF* NE16 ... **95** F2 ③
Tennyson Rd *CLSW/PEL* DH2......... **152** A5
  PLEE/EAS SR8 .... **200** C2 ②
Tennyson St *SWCK/CAS* SR5 .... **125** F2 ③
Tennyson Ter *NSHW* NE29 .... **71** D2 ①
Tenter Ter *DHAM* DH1 .... **194** B4
Tenth Av *BLYTH* NE24 .... **16** C1
  BYK/HTN/WLK NE6 .... **65** E6
  DUN/TMV NE11 .... **116** C2
Tenth Av West *DUN/TMV* NE11...... **116** B2
Tenth St *PLEE/EAS* SR8 .... **209** F1
Tern Cl *BLYTH* NE24 .... **17** E2
Terrace Pl *CNUT* NE1 .... **2** B2
Terrier Cl *BDLGTN* NE22 .... **8** B3
Territorial La *DHAM* DH1 .... **194** C5
Tetford Pl *LGB/KIL* NE12......... **49** E5
Teviot *WASHS* NE38......... **137** F5
Teviotdale Gdns *LGB/HTN* NE7 ...... **65** D3
Teviot St *GATE* NE8 .... **99** F2 ⑬
  HLH DH5 .... **186** B4 ①
Teviot Wy *JRW* NE32 .... **85** F3 ③
Tewkesbury *LGB/KIL* NE12 .... **35** F6 ⑩
Tewkesbury Rd
  BW/LEM/TK/HW NE15......... **76** D1
Thackeray Rd *SUNDSW* SR3......... **142** C4
Thames Av *JRW* NE32......... **86** B5
Thames Crs *HLS* DH4......... **169** F2
  STLY/ANP DH9 .... **148** B4
Thames Gdns *WLSD/HOW* NE28 ... **67** D5 ⑪
Thames Rd *HEBB* NE31 .... **85** E4
  PLEE/EAS SR8 .... **208** B3
  SUNDSW SR3 .... **142** B6 ③
Thames St *GATE* NE8 .... **99** F2
  HLH DH5 .... **186** B4
Thanet Rd *SUNDSW* SR3 .... **142** C5
Tharsis Rd *HEBB* NE31 .... **84** C3
Thatcher Cl *WICK/BNPF* NE16 .... **95** F5
Thelma St *MLFD/PNYW* SR4......... **126** A6
Theme Rd *SUNDSW* SR3 .... **142** B6
Theresa St *BLAY* NE21 .... **76** B5
Third Av *BLYTH* NE24 .... **10** C6
  BYK/HTN/WLK NE6 .... **82** B1
  CLSW/PEL DH2 .... **153** D1
  DUN/TMV NE11 .... **98** B5
  NSHW NE29 .... **69** D1
Third St *PLEE/EAS* SR8 .... **209** F1
Thirkeld Pl *HLS* DH4 .... **157** D1 ③

Thirlington Cl *WD/WHPE/BLK* NE5... **61** D3
Thirlmere *CLDN/WHIT/ROK* SR6 ... **107** F1
  CLS/BIR/GTL DH3 .... **137** D4
  FELL NE10 .... **101** F2 ③
Thirlmere Av *CLSW/PEL* DH2......... **166** A1
  HLH DH5 .... **186** B4
  TYNE/NSHE NE30 .... **54** C2
Thirlmere Cl *LGB/KIL* NE12 .... **50** B1
Thirlmere Ct *HEBB* NE31 .... **85** E4 ③
Thirlmere Crs *BLAY* NE21 .... **94** A2 ③
  HLS DH4 .... **157** D2
Thirlmere Rd *PLEE/EAS* SR8 .... **209** D1
Thirlmere Wy *BLYTH* NE24 .... **9** F3
  WD/WHPE/BLK NE5 .... **61** D5
Thirlmoor *WASHN* NE37 .... **119** F6
Thirlwell Gv *JRW* NE32 .... **85** F5
Thirlwell Rd *GATE* NE8 .... **81** F5 ①
Thirsk Rd *SUNDSW* SR3 .... **142** C4 ③
Thirston Dr *CRAM* NE23 .... **22** B2
Thirston Pl *NSHW* NE29 .... **53** F5 ④
Thistlecroft *HLH* DH5 .... **171** D3
Thistledon Av *WICK/BNPF* NE16 ... **95** E5
Thistle Rd *BDN/LAN/SAC* DH7 ... **204** B4
Thistle St *SUNDSW* SR3 .... **142** B5
Thistley Cl *BYK/HTN/WLK* NE6 ... **66** A6 ①
Thomas Hawksley Pk
  SUNDSW SR3......... **143** F3
Thomas St *ASHBK/HED/RY* SR2 ... **162** B2
  LWF/SPW/WRK NE9......... **118** C3
  PLEE/EAS SR8 .... **201** D1
  SSH NE33 .... **71** E3 ⑩
  STLY/ANP DH9 .... **149** F5
  WICK/BNPF NE16 .... **95** F3 ⑪
Thomas St North
  CLDN/WHIT/ROK SR6 .... **126** C4
Thomas St South
  ASHBK/HED/RY SR2 .... **162** B2
  SWCK/CAS SR5 .... **125** F3
Thompson Av *LGB/KIL* NE12 .... **35** E6 ⑫
Thompson Crs *SWCK/CAS* SR5 ... **124** A3 ③
Thompson Gdns
  WLSD/HOW NE28 .... **67** D4 ⑦
Thompson Pl *FELL* NE10 .... **100** C2 ⑦
Thompson Rd *SWCK/CAS* SR5 ...... **126** B2
Thompson St *BLYTH* NE24 .... **10** C4 ⑤
  BLYTH NE24 .... **11** D3 ⑪
  BLYTH NE24 .... **11** D3 ②
  HAR/WTLS NE34 .... **88** A3 ③
  PLEE/EAS SR8 .... **201** F6
Thorburn St
  CLDN/WHIT/ROK SR6 .... **108** C6 ⑦
Thornbank Cl *SUNDSW* SR3......... **160** C4 ⑤
Thornbridge *WASHS* NE38 .... **139** F1
Thornbury Av *CRAM* NE23......... **23** E6
Thornbury Cl *BOLCOL* NE35 .... **105** D3 ③
  DIN/WO NE13 .... **45** D6
Thornbury Dr *MONK* NE25......... **39** E4
Thornbury St *MLFD/PNYW* SR4 ... **125** F5
Thorncliffe Pl *NSHW* NE29 .... **70** A1 ③
Thorn Cl *DIN/WO* NE13 .... **32** C5 ③
Thorndale Pl *BLYTH* NE24 .... **9** F4 ③
Thorndale Rd
  BW/LEM/TK/HW NE15......... **77** E3
  DHAM DH1 .... **196** C3
  SUNDSW SR3......... **142** B5
Thorne Av *FELL* NE10 .... **102** A2
Thorne Brake *FELL* NE10 .... **101** F3 ①
Thorne Rd *SUNDSW* SR3 .... **142** B5 ②
Thornes Cl *PLEE/EAS* SR8 .... **209** E5 ③
Thorne Sq *SUNDSW* SR3......... **142** B5
Thorne Ter *BYK/HTN/WLK* NE6 ...... **83** D1
Thorneyburn Cl *HLS* DH4 .... **157** E6 ③
Thorneyburn Wy *BLYTH* NE24 ...... **10** B5 ②
Thorney Close Rd *SUNDSW* SR3 ... **142** C5
Thorneyford Pl *PONT/DH* NE20 ... **28** A3 ①
Thorneyholme Ter *STLY/ANP* DH9 ... **148** A2
Thornfield Gv
  ASHBK/HED/RY SR2 .... **145** D4 ①
Thornfield Pl *ROWG* NE39 .... **111** D1 ④
Thornfield Rd *GOS/KPK* NE3 .... **63** D2 ④
Thorngill *WASHN* NE37 .... **120** A6
Thornhaugh Av
  WICK/BNPF NE16 .... **95** E4 ①
Thornhill Cl *MONK* NE25......... **24** C6
Thornhill Gdns
  ASHBK/HED/RY SR2 .... **144** B2
Thornhill Pk *ASHBK/HED/RY* SR2 ... **4** A6
  PONT/DH NE20 .... **28** A3 ②
Thornhill Rd *LGB/KIL* NE12......... **49** F6
  PONT/DH NE20 .... **28** A3
  RDHAMSE DH6 .... **206** B2
Thornhill St *HLS* DH4 .... **170** C2
Thornhill Ter *ASHBK/HED/RY* SR2 ... **4** A5
Thornholme Av *HAR/WTLS* NE34 ... **90** A2
Thornholme Rd
  ASHBK/HED/RY SR2 .... **144** A1
Thornhope Cl *WASHS* NE38 .... **121** E6 ①
Thornlea Gdns *LWF/SPW/WRK* NE9 ... **99** E4
Thornleigh Gdns
  CLDN/WHIT/ROK SR6......... **89** F6
Thornleigh Rd *JES* NE2 .... **64** A3 ③
Thornley Av *CRAM* NE23 .... **22** B2
  FELL NE10 .... **102** A4 ①
Thornley Cl *BDN/LAN/SAC* DH7 ... **192** A5 ④

WICK/BNPF NE16 .... 95 F6
Thornley La *BLAY* NE21 .... 93 F4
ROWG NE39 .... 93 F6
Thornley Rd *WD/WHPE/BLK* NE5 .. 60 A5
Thornley Vw *ROWG* NE39 ...... 111 E2
Thornton Cl *HLS* DH4 .... 156 C1
Thornton Crs *BLAY* NE21 .... 76 B5
Thornton Lea *CLDN/WHIT/ROK* DH2 .. 151 F1
Thornton St *CNUT* NE1 .... 2 B5
Thorntree Av *DIN/WO* NE13 ...... 33 D1
Thorn Tree Dr *BDLGTN* NE22 ...... 7 E2
Thorntree Dr
  BW/LEM/TK/HW NE15 .... 77 F1
  MONK NE25 .... 39 D6
Thorntree Ter *STLY/ANP* DH9 .. 149 D1
Thorntree Wy *BLYTH* NE24 .... 9 E5
Thornwood Gdns *DUN/TMV* NE11 .. 98 A5
Thornygarth *FELL* NE10 .... 101 D3 ⑦
Thorp Cl *BLYTH* NE24 .... 16 A1 ⑩
Thorpe Cl *ELS/FEN* NE4 .... 79 F2
Thorpe Dr *RYTON* NE40 .... 74 C3
Thorpeness Rd *SWCK/CAS* SR5 .. 142 B5 ⑨
Thorpe Rd *PLEE/EAS* SR8 ...... 200 A3 ④
Thorpe St *PLEE/EAS* SR8 .... 201 D1
  PLEE/EAS SR8 .... 209 F1 ⑧
Threap Gdns *WLSD/HOW* NE28 .... 68 A2
Three Rivers Ct *BOL* NE36 ..... 105 F3 ⑧
Threlkeld Cv
  CLDN/WHIT/ROK SR6 .... 108 B5 ⑤
Thrift St *NSHW* NE29 .... 70 C2 ⑦
Thristley Gdns
  ASHBK/HED/RY SR2 .... 144 B3
Throckley Wy *HAR/WTLS* NE34 ... 88 A2
Thropton Av *BLYTH* NE24 .... 16 B1 ⑤
  LGB/HTN NE7 .... 65 D1
Thropton Cl *FELL* NE10 .... 102 B3
Thropton Ct *BLYTH* NE24 .... 10 B6 ⑧
Thropton Crs *GOS/KPK* NE3 ...... 47 D6
Thropton Pl *NSHW* NE29 .... 53 F5
Thropton Ter *LGB/HTN* NE7 ...... 65 D4
Thrush Gv *SWCK/CAS* SR5 ..... 124 B3 ⑦
Thursby Av *TYNE/NSHE* NE30 .... 55 D2
Thurso Cl *SUNDSW* SR3 .... 142 A5 ①
Tiberius Cl *WLSD/HOW* NE28 .... 67 D5
Tilbeck Sq *SWCK/CAS* SR5 .... 160 C2 ⑬
Tilbury Cl *HLS* DH4 .... 157 E3
Tilbury Gdns *SUNDSW* SR3 .... 142 B6 ④
Tilbury Gv *MONK* NE25 .... 54 C1
Tilbury Rd *SUNDSW* SR3 .... 142 B6
Tileshed La *BOL* NE36 .... 106 B1
Till Av *BLAY* NE21 .... 76 A6
Tilley Rd *WASHS* NE38 .... 137 E1
Tillmouth Av *MONK* NE25 .... 24 C6
Tillmouth Gdns *ELS/FEN* NE4 .. 78 B2
Tillmouth Park Rd
  BW/LEM/TK/HW NE15 .... 57 F5
Till St *BYK/HTN/WLK* NE6 ...... 82 B4
Tilson Wy *GOS/KPK* NE3 .... 46 B6 ⑤
Timber Beach Rd *SWCK/CAS* SR5 .. 124 C3
Timber Rd *PLEE/EAS* SR8 ...... 201 F5
Timlin Gdns *WLSD/HOW* NE28 .. 69 D3
Tindal Cl *ELS/FEN* NE4 .... 80 A3 ⑬
Tindale Av *CRAM* NE23 .... 22 B2
Tindale Dr *WICK/BNPF* NE16 .... 95 F4
Tindal St *ELS/FEN* NE4 .... 80 A3 ⑲
Tintagel Cl *CRAM* NE23 .... 14 A6
  SUNDSW SR3 .... 142 A5 ②
Tintagel Dr *SEA/MUR* SR7 ..... 176 B2
Tintern *WASHS* NE38 .... 138 B3
Tintern Cl *HLS* DH4 .... 157 E6
Tintern Crs *BYK/HTN/WLK* NE6 .. 82 A1
  NSHW NE29 .... 53 F4
Tintern St *MLFD/PNYW* SR4 ... 126 A6 ⑬
Tiree Cl *BDN/LAN/SAC* DH7 .... 203 E3
Tiree Ct *SUNDSW* SR3 .... 160 C2 ⑬
Tirril Pl *WD/WHPE/BLK* NE5 .... 60 C5
Titan Rd *BYK/HTN/WLK* NE6 .... 83 F2
Titchfield Rd *WASHS* NE38 .... 138 B2
Titian Av *HAR/WTLS* NE34 ...... 88 B6
Titlington Gv *HEBB* NE31 .... 84 C5
Tiverton Av *ELS/FEN* NE4 .... 79 D3
  NSHW NE29 .... 53 E4
Tiverton Cl *WLSD/HOW* NE28 ... 68 B1
Tiverton Gdns
  LWF/SPW/WRK NE9 .... 117 E1
Tiverton Pl *CRAM* NE23 .... 14 A6
Tiverton Sq *SUNDSW* SR3 ..... 142 B5
Toberty Gdns *FELL* NE10 ...... 102 A2
Toft Crs *SEA/MUR* SR7 .... 188 C1
Togstone Pl *WD/WHPE/BLK* NE5 .. 61 E5 ⑨
Toll *WLSD/HOW* NE28 .... 69 D5
Toll Bar Rd *ASHBK/HED/RY* SR2 .. 144 C5
Toll Bridge Rd *BLAY* NE21 ...... 77 E5
Tollerton Dr *SWCK/CAS* SR5 ... 123 E3
Tollgate Flds *HLS* DH4 .... 183 E3 ②
Toll House Rd *DHAM* DH1 ...... 193 E4
Tolls Cl *MONK* NE25 .... 39 E5
Toll Sq *TYNE/NSHE* NE30 .... 55 E6
Tomlea Av *BDLGTN* NE22 .... 8 C3
Tonbridge Av *NSHW* NE29 .... 70 A1
Toner Av *HEBB* NE31 .... 84 C5
Topaz St *SEA/MUR* SR7 .... 175 F3
Topcliff *CLDN/WHIT/ROK* SR6 .. 127 D4
Torcross Wy *CRAM* NE23 .... 14 A6

Toronto Rd *SUNDSW* SR3 ...... 142 C4
Toronto Sq *SUNDSW* SR3 ...... 142 C4
Torquay Gdns *LWF/SPW/WRK* NE9 .. 117 E1
Torquay Rd *SUNDSW* SR3 ...... 142 C4
Torrens Rd *SUNDSW* SR3 .... 142 C4
Torrington Cl *HLS* DH4 .... 157 E4 ⑥
Torver Cl *DIN/WO* NE13 .... 32 C5
Torver Crs *CLDN/WHIT/ROK* SR6 .. 108 B5
Torver Pl *LWF/SPW/WRK* NE9 .. 100 A6
Torver Wy *TYNE/NSHE* NE30 .... 54 B2
Tosson Pl *NSHW* NE29 .... 69 F1 ⑭
Tosson Ter *BYK/HTN/WLK* NE6 .. 65 E5 ④
Totnes Dr *CRAM* NE23 .... 14 A6
Toward Rd *ASHBK/HED/RY* SR2 .. 5 E5
  SUND SR1 .... 14 D4
Toward St *BYK/HTN/WLK* NE6 .. 82 A2 ⑩
Tower Gdns *RYTON* NE40 .... 74 B3
Tower Pl *ASHBK/HED/RY* SR2 .... 5 F6 ③
Tower Rd *STLY/ANP* DH9 .... 144 A1
  WASHN NE37 .... 121 D5
Towers Av *JES* NE2 .... 64 A3
Towers Cl *BDLGTN* NE22 .... 7 F4
Towers Pl *HAR/WTLS* NE34 ..... 87 D3
Tower St *ASHBK/HED/RY* SR2 .... 5 G6
  CNUT NE1 .... 3 F4
  PLEE/EAS SR8 .... 201 E1
Tower St West
  ASHBK/HED/RY SR2 .... 145 D2
The Towne Ga
  BW/LEM/TK/HW NE15 .... 56 A4
Townend Ct *HAR/WTLS* NE34 ... 88 B3
Townfield Gdns
  BW/LEM/TK/HW NE15 .... 58 B6
Townley Flds *ROWG* NE39 ..... 111 E2
Townley Rd *ROWG* NE39 .... 110 C2 ④
Townsend Rd *SUNDSW* SR3 ... 142 B6
Townsville Av *MONK* NE25 ...... 53 F1
Towton *LGB/KIL* NE12 .... 35 F6 ⑪
Toynbee *WASHS* NE38 .... 139 F1
Tracey Av *BOL* NE36 .... 106 A2
Trafalgar Rd *WASHN* NE37 .... 121 E3 ②
Trafalgar St *CNUT* NE1 .... 3 F3 ⑪
Trafford *LWF/SPW/WRK* NE9 .. 117 F2
Trafford Rd *SWCK/CAS* SR5 .. 125 F3
Trafford *WD/WHPE/BLK* NE5 .. 60 A3 ③
Trajan Av *SSH* NE33 .... 71 F2
Trajan St *SSH* NE33 .... 71 F2
Tranwell Cl *GOS/KPK* NE3 ...... 46 B4 ⑤
Tranwell Dr *MONK* NE25 .... 25 D6
Treby St *MLFD/PNYW* SR4 .... 125 F5
Tredegar Cl
  WD/WHPE/BLK NE5 .... 61 D2 ⑬
Treecone Cl *SUNDSW* SR3 ..... 160 C3
Treen Crs *SEA/MUR* SR7 .... 188 C1 ⑪
Trefoil Rd *STLY/ANP* DH9 ...... 130 C6
Tregoney Av *SEA/MUR* SR7 .... 188 C1
Treherne Rd *JES* NE2 .... 63 F3 ③
Trent Av *HEBB* NE31 .... 85 D5
Trent Dr *JRW* NE32 .... 86 B6
Trent Gdns *GATE* NE8 .... 100 A2 ⑥
Trentham Av *LGB/HTN* NE7 ..... 65 D1
Trenton Av *WASHS* NE38 ..... 120 C6 ⑬
Trent Rd *SUNDSW* SR3 .... 142 B5
Trent St *HLH* DH5 .... 186 B4
Trevarren Dr *ASHBK/HED/RY* SR2 .. 145 E6
Trevelyan Av *BDLGTN* NE22 ..... 8 A3
  BLYTH NE24 .... 10 B6
Trevelyan Cl *SUNDSW* SR3 ... 142 A5 ③
Trevelyan Dr *WD/WHPE/BLK* NE5 .. 60 C3
Trevethick St *GATE* NE8 .... 98 C2
Trevone Pl *CRAM* NE23 .... 23 F6
Trevone Sq *SEA/MUR* SR7 .... 188 C1
Trevor Gv *CLDN/WHIT/ROK* SR6 .. 107 F2
Trevor Ter *TYNE/NSHE* NE30 ... 54 C5
Trewhitt Rd *BYK/HTN/WLK* NE6 .. 65 E6 ③
Tribune Pl *LWF/SPW/WRK* NE9 .. 100 A4
Trident Av *SUNDSW* SR3 ...... 160 C1
Trimdon St *MLFD/PNYW* SR4 .. 126 A5
Trinity Ctyd *BYK/HTN/WLK* NE6 .. 82 C4 ④
Trinity Crt *CRAM* NE23 .... 23 F6
Trinity Pk *HLS* DH4 .... 157 D3
Trinity Pl *NSHW* NE29 .... 70 C2 ③
Trinity St *NSHW* NE29 .... 70 C2
  SWCK/CAS SR5 .... 125 E2
Trinity Wk *SSH* NE33 .... 71 D5
Trojan Av *BYK/HTN/WLK* NE6 .. 83 D1
Tromso Cl *NSHW* NE29 .... 69 D1
Trool Ct *SUNDSW* SR3 .... 160 C3
Troon Cl *WASHN* NE37 .... 120 B2 ⑧
Trotter Gv *BDLGTN* NE22 .... 8 B3 ③
Trotter Ter *ASHBK/HED/RY* SR2 .. 162 B2
Troutbeck Av *BYK/HTN/WLK* NE6 .. 83 E3 ④
Troutbeck Rd
  CLDN/WHIT/ROK SR6 .... 108 B5 ⑦
Troutbeck Wy *HAR/WTLS* NE34 .. 87 E5
  PLEE/EAS SR8 .... 209 D1 ④
Troutdale Pl *LGB/KIL* NE12 .... 48 B6 ④
Trout's La *DHAM* DH1 .... 178 C5
Trowbridge Wy *GOS/KPK* NE3 .. 62 B1
Truro Av *SEA/MUR* SR7 .... 174 C6
Truro Gv *NSHW* NE29 .... 53 F4
Truro Rd *SUNDSW* SR3 .... 142 C5 ①
Tuart St *CLS/BIR/GTL* DH3 .... 153 E5
Tudor Av *NSHW* NE29 .... 54 A6
Tudor Ct *RDHAMSE* DH6 .... 206 C2

Tudor Dr *STLY/ANP* DH9 ...... 130 C3 ①
Tudor Gra *PLEE/EAS* SR8 ..... 199 F3
Tudor Gv *SUNDSW* SR3 .... 143 E3
Tudor Rd *CLS/BIR/GTL* DH3 ... 153 F3
  SSH NE33 .... 71 E4
Tudor Wy *GOS/KPK* NE3 .... 45 E6
  WD/WHPE/BLK NE5 .... 61 D1
Tudor Wynd *BYK/HTN/WLK* NE6 .. 65 F5
Tulip St *GATE* NE8 .... 100 A1
Tumulus Av *BYK/HTN/WLK* NE6 .. 66 C6
Tunbridge Rd *SUNDSW* SR3 .. 142 C4
Tundry Wy *BLAY* NE21 .... 77 E4
Tuneside *FELL* NE10 .... 102 A3
Tunis Rd *SUNDSW* SR3 .... 143 D4 ③
Tunstall Av *BYK/HTN/WLK* NE6 .. 82 C2 ③
  HAR/WTLS NE34 .... 90 A2
Tunstall Bank *SUNDSW* SR3 .. 161 E1
Tunstall Hill Cl
  ASHBK/HED/RY SR2 .... 144 B4 ⑦
Tunstall Pk *ASHBK/HED/RY* SR2 .. 144 B2
Tunstall Rd *ASHBK/HED/RY* SR2 .. 144 B4
  ASHBK/HED/RY SR2 .... 144 B4
  SUNDSW SR3 .... 144 A5
Tunstall Ter *ASHBK/HED/RY* SR2 .. 4 B4
Tunstall Ter West
  ASHBK/HED/RY SR2 .... 4 A4
Tunstall V *ASHBK/HED/RY* SR2 .. 144 B2
Tunstall Vw *SUNDSW* SR3 .... 144 A6
Tunstall Village Gn *SUNDSW* SR3 .. 161 D1
Tunstall Village Rd *SUNDSW* SR3 .. 161 D1
Tunstall Vis *SUNDSW* SR3 .... 161 D1 ③
Turbinia Gdns *LGB/HTN* NE7 .. 65 E4
Turnberry *CLSW/PEL* DH2 .... 135 E4
  MONK NE25 .... 39 E5
  SSH NE33 .... 72 A5 ⑨
Turnberry Cl *WASHN* NE37 ... 120 B2 ③
Turnberry Wy *GOS/KPK* NE3 ... 48 A6 ①
Turner Av *HAR/WTLS* NE34 ..... 88 C5
Turner Cl *RYTON* NE40 .... 74 C4
Turner Crs *GOS/KPK* NE3 ...... 62 C1 ⑨
Turner St *SMOOR* NE27 .... 52 A3
Turnham Rd *SUNDSW* SR3 .... 142 B5
Turnstone Dr *WASHS* NE38 ... 137 E3
Turret Rd *BW/LEM/TK/HW* NE15 .. 77 E1
Tuscan Cl *BDN/LAN/SAC* DH7 .. 202 A1
Tuscan Rd *SUNDSW* SR3 ...... 142 B5
Tweed Cl *ASHBK/HED/RY* SR2 .. 145 E6
  CLSW/PEL DH2 .... 135 E6
  PLEE/EAS SR8 .... 208 B3
Tweed Gv *BW/LEM/TK/HW* NE15 .. 76 B1
Tweed St *ELS/FEN* NE4 .... 79 C5
  HEBB NE31 .... 84 C2
  HLH DH5 .... 186 B4 ②
  JRW NE32 .... 85 F3
  WASHS NE38 .... 139 D2
Tweed Ter *STLY/ANP* DH9 ..... 148 B3
Tweedy St *BLYTH* NE24 .... 9 F4 ④
Tweedy Ter *BYK/HTN/WLK* NE6 .. 83 E3 ④
Twelfth Av *BLYTH* NE24 .... 10 C6
  CLSW/PEL DH2 .... 153 D4
Twelfth St *PLEE/EAS* SR8 .... 209 E1 ④
Twentieth Av *BLYTH* NE24 .... 16 C1 ⑤
Twentyfifth Av *BLYTH* NE24 .. 16 C1 ⑥
Twentysecond Av *BLYTH* NE24 .. 16 B1 ⑤
Twentysixth Av *BLYTH* NE24 ... 16 B1
Twentythird Av *BLYTH* NE24 ... 16 B1
Twickenham Ct *CRAM* NE23 .... 23 E6
Twickenham Rd *SUNDSW* SR3 .. 142 B4
Twizell La *STLY/ANP* DH9 .... 150 A3
Twizell Pl *PONT/DH* NE20 ...... 28 A3
Twizell St *BLYTH* NE24 .... 11 E6 ③
Twyford Cl *CRAM* NE23 .... 14 A6
Tyldesley Sq *SUNDSW* SR3 .. 142 B5 ⑤
Tyne Ap *JRW* NE32 .... 68 C6
Tynebank *BLAY* NE21 .... 76 A6
Tyne Br *CNUT* NE1 .... 3 F5
Tynedale Av *WBAY* NE26 .... 40 B4
  WLSD/HOW NE28 .... 67 D1
Tynedale Crs *HLS* DH4 .... 157 D1
Tynedale Dr *BLYTH* NE24 .... 9 F5
Tynedale Rd *HAR/WTLS* NE34 .. 72 A6
Tynedale St *HLH* DH5 .... 185 D3
Tynedale Ter *LGB/KIL* NE12 ... 49 F6 ⑦
Tyne Gdns *WASHN* NE37 .... 120 C3
Tyne Main Rd *FELL* NE10 ...... 82 B5
Tynemouth Rd *BYK/HTN/WLK* NE6 .. 82 A2
  JRW NE32 .... 85 F6
  TYNE/NSHE NE30 .... 55 E6
  WLSD/HOW NE28 .... 68 B4
  WLSD/HOW NE28 .... 69 D3 ④
Tynemouth Sq *SUNDSW* SR3 .. 142 C5 ②
Tynemouth Ter
  TYNE/NSHE NE30 .... 55 F5 ③
Tyne Rd *STLY/ANP* DH9 .... 148 A3
Tyne Rd East *GATE* NE8 .... 80 B6
  STLY/ANP DH9 .... 148 A3
Tyneside Rd *ELS/FEN* NE4 ..... 80 A5 ⑨
Tyne St *BLAY* NE21 .... 76 B4
  CNUT NE1 .... 81 F3
  FELL NE10 .... 83 E6
  HLH DH5 .... 186 B4
  JRW NE32 .... 69 D6
  SEA/MUR SR7 .... 176 C3 ⑬
  TYNE/NSHE NE30 .... 71 D1
Tyne Ter *HAR/WTLS* NE34 ..... 88 C3

Tynevale Av *BLAY* NE21 .... **94** A1
Tyne Vw *BW/LEM/TK/HW* NE15 .... **76** B2
  HEBB NE31 .... **84** B2
Tyne View Av *WICK/BNPF* NE16 ...... **96** B2
Tyne View Ter *WLSD/HOW* NE28...... **69** D5
Tyne-Wear Trail *DUN/TMV* NE11...... **96** C1
  WICK/BNPF NE16 .... **96** C5

U

Ugly La *CLSW/PEL* DH2.................... **165** E6
Uldale Ct *GOS/KPK* NE3 .... **46** A5 🟦
Ullerdale Cl *DHAM* DH1.................... **197** D2
Ullswater Av *HLH* DH5 .... **186** B4
  JRW NE32 .... **86** C5
Ullswater Cl *BLYTH* NE24 .... **9** D4
Ullswater Crs *BLAY* NE21 .... **94** A2 🟦
Ullswater Dr *LGB/KIL* NE12 .... **50** B1
Ullswater Gdns *HAR/WTLS* NE34 ...... **88** C1
Ullswater Gv *SWCK/CAS* SR5 .... **108** B6 🟦
Ullswater Rd *CLSW/PEL* DH2............ **166** A1
Ulverstone Ter *BYK/HTN/WLK* NE5 .... **61** D5
Ulwater Wy *WD/WHPE/BLK* NE5 ...... **83** D1
Ulverston Gdns
  LWF/SPW/WRK NE9.......................... **118** A1
Underhill Rd *CLDN/WHIT/ROK* SR6... **107** E2
Underwood Gv *CRAM* NE23 .... **13** F5
Union Aly *SSH* NE33 .... **71** E3
Union Hall Rd
  BW/LEM/TK/HW NE15 .... **59** E6
Union La *CLSW/PEL* DH2...................... **5** E1
  SUND SR1 .... **5** F1 🟦
Union Quay *TYNE/NSHE* NE30.......... **71** E1
Union Rd *BYK/HTN/WLK* NE6 .... **82** B2
  TYNE/NSHE NE30 .... **55** E6
Union St *BLYTH* NE24 .... **11** D4
  HLH DH5 .... **171** F6
  JES NE2 .... **3** H2
  JRW NE32 .... **69** D6
  MLFD/PNYW SR4 .... **123** F6 🟦
  NSHW NE29 .... **71** D1
  SEA/MUR SR7 .... **176** C2 🟦
  SSH NE33 .... **88** A2 🟦
  SUND SR1 .... **4** C2
  WLSD/HOW NE28 .... **67** D6
Unity Ter *STLY/ANP* DH9.................. **130** A4
  STLY/ANP DH9 .... **146** A1
Uplands *MONK* NE25 .... **39** F5
The Uplands *CLS/BIR/GTL* DH3 .... **136** C1
  GOS/KPK NE3 .... **62** B2
Uplands Wy *LWF/SPW/WRK* NE9 .... **119** E3
Upper Camden St
  TYNE/NSHE NE30 .... **54** C6 🟦
Upper Elsdon St *NSHW* NE29 .... **70** C2 🟦
Upper Norfolk St
  TYNE/NSHE NE30 .... **55** D6 🟦
Upper Pearson St
  TYNE/NSHE NE30 .... **55** D6 🟦
Upper Queen St *TYNE/NSHE* NE30... **55** D6
Upton St *GATE* NE8 .... **98** B1 🟦
Urswick Ct *SWCK/CAS* SR5 .... **61** D1
Urwin St *HLH* DH5 .... **186** A1
Usher Av *ROHAMSE* DH6 .... **197** E4
Usher St *SWCK/CAS* SR5 .... **126** A3 🟦
Usk Av *JRW* NE32 .... **86** B5
Usworth Station Rd
  WASHN NE37 .... **121** D4 🟦

V

Valebrooke Av
  ASHBK/HED/RY SR2 .... **144** B2
Valebrooke Gdns
  ASHBK/HED/RY SR2 .... **144** B2
Valehead *MONK* NE25 .... **39** F5
Valentia Av *BYK/HTN/WLK* NE6........ **83** D1
Valeria Cl *WLSD/HOW* NE28 .... **51** F6
Valerian Av *BW/LEM/TK/HW* NE15.... **56** B4
Valeside *BW/LEM/TK/HW* NE15 .... **57** E4
Vale St *HLH* DH5 .... **186** A1
  MLFD/PNYW SR4 .... **144** A1 🟦🟦
Vale Wk *JES* NE2 .... **71** F1
Valley Crs *BLAY* NE21 .... **75** F1
Valley Dr *LWF/SPW/WRK* NE9 .... **99** F3
  WICK/BNPF NE16 .... **95** F2
Valley Forge *WASHS* NE38 .... **120** C6
Valley Gdns *LWF/SPW/WRK* NE9...... **99** F3
  MONK NE25 .... **39** F5
  WLSD/HOW NE28 .... **67** F3
Valley La *HAR/WTLS* NE34 .... **90** B2
Valley Rd *CLSW/PEL* DH2 .... **152** A4
  MONK NE25 .... **25** E6
Valley Vw *BDN/LAN/SAC* DH7 .... **178** A2
  BDN/LAN/SAC DH7 .... **192** A5
  BW/LEM/TK/HW NE15...................... **76** B1
  CLS/BIR/GTL DH3 .... **118** A5
  JES NE2 .... **64** B5
  JRW NE32 .... **86** A4
  ROWG NE39.. **110** C2

WASHS NE38 .... **139** D5
WICK/BNPF NE16 .... **111** E5
Vallum Rd *BW/LEM/TK/HW* NE15.... **58** A4
  BYK/HTN/WLK NE6 .... **83** D2
Vanborough Ct *MONK* NE25 .... **24** C6 🟦
Vancouver Dr *LGB/HTN* NE7 .... **65** F4
Vane St *PLEE/EAS* SR8 .... **201** D2
  SUNDSW SR3 .... **160** C1 🟦
Vane Ter *ASHBK/HED/RY* SR2 .... **5** H5
  SEA/MUR SR7 .... **176** C2 🟦
Van Mildert Cl *PLEE/EAS* SR8 .... **208** A4 🟦
Vardy Ter *HLS* DH4............................ **158** A1
Vauxhall Rd *BYK/HTN/WLK* NE6 ...... **66** C6
Vedra St *SWCK/CAS* SR5 .... **126** A3 🟦
Velville Ct *WD/WHPE/BLK* NE5 .... **45** D6
Ventnor Av *ELS/FEN* NE4 .... **79** E3
Ventnor Crs *LWF/SPW/WRK* NE9 ...... **99** D4
Ventnor Gdns *LWF/SPW/WRK* NE9 .... **99** D4
  WBAY NE26.. **40** C4
Verdun Av *HEBB* NE31 .... **85** D2
Vermont *WASHN* NE37 .... **120** C4
Verne Rd *NSHW* NE29 .... **69** F1
Vernon Cl *SSH* NE33 .... **71** D6
Vernon Dr *MONK* NE25...................... **40** A6
Vernon St *WASHN* NE37 .... **120** C4
Veryan Gdns *SUNDSW* SR3 .... **144** A3
Vespasian Av *SSH* NE33 .... **71** F2
Viador *CLS/BIR/GTL* DH3 .... **153** E4
Viaduct St *WLSD/HOW* NE28 .... **68** A4
Vicarage Ct *CLSW/PEL* DH2 .... **152** A1 🟦
  SUNDSW SR3 .... **160** B1
Vicarage Flats
  BDN/LAN/SAC DH7 .... **203** D4 🟦
Vicarage La *MLFD/PNYW* SR4 .... **123** F6 🟦
Vicarage Rd *SUNDSW* SR3 .... **160** C1
Vicarage St *NSHW* NE29 .... **70** C1
Vicarsholme Cl *SUNDSW* SR3.......... **160** A3
Vicars' La *LGB/HTN* NE7 .... **64** C1
Vicars Wy *LGB/KIL* NE12 .... **48** B6
Viceroy St *SEA/MUR* SR7 .... **176** C3
Victoria Av *ASHBK/HED/RY* SR2 ...... **145** D4
  BDN/LAN/SAC DH7 .... **203** E4
  FELL NE10 .... **100** B2
  LGB/KIL NE12 .... **49** F5
  MLFD/PNYW SR4 .... **124** A6
  WLSD/HOW NE28 .... **67** D4 🟦
Victoria Av West
  ASHBK/HED/RY SR2 .... **145** D4
Victoria Crs *NSHW* NE29.................... **70** A3
Victoria Ms *BLYTH* NE24 .... **10** C6
Victoria Rd *GATE* NE8 .... **98** B2
  SSH NE33 .... **71** E5
  WASHN NE37...................................... **120** C4
Victoria Rd East *HEBB* NE31 .... **85** E2
Victoria Rd West *FELL* NE10 .... **84** B6
  HEBB NE31 .... **84** B6
Victoria St *DUN/TMV* NE11 .... **97** F1
  ELS/FEN NE4 .... **80** A4 🟦
  HLH DH5 .... **171** F6 🟦
  NSHW NE29 .... **70** C2
  RDHAMSE DH6 .... **206** C2
  SEA/MUR SR7 .... **176** B3
Victoria Ter *JRW* NE32 .... **85** F2
  WBAY NE26.. **41** D5
Victor St *CLS/BIR/GTL* DH3.............. **153** E5
Victory St East *HLH* DH5 .... **172** A6 🟦
Victory St West *HLH* DH5 .... **172** A6 🟦
Victory Wy *SUNDSW* SR3 .... **159** E3
Viewforth Dr *SWCK/CAS* SR5............ **126** B1
Viewforth Rd *ASHBK/HED/RY* SR2 .. **162** B3
Viewforth Ter *SWCK/CAS* SR5 .... **126** A1
View La *STLY/ANP* DH9...................... **148** B1
View Pk *MONK* NE25............................ **24** C5
Vigo La *CLS/BIR/GTL* DH3................ **136** C5
  CLS/BIR/GTL DH3 .... **154** A2
  WASHS NE38...................................... **137** E6
Village Centre *WASHS* NE38 .... **138** C2 🟦
Village Ct *WBAY* NE26.......................... **40** B5
Village East *RYTON* NE40 .... **74** B2
Village Farm
  BW/LEM/TK/HW NE15 .... **58** C5 🟦
Village La *WASHS* NE38 .... **120** A5
Village Rd *CRAM* NE23 .... **22** B2
The Village *ASHBK/HED/RY* SR2 .... **162** C2
Villa Pl *GATE* NE8 .... **99** D1 🟦
Villa Vw *LWF/SPW/WRK* NE9 .... **99** F4 🟦
Villette Brook St
  ASHBK/HED/RY SR2 .... **145** D2 🟦
Villette Pth *ASHBK/HED/RY* SR2 .... **145** D2
Villette Rd *ASHBK/HED/RY* SR2 ...... **145** D2
Villiers St *SUND* SR1 .... **5** E2
Villiers St South *SUND* SR1 .... **5** E5
Vimy Av *HEBB* NE31 .... **85** D2
Vincent St *PLEE/EAS* SR8 .... **201** D2 🟦
  SEA/MUR SR7 .... **176** C4 🟦
Vine La *CNUT* NE1 .... **2** D1
Vine Pl *HLS* DH4 .... **171** D2
  SUND SR1 .... **4** B4
Vine St *SSH* NE33 .... **88** B2
  WLSD/HOW NE28 .... **67** E5
Viola Crs *BDN/LAN/SAC* DH7 .... **178** B2
  CLSW/PEL DH2 .... **135** E4
Viola St *WASHN* NE37 .... **120** C4
Violet Cl *ELS/FEN* NE4 .... **78** C4 🟦

Violet St *HLS* DH4 .... **170** C2
  MLFD/PNYW SR4 .... **123** F6
  MLFD/PNYW SR4 .... **126** A5
Viscount Rd *SUNDSW* SR3 .... **160** C1 🟦
Vivian Crs *CLSW/PEL* DH2 .... **153** E6
Vivian Sq *CLDN/WHIT/ROK* SR6 .... **126** C1 🟦
Voltage Ter *HLS* DH4 .... **157** F4 🟦
Vulcan Pl *BDLGTN* NE22 .... **7** F4

W

Waddington St *DHAM* DH1 .... **194** A4
Wadsley Sq *ASHBK/HED/RY* SR2.... **145** D3
Wagon Wy *WLSD/HOW* NE28 .... **67** F4
Wagonway Rd *HEBB* NE31 .... **84** C1
Wagtail La *STLY/ANP* DH9 .... **149** E6
Wagtail Ter *STLY/ANP* DH9.............. **149** E6
Wakefield Av *HAR/WTLS* NE34 .... **90** A3
Wakenshaw Rd *DHAM* DH1 .... **195** E3
Walbottle Rd
  BW/LEM/TK/HW NE15...................... **58** B5
Walden Cl *CLSW/PEL* DH2................ **134** C5
Waldo St *NSHW* NE29 .... **70** C1
Waldridge La *CLSW/PEL* DH2 .... **152** C6
Waldridge Rd *CLSW/PEL* DH2 .... **153** D6
Waldron Sq *ASHBK/HED/RY* SR2.... **145** D3
Walkerburn *CRAM* NE23 .... **22** A5
Walkergate *DHAM* DH1 .... **194** B4 🟦
Walker Pl *TYNE/NSHE* NE30 .... **55** E6 🟦
Walker Rd *BYK/HTN/WLK* NE6 .... **82** A4
Wallace Av *WICK/BNPF* NE16 .... **96** B2
Wallace Gdns *LWF/SPW/WRK* NE9 .. **101** D2
Wallace St *DUN/TMV* NE11 .... **97** F1 🟦
  HLS DH4.. **170** C2
  JES NE2 .... **80** A1
  SWCK/CAS SR5 .... **126** B3
Wallingford Av
  ASHBK/HED/RY SR2 .... **145** D4
Wallington Av *DIN/WO* NE13.............. **32** C4
  TYNE/NSHE NE30 .... **54** C3
Wallington Cl *BDLGTN* NE22 .... **8** B2
Wallington Ct *MONK* NE25 .... **24** C5 🟦
Wallington Dr
  BW/LEM/TK/HW NE15...................... **60** A6
Wallis St *HLS* DH4 .... **140** A6 🟦
  SSH NE33 .... **71** D3 🟦
Wallridge Dr *MONK* NE25.................. **38** A1
Wallsend Rd *NSHW* NE29 .... **69** E3
  WLSD/HOW NE28 .... **69** E3
Wall St *GOS/KPK* NE3 .... **62** C1
Wall Ter *BYK/HTN/WLK* NE6.............. **83** D1
Walnut Gdns *GATE* NE8 .... **98** B2 🟦
Walnut Pl *GOS/KPK* NE3 .... **62** B3
Walpole Cl *SEA/MUR* SR7 .... **175** E4
Walpole St *MLFD/PNYW* SR4 .... **125** E6 🟦
Walpole St *BYK/HTN/WLK* NE6 .... **66** A6 🟦
Walsham Cl *BLYTH* NE24 .... **16** A1
Walsh Av *HEBB* NE31 .... **85** D1
Walsingham *WASHS* NE38 .... **138** B3
Walter St *JRW* NE32 .... **69** D6
Walter Ter *ELS/FEN* NE4 .... **79** F2
  HLH DH5 .... **186** A3
Walter Thomas St
  SWCK/CAS SR5 .... **125** E2 🟦
Waltham *WASHS* NE38 .... **138** C2
Waltham Cl *WLSD/HOW* NE28 .... **66** B3 🟦
Waltham Pl *WD/WHPE/BLK* NE5 ...... **61** D4 🟦
Walton Av *BLYTH* NE24...................... **10** B4
  NSHW NE29 .... **54** B5
  SEA/MUR SR7 .... **175** E4
Walton Cl *STLY/ANP* DH9 .... **148** C3
Walton La *SUND* SR1 .... **5** F1
Walton Pk *NSHW* NE29 .... **54** B4
Walton Rd *WASHS* NE38 .... **140** A1
  WD/WHPE/BLK NE5.......................... **60** C5
Walworth Av *HAR/WTLS* NE34 .... **90** B2
Walworth Gv *JRW* NE32 .... **86** A5
Wandsworth Rd
  BYK/HTN/WLK NE6 .... **82** A1
Wanebeck *WASHS* NE38 .... **137** F5
Wanless Ter *DHAM* DH1 .... **194** C4
Wanley St *BLYTH* NE24...................... **11** D4
Wanlock Cl *CRAM* NE23 .... **22** A5
Wanny Rd *BDLGTN* NE22 .... **8** A3 🟦
Wansbeck Av *BLYTH* NE24................ **11** D6
  STLY/ANP DH9 .... **148** B3
  TYNE/NSHE NE30 .... **55** E1
Wansbeck Cl *CLSW/PEL* DH2 .... **135** E6
  WICK/BNPF NE16 .... **113** F1
Wansbeck Gv *MONK* NE25 .... **24** C2 🟦
Wansbeck Rd *CRAM* NE23 .... **34** B2
  JRW NE32 .... **86** B3
Wansbeck Rd North
  GOS/KPK NE3 .... **46** C5 🟦
Wansbeck Rd South
  GOS/KPK NE3 .... **46** C6 🟦
Wansfell Av *WD/WHPE/BLK* NE5 ...... **61** F3
Wansford Av *WD/WHPE/BLK* NE5 .... **61** D5
Wantage Av *NSHW* NE29 .... **69** F2
Wantage Rd *DHAM* DH1.................... **196** C1
Wantage St *SSH* NE33 .... **88** C1

Wapping St *SSH* NE33 .... 71 D2
Warbeck Cl *WD/WHPE/BLK* NE5 .... 45 D6
Warburton Crs
  LWF/SPW/WRK NE9 .... 99 F2 14
Warcop Ct *GOS/KPK* NE3 .... 46 A5
Warden Law La *SUNDSW* SR3 ...... 160 A2
Wardill Gdns *LWF/SPW/WRK* NE9.... 100 A3
Wardle Av *SSH* NE33 .... 72 A5
Wardle Dr *CRAM* NE23 .... 35 D2
Wardle Gdns *FELL* NE10 .... 101 D3
Wardle St *GOS/KPK* NE3 .... 64 A1 8
  STLY/ANP DH9 .... 148 A5
Wardley Ct *FELL* NE10 .... 102 C2
Wardley Dr *FELL* NE10 .... 102 C2
Wardley La *FELL* NE10 .... 102 B1
Warenford Cl *CRAM* NE23 .... 22 B4 3
Warenford Pl
  WD/WHPE/BLK NE5 .... 78 B1 3
Warenmill Cl
  BW/LEM/TK/HW NE15 .... 76 A1
Warennes St *MLFD/PNYW* SR4 .... 125 D5 7
Warenton Pl *NSHW* NE29 .... 53 D3
Waring Av *WBAY* NE26 .... 26 A1
Waring Ter *SEA/MUR* SR7 .... 175 E4
Wark Av *NSHW* NE29 .... 53 E6
  SMOOR NE27 .... 38 B6
Wark Crs *JRW* NE32 .... 86 A6
Warkdale Av *BLYTH* NE24 .... 9 F6 2
Warkworth Av *BLYTH* NE24 .... 17 D1
  HAR/WTLS NE34 .... 90 A1
  WLSD/HOW NE28 .... 67 E2
Warkworth Cl *WASHS* NE38 .... 138 A2
Warkworth Crs *GOS/KPK* NE3 ..... 47 D6
  SEA/MUR SR7 .... 175 D3
Warkworth Dr *CLSW/PEL* DH2 .... 165 F2
  DIN/WO NE13 .... 33 E3
Warkworth Gdns *FELL* NE10 ...... 100 B3 8
Warkworth Rd *DHAM* DH1 .... 180 B5
Warkworth St
  BW/LEM/TK/HW NE15 .... 76 B2
  BYK/HTN/WLK NE6 .... 82 B2 8
Warkworth Ter *JRW* NE32 .... 86 A6
  TYNE/NSHE NE30 .... 55 F4 7
Warnham Av *ASHBK/HED/RY* SR2 .. 145 D4
Warnhead Rd *BDLGTN* NE22 ...... 8 A3
Warren Av *BYK/HTN/WLK* NE6 ..... 66 C6
Warren Cl *HLS* DH4 .... 157 E4 9
Warrenmor *FELL* NE10 .... 101 F3
Warren St *PLEE/EAS* SR8 .... 209 F2
Warrington Rd *ELS/FEN* NE4 .... 79 F4
  GOS/KPK NE3 .... 46 A6
Warton Ter *BYK/HTN/WLK* NE6 ... 65 E6 5
Warwick Av *WICK/BNPF* NE16 ..... 95 F5
Warwick Cl *CRAM* NE23 .... 36 A1 3
  WICK/BNPF NE16 .... 95 F5 1
Warwick Ct *DHAM* DH1 .... 204 C1 8
  GOS/KPK NE3 .... 45 F5
Warwick Dr *HLH* DH5 .... 171 D4
  SUNDSW SR3 .... 159 E1
  WASHN NE37 .... 120 C2
  WICK/BNPF NE16 .... 96 A5
Warwick Gv *BDLGTN* NE22 .... 6 C3
Warwick Hall Wk *LGB/HTN* NE7 .. 65 F4
Warwick Pl *PLEE/EAS* SR8 .... 200 A6
Warwick Rd *HAR/WTLS* NE34 ...... 88 C1
  HEBB NE31 .... 85 E5 4
  WD/WHPE/BLK NE5 .... 60 A6 8
  WLSD/HOW NE28 .... 67 D5
Warwickshire Dr *DHAM* DH1 ...... 196 C4 1
Warwick St *BLYTH* NE24 .... 16 A2
  GATE NE8 .... 81 E6
  JES NE2 .... 81 E1
  SWCK/CAS SR5 .... 126 C3
Warwick Ter *SUNDSW* SR3 .... 143 F6
Wasdale Cl *CRAM* NE23 .... 22 A5
  PLEE/EAS SR8 .... 209 D2
Wasdale Ct *CLDN/WHIT/ROK* SR6 108 B5 8
Wasdale Rd *WD/WHPE/BLK* NE5 .. 61 D6
Washington Hwy *WASHN* NF37 ... 119 F4
  WASHS NE38 .... 138 B4
Washington Rd *SWCK/CAS* SR5... 123 E1
Washington St
  MLFD/PNYW SR4 .... 125 E6 8
Washingwell La *WICK/BNPF* NE16 .. 96 C3
Washingwell Pk *WICK/BNPF* NE16 .. 96 B4
Waskdale Crs *BLAY* NE21 .... 94 A2 7
Waskerley Cl *WICK/BNPF* NE16..... 113 F1
Waskerley Dr *RDHAMSE* DH6 ..... 206 A1
Waskerley Rd *WASHS* NE38 .... 139 E1
Watch House Cl *WASHN* NE37 ..... 70 C3 4
Watcombe Cl *WASHN* NE37 .... 121 E2 1
Waterbeach Pl *WD/WHPE/BLK* NE5.. 60 C4
Waterbeck Cl *CRAM* NE23 .... 22 A5
Waterbury Rd *GOS/KPK* NE3 ...... 47 D3
Waterford Cl *HLH* DH5 .... 170 C6 3
  WBAY NE26 .... 26 C2 3
Waterford Pk *DIN/WO* NE13 .... 32 B4
  SUND SR1 .... 4 C3
Waterloo Rd *BLYTH* NE24 .... 11 D5
  MONK NE25 .... 38 C5
  WASHN NE37 .... 121 D3
Waterloo Sq *SSH* NE33 .... 71 E3 12
Waterloo St *BLAY* NE21 .... 93 F1 9
  CNUT NE1 .... 2 B5

Waterloo V *SSH* NE33 .... 71 E3 13
Waterlow Cl *SWCK/CAS* SR5 ..... 107 E6 3
Watermill *RYTON* NE40............... 74 C3
Watermill La *FELL* NE10 .... 101 D2
Water Rw *BW/LEM/TK/HW* NE15 .... 75 D1
Waterside Dr *DUN/TMV* NE11 ..... 79 D6
Waterside Elvet *DHAM* DH1 ...... 194 C5 3
Waterson Crs *BDN/LAN/SAC* DH7 ... 178 A3
Water St *BDN/LAN/SAC* DH7 ...... 178 B1
  ELS/FEN NE4.......................... 80 A5
Waterville Rd *NSHW* NE29 .... 69 F2
Waterworks Rd *SUND* SR1 .... 126 A6 14
Watford Cl *SWCK/CAS* SR5 .... 107 E6 6
Watkin Crs *SEA/MUR* SR7 .... 188 B1
Watling Av *SEA/MUR* SR7 .... 175 E4
Watling Pl *LWF/SPW/WRK* NE9 ... 100 A6 6
Watling St *HAR/WTLS* NE34 .... 88 A3 7
Watson Av *HAR/WTLS* NE34 .... 90 A3
Watson Cl *SEA/MUR* SR7 .... 175 E4
Watson Gdns *WLSD/HOW* NE28 .. 68 C3 1
Watson Pl *HAR/WTLS* NE34 .... 90 A3 5
Watson St *JRW* NE32 .... 69 E6
  STLY/ANP DH9 .... 131 E6
  WICK/BNPF NE16 .... 112 A6 2
Watt's Rd *WBAY* NE26 .... 40 C4
Watts St *SEA/MUR* SR7 .... 188 B1 6
Watt St *GATE* NE8 .... 98 C3
Wavendon Crs *MLFD/PNYW* SR4 .. 142 C2
Waveney Gdns *STLY/ANP* DH9 ... 148 A4
Waveney Rd *PLEE/EAS* SR8 .... 208 A4
Waverdale Av *BYK/HTN/WLK* NE6 .. 83 F1
Waverdale Wy *SSH* NE33 .... 88 A2
Waverley Cl *BLAY* NE21 .... 93 E2 2
  RDHAMSE DH6 .... 206 A1
Waverley Crs
  BW/LEM/TK/HW NE15 .... 76 C1
Waverley Dr *BDLGTN* NE22 .... 8 B2
Waverley Rd *ELS/FEN* NE4 .... 80 A4 10
  LWF/SPW/WRK NE9 .... 117 F2
Waverley Ter *MLFD/PNYW* SR4..... 125 D5
Waverton Cl *CRAM* NE23 .... 22 A5
Wawn St *SSH* NE33 .... 71 F6 8
Wayfarer Rd *SWCK/CAS* SR5 ..... 125 F3
Wayland Sq *ASHBK/HED/RY* SR2 .. 145 D5
Wayman St *SWCK/CAS* SR5 .... 126 B3
Wayside *ASHBK/HED/RY* SR2 ..... 144 A2 3
  BW/LEM/TK/HW NE15............ 78 A3
Wealcroft *FELL* NE10 .... 101 E5 0
Wear Ct *HAR/WTLS* NE34 .... 88 B3
Weardale Av *BLYTH* NE24 .... 9 E4
  BYK/HTN/WLK NE6 .... 83 F1
  CLDN/WHIT/ROK SR6 .... 109 D3
  LGB/KIL NE12 .... 49 F4
  WASHN NE37 .... 120 B4
  WLSD/HOW NE28 .... 67 D2 4
Weardale Crs *HLS* DH4 .... 157 F1
Weardale St *HLH* DH5 .... 185 D3
Wearfield *SWCK/CAS* SR5 .... 125 D5
Wear Ldg *CLS/BIR/GTL* DH3 .... 125 D3
Wearmouth Av *SWCK/CAS* SR5 .. 126 C2 6
Wearmouth Br *SUND* SR1 .... 4 C1
Wearmouth Dr *SWCK/CAS* SR5 .. 126 B2
Wearmouth St *SWCK/CAS* SR5 .. 126 C3 10
Wear Rd *HEBB* NE31 .... 85 D4
  STLY/ANP DH9 .... 148 B3
Wearside Dr *DHAM* DH1 .... 194 C4
Wear St *HLH* DH5 .... 185 F1
  HLS DH4 .... 169 F3
  JRW NE32 .... 86 A1 10
  MLFD/PNYW SR4 .... 143 F5
  SEA/MUR SR7 .... 176 C3 13
  SUND SR1 .... 5 G5
  SWCK/CAS SR5 .... 125 F3
Wear Vw *DHAM* DH1.................. 194 C4
Weathercock La
  LWF/SPW/WRK NF9 .... 99 E5 10
Weatherside *BLAY* NE21 .... 94 A3 3
Webb Av *SEA/MUR* SR7 .... 174 B6
  SEA/MUR SR7 .... 175 D3
Webb Gdns *FELL* NE10 .... 101 F2 6
Webb Sq *PLEE/EAS* SR8 .... 201 D5
Wedgewood Cottages
  BW/LEM/TK/HW NE15 .... 76 C2 2
Wedgwood Rd *SEA/MUR* SR7 ..... 175 D4
Wedmore Rd *WD/WHPE/BLK* NE5 .. 59 F4
Weetman St *SSH* NE33 .... 71 D5 2
Weetslade Crs *CRAM* NE23 .... 34 C3
Weetslade Rd *CRAM* NE23 .... 34 C3
Weetwood Rd *CRAM* NE23 .... 22 B4 0
Weidner Rd *BW/LEM/TK/HW* NE15 .. 78 C3
Welbeck Rd *BYK/HTN/WLK* NE6 ... 82 B3
Weldon Av *ASHBK/HED/RY* SR2 .. 145 D4 3
Weldon Crs *LGB/HTN* NE7 .... 65 D4
Weldon Pl *NSHW* NE29 .... 53 F4
Weldon Rd *CRAM* NE23 .... 23 D3 1
  LGB/KIL NE12 .... 49 D6
Weldon Ter *CLS/BIR/GTL* DH3 .... 153 F6
Weldon Wy *GOS/KPK* NE3 .... 47 D6
Welfare Cl *PLEE/EAS* SR8 .... 201 D2
Welfare Rd *HLH* DH5 .... 171 F6
Welford Av *GOS/KPK* NE3 .... 62 C1
Welland Cl *PLEE/EAS* SR8.......... 208 B4
Welland La *CLDN/WHIT/ROK* SR6 .. 109 D1

Wellands Cl *CLDN/WHIT/ROK* SR6.. 109 D1
Wellands Ct *CLDN/WHIT/ROK* SR6 .. 109 D1
Well Bank Rd *WASHN* NE37 ...... 120 A4
Wellburn Rd *WASHN* NE37 .... 120 A3
Well Close Wk *WICK/BNPF* NE16 .. 95 F4 2
Wellesley St *JRW* NE32............... 86 A3
Wellfield Cl *BW/LEM/TK/HW* NE15... 57 E5
Wellfield La *WD/WHPE/BLK* NE5 .. 61 D4 2
Wellfield Rd *ELS/FEN* NE4 .... 78 C3
  ROWG NE39.......................... 110 B2
  SEA/MUR SR7 .... 188 A1
Wellington Av *MONK* NE25 .... 38 C5 2
Wellington Dr *SSH* NE33 .... 71 C2
Wellington La *MLFD/PNYW* SR4 .. 126 A4
Wellington Rd *DUN/TMV* NE11 .... 96 C1
Wellington St *BLYTH* NE24 .... 11 E5 3
  ELS/FEN NE4.......................... 2 A2
  FELL NE10 .... 100 B2
  HEBB NE31 .... 84 C3
Well La *SMOOR* NE27 .... 53 D2
Well Ridge Cl *MONK* NE25 .... 39 E4
Well Ridge Pk *MONK* NE25 .... 39 E3
Wells Cl *LGB/KIL* NE12 .... 65 F2 1
Wells Crs *SEA/MUR* SR7 .... 175 D3
Wells Gdns *LWF/SPW/WRK* NE9 .. 117 E2
Wells Gv *HAR/WTLS* NE34 .... 89 F1
Well St *MLFD/PNYW* SR4 .... 125 E5
Welsh Ter *STLY/ANP* DH9 .... 146 C5
Welwyn Cl *SWCK/CAS* SR5 .... 123 F4
  WLSD/HOW NE28 .... 66 B2
Wembley Av *MONK* NE25 .... 40 A6
Wembley Rd *SWCK/CAS* SR5 ..... 125 E1
Wendover Cl *SWCK/CAS* SR5 ..... 107 D6
Wendover Wy *SWCK/CAS* SR5 .... 107 D6
Wenham Sq
  ASHBK/HED/RY SR2 .... 144 A2 4
Wenlock *WASHS* NE38 .... 138 C3
Wenlock Dr *NSHW* NE29 .... 54 A4
Wenlock Rd *HAR/WTLS* NE34 ..... 87 F3
Wensley Cl *CLSW/PEL* DH2 .... 135 D5
Wensleydale *WLSD/HOW* NE28 .. 66 B1 4
Wensleydale Av *HLS* DH4........... 156 C1
  WASHN NE37 .... 120 B4 2
Wens Leydale Dr *LGB/KIL* NE12 .. 49 F4 10
Wensleydale Ter *BLYTH* NE24 .... 11 E6
Wentworth *SSH* NE33 .... 72 A5
Wentworth Cl *FELL* NE10 .... 100 C3 4
Wentworth Dr *WASHN* NE37 ..... 120 B2
Wentworth Gdns *MONK* NE25 .... 39 E5
Wentworth Pl *ELS/FEN* NE4 .... 80 A4 11
Wentworth Ter *MLFD/PNYW* SR4 .. 126 A5
Werhale Gn *FELL* NE10 .... 100 C2 8
Wesley Dr *LGB/KIL* NE12 .... 51 D3
Wesley St *LWF/SPW/WRK* NE9 ... 99 E5 11
Wesley Wy *BW/LEM/TK/HW* NE15 .. 57 F4
  LGB/KIL NE12 .... 51 D3
  SEA/MUR SR7 .... 175 E3
Wessex Cl *SWCK/CAS* SR5......... 107 E6
Wessington Wy *SWCK/CAS* SR5 .. 123 E5
  SWCK/CAS SR5 .... 125 F3 1
  SWCK/CAS SR5 .... 125 D3
Westacre Gdns
  WD/WHPE/BLK NE5 .... 78 B1 4
West Acres *DIN/WO* NE13 .... 31 D2 1
Westacres Av *WICK/BNPF* NE16 ... 96 A6
Westacres Crs
  BW/LEM/TK/HW NE15 .... 78 B2 3
West Av *CLDN/WHIT/ROK* SR6 ... 109 D5
  GOS/KPK NE3 .... 63 C2
  HAR/WTLS NE34 .... 89 D2
  LGB/KIL NE12 .... 49 F6
  NSHW NE29.......................... 69 F1
  PLEE/EAS SR8 .... 201 D1
  ROWG NE39.......................... 110 C3 2
  SEA/MUR SR7 .... 188 B1 7
  WASHS NE38 .... 138 A5
  WD/WHPE/BLK NE5............... 60 B4
West Bailey *LGB/KIL* NE12 .... 35 F6 12
  LGB/KIL NE12 .... 49 F1 3
Westbourne Av *BYK/HTN/WLK* NE6.. 66 B6
  GATE NE8 .... 99 D2
  GOS/KPK NE3 .... 47 E5
Westbourne Dr *HLS* DH4 .... 156 C2
Westbourne Rd *SUND* SR1 .... 126 A6
Westburn Gdns
  WLSD/HOW NE28 .... 66 B2 2
Westburn Ter
  CLDN/WHIT/ROK SR6............. 127 D2
Westbury Av *BYK/HTN/WLK* NE6 .. 66 B6
Westbury Rd *NSHW* NE29 .... 54 B4 1
Westbury St *MLFD/PNYW* SR4 ... 126 A5
Westcliff Cl *PLEE/EAS* SR8 .... 199 F3 3
Westcliffe Rd
  CLDN/WHIT/ROK SR6 .... 109 E6 2
Westcliffe Wy *HAR/WTLS* NE34 ... 87 E5
West Clifton *LGB/KIL* NE12 .... 35 E6 13
West Copperas
  BW/LEM/TK/HW NE15 .... 77 D3 5
Westcott Av *SSH* NE33 .... 72 A5
Westcott Dr *DHAM* DH1 .... 193 F5
Westcott Rd *HAR/WTLS* NE34 .... 88 B3
  PLEE/EAS SR8 .... 208 C1
West Crs *FELL* NE10 .... 102 B2
Westcroft Rd *LGB/KIL* NE12 ...... 50 A4
West Dene Dr *TYNE/NSHE* NE30 .. 54 C4

West Denton Cl
BW/LEM/TK/HW NE15............ **59** F6
West Denton Rd
BW/LEM/TK/HW NE15............ **59** F6
West Denton Wy
WD/WHPE/BLK NE5................. **59** F4
WD/WHPE/BLK NE5................. **60** C4
West Dr *BLYTH* NE24 .... **16** B2 **6**
CLDN/WHIT/ROK SR6.............. **107** D1
CLSW/PEL DH2 .... **152** B6
West End Front St *BDLGTN* NE22 ... **7** E4 **5**
Westerdale *HLS* DH4 .... **139** D6
WLSD/HOW NE28 .... **66** B2
Westerdale Pl *BYK/HTN/WLK* NE6 ... **84** A2
Westerham *CI SWCK/CAS* SR5 .... **107** E6
Westerhope Gdns
WD/WHPE/BLK NE5 .... **61** F5 **10**
Westerhope Rd *WASHS* NE38 ... **139** E1
Westerkirk *CRAM* NE23 .... **22** A4
Western Ap *SSH* NE33 .... **71** E5
Western Av *ELS/FEN* NE4............ **79** E3
MONK NE25............................. **24** B5
WD/WHPE/BLK NE5 .... **59** F5
Western Dr *ELS/FEN* NE4............ **79** E3
Western Hwy *WASHS* NE38 .... **137** F4
Western Hl
ASHBK/HED/RY SR2 .... **144** A1 **13**
ASHBK/HED/RY SR2 .... **162** A1
MLFD/PNYW SR4 .... **126** A6 **15**
MLFD/PNYW SR4 .... **144** A1
Westernmoor *WASHN* NE37 ...... **119** E6
Western Rd *JRW* NE32 .... **85** F1
WLSD/HOW NE28 .... **68** B4
Western Ter *BOL* NE36 .... **105** F3
CRAM NE23 .... **34** B2
Western Wy *BLAY* NE21 .... **77** D6
RYTON NE40 .... **74** B4
WBAY NE26 .... **40** B2
West Farm Av *LGB/KIL* NE12 .... **48** B6 **5**
West Farm Ct *CRAM* NE23 .... **22** A1 **3**
West Farm Rd *BYK/HTN/WLK* NE6 ... **83** D1
CLDN/WHIT/ROK SR6................ **108** A2
WLSD/HOW NE28 .... **68** A3
West Farm Wynd *LGB/KIL* NE12 ..... **64** B1
Westfield *GOS/KPK* NE3 .... **63** D4
Westfield Av *DIN/WO* NE13 .... **32** C4
GOS/KPK NE3 .... **63** E3
MONK NE25............................. **39** F6
Westfield Ct *MLFD/PNYW* SR4 ... **143** D2 **4**
WLSD/HOW NE28 .... **67** D6
Westfield Dr *GOS/KPK* NE3 .... **63** D5
Westfield Gv *GOS/KPK* NE3 .... **63** D5
MLFD/PNYW SR4 .... **143** D2
Westfield La *RYTON* NE40 .... **74** A2
Westfield Pk *WLSD/HOW* NE28... **66** C4
Westfield Rd
BW/LEM/TK/HW NE15............... **78** B3
Westfield Ter *GATE* NE8 .... **99** D2 **11**
Westgarth *WD/WHPE/BLK* NE5 ... **60** A2
Westgarth Gv *RDHAMSE* DH6 ... **206** A1
Westgate Av *SUNDSW* SR3 .... **143** F6
Westgate Cl *MONK* NE25 .... **39** E4
Westgate Gv *SUNDSW* SR3 .... **143** F6
Westgate Hill Ter *CNUT* NE1 ...... **2** A5
Westgate Rd *CNUT* NE1 .... **2** A4
ELS/FEN NE4............................ **79** D2
West George Potts St
SSH NE33 .... **71** F5 **12**
West Gra *SWCK/CAS* SR5 .... **126** B1
West Gv *MLFD/PNYW* SR4 .... **142** A1
Westheath Av
ASHBK/HED/RY SR2................ **145** D5
West High Horse *CI ROWG* NE39..... **93** E6
West Hl *MLFD/PNYW* SR4........... **143** D2
Westhills *STLY/ANP* DH9 .... **129** F4 **1**
Westhills *CI BDN/LAN/SAC* DH7 ... **164** A6
West Holborn *SSH* NE33 .... **71** D5
Westholme Gdns
BW/LEM/TK/HW NE15............... **78** C2
Westhope *CI HAR/WTLS* NE34 ...... **89** F1
Westhope Rd *HAR/WTLS* NE34 ...... **89** F1
West Jesmond Av *JES* NE2 .... **64** A4 **5**
Westlands *BW/LEM/TK/HW* NE15 ... **59** E5
JRW NE32 .... **104** C1
LGB/HTN NE7 .... **64** C3
TYNE/NSHE NE30 .... **55** D3
WBAY NE26 .... **26** A2
West La *BLAY* NE21 .... **93** F2
CLS/BIR/GTL DH3 .... **153** E6
LGB/KIL NE12 .... **49** F3
RDHAMSE DH6 .... **188** C6
SEA/MUR SR7 .... **189** E5
WICK/BNPF NE16 .... **112** B3
West Lawn *ASHBK/HED/RY* SR2 ... **144** B2
West Lawson St *NSHW* NE29 .... **70** C2 **10**
West Lea *BLAY* NE21 .... **94** B2
Westleigh Ct *MLFD/PNYW* SR4 ... **125** E6 **10**
Westleigh Rd *HLS* DH4 .... **157** E4
Westley Av *WBAY* NE26 .... **40** A1
Westley Cl *WBAY* NE26 .... **40** A1
Westloch Rd *CRAM* NE23 .... **22** A5
Westmacott St
BW/LEM/TK/HW NE15............ **58** A6 **1**
West Mdw *WD/WHPE/BLK* NE5 ..... **59** F2 **2**

West Meadows Dr
CLDN/WHIT/ROK SR6 .... **107** F2
West Meadows Rd
CLDN/WHIT/ROK SR6 .... **107** F2
Westminster Av *NSHW* NE29....... **70** C3
Westminster Crs *HEBB* NE31 .... **85** D6
Westminster Dr *DUN/TMV* NE11 ... **97** E4 **5**
Westminster St *GATE* NE8 .... **98** C2
Westminster Wy *LGB/HTN* NE7 ..... **65** E2
West Moffett St *SSH* NE33 .... **71** F5 **13**
West Moor Dr
LGB/KIL NE12 .... **107** F3
Westmoor Dr *LGB/KIL* NE12 .... **49** D3
Westmoor Rd *MLFD/PNYW* SR4 ... **124** C5
Westmoreland St
WLSD/HOW NE28 .... **67** E4
Westmorland Av *BDLGTN* NE22 ..... **7** F2
WASHN NE37.......................... **120** C2
WLSD/HOW NE28 .... **69** D5 **4**
Westmorland Gdns
LWF/SPW/WRK NE9 .... **99** E5 **12**
Westmorland La *CNUT* NE1.......... **2** B5
Westmorland Rd *CNUT* NE1 .... **2** A5
ELS/FEN NE4............................ **79** E4
HAR/WTLS NE34 .... **90** B1
NSHW NE29............................. **53** D5
Westmorland Wy *CRAM* NE23 ..... **21** E2
West Mt *MLFD/PNYW* SR4 .... **143** D1
Westoe Av *SSH* NE33 .... **72** A5
Westoe Dr *SSH* NE33 .... **72** A5
Westoe Rd *SSH* NE33 .... **71** F4
Westoe Village *SSH* NE33 .... **72** A6
Weston Av *WICK/BNPF* NE16........ **95** E5
Weston Vw *PLEE/EAS* SR8......... **208** B1
West Ousterley Rd *STLY/ANP* DH9 ... **148** C6
Westover Gdns
LWF/SPW/WRK NE9 .... **99** E3
West Pde *ELS/FEN* NE4 .... **80** A4
HEBB NE31 .... **84** C4
West Pk *SUNDSW* SR3.............. **159** D2
West Park Gdns *BLAY* NE21 .... **94** B1
West Park Rd
CLDN/WHIT/ROK SR6 .... **107** F1
LWF/SPW/WRK NE9 .... **99** E5
SSH NE33............................... **71** E6
West Park Vw *CRAM* NE23 .... **34** B2
West Pastures *BOL* NE36 .... **104** B5
West Percy Rd *NSHW* NE29 .... **70** B2
TYNE/NSHE NE30 .... **54** C6 **13**
West Percy St *NSHW* NE29 .... **70** C1 **14**
Westport Cl *SWCK/CAS* SR5 ...... **107** E6 **9**
West Riggs *BDLGTN* NE22 .... **7** F4
The West Rig *GOS/KPK* NE3.......... **62** A2
West Rd *BDLGTN* NE22 .... **8** C2
STLY/ANP DH9 .... **129** F5
STLY/ANP DH9 .... **146** B5
West Salisbury St *BLYTH* NE24 ... **10** C4
West Stainton St *SSH* NE33 ..... **71** F5 **14**
West Stevenson St *SSH* NE33 ... **71** F5 **15**
West Stoneycroft *LGB/KIL* NE12 ... **50** A2 **2**
West St *CLS/BIR/GTL* DH3 .... **136** B2
CLSW/PEL DH2 .... **150** C3
GATE NE8 .... **81** D5
HEBB NE31 .... **85** D1
RDHAMSE DH6 .... **206** B2
SEA/MUR SR7 .... **176** C3
SMOOR NE27........................... **51** F3
STLY/ANP DH9 .... **130** C6
SUND SR1................................ **4** B2
SUNDSW SR3 .... **143** F6 **6**
WICK/BNPF NE16 .... **95** F3
WLSD/HOW NE28 .... **66** C4
West Sunniside *SUND* SR1........... **4** D2
West Ter *WBAY* NE26 .... **26** C2
West Thorp *WD/WHPE/BLK* NE5 ... **60** B1
West Vallum
BW/LEM/TK/HW NE15 .... **77** E3 **8**
West Vw *BDLGTN* NE22 .... **8** B1
BDN/LAN/SAC DH7 .... **203** E5
BLAY NE21 .... **76** B5
BW/LEM/TK/HW NE15................ **76** B2
CLDN/WHIT/ROK SR6 .... **126** C1
DHAM DH1 .... **195** D4
DUN/TMV NE11 .... **116** C6
ELS/FEN NE4............................ **79** E4
HLS DH4................................ **157** D4
LGB/KIL NE12 .... **49** F4 **10**
SWCK/CAS SR5 .... **124** A5 **10**
West Walls *CNUT* NE1 .... **2** C5
West Walpole St *SSH* NE33 .... **71** D5
Westward Ct
WD/WHPE/BLK NE5 .... **60** A3 **9**
Westward Pl *WASHS* NE38......... **138** A5
West Wy *DUN/TMV* NE11 .... **97** F2
SSH NE33................................ **88** B1
Westway *BLAY* NE21 .... **76** A4 **2**
BW/LEM/TK/HW NE15................ **57** F3
PLEE/EAS SR8 .... **208** B3 **2**
West Wear St *SUND* SR1............. **4** C1
Westwell Ct *LGB/HTN* NE7 .... **64** B2 **5**
West Wellington St
NSHW NE29 .... **70** C1 **15**
Westwood Av
BYK/HTN/WLK NE6 .... **85** E5 **5**

Westwood Cl *WICK/BNPF* NE16 ... **112** A5
Westwood Gdns *GOS/KPK* NE3...... **62** A3
Westwood Rd *GOS/KPK* NE3......... **47** E3
Westwood St
MLFD/PNYW SR4 .... **125** E6 **11**
West Wynd *LGB/KIL* NE12 .... **49** F1
Wetheral Gdns
LWF/SPW/WRK NE9 .... **117** F1
Wetheral Ter *BYK/HTN/WLK* NE6 ... **83** E4 **5**
Wetherburn Av *SEA/MUR* SR7 ..... **188** A1
Wetherby Gv *GATE* NE8 .... **98** C3 **5**
Wetherby Rd *ASHBK/HED/RY* SR2 ... **145** F5
Wettondale Av *BLYTH* NE24 .... **9** F5
Weybourne Sq
ASHBK/HED/RY SR2 .... **145** D4 **3**
Weyhill Av *NSHW* NE29............... **69** F2
Weymouth Dr *SEA/MUR* SR7 ...... **175** F4
Weymouth Gdns
LWF/SPW/WRK NE9 .... **117** E2
Whaggs La *WICK/BNPF* NE16 .... **96** A4
Whalton Av *GOS/KPK* NE3 .... **46** C6
Whalton Cl *FELL* NE10 .... **102** B3
RDHAMSE DH6 .... **197** F5
Whalton Ct *HAR/WTLS* NE34 ...... **89** D2 **5**
Wharfdale Pl *BYK/HTN/WLK* NE6 ... **83** F2
Wharfedale *HLS* DH4 .... **139** F6 **5**
WLSD/HOW NE28 .... **66** B1
Wharfedale Av *WASHN* NE37 ...... **120** A4
Wharfedale Dr *SSH* NE33 .... **88** B1 **4**
Wharfedale Gdns *BLYTH* NE24 .... **9** F4
Wharmlands Rd
BW/LEM/TK/HW NE15................ **77** E1
Wharncliffe St *SUND* SR1.......... **126** A6
Wharrier St *BYK/HTN/WLK* NE6 ... **83** E4
Wharton St *BLYTH* NE24 .... **16** A2
SSH NE33............................... **71** F4
Wheatall Dr *CLDN/WHIT/ROK* SR6 ... **91** E6
Wheatfield Gv *LGB/KIL* NE12........ **49** D5
Wheatfield Rd *WD/WHPE/BLK* NE5 ... **60** B3
Wheatley Gdns *BOL* NE36 .... **105** F3
Wheatleywell La
CLS/BIR/GTL DH3 .... **166** B5
Whernside Pl *CRAM* NE23 .... **22** A5 **2**
Whernside Wk *RYTON* NE40 .... **74** C4 **3**
Whickham Cl *HLS* DH4 .... **170** B2
Whickham Hwy *DUN/TMV* NE11 ... **97** D3
WICK/BNPF NE16 .... **96** C3
Whickham Ldg *WICK/BNPF* NE16 ... **96** B3 **4**
Whickham Pk *WICK/BNPF* NE16 ... **96** B3 **4**
Whickham Rd *HEBB* NE31 .... **84** C3
Whickham St
CLDN/WHIT/ROK SR6 .... **127** D3
PLEE/EAS SR8 .... **200** C2 **3**
Whickham St East
CLDN/WHIT/ROK SR6 .... **127** D3
Whickham Vw
BW/LEM/TK/HW NE15................ **77** F2
LWF/SPW/WRK NE9 .... **99** F5
Whickhope *WASHS* NE38 .... **139** D4
Whinbrooke *FELL* NE10 .... **101** F4
Whinbush Pl
BW/LEM/TK/HW NE15................ **77** F3
Whinfell Cl *CRAM* NE23 .... **22** B5
Whinfield Av *RDHAMSE* DH6 ...... **206** B2
Whinfield Ter *ROWG* NE39 .... **110** C2
Whinfield Wy *ROWG* NE39 .... **110** B3
Whinlatter Gdns
LWF/SPW/WRK NE9 .... **99** F6
Whinmoor Pl *WD/WHPE/BLK* NE5 ... **62** A5
Whinney Cl *BLAY* NE21 .... **93** F2 **7**
Whinneyfield Rd
BYK/HTN/WLK NE6 .... **66** B6
BYK/HTN/WLK NE6 .... **83** E1
Whinney Hl *DHAM* DH1 .... **194** C6
Whinshaw *FELL* NE10 .... **101** E3
Whistler Gdns *HAR/WTLS* NE34...... **88** C5
Whitbay Crs *LGB/KIL* NE12........... **49** E6
Whitbeck Rd *WD/WHPE/BLK* NE5 ... **60** C6
Whitbourne Cl *WASHN* NE37 ..... **121** D2 **2**
Whitburn Bents Rd
CLDN/WHIT/ROK SR6 .... **109** E3 **1**
Whitburn Gdns
LWF/SPW/WRK NE9 .... **118** C1
Whitburn Pl *CRAM* NE23 .... **22** A5
Whitburn Rd
CLDN/WHIT/ROK SR6 .... **107** E2
CLDN/WHIT/ROK SR6 .... **109** E6
Whitburn Rd East
CLDN/WHIT/ROK SR6 .... **108** A1
Whitburn St
CLDN/WHIT/ROK SR6 .... **126** C4 **11**
Whitburn Ter *BOL* NE36 .... **106** C3
CLDN/WHIT/ROK SR6 .... **108** C6 **3**
Whitby Av *CLDN/WHIT/ROK* SR6... **109** E4
Whitby Cl *GATE* NE8 .... **99** E1 **16**
Whitby Dr *WASHS* NE38 .... **138** C3
Whitby Gdns *WLSD/HOW* NE28..... **68** A2
Whitby St *TYNE/NSHE* NE30 .... **55** D6
Whitchurch Cl *BOLCOL* NE35 .... **105** D1 **8**
SWCK/CAS SR5 .... **107** E6
Whitchurch Rd *SWCK/CAS* SR5 ... **107** E6
Whitebark *SUNDSW* SR3 .... **160** A4 **11**
Whitebeam Pl *ELS/FEN* NE4 .... **80** A5 **10**
Whitebridge Cl *GOS/KPK* NE3 ...... **47** E4
Whitebridge Ct *GOS/KPK* NE3 ..... **47** E5 **5**

Whitebridge Pk *GOS/KPK* NE3 ...... **47** F5
White Cedars *BDN/LAN/SAC* DH7 ... **202** C5
Whitecliff Cl *NSHW* NE29 .... **54** B4
Whitecroft Rd *LGB/KIL* NE12............ **48** C2
Whitefield Crs *HLS* DH4 .... **156** C1
Whitefield Gv *HLS* DH4 .... **100** C2
Whitefield Ter *BYK/HTN/WLK* NE6 .... **65** F5
Whiteford Pl *CRAM* NE23................. **23** F6
Whitefriars Wy *LGB/KIL* NE12 .... **64** C1
White Gates Dr *HLH* DH5 .... **186** A2 **2**
Whitegates Rd *RDHAMSE* DH6 ... **197** E3
Whitehall Rd
  BW/LEM/TK/HW NE15............. **58** B4
  GATE NE8.................................... **99** D2
Whitehall St *SSH* NE33 .... **88** B2
Whitehead St *SSH* NE33 .... **88** A1 **4**
Whitehill Fell NE10 .... **101** E5
Whitehill Crs *CLSW/PEL* DH2 ..... **152** A4
Whitehill Dr *FELL* NE10................ **100** C4
Whitehill Hall Gdns
  CLSW/PEL DH2 .... **152** C4
Whitehill Rd *CRAM* NE23 .... **13** F5 **5**
White Hill Rd *HLH* DH5 .... **186** B4
Whitehorn Crs *WD/WHPE/BLK* NE5... **61** F4
White Horse Vw
  HAR/WTLS NE34 .... **90** B2 **1**
Whitehouse Crs
  LWF/SPW/WRK NE9................ **101** D6
Whitehouse La *NSHW* NE29 .... **53** F4
White House Pl
  ASHBK/HED/RY SR2 .... **5** G4 **1**
White House Rd
  ASHBK/HED/RY SR2 .... **5** F5 **4**
Whitehouse Rd
  BW/LEM/TK/HW NE15 .... **78** A4
White House Wy *FELL* NE10 ...... **101** D5
Whitehouse Wy *PLEE/EAS* SR8 ... **207** E2
  RDHAMSE DH6 .... **207** E4
Whitelaw Pl *CRAM* NE23 .... **22** B4 **9**
White Lea Cl *PLEE/EAS* SR8 ...... **209** E3
Whiteleas Wy *HAR/WTLS* NE34....... **88** C6
Whiteleees Ct *GOS/KPK* NE3 .... **46** A5 **9**
White Le Head Gdns
  STLY/ANP DH9 .... **129** F4 **2**
Whiteley Rd *BLAY* NE21 .... **77** D4
Whitemere Cl *ASHBK/HED/RY* SR2.. **145** D4
White Mere Gdns *FELL* NE10 .... **102** B2
Whiteoak Av *DHAM* DH1 .... **196** A3
White Oaks *FELL* NE10 .... **101** D5
White Rocks Gv
  CLDN/WHIT/ROK SR6.............. **91** E5
Whites Gdns *HEBB* NE31 .... **84** B2
Whitesmocks *DHAM* DH1 .... **193** F2
Whitesmocks Av *DHAM* DH1 .... **193** E3
White St *BYK/HTN/WLK* NE6 .... **84** A3
Whitewell Rd *BLAY* NE21 .... **76** B6
Whitfield Dr *LGB/KIL* NE12............ **49** E6
Whitfield Rd *BW/LEM/TK/HW* NE15.. **77** E3
  LGB/KIL NE12 .... **49** F6 **3**
  MONK NE25............................. **24** C5
Whitgrave Rd *WD/WHPE/BLK* NE5 ... **61** F3
Whithorn Ct *BLYTH* NE24 .... **10** B5 **3**
Whitley Rd *LGB/KIL* NE12............. **50** A6
  MONK NE25.............................. **38** C5
  WBAY NE26 .... **41** D6
Whitmore Rd *BLAY* NE21 .... **76** B5
Whittingham Rd *TYNE/NSHE* NE30 .. **55** E2
  WD/WHPE/BLK NE5 .... **60** B2 **7**
Whittington Gv
  WD/WHPE/BLK NE5................. **78** B1
Whittleburn *FELL* NE10 .... **101** E5
Whitton Av *BLYTH* NE24 .... **16** A1
Whitton Gdns *NSHW* NE29 .... **53** F5 **3**
Whitton Pl *LGB/HTN* NE7 .... **64** C2
  MONK NE25.............................. **24** C5
Whittonstall *WASHS* NE38 .... **139** E5
Whitton Wy *GOS/KPK* NE3........... **47** D6
Whitworth Pl *BYK/HTN/WLK* NE6 ... **83** F5 **6**
  GATE NE8................................. **98** C3 **4**
Whitworth Rd *PLEE/EAS* SR8 ..... **207** E2
  WASHS NE37 .... **119** E5
Whorlton Pl
  WD/WHPE/BLK NE5 .... **60** A3 **10**
Whyndyke *FELL* NE10................... **101** D5
Whytrigg Cl *MONK* NE25 .... **24** A4
Widdrington Av *HAR/WTLS* NE34.... **73** D6
Widdrington Gdns *DIN/WO* NE13 ... **33** E4 **2**
Widdrington Rd *BLAY* NE21........... **76** B6
Widnes Pl *LGB/KIL* NE12............... **49** E5
Wigeon Cl *WASHS* NE38 .... **137** E4
Wigmore Av *BYK/HTN/WLK* NE6..... **83** D4
Wilber Ct *MLFD/PNYW* SR4 .... **125** E6 **4**
Wilberforce St *JRW* NE32 .... **86** D1
  WLSD/HOW NE28 .... **67** D6 **3**
Wilber St *MLFD/PNYW* SR4 .... **125** E6 **13**
Wilbury Pl *WD/WHPE/BLK* NE5 .... **61** E4 **4**
Wilden Ct *SUNDSW* SR3 .... **144** A4 **6**
Wilden Rd *WASHS* NE38 .... **139** E3
Wildshaw Cl *CRAM* NE23 .... **22** B5
Wilfred St *BOLCOL* NE35............. **105** E3
  BYK/HTN/WLK NE6 .... **81** F2 **10**
  CLS/BIR/GTL DH3 .... **153** E6
  MLFD/PNYW SR4 .... **125** D5 **8**
Wilfrid St *CLS/BIR/GTL* DH3 ..... **136** B3

Wilkes Cl *WD/WHPE/BLK* NE5 ...... **60** B4 **7**
Wilkinson Av *HEBB* NE31 .... **84** C5 **3**
Wilkinson Rd *PLEE/EAS* SR8 ..... **201** D5
Wilkwood Cl *CRAM* NE23 .... **22** B4 **6**
Willerby Dr *GOS/KPK* NE3 .... **47** D4
Willerby Gv *PLEE/EAS* SR8 .... **208** B1 **2**
William Armstrong Dr
  ELS/FEN NE4............................ **79** D5
William Cl *LGB/KIL* NE12 .... **50** C4 **3**
William Morris Av *ROWG* NE39 ... **110** A2
William Pl *DHAM* DH1 .... **195** E4
William Cl *STLY/ANP* DH9 .... **148** C3
Williamson Ter
  CLDN/WHIT/ROK SR6 .... **126** C4 **12**
Williams Rd *SEA/MUR* SR7 .... **188** B1
William St *BLYTH* NE24 .... **11** D5
  FELL NE10 .... **100** C1
  GOS/KPK NE3 .... **64** A1
  HEBB NE31 .... **84** C1
  NSHW NE29 .... **70** C1 **16**
  SUND SR1 .... **4** D1
  WICK/BNPF NE16 .... **95** F5 **12**
William St West *HEBB* NE31 .... **84** C2
  NSHW NE29 .... **70** C1
Willington St *WLSD/HOW* NE28 .... **68** A3
Willis St *HLH* DH5 .... **171** F5 **3**
Willmore St *MLFD/PNYW* SR4 .... **125** F6
Willoughby Dr *WBAY* NE26 .... **40** A3
Willoughby Rd *NSHW* NE29......... **53** F6
Willow Av *BLYTH* NE24 .... **10** C3
  DUN/TMV NE11 .... **97** E2 **3**
  ELS/FEN NE4............................. **61** F6
Willowbank Gdns *JES* NE2 .... **64** A2 **8**
Willow Bank Rd
  ASHBK/HED/RY SR2 .... **144** B3 **10**
Willow Cl *BDN/LAN/SAC* DH7 ..... **203** D4
Willow Ct *RYTON* NE40................. **74** C2
Willow Crs *BLYTH* NE24 .... **16** B2
  HLH DH5 .... **186** C3
Willowdene *LGB/KIL* NE12 .... **50** A3 **4**
Willowfield Av *GOS/KPK* NE3 ...... **46** B6
Willow Gdns *LGB/KIL* NE12 ...... **35** E6 **14**
Willow Gra *JRW* NE32 .... **85** F1 **2**
Willow Gv *HAR/WTLS* NE34 .... **89** E3
  WLSD/HOW NE28 .... **67** F4
Willow Pl *PONT/DH* NE20............. **28** A6
Willow Rd *BLAY* NE21 .... **76** C6
  HLS DH4 .... **170** B2
Willows Cl *DIN/WO* NE13 .... **32** C5 **9**
The Willows *BW/LEM/TK/HW* NE15.. **57** F5
  WASHS NE38 .... **139** E2
Willowtree Av *DHAM* DH1 .... **195** F2
Willow Wy *PONT/DH* NE20 .... **42** A2
Wilmington Cl *WD/WHPE/BLK* NE5 **45** D6
Wilson Av *CLS/BIR/GTL* DH3........ **136** B1
Wilson Dr *BOL* NE36 .... **106** A2 **1**
Wilson Gdns *GOS/KPK* NE3 .... **63** D3
Wilson Pl *PLEE/EAS* SR8 .... **200** D5
Wilson's La *LWF/SPW/WRK* NE9 .... **99** E5
Wilson St *DUN/TMV* NE11 .... **97** E2
  MLFD/PNYW SR4 .... **125** F5
  SSH NE33.................................. **71** E5
  WLSD/HOW NE28 .... **67** D4
Wilson St North *SWCK/CAS* SR5 ... **126** B4
Wilson Ter *LGB/KIL* NE12 .... **49** F4 **13**
  SUNDSW SR3............................ **143** F6
Wilsway *BW/LEM/TK/HW* NE15 ..... **57** E4
Wilton Av *BYK/HTN/WLK* NE6 .... **83** D3
Wilton Cl *CRAM* NE23 .... **22** B5
  MONK NE25.............................. **39** D5
Wilton Dr *MONK* NE25 .... **39** D5
Wilton Gdns North *BOLCOL* NE35.. **87** D6 **3**
Wilton Gdns South *BOLCOL* NE35.. **105** D1
Wiltshire Cl *DHAM* DH1 .... **196** B3 **5**
  SWCK/CAS SR5 .... **107** D6 **1**
Wiltshire Dr *WLSD/HOW* NE28 ...... **66** B1
Wiltshire Gdns *WLSD/HOW* NE28 .. **66** B3
Wiltshire Pl *WASHN* NE37 .... **120** C2
Wiltshire Rd *SWCK/CAS* SR5 .... **107** E6 **7**
Wimbledon Cl *SWCK/CAS* SR5 ... **125** E1 **1**
Wimborne Cl *BOLCOL* NE35 ...... **105** D2 **2**
Wimbourne Av
  MLFD/PNYW SR4 .... **143** D2 **5**
Wimbourne Gn
  WD/WHPE/BLK NE5 .... **60** B3 **8**
Wimpole Cl *WASHN* NE37........... **121** D2 **3**
Wimslow Cl *WLSD/HOW* NE28....... **66** B3
Winalot Av *ASHBK/HED/RY* SR2 ... **145** D4
Wincanton Pl *NSHW* NE29 .... **70** A2 **4**
Winchcombe Pl *LGB/HTN* NE7 ..... **64** C3 **3**
Winchester Av *BLYTH* NE24 .... **11** D5
Winchester Cl *CLS/BIR/GTL* DH3 .. **167** F3
Winchester Ct *JRW* NE32 .... **104** A1
  MLFD/PNYW SR4 .... **125** E6 **8**
Winchester Dr *BDN/LAN/SAC* DH7 .. **202** C6
  PLEE/EAS SR8 .... **207** E3 **1**
Winchester Rd *DHAM* DH1 .... **181** D5
Winchester St *SSH* NE33 .... **71** F3 **7**
Winchester Wk *DIN/WO* NE13 ...... **33** D5
Winchester Wy *BDLGTN* NE22........ **7** E2
Wincomblee Rd
  BYK/HTN/WLK NE6 .... **84** A5
Windburgh Dr *CRAM* NE23 .... **22** A5
Windermere
  CLDN/WHIT/ROK SR6 .... **107** F1 **3**

Windermere Av *CLSW/PEL* DH2 .. **166** B1
  FELL NE10 .... **101** E2
  HLH DH5 .... **186** B4
Windermere Cl *CRAM* NE23........... **22** A5
Windermere Crs *BLAY* NE21 .... **94** A3 **8**
  HAR/WTLS NE34 .... **89** D2
  HEBB NE31 .... **85** E3
  HLS DH4.................................. **157** D2
  JRW NE32 .... **86** C5
Windermere Gdns
  WICK/BNPF NE16.................... **96** B3
Windermere Rd *RDHAMSE* DH6 ... **188** A4
  SEA/MUR SR7 .... **175** D3
  WD/WHPE/BLK NE5................. **61** D6 **4**
Windermere St
  ASHBK/HED/RY SR2 .... **145** E4
Windermere Ter *NSHW* NE29 .... **54** B6
Windhill Rd *BYK/HTN/WLK* NE6 ..... **83** C5
The Winding *DIN/WO* NE13 .... **31** D3 **4**
Windlass Ct *HAR/WTLS* NE34 ..... **88** B3 **13**
Windlass La *WASHN* NE37 .... **120** B5
Windmill Ct *JES* NE2 .... **63** E6 **1**
  JES NE2 .... **80** B1 **2**
Windmill Gv *BLYTH* NE24 .... **9** F4
Windmill Hl *SSH* NE33 .... **71** D5 **3**
Windmill Sq *SWCK/CAS* SR5 ..... **108** B6 **5**
Windmill Wy *HEBB* NE31 .... **68** A6
Winds La *SEA/MUR* SR7 .... **188** A2
Winds Lonnen Est *SEA/MUR* SR7 ... **187** F1
Windsor Av *GATE* NE8.................. **99** D2
Windsor Cl *WICK/BNPF* NE16........ **95** E6
Windsor Cottages
  WLSD/HOW NE28 .... **68** C2 **3**
Windsor Ct *BDLGTN* NE22 .... **7** E4
  CRAM NE23 .... **13** F5
  GOS/KPK NE3 .... **46** A5
Windsor Crs *HEBB* NE31.............. **85** E2
  HLH DH5 .... **171** E2
  WBAY NE26 .... **41** E6
  WD/WHPE/BLK NE5 .... **60** C3
Windsor Dr *CLDN/WHIT/ROK* SR6 .. **107** D1
  HLH DH5 .... **171** D4
  RDHAMSE DH6 .... **187** E4
  STLY/ANP DH9 .... **146** B3
  SUNDSW SR3 .... **160** C1
  WLSD/HOW NE28 .... **68** C3
Windsor Gdns *BDLGTN* NE22 .... **7** E4
  FELL NE10 .... **100** B2 **7**
  HAR/WTLS NE34 .... **89** D1
  NSHW NE29 .... **54** C5
  WBAY NE26 .... **40** B4
Windsor Pk *WLSD/HOW* NE28....... **66** B3
Windsor Pl *JES* NE2 .... **81** D1 **3**
  RDHAMSE DH6 .... **206** C1
  SMOOR NE27 .... **51** E3
Windsor Rd *CLS/BIR/GTL* DH3 .... **118** A6
  LWF/SPW/WRK NE9 .... **119** D3
  MONK NE25............................. **40** A5
  SEA/MUR SR7 .... **175** E3
Windsor St *WLSD/HOW* NE28 .... **67** D4
Windsor Ter *GOS/KPK* NE3............ **64** A2
  JES NE2 .... **80** C1
  SEA/MUR SR7 .... **188** C1 **2**
  SEA/MUR SR7 .... **188** C2 **1**
  WBAY NE26 .... **41** E6
Windsor Wy *GOS/KPK* NE3 .... **45** E5
Windt St *DIN/WO* NE13 .... **32** C5 **10**
Windy Nook Rd
  LWF/SPW/WRK NE9................ **100** A4
Windy Ridge Vls *FELL* NE10 ...... **100** B3 **4**
Wingate Cl *BW/LEM/TK/HW* NE15 ... **77** D2
  HLS DH4 .... **170** C2
Wingate Gdns
  LWF/SPW/WRK NE9................ **100** C6
Wingrove *ROWG* NE39 .... **110** C3 **3**
Wingrove Av
  CLDN/WHIT/ROK SR6.............. **109** D6
  ELS/FEN NE4............................ **79** E2
Wingrove Gdns *ELS/FEN* NE4........ **79** E2
Wingrove Rd *ELS/FEN* NE4 .... **62** A5
Winifred St *CLDN/WHIT/ROK* SR6... **127** D1
Winifred Ter *SUND* SR1 .... **5** E4 **1**
Winshields *CRAM* NE23 .... **22** B4
Winship Cl *HAR/WTLS* NE34......... **88** B6
Winship St *BLYTH* NE24 .... **16** B1
Winskell Rd *HAR/WTLS* NE34 ...... **87** E4
Winslade Cl *SUNDSW* SR3 .... **144** A6 **2**
Winslow Cl *BOLCOL* NE35............. **87** E6
  BYK/HTN/WLK NE6 .... **83** F2 **3**
  SWCK/CAS SR5 .... **107** E6
Winslow Crs *SEA/MUR* SR7 .... **175** E3
Winslow Gdns
  LWF/SPW/WRK NE9................. **99** D5 **3**
Winslow Pl *BYK/HTN/WLK* NE6...... **83** F2
Winsten WASHS NE38 .... **137** F5
Winston Crs *MLFD/PNYW* SR4 ... **143** D2 **8**
Winston Gn *HLS* DH4 .... **139** E6
Winton Cl *CRAM* NE23 .... **23** F6
Winton Wy *GOS/KPK* NE3 .... **62** B3 **3**
Wishaw Cl *CRAM* NE23 .... **22** B4
Wishaw Ri *BW/LEM/TK/HW* NE15 ... **77** D1
Witham Rd *HEBB* NE31 .... **85** E5
Witherington Cl *LGB/HTN* NE7 ... **66** A3 **5**
Withernsea Gv
  ASHBK/HED/RY SR2 .... **161** F1

Witney CI *SWCK/CAS* SR5 .... 107 D6
Witney Wy *BOL* NE36 .... 105 D3
Witton Av *BDN/LAN/SAC* DH7 ...... 178 B1
  HAR/WTLS NE34 .... 89 F2
Witton Ct *GOS/KPK* NE3 .... 46 A6
  SUNDSW SR3 .... 144 A4
Witton Gdns *JRW* NE32 .... 86 A5
Witton Garth *PLEE/EAS* SR8 ...... 208 B5
Witton Gv *DHAM* DH1 .... 193 E2
  HLS DH4 .... 170 B3
Witton Rd *BDN/LAN/SAC* DH7 ...... 178 A2
  HEBB NE31 .... 68 B6
  SMOOR NE27 .... 52 B1
Witty Av *HEBB* NE31 .... 85 E3
Woburn CI *WASHS* NE38 .... 138 C2
Woburn CI *CRAM* NE23 .... 13 F5
  WLSD/HOW NE28 .... 66 B3 ⑤
Woburn Dr *BDLGTN* NE22 .... 8 B2
  SUNDSW SR3 .... 160 C2
Wolmer Rd *BLYTH* NE24 .... 17 E1
Wolseley CI *GATE* NE8 .... 98 B1
Wolseley Gdns *JES* NE2 .... 64 C6 ⑥
Wolseley Ter *MLFD/PNYW* SR4 .. 143 F1 ⑦
Wolsey Ct *HAR/WTLS* NE34 .... 88 B2
Wolsey Rd *SEA/MUR* SR7 .... 175 D4
Wolsingham Ct *CRAM* NE23 ...... 21 E1
Wolsingham Dr *DHAM* DH1 ...... 180 C6
Wolsingham Rd *GOS/KPK* NE3 .. 55 D2
Wolsingham St *ELS/FEN* NE4 ..... 79 F5
Wolsley Rd *BLYTH* NE24 .... 11 D4
Wolveleigh Ter *GOS/KPK* NE3 ... 63 F1
Woodbine Av *WLSD/HOW* NE28 .. 67 D4
Woodbine Rd *DHAM* DH1 .... 179 F5
  GOS/KPK NE3 .... 63 E2
Woodbine St *GATE* NE8 .... 99 D1
  SSH NE33 .... 71 F3 ⑧
  SUND SR1 .... 5 G3
Woodbine Ter *BLYTH* NE24 .... 11 E6
  FELL NE10 .... 100 A2
  MLFD/PNYW SR4 .... 125 E4
Woodbrook Av
  WD/WHPE/BLK NE5 .... 60 C6
Woodburn Fell NE10 .... 101 D5
  STLY/ANP DH9 .... 130 B6
Woodburn Av *ELS/FEN* NE4 .... 62 A5
Woodburn CI *BLAY* NE21 .... 93 F2 ⑧
Woodburn Dr *HLS* DH4 .... 170 B1
  WBAY NE26 .... 40 A3
Woodburn Gdns *DUN/TMV* NE11 .. 97 F4
Woodburn Sq *WBAY* NE26 .... 39 F3
Woodburn St
  BW/LEM/TK/HW NE15 .... 76 B1 ⑨
Woodchurch CI *LGB/KIL* NE12 ... 65 F2
Woodcroft CI *CRAM* NE23 .... 34 C1
Woodend Wy *GOS/KPK* NE3 .... 45 E4
Woodfield *PLEE/EAS* SR8 .... 208 B2 ⑧
Wood Flds *PONT/DH* NE20 .... 28 D4
Woodford *LWF/SPW/WRK* NE9 .. 117 E3
Woodford CI *SWCK/CAS* SR5 .... 107 E6 ⑧
Woodgate Gdns *FELL* NE10 ...... 102 A1
Woodgate La *FELL* NE10 .... 84 A6
Wood Gv *BW/LEM/TK/HW* NE15 .. 77 E1
Woodhall Spa *HLS* DH4 .... 156 C4
Woodhead Rd *BYK/HTN/WLK* NE6 .. 66 A6
Woodhill Rd *CRAM* NE23 .... 22 B4 ⑦
Woodhorn Gdns *DIN/WO* NE13 ... 33 D4
Woodhouses La
  WICK/BNPF NE16 .... 95 D6 ⑨
Woodhurst Gv
  MLFD/PNYW SR4 .... 141 F4 ⑨
Woodland Crs
  BW/LEM/TK/HW NE15 .... 78 A4
Woodland Dr *MLFD/PNYW* SR4 .. 143 D2
Woodland Gra *HLS* DH4 .... 169 E1
Woodland Ri *SUNDSW* SR3 ...... 160 A2
Woodlands *BW/LEM/TK/HW* NE15 .. 57 C4
  GOS/KPK NE3 .... 63 E3
  NSHW NE29 .... 54 A4
  WASHS NE38 .... 137 D6
Woodlands CI *MONK* NE25 .... 38 C5
Woodlands Dr
  CLDN/WHIT/ROK SR6 .... 107 F2
Woodlands Gra *LGB/KIL* NE12 .. 50 A3
Woodlands Park Dr *BLAY* NE21 .. 76 C6
Woodlands Rd
  BW/LEM/TK/HW NE15 .... 76 C1 ④
  CLDN/WHIT/ROK SR6 .... 107 E2
  ROWG NE39 .... 110 C2
Woodlands Ter *FELL* NE10 .... 100 B2 ⑧
Woodlands Vw
  CLDN/WHIT/ROK SR6 .... 107 F2
Wood La *BDLGTN* NE22 .... 8 A3
Wood Lea *HLH* DH5 .... 171 F3
Woodlea *LGB/KIL* NE12 .... 49 F3
Woodlea CI *HLH* DH5 .... 171 F6
Woodlea Ct *NSHW* NE29 .... 70 A3 ⑨
Woodlea Gdns *GOS/KPK* NE3 .... 48 A5
Woodlea Sq *NSHW* NE29 .... 70 A3
Woodleigh Rd *MONK* NE25 .... 40 A6
Woodleigh Vw
  WD/WHPE/BLK NE5 .... 62 A3 ⑨
Woodman St *WLSD/HOW* NE28 .. 69 D3
Woodmans Wy *WICK/BNPF* NE16 .. 95 D6
Woodnansey CI *PLEE/EAS* SR8 .. 208 A1

Woodpack Av *WICK/BNPF* NE16 .. 95 E4
Woodside *ASHBK/HED/RY* SR2 ..... 4 B6
  BDLGTN 8 B3
  BLYTH NE24 .... 11 E6 ⑥
Woodside Av
  BW/LEM/TK/HW NE15 .... 58 A4
  MONK NE25 .... 24 C6
Woodside CI *RYTON* NE40 .... 74 A3
Woodside Crs *LGB/KIL* NE12 ...... 50 A4
Woodside Gdns *DUN/TMV* NE11 ... 97 E2
  STLY/ANP DH9 .... 149 D5
Woodside La *HLS* DH4 .... 183 D3
  RYTON NE40 .... 74 A4
Woodside Rd *RYTON* NE40 .... 74 A3
Woodside Ter *SUNDSW* SR3 ...... 159 E2
Woodside Wk *ROWG* NE39 .... 110 B3
Woodside Wy *RYTON* NE40 .... 74 A3 ②
  SSH NE33 .... 88 A1
Woods Ter *GATE* NE8 .... 99 E1
  SEA/MUR SR7 .... 188 C1
Woodstock Rd
  BW/LEM/TK/HW NE15 .... 77 F3
  LWF/SPW/WRK NE9 .... 117 F2
Wood St *CLSW/PEL* DH2 .... 152 A1
  DUN/TMV NE11 .... 97 E2
  MLFD/PNYW SR4 .... 125 F5 ⑦
Wood Ter *FELL* NE10 .... 84 A6 ⑧
  JRW NE32 .... 85 F4
  SSH NE33 .... 71 F6
Woodthorne Rd *JES* NE2 .... 64 A3 ①
Woodvale Dr *HEBB* NE31 .... 84 B4
Woodvale Gdns
  LWF/SPW/WRK NE9 .... 100 B4 ③
Woodvale Rd *BLAY* NE21 .... 94 C1
  LGB/KIL NE12 .... 35 E6
Woodville CI *MLFD/PNYW* SR4 ... 143 D2 ⑧
Woodville Crs *MLFD/PNYW* SR4 .. 143 D2 ⑧
Woodville Rd
  BW/LEM/TK/HW NE15 .... 59 F6
Wooler Av *NSHW* NE29 .... 69 F2
Wooler Crs *GATE* NE8 .... 98 B2 ⑤
Wooler Sq *ASHBK/HED/RY* SR2 .. 145 D3
  DIN/WO NE13 .... 33 E2 ①
Woolerton Dr
  BW/LEM/TK/HW NE15 .... 77 D1
  LWF/SPW/WRK NE9 .... 100 A4 ⑦
Wooler Wk *JRW* NE32 .... 85 F4
Wooley Dr *BDN/LAN/SAC* DH7 .. 192 B5
Wooley St *WLSD/HOW* NE28 ...... 67 D5
Woolmer Ct *LGB/HTN* NE7 .... 66 A3 ⑥
Woolsington Ct
  MLFD/PNYW SR4 .... 125 E6 ⑮
Woolsington Gdns *DIN/WO* NE13 ... 44 B4
Woolsington Pk South
  DIN/WO NE13 .... 44 B4
Woolsington Rd *NSHW* NE29 ...... 53 E5
Woolwich CI *SWCK/CAS* SR5 ... 107 E6
Woolwich Rd *SWCK/CAS* SR5 ... 107 E6
Wooperton Gdns
  WD/WHPE/BLK NE5 .... 78 B1
Worcester CI *CLS/BIR/GTL* DH3 .. 167 F3
Worcester Rd *DHAM* DH1 .... 180 C5
Worcester St *ASHBK/HED/RY* SR2 .. 4 B5 ①
Worcester Ter
  ASHBK/HED/RY SR2 .... 4 B5 ②
Worcester Wy *DIN/WO* NE13 ...... 33 D5
Wordsworth Av *BLYTH* NE24 ...... 16 B1
  CLSW/PEL DH2 .... 152 A6
  HEBB NE31 .... 85 D2
  HLH DH5 .... 186 C4 ④
  SEA/MUR SR7 .... 175 D3
  WICK/BNPF NE16 .... 96 A2
Wordsworth Rd *PLEE/EAS* SR8 .. 200 B2
Wordsworth St *GATE* NE8 .... 99 F1
Worley CI *ELS/FEN* NE4 .... 80 A3 ⑳
Worley St *ELS/FEN* NE4 .... 80 A3 ㉑
Worm Hill Ter *WASHS* NE38 ..... 139 D5
Worsdell St *BLYTH* NE24 .... 11 D3 ⑦
Worsley CI *WLSD/HOW* NE28 ..... 66 B3
Worswick St *CNUT* NE1 .... 3 E3
Worthing CI *WLSD/HOW* NE28 ... 66 B3 ⑥
Worton CI *RDHAMSE* DH6 ...... 206 B1
Wouldhave Ct *SSH* NE33 .... 72 A3 ①
Wraysbury Ct *GOS/KPK* NE3 ..... 45 F5 ⑤
Wreigh St *HEBB* NE31 .... 84 C2
Wrekenton Rw
  LWF/SPW/WRK NE9 .... 118 B2
Wren CI *WASHS* NE38 .... 137 F3
Wren Gv *SWCK/CAS* SR5 .... 124 B3 ⑨
Wretham PI *JES* NE2 .... 3 C1
Wright Dr *CRAM* NE23 .... 34 C3
Wrightson St *CRAM* NE23 .... 14 A3
Wright St *BLYTH* NE24 .... 10 C4
Wright Ter *HLS* DH4 .... 156 C3
Wroxham Ct *ASHBK/HED/RY* SR2 .. 145 D4
  WD/WHPE/BLK NE5 .... 61 D2 ⑭
Wroxton *WASHS* NE38 .... 138 B3
Wuppertal Ct *JRW* NE32 .... 86 A2
Wychcroft Wy
  WD/WHPE/BLK NE5 .... 61 E4 ⑨
Wych Elm Crs *LGB/HTN* NE7 ..... 65 E3
Wycliffe Av *GOS/KPK* NE3 .... 62 B3
Wycliffe Rd *MLFD/PNYW* SR4 ... 143 E2
  SEA/MUR SR7 .... 175 D3

Wye Av *JRW* NE32 .... 86 B5
Wye Rd *HEBB* NE31 .... 85 D5
Wylam Av *MONK* NE25 .... 25 E6
Wylam CI *HAR/WTLS* NE34 .... 89 D3 ②
  WASHN NE37 .... 121 D3 ①
Wylam Gdns *WLSD/HOW* NE28 .. 68 B2
Wylam Gv *SUND* SR1 .... 5 F4
Wylam Rd *NSHW* NE29 .... 70 B3
  STLY/ANP DH9 .... 148 C1
Wylam St *JRW* NE32 .... 86 A1
  STLY/ANP DH9 .... 149 E6
Wylam Ter *STLY/ANP* DH9 ...... 131 E6 ⑦
Wylam Vw *BLAY* NE21 .... 76 A6
Wynbury Rd *LWF/SPW/WRK* NE9 .. 99 F5 ⑤
Wyncote Ct *LGB/HTN* NE7 .... 65 D4 ②
The Wynde *HAR/WTLS* NE34 ...... 88 B3
Wyndfall Wy *GOS/KPK* NE3 .... 62 C3
Wyndham Av *GOS/KPK* NE3 ...... 62 B3
Wyndham Wy *NSHW* NE29 .... 53 D4
The Wynding *BDLGTN* NE22 .... 7 D2
  CRAM NE23 .... 34 C1
Wyndley CI *WICK/BNPF* NE16 .... 95 E6
Wyndley PI *GOS/KPK* NE3 .... 62 B3
Wyndsail PI *GOS/KPK* NE3 .... 62 C3 ⑧
The Wynd *BW/LEM/TK/HW* NE15 .. 57 F3 ⑧
  CLSW/PEL DH2 .... 152 A2
  GOS/KPK NE3 .... 62 C2
  TYNE/NSHE NE30 .... 54 C4
Wyndtop PI *GOS/KPK* NE3 .... 62 C3 ③
Wyndways Dr *STLY/ANP* DH9 ... 129 D5
Wynn Gdns *FELL* NE10 .... 101 E1
Wynyard *CLSW/PEL* DH2 .... 152 C5
Wynyard Dr *BDLGTN* NE22 .... 8 B1
Wynyard Gdns
  LWF/SPW/WRK NE9 .... 118 B2
Wynyard Sq *ASHBK/HED/RY* SR2 .. 145 D3
Wynyard St *DUN/TMV* NE11 ...... 97 C2
  HLS DH4 .... 169 F2
  SEA/MUR SR7 .... 176 C5
  SUNDSW SR3 .... 160 C1
Wyvern Sq *ASHBK/HED/RY* SR2 .. 145 D4

Y

Yardley CI *SUNDSW* SR3 .... 160 C3
Yardley Gv *CRAM* NE23 .... 13 F6 ①
Yarmouth CI *HAR/WTLS* NE34 .... 89 D3 ①
Yarmouth Dr *CRAM* NE23 .... 13 F6
Yatesbury Av *WD/WHPE/BLK* NE5 .. 61 D4
Yelverton Ct *CRAM* NE23 .... 13 F6
Yelverton Crs *BYK/HTN/WLK* NE6 ... 83 E5
Yeoman St *NSHW* NE29 .... 71 D2
Yeovil CI *CRAM* NE23 .... 13 F6 ②
Yetholm Av *CLSW/PEL* DH2 ...... 153 D6
Yetholm PI *WD/WHPE/BLK* NE5 ... 60 C2 ⑤
Yetholm Rd *GATE* NE8 .... 98 A1
Yetlington Dr *GOS/KPK* NE3 ...... 62 C2
Yewbank Av *DHAM* DH1 .... 196 A3
Yewburn Wy *LGB/KIL* NE12 .... 49 D6
Yewcroft Av *BW/LEM/TK/HW* NE15 .. 77 E2
Yewdale Gdns
  LWF/SPW/WRK NE9 .... 99 F6 ①
Yewtree Av *SWCK/CAS* SR5 ..... 125 E2
Yew Tree Dr *BDLGTN* NE22 .... 7 E2
Yewtree Gdns *BYK/HTN/WLK* NE6 .. 66 C5
Yewtrees *FELL* NE10 .... 101 D5 ③
Yewvale Rd *WD/WHPE/BLK* NE5 .. 61 F5
Yoden Av *PLEE/EAS* SR8 .... 201 E6
Yoden Crs *PLEE/EAS* SR8 .... 201 E6
Yoden Rd *PLEE/EAS* SR8 .... 208 C1
Yoden Wy *PLEE/EAS* SR8 .... 209 E2 ①
York Av *JRW* NE32 .... 86 A5 ⑤
York CI *CRAM* NE23 .... 13 F6
York Crs *DHAM* DH1 .... 180 C4
  HLH DH5 .... 171 E6
Yorkdale PI *BYK/HTN/WLK* NE6 ... 81 F3 ⑧
York Dr *WLSD/HOW* NE28 .... 66 C5
York Rd *CLS/BIR/GTL* DH3 ...... 156 B6
  PLEE/EAS SR8 .... 200 D6
  WBAY NE26 .... 41 D5
Yorkshire Dr *DHAM* DH1 .... 196 C3
York St *ELS/FEN* NE4 .... 80 A3
  FELL NE10 .... 101 F1
  HLH DH5 .... 185 D3
  JRW NE32 .... 85 F2
  SUND SR1 .... 4 C2
York Ter *CLS/BIR/GTL* DH3 ...... 153 F6
York Wy *HAR/WTLS* NE34 .... 89 F2
Yorkwood *HEBB* NE31 .... 84 B1
Young Rd *LGB/KIL* NE12 .... 50 B3
Young St *DHAM* DH1 .... 195 E4 ②

Z

Zetland Dr *MONK* NE25 .... 54 B2
Zetland St *CLDN/WHIT/ROK* SR6 .. 127 D3
Zion St *SUND* SR1 .... 5 F2 ④
Zion Ter *SWCK/CAS* SR5 .... 126 B1

Abbey Sports Centre
  DHAM DH1 180   B4
Acre Rigg Junior & Infant School
  PLEE/EAS SR8 200   A6
Adamsez West Industrial Estate
  BLAY NE21 77   E4
Adelaide Row Medical Centre
  SEA/MUR SR7 176   C3
Airport Church
  WD/WHPE/BLK NE5 61   E4
Akhurst Preparatory School
  JES NE2 64   B4
Albert Elliott County Junior Mixed
  School
  HAR/WTLS NE34 88   B6
Albert Road Surgery
  JRW NE32 86   A2
Alexandra Business Park
  MLFD/PNYW SR4 125   D4
Algernon Industrial Estate
  SMOOR NE27 52   B3
All Saints Junior Mixed School
  HAR/WTLS NE34 88   A4
Amberley First School
  LGB/KIL NE12 36   A6
AMF Bowling
  ELS/FEN NE4 79   F3
AMF Bowling
  WASHS NE38 138   B1
Amphitheatre
  SSH NE33 72   A3
Annfield Plain County
  Junior Mixed School
  STLY/ANP DH9 146   C5
Annfield Plain Cricket Club
  STLY/ANP DH9 146   A5
Annfield Plain Infants School
  STLY/ANP DH9 146   B5
Appletree Gardens First School
  MONK NE25 40   A6
Arbeia Roman Fort & Museum
  SSH NE33 71   E2
Archbishop Runcie C of E School
  GOS/KPK NE3 47   F6
Archibald First School
  GOS/KPK NE3 63   D1
Arena Business Park
  HLS DH4 170   C4
Argyle House School
  ASHBK/HED/RY SR2 4   A6
The Art Gallery
  SUND SR1 4   C3
Arthurs Hill Clinic
  ELS/FEN NE4 80   A2
Ascham House School
  GOS/KPK NE3 63   E2
Ashburne Medical Centre
  ASHBK/HED/RY SR2 145   D2
Ashleigh School
  TYNE/NSHE NE30 71   D1
Ashley Road County JMI School
  HAR/WTLS NE34 88   B2
Astley Community High School
  MONK NE25 24   B5
Atkinson House School
  CRAM NE23 23   E6
Atkinson Road Primary School
  BW/LEM/TK/HW NE15 78   B4
The Avenues Medical Practice
  GOS/KPK NE3 63   E3
Aykley Heads Business Centre
  DHAM DH1 194   A2
Ayton Primary School
  WASHS NE38 137   E3
Backworth County First School
  SMOOR NE27 37   E5
Bailey Green First School
  LGB/KIL NE12 35   E6
Balliol Business Park
  LGB/KIL NE12 48   C4
Balliol First School
  LGB/KIL NE12 49   D6
Barbara Priestman School
  ASHBK/HED/RY SR2 144   A2
Barley Mow Primary School
  CLS/BIR/GTL DH3 136   C4
Barmston Medical Centre
  WASHS NE38 121   E6
Barmston Village Primary School
  WASHS NE38 139   E1
Barnes Junior School
  MLFD/PNYW SR4 143   E2
Barnwell Primary School
  HLS DH4 140   A6

Battle Hill First School
  WLSD/HOW NE28 67   F1
BBC North & Radio Newcastle
  ELS/FEN NE4 79   F1
Beaconhill County First School
  CRAM NE23 21   D2
Beamish County School
  STLY/ANP DH9 149   F1
Beamish Park Golf Club
  STLY/ANP DH9 132   B4
Beaumont Park Surgery
  MONK NE25 39   F4
Bebside County Middle School
  BLYTH NE24 9   E4
Bebside Social Club House
  BLYTH NE24 8   C5
Bede Infant School
  FELL NE10 82   A6
Bedewell School
  HEBB NE31 85   D4
Bedlington Community
  High School
  BDLGTN NE22 8   C2
Bedlington Station County
  First School
  BDLGTN NE22 8   C1
Bedlington Stead County
  First School
  BDLGTN NE22 8   B3
Belford House Sports Club
  ASHBK/HED/RY SR2 144   C3
Bellway Industrial Estate
  LGB/KIL NE12 50   B5
Belmont C of E (Controlled)
  Junior School
  DHAM DH1 196   B3
Belmont Comprehensive School
  DHAM DH1 196   B3
Belmont County Infant School
  DHAM DH1 196   B3
Belmont Grange Clinic
  DHAM DH1 196   B2
Belvedere Retail Park
  GOS/KPK NE3 45   E6
Benedict Biscop C of E School
  SUNDSW SR3 159   F3
Benfield Comprehensive School
  BYK/HTN/WLK NE6 66   A5
Bensham District Clinic
  GATE NE8 98   C2
Bensham Family Practice
  GATE NE8 98   C1
Bensham Synagogue
  GATE NE8 98   C1
Benton Park Primary School
  LGB/HTN NE7 65   D2
Benwell Hill Cricket Club
  BW/LEM/TK/HW NE15 78   A1
Bernard Gilpin Primary School
  HLH DH5 171   D2
Bessie Surtees House
  CNUT NE1 3   E5
Bewicke Health Centre
  WLSD/HOW NE28 68   C4
Bewick Road Medical Centre
  GATE NE8 81   E6
Bexhill Primary School
  SWCK/CAS SR5 123   E1
Biddick Hall County Infant School
  HAR/WTLS NE34 87   F5
Biddick Hall County Junior School
  HAR/WTLS NE34 88   A4
Biddick School
  WASHS NE38 139   D3
Bill Quay Cricket Club
  FELL NE10 84   A6
Birtley East First School
  CLS/BIR/GTL DH3 118   B6
Birtley Lane Surgery
  CLS/BIR/GTL DH3 136   B2
Birtley Medical Group Practice
  CLS/BIR/GTL DH3 136   B3
Birtley St Josephs RC School
  CLS/BIR/GTL DH3 136   B2
Birtley Swimming Baths
  CLS/BIR/GTL DH3 136   B3
Blackfell Primary School
  WASHN NE37 119   F6
Blackfriars Craft Centre
  CNUT NE1 2   B3
Black Gate
  CNUT NE1 2   D5
Blakelaw Health Centre
  WD/WHPE/BLK NE5 61   E4

Blakelaw School
  WD/WHPE/BLK NE5 61   E4
Blaydon Business Centre
  BLAY NE21 77   D5
Blaydon Business Park
  BLAY NE21 77   E4
Blaydon Cricket Club
  BLAY NE21 76   B6
Blaydon Haugh Industrial Estate
  BLAY NE21 77   D5
Blaydon Industrial Park
  BLAY NE21 76   C5
Blaydon Rugby Football Club
  WICK/BNPF NE16 95   E1
Blaydon Swimming Pool
  BLAY NE21 77   D6
Blaydon West Primary School
  BLAY NE21 76   B5
Bloemfontein County
  Junior Mixed School
  STLY/ANP DH9 148   C5
Blyth Delaval County
  Middle School
  BLYTH NE24 16   C3
Blyth New Delaval County
  First School
  BLYTH NE24 16   A2
Blyth Newsham County
  First School
  BLYTH NE24 16   B1
Blyth Plessey Road County
  First School
  BLYTH NE24 11   E5
Blyth Spartans AFC
  BLYTH NE24 11   D6
Blyth Sports Centre
  BLYTH NE24 10   C5
Blyth Tyndale County
  High School
  BLYTH NE24 9   F5
Blyth Tyndale County
  Middle School
  BLYTH NE24 9   F5
Blyth Valley Borough Council
  BLYTH NE24 10   A3
Blyth Valley Borough Council
  MONK NE25 24   B5
Boker Lane Health Centre
  BOLCOL NE35 106   A2
Bolam Business Park
  CRAM NE23 12   C6
Boldon Comprehensive School
  BOLCOL NE35 105   F2
Boldon Lane Health Centre
  HAR/WTLS NE34 88   B4
Bow School
  DHAM DH1 205   E1
Brandling Primary School
  FELL NE10 100   C1
Brandon & Byshottles
  Parish Council
  BDN/LAN/SAC DH7 203   F3
Brandon Cricket Club
  BDN/LAN/SAC DH7 203   F3
Brandon Modern School
  BDN/LAN/SAC DH7 203   D4
Brandon United Football Club
  BDN/LAN/SAC DH7 203   E3
Brewery
  ELS/FEN NE4 2   A3
Brewery
  SUND SR1 4   B1
Bridges Shopping Centre
  SUND SR1 4   B3
Brighton Avenue Primary School
  GATE NE8 98   C1
Brinkburn First School
  HAR/WTLS NE34 88   C3
Broadway East First School
  GOS/KPK NE3 47   F5
Broadway Junior School
  MLFD/PNYW SR4 142   C2
Broadwood Junior &
  Infant School
  BW/LEM/TK/HW NE15 77   E1
Brockwell Clinic
  CRAM NE23 14   A6
Brockwell County Middle School
  CRAM NE23 14   A6
Broomside Lane Surgery
  DHAM DH1 196   B2
Browney County Primary School
  BDN/LAN/SAC DH7 203   F5

Browns Gallery
JES NE2 .... **64** A4

Brunswick Beech Special School
DIN/WO NE13 .... **32** C4

Buddle Industrial Estate
WLSD/HOW NE28 .... **67** D6

Bugatti Industrial Park
NSHW NE29 .... **69** E1

Bullion Lane Primary School
CLSW/PEL DH2 .... **153** D6

Burnmoor Cricket Club
HLS DH4 .... **156** A4

Burnopfield Primary School
WICK/BNPF NE16 .... **111** E6

Burnside County First School
CRAM NE23 .... **14** B5

Burnside High School
WLSD/HOW NE28 .... **67** F4

Burnside JMI School
STLY/ANP DH9 .... **149** D3

Burnside Primary School
HLS DH4 .... **170** C1

Burradon First School
CRAM NE23 .... **35** E5

Byermoor RC Aided Junior &
Infant School
WICK/BNPF NE16 .... **112** C5

Byker Primary School
BYK/HTN/WLK NE6 .... **82** A3

Caedmon Primary School
GATE NE8 .... **99** D1

Camden Square
Secondary School
SEA/MUR SR7 .... **176** B3

Carr Hill Infant & Junior School
LWF/SPW/WRK NE9 .... **100** A2

Cartmel Business Centre
FELL NE10 .... **101** F1

Carville First School
WLSD/HOW NE28 .... **67** D6

Castle
DHAM DH1 .... **194** B5

Castle Dene Special School
GOS/KPK NE3 .... **64** B2

Castle Keep
CNUT NE1 .... **3** E5

Castle Leazes Halls
JES NE2 .... **80** A1

Castle View School
SWCK/CAS SR5 .... **123** F3

Catchgate Primary School
STLY/ANP DH9 .... **146** A4

Cedars Special School
LWF/SPW/WRK NE9 .... **117** F1

Central First School
WLSD/HOW NE28 .... **67** F4

Central High School
GOS/KPK NE3 .... **63** E2

Central Newcastle High School
JES NE2 .... **64** A6

Central Surgery
SUND SR1 .... **4** D3

Cestria Health Centre
CLSW/PEL DH2 .... **152** B6

Cestria Primary School
CLS/BIR/GTL DH3 .... **153** F5

Chapel House Middle School
WD/WHPE/BLK NE5 .... **59** D4

Chapel Park Shopping Centre
WD/WHPE/BLK NE5 .... **59** F2

Chase School
WICK/BNPF NE16 .... **96** A3

Chastleton Surgery
DHAM DH1 .... **180** A6

Chester Le Street Leisure Centre
CLS/BIR/GTL DH3 .... **153** F5

Chester Le Street C of E
Junior School
CLSW/PEL DH2 .... **153** D4

Chester Le Street Cricket Club
CLS/BIR/GTL DH3 .... **153** F6

Chester Le Street District Council
CLS/BIR/GTL DH3 .... **153** E4

Chester Le Street District Council
CLSW/PEL DH2 .... **152** C5

Chester Le Street Health Centre
CLS/BIR/GTL DH3 .... **153** F4

Chester Road Surgery
MLFD/PNYW SR4 .... **125** F6

Cheveley Park Medical Centre
DHAM DH1 .... **196** C3

Cheveley Park Primary School
DHAM DH1 .... **196** C2

Cheviot County Junior
Mixed School
HAR/WTLS NE34 .... **72** C6

Cheviot First School
WD/WHPE/BLK NE5 .... **60** C2

Chevyside Middle School
WD/WHPE/BLK NE5 .... **60** C2

Childrens Hospital
SUNDSW SR3 .... **143** F2

Chillingham Industrial Estate
BYK/HTN/WLK NE6 .... **82** C1

Chillingham Road Primary School
BYK/HTN/WLK NE6 .... **65** E6

The Chorister School
DHAM DH1 .... **194** B6

Christ Church C of E
Primary School
JES NE2 .... **3** F2

Church of England
Primary School
WLSD/HOW NE28 .... **68** A4

Church View Medical Centre
SUNDSW SR3 .... **160** C1

Cinema
SUND SR1 .... **4** C4

City Hall
CNUT NE1 .... **3** E1

City of Sunderland College
ASHBK/HED/RY SR2 .... **145** D4

City of Sunderland College
HLS DH4 .... **157** D3

City of Sunderland College
SUND SR1 .... **4** C2

City of Sunderland College
SWCK/CAS SR5 .... **124** C2

City Pool
CNUT NE1 .... **2** D1

Civic Centre
CLS/BIR/GTL DH3 .... **153** F4

Civic Centre
CNUT NE1 .... **2** D1

Civic Centre
GATE NE8 .... **81** D6

Civic Centre
SUND SR1 .... **4** C4

Civic Hall
WLSD/HOW NE28 .... **67** D4

Civil Service Sports Club
LGB/KIL NE12 .... **66** A1

Claremont Footcare Surgery
WBAY NE26 .... **40** A3

Claypath Medical Practice
DHAM DH1 .... **194** C4

Clayton Street Indoor
Mini Market
CNUT NE1 .... **2** C4

Cleadon Village C of E
Infant School
CLDN/WHIT/ROK SR6 .... **108** A1

Cleadon Village County JM
School
CLDN/WHIT/ROK SR6 .... **107** E1

Club House
DHAM DH1 .... **205** D2

Club House
HLH DH5 .... **172** A2

Collierley County Primary School
STLY/ANP DH9 .... **128** B6

Collingwood Primary School
NSHW NE29 .... **69** F1

Community College
SEA/MUR SR7 .... **176** B2

Coquet Park First School
WBAY NE26 .... **40** C4

Corpus Christi RC Primary School
GATE NE8 .... **99** D2

Corrymella Scott Gallery
JES NE2 .... **63** F6

County Durham Health Authority
PLEE/EAS SR8 .... **208** C2

County Hall Durham
County Council
DHAM DH1 .... **194** A2

County Hospital
DHAM DH1 .... **194** A4

County Junior & Infant School
BDN/LAN/SAC DH7 .... **192** A3

County Junior Middle &
Infant School
STLY/ANP DH9 .... **150** B2

Cowgate Leisure Centre
WD/WHPE/BLK NE5 .... **61** F3

Cowgate Primary School
ELS/FEN NE4 .... **62** A5

Cragside County First School
CRAM NE23 .... **22** A4

Cragside Primary School
LGB/HTN NE7 .... **64** C3

Craigievar School
CLDN/WHIT/ROK SR6 .... **127** D1

Cramlington Football Club
CRAM NE23 .... **22** C2

Crook Hall
DHAM DH1 .... **194** B3

Crookhill Junior School
RYTON NE40 .... **75** D3

Crown Court
CNUT NE1 .... **3** E5

Crowtree Leisure Centre
SUND SR1 .... **4** B3

Cruddas Park Health Centre
ELS/FEN NE4 .... **79** F4

Cruddas Park Surgery
ELS/FEN NE4 .... **80** A4

Cullercoats Primary School
TYNE/NSHE NE30 .... **55** E1

Custom House
CNUT NE1 .... **3** F5

Dame Allans Boys School
ELS/FEN NE4 .... **79** D1

Dame Dorothy Street School
CLDN/WHIT/ROK SR6 .... **127** D4

Davenport School
HLH DH5 .... **171** D4

Deerness Park Medical Centre
ASHBK/HED/RY SR2 .... **5** F5

Delaval Primary School
BW/LEM/TK/HW NE15 .... **78** A3

Denbigh Community First School
WLSD/HOW NE28 .... **68** C3

Dene House County
Mixed Modern School
PLEE/EAS SR8 .... **209** F2

Deneside Junior & Infant School
SEA/MUR SR7 .... **175** F4

Deneside Medical Centre
SEA/MUR SR7 .... **176** A3

Denton Park Middle School
WD/WHPE/BLK NE5 .... **60** B4

Denton Road Primary School
BW/LEM/TK/HW NE15 .... **77** E3

Derwenthaugh Industrial Estate
BLAY NE21 .... **77** E5

Derwent Infant School
GATE NE8 .... **98** B1

Derwentside District Council
STLY/ANP DH9 .... **146** C6

Derwentside District Council
STLY/ANP DH9 .... **148** B2

Diamond Hall Junior &
Infant School
MLFD/PNYW SR4 .... **125** E5

Dinnington Village First School
DIN/WO NE13 .... **31** E3

Dipton Surgery
STLY/ANP DH9 .... **128** B6

DLI Museum & Arts Centre
DHAM DH1 .... **194** B3

Donwell Primary School
WASHN NE37 .... **120** B3

Downhill Primary School
SWCK/CAS SR5 .... **106** A6

Dragonville Industrial Park
DHAM DH1 .... **196** A4

Dr Chandy's Surgery
PLEE/EAS SR8 .... **209** F1

Dr Dhuny's Surgery
STLY/ANP DH9 .... **149** D5

The Drive Primary School
FELL NE10 .... **101** D2

Dr Krishnans Surgery
GATE NE8 .... **98** C2

Dr Rannus Surgery
DUN/TMV NE11 .... **97** F2

Dr Reg Carrs Surgery
BLYTH NE24 .... **11** E5

Dryburn Hospital
DHAM DH1 .... **193** F2

DSS
SUND SR1 .... **4** A2

Dubmire County Junior &
Infant School
HLS DH4 .... **169** F2

Dudley Surgery
CRAM NE23 .... **35** D2

Dunelm Medical Practice
BDN/LAN/SAC DH7 .... **192** A3

Dunelm Medical Practice
DHAM DH1 .... **195** E4
Dunholme School
DHAM DH1 .... **194** A1
Dunston Federation
Football Club
DUN/TMV NE11 .... **97** D1
Dunston Health Centre
DUN/TMV NE11 .... **97** D2
Dunston Hill Hospital
WICK/BNPF NE16 .... **96** C3
Dunston Hill Junior &
Infant School
DUN/TMV NE11 .... **97** D2
Dunston Industrial Estate
DUN/TMV NE11 .... **97** D1
Dunston Riverside Primary School
DUN/TMV NE11 .... **97** E1
Dunston Swimming Pool
DUN/TMV NE11 .... **97** D3
Durham Baths
DHAM DH1 .... **194** C5
Durham Blue Coat C of E
(Aided) Junior School
DHAM DH1 .... **180** B6
Durham Business Centre
BDN/LAN/SAC DH7 .... **204** A3
Durham Cathedral
DHAM DH1 .... **194** B5
Durham City Amateur
Football Club
DHAM DH1 .... **196** A2
Durham City Cricket Club
DHAM DH1 .... **195** D5
Durham City Rugby Club
DHAM DH1 .... **195** D5
Durham County Constabulary
PLEE/EAS SR8 .... **208** C2
Durham County Council
CLS/BIR/GTL DH3 .... **168** A3
Durham County Council
DHAM DH1 .... **194** A1
Durham County Council
DHAM DH1 .... **196** B4
Durham County Council
PLEE/EAS SR8 .... **200** B5
Durham County Council
SEA/MUR SR7 .... **188** B1
Durham County Council
STLY/ANP DH9 .... **148** A2
Durham County Cricket Club
DHAM DH1 .... **154** A6
Durham County NHS Trust
DHAM DH1 .... **179** D5
Durham Crown Court
DHAM DH1 .... **194** C5
Durham Gilesgate
Comprehensive School
DHAM DH1 .... **195** F3
Durham High School
DHAM DH1 .... **205** D3
Durham Johnston
Comprehensive School
DHAM DH1 .... **193** F4
Durham Johnston
Comprehensive School
DHAM DH1 .... **195** D6
Durham Markets Co
DHAM DH1 .... **194** B4
Durham Newton Hall
County Infant School
DHAM DH1 .... **180** B6
Durham St Hilds C of E (Aided)
Primary School
DHAM DH1 .... **195** F4
Durham School
DHAM DH1 .... **194** A6
Durham Sixth Form Centre
DHAM DH1 .... **194** B4
Earls House Hospital
DHAM DH1 .... **179** D6
Easington C of E School
PLEE/EAS SR8 .... **199** F3
Easington Colliery
Primary School
PLEE/EAS SR8 .... **200** B2
Easington
Comprehensive School
PLEE/EAS SR8 .... **199** F3
Easington District Council
PLEE/EAS SR8 .... **200** A2
Easington District Council
SEA/MUR SR7 .... **175** F3

Easington District Council
SEA/MUR SR7 .... **188** C1
Easington District Leisure Centre
SEA/MUR SR7 .... **176** A3
Easington Lane Primary School
HLH DH5 .... **186** C4
East Boldon Junior School
BOL NE36 .... **106** B3
Eastcliffe Grammar School
GOS/KPK NE3 .... **63** F2
East Durham Community College
PLEE/EAS SR8 .... **208** C2
East Herrington Primary School
SUNDSW SR3 .... **159** E1
Eastlea First School
CRAM NE23 .... **14** B6
East Rainton JMI School
HLH DH5 .... **170** B6
Eden Hall Infant School
PLEE/EAS SR8 .... **209** D1
Edmondsley JMI School
BDN/LAN/SAC DH7 .... **164** A3
Eldon Square Shopping Centre
CNUT NE1 .... **2** D2
Elemore Leisure Centre
HLH DH5 .... **186** B3
Ellison C of E JMI School
JRW NE32 .... **86** A2
Elswick Way Industrial Estate
HAR/WTLS NE34 .... **87** F2
Emmanuel College
DUN/TMV NE11 .... **97** E5
Empire Theatre
SUND SR1 .... **4** A2
English Martyrs RC
Primary School
SWCK/CAS SR5 .... **125** D2
Epinay Special School
JRW NE32 .... **86** B2
Eppleton Cricket Club
HLH DH5 .... **171** F4
The Evergreen Gallery
CNUT NE1 .... **2** C5
Eye Clinic
CNUT NE1 .... **2** D1
Farne First School
WD/WHPE/BLK NE5 .... **60** C3
Farnham Medical Centre
HAR/WTLS NE34 .... **88** B2
Farringdon School
SUNDSW SR3 .... **159** F1
Farrington Infant School
SUNDSW SR3 .... **142** C6
Farrington Junior School
SUNDSW SR3 .... **142** C6
Fatfield Junior & Infant School
WASHS NE38 .... **138** C4
Felldyke Primary & Infant School
LWF/SPW/WRK NE9 .... **118** C1
Fellgate JMI School
JRW NE32 .... **104** A1
Felling Business Centre
FELL NE10 .... **82** C6
Fellrose Surgery
CLSW/PEL DH2 .... **152** A4
Fellside County Primary School
WICK/BNPF NE16 .... **95** F4
Fell Tower Medical
Centre Whereis Building
LWF/SPW/WRK NE9 .... **99** E6
Felstead School
MLFD/PNYW SR4 .... **124** C6
Fence Houses Surgery
HLS DH4 .... **156** A6
Finchale County Infant School
DHAM DH1 .... **181** D5
Finchale Priory
DHAM DH1 .... **182** A1
Fire Station
CNUT NE1 .... **3** E3
Fire Station
SUND SR1 .... **126** A5
First School
MONK NE25 .... **24** A4
Fordley Clinic
CRAM NE23 .... **34** C2
Formica Social & Sports Club
NSHW NE29 .... **53** D5
Framwellgate Moor
Comprehensive School
DHAM DH1 .... **180** A6
Framwellgate Moor
Junior & Infant School
DHAM DH1 .... **180** A6

Freeman Hospital
LGB/HTN NE7 .... **64** C2
Front Street Industrial Estate
RDHAMSE DH6 .... **187** E5
Front Street Junior &
Infant School
WICK/BNPF NE16 .... **95** F3
Front Street Surgery
BLAY NE21 .... **94** A1
Fulwell Grange Christian School
SWCK/CAS SR5 .... **126** B1
Fulwell Junior School
CLDN/WHIT/ROK SR6 .... **109** D6
Fulwell Medical Centre
CLDN/WHIT/ROK SR6 .... **108** C6
Fyndoune Community College
BDN/LAN/SAC DH7 .... **178** B2
The Gables Medical Group
BDLGTN NE22 .... **8** C2
Galactic Zoo
CNUT NE1 .... **2** B5
Gallery of Fine Art
CNUT NE1 .... **2** C2
The Gallery
CLSW/PEL DH2 .... **166** A3
The Gambling Man Gallery
TYNE/NSHE NE30 .... **71** D2
Garden Park Surgery
WLSD/HOW NE28 .... **68** C2
The Garrick Gallery
STLY/ANP DH9 .... **148** A2
Gateshead Area Health Authority
BLAY NE21 .... **77** E6
Gateshead Area Health Authority
DUN/TMV NE11 .... **97** F4
Gateshead Area Health Authority
GATE NE8 .... **81** D6
Gateshead Area Health Authority
GATE NE8 .... **98** B1
Gateshead Area Health Authority
LWF/SPW/WRK NE9 .... **100** A4
Gateshead Area Health Authority
WICK/BNPF NE16 .... **96** A3
Gateshead College
LWF/SPW/WRK NE9 .... **99** E3
Gateshead Complimentary Health
Centre
GATE NE8 .... **99** D1
Gateshead Fell Cricket Club
LWF/SPW/WRK NE9 .... **99** F4
Gateshead Health Care
FELL NE10 .... **102** A4
Gateshead Health NHS Trust
LWF/SPW/WRK NE9 .... **99** E3
Gateshead Hospitals NHS Trust
GATE NE8 .... **98** C3
Gateshead International Stadium
FELL NE10 .... **82** B5
Gateshead Jewish Boys School
GATE NE8 .... **99** D1
Gateshead Leisure Centre
GATE NE8 .... **99** E2
Gateshead Little Theatre
LWF/SPW/WRK NE9 .... **99** E3
Gateshead Magistrates Court
GATE NE8 .... **81** E6
Gateshead Metropolitan Borough
Council
BLAY NE21 .... **76** C5
Gateshead Metropolitan Borough
Council
CLS/BIR/GTL DH3 .... **136** B1
Gateshead Metropolitan Borough
Council
DUN/TMV NE11 .... **116** C1
Gateshead Metropolitan Borough
Council
FELL NE10 .... **100** C2
Gateshead Metropolitan Borough
Council
GATE NE8 .... **80** C2
Gateshead Metropolitan Borough
Council
GATE NE8 .... **82** A5
Gateshead Metropolitan Borough
Council
LWF/SPW/WRK NE9 .... **99** E5
Gateshead Metropolitan Borough
Council
LWF/SPW/WRK NE9 .... **117** F1
Gateshead Metropolitan Borough
Council
ROWG NE39 .... **110** B2

Gateshead Metropolitan Borough Council
WICK/BNPF NE16 .... **96**   A3

Gateshead & South Tyneside Health Authority
SSH NE33 .... **71**   F5

Gateshead Talmudical College
GATE NE8 .... **99**   D1

George Stephenson High School
LGB/KIL NE12 .... **49**   F2

Gibside School
WICK/BNPF NE16 .... **95**   F5

Gilesgate County Infant School
DHAM DH1 .... **195**   F3

Gilesgate County Junior School
DHAM DH1 .... **195**   F3

Glebe School
WBAY NE26 .... **40**   A2

Glebe Village Primary School
WASHS NE38 .... **138**   C1

Glen Dene School
PLEE/EAS SR8 .... **199**   F2

The Globe Gallery
TYNE/NSHE NE30 .... **71**   D1

Glover Industrial Estate
WASHN NE37 .... **121**   E5

Glynwood Primary School
LWF/SPW/WRK NE9 .... **99**   F5

Coathland Primary School
LGB/KIL NE12 .... **49**   E6

Gosforth Central Middle School
GOS/KPK NE3 .... **47**   E6

Gosforth Cricket Club
GOS/KPK NE3 .... **63**   E2

Gosforth High School
GOS/KPK NE3 .... **47**   E6

Gosforth Industrial Estate
GOS/KPK NE3 .... **47**   F6

Gosforth Memorial Health Centre
GOS/KPK NE3 .... **63**   F1

Gosforth West Middle School
GOS/KPK NE3 .... **63**   D1

Grainger Market
CNUT NE1 .... **2**   C3

Grange First School
GOS/KPK NE3 .... **47**   D6

Grange Park Primary School
SWCK/CAS SR5 .... **126**   B2

Grange Terrace Surgery
ASHBK/HED/RY SR2 .... **4**   B5

Grangetown Family Dental Health Centre
ASHBK/HED/RY SR2 .... **145**   D4

Grangetown Junior & Infant School
ASHBK/HED/RY SR2 .... **145**   E3

Grangewood Surgery
HLS DH4 .... **156**   C2

Greencroft Comprehensive School
STLY/ANP DH9 .... **146**   A4

Greenesfield Business Centre
GATE NE8 .... **81**   D5

Greenfields Special School
HEBB NE31 .... **85**   E1

Greenland County JMI School
STLY/ANP DH9 .... **147**   F4

Grey College
DHAM DH1 .... **205**   E1

Grindon Infants School
MLFD/PNYW SR4 .... **142**   A3

Hadrian JMI School
SSH NE33 .... **71**   E2

Hadrian Park First School
WLSD/HOW NE28 .... **52**   A5

Hadrian Park Middle School
WLSD/HOW NE28 .... **52**   A5

Hadrian School
BW/LEM/TK/HW NE15 .... **78**   B2

Halls of Residence
MLFD/PNYW SR4 .... **126**   A6

Hancock Museum
CNUT NE1 .... **80**   C1

Harlow Green Infant School
LWF/SPW/WRK NE9 .... **117**   F2

Harraton Primary School
WASHS NE38 .... **138**   A5

Hartlepool Community Care NHS Trust
PLEE/EAS SR8 .... **208**   C2

Harton School
HAR/WTLS NE34 .... **89**   F2

Hatfield College
DHAM DH1 .... **194**   B5

Havelock Primary School
MLFD/PNYW SR4 .... **124**   C6

Hawthorn House Medical Centre
BYK/HTN/WLK NE6 .... **82**   B2

Hawthorn Primary School
ELS/FEN NE4 .... **79**   F4

Hawthorns Hospital
PLEE/EAS SR8 .... **209**   D3

Hazlewood Community Primary School
DIN/WO NE13 .... **33**   D5

Headway Theatre
BLYTH NE24 .... **11**   E4

Heaton Manor Lower School
LGB/HTN NE7 .... **64**   C4

Heaton Manor Upper School
LGB/HTN NE7 .... **65**   E2

Hebrew Synagogue
WBAY NE26 .... **40**   C5

Heddon on the Wall C of E Controlled First School
BW/LEM/TK/HW NE15 .... **56**   A4

Hedworthfield Comprehensive School
JRW NE32 .... **104**   A1

Heritage Centre
DHAM DH1 .... **194**   C5

Herrington Medical Centre
HLS DH4 .... **157**   E2

Hetton Health Centre
HLH DH5 .... **171**   F6

Hetton Lyons School
HLH DH5 .... **185**   F2

Hetton Primary School
HLH DH5 .... **185**   E1

Hetton Secondary School
HLH DH5 .... **185**   E1

Hetton UDC Swimming Baths
HLH DH5 .... **185**   E1

Heworth Grange Comprehensive School
FELL NE10 .... **101**   E2

High Farm Middle School
WLSD/HOW NE28 .... **67**   D1

High Fell Special School
LWF/SPW/WRK NE9 .... **99**   F3

Highfield County Infant School
HAR/WTLS NE34 .... **72**   C5

Highfield Hospital
CLS/BIR/GTL DH3 .... **153**   E3

Highfield Junior & Infant School
ROWG NE39 .... **110**   A2

High Spen Industrial Estate
ROWG NE39 .... **111**   E1

Hillcrest Day Special School
CRAM NE23 .... **22**   A2

Hillsview Surgery
GOS/KPK NE3 .... **46**   A6

Hill Top School
LWF/SPW/WRK NE9 .... **101**   D6

Hillview Clinic
ASHBK/HED/RY SR2 .... **144**   C4

Hill View Infant School
ASHBK/HED/RY SR2 .... **144**   C4

Hill View Junior School
ASHBK/HED/RY SR2 .... **144**   C4

Hilton Primary School
WD/WHPE/BLK NE5 .... **61**   D4

Hindu Temple
ELS/FEN NE4 .... **78**   C2

HM Prison
DHAM DH1 .... **194**   C5

HMS Calliope Cadet Training Centre
GATE NE8 .... **3**   G5

The Hobart Gallery
GOS/KPK NE3 .... **63**   G2

Hollyhurst Medical Centre
BLAY NE21 .... **94**   A1

Holly Park Primary School
WASHS NE38 .... **137**   E3

Holmside & South Moor Hospital
STLY/ANP DH9 .... **148**   C4

Holy Cross RC Primary School
WLSD/HOW NE28 .... **68**   B2

Holystone First School
SMOOR NE27 .... **51**   E2

Holywell County First School
MONK NE25 .... **25**   E6

Hookergate Comprehensive School
ROWG NE39 .... **110**   A1

Horden & Easington RC Primary School
PLEE/EAS SR8 .... **201**   E5

Horton Grange First School
BLYTH NE24 .... **9**   E4

Hotspur Primary School
BYK/HTN/WLK NE6 .... **81**   F2

Houghton Colliery Welfare Cricket Club
HLS DH4 .... **170**   B1

Houghton Health Centre
HLH DH5 .... **171**   D2

Houghton Kepier School
HLS DH4 .... **170**   C2

Howden Green Industrial Estate
WLSD/HOW NE28 .... **69**   D4

Howletch Lane Junior & Infant School
PLEE/EAS SR8 .... **208**   A2

Hudson Road Primary School
SUND SR1 .... **5**   E4

Hylton Castle
SWCK/CAS SR5 .... **124**   A2

Hylton Castle Health Centre
SWCK/CAS SR5 .... **124**   A2

Hylton Castle Junior School
SWCK/CAS SR5 .... **123**   E2

Imex Business Centre
DHAM DH1 .... **180**   A4

Industrial Estate
BDN/LAN/SAC DH7 .... **178**   B1

Ivy Road Primary School
LGB/KIL NE12 .... **50**   A4

Jewish High School
GATE NE8 .... **99**   D1

Jewish Infant School
GATE NE8 .... **99**   E1

John Spence Community High School
TYNE/NSHE NE30 .... **54**   C4

Joseph Swan School
LWF/SPW/WRK NE9 .... **117**   D1

Jubilee Infant School
SEA/MUR SR7 .... **188**   C1

Kenton Comprehensive School
GOS/KPK NE3 .... **61**   F2

Kenton Lodge Residential School
ELS/FEN NE4 .... **63**   D4

Kepier Clinic
DHAM DH1 .... **195**   F3

Kibblesworth Primary School
DUN/TMV NE11 .... **116**   C6

Killingworth Middle School
LGB/KIL NE12 .... **49**   F2

King Edward Junior & Infant School
TYNE/NSHE NE30 .... **55**   D5

Kingfisher Industrial Estate
SEA/MUR SR7 .... **175**   F2

King George Comprehensive School
HAR/WTLS NE34 .... **89**   E5

Kingsmeadow Comprehensive School
DUN/TMV NE11 .... **97**   D2

Kings School
TYNE/NSHE NE30 .... **55**   F5

Kingston Park Primary School
GOS/KPK NE3 .... **45**   F6

Kingsway First School
BLYTH NE24 .... **11**   D6

Knoplaw First School
WD/WHPE/BLK NE5 .... **59**   E4

Laing Art Gallery
CNUT NE1 .... **3**   E2

Lancaster University
CNUT NE1 .... **2**   D5

Langley Moor Primary School
BDN/LAN/SAC DH7 .... **204**   A2

Larkspur Primary School
LWF/SPW/WRK NE9 .... **100**   B6

La Sagesse Convent High School
JES NE2 .... **64**   A3

Laurel Avenue County Junior & Infant School
DHAM DH1 .... **195**   E5

Law Courts
CNUT NE1 .... **3**   F4

Laygate Lane County Infant School
SSH NE33 .... **71**   E5

Laygate School
SSH NE33 .... **71**   E5

Leafield House School
CLS/BIR/GTL DH3 .... 136 C3

Lemington Clinic
BW/LEM/TK/HW NE15.................. 76 C2

Lemington First School
BW/LEM/TK/HW NE15.................. 76 C2

Lemington Middle School
BW/LEM/TK/HW NE15.................. 59 F6

Linden School
LGB/KIL NE12 .... 49 F4

**Lindisfarne County
Primary School**
GATE NE8.. 81 E6

Lingey House Primary School
FELL NE10 .... 102 A3

Linhope First School
WD/WHPE/BLK NE5..................... 60 B4

Little Theatre
CLDN/WHIT/ROK SR6 .... 107 F1

Live Theatre
CNUT NE1 .... 3 F5

Lobley Hill Junior & Infant School
DUN/TMV NE11 .... 97 F5

Longbenton Community College
LGB/KIL NE12 .... 49 E5

Longrigg Medical Centre
FELL NE10 .... 101 F3

Lord Chancellors Department
CNUT NE1 .... 2 C5

Lord Chancellors Department
GATE NE8.. 81 D5

**Lord Lawson of Beamish
Secondary School**
CLS/BIR/GTL DH3 .... 136 C3

Louisa Surgery
STLY/ANP DH9 .... 148 A2

Low Fell Clinic
LWF/SPW/WRK NE9..................... 99 F6

Low Fell Junior & Infant School
LWF/SPW/WRK NE9..................... 99 E5

Lumley County Infant School
CLS/BIR/GTL DH3 .... 167 F2

**Lumley Junior Middle &
Infant School**
CLS/BIR/GTL DH3 .... 168 A3

Lynnwood Business Centre
ELS/FEN NE4................................... 79 E3

Malvins Close County First School
BLYTH NE24.................................... 10 B4

Maplewood School
SWCK/CAS SR5 .... 125 D1

Marden Bridge Middle School
MONK NE25.................................... 40 C6

Marden High School
TYNE/NSHE NE30 .... 55 D3

Marine Avenue Medical Centre
WBAY NE26 .... 40 B5

Marine Park JMI School
SSH NE33.. 71 F3

Market Place Industrial Estate
HLH DH5 .... 171 E1

Marlborough Clinic
SEA/MUR SR7 .... 176 B3

Marley Hill Primary School
WICK/BNPF NE16......................... 113 F4

Mary Trevelyan Primary School
ELS/FEN NE4................................... 79 F5

Masonic Temple
ASHBK/HED/RY SR2...................... 4 C5

Mayfield Medical Centre
JRW NE32.. 85 F2

Meadowfield Clinic
BDN/LAN/SAC DH7 .... 203 F4

Meadowfield Sports Centre
BDN/LAN/SAC DH7 .... 203 F4

Meadow Well Primary School
NSHW NE29 .... 69 F2

Megabowl
LGB/KIL NE12 .... 50 C5

Metrocentre East Business Park
DUN/TMV NE11 .... 78 C6

The Metro Centre
WICK/BNPF NE16........................... 96 B1

Millburngate Shopping Precinct
DHAM DH1 .... 194 B4

Modern Mixed School
RDHAMSE DH6 .... 206 B1

Monkhouse Primary School
TYNE/NSHE NE30 .... 55 D3

Monkseaton Clinic
MONK NE25.................................... 40 A6

Monkseaton High School
MONK NE25.................................... 54 A2

Monkseaton Medical Centre
MONK NE25..................................... 39 F6

Monkseaton Middle School
MONK NE25..................................... 40 A6

Monkton County Infant School
HAR/WTLS NE34 .... 87 F4

**Monkton County Junior
Mixed School**
HAR/WTLS NE34 .... 87 E4

Monkton Hall Hospital
HEBB NE31 .... 85 E4

Monkwearmouth Health Centre
SWCK/CAS SR5 .... 126 C4

Monkwearmouth Hospital
SWCK/CAS SR5 .... 126 B2

**Monkwearmouth
Railway Station Museum**
CLDN/WHIT/ROK SR6 .... 126 C4

Montagu Junior & Infant School
WD/WHPE/BLK NE5..................... 62 A3

Moor Edge First School
LGB/KIL NE12 .... 49 D1

**Moorside Community
Primary School**
ELS/FEN NE4................................... 79 F2

**Mortimer
Comprehensive School**
HAR/WTLS NE34 .... 88 C1

Mosque
BYK/HTN/WLK NE6 .... 65 D6

Mosque
MLFD/PNYW SR4 .... 126 A6

Mosque
SSH NE33.. 71 D5

Mountbatten Medical Centre
HEBB NE31 .... 84 C3

Mountfield Primary School
GOS/KPK NE3 .... 62 A1

Murton Primary School
SEA/MUR SR7 .... 188 C1

Museum & Art Gallery
SSH NE33.. 71 E3

Museum of Science and Industry
ELS/FEN NE4................................... 80 A4

Music School
DHAM DH1 .... 194 B5

The Natural Therapy Clinic
TYNE/NSHE NE30 .... 54 C6

Nature Reserve
LGB/KIL NE12 .... 51 E5

Nelson Health Centre
NSHW NE29 .... 54 C6

Nettlesworth Primary School
CLSW/PEL DH2 .... 165 E6

Nevilles Cross Primary School
DHAM DH1 .... 193 E5

Newbottle Primary School
HLS DH4.. 157 E5

New Brancepeth Primary School
BDN/LAN/SAC DH7 .... 202 B1

Newburn Hall Motor Museum
BW/LEM/TK/HW NE15.................. 58 B6

Newburn Industrial Estate
BW/LEM/TK/HW NE15.................. 75 F2

Newburn Leisure Centre
BW/LEM/TK/HW NE15.................. 58 A6

Newburn Manor First School
BW/LEM/TK/HW NE15.................. 58 B6

**Newcastle Antiques &
Independent Museum**
CNUT NE1 .... 2 C4

Newcastle Area Health Authority
BW/LEM/TK/HW NE15.................. 78 A3

Newcastle Area Health Authority
ELS/FEN NE4................................... 79 F4

Newcastle Area Health Authority
JES NE2 .... 80 B1

Newcastle Arena
ELS/FEN NE4................................... 80 B5

Newcastle City Council
BW/LEM/TK/HW NE15.................. 57 F5

Newcastle City Council
BW/LEM/TK/HW NE15.................. 58 B6

Newcastle City Council
BW/LEM/TK/HW NE15.................. 78 A4

Newcastle City Council
BYK/HTN/WLK NE6 .... 82 B4

Newcastle City Council
BYK/HTN/WLK NE6 .... 83 E5

Newcastle City Council
CNUT NE1 .... 2 C2

Newcastle City Council
ELS/FEN NE4................................... 78 C3

Newcastle City Council
ELS/FEN NE4................................... 79 D4

Newcastle City Council
ELS/FEN NE4................................... 79 E4

Newcastle City Council
GOS/KPK NE3 .... 62 B3

Newcastle City Council
JES NE2 .... 64 A3

Newcastle City Council
JES NE2 .... 64 A3

Newcastle City Council
JES NE2 .... 81 E1

Newcastle City Council
JES NE2 .... 81 F1

Newcastle City Council
JES NE2 .... 81 F2

Newcastle City Council
JES NE2 .... 81 D1

Newcastle City Council
WD/WHPE/BLK NE5..................... 60 B3

Newcastle City Council
WD/WHPE/BLK NE5..................... 61 D5

Newcastle City Council
WD/WHPE/BLK NE5..................... 61 F4

Newcastle City Council
WD/WHPE/BLK NE5..................... 61 F5

Newcastle Clinic
JES NE2 .... 64 A3

Newcastle College
ELS/FEN NE4................................... 80 A4

Newcastle College Concert Hall
ELS/FEN NE4................................... 80 A4

**Newcastle Falcons Rugby
Football Club**
DIN/WO NE13 .... 45 D5

Newcastle General Hospital
ELS/FEN NE4................................... 79 E3

Newcastle Nuffield Hospital
JES NE2 .... 64 A6

**Newcastle Playhouse &
Gulbenkian Studio Theatre**
CNUT NE1 .... 80 C1

Newcastle Preparatory School
JES NE2 .... 81 D1

Newcastle Reform Synagogue
GOS/KPK NE3 .... 62 C2

The New City Medical Centre
SUND SR1 .... 5 E3

New College Durham
DHAM DH1 .... 193 F6

New College Durham
DHAM DH1 .... 193 F1

New College Durham
DHAM DH1 .... 194 A6

Newgate Shopping Mall
CNUT NE1 .... 2 C4

Newker Junior & Infant School
CLSW/PEL DH2 .... 153 D6

New Seaham Primary School
SEA/MUR SR7 .... 175 E1

Newsham Surgery
BLYTH NE24.................................... 16 B2

NHS Clinic
SEA/MUR SR7 .... 188 C1

Norfolk Clinic
SUND SR1 .... 4 D2

Norham Community High School
NSHW NE29 .... 69 F1

North Biddick Club House
WASHS NE38 .... 138 C6

North Blunts Primary School
PLEE/EAS SR8 .... 208 C2

Northburn County First School
CRAM NE23 .... 14 A5

North Durham NHS Trust
CLS/BIR/GTL DH3 .... 153 E6

North East Aircraft Museum
SWCK/CAS SR5 .... 122 C2

Northern Land & Leisure Centre
DHAM DH1 .... 194 A2

Northern Rugby Club
GOS/KPK NE3 .... 47 E4

North Fawdon Primary School
GOS/KPK NE3 .... 46 B5

North Heaton Sports Club
BYK/HTN/WLK NE6 .... 65 E6

North Sands Business Centre
CLDN/WHIT/ROK SR6 .... 127 D4

North Shields Rugby Club
NSHW NE29 .... 54 B4

North Tyne Industrial Estate
LGB/KIL NE12 .... 50 C4

North Tyneside Area Health
Authority
LGB/KIL NE12 .... **49** F1
North Tyneside Area
Health Authority
NSHW NE29 .... **54** B6
North Tyneside Area
Health Authority
WLSD/HOW NE28 .... **52** A5
North Tyneside Area
Health Authority
WLSD/HOW NE28 .... **67** E3
North Tyneside Borough Council
NSHW NE29 .... **70** C1
North Tyneside College
WLSD/HOW NE28 .... **68** A1
North Tyneside Council
LGB/KIL NE12 .... **48** C6
North Tyneside Council
LGB/KIL NE12 .... **49** D1
North Tyneside Council
LGB/KIL NE12 .... **49** F4
North Tyneside Council
TYNE/NSHE NE30 .... **55** D6
North Tyneside Council
WLSD/HOW NE28 .... **67** F5
North Tyneside Council
WLSD/HOW NE28 .... **69** D5
North Tyneside Council Offices
WBAY NE26 .... **41** D5
North Tyneside
Metropolitan Borough Council
NSHW NE29 .... **70** B2
Northumberland Area
Health Authority
BLYTH NE24 .... **10** A5
Northumberland County Council
BLYTH NE24 .... **9** E4
Northumberland County Council
BLYTH NE24 .... **11** E5
Northumberland County Council
BLYTH NE24 .... **16** B1
Northumberland County Council
CRAM NE23 .... **21** D1
Northumberland County Council
GOS/KPK NE3 .... **47** F3
Northumberland County
Cricket Club
JES NE2 .... **64** B6
Northumberland Mental
Health NHS Trust
CRAM NE23 .... **22** A1
Northumbria Sports Centre
WASHN NE37 .... **121** D1
Novacastrians Rugby
Football Club
LGB/HTN NE7 .... **65** D2
Oakfield College
ELS/FEN NE4 .... **78** C2
Oakfield Junior School
LWF/SPW/WRK NE9 .... **117** E1
Oakleigh Gardens School
CLDN/WHIT/ROK SR6 .... **90** A6
The Old Forge Surgery
MLFD/PNYW SR4 .... **125** E5
The Open University
GOS/KPK NE3 .... **47** E6
The Osborne Clinic
JES NE2 .... **64** B5
Our Lady of Peace RC School
HLS DH4 .... **156** C1
Our Lady & St Annes
Primary School
ELS/FEN NE4 .... **80** A3
Ouston County Infant School
CLSW/PEL DH2 .... **135** E5
Ouston Junior School
CLSW/PEL DH2 .... **135** D5
Oxclose Community School
WASHS NE38 .... **137** F2
Pallion Health Centre
MLFD/PNYW SR4 .... **125** E6
Pallion Primary School
MLFD/PNYW SR4 .... **125** D4
Palmer Community Hospital
JRW NE32 .... **86** A1
Parkside Infant School
SEA/MUR SR7 .... **176** A5
Parkside Middle School
CRAM NE23 .... **22** A1
Parkside School
CRAM NE23 .... **66** C1
The Parks Sports Centre
NSHW NE29 .... **70** B2

Park View Community School
CLS/BIR/GTL DH3 .... **153** F5
Park View
Comprehensive School
CLS/BIR/GTL DH3 .... **153** E1
Parkway Medical Centre
WD/WHPE/BLK NE5 .... **59** E4
Parkway School
WD/WHPE/BLK NE5 .... **59** F4
Pelaw County Infant School
CLSW/PEL DH2 .... **153** D3
Pelton County Junior &
Infant School
CLSW/PEL DH2 .... **152** B1
Pelton Fell Surgery Building
CLSW/PEL DH2 .... **152** A4
Pelton Health Clinic
CLSW/PEL DH2 .... **152** B1
Pendower Clinic
BW/LEM/TK/HW NE15 .... **78** A3
Pennywell Comprehensive School
MLFD/PNYW SR4 .... **142** A1
Percy Main Cricket Club
NSHW NE29 .... **69** F3
Percy Main Primary School
NSHW NE29 .... **69** F4
Percy St Johns Primary School
NSHW NE29 .... **70** A3
Peterlee College
PLEE/EAS SR8 .... **208** B1
Peterlee Leisure Centre
PLEE/EAS SR8 .... **208** C3
Peterlee Town Council
PLEE/EAS SR8 .... **208** A4
Philadelphia Cricket Club
HLS DH4 .... **157** E3
Phoenix Theatre
BLYTH NE24 .... **11** E5
Plawsworth Road County
Infant School
BDN/LAN/SAC DH7 .... **178** B1
Plessey Road County
Junior School
BLYTH NE24 .... **11** E5
Police Headquarters and
Magistrates Court
SUND SR1 .... **4** B2
Ponteland County First School
PONT/DH NE20 .... **28** B3
Ponteland County High School
PONT/DH NE20 .... **28** A5
Ponteland County Middle School
PONT/DH NE20 .... **28** B5
Ponteland Health Centre
PONT/DH NE20 .... **28** A3
Ponteland Leisure Centre
PONT/DH NE20 .... **28** B4
Ponteland Parish Council
PONT/DH NE20 .... **28** A4
Portland School
SUNDSW SR3 .... **143** F4
Portobello County Junior
Infant School
CLS/BIR/GTL DH3 .... **136** C4
Primary School
NSHW NE29 .... **70** B1
Primrose Hill Hospital
JRW NE32 .... **86** D4
Princess Louise First School
BLYTH NE24 .... **10** C5
Princess Road Junior School
SEA/MUR SR7 .... **176** B3
Priory Primary School
TYNE/NSHE NE30 .... **55** F4
Priory Theatre
TYNE/NSHE NE30 .... **55** F4
Queen Elizabeth Hospital
LWF/SPW/WRK NE9 .... **100** A5
Raby Cross Medical Centre
BYK/HTN/WLK NE6 .... **82** A2
Ramside Hall (Hotel)
DHAM DH1 .... **183** D6
Ravenswood Infant &
Primary School
BYK/HTN/WLK NE6 .... **65** E5
Ravensworth Surgery
SSH NE33 .... **72** A5
Ravensworth Terrace
Primary School
CLS/BIR/GTL DH3 .... **136** B2
RC JMI School
BDN/LAN/SAC DH7 .... **164** A6
Recreation Centre
CNUT NE1 .... **2** D3

Redesdale First School
WLSD/HOW NE28 .... **66** B2
Red House Junior Mixed School
SWCK/CAS SR5 .... **124** C2
Red Rose Primary School
CLS/BIR/GTL DH3 .... **166** C1
Regent Farm First School
GOS/KPK NE3 .... **46** C6
Regional National Blood
Transfusion Centre
JES NE2 .... **80** A1
Richard Avenue Primary School
MLFD/PNYW SR4 .... **143** F2
Richard Coates Church of
England Middle School
PONT/DH NE20 .... **28** A3
Richardson Dees First School
WLSD/HOW NE28 .... **67** F4
Rickleton Primary School
WASHS NE38 .... **137** E6
Riverview House Business Centre
SUND SR1 .... **4** D1
Roman Road Primary School
FELL NE10 .... **101** F5
Ronald Moore Gallery
TYNE/NSHE NE30 .... **55** D5
Ropery Walk Primary School
SEA/MUR SR7 .... **177** D5
Roseberry Primary School
CLSW/PEL DH2 .... **151** E3
Rowlands Gill Infant School
ROWG NE39 .... **111** E1
Rowlands Gill Junior School
ROWG NE39 .... **111** E1
Rowletch Burn Industrial Estate
CLS/BIR/GTL DH3 .... **136** A2
Royal College of Nursing
CNUT NE1 .... **2** D4
Royal Grammar School
JES NE2 .... **81** D1
Royalty Theatre
MLFD/PNYW SR4 .... **126** A6
Royal Victoria Infirmary
JES NE2 .... **80** B1
Rye Hill Sports Centre
ELS/FEN NE4 .... **80** A4
Ryhope General Hospital
ASHBK/HED/RY SR2 .... **162** B3
Ryhope Health Centre
ASHBK/HED/RY SR2 .... **162** A1
Ryhope Junior & Infant School
ASHBK/HED/RY SR2 .... **162** A1
Ryhope Village C of E
Primary School
ASHBK/HED/RY SR2 .... **162** B2
Ryton Industrial Estate
BLAY NE21 .... **75** F3
Sacred Heart Primary School
ELS/FEN NE4 .... **78** C1
Sacriston Cricket Club
BDN/LAN/SAC DH7 .... **178** A1
Sacriston Junior School
BDN/LAN/SAC DH7 .... **178** B2
Sacriston Swimming Baths
BDN/LAN/SAC DH7 .... **178** A1
St Aidans College
DHAM DH1 .... **205** D1
St Aidans RC Comprehensive
School
ASHBK/HED/RY SR2 .... **144** B2
St Albans Medical Group
FELL NE10 .... **100** C2
St Aloysius RC Infants School
HEBB NE31 .... **85** D1
St Aloysius RC Junior School
HEBB NE31 .... **85** D1
St Andrews RC Aided First School
BLYTH NE24 .... **10** B5
St Annes Mixed High School
SSH NE33 .... **72** A6
St Annes RC Primary School
MLFD/PNYW SR4 .... **142** A1
St Anthonys Health Centre
BYK/HTN/WLK NE6 .... **83** E4
St Anthonys RC School
ASHBK/HED/RY SR2 .... **4** A5
St Augustines RC Infant School
FELL NE10 .... **101** E4
St Bede Medical Centre
CLDN/WHIT/ROK SR6 .... **127** D4
St Bedes First School
BDLGTN NE22 .... **7** D3

St Bedes RC
Comprehensive School
PLEE/EAS SR8 .... **208** B2
St Bedes RC Infants School
JRW NE32 .... **86** B1
St Bedes RC Jmi School
JRW NE32 .... **86** B1
St Bedes RC Primary School
BW/LEM/TK/HW NE15 .... **77** E1
St Bedes RC Primary School
SSH NE33 .... **71** E4
St Bedes RC Primary School
WASHN NE37 .... **120** C3
St Benet Biscops RC High School
BDLGTN NE22 .... **7** D4
St Benets Primary RC School
CLSW/PEL DH2 .... **135** E5
St Benets RC Primary School
CLDN/WHIT/ROK SR6 .... **126** C2
St Bernadettes RC First School
WLSD/HOW NE28 .... **67** D1
St Catherines RC Primary School
JES NE2 .... **64** B6
St Chads College
DHAM DH1 .... **194** B5
St Charles RC Primary School
GOS/KPK NE3 .... **47** D6
St Columbas RC First School
WLSD/HOW NE28 .... **66** C4
St Cuthberts C of E Junior School
GATE NE8 .... **98** B1
St Cuthberts High School
BW/LEM/TK/HW NE15 .... **78** A2
St Cuthberts RC Lower School
BW/LEM/TK/HW NE15 .... **78** A2
St Cuthberts RC Primary School
BW/LEM/TK/HW NE15 .... **58** B4
St Cuthberts RC Primary School
CLS/BIR/GTL DH3 .... **153** F6
St Cuthberts RC Primary School
GOS/KPK NE3 .... **61** F2
St Cuthberts RC Primary School
NSHW NE29 .... **70** C1
St Cuthberts RC School
SEA/MUR SR7 .... **175** D2
St Edmunds RC
Comprehensive School
LWF/SPW/WRK NE9 .... **100** C6
St Georges RC Primary School
BW/LEM/TK/HW NE15 .... **76** C3
St Godrics RC Junior &
Infant School
DHAM DH1 .... **180** B6
St Hilda Industrial Estate
SSH NE33 .... **71** E4
St Hildas RC School
SWCK/CAS SR5 .... **125** F2
St Hild & St. Bede College
DHAM DH1 .... **195** D4
St James Park
(Newcastle United FC)
CNUT NE1 .... **2** B2
St John Bosco RC Primary School
SWCK/CAS SR5 .... **105** F6
St John Boste RC Primary School
WASHS NE38 .... **137** F1
St John Vianney School
WD/WHPE/BLK NE5 .... **59** F5
St Joseph RC Junior
Primary School
BW/LEM/TK/HW NE15 .... **78** B4
St Josephs Infant School
CLS/BIR/GTL DH3 .... **136** A1
St Josephs RC School
DHAM DH1 .... **195** F4
St Josephs RC School
MLFD/PNYW SR4 .... **125** E5
St Josephs RC School
SEA/MUR SR7 .... **188** B2
St Josephs School
NSHW NE29 .... **70** A2
St Josephs School
ROWG NE39 .... **110** A2
St Josephs School
WASHS NE38 .... **120** C6
St Lawrence RC Primary School
BYK/HTN/WLK NE6 .... **82** B2
St Leonards Junior &
Infants School
SUNDSW SR3 .... **144** A6
St Leonards RC
Comprehensive School
DHAM DH1 .... **194** A3

St Margarets C of E
Infants School
DHAM DH1 .... **193** F6
St Margarets C of E
Primary School
DHAM DH1 .... **194** A6
St Marks RC Primary School
WD/WHPE/BLK NE5 .... **60** B2
St Mary Magdalene RC
Primary School
SEA/MUR SR7 .... **176** B2
St Marys College
ELS/FEN NE4 .... **78** C1
St Marys Junior & Infant School
STLY/ANP DH9 .... **148** B4
St Marys RC
Comprehensive School
LGB/HTN NE7 .... **64** C1
St Marys RC Primary School
ASHBK/HED/RY SR2 .... **144** A2
St Marys RC Primary School
JRW NE32 .... **86** C5
St Marys RC Primary School
TYNE/NSHE NE30 .... **54** C2
St Marys RC Primary School
WICK/BNPF NE16 .... **96** B3
St Mary's Roman Catholic
Cathedral
CNUT NE1 .... **2** B5
St Michaels Industrial Estate
BYK/HTN/WLK NE6 .... **82** A3
St Michaels RC Primary School
ELS/FEN NE4 .... **79** F5
St Nicholas Cathedral
CNUT NE1 .... **3** E5
St Oswalds CE Junior Mixed &
Infant School
HEBB NE31 .... **85** E1
St Oswalds Clinic
FELL NE10 .... **100** C2
St Oswalds C of E Infants School
DHAM DH1 .... **194** C6
St Oswalds RC Infant &
Junior School
LWF/SPW/WRK NE9 .... **118** B1
St Patricks RC School
ASHBK/HED/RY SR2 .... **162** B2
St Patricks RC School
BDN/LAN/SAC DH7 .... **204** A3
St Pauls RC First School
CRAM NE23 .... **22** A3
St Peter RC Junior &
Infant School
LWF/SPW/WRK NE9 .... **99** F4
St Peters JMI School
JRW NE32 .... **69** E6
St Peters RC Middle School
CRAM NE23 .... **22** A4
St Robert of Newminster RC
Comprehensive School
WASHS NE38 .... **138** C4
St Stephens RC Primary School
LGB/KIL NE12 .... **49** D5
St Teresas RC Primary School
BYK/HTN/WLK NE6 .... **65** D6
St Thomas More RC (Aided)
Comprehensive School
BLAY NE21 .... **76** A5
St Thomas Mores RC School
DHAM DH1 .... **196** C3
St Thomas Street Business Centre
CNUT NE1 .... **2** C2
St Vincents RC Primary School
BYK/HTN/WLK NE6 .... **83** D4
St Wilfreds RC Junior &
Infant School
FELL NE10 .... **82** A6
St Wilfrids Middle School
BLYTH NE24 .... **10** C5
St Wilfrids RC
Comprehensive School
HAR/WTLS NE34 .... **88** C2
Sam Smiths Sports Ground
BYK/HTN/WLK NE6 .... **66** A5
Sanderson Hospital
GOS/KPK NE3 .... **63** D2
Saville Clinic
CNUT NE1 .... **2** D2
Seaburn Dene Primary School
CLDN/WHIT/ROK SR6 .... **108** C5
Seaham College
SEA/MUR SR7 .... **176** C3
Seaham Comprehensive School
SEA/MUR SR7 .... **175** E1

Seaham Town Council
SEA/MUR SR7 .... **176** C3
Seaton Delaval
Whytrig County Middle School
MONK NE25 .... **24** A4
Seaton Sluice Middle School
WBAY NE26 .... **26** A1
Segedunum Business Centre
WLSD/HOW NE28 .... **67** E5
Seghill County First School
CRAM NE23 .... **36** B1
Shanklea First School
CRAM NE23 .... **22** A1
Sherburn Hospital
DHAM DH1 .... **196** C6
Shieldfield Health Centre
JES NE2 .... **3** G1
Shield Row Junior & Infants School
STLY/ANP DH9 .... **131** F6
Shiney Row Primary School
HLS DH4 .... **157** D2
Shipley Art Gallery
GATE NE8 .... **99** E2
Shiremoor First School
SMOOR NE27 .... **52** A1
Shiremoor Middle School
SMOOR NE27 .... **38** B6
The Shopping Centre
STLY/ANP DH9 .... **148** B3
Shotton Colliery Primary School
RDHAMSE DH6 .... **206** B1
Shotton Hall
Comprehensive School
PLEE/EAS SR8 .... **208** A4
Shotton Hall Junior School
PLEE/EAS SR8 .... **208** A4
Shotton Parish Council
RDHAMSE DH6 .... **206** C2
Shotton RC JMI School
RDHAMSE DH6 .... **206** A1
The Side Gallery
CNUT NE1 .... **3** E5
Sidegate Gallery
WICK/BNPF NE16 .... **114** A1
Sikh Temple
ELS/FEN NE4 .... **80** A3
Silksworth Health Centre
SUNDSW SR3 .... **160** C1
Silverlink Business Park
WLSD/HOW NE28 .... **52** C6
Simonside First School
WD/WHPE/BLK NE5 .... **60** B1
Simonside Industrial Estate
HAR/WTLS NE34 .... **87** D3
Sir G B Hunter Memorial Hospital
WLSD/HOW NE28 .... **67** E4
Smiths Surgery
BOLCOL NE35 .... **105** D2
South Benwell Primary School
ELS/FEN NE4 .... **79** D4
Southdene Medical Centre
RDHAMSE DH6 .... **206** C1
South Gosforth First School
JES NE2 .... **64** A2
South Hetton Health Centre
RDHAMSE DH6 .... **187** E5
South Hetton Primary School
RDHAMSE DH6 .... **187** E5
South Hylton Primary School
MLFD/PNYW SR4 .... **123** F6
Southlands Middle School
CRAM NE23 .... **22** A5
Southlands School
TYNE/NSHE NE30 .... **54** C4
Southmoor School
ASHBK/HED/RY SR2 .... **145** D3
Southridge First School
MONK NE25 .... **39** F4
South Shields FC
JRW NE32 .... **87** D2
South Stanley
Comprehensive School
STLY/ANP DH9 .... **148** A3
South Stanley County
Junior Mixed School
STLY/ANP DH9 .... **148** A3
South Street County
Primary School
GATE NE8 .... **99** E1
South Tyneside Area
Health Authority
HAR/WTLS NE34 .... **89** F1
South Tyneside Borough Council
HEBB NE31 .... **84** C3

South Tyneside College
HEBB NE31 .... **84** C6

South Tyneside College
SSH NE33 .... **72** A6

South Tyneside Health Care Trust
HAR/WTLS NE34 .... **88** C3

South Tyneside Health Care Trust
HEBB NE31 .... **85** D3

South Tyneside Health Care Trust
SSH NE33 .... **71** F4

South Tyneside Magistrates Court
SSH NE33 .... **71** D4

South Tyneside
Metropolitan Borough Council
HAR/WTLS NE34 .... **90** A1

South Tyneside
Metropolitan Borough Council
SSH NE33 .... **71** F4

South Wellfield First School
MONK NE25 .... **39** D6

Southwick Health Centre
SWCK/CAS SR5 .... **125** F3

Sports Centre
RDHAMSE DH6 .... **197** E5

Springfield Clinic
GATE NE8 .... **99** E2

Springfield Comprehensive School
JRW NE32 .... **86** A3

Spring Terrace Health Centre
NSHW NE29 .... **54** C6

Springwell Health Centre
SUNDSW SR3 .... **143** D3

Springwell House Surgery
SUNDSW SR3 .... **143** D4

Springwell Village Primary School
LWF/SPW/WRK NE9 .... **119** E3

Stanhope County Infants School
SSH NE33 .... **88** B1

Stanhope County Junior
Mixed School
SSH NE33 .... **88** A2

Stanhope Parade Health Centre
SSH NE33 .... **71** E6

Stanley Health Centre
STLY/ANP DH9 .... **148** A2

Stanley RC Junior Mixed &
Infants School
STLY/ANP DH9 .... **148** B1

Star Clinic
DHAM DH1 .... **194** B4

Stephenson Railway Museum
SMOOR NE27 .... **52** C5

Stonelaw County Middle School
CRAM NE23 .... **21** F4

Studio Gallery
TYNE/NSHE NE30 .... **55** F5

Sunderland AFC Club Shop
SUND SR1 .... **4** C2

Sunderland Bowling Centre
SWCK/CAS SR5 .... **126** B3

Sunderland City Council
HLS DH4 .... **170** C2

Sunderland City Council
SUND SR1 .... **4** D3

Sunderland Counselling Services
MLFD/PNYW SR4 .... **142** B1

Sunderland County Court
SUND SR1 .... **4** D3

Sunderland Cricket &
Rugby Football Club
ASHBK/HED/RY SR2 .... **144** B2

Sunderland Cricket &
Rugby Football Club House
ASHBK/HED/RY SR2 .... **144** B2

Sunderland District General
Hospital
MLFD/PNYW SR4 .... **125** E6

Sunderland Eye Infirmary
ASHBK/HED/RY SR2 .... **144** C3

Sunderland Football Club
SWCK/CAS SR5 .... **126** B4

Sunderland High School
ASHBK/HED/RY SR2 .... **4** D6

Sunderland Museum & Art Gallery
SUND SR1 .... **4** D4

Sunderland Retail Park
CLDN/WHIT/ROK SR6 .... **126** C3

Sunderland Royal Hospital
MLFD/PNYW SR4 .... **125** E6

Sunderland Royal Infirmary
ASHBK/HED/RY SR2 .... **126** A6

Sunderland Talmudical College
GATE NE8 .... **99** E2

Sunderland University
SUND SR1 .... **4** D2

Swalwell Cricket Club
WICK/BNPF NE16 .... **95** E1

Talbot House Special School
BW/LEM/TK/HW NE15 .... **58** A4

Tanfield Lea County
Junior Mixed & Infant School
STLY/ANP DH9 .... **130** C6

Tanfield Lea County
Junior Mixed & Infantschool
STLY/ANP DH9 .... **130** B5

Tanfield View Surgery
STLY/ANP DH9 .... **148** A2

Tax Office
SUND SR1 .... **4** B2

Team Valley Business Centre
DUN/TMV NE11 .... **98** C4

Team Valley Trading Estate
Post Office
DUN/TMV NE11 .... **117** D2

Tedco Business Centre
HEBB NE31 .... **68** B6

Tedco Business Park
JRW NE32 .... **68** C6

Theatre Royal
CNUT NE1 .... **2** D3

Thockley First School
BW/LEM/TK/HW NE15 .... **57** E4

Thomas Bewick Special School
WD/WHPE/BLK NE5 .... **59** E4

Thomas Hepburn
Community School
FELL NE10 .... **101** D3

Thornhill
Comprehensive School
ASHBK/HED/RY SR2 .... **144** A2

Throckley Industrial Estate
BW/LEM/TK/HW NE15 .... **57** F3

Throckley Middle School
BW/LEM/TK/HW NE15 .... **57** E4

Throckley Surgery
BW/LEM/TK/HW NE15 .... **57** F4

The Toco Gallery
JES NE2 .... **64** A4

Toner Avenue County
Infant School
HEBB NE31 .... **84** C5

Townend Primary School
SWCK/CAS SR5 .... **105** E6

Town Hall & Civic Offices
SSH NE33 .... **71** F4

Trevelyan College
DHAM DH1 .... **205** E1

Trinity Maritime Museum
CNUT NE1 .... **3** F4

Trinity Medical Centre
SSH NE33 .... **71** E5

Trinity School
BLAY NE21 .... **95** D1

Trouts Lane School
DHAM DH1 .... **179** D5

Tynemouth Business Centre
TYNE/NSHE NE30 .... **55** D6

Tynemouth College
NSHW NE29 .... **54** B6

Tynemouth Cricket Club
TYNE/NSHE NE30 .... **55** D4

Tyne Point Industrial Estate
JRW NE32 .... **87** D2

Tyne Tees TV Studios
CNUT NE1 .... **3** H4

Tyne Theatre and Opera House
CNUT NE1 .... **2** A4

Tyneview Primary School
BYK/HTN/WLK NE6 .... **83** F3

Tyne View Primary School
GATE NE8 .... **80** B6

Tyne & Wear County Council
SSH NE33 .... **71** E3

Univeristy Halls of Residence
CLDN/WHIT/ROK SR6 .... **126** C4

Univeristy Halls of Residence
SUND SR1 .... **5** E1

University College
DHAM DH1 .... **194** B5

University for Industry
SUND SR1 .... **4** C2

University Library
DHAM DH1 .... **194** B5

University of Durham
DHAM DH1 .... **194** C4

University of Durham
DHAM DH1 .... **194** B5

University of Durham
DHAM DH1 .... **194** C5

University of Durham
DHAM DH1 .... **195** D5

University of Durham
DHAM DH1 .... **196** A1

University of Durham
DHAM DH1 .... **205** D1

University of Newcastle
Upon Tyne
JES NE2 .... **2** A1

University of Newcastle
Upon Tyne
JES NE2 .... **64** A6

University of Newcastle
Upon Tyne
JES NE2 .... **80** B1

University of Newcastle
Upon Tyne
LGB/HTN NE7 .... **65** E3

University of Northumbria
at Newcastle
CNUT NE1 .... **3** E1

University of Northumbria
at Newcastle
CNUT NE1 .... **81** D1

University of Northumbria
at Newcastle
LGB/HTN NE7 .... **65** E2

University of Sunderland
ASHBK/HED/RY SR2 .... **4** D6

University of Sunderland
ASHBK/HED/RY SR2 .... **4** C5

University of Sunderland
ASHBK/HED/RY SR2 .... **144** C2

University of Sunderland
CLDN/WHIT/ROK SR6 .... **127** D4

University of Sunderland
CLDN/WHIT/ROK SR6 .... **127** D3

University of Sunderland
MLFD/PNYW SR4 .... **125** D4

University of Sunderland
SUND SR1 .... **4** A3

University of Sunderland
SUND SR1 .... **126** A6

University of Sunderland
SWCK/CAS SR5 .... **124** A4

University of Sunderland
WASHN NE37 .... **119** F5

University of Sunderland (Library)
SUND SR1 .... **4** A4

University Technology Park
ASHBK/HED/RY SR2 .... **4** A4

Usworth Colliery Junior School
WASHN NE37 .... **121** D3

Usworth Grange Primary School
WASHN NE37 .... **121** E3

Usworth Secondary School
WASHN NE37 .... **120** C2

Valley Road Infant School
ASHBK/HED/RY SR2 .... **145** E2

Valley Road Junior School
ASHBK/HED/RY SR2 .... **145** E2

Valley View County Infant School
JRW NE32 .... **86** A4

Van Mildert College
DHAM DH1 .... **205** D2

Victoria Industrial Estate
FELL NE10 .... **84** B5

Victoria Medical Centre
HEBB NE31 .... **84** C2

Victoria Road Health Centre
WASHN NE37 .... **120** C4

Viking Gallery
JRW NE32 .... **86** A1

Village Gallery
WICK/BNPF NE16 .... **96** A3

Wagonway Industrial Estate
HEBB NE31 .... **68** A6

Walker Comprehensive School
BYK/HTN/WLK NE6 .... **83** E2

Walkerdene Special School
BYK/HTN/WLK NE6 .... **83** E2

Walkergate Hospital
BYK/HTN/WLK NE6 .... **66** A6

Walkergate Infant School
BYK/HTN/WLK NE6 .... **66** A6

Wallsend Business Centre
WLSD/HOW NE28 .... **67** E5

Wallsend Sports Centre
WLSD/HOW NE28 .... **66** B4

Wansbeck District Council
BDLGTN NE22 .... **7** E4

Wardley Primary School
FELL NE10 .... **101** F2
War Memorial
SUND SR1 .... **4** D4
Washington Albany
Infants School
WASHN NE37 .... **120** A5
Washington Football Club
WASHN NE37 .... **120** C5
Washington F Pit Museum
WASHN NE37 .... **120** B5
Washington Hospital
WASHS NE38 .... **137** D6
Washington Secondary School
WASHN NE37 .... **120** C5
Washington Village
Primary School
WASHS NE38 .... **121** D6
Washingwell Primary School
WICK/BNPF NE16 .... **96** B4
Waterloo Medical Group
BLYTH NE24 .... **10** C4
Waterville Primary School
NSHW NE29 .... **70** B2
Waverley First School
BW/LEM/TK/HW NE15 .... **77** D2
Waygood Gallery & Studios
CNUT NE1 .... **2** D4
Wearside College
SUNDSW SR3 .... **143** E3
Welbeck Primary School
BYK/HTN/WLK NE6 .... **82** C3
Wellbank Special School
WASHN NE37 .... **120** A3
West Boldon Junior
Mixed School
BOL NE36 .... **105** F2
Westbourne Surgery
HLS DH4 .... **156** C2
West Denton First School
WD/WHPE/BLK NE5 .... **59** F5
West Denton High School
WD/WHPE/BLK NE5 .... **60** A4
Westerhope Clinic
WD/WHPE/BLK NE5 .... **60** B3
Westerhope First School
WD/WHPE/BLK NE5 .... **60** A3

Westerhope Small Business Park
WD/WHPE/BLK NE5 .... **60** A2
Western First School
WLSD/HOW NE28 .... **66** C4
Western Infant School
NSHW NE29 .... **70** B2
Western Middle School
WLSD/HOW NE28 .... **66** C5
Westfield School
GOS/KPK NE3 .... **63** D3
West Gate Community College
ELS/FEN NE4 .... **78** C2
Westgate Hill Primary School
ELS/FEN NE4 .... **79** F3
West Jesmond Junior School
JES NE2 .... **64** A5
West Lane Junior & Infant School
BLAY NE21 .... **93** F2
Westlea Junior School
SEA/MUR SR7 .... **175** D2
West Moor First School
LGB/KIL NE12 .... **49** E3
Westmoor Middle School
LGB/KIL NE12 .... **49** D3
Westmorland Business Centre
ELS/FEN NE4 .... **2** A5
Westmorland Business Centre
ELS/FEN NE4 .... **80** A4
Westoe Gallery
SSH NE33 .... **71** F4
Westovian Theatre Society
SSH NE33 .... **72** A2
West Rainton Primary School
HLS DH4 .... **183** E2
West Walker School
BYK/HTN/WLK NE6 .... **83** F4
Whickham Comprehensive School
WICK/BNPF NE16 .... **95** F4
Whickham Parochial C of E
Junior & Infant School
WICK/BNPF NE16 .... **95** E5
Whinfield Industrial Estate
ROWG NE39 .... **110** B3
Whitburn
Comprehensive School
CLDN/WHIT/ROK SR6 .... **109** F2

Whitburn Cricket Club
CLDN/WHIT/ROK SR6 .... **109** E2
Whitburn Junior Mixed School
CLDN/WHIT/ROK SR6 .... **109** D2
Whitburn Surgery
CLDN/WHIT/ROK SR6 .... **109** D2
Whitehouse Industrial Estate
BW/LEM/TK/HW NE15 .... **78** B4
Whitehouse Primary School
NSHW NE29 .... **53** E5
Whitley Bay Cricket Club
MONK NE25 .... **54** C1
Whitley Bay Football Club
MONK NE25 .... **54** C1
Whitley Bay High School
MONK NE25 .... **40** A4
Whitley Bay Ice Rink
MONK NE25 .... **54** B1
Whitley Bay Rockcliff RFC
MONK NE25 .... **54** C1
Whitley Lodge First School
WBAY NE26 .... **40** A2
Whitley Memorial School
BDLGTN NE22 .... **7** F4
Willington High School
WLSD/HOW NE28 .... **68** B1
Windy Nook Primary School
FELL NE10 .... **100** C4
Wingrove Primary School
ELS/FEN NE4 .... **79** D2
Winlaton Park Junior School
BLAY NE21 .... **94** B2
Winlaton Vulcans Rugby Club
BLAY NE21 .... **94** B1
Witherwack Primary School
SWCK/CAS SR5 .... **107** E6
Woodlands Park Health Centre
DIN/WO NE13 .... **33** D5
Woodlea County Primary School
HLS DH4 .... **169** D1
Wrekenton Health Centre
LWF/SPW/WRK NE9 .... **118** C1
Yates Jewish School for Girls
GATE NE8 .... **99** D1
The Yemeni School
SSH NE33 .... **71** D5

Page 5

E4
1 Winifred Ter

Page 35

F5
1 Algernon
2 Callerton
3 Hauxley
4 Havanna

F6
1 Agincourt
2 Alresford
3 Bannockburn
4 Blenheim
5 Cannock
6 Culloden Wk
7 East Bailey
8 Falkirk
9 Marston
10 Tewkesbury
11 Towton
12 West Bailey

Page 46

A5
1 Alnham Ct
2 Cartington Ct
3 Espley Ct
4 Fawdon Park Rd
5 Hesket Ct
6 Ludlow Ct
7 Pelham Ct
8 Uldale Ct
9 Whiteleas Ct

Page 49

D5
1 Ashdown Cl
2 Aylesbury Pl
3 Myreside Pl
4 The Roundway

F4
1 Albany Av
2 Avondale Av
3 Cambridge Av
4 Lynholm Gv
5 North Vw
6 Park Vw
7 Percy Gdns
8 Station Rd North
9 Teesdale Gv
10 Wens Leydale Dr
11 West Vw
12 Whitfield Rd
13 Wilson Ter

F6
1 Belvedere Gdns
2 Eastfield Ter
3 Oakhurst Ter
4 Parkland
5 St Margarets Av
6 Station Ap
7 Tynedale Ter

Page 54

C5
1 Medway Gdns
2 Osborne Gdns

C6
1 Albion Ter
2 Ashfield Gv
3 Ayre's Ter
4 Church Wy
5 Cleveland Crs
6 Cleveland Ter
7 Frank Pl
8 Lovaine Ter
9 Northumberland Sq
10 Springfield
11 Spring Ter
12 Upper Camden St
13 West Percy Rd

Page 55

F5
1 Northumberland Ter
2 Percy St
3 Silver St
4 Stephenson St
5 Tynemouth Ter

Page 59

D2
1 Abbey Dr
2 Ashford Gv
3 Callerton Vw
4 Claverdon St
5 Lilac Cl
6 Nedderton Ct
7 Newsham Cl

Page 60

A3
1 Bamburgh Rd
2 Baybridge Rd
3 Counden Rd
4 Kendale Wk
5 Marsham Rd
6 Mitford Dr
7 Norham Dr
8 Trafford Wk
9 Westward Ct
10 Whorlton Rd

A6
1 The Close
2 Hedgeley Rd
3 Ilderton Pl
4 Layburn Gdns
5 Northlea
6 St Vincents Ct
7 Sandringham Rd
8 Warwick Rd

B4
1 Barents Cl
2 Bruce Cl
3 Frankham St
4 James St
5 Lordenshaw
6 Nansen Cl
7 Wilkes Cl

Page 61

D3
1 Hendersyde Cl
2 Lynfield Ct
3 Lynfield Pl
4 Marlfield Ct
5 Melkington Ct
6 Mellendean Cl
7 Pallinsburn Ct
8 Stonefold Cl

D5
1 Buttermere Cl
2 Cotehill Rd
3 Finsmere Av
4 Finsmere Pl
5 Fulwell Gn
6 Loweswater Rd

F4
1 Brieryside
2 Coldingham Gdns
3 Crossbrook Rd
4 Fallodon Gdns
5 Fuchsia Pl
6 Hauxley Gdns
7 Holden Pl
8 Middlegarth
9 Monroe Pl
10 Radcliffe Pl

F5
1 Bondicarr Pl
2 Broomhill Gdns
3 Chevington Gdns
4 Doxford Gdns
5 Embleton Gdns
6 Mauifin Pl
7 Morwick Pl
8 Rennington Pl
9 Stamfordham Ms
10 Westerhope Gdns

F6
1 Genister Pl

Page 62

C2
1 Delaval Ter
2 Dunmoor Cl
3 Hownam Cl

Page 64

A1
1 Bowes St
2 Bowsden Ct
3 Christon Cl
4 Commercial Rd
5 Donald St
6 Ridgewood Gdns
7 Ridgewood Vls
8 Wardle St

C6
1 Granville Gdns
2 Grosvenor Gdns
3 Jesmond Rd
4 Kimberley Gdns
5 Northumberland Gdns
6 Wolseley Gdns

Page 66

A3
1 Allingham Ct
2 Highworth Dr
3 Kilburne Ct
4 Stanfield Ct
5 Witherington Ct
6 Woolmer Ct

D5
1 Atkinson St
2 Benton Wy
3 Border Rd
4 Chadwick St
5 Curzon Rd West
6 Eden St
7 Equitable St
8 Hedley Pl
9 James Ter
10 Portugal Pl
11 Thames Gdns

E2
1 Baildon Cl
2 Boscombe Dr
3 Bridgewater Cl

F2
1 Bellingham Cl
2 Blanchard Cl

Page 67

Page 68

C5
1 Addison Ct
2 Carlyle Ct
3 Carlyle St
4 Douglas St
5 Smeaton Ct
6 Smeaton St

Page 71

E4
1 Mount Ter
2 Old Coronation St

E5
1 Beethoven St
2 Berkely St
3 Bolingbroke St
4 Burleigh St
5 Dunelm St
6 Elizabeth St
7 Graham St
8 Handel St
9 Lyndhurst St
10 Percy St
11 Salisbury St
12 Selbourne St

F5
1 Chichester Rd
2 East George Potts St
3 East Moffett St
4 East Stevenson St
5 Imeary Gv
6 John Clay St
7 May St
8 Newburn Ct
9 Robinson St
10 Shakespeare St
11 Stainton St East
12 West George Potts St
13 West Moffett St
14 West Stainton St
15 West Stevenson St

F6
1 Alansway Gdns
2 Albany St East
3 Albany St West
4 Marlborough St North
5 Oxford Av
6 Southey St
7 Stanhope Pde
8 Wawn St

Page 76

B4
1 Cochran St

Page 79

F4
1 Bristol Ter
2 Gloucester Ter
3 Hawthorn Ter
4 Kenilworth Rd
5 Park Cl
6 Portland St

Page 80

A2
1 Avison Pl
2 Avolon Pl
3 Bassington Cl
4 Frosterley Pl
5 Hamilton Crs
6 Holywell Ct
7 Jefferson Pl
8 Monday Crs
9 Monday Pl
10 Spring Garden La

A4
1 Belgrave Pde
2 Cambridge St
3 Cross Pde
4 Hawthorn Pl
5 Houston Ct
6 Kirkdale Gn
7 Mather Rd
8 Palace St
9 Victoria St
10 Waverley Rd
11 Wentworth Pl

A5
1 Back Mitford St
2 Blackthorn Pl
3 Charlotte Cl
4 Clasper St
5 Dobson Ct
6 Hornbeam Pl
7 Maiden St
8 Mulberry Pl
9 Tyneside Rd
10 Whitebeam Pl

B5
1 Ord St
2 Redheugh Bridge Rd

Page 81

D1
1 Archbold Ter
2 Eslington Rd
3 Gladstone Pl
4 Gladstone Ter
5 Harrison Pl
6 Osborne Ter
7 Sandyford Rd
8 Windsor Pl

Page 82

A2
1 Albion Rw
2 Back Heaton Park Rd
3 Brinkburn St
4 Dalton St
5 Edwin St
6 Flora St
7 Grafton St
8 Matthew St
9 Molineux St
10 Toward St

Page 83

F5
1 Burwood Cl

Page 86

A1
1 Albert Rd
2 Burns St
3 Clayton St
4 Ellison St
5 Hibernian Rd
6 Market Rd
7 Monkton Rd
8 Napier St
9 St John's Ter
10 Wear St

Page 88

B4
1 Carnegie Ct
2 Douglas Cl

Page 95

F4
1 Redewater Gdns
2 Well Close Wk

Page 99

D1
1 Claremont St
2 Ely St
3 Grasmere St
4 Grasmere St West
5 Lincoln St
6 Sedgewick Pl
7 Villa Pl

E2
1 Patterdale Ter
2 Perry St
3 Silverdale Ter

E6
1 Albert Pl

F3
1 Baden Powell St
2 Prefect Pl
3 Stavordale Ter

Page 100

A1
1 Allhusen Ter
2 Beaufront Gdns
3 Bronte St
4 Elliot Rd
5 Emily St
6 Ford St
7 Howard St
8 Jane Eyre Ter
9 King Edward Pl
10 Kings Cl
11 Old Fold Rd
12 St James Ct

Page 120

B2
1 Blackheath Cl
2 Ganton Cl
3 Lytham Cl
4 Portrush Cl
5 Prestwick Cl
6 Rosemount Cl
7 Sunningdale Dr
8 Troon Cl
9 Turnberry Cl

Page 123

E1
1 Barking Sq
2 Bathgate Sq
3 Batley St
4 Beeston Av
5 Belgrade Sq
6 Berwick Sq
7 Craigshaw Rd

F6
1 Cambria Gn
2 Frederick St
3 Kepier Gdns
4 New St
5 Primrose St
6 Union St
7 Vicarage La

Page 124

A5
1 Claxheugh Rd
2 Mailing Pk

B2
1 Bowburn Av
2 Howley Av
3 Ribble Rd
4 Shincliffe Av
5 Stockley Av

B4
1 Defender Ct

Page 125

E6
1 Arlington St
2 Bell St
3 Brookland Rd
4 Hazledene Ter
5 Kimberley St
6 Romford St
7 Tamerton St
8 Walpole Ct
9 Washington St
10 Westleigh Ct
11 Westwood St
12 Wilber St
13 Wilber St
14 Winchester St
15 Woolsington Ct

F2
1 Cato St
2 Churchill Av
3 Clarence St
4 James St
5 Jowett Sq
6 Julius Caesar St
7 Keats Av
8 Tennyson St

F5
1 Gilsland St
2 Handel St
3 Oswald St
4 Paxton Ter
5 Pickard St
6 Shepherd St
7 Wood St

Page 126

A2
1 Amy St
2 Chester St
3 Coldstream Av
4 Collingwood St
5 Columba St
6 Cornhill Rd
7 Edward Burdis St
8 Frank St
9 James Armitage St
10 Ridley St
11 Schimel St
12 Sophy St

A4
1 Priestly Crs

A6
1 Chepstow St
2 Chester St East
3 Chester Ter North
4 East Cleft Rd
5 Gilhurst Gra
6 Harlow St
7 Langton Cl
8 The Leazes
9 The Retreat
10 The Royalty
11 St Mark's St
12 St Mark's Ter
13 Tintern St
14 Waterworks Rd
15 Western Hl

C1
1 Alexander Ter
2 Foildon Av
3 Friarage Av
4 Hilda St
5 Laburnam Rd
6 Laburnum Rd
7 Marcia Av
8 Marina Ct
9 Marina St
10 Melbury Ct
11 Montague St
12 Ormesby Rd
13 Pauline Av
14 Primrose Prec
15 Ronald Sq
16 Vivian Sq

C3
1 Abbs St
2 Dixon's Sq
3 Fulwell Rd
4 Howard St
5 Monk St
6 Oriel Ct
7 Rosebery St
8 Shore St
9 Southwick Rd
10 Wearmouth St

C4
1 Barclay St
2 Causeway
3 Dundas St
4 George St North
5 Liddell St
6 Lower Dundas St
7 North Bridge St
8 Sheepfolds North
9 Sheepfolds St
10 Southwick Rd
11 Whitburn St
12 Williamson Ter

C5
1 Back Bridge St
2 Bedford St
3 Bridge Crs
4 Bridge St
5 Charman St
6 Cumberland St
7 Fawcett St
8 Frederick Rd
9 Green St
10 John St
11 Lambton St
12 Pann La
13 Press La
14 Prince St
15 Queen St
16 Sheepfolds South
17 Station St
18 Union St
19 West Sunniside
20 York St

C6
1 Athenaeum St
2 Cowan Ter
3 Fawcett St
4 Frederick St
5 King St
6 Maritime St
7 Park La
8 Tavistock Pl
9 Waterloo Pl

Page 142

A5
1 Thurso Cl
2 Tintagel Cl
3 Trevelyan Cl

C6
1 Truro Rd
2 Tynemouth Sq

C6
1 Alloa Rd
2 Archer Sq

Page 143

D2
1 Arncliffe Av
2 Corry Ct
3 Ingoldsby Ct
4 Westfield Ct
5 Wimbourne Av
6 Winston Crs
7 Woodville Ct
8 Woodville Crs

D6
1 Buckingham
2 Knightsbridge
3 Piccadilly
4 The Strand

F5
1 Somerset St

Page 144

A1
1 Beachcross Rd
2 Beachville St
3 Beresford Pk
4 Burnville Rd South
5 Elmwood St
6 Ewing Rd
7 Fernville St
8 Havelock Ter
9 Hunters Hall Rd
10 Oakwood St
11 Roseville St
12 Vale St
13 Western Hl

B4
1 Brackenwood Gv
2 Glenesk Gdns
3 Greybourne Gdns
4 Larchwood Gv
5 Ringmore Ct
6 Stannington Gdns
7 Tunstall Hill Cl

Page 160

C3
1 Fairgreen Cl
2 Fernwood Cl
3 Hightree Cl
4 Katrine Ct

Notes